GORONWY REES

GORONWY REES

Sketches in Autobiography

A Bundle of Sensations and *A Chapter of Accidents*

with 'A Winter in Berlin', a further autobiographical essay

Edited with Introduction and Notes

by

JOHN HARRIS

UNIVERSITY OF WALES PRESS
CARDIFF
2001

A Bundle of Sensations was originally published by Chatto & Windus in 1960.
A Chapter of Accidents was originally published by Chatto & Windus and Library Press of New York in 1972.

British Library Cataloguing-in-Publication Data.
A catalogue record for this book is available from the British Library.

ISBN 0–7083–1676–X

Published with the financial support of the Arts Council of Wales

Typeset at University of Wales Press
Printed in Great Britain by Bookcraft Ltd, Avon

To Jan and Leon

Contents

Preface

❧

This edition offers, with full background and explanatory notes, Goronwy Rees's two volumes of autobiography, together with 'A Winter in Berlin', a closely related essay that has recently come to light. An introduction sets these volumes in the context of Rees's other books: here no comprehensive survey of Rees the writer has been attempted, my short monograph in the Writers of Wales series going some way towards providing such a study (besides his books, it pays attention to Rees's journalism, an integral part of his output extending over five decades). Rees's autobiographies skate over his writings, as they do over his professional career and almost every aspect of his private life. 'Of what interest to me is anything, if it only interest me?' asked André Malraux at the outset of his own autobiography. Rees applauded *Antimémoires* and, in similar spirit, aimed at an account of events that were not purely personal to the author but which carried a wider public significance. This wish to bring to the fore the experiences of a generation led inevitably to some distortion of the biographical record, a matter taken up in the preliminary essay, 'Goronwy Rees: The Memoirist', and from time to time in the notes. Rees readily acknowledged the fictive element in autobiography – to the extent that his publishers, when devising the blurb for *A Chapter of Accidents*, could describe it as a sequel to his earlier 'autobiographical novel', *A Bundle of Sensations*.

The texts of both these volumes are as Chatto & Windus first published them, except for a few editorial changes. These mostly relate to quotations, where Rees's memory sometimes played him false. Misquotations have been silently corrected, as has the occasional misspelling and obvious error of fact. Styling too has undergone some change, so as to bring capitalization, italicization and hyphenation in particular into line with modern practice. Here, as elsewhere, I am indebted to the team at the University of Wales Press for their careful scrutiny and expert guidance, and for the patience they have shown me.

In preparing this edition I have approached a number of individuals concerning Rees; I am grateful for their ready response, and most particularly to Jack Wanger, a teacher at Cardiff High School for Boys in the 1930s, who spoke revealingly of Goronwy's time there. Caroline Dalton (New College, Oxford), Roger Hallett (Friends of Hafod),

Christina Harris (BBC Written Archives Centre), Sylvia Harris (Welsh School of Architecture), Christopher Hunt (Imperial War Museum), Dr Lothar Kettanacker (German Historical Institute), Nicholas R. Mays (News International plc), Sue Neville (Cambridgeshire County Record Office), and Jacqueline Sen (John Rylands University Library) all supplied useful information, for which I offer my thanks; as I do to Jenny Naipaul, who granted me valuable access to the in-house records of the *Spectator*, and to Daniel Gruffydd Jones, formerly registrar of the University of Wales, Aberystwyth, who kindly allowed me to consult the Willink Report. My greatest debt of gratitude must be to Jenny Rees. Her *Looking for Mr Nobody: The Secret Life of Goronwy Rees* (1994) is an intimate, unwavering biography from which I have benefited greatly, as indeed I have from our many conversations about her father. Her help has been unfailing and it is a pleasure here to acknowledge it.

John Harris
Aberystwyth, July 2001

Introduction

On 3 November 1931, shortly before his twenty-second birthday, an excited Goronwy Rees wrote home to Cardiff from Oxford with news that he had gained the first All Souls prize fellowship of that year. 'I'm very bewildered & don't know quite what to think about it. I go & dine there as a Fellow tonight! The other fellow elected was Quintin Hogg.' Hogg was an old Etonian, son of a Lord Chancellor, whereas Rees was a state-educated Welshman, the first of his kind to be elected to All Souls. At Cardiff High School for Boys the success of a former pupil warranted a rare half-holiday while in Wales a wider public shared a moment of national pride. As for his family background, Elizabeth Bowen thought it 'obscure' – 'the brilliant child of an obscure home' runs her fictional portrait of Rees[1] – but hers is a metropolitan perspective; in the eyes of his compatriots Rees was elect of the elect, the younger son of the Revd Richard Jenkin Rees, a distinguished Calvinistic Methodist minister, and of his wife Apphia (née James) who shared her husband's north Cardiganshire farming roots. Their son's scholastic brilliance, remarkable though it was, accords with a family accustomed to academic success; Goronwy's father and brother gained first-class degrees (from Oxford and Cambridge respectively), while an elder sister graduated in history at Aberystwyth. As a youth consumed by literature Rees inevitably rebelled against his upbringing but he always readily acknowledged an intellectual debt to his father, to the minister's house of books, as he did to his grammar school teachers at Cardiff. Knowledge was perhaps the greatest and most enduring of life's pleasures: 'that it should become one in childhood is the greatest service a system of education can give'. Progress at New College confirmed his school's assurances that academically he had nothing to fear at Oxford since his preparation had been of the best. Social success was another matter; this, he quickly realized, depended on something more than brain power.

Rees's time at Oxford became the stuff of legend. 'Poet, scholar, seducer' is Douglas Jay's description of a friend full of Celtic charm and fluency. Though examples of Rees's versifying made the *Oxford Poetry* anthologies, it was his undergraduate novel that he valued and that offered some distraction from the desolating loss of a mother: Apphia Rees died suddenly, aged sixty-one, a little before the All Souls triumph. 'Writing books is the only thing I'm serious about', he confided to a girlfriend, adding, 'and I think mine is good.' Fortunately Geoffrey Faber thought so too; London publisher cum All Souls bursar, he kept a watch on Oxford hopefuls and in July 1932 added *The Summer Flood* to his firm's fiction list. Treating of a dismal passion for a Bangor cousin by marriage, Rees's novel projects what he described as 'the somnambulance of youth', an adolescent dream-state in which the external world loses shape and substance and only that which originates in the self seems to possess reality. If the novel overplayed teenage angst, the reviewers in general were kind, L. P. Hartley and L. A. G. Strong particularly, the latter speaking of 'its complete surrender to the freshness and thoughts of youth'. Rees came to dislike the book and all its solemn introspection as the pressures of the outside world inexorably broke in upon him. He became a man of the thirties, a *Marxisant* literary intellectual caught up with the urgent questions of the time, in politics, literature and society, and finding an outlet for his opinions in the editorial columns of the *Spectator* (a journalism of bite and brilliance largely published anonymously).

Tracking Rees through his golden decade is no easy matter: the travels around Europe, the longer stays in Vienna and Berlin, his spells with the *Manchester Guardian* and *The Times*, the string of notable affairs, his engagement in radical politics. Rees himself provides scant help. He kept no diaries and no correspondence, and was habitually uncommunicative on the particularities of his life; what little he lets slip in print is invariably vague, or careless regarding date. And his persona is only a half-truth – the man of modest abilities, frivolous, irresponsible, pleasure-seeking. Cyril Connolly knew a different Rees, one capable of intellectual arrogance and moral outrage, and there is ready evidence of such qualities, the marks of a Calvinist upbringing. 'Contradictory', 'enigmatic', 'secretive', these are the words applied to Rees throughout what proved to be an extraordinary career. For a man with no ambition for office he found himself strategically positioned in an amazing variety of fields; in journalism, in the army, in the worlds of business and university administration (not to mention his work for MI6 – the Secret Intelligence Service – or the pre-war dabbling in espionage that clouded the rest of his life). Rees was all for shedding skins, for periodic self-renewals drawing upon that element of the unexpected and irrational which he saw as absolutely native to our make-up, preventing any human being from conforming completely to rule.

His ambitions as novelist barely survived *A Bridge to Divide Them* (1937), his second published book,[2] in which he sought to connect the inner life with the external world or, as he put it, to move outside the heads of his characters, turning 'all the doubts, conflicts and desires inside them into a real world of people and events'. Though the new canvas is suitably broad, both geographically and in its class dimensions, in no particular setting does Rees seem fully at ease, and improbabilities of plotting heighten the over-literary feel. Proletarian novel, study of bourgeois manners, a Lawrentian blending of the two (English rich girl falls for Welsh stoker), *A Bridge to Divide Them* satisfied no one. 'Mr Rees will probably write some fine novels, but he must avoid the clichés not only of phrasing but of vision', wrote his friend Louis MacNeice. One fine novel came, though more than a decade later. *Where No Wounds Were* (1950) is unashamedly a novel of ideas, centred on a succession of interviews between a captured Luftwaffe pilot, the young arrogant Lipansky, and a world-weary British army officer whose job it is to interrogate him. Free of all physical intimidation, their exchanges become an exploration of Nazi ideology and the German cast of mind. Here Rees – a serious Germanist – covers solid ground ('Nazi Germany was precisely thus', declared James Hanley's review) and the book is further authenticated by the author's background in military interrogation. Also, in a sequence of conventional action Lipansky escapes to Wales, to Rees's own bald Welsh hills, a spiritual location enshrining the Christian idea of the equality of all men (our surest protection against fascism). *Where No Wounds Were* remains a highly readable novel, its excitements largely stemming from the mental battle fought between intimate enemies and, more deeply, within one man's mind which is also the mind of a nation. Reviews were universally welcoming, sales moved nicely along, and the publishers Chatto & Windus looked forward to Rees's next offering.

It arrived in 1960, though the beginnings of *A Bundle of Sensations* date back to Rees's time at Aberystwyth, the place of his birth to which he returned as university college principal in 1953. His trials in the town are well known; less well known is the fact that he enjoyed there two or more relatively trouble-free years during which his writing changed direction. First, he contributed a radio talk on an aspect of his childhood and, pleased with the result, he set about composing other autobiographical pieces. One of these, 'Innocent Abroad', an account of an undergraduate vacation spent amid the Silesian wheatfields, greatly impressed Stephen Spender, then joint editor of *Encounter*, who made it the lead essay in the issue of April 1956, at the same time assuring Rees that he would welcome further pieces of this kind. It is possible that 'A Winter in Berlin' was prepared with *Encounter* in mind, though it never appeared in that journal, or seemingly anywhere else during the author's lifetime.[3] By the time of his next *Encounter* showing Rees's world had been blown apart; he had lost his job at Aberystwyth as a consequence of the Burgess furore and suffered a motor accident that brought him close to death. Henceforth, from 1957 onwards, he would have to survive by full-time writing. In August 1958, appointed the *Listener*'s new fiction reviewer, he gave Spender 'The Great Good Place' (a picture of the Ascot hospital from which he had recently emerged) and sounded Chatto & Windus about the possibility of another book. This would be a collection of sketches centred on his experiences as a soldier and prefaced by a more general essay on the nature of autobiography. The book would also contain 'A Childhood in the Chapel' (his radio script expanded) and possibly 'The Blood Letting', a long unpublished story written before the war. In discusssion it was agreed that the story be dropped in favour of the two *Encounter* pieces, 'Innocent Abroad' and 'The Great Good Place', with the latter standing by way of an epilogue. Rees submitted a typescript recast along these lines but without the prefatory essay. This arrived some months later: 'I hope it will serve its purpose and I don't mind saying that it has taken me almost more trouble than the rest of the book put together', he wrote in August 1959. With the essay came some sentences for the blurb, designed to underline the volume's consciously distinctive approach:

> This is not an Autobiography but a collection of 'autobiographies', in which the author's character varies with, and takes the colour of, the circumstances in which it finds itself. It is an attempt to recover from the past some of the most vivid chapters in the author's life . . . These incidents and scenes are presented for their own intrinsic interest and do not attempt to present any coherent account of the author's personality; indeed the effect is, with intention, rather the opposite.

A Bundle of Sensations: Sketches in Autobiography duly appeared on 14 July 1960. Rees's blurb was printed, as was his expression of gratitude to the journal that had helped revive his fortunes after the Aberystwyth débâcle; to the editors of *Encounter* he owed 'more than a formal acknowledgment for their generous help and encouragement at a time when these were not easy to find'.[4] The book captivated the critics. Connolly's praise in the *Sunday Times* ('delightfully refreshing and intelligent . . . so cool, so collected, so analytical an arrangement of consciousness') was echoed by senior reviewers: *A Bundle of Sensations* was brilliantly effective, sensitive and exact, amusing and touching in its accounts of high and low life, and written in unforced prose of enviable elegance and clarity. What is more, it sold – 2,600 copies by the close of 1960, with a further thousand going to the American market. In all, it seemed a brilliant breakthough at the start of a new writing career.

Yet throughout the 1960s financial pressures led Rees towards quite different kinds of book: some repackaged *Sunday Times* articles (*The Multi-Millionaires: Six Studies in Wealth*, 1961), a historical guide (*The Rhine*, 1967), and *St Michael: A History of Marks & Spencer* (1969). None of these works is negligible, *St Michael* least of all. Sir Simon Marks, chairman of Marks & Spencer, greatly warmed to Rees – they had met in connection with *The Multi-Millionaires* – and commissioned him to write a full company history. It was a world which fascinated Rees; he shadowed Sir Simon on his company visits ('like a very good battalion commander carrying out an inspection') and drafted his chairman's speeches. And if *St Michael* veered towards hagiology – Marks & Spencer as a characteristically Jewish concern, transcending the limits of business and evolving into a general philosophy of enterprise and human relations of significance to society as a whole – its factual research was thorough and ably presented (Rees had access to in-house researchers). *The Great Slump: Capitalism in Crisis, 1929–33* (1970) was an altogether more ambitious undertaking, a study of the Great Depression, that international economic crisis which began with the Wall Street crash of 1929 and came to a close (so Rees would argue) in 1933, with Roosevelt's inauguration as president and Hitler's assumption of power. Confining his account to three leading countries – the United States, Germany and Britain – Rees considered the capitalist breakdown not exclusively in terms of economics but within the social and political conditions which had produced it. As A. J. P. Taylor observed, besides his technical grasp of banking and financial systems, the author had a real feel for the period, having lived through it himself. It was the Great Depression, Rees suggested, more than the Great War, that 'fixed a gulf between what went before and what came after; . . . like some seismological disturbance it shifted the ground on which men stood'. An accessible study, with much vivid detail and a breadth of literary reference, *The Great Slump* was generally ap-plauded, notwithstanding its frequent inaccuracies; shorn of his researchers, Rees, in Taylor's words, was 'a somewhat slapdash historian'.

Besides his authored books, Rees periodically produced translations from the German. In 1937 he published *Danton's Death*, a version (with Stephen Spender) of Georg Büchner's *Dantons Tod*, the epic drama by the author of *Wozzeck* which spoke to the British Left as it had done, a decade previously, to the German expressionist theatre. Then came *Conversations with Kafka* (1953), Rees's rendition of Gustav Janouch's book of reminiscences (a much expanded edition appeared in 1971 though lacking Rees's magisterial preface). The immediate post-Aberystwyth period saw a flurry of radio commissions, including translations and adaptations by Rees of Brecht's political morality *Die Ausnahme und die Regel*, Georg Büchner's novella *Lenz*, and Heinrich von Kleist's verse drama *Das Käthchen von Heilbronn*, all these in Third Programme productions.

A Chapter of Accidents (1972) was long in the making. As early as 1955, while Rees was at Aberystwyth, he contemplated a book about his relations with Guy Burgess, from the moment of their first meeting in the thirties to the point of the diplomat's defection to Moscow. As he explained to Chatto & Windus:

> Burgess was my oldest friend, and in one way and another I think I knew more about him than any one else; and what I did know was in many ways very strange indeed. So much so that, given his strange end, my knowledge has become rather an obsession, and until I write it down I feel I shall never get rid of it. The greater part of the story is concerned with his past, and with my own past, and other people's pasts, rather than with his melodramatic end. It seems to me to reflect some strange and rather lurid lights on the society we live in . . . In any case I feel I have to write it down, and am doing so at great speed, and very soon will send you some of what I have written. One of the troubles is that I feel I cannot finish anything else until I have done this.

The Burgess material lent itself to different treatments, some of which he suggested to his literary agent David Higham as soon as Burgess and Maclean resurfaced in Moscow (11 February 1956). The immediate upshot was the notorious version rewritten by a professional journalist and published with shattering consequences by the *People* newspaper (April–May 1956). When the dust had settled, Rees returned to an earlier idea of recasting his reminiscences as fiction – for whenever he thought of Guy it was as an extraordinary character in a novel or a play – and in 1959 he accepted an advance for a novel about Burgess and Maclean. Ten years later talk had turned to some kind of sequel to *A Bundle of Sensations*; the new book would be 'both a chapter of autobiography and a reflection of English (and also Welsh) life between 1930 and 1955'. Chatto warmed to the proposal, advancing the author a further £500 but incorporating a deadline for completion. This passed with no sign of a text, as did other 'absolutely cast-iron' delivery dates as Rees worked to finish *The Great Slump*, the revised *Conversations with Kafka*, and a fascinating edition of Koestler's

Darkness at Noon.[5] Rees now promised Chatto a greatly expanded manuscript, a prospect which excited them while not wholly dispelling the feeling that they were once more being taken for a ride. However this time Rees delivered, if again a year or so late.

The wait had been worthwhile; as with *A Bundle of Sensations*, the *Sunday Times* purchased serial rights, printing three controversial extracts in advance of 10 February 1972, the date when *A Chapter of Accidents* appeared to high critical acclaim. The book was a superb performance and made compulsive reading: A. J. P. Taylor devoured it at one sitting ('a fascinating story'); Michael Foot spoke of a tale superbly told, 'with a suave and subtle brilliance which carries all before it'; Geoffrey Grigson – not an easy man to please – found the book 'extraordinarily occupying and suggestive', while to Philip Toynbee it was 'as full of fine *obiter dicta* as . . . of vivid descriptions'. Hugh Trevor-Roper thought the social analysis perceptive and just: 'Nowhere have I read a better exposure of "the liberal illusion" of the 1930s . . . as literature and as autobiography this book is unique' – a viewpoint challenged in part by Richard Crossman, who questioned Rees's reading of political history and the handling of his relations with Burgess. Still, the book was brilliantly readable: 'Treated as a *nouvelle* – fiction based on fact – it is without doubt a minor masterpiece' (both he and Noël Annan agreed that the portrait of Burgess was masterly). Buoyed up by such reviews, Rees took part in televised discussions and gave press and radio interviews, and on the back of this kind of promotion *A Chapter of Accidents* reached fourth place in the *Evening News*'s bestselling non-fiction list. Not everyone was impressed. What was brilliant social analysis for Trevor-Roper was for Harri Webb, incensed by the pages on Wales, the 'obsessive chronicles of snobbery, sodomy and treachery', with the author resembling 'nothing so much as an ageing daughter of the night . . . parading in the pathetic finery of a bygone day on some windy corner long deserted by the traffic of pleasure'. Rees took offence at this *Planet* review, to the point of threatening legal action; and he must have been particularly repelled by Webb's reference to one of Rees's early Oxford friends, the German patriot Adam von Trott, who was executed for his part in the plot to assassinate Hitler. Webb likened Rees to Trott, the man 'who played with fire and only had himself to blame for getting burnt, an empty character, with no loyalty or sensibility'.

Though at heart a Chatto author, Rees during the sixties had published four books with Weidenfeld & Nicolson, who paid him particularly well. Now he appeared with Hutchinson as the unlikely editor of John McVicar's prison writings.[6] At the core of *McVicar by*

Himself (1974) is McVicar's insistence that 'all the penal measures adopted in this country are, as a means of reformation, a joke'. Rees's introduction dwells on this, and on the 'machismo' which McVicar believed to be the basis of his own criminality; far from exposing machismo as 'a kind of romantic illusion, a form of false consciousness', his experience of long-term imprisonment reinforced it. McVicar's change of mind and heart (his 'conversion' as Rees depicted it) arose from the discovery of 'a higher order and value' in the life he was able to live for two years with his wife and child, after his sensational escape from Durham. Regarding his role as editor, Rees is characteristically modest: McVicar's manuscripts were 'a considerable literary achievement' requiring little attention from himself; he did not consult the author, having been refused permission to visit him in prison. McVicar judged things differently, insisting that the book would never have been published but for Rees.

By the early 1970s Goronwy Rees was a fixture at *Encounter*, the prestigious politico-cultural monthly he had joined in February 1966, shortly before it was confirmed beyond doubt that the CIA had backed the magazine financially. Rees survived the ensuing tumult, to flourish under the beneficent eye of Melvin Lasky, the long-serving American joint editor: 'he was enormously talented and he represented the spirit of the magazine', said Lasky of Rees. *Encounter* indeed became his spiritual home; he liked the people and the atmosphere there, and he endorsed the journal's ethos: its cosmopolitan breadth, its wish not to departmentalize literature and politics and, most crucially, its anti-communist line. As regular monthly columnist Rees eschewed displays of personality for cool, dispassionate analysis (he signed himself simply 'R'); the tone is civilized, his pieces beautifully crafted. *Brief Encounters* (1974), a selection from Rees's column urged on him by others, exhibits some dominant themes: the counter-culture and the cult of Permissiveness; education and the universities; the condition of the media (Pope's goddess Dulness still reducing 'life, society, literature, art, to an indiscriminate assemblage of bits and pieces in which nothing is of more value than anything else'); violence in books and films – when Bernard Levin alluded to psychological studies questioning the link between 'sado-pornographic *reading* and similar *doing*', Rees asked whether he would place much faith in such researches, 'if they assured him that a reading of *Der Stürmer* had no practical effect on those who carried out its sadistic recommendations'. Though an ardent cold warrior, Rees could not be classified as of the Right or the Left. He stood by the Western intellectual tradition ('reasonable men in reasonable discourse about common themes') in opposition to political autocracy, and the flight from rationalism dismayed him – in the eyes of the counter-culture, the commitment to reason was the original sin of the West.

Outstanding in *Brief Encounters* are the essays on the world of Lytton Strachey (importantly homosexual, though this dimension is commonly overlooked) and on Berlin in the twenties, a reminder that the glamorous veil thrown over the epoch by cultural historians hides a rotting dung-heap of human suffering. Both essays draw on personal experience and lifelong interest, as do most of Rees's more valuable *Encounter* pieces. He is always impressive on Germany (its literature and modern history), on the Soviet Union and the dissidents (Solzhenitsyn especially, a hero of his), on English intellectuals and the political climate of the thirties. America featured regularly in his columns and, at a time of great anti-Americanism prompted by the Vietnam war, he struggled to make intelligible 'the contradictions between what Americans are at heart and what their government does in their name and what they do in the service of their government'. Rees's knowledge of the political culture of the United States astonished Diana Trilling, yet this was merely one field in which he read voraciously. For Rees lived in books and literature, as Jenny Rees attests: her abiding memory is of him working at his desk each morning before a lunchtime trip to the pub; then afternoons spent reading in his armchair, book in the left hand, cigarette in the right, a glass of whisky at his side, 'in his little oasis of calm'.

In 1973 he agreed a £2,000 advance for a book entitled 'In the Thirties', a commission swept aside by a far more lucrative undertaking, a company history for a multinational corporation at a fee of £15,000, plus expenses. Research for *Dalgety: The History of a Merchant House* took Rees to America, Canada and Australia in 1975, after which the work appeared in a private printing for the benefit of the directors only. Rees produced no more books, though he kept up his *Encounter* column to the end, despite his failing health. For the October 1979 issue he turned in a review of Isaiah Berlin's *Against the Current*. It was to be Rees's last piece, and it suggests a growing hospitality towards a view of life and the world which is at odds with the main current of classical Western thought; meditating on Berlin's essays, Rees speaks of 'the unique reality of the individual human being as the centre of the experience which streams in on him from within and without. This belief has no logical or rational foundation; yet it is this alone which ultimately gives meaning and significance to human life.' Isaiah Berlin was one of a few old friends who visited Rees towards the end, as he lay in strike-bound Charing Cross hospital (there, in November 1979, *Encounter* marked his seventieth birthday with a party in his room). It was to a newer friend that Rees, prompted by a remark of Cromwell's close to death, looked back on his life and confessed the influence of his father's religion: 'I was brought up a Calvinist and taught that if one was born one of the elect, one never ceased to belong – a doctrine which had strange effects on me . . .' These words, as good a guide as any to a complex, baffling man, were written on 7 December, five days before he died.

Goronwy Rees: The Memoirist

Rees, like every memoirist, purposefully reshaped his past. The publishers' report on *A Bundle of Sensations* voiced an immediate concern: the book was not strictly an autobiography because it lacked a continuous thread and was short on personal detail – 'one learns nothing of the writer besides the clear fact that he is a very acute observer'. Rees's reply, in the prefatory essay submitted some time later, made clear that for him conventional autobiography was an impossibility; he could not provide what the form demanded, a created character or personality with its own continuous history. If novelists invented other people, autobiographers invented themselves, a far more difficult task for one who did not enjoy the conviction of an integrated, enduring self – something over and above the moderately consistent persona we all present to the outside world. On the contrary, fundamental to his make-up was the feeling that he existed only in the moment, a disposition which set him oddly apart (except – the implication is – that others might find themselves in his company if they were to acknowledge the vagaries of their own behaviour). In support Rees called on David Hume (the self as 'a bundle of different perceptions'); he might have mentioned Walter Pater, an early hero (all we have is 'a drift of momentary acts of sight and passion and thought'), or André Gide, whose capacity for self-transformation excited him. He did quote Whitman approvingly, as he had done as an undergraduate, moving between Oxford's sweet life and serious study at home: 'Do I contradict myself? / Very well then I contradict myself, / (I am large, I contain multitudes.)'

The comments on personal identity may strike us as mischievously provocative – in admitting our contradictory natures we do not lose our sense of self – but they are of a piece with a credo that elevated the collective as distinct from the individual experience; Rees's daughter Jenny recalls how he might dismiss an argument with, 'You are simply making a statement about yourself. It is not interesting.' Likewise he refused to put selfness at the centre of his book; he would instead look outwards on a life of dramatic turnings, selecting 'detached episodes arbitrarily abstracted from the changing current of experience, like pieces of driftwood which someone drags ashore from a flood in order to make a fire'. His bonfire burns so beautifully because it has been carefully laid, and in accordance with his expectations both of autobiography and of fiction proper; for as the novelist of worth looks on men and women as 'types' not 'characters', as embodiments of social and historical forces transcending the individual, so Rees as autobiographer strives for the representative status that would relate him to his generation and its times.

A feeling of being bound up in history must have come naturally to one who had witnessed the triumph of Nazism at first hand, and Samuel Hynes has commented that writers who came of age in the thirties were more than usually generation-conscious;[1] uniquely challenged by social realities, they gravitate in their autobiographies towards accounts that would explain their generation's predicament. 'Innocent Abroad', one of the two German chapters in *A Bundle of Sensations*, admirably illustrates this; engagingly intimate, it nonetheless defines the attitude of young left-wing intellectuals to developments in Germany. Like many of his literary contemporaries, Rees was compulsively drawn to Weimar, 'a country of the imagination', as he describes it – a culture not circumscribed by place or by any one sphere of interest. In art, literature, music and theatre, in philosophy and science, in social progressiveness and sexual freedom, Weimar caught the spirit of modernism, an antidote to bourgeois Britain and Oxford's dusty wisdom. Immensely creative and immensely destructive in its search for new values and systems, Weimar met all the aspirations of the young, who under its influence extended their sympathy to the German people at large. Thus Versailles became an iniquitous treaty, the upshot of a hideous war fought between rival forces of indistinguishable guilt. Yet German socialism was liquidated and Weimar killed stone dead. On the estate of a Silesian baron Rees hears a reading of history that became the myth binding Hitler to his people: the belief that Germany had not been defeated in battle, that she had lost through the treachery of politicians at home. In the Prussian east, home of militarism and autocracy, they spoke of the old German virtues – simplicity, loyalty and truth – and of a poison in the blood, an alien virus carried by communists and Jews. Drinking schnapps in a forest cabin, Graf Felix Waldstein and his military comrades contemplate the revenge that will allay their hatred and humiliation; in such a setting it had a dream-like quality, akin to the political silliness Rees heard from the Baron's son. Except that Germany awoke to this nightmare – 'it was Weimar which was the dream'.

The *TLS* believed that 'Innocent Abroad', more clearly than anything in Isherwood, conveyed the reasons for 1939. Rees lays down some significant markers: the traumatizing effect of 1918; the semi-mystical belief that German strength and values derived from native soil; the appeal of pan-German *völkisch* nationalism and of the soldierly ideal; above all, the inability of outsiders to come to grips with the German mind – witness the delegations of British gentlemen who would do pilgrimage to Germany in the hope of reaching some understanding with the Nazis. Rees casts himself as another innocent, a stance which the drama critic Harold Hobson felt inclined to query, together with other aspects of Rees's narrative; in a discussion of the book on radio he interestingly suggested that the entire admirable essay had been directed not by factual recollection of what the author had heard and felt at the time but by artistic motives – predominantly a wish to explain the path to Hitler. Truth is different from facts; Rees's essay was a work of art, and also of artifice.

'Scenes from Military Life' adopts the position of socialist intellectuals on the eve of the Second World War, their faith and optimism exhausted by a decade of civil and military turmoil. Belief in justice and co-operation as agents in international diplomacy had all but been destroyed, while in Europe the forces of democracy and progressive socialism, which would carry the working classes to victory, were in disarray. War was to be resisted precisely because the working classes most stood to lose by it; the pacifist strain, running back to the costly, indecisive battles at the outset of the First World War, was deepened by the belief that once again the little man was being asked to put his life on the line for a system that offered him nothing. Once again there seemed to be no distinction of guilt between opponents: Hitler and Chamberlain were two sides of the same coin, so that to serve in the British army under a Conservative government was close to mortal sin ('like going to battle for the devil himself'). Though this might have been true for others, Rees's claims of identification with them are not wholly supported by the facts. Six months before war was declared he had volunteered for military service, an act without parallel among his friends and one they regarded with horror. Yet it was a principled action, wholly consistent with his understanding of affairs. Since the early thirties he had felt convinced that war was coming, that Hitler was bent on world domination, and that appeasement, far from slaking his appetite, simply inflamed it. (Rees resigned his post on *The Times* over Dawson's policy of appeasement.) Meanwhile, Britain was disastrously ill prepared for any serious military confrontation and had to achieve a position from which she could fight effectively. All this Rees had argued in his journalism, and far from slinking off guiltily into the Territorials, he set out his position with great moral persuasiveness in an article for *Horizon* which made plain how at odds he was with his literary contemporaries.[2]

His immediate experience of the Territorials seemed to confirm their warnings, that the whole business of military service was a ridiculous waste of time. He met boredom and futility in an ill-directed unit composed of two London tribes: City gents and East-Enders, bank clerks and barrow boys, and wandering between them, misfits like Whitey and himself. The intractable Whitey is far removed from Rees's working-class saviours, yet towards the protective ex-boxer from Whitechapel he develops a firm attachment. This heavily fictionalized chapter wonderfully captures the spirit of army life, the camps as oases of peace for men 'not fit to face the harsh realities of ordinary life'; bowling along Holborn Rees's comrades are 'like schoolboys on holiday', for with the loss of identity upon which any army depends comes an exhilarating sense of release from the cares of the outside world (a world which nonetheless regards its soldiers as heroes). Rees has a telling eye for soldiers in groups, as he does for lower-rank psychology: the skiving and manœuvring for small material gain (he himself joins Whitey in the cookhouse). If Whitey is a natural anarchist predestined for the glasshouse, Sergeant Bulford is a classic veteran – the foul-mouthed drill instructor for whom the glories of the regiment are its prodigious drinking bouts. He usurps Whitey's position as mentor, introducing Rees to the military *demi-monde* once it is learnt that this aesthete of squalor is actually bound for Sandhurst. Gunner M. G. Rees shares in the general amazement; All Souls fellow he might be, but with no wish to become an officer. (In reality he swiftly applied for a commission: 'You've got all the brains and guts and leadership necessary, so do not give the impression of slackness and casualness!', advised his referee, Major-General Sir Ernest Swinton.)

That Rees should choose to emphasize his brief experience as squaddie is explicable in the light of his feelings, publicly expressed at the time, and here set down in a paragraph at odds with an otherwise urbanely amusing account, that Britain in the first twelve months of the war found its army in no condition to fight; as a preparation for battle its so-called training camps were an utter waste of time. Dunkirk revealed the deficiencies of a military machine officered by men who had been commissioned, and promoted, for reasons that had nothing to do with the conduct of war and everything to do with class. 'No army ever received a more inadequate education for war or for peace; war itself had to eradicate its results, which were disastrous.' The turn-about was accomplished through an intensive programme of education for all ranks, one in which Rees as intelligence officer played an active part. By recruiting officers from non-traditional sources, by developing new techniques of training, by acknowledging that science and technology had revolutionized the art of war, the British army had so professionalized itself that by 1944 it was able to carry out the invasion of Normandy. But before Operation Overlord came Dieppe, subject of Rees's most controversial chapter.

'A Day at the Seaside' stands out among the writings on the combined air, sea and land operation of 19 August 1942 against the German-occupied port of Dieppe. Rees participated from start to finish; from the initial planning of Operation Rutter to final action on board HMS *Garth*, one of eight naval destroyers allotted to the Operation Jubilee landing (as the aborted Rutter became). Consequently he can provide a fully rounded picture of a calamitous episode – one deemed all too representative of war, where thousands of men, released into the business of killing each other in accordance with the plans of professional strategists, find themselves stumbling through a blur of confused and meaningless action. Risky under optimum conditions, the Dieppe raid was thought necessary in order to gain experience of the problems that would be encountered in any land invasion of Europe; additionally, the German air force would be brought into battle and defeat inflicted upon it. Thus the Canadian troops assigned to the assault were 'not only guinea pigs. They were also bait, the victims of a murderous laboratory experiment designed to arrive at certain results which might have been achieved less expensively, certainly in blood, by other means.' The plan provided for a preliminary bombing of German gun positions, as well as for fire power from battleships moving in support. When it was learnt that such air and sea assistance would not be forthcoming the operation became unfeasible, but at Combined Operations Headquarters Admiral Mountbatten, 'handsome and breezy, like Brighton at its best', so successfully allayed misgivings that 'the operation would have proceeded even if the troops had been asked to land with no better weapons than their bare hands and fists; in the event, they had very little more'.

Analysis of such trenchancy understandably ruffled feathers. In a letter to the *Sunday Times* (which was serializing Rees's chapter) Brigadier Bernard Fergusson, while agreeing that a frontal assault on Dieppe without any covering fire was a risky business, thought Rees seriously deficient in his understanding of how Jubilee had arrived at this position. Fergusson could not speak of the dreadful consequences ('Mr Rees was at Dieppe, and I was not'), and he found Rees's account of them 'moving and magnificent'; it was his background knowledge that was lacking. Rees responded crisply: he had spoken of what personally he had seen and heard; Fergusson objected to his description of the Canadian ground forces as both guinea-pigs and bait, though he could not deny that the operation had been designed to gain experience of a large-scale assault and to provoke an aerial battle; 'in what sense, therefore, is my statement untrue?'[3]

Rees's background knowledge came from Combined Operations HQ where he served as a liaison officer under General Montgomery. The Monty of this essay is strikingly at odds with the intimidating show-off of common repute; it brings out a courtesy and charm largely lost on others – but then others had not met the General at home after dinner, or seen him propped up in bed in his flannelette pyjamas. Rees's much praised cameo pinpoints a donnish aspect in the man, his priest-like air of tranquillity, his ability to listen and to explain (so rare in generals as a class). The calmness is in keeping with the lucidity of mind he brought to his profession – as though the art of war was amenable to rational analysis (the contrasting procedures at Combined Operations tell to Montgomery's advantage). If anything, Rees's respect for Monty increased over time, so that Lord Chalfont would come to call him a 'devoted disciple', a description Rees thought not inapppropriate because Montgomery was indeed a great teacher and communicator – this had been a constant source of assurance to those who served under him. His cautiousness as commander, his meticulous preparation, his careful avoidance of risks, all this was legendary, and attributed by Chalfont to Monty's unhappy relations with his mother. This caused Rees to reply that if this were the case, 'one would be inclined to wish that all appointments to the higher command were reserved for generals with unhappy childhoods'.[4] The British soldier gave his heart to Montgomery and the trust was not misplaced; the survivors of Dieppe, on the other hand, railed against those who they felt had betrayed them. 'I thought that this is what a beaten army looks like', Rees reflected, 'for no army is beaten until it has lost faith and confidence in those who command it.'

'Victory' completes the military triptych. This comi-tragic essay broaches the problems, physical and moral, that faced the Atlantic powers in Germany at the end of the war: the apocalyptic townscapes of a devasted Ruhr and the unscathed psyches of a people who lock away their past – as in smug, respectable Bad Oenhausen where a terminally indoctrinated grandfather is shut in the cage of his room. There is also the Russian presence, ambiguous and unsettling, whether as displaced persons (one-time slaves of the Reich) or as friendly warm-hearted soldiers, the drinking companions of Rees. Ironies abound. The good burghers of Bad Oenhausen and Lübbecke, less shattered by war than the British, cloak themselves in self-pity; are *they* who risked so much in defence of the Jews to be punished by an army of liberation? They do not plead in vain. The victorious forces have become the military government and a British officer-turned-administrator now 'endeavours to succour a people whom, a short time ago, he had been doing his best to destroy'. Rees's first honest German is an unreconstructed Nazi who in a drunken argument becomes an improbable friend. Rees meets him during a Rhineland wine hunt ('I was once again on a war footing'), and his capture of a precious hock establishes British credentials among the Allies.

Evocative of a strange interregnum, 'Victory' plays down Rees's concern with the wider German question – how far should Germany be punished? and at what cost to Europe? – a problem he discussed perceptively in the first few months of demobilization. His disposition in this chapter is once more to stand with the common soldier, with the men who, though dehumanized and degraded by the army fighting machine, instinctively revert to friendship when the conflict has ceased. There was little real hatred of the enemy, even in time of war: rather, a detached respect for others forced to perform the same appalling task. 'But most went glumly through it / Dumbly doomed to rue it.' Siegfried Sassoon's lines on the Great War were more truthful than the rhetoric of war correspondents: the talk of battlefield heroics, of games of strategy, or of a struggle between good and evil. Once the combatants are joined, 'they form a single pattern to which conflicting political and spiritual aims are curiously irrelevant'.[5]

Rees felt a natural kinship with the group of Welsh writers in English who came to prominence in the 1930s. 'A Childhood in the Chapel', the opening chapter of *A Bundle of Sensations*, finely delineates the cradle gifts of the Anglo-Welsh. No doubt his personal circumstances threw them into sharper relief: son of a Calvinist minister in theocratic Aberystwyth, he endured a more than usually gruelling religious education, one spilling over from Sundays into evenings of the working week. A schooling of such intensity left its permanent mark, not least in a love of communication and of rational debate. Rees's father exhibited these qualities, that is, most of the time, for, as if to exemplify Hume, he had no single personality. Sundays transformed him from a man of reason and tolerance into the type of minor prophet who with arms outstretched, like the wings of some great bird, abandoned sense for sound, for studied theatricality ('his voice . . . nicely tuned to crack with grief and passion'). Goronwy adored his weekday father; the Sunday shaman terrified him. The evening service is beautifully captured: the heightened emotions, the overwrought nerves, the rocking harmonies of song. 'I sat in the corner of my pew overwhelmed by some strange bitter-sweet emotion in which happiness and sorrow were equally mixed.' Late sunlight flooding the chapel dissolved the gloom of Nonconformity and all the sadness of Wales, shedding a warmth and radiance that Rees would forever associate with childhood and home. Nature was an unfailing protection in the country-and-seaside town, as was the world of the imagination, whether fed by books or by the flesh-and-blood characters who flocked to his mother's back door. They were the disreputables, the underdogs and outsiders, and their appeal for the minister's wife communicated itself to her son. They offered relief from the respectability of chapel and an assurance that outside its walls lay a realm of 'fabulous freedom and adventure'.

Standing last in the collection, 'The Great Good Place' is in a different key, the most introspective of the essays. Rees lies becalmed in an Ascot hospital following the dreadful accident that brought him close to death. One might say that by May 1957, in the aftermath of Aberystwyth, he was already dead, at least to establishment circles – socially unacceptable, as he puts it, his career and reputation in ruins. His fall had a Wildean dimension: the favourite of fortune brought down by his own hand, his double life exposed, his association with a sordid underworld of deceit and sexual decadence revealed. Now boyish terrors resurface, those issues of sin and hell about which his father preached. He has night-time hallucinations of being steeped in vice and crime, and of desperately seeking escape or else meeting exposure and shame (the imagined backdrop, of unnameable acts in sinister surroundings, suggests a guilt at having succumbed to Burgess). Recovery comes about through the therapy of nature, through the healing powers of the hospital garden contemplated with intense absorption. With the same quiet watchfulness he turns to his fellow patients, discovering the variety and richness of their individual lives. Illness is a democratizing condition, and the public ward a forcing ground for personal revelations offered with a profusion and intensity that leaves Rees exhausted, 'as if, in the course of a day, I had lived twenty men's lives as well as my own'. He discovers the oxygen of such lives: not literature or politics but the 'adventures, and especially disasters, of individual human beings, known not at second-hand, as from literature or from the press, but from the direct experience of daily life'. As if to reinforce all this, Rees concludes with a memorable life portrait of Jock, an institutionalized patient of looks, charm and vitality who awaits a surgical boot for his amputated limb. In Jock, as in Whitey, Rees divines 'a principle of anarchy . . . as much deserving of respect as any other principle by which a man, or boy, may live'. But he fears for Jock as he did for Whitey – another aged boy with the finger of doom upon him – and in truth as he did for himself when he too left the hospital sanctuary for a wholly uncertain future.

One wonders how much Rees offered in exchange for those hospital confidences. He reveals precious little in *A Bundle of Sensations*: nothing about love and marriage, next to nothing of his professional career (though this was as arresting as his love life). He makes no mention of his writings, casually alludes to his Oxford college, and maintains an absolute silence on Burgess and the Aberystwyth débâcle. The selectiveness is typical of a highly secretive man, one who remained an enigma even to someone like Geoffrey Grigson who had known him for thirty years; 'I could say only that he was a slight, quick-moving, engagingly smiling, enviably handsome Welshman, who never seems to age, and always seems to know a great deal more – about exactly what? – than others know.'[6] The kind of person emerging from the book was a matter which preoccupied reviewers. They judged him refreshingly free of rancour towards the Welsh and English establishments that had recently rejected him. Bedazzled by neither, he could endure their loss: indeed, he seemed happier in lesser company. Such modesty of manner was rare in autobiographical writing and warmly to be welcomed, whether a pose or not. Reviewers also took up the challenge of detecting in Rees's bundle of perceptions a greater degree of continuity than he himself had been able to find, some consensus developing around the view that here was a man born to an important father who throughout his life had sought for, and rebelled against, other father figures, both personal and institutional. He had gravitated towards centres of power only to end up in conflict with them. 'The Great Good Place' signalled a change: now a more integrated personality, Rees in turn begins to feel paternal.

With *A Bundle of Sensations* Rees found his true literary voice. Released from the constraints of the novel, from plotting and character particularly, he became more freely creative. Now within an auto-biographical framework – the recollections of an imagined self – he blended the personal and the public, his memorable snapshots of people with acute social analysis. 'A Winter in Berlin' demonstrates the new-found power, skilfully building a sense of menace around visits to individual friends – each one a phenomenon – and against the heightened backdrop of a terrifying historical moment.

Even before *A Bundle of Sensations* Rees had contemplated a book on his relationship with Burgess. He had supplied material on the defect-ing diplomat for five incendiary articles published by the *People* news-paper in 1956. The material, Rees recognized, might also be worked as a novel, and this he attempted to do, only to settle a decade later for a combination of autobiography and cultural history embracing both England and Wales. His much debated reminiscences of Burgess are palpably jumbled in places and his memory for dates here no more reliable than for other periods of his life; additionally, there are discrepancies between his various retellings of the story, and overhanging each one of them, the need to conceal his own pre-war co-operation with the spy. Thanks to the opening up of KGB archives, we know how brief this was and something of what it entailed.[7] It appears that Rees for a little more than a year (1938–9), and in the anti-fascist cause, supplied political hearsay gathered from weekends at All Souls – most probably on Cabinet attitudes to Hitler and the likelihood of a British stand against him. It was material slight in itself, and almost certainly accessible to any assiduous enquirer or reader of the political press, but, as the last professional KGB officer in control of the Cambridge spy ring explains, his colleagues were 'gluttons for information' who valued 'oral material' passed on through an agent such as Burgess. 'In the world of espionage, the greater the prolifera-tion of source material defining the same subject, the greater its credibility.'[8] Burgess had high hopes of his new recruit, only to be disappointed; he puffed him before his Soviet handlers, painting a picture of Rees and Blunt assisting in talent-spotting, at Oxford and Cambridge respectively.

A reader of *A Chapter of Accidents* might sense that Rees was to some degree complicit in Burgess's activities – he reports Maclean's near-the-knuckle remark at the Gargoyle, and his account of the fateful evening when Burgess tried to recruit him has him reacting, not with horrified refusal, but with puzzlement as to how he might help. Yet Rees felt able to affirm that he had never been a spy. He stressed the distinction between public and covert sources of information, main-taining that, though aware of Burgess's Moscow contacts, he imagined it was political intelligence he was after, not Britain's secrets. 'I did nothing', Rees would insist, a defensible position for himself – and apparently also for others in the pre-war period when the recalling of professional Soviet agents as a consequence of Stalin's purges disrupted espionage operations in London. But however slight his involvement, Rees remained important because of what he knew about Burgess and Blunt. In 1939 he promised never to reveal their past connections, on the understanding that these were truly past, that they too, like himself, had thrown in their cards in protest at the Nazi–Soviet Pact. It was a crisis, reported Burgess to his KGB handler, which showed that Rees 'was no Marxist at all'; from the time of the Seventh Congress of the Communist International (1935) 'he began laying his criticism on thick'.[9] How far could he now be trusted? Burgess banked on their friendship – there seems to have been no feeling that Rees's own dip into espionage was sufficient to ensure his silence – but the risk he posed became more worrying as the productivity of the Cambridge agents increased. This is why in July 1943 Burgess advanced the extraordinary suggestion that Rees be physically liquidated; and as the person who had recruited him, Burgess offered to do the job himself.[10]

The Rees–Burgess friendship puzzled a great many people. Interviewed on radio, Rees made it seem quite natural: 'First of all, he was extremely clever by nature: he was full of ideas, and very odd and original ideas always. He looked at the world in a rather different way from most people and this had a charm of its own. He was also extremely funny and I would really do almost anything for people who make me laugh.' But the charm was a hit-or-miss weapon: 'There were some people who were really quite impervious to it and really detested him, but those who fell for it fell for it very strongly.' Another displaced anarchist, one might suppose, of a type that appealed to Rees. Additionally, Burgess was a liberator, as Noël Annan attests: 'one of those students who appear to their contemporaries to be more assured, more able to liberate them from the conventions of family, school or class'.[11] Shiela Grant Duff recognized this dimension, though she judged it differently: Guy brought to mind Rees's Oxford friends, 'all brilliant and clever, but also somehow cynical and amoral', and his reappearance in 1936 cast a warning shadow across her own close relationship with Rees. The attraction to Burgess she linked with Rees's love of Baudelaire. As he explained, Baudelaire saw evil as a quality like colour or sound, and as colour had its particular beauty, so had evil also; what was disgusting morally could be satisfying aesthetically. This was not Shiela's way: 'You think of evil as something to be known and learnt from and almost made part of your life', ran her parting letter to Rees.[12]

The Burgess of *A Chapter of Accidents* is a monstrous hero-villain whose habitual element is near-farce and fantasy: like 'some great actor in a comic role invented by a dramatist of genius', thought Rees, confessing an inability to take Guy seriously. The domestic surrealism, the drunkenness and promiscuity, the lack of self-control – was this the stuff of spies? Rees's failure in the forties to recognize that his friend was still an agent of the Russians has staggered certain critics: did he not know this in his heart of hearts? How else could Burgess's succession of appointments possibly make sense? The careers of the Cambridge spies indeed were classically shaped – they advanced in the service of their country so as better to serve their masters – yet even his Soviet masters had occasional doubts about Burgess. Might he not even be a double-agent planted by British Intelligence? And was the murder plot against Rees really a means of learning about Soviet techniques of liquidation? He was 'a very peculiar person', distinguished from other agents by 'bohemianism in its most unattractive form'.[13] Nonetheless they agreed that he was 'well grounded politically and theoretically'. It is an aspect confirmed by Rees, who speaks of a qualitative difference between the kind of political conversion undergone by Burgess and the experience of other university contemporaries drawn for a while to communism: for them it proved impossible to abandon their liberal consciences in favour of a new morality founded on revolutionary faith and Soviet Party diktat. Burgess despised such fellow-travellers; they saw in communist philosophy some message of hope for their own stricken society whereas he believed England was done for, that no more could be expected of her. Far from a message of hope, his communism reflected a conviction that the world he had been brought up in was totally and irredeemably lost. He deprecated, not celebrated, its passing, so that Rees would come to speak of him as a perverted imperialist who having witnessed the death of one empire now attached himself to another; 'and from such a decision there could be no turning back'.[14]

Rees's own political odyssey is a matter for some debate. He was teased as a 'parlour Bolshevik', for claims by literary Marxists of oneness with the workers had their amusing aspects, especially for each other – as when Stephen Spender reported how Goronwy, at a meeting in support of the Popular Front, 'insisted that he had sprung from the working classes and would at this moment be a miner but for the extenuating circumstances (perhaps to be regretted after all!) of a scholarship to Oxford'. Oxonian he might have been but he was not the upper-middle-class public-school boy. From his time at Cardiff, and his father's work in the Valleys, he knew something of the industrial Depression and the working-class communities it threatened to destroy. In September 1931, soon after his mother's death (a loss which damaged him severely), Rees made a visit to Merthyr, the once prosperous colliery town where crowds lounged listlessly in the streets because there was nothing else to do. 'I can't stop thinking about that incredible town', he wrote to Douglas Jay:

> To talk about goodness and beauty and truth when such things exist seems to me complete hypocrisy. All this worries and saddens me, I think, more than my mother's death . . . Merthyr seems to me a complete negation of life. I can't

really express its significance . . . What one can do I don't know, but one needn't live as if it didn't exist. That's a sort of final treachery to everything one admires.

Merthyr epitomized the chronic condition of the depressed areas, a subject of numerous reports to the National Government. Some time later in the Conservative *Spectator* Rees would press the case for state intervention to create employment, via schemes like the Severn Bridge (a project he incorporated into his second novel). By April 1937 he was urging the need for a minimum wage: every democracy assumed that its working citizens were entitled to lives which were not a burden to themselves or to the state. 'It is idle to argue whether such a belief is true or false; to modern consciences a society which does not fulfil this condition is intolerable.'

But his true political awakening came about in post-1933 Germany. No one who had witnessed directly the consequences of Hitler's seizure of power – 'the betrayal and death of every human virtue; no mercy, no pity, no peace; . . . and sixty million people pleased and proud to be governed by a gang of murderous animals' – could have doubted its historical momentousness. The Nazis were quite obviously criminals who somehow had to be stopped, and this could best be done through a broad alliance of the Left. Rees became active in the Popular Front and embraced a doctrine of salvation through the working classes; the international working-class movement was the real bulwark against fascism and the true vehicle for peace and social progress. In 1937 he was chastising Orwell's inability to conceive of a socialism not essentially driven by middle-class intellectuals: his otherwise admirable *The Road to Wigan Pier* scarcely mentioned a trade union or local Labour Party except to deride them, yet it was through the Labour Party and the trade union movement that the British working class had built up its industrial and political power. The natural complement to Orwell's account of Welsh mining life was not his appeal to London intellectuals, 'but an account of the collier's struggles, as difficult and heroic as his life in the pit, to create the South Wales Miners' Federation'.[15]

By the time of *A Chapter of Accidents* the committed cold warrior (the only Westerner, according to Robert Conquest, to be quoted at length in the Soviet underground press) was blackening his thirties past with talk of the unconditional support and approval he had given to Soviet communism. One might ask for evidence of such backing because it is not apparent in the journalism. True, Rees accepted that Soviet communism was genuinely opposed to fascism – this allowed his co-operation with Burgess – but otherwise he was not duped by the Stalinist dictatorship. For a moment in 1936, influenced by Sir Bernard Pares's witness accounts, he allowed himself to believe that Russia was moving towards greater freedom and democratization. One year later all such hope had evaporated. The execution of eight Soviet army generals defied rational explanation, though 'the sinister routine of arrest by secret police, secret cross-examination, public confession and execution is so familiar that it is rather the prominence of the victims than the methods invoked that creates astonishment. By now it is accepted that M. Stalin governs like an Asiatic despot, who strikes suddenly and swiftly where he will' (*Spectator*, 18 June 1937). Russian communism never had been an expression of the masses; on the contrary, it was a movement for directing the masses, led by professional revolutionaries who embraced an iron framework of ideology and discipline ('It is vitality and desire which makes it impossible to be a communist', suggested Rees in a letter of this period). Post-First World War events in Russia might as well have been the work of criminals as of political revolutionaries, 'for one of the purposes of a revolutionary morality, such as Lenin tried to instil, is to create a standard of virtue which will impel men of the highest character to commit acts which by any other standard must be judged atrocious' (9 September 1938).

Rees had visited Russia and beheld no radiant tomorrow: rather, 'a waggoner standing over a starved horse and flogging it as it died between the shafts . . . a hospital where flies crawled undisturbed over children's eyelids because the Five Year Plan had not allowed for gauze . . . jerry-built tenements run up without plan and without beauty' (13 December 1935). He had read the crucial texts, including Trotsky's *The Revolution Betrayed*. But communism was a house with many mansions and Rees looked to a non-Russian variety that might be something more than gullible young people in the West accepting, out of ignorance or idealism, acts of political violence belonging to a different moral sphere from their own. Courage, devotion and self-sacrifice were not exclusive to Russian revolutionaries: 'in the last two years, in Great Britain itself, communism has inspired no less a devotion and courage in young men like John Cornford and Ralph Fox, than whom none could have been more English' (9 September 1938). With its appeal to human dignity and equality, and to faith in human reason, communism was moving westwards, and in the process surrendering what was purely Russian (a Bolshevist principle of authoritarianism) for what was more fully European. This had happened in France and Spain, where it propelled genuine working-

class movements that frustrated the victory of fascism and were led by
men and women like La Pasionaria, 'through whom Communism
speaks not with the voice of Moscow or of a revolutionary sect but
with the voice of suffering peoples'. Burgess reported his friend's
disillusionment with the Soviet Party and in key political areas Rees
dismissed the Party line: the United States for instance, a country
demonized by Soviet apologists, he saw as a decisive new force in the
modern world. The English public had become accustomed to talk of
the USSR as 'a momentous experiment' but the American attack on
mass unemployment, Roosevelt's New Deal, was infinitely more
important. And Rees looked further:

> At a time when Europe . . . threatens to lapse into barbarism, when the ordinary
> man fears for his security, for the future of himself and his children and of
> civilisation itself, there is some alleviation to despair in the knowledge that on
> the other side of the Atlantic is a great and young nation which may inherit what
> Europe has not known how to preserve, which may help to save Europe itself
> from ruin. (18 March 1938)

Rees stood by capitalism, and by democracy, a capitalist institution;
though 'only states which at home pursue programmes of fundamental
social reform, which will abolish poverty, depressed areas, social
privilege, economic inequality, malnutrition, can hope to oppose the
totalitarian States with a passion and courage equal to or greater than
theirs' (25 March 1938).

Contemplating the near-obsessive public interest in the case of
Burgess and Maclean, Rees noted its adventure-book elements: sex
and politics, treachery and betrayal, suspense, escape and pursuit.
Additionally, there was the feeling that it possessed a higher significance; that like the Hiss case in America or the Dreyfus affair in
France, 'it revealed an aspect of society which would not otherwise have
been so nakedly and harshly exposed. Such cases hold up to society a
mirror into which it gazes with a kind of fascinated horror.'[16] In his
framing of the Burgess story Rees draws out these social dimensions;
oddball though he might have been, Burgess was also a representative
product of English ruling-class society and of the education it received
before the war – or so it seemed to an observer from a totally different
background. What struck a state-educated Welshman was the social
cohesiveness of his Oxford contemporaries: sons of Keynes's 'great
capitalist class', their individual differences – even in politics – were
superficial compared with the underlying likenesses, stemming from a
shared social and family environment. At university class affinities were
consolidated, in great part by a cult of personal relationships deriving

from Forster and the Cambridge Moralists and exhibiting strong homosexual overtones; for in an almost exclusively male society homosexuality flourished as a badge of rebellion and 'among undergraduates and dons with pretensions to culture and a taste for the arts, at once a fashion, a doctrine, and a way of life'.[17] (Rees himself struck Maurice Bowra as a 'normally-sexed pansy'.) Social kinship, caste solidarity, the togetherness of an establishment élite, helped even the renegade Burgess make headway in his career and, so Rees became convinced, shielded him at critical moments.[18]

The sturdier world of Wales is the subject of Rees's opening chapter, warmed by a generous portrait of the loving, godly family in which he grew up, the youngest and favourite child. The Revd R. J. Rees, ecclesiastical scholar and statesman, showed many of the qualities discernible in his son, not least a lack of parochialism, and that 'mysterious, irrational element' which removed him from 'the arena in which worldly success or failure is important'. (It is interesting, too, that Rees *père* should have left Aberystwyth following a bitter dispute within the institution he directed.) Aberystwyth was the childhood Eden out of which Goronwy was cast when in summer 1922 his parents moved to Cardiff. There he was rescued by a grammar school that wonderfully nurtured his talents and by a public library that fed his love of reading. Literature and history naturally partnered the active life; 'we need it for life and action', said Nietzsche of history in an essay much admired by Rees. He approached Welsh history in Nietzschean spirit, fashioning a Welsh identity through his under-standing of the past. The qualities so manifest in his family belonged to the nation at large, the finer gifts of Liberal Nonconformity in its golden age. The common people of Wales, affirmed Rees in 1938, have more 'of passion, intelligence, individualism, and of natural devotion to culture than almost any other I have known' (the Jews were his exception, a people among whom he found many friends).[19] A common language, a widely disseminated literary culture, a fund-amentally democratic disposition, all had flowed from a form of religion by which the Welsh became, no less than the Jews, a people of the book ('literate perhaps even to the point of oversophistication, so that nowhere in the world is the word more easily taken for the deed', Rees would add – attachment to homeland never blinded him to the nation's vices and follies). He praised Welsh educational achievements, crowned by university colleges which, in striking contrast to England, were accessible to the poorest. The Welsh were radicals by instinct, united by 'our common wish for social change and progress', and in Lloyd George they had produced a politician of genius, one truly representative of Welsh rural culture, both in his early triumphs and his later decline. For that rural culture was a thing of the past, a Land-of-Heart's-Desire to which the Welsh intelligentsia were still damagingly addicted. As Rees would later write:

> a people cannot live upon its past, and that past itself, however well loved, ceases to have any meaning unless it is continuously transformed and transmuted in the light of the present. This is a task which modern Wales has conspicuously failed to discharge, and the responsibility for this failure falls pre-eminently upon those who would claim to be its spiritual and intellectual leaders, who, having little virtue in themselves, continue to live on the little that is left of the faith and energy of their fathers.[20]

Harsh on the myths of others, he extravagantly advanced his own in paeans to industrial Wales. He describes how its spirit first touched him as a schoolboy when, on summer camp from Aberystwyth, he met some lads from the Valleys. It was like a Roman confronting the Goths; they were rougher, tougher, jeering and foul-mouthed, 'but they also seemed freer and more adult and less inhibited than the boys I had known, scornful of authority, untouched by the miasma of bigotry and hypocrisy which emanated from the twenty-four chapels of our little town'.[21] South Wales working-class culture had come to exemplify all that was best in the Welsh. 'The life has gone out of the chapel', Rees insisted in the midst of the Depression, and 'the same passion which once characterised Welsh religious life is now to be found in the socialist struggles of the miners'.[22] They epitomized a radical tradition whose principles were more moral than political, owing much to Christian notions of equality and the belief that man does not live by bread alone. The miners' passion for self-improvement encompassed cultural and intellectual matters as well as material conditions – they would never agree with Brecht that food came first and culture a long way behind. The shapers of capitalism, they now led the industrial worker's struggle for a life which recognized his human dignity, and the dignity of collective labour; through them Wales at last was connected to the wider modern world. This remained Rees's perspective. Wales was a land of conflicting cultures: that of the vibrant industrial south, whose resources – political, intellectual and spiritual – owed nothing to traditional culture; and that of an ossified north and west, stultifying and puritanical, sealed off from progressive forces by language and religion. He would recognize no interpenetration of the two, or see the gulf between rural and industrial as anything but unbridgeable.

By his own admission, the Rees who arrived at Oxford was an odd and contrary person, an outsider who would seem to have internalized all the ambiguities and contradictions of Wales. He said as much of Dylan Thomas, remarking the strains attendant upon the loss of a language his parents spoke. Confronted by a neighbouring society that appeared immeasurably more powerful and stable, Thomas 'had tried to take it by storm, and to a certain extent succeeded, but never so much that he ever really felt at home in it'.[23] Rees likewise found no resting place, not in Wales, not truly in Oxford (though seeming to fit him well, it deepened the internal conflicts), not in the certainties of class or the comforts of a settled profession. He remained placeless and disconnected, rarely lonely but not fully absorbed. The condition did not displease him; it provided the psychological core for a promising undergraduate novel and made him the delicate anatomist of an upper-class educational preserve, 'a kind of pheasantry in which the products of the English public school were reared like game birds'.[24]

The same critical gaze he trained on his native Wales when, in 1953, he became Principal of the University College of Wales at Aberystwyth – his greatest mistake, as he later would admit. One understands the appeal of the post to a son of the town who moved in academic circles and had a lifelong interest in education. Rees's further explanation, that he wished to commit himself more fully, both professionally and in the cause of Wales, also rings true. On paper it all looked so promising: as the College's historian writes: 'Exceptionally able, distinguished in appearance, impressively sophisticated, blessed with a winning charm, and brilliantly articulate, Principal Rees seemed ideally equipped for his new responsibility.'[25] Except in the matter of temperament, his closest friends might have said. Would Rees be able to stand it? Could a man who flourished on the London–Oxford axis adapt to life in a small Welsh town where, as he remembered, 'certain standards of conduct and belief commanded, in public at least, almost universal assent'. Was not some strange ancestral impulse returning him to the land of bondage? For Rees, as for many of his generation, Wales remained alive as an emotional compound of childhood, family and landscape – 'in these we find a sense of actuality, because they have made us what we are' – but had featured little in his thinking since the time in the 1930s when he urged the nationalist position. He did so, fundamentally, on the grounds that 'no culture is safe, or can prosper, which is divorced from political responsibility'; a parliament in Wales, 'the natural centre of men's minds and hearts, and of their activities, would bring the values of our culture into the very heart of practical life'.[26] Nationalism could be readily defended, less so its representatives in Wales, especially after Saunders Lewis, accepting (so one hopes) the old saw about mine enemy's enemy, published some flattering remarks on Hitler, a latterday Samson who would bring down the English edifice. This, and Plaid Cymru's assumption of a superior Welshness in its dismissal of the industrial south, deeply offended Rees: to the end he advocated Welsh self-government, while warning that it must bring into prominence 'the most intellectually narrow class of people I think I know'. Inevitably during his principalship the College became a cultural battleground, with Rees at bay for his unorthodox views on Welsh life. He clashed fundamentally with the nationalists over the role of the university in nation-building: the College was rightly a national institution, with two-thirds of its students from Wales, but one function of a university, so Rees insisted, was to help produce people who would be able to look critically at their own society, as it were from the outside and in relation to other societies; the intellectual life precluded blind loyalty to nation. Rees found himself at odds over other issues, especially with the tradition-alists who treated university students strictly as children. The students warmed to him hugely: they loved his approachability, his liberalizing spirit and his intellectual profile; he brought big names to the College and appeared in print and on radio discussing non-Welsh issues. 'The examination room at the College was crowded with students when Mr Rees turned up to address them for the last time', recounted the local *Cambrian News.* 'He was cheered to the echo but despite his popularity among the students there is no doubt that he left Aberystwyth – his home town – a bitter and disappointed man.' Emotional hurt com-pelled an unforgettable portrait of Rees's 'town of the middle-aged', the only instance of his looking back on the past with any degree of bitterness.

No one emerged with credit from the long drumming out of the Principal. He left in humiliating circumstances in the spring of 1957, one year after the senseless moment that permitted a butchered version of his Burgess story to appear in the Sunday press. He had made powerful enemies at Aberystwyth and with the publication of the *People* articles he handed them a knife ('a trigger to fire the rifle of intrigue right in his face', as the Student President expressed it). They used it clumsily, eventually managing to arraign him before a com-mittee of inquiry. The resulting Willink Report found his Burgess narrative appalling – 'more reminiscent of a scandalous novel than of a serious record or a balanced biographical sketch. The description of Burgess's homosexual adventures is flippant and the attitude of the author a-moral.'[27] The Principal, so it judged, 'both in the making of his contract and in its performance, acted in a manner incompatible with the standard required of his office'. Why he had done so remained a mystery but, picking up on Oxford thinking, Willink imagined that the articles might have beeen some kind of pre-emptive strike: by painting his erstwhile friend as utterly depraved and untrustworthy, Rees was seeking to defend himself, and maybe others, against the possibility of embarrassing revelations. His motive was thus 'self-regarding'; there was not 'from first to last any hint or suggestion that he gave a thought to the effect upon the College'. His 'patriotic' argument was rejected: that Rees, fearing Burgess's continuing usefulness as part of an espionage network, had exposed him in the interests of national security (and, so he seemed to imply, with the tacit approval of the Security authorities).

Security was Rees's defence from the outset. His articles would serve as an answer to a Privy Council report finding 'nothing organically wrong or unsound' in the government's security arrangements (a verdict welcomed by *The Times* as 'refreshingly calm and sensible . . . in contrast to the hysterical nonsense poured out in various quarters during the Burgess and Maclean story'). Rees saw a government cover-up of their friends in high places, for Burgess and Maclean, he would insist, were not the only Britons in positions of trust to have been recruited into a Soviet spy ring. The staged reappearance in Moscow was by way of long-range blackmail, a warning to others that they might be exposed if they did not continue in their work. Rees hoped that his *People* articles might lead to a public inquiry which would unmask the fellow conspirators: 'Instead, I was hounded down.' And here one has to endorse Diana Trilling's observation, that beneath Rees's frivolous manner lay a deep political seriousness.[28] His anti-communism was genuine, as genuine as his anti-fascism, and it took root equally early, ineradicably in the post-war years when the Soviet Union turned the countries of eastern Europe into brutal puppet states. In Rees's opinion, anyone who remained in the Communist Party after the 1948 Soviet *putsch* in Prague hardly qualified as a human being. In 1953, to the disgust of the pro-Hiss British Left, he was lauding Whittaker Chambers, the shady apostate from communism; a year later he was speaking of communism as one of the two great heresies of the age. It was to be feared, not on account of Soviet military might, but because it appealed in millions of men and women to the sense of their own human dignity and to the idea that all are capable of achieving it.[29]

> The catastrophe for the Western World today is that the Soviet Union has captured for its own those very ideas of human dignity, of human equality, of faith in the human reason, whatever its limitations, of confidence in the human

spirit, which were the finest fruits of our own civilisation, and thereby has discredited them even in our own eyes. Indeed, in the unceasing intellectual war which the West is now waging with Communism it is very often its own discarded ideals which it is attacking.

If Rees struck openly at Burgess, Blunt was the hidden quarry – the agent who in 1951 had deflected suspicion when Rees first pointed the finger at him and would triumphantly do so again (two months after the *People* furore he received his knighthood). By 1964 Blunt was seemingly safe, with a promise of immunity in return for a full confession; henceforth MI5 (the Security Service) and the British government would do everything to protect him. Meanwhile the Oxford establishment continued to ostracize Rees, the ratter on friends – 'Give Guy my warmest love, and tell him that none of us are speaking to Goronwy' was Isaiah Berlin's message passed on by Tom Driberg in Moscow. As Robert Conquest remarked, 'the moral lunacy of Rees's critics hardly needs rubbing in'. Whatever his delays and evasions, his failure when denouncing others to come clean about his own past involvement in espionage, Rees proved to be right about Blunt, and about Burgess also. Rees insisted that Burgess had 'wrought more damage to Britain than any traitor in our history', a judgement at odds with the surprisingly widespread feeling that Cambridge espionage, though active for fifteen years, did little serious harm, but one now seemingly confirmed by Soviet sources: 'Undoubtedly, the damage inflicted by Philby, Burgess and Blunt can only be described as colossal, and on a much greater scale than has ever been publicly admitted.'[30]

The post-Aberystwyth period tried Rees to the very limit and he suffered a mental breakdown that needed hospitalization. A psychiatrist's report attributed his illness to feelings of guilt and shame at having let down his father and the rest of the family. Whatever its specific source – and Jenny Rees sees the guilt as largely deriving from his brief surrender to the Soviet Union – there seems no denying the sense of guilt that Rees carried within him. It must have been bound up also with his failure to act more properly, more decisively and more honestly, concerning his knowledge of Burgess: *A Chapter of Accidents* conveys the turmoil of conscience surrounding the long suppression of dangerous facts. There was a difference between right and wrong, and the son of a Calvinist manse wished to do what was right. No matter friends and country, Rees had betrayed himself. 'Nothing is really valuable but integrity', he had written to Shiela Grant Duff, 'but it is very elusive and once you have lost it, I think you will never see it again.'

In Wales the cultural establishment rejoiced at Rees's downfall, Alun Richards remarking how his reputation came to resemble Keidrych Rhys's – consorting with them even was 'somehow a danger to one's chances of respectability . . . These were not men who would enhance your career.'[31] The obloquy surrounded Rees's perceived anti-Welshness, a state of affairs which did nothing to silence him though in truth Wales was never at the centre of his interests; he had always, since before his time at Oxford, sought to attach himself to broader cultural flows ('I think it terrible this feeling that the most important thing about you is being a Welshman'). Even so, he wrote of 'the fatal Welsh instinct for sentimentalising, sweetening and vulgarising whatever is best in their own people'; of the absence of self-criticism ('the Welsh fall easily into complacency and flatter themselves interminably'); of the language question as diverting intellectual energy from other more creative things (and of 'the illusions and evasions which make any serious discussion of the Welsh language almost impossible within Wales').[32] In the 1960s he failed to recognize any popular groundswell of support for the language, and seemed perplexed by the wish of younger people to make a life for themselves in Wales – the Welsh would really have to go through an internal revolution if the country was to become a place fit to live in. By the late seventies he sensed they were doing so, and in ways he had not expected; Wales had decidedly changed for the better – 'hardly the same country as we once knew . . . a happier place than it used to be'.[33]

Interviewed by the *Scotsman* in 1972, Rees summed up his life as 'a restless one, with far too many jobs taken on, too many worlds either conquered or left in a mild state of chaos because of [my] arrival on the scene'. A fair assessment, one would have to say, of the post-war years in particular. The war was the crucial turning-point, for after six good years in the army Rees turned his back on intellectual journalism, the field that suited him best. Here was one world conquered then quitted too soon (though reoccupied again with distinction for the last fourteen years of his life). From university he had drifted into journalism, and, at a time when good openings were rare, parted company with both the *Manchester Guardian* and *The Times*, excellent nurseries for budding journalists, especially if they came from All Souls and sought to make an impact beyond the academic sphere. Then in 1936 the *Spectator* rescued him with a part-time post that perfectly matched his interests and gave him entrance to London intellectual life. Besides a passion for literature, and a keen engagement in political issues (as opposed to party politics), Rees brought to the assistant editorship a technical grasp of economics and a knowledge of foreign affairs that in relation to Germany placed him in the category of expert.[34] Though reluctant to admit it, he proved an accomplished professional whose frank, clear-sighted leaders regularly stirred up debate. Nor should one overlook his literary criticism, which made much of the writer's function and notions of artistic responsibility. Rees insisted that this did not mean a commitment to any particular political position, or to any kind of overt social activity; but 'it does imply, while imposing no restraint on forms of expression or even the most ambiguous machinery of mythology, or fantasy or imagery, that the content of the artist's imagination should be the reality of his time'. Generally Rees found the requirement better met in European literature – he was a great comparatist – and pre-eminently in the nineteenth-century French masters whom he admired both as writers and as social critics. On demobilization Rees rejoined the *Spectator*, only to resign in a matter of weeks for an opening in the engineering business managed by his great crony, Henry Green. It was a startling departure, even by Rees's standards and albeit at the end of the war, a natural moment for change. No doubt his success as a soldier encouraged him, since military service had uncovered new strengths and confirmed that the known ones were fluid and might run into other channels; as senior intelligence officer he had used his journalistic skills, as he would shortly do again, on afternoons away from Pontifex intelligence-gathering for MI6. Rees could be many things by turn, and nothing for very long. His sense of himself as a writer evaporated in 1937 with the failure of *A Bridge to Divide Them*, the book intended to signal a central shift in his fiction away from psychological drama towards 'a real world of people and events'. The challenge proved beyond him. 'My new book promises well, but I can't get on with it', Rees confessed to Douglas Jay; 'no satisfactory style, the old will not do and there is an embarrassment of a vague, unformed mass of material.' Before Shiela Grant Duff he was more despairing: 'I try to describe very complicated things when I can't even describe a man walking down the street'; 'that damned book' had damaged his confidence but not destroyed it completely. 'I will be very good one day', he felt able to assure her. Two decades later, freed from fiction, how magnificently he delivered on his promise.

❧

A Bundle of Sensations

❧

Foreword

I

For as long as I can remember it has always surprised and slightly bewildered me that other people should take it so much for granted that they each possess what is usually called 'a character'; that is to say, a personality with its own continuous history which can be described as objectively as the life cycle of a plant or an animal. I have never been able to find anything of that sort in myself, and in the course of my life this has been the source of many misunderstandings, since other people persist in expecting of one a kind of consistency which, in the last resort, they really have no right to demand. It has also given me, in the practical affairs of life, a certain sense of inferiority to my fellows, who have always seemed to me to possess something which I lacked, as if I were short of an arm or a leg or were otherwise deficient in what is usually regarded as constituting a normal human being. How much I admire those writers who are actually able to record the growth of what they call their personality, describe the conditions which determined its birth, lovingly trace the curve of its development and accurately assign to nature and nurture their exact part in this process; and how satisfactory it must be to be able to say at the end of the story (and no autobiographer is quite without a certain pride in saying it): 'Here I am; this is what made me and what I made of myself, and now you can see exactly why I am as I am, and could not conceivably be any other.'

For myself it would be quite impossible to tell such a story, because at no time in my life have I had that enviable sensation of constituting a continuous personality, of being something which, in the astonishing words of T. H. Green, 'is eternal, self-determined, and thinks'.* As a child this did not worry me, and if indeed I had known at that time of *Der Mann ohne Eigenschaften,** the man without qualities, I would have greeted him as my blood brother and rejoiced because I was not alone in the world; as it was, I was content with a private fantasy of my own in which I figured as Mr Nobody. For I was quite certain that I had no character of my own, good or bad, that I existed only in the particular circumstances of the moment, and since circumstances were always changing, so fast, so bewilderingly, so absorbingly, how could it not follow that I must change with them? I was quite content, even blissfully happy, that this should be so; the notion of a self, a character, a personal identity, if it had ever occurred to me, would have seemed strictly one of those things which only adults possess, like bowler hats, or umbrellas, or long trousers. For myself I had no need of it and was happy to enjoy an existence in which I hardly distinguished myself from the natural objects around me, and was as safely, as deeply, as warmly embedded in the physical world as a child is in the womb. If I could have found any metaphor to describe what that kind of life was like, it would have been that of a single wave of some boundless ocean which incessantly changes with the ebb and flow of its tides and the passage of sun and cloud across the heavens which it reflects.

But of course this kind of thing could not go on. The entire structure of our society depends upon the fiction of an individual and responsible 'I' which shall be the object of rewards and punishments, and into such a society even a child like myself had one day to be inducted. From time to time I was punished, for actions which seemed to me in no way different in kind or quality from others for which I was quite as unreasonably praised. There were rules, it was explained to me, there were conventions, there was a system of morality, which it was one's duty to follow; how could I explain, at that age, or even now, that in my case, as far as I could see, there was no one to follow them?

One of my misdemeanours was so grave that my father for the only time in his life beat me, and my mother prayed on her knees beside me that God would save me from the bottomless pit into which I was so inevitably falling. But I wanted to say that this was all nonsense; there was no such thing as the soul they hoped to save, either by beating or by praying; who were they, although I loved them, to thrust upon me this intolerable burden of an 'I' which, so far as I could understand it at all, was nothing but a fiction invented by adults to justify the tedious and colourless world, so different from my own, which they chose or were forced to inhabit? But to say this was well beyond any powers of thought or expression which I then possessed; even as it still is, for the notion of a continuous, identical, responsible self is so much a part of the structure of our language that to describe the bliss of existence in which 'I' has no part is to invite self-contradiction. And yet life is not governed by the conventions of grammar. What I cannot do now, I could not do then; all I could do then was to cry, both because of what I felt myself in danger of losing, and because I hoped that my fears might be taken as an act of contrition by the person my parents expected me to be. And perhaps for me this was the first act of hypocrisy which all children are asked to commit at some time or other.

II

When I was an undergraduate at Oxford, I was misguided enough to read philosophy, for which I had no talent; and only a highly developed faculty for imitation and mimicry allowed me to satisfy the examiners in the schools. My lack of talent depressed me, and all the more, perhaps, because of my persisting conviction that I had no real existence except for the sensations which I enjoyed or suffered at the moment. For I had learnt by now that if I ventured to make such an assertion, no one would take what I said seriously, or, if they did, took it merely as one more proof of my total incapacity for philosophic studies. They may indeed have been right, yet it was with a sense of blinding revelation that one day I read in Hume's *Treatise of Human Nature* the words: 'But setting aside some metaphysicians . . . I may venture to affirm of the rest of mankind, that they are nothing but a bundle or collection of perceptions, which succeed each other with an inconceivable rapidity, and are in a perpetual flux and movement.' This seemed to me to describe exactly my own experience; I felt as if I were no longer alone in the world; and I read Hume's chapter on *Personal Identity*⋆ with the same feeling of joy as Robinson Crusoe came across the footprint of Man Friday, and all the more because Hume was after all no naked savage but himself a philosopher whose views demanded a good deal more respect than mine.

But alas! I soon found that it was even worse to profess Hume's views about the identity of the self than to put them forward as my own. In the one case they could be taken merely as a sign of stupidity which might be curable; in the other they were a mark of downright wrongheadedness which might well prove to be incorrigible. For Hume has always been regarded, particularly at Oxford, as a kind of rogue elephant which has run amok in the fields of speculation, and anyone who chose to imitate his example laid himself open to the severest censure. I was soon taught that Hume's error had been finally exposed by Bradley's retort to the psychologist Bain: 'Mr Bain collects that the mind is a collection. Has he ever thought who collects Mr Bain?'⋆ This seemed to me witty but not conclusive; yet I soon realised that if, in spite of Bradley, I persisted in following Hume, I should inevitably involve myself in the most serious trouble with my tutor, H. W. B. Joseph,⋆ who for three years wheedled, cajoled, threatened, and bullied me into holding the philosophical views which he thought appropriate to a scholar of New College; that is to say, into a curious form of Platonism which seemed to have received the personal blessing of William of Wykeham.⋆

Joseph was one of the last, and certainly one of the most ferocious *epigones* of the old-fashioned Oxford school of realism, and I imagine that now no one takes his views seriously except for a few pious disciples. But as an educator of youth he was an alarming figure, or at least he was to me. His methods of argument were peculiar in that he combined with a powerful and ingenious mind an uncanny capacity for making one feel that if one disagreed with him one was not only intellectually but morally at fault. For Joseph, the true was the good and the good was the beautiful and anyone who had empirical difficulties in reconciling these propositions was either mad or bad or both, and I was often in great danger of being relegated into one of these categories, though with a kind of unwilling affection Joseph persisted in trying to look after my spiritual welfare. There was certainly no place in Joseph's philosophy for Hume's scepticism about the self, and when I was tempted to wonder, as I still wonder today, whether Hume may not after all have been right, I put the thought away with a guilty feeling that I had been near to committing not merely an error but a sin; for Joseph they were really indistinguishable.

Yet in spite of Joseph, my childish fantasy of existing only in the moment, and of being only what the moment dictated, still lingered in some deeper stratum of the mind than he had been able to reach; it was so native and so fundamental to me that I would have said it lingered in the subconscious, if Joseph had not explained to me that the subconscious mind is a contradiction in terms and hence an illusion foisted upon the world by a wicked Viennese called Freud. (All Viennese were wicked to Joseph.) In the same way he had refuted Einstein, crying triumphantly, when some lecturer on the theory of relativity had incautiously used the metaphor that space is curved: 'But curved in what?'*

But as I trudged loyally behind Joseph along the dusty paths mapped out by Plato, T. H. Green, and Cook Wilson,* from time to time Hume's words recurred to me, and in the privacy of my rooms, like an Early Christian in the catacombs, I opened the proscribed texts: 'The mind is a kind of theatre, where several perceptions successively make their appearance; pass, re-pass, glide away, and mingle in an infinite variety of postures and situations. There is properly no *simplicity* in it at one time, nor *identity* in different; whatever natural propension we may have to imagine that simplicity and identity. The comparison of the theatre should not mislead us. They are the successive perceptions only, that constitute the mind; nor have we the most distant notion of the place where the scenes are represented, or of the material of which it is composed.' How delightful it was to think that, after all, Joseph was only the victim of a *natural propension* to an illusion; and often after a more than usually censorious tutorial from him, how comforting it was to read Hume's ironic dismissal of the metaphysician: 'He may, perhaps, perceive something simple and continu'd, which he calls *himself*; tho' I am certain there is no such principle in me.' But even as I write these words my hand trembles, and I hear the high-pitched, admonitory querulous voice of Joseph, sitting in his armchair beneath his Indian fretwork over-mantel, as ugly and persistent as Socrates, and know that once again I have fallen into error and sin.

III

I offer these reminiscences of my childhood and education, certainly not because I believe them to have any philosophic value, but simply as some explanation for the chapters of autobiography which make up this book. Like Hume, I find no trace in myself of that *something* simple and continued which most autobiographies take for granted; and I find it difficult to believe that a continuous history of any person can be written without a degree of falsification which must make it, however dull or trivial it may be, in some sense a work of art. Indeed, one might define autobiography as the art of creating a self which does not exist, of applying to oneself the trick, which every novelist uses, of constructing out of the flux of impressions which is all that experience offers us the illusion of a continuous personality which is identical with itself through all the changes it suffers in time. But if the trick is to be performed at all, one would rather it were performed by an expert. After all, we do not expect of an autobiographer, as we do of a novelist, that he should invent incidents and scenes which are in themselves interesting, moving, or delightful; all we expect of him is to invent *himself*.

So that there is, and with intention, little or no continuity between the various episodes I have tried to describe; they are to be taken simply as a few of the scenes which make their appearance in that theatre of which Hume says that we have no notion of the place in which they are represented or the materials of which it is composed. The most one can say of these episodes, so far as continuity goes, is that a large part of them are concerned with the war and its aftermath; but I do not think that anyone could find any logical thread between my experiences in the military labyrinth through which I strayed in such bewilderment for nearly six years. Here all is chance, accident, absurdity. Perhaps indeed the only profitable aspect of the atrocious business of war is that it exposes the principle of indeterminacy which governs all our lives in all its nakedness and simplicity; for war makes such a mockery of all personal pretensions that for ever after we recognise them, or should recognise them, for the illusions that they are.

If it is not possible to find any logical sequence in the incidents of my military career, it is, so far as I am concerned, even harder to find any connection between the boy who attended chapel three times a Sunday in Wales and the unrecognisable, almost anonymous, victim of a motor accident who lay in a hospital bed at Ascot nearly forty years later. If I were to suggest that I could find any continuous process of growth which united the one person with the other, I should be guilty of what would be in my case a conscious act of hypocrisy. No doubt, as the admirable Hume would accept, it may be necessary for us for practical purposes to present to the world a *persona*, a public image, which is reasonably self-consistent and may support the legal and moral obligations which society imposes on us; but it is useless to pretend that such an image has anything to do with the reality of subjective experience.

So that the chapters which follow are simply to be taken as detached episodes arbitrarily abstracted from the changing current of experience, like pieces of driftwood which someone drags ashore from a flood in order to make a fire. If they have any value it is only because, at the moment they were lived, one's sensations seemed particularly vivid and awareness of them particularly heightened; also perhaps because one has tried to set them down without any of the falsification which would be required if one were to represent oneself as something which is 'eternal, self-determined, and thinks'. But perhaps, in putting these episodes together, I have not been entirely free from a certain curiosity whether someone else may not be able to find in this bundle of sensations a greater degree of continuity than I have been able to do.

A Childhood in the Chapel

I was born in Cardiganshire, in the small seaside town of Aberystwyth, which had the distinction of being the seat both of the first Welsh university college and of the National Library of Wales. So much learning was almost too much for its inhabitants; they felt as if Providence had selected them to be the intellectual leaders of their nation, and this seemed only natural to them. This gave them a kind of smugness, which was increased because the little town also had thirty or forty churches and chapels, mostly chapels, which gave it the astonishing proportion of one place of worship for every two or three hundred people.* When I returned to Aberystwyth in later life, the decay of faith even in that remote corner of Wales had reduced the number of chapels to about twenty-five and the proportion of chapels to population had slightly but not noticeably decreased, but the provision of the means of grace was still far more lavish than anywhere else in the British Isles; perhaps they were more needed.

For a child this gave the town a rather forbidding aspect. On my way to school every day I passed a Salem, a Shiloh, a Tabernacle, a Bethel, and a Moriah; it was like taking a walk through the Middle East, and indeed I cannot think of Israel today except as a Welsh-speaking, Nonconformist country. My father was the minister of one of the largest Nonconformist chapels, of the Calvinistic Methodist denomination, and this made him a person of considerable importance in the town.* Ours was a theocratic society, ruled by priests and elders; they formed a sort of unofficial Sanhedrin which exercised an absolute dictatorship over the morals and behaviour of the town. My father shared in the respect and devotion which was shown to all ministers of religion; they ranked in society even higher than Professors at the University College, being less learned perhaps but more holy, and being armed moreover with all the authority of the law and the prophets. There were some Professors, of course, who were also ministers of religion and preached regularly every Sunday in the chapels of the town and the surrounding countryside, but strangely enough they were not highly thought of; they were like unlicensed amateurs breaking into the strictly professional mysteries of religion.

For his children my father's position had serious and, as it seemed to us, unfortunate consequences, for we were expected to practise our religious observances even more strictly than other children, who were, after all, children of the world. On Sundays, when we were very small, we only attended chapel twice, for the morning service and for Sunday school in the afternoon; as we grew older, we were allowed to attend the evening service, and there were also additional forms of observance to begin and end the long day, like *hors-d'œuvre* and savouries to give variety to some immense and wearisome banquet. The morning service involved learning a few verses of scripture, which the children recited to the congregation; this was an opportunity for exhibitionism, and I always felt that I had a special responsibility, as my father's child, to learn longer and more difficult passages than anyone else. I once learned the whole of the One Hundred-and-Nineteenth Psalm,* but to my chagrin was not allowed to recite it all through, though my feat of memory and piety was warmly commended.

For Sunday school we prepared during the week by studying selected passages of scripture, together with a printed commentary which was provided in the form of little pink, blue, or green booklets circulated at the beginning of the year throughout all the Sunday schools of Wales. The religious sects in Wales at that time had really achieved the kind of object which Napoleon set himself in his reform of the French educational system; at half-past two on a fine Sunday afternoon any minister of religion could look at his watch and assure himself that every properly brought up child was at that moment reading, studying, expounding, discussing, the eleventh verse of the sixth chapter of the Epistle to the Hebrews, together with the appropriate notes from the learned commentary of the Rev. Elias Jones, DD.*

Sunday was followed by Monday when in the evening after school we attended, as a kind of refresher, the Band of Hope; this was primarily a temperance association, designed to strengthen one against all kinds of temptation, where we took solemn oaths to abjure all forms of gambling, swearing, and alcoholic liquor; for some reason no oath was required of us against sexual indulgence, and I could not understand whether this was because it was too trivial to mention or too serious to be contemplated. We also studied a little catechism in a red paper cover called *Y Rhôdd Mam, The Mother's Gift*, of which I can now remember only some of the opening words:

Q. Beth yw Creadigaeth?
A. Gwneud peth o ddim.

Q. What is Creation?
A. Making something out of nothing.

As we grew older we also attended, on Wednesday, the Prayer Meeting, when to our alarm our elders exercised themselves spontaneously in prayer, and on Thursday night there was the *Seiat,* or Session, a fellowship meeting which was also a kind of public confessional, in which they discussed various aspects of religious experience, usually of a highly personal and embarrassing kind. The Prayer Meeting and the *Seiat* could often be very frightening to a child; it was alarming to see one's elders beat their breasts and bare their hearts, violently proclaiming and denouncing their sins, which were often of so complicated a kind that we could not understand why they should arouse so much emotion. For a child, however, there was always the possibility of a diversion, because some of the most devout of our members were subject to fits, and one knew that these were likely to be brought on by any particularly violent explosion of religious passion. As the speaker's eye rolled more wildly, and his discourse grew in intensity, one kept one's eye nervously on one's elderly neighbour for any signs of those convulsive tics, the agitated movements of head and body, which meant that at any moment he would be seized by two devout and stalwart chuckers-out, recruited for this very purpose, and dragged foaming at the mouth from the meeting place. Somehow one did not regard such incidents as in any way abnormal; they seemed a part of religion itself, only more exciting than most of it, and had a kind of horrible fascination in which repulsion and curiosity were equally combined.

All these services and meetings involved study and application and often the ability to follow theological arguments of considerable complexity and refinement. They formed an entire course of religious instruction which was superimposed on the secular processes of education and left a much deeper mark on one. They also involved the use of a different language, because they were conducted in Welsh, while in school in those days we were taught in English. English was the language of the world; God spoke in Welsh, and it was a puzzle why the Bible had been composed in Hebrew and in Greek.

One of the effects of this precocious training in theology and dialectics, conducted entirely through the spoken and written word, which made no appeal to the senses and despised the frivolous charms of ritual and ceremony, was to make all of us children intensely argumentative. Our house was the scene of an endless debate in which we all, including my father, who was the eldest and most reasonable, and myself, who was the youngest and most violent, took part on terms of equality. Like a French revolutionary assembly, we were in permanent session and we never adjourned; to the most ordinary and trivial affairs of daily life we applied the pedantry and acrimoniousness of textual scholars. But if in these disputations my father revealed himself as the wisest and most tolerant of us, on Sundays he became completely transformed, and to a child like me in the most alarming way. For on that day he seemed to lose the personal and individual character by which we knew him and for which we loved him during the week; he put on the mantle of the prophets, and became merely one in the long succession of preachers of the Gospel who from time to time occupied the pulpit in our chapel.

In memory I see myself now as a very small and rather stout child seated in the corner of our family pew. Facing me, at about the height of my eyes, is a small locker fixed in the corner of the pew, in which we kept our Bibles and hymn books, and where my brother and I secreted toys, sweets, and picture books which we had managed to smuggle into chapel. At this moment, I have just ceased playing with a long-eared mouse made out of my pocket handkerchief, and deprived of distraction I swivel my eyes half right to where, high in the pulpit, towering over me, a huge black figure, angry and eloquent, its arms outstretched like the wings of a great bird, is preaching endlessly on the tremendous themes of sin, grace, redemption, and eternal punishment.

In those days, it was usual for the Welsh preacher in the peroration of his sermon to enter into what is called in Welsh the *hwyl*, which is a special form of impassioned utterance half-way between speech and song, and so rhythmical and emotional that sense gives way entirely to sound. A Welsh preacher in the *hwyl* would not shrink from the most grotesque and bizarre effects; a simple appeal for funds for the mission field would become an elaborate play with the musical values of the words *Shilling, Patagonia,* and *Timbuctoo.* When the preacher moved into the *hwyl*, it was formal notification that he had become possessed of the living Word, that the *afflatus* had descended upon him; he spoke as if with the gift of tongues, but the tongue was Welsh embellished with the most striking and esoteric words which happened to fit in with whatever rhythmical scheme the preacher was pursuing at the moment. This peculiar form of oratory, more closely allied to the tricks of tribal magic than the theology of Calvin and Augustine, could sometimes be strangely moving and impressive, even though the element of art and of artifice in it was always apparent.* But every art has its decadence, and even as a child I was already living in the silver age of Welsh preaching; as practised by those who were merely performing a technical trick which was part of the stock-in-trade of every Welsh preacher, the *hwyl* could seem merely cynical, a cold-blooded imitation of old masters in whom it had been the genuine voice of passion. In the mouths of novices merely following the style of their elders it could be ludicrous and embarrassing; but whatever form it took, the *hwyl* was, for a child, terrifying.

One saw before one's eyes a man, whom one had taken to be a man like any other man, quite suddenly transformed into a kind of witch-doctor, demoniac and possessed; it was as if, without any warning, he had gone off his head. As a child I saw this happen on innumerable occasions and in a variety of forms; indeed, amongst our preachers, it was the rule and not the exception. Sometimes the trick was performed by one of the great popular artists of the Welsh pulpit, a man with the looks, the exquisitely arranged and silvered locks, the beautifully modulated voice, of a tragic actor; sometimes by men who had the violent passion and bitter eloquence of prophets; sometimes by some naïve, unlettered minister from an isolated chapel in the hills of Cardiganshire, whose sermon was quaint and touching like a primitive painting. But whatever form it took, the *hwyl* inspired fear and terror in me, and a kind of shuddering shrinking from such a bare-faced, bare-breasted display of real or simulated emotion; and also a kind of alarm, because my father also could become, whenever he chose, a victim of this kind of possession. I resented it because in my heart I felt him to be a great man, too good for this kind of thing. Now I never like to read the chapter in the Acts* which describes how the gift of tongues descended on the Apostles; I feel that I know how they looked and spoke.

And I remember that once I seemed to have incurred the direct displeasure of whatever power it was which moved men to behave in this mysterious way. My brother and I were not always as attentive as we should have been to my father's eloquence, particularly when he swung into the *hwyl*; we were apt to avert our eyes, because we knew we should have to meet him again at lunch. In the shadow of our pew, behind a barrage of Bibles and hymn books, we could nearly always organise some distraction like noughts-and-crosses. But this Sunday our game, whatever it was, gave rise to a whispered quarrel, which developed into a scuffle, and finally degenerated into an open brawl. At the climax of his sermon, my father found that the attention of his congregation was being drawn gradually, irresistibly, away from him to the scene that was being enacted in our family pew. It was no good that the *hwyl* was upon him, no good that his voice was nicely tuned to crack with grief and passion, no good that he was ready to strike just those rhythms most calculated to move his audience; all these effects were destroyed by my scandalous behaviour.

My father paused in the flood of his argument; he frowned; he lifted his hand to silence me; he directed at me all the unspoken condemnation of which he was capable. It was quite useless. I was beside myself, provoked to indignation or frenzy by some imagined offence of my brother's against the rules of our game. Finally, with a terrible gesture of his left hand, like the hand of God himself, my father pointed at me with his forefinger and with the voice of one casting out devils spoke the words: 'Remove that child.' I suppose that his voice, his manner, his gesture brought home to me the enormity of my offence, and terror and panic began to enter into my frenzy of indignation. I screamed, I howled, I kicked, I clung to the pew, I refused to be removed. I wonder how many endless sermons, how much Bible reading, I was avenging by this act of rebellion; but at last I was overpowered by my elder sister and carried, still screaming, down the aisle and into the street.

I suppose that my father, who was incapable of being cruel or unjust, was on this occasion provoked to desperation by the shame I had brought upon him, and decided that my offence required some exceptional punishment. He adopted the expedient of totally ignoring my existence during the days that followed. He could not have done anything more effective or more terrible. It seemed to me that this time I had really committed the sin against the Holy Ghost, that I was beyond forgiveness, that I was expelled for ever from my Father's presence. I hardly knew indeed whether it was my heavenly or my earthly father who was punishing me in this way. When I saw my father in the pulpit, I hardly distinguished between him and the God whose religion he preached, and somehow I always felt that during the week God also, like my father, took time off, as it were, from the more frightening aspects of his work. Calvinism is not an easy or a comforting religion, but at least it has for the elect the knowledge that they can never fall from God's grace, whatever their sins. All my childhood I had had the comfortable confidence that, as my father's child, I could not fail to be among the elect; it was as if I had been put down from birth as a member of my father's club. But now, when my father turned his face away from me in such displeasure, it seemed as if grace had been taken away from me as finally and mysteriously as it had been given, and for days I trotted like a puppy at my father's heels, vainly trying to make him recognise that I existed, sinful though I was.

Fortunately my father was never as harsh as Calvin would have had him be. In the end he relented, he spoke to me again, I was forgiven, and permitted to enter the chapel I had disgraced. Once again I could listen to the sermons and to the Welsh hymns which used to stimulate my childish nerves and emotions to an intolerable pitch. In summer especially, at the Sunday evening service, the tension they created sometimes seemed to be unbearable. The late sunlight used to fall through the tall windows in great golden waves that washed against the green and gilt Corinthian columns that supported the gallery; it was as if sea and the sunset were flooding the chapel. Welsh voices singing raised one and rocked one on a flood of harmony; the air inside the chapel was close and warm and drowsy; I sat in the corner of my pew overwhelmed by some strange bitter-sweet emotion in which happiness and sorrow were equally mixed, while above me in the pulpit the preacher continued to denounce our sins and expound our need of grace. And afterwards we walked through the grey streets of the ugly little town, now crowded with chapelgoers returning home, to Sunday supper at my grandmother's, where my brother and I stared at the Victorian illustrations in the bound copies of *The Quiver* and *The Strand Magazine,* until after supper we all collected round the piano and I stood, half-asleep, holding my mother's hand while we all sang once again the hymns we had sung all day in chapel; until at last the pressure of feeling seemed to grow so huge within me that I burst into inconsolable, inexplicable tears. My mother kissed me and caressed me, murmuring that I was tired, and took me on her knee where I fell asleep with the tinkling notes of the piano still in my ears.

Years later I came across a poem* which seemed to express so exactly the mood of those Sunday evenings in my grandmother's little parlour that I wondered who its author could be; for what English writer could have had precisely that experience which for me was so deeply coloured by the sadness of Wales and Nonconformity?

> Softly, in the dusk, a woman is singing to me;
> Taking me back down the vista of years, till I see
> A child sitting under the piano, in the boom of the tingling strings
> And pressing the small, poised feet of a mother who smiles as she sings.
>
> In spite of myself, the insidious mastery of song
> Betrays me back, till the heart of me weeps to belong
> To the old Sunday evenings at home, with winter outside
> And hymns in the cosy parlour, the tinkling piano our guide.
>
> So now it is vain for the singer to burst into clamour
> With the great black piano appassionato. The glamour
> Of childish days is upon me, my manhood is cast
> Down in the flood of remembrance, I weep like a child for the past.

Yet strangely enough even the near-hysteria of such evenings is drowned for me by the particular golden-yellow haze of evening sunlight in the chapel, so that even the gloom of Nonconformity seems to dissolve in its glow. And children have strange ways of protecting themselves against too violent an assault on their emotions. Sometimes, for whatever reason, we were allowed to stay at home on Sunday evenings instead of going to chapel and then our favourite game was to stage our own version of the evening service. My brother took the part of the preacher and conducted the service from a pulpit constructed out of a massive armchair; his sermon, flavoured with childish smut, seemed to me the wittiest parody in the world, and himself the most brilliant and charming of parodists, and I laughed as much as I sometimes cried in chapel. My sister sat at the bookcase and with wonderful dexterity manipulated the books as organ stops; I, being the youngest, formed the delighted congregation, staring up open-mouthed as my brother went through the points of his sermon. It was best of all when he gave his own version of our favourite sermon by one of the greatest actors and exhibitionists of the Welsh pulpit.* It was a sermon about Noah and the Ark, in which the preacher re-enacted the whole story of the Flood, taking in turn the parts of Noah himself, then of his sons, then of the animals entering the Ark, giving to each part its appropriate dialogue, human and animal, and with wonderful and primitive realism transforming the Bible story into a drama that could have taken place in any farmyard of any little Welsh farm in the hills.

This was by far my favourite game, and the element of mockery in it provided a release for nerves and emotions overwrought by so many religious exercises. But there were also other forms of release; for though the shadows of so many chapels fell across our little town, it also lay in the centre of a wonderful bay at the mouth of two rivers which flowed torrentially down from the hills in a series of waterfalls and cascades. The coast stretched immediately north and south in a crescent of jagged cliffs broken by little coves, and every Saturday in summer my brother and I set out with billy-cans and haversacks to cross the cliff to a little bay a few miles away. There we bathed and explored the rock pools and barbarously cooked our food and made tea, and finally, warm with sun and sea, we lay in the sand and read for hours and hours until the sun had gone down.

For our precocious education in Biblical criticism had made us passionately, inordinately, fond of reading any book that was not the Bible and did not require a commentary. Our preparations for our excursions always began with a walk into the town to buy our supplies and visit the Public Library to borrow enough books to last throughout the day. Then we walked home, only our desire to read our books was so urgent, that we read them as we dragged at a snail's pace through the town, holding them before our eyes as we walked, so that sometimes when we reached home the book was already finished and we were no better off than when we started.

We read so blindly and so voraciously that at a very early age I became a kind of literary adviser to my uncle, who was a Professor of

Philosophy at the University College* and a hopeless addict of thrillers and adventure stories; today he would have loved science fiction. I was responsible for introducing him to the works of Edgar Rice Burroughs and together, a small boy and a tall thin absent-minded man, we would gravely discuss the merits of each of the *Tarzan* books as they appeared; he would eagerly ask me whether I could put him on to anything else that was equally as good. But whatever the books we read, for me they populated the shores and cliffs and the great shining semicircle of the sea with a crowd of fabulous figures; on the long golden sands that lay a few miles away from us I looked for the dark-skinned Italians of *The Pavilion on the Links*.* For me these creatures of the imagination seemed to merge and become confused with the real figures of flesh and blood who inhabited our town, and all the more so because my mother had an instinctive and intuitive sympathy with all the unfortunates, the eccentrics, and the failures of life; they were her own form of release from the intolerably oppressive respectability of the chapel, and, sometimes to my father's irritation, she attracted them as flies to the honey pot. So that to the back door of our house flowed an endless stream of fantastic and disreputable characters, never seen in chapel, who called in the certain confidence that they could depend on my mother's inexhaustible love and charity. Such creatures, gypsies, tramps, drunks, the outcasts and ne'er-do-wells of the town and the wild country behind, often in rags and always penniless, offering for sale worthless objects which my mother always bought, performing useless services which only my mother would have invented for them, were an assurance to a child that somewhere outside the walls of the chapel there existed another world of fabulous freedom and adventure. And for me this world was in some strange way both the world which I read of in my books and the world which existed on the hills and the shores and the sea which surrounded our priest-and-professor-ridden little town.

Innocent Abroad*

I

It is hard now, nearly thirty years later, to explain even to myself the kind of attraction which Germany exerted on young men of my generation at Oxford. The image of Germany which we found so seductive has been irretrievably shattered by the events of the last twenty-five years; at the most a few scattered splinters are left, like the shards and fragments from which an archaeologist tries to reconstruct a lost civilisation. To try to recover the original image of Weimar Germany by which I, and so many others, were attracted is like trying to restore some lost masterpiece which has been painted over by a succession of brutal and clumsy artists; and in this case the task is all the harder because the masterpiece never really existed and the Germany of Weimar in which we believed was really only a country of the imagination.

First of all, one would have to reconstruct the illusions under which we suffered at that time; the illusion, for instance, that in the war of 1914–18 there was no distinction of guilt between the Allies and the Central Powers, and that both sides were equally responsible for that appalling catastrophe; to which we added the emotional and irrational corollary that somehow or other the defeated were less responsible than the victors. In this illusion we were happily confirmed by reading Brandenburg, Lowes Dickinson, and Sidney Fay.* It followed, for us, that the terms of the Versailles Treaty, which was then hardly older than the Potsdam agreement is now, were manifestly unjust, a pure assertion of the rights of the strong over the weak, and of the victor over the vanquished; and for this reason it was clear that Germany deserved our sympathy and our understanding more than any other country, including our own. It must be remembered that we were very young men, who will always respond to ideas of this kind. The young dislike power, because they do not share it; the middle-aged adore it, because it gives them some assurance that the world will continue to be as they have known it.

We were all agreed, therefore, that the terms of the Treaty were unjust; it was equally obvious that they were futile. This illusion was firmly founded on Maynard Keynes's *Economic Consequences of the Peace*.* Thus the Treaty was evidence not only of the brutality of the Allies, but of their stupidity. By contrast, Germany, still suffering under the injustices of the Treaty and without power to redress her wrongs, appeared as an innocent victim calculated to appeal to all our liberal and progressive instincts.

To those who said that, whether the Treaty was just or unjust, Germany might one day try to redress her defeat by force of arms, we replied scornfully that such fears ignored all the realities of the international situation; for we set great store by realities. For did not the League of Nations, supported by all the power of the Allies, exist to prevent the recurrence of war? We could not refrain from adding that even to question the power and intention of the League only threw further suspicion on the post-war policies of the Allies. But even if the League, as an instrument of Anglo-French capitalism, could not be trusted, was it not clear that there was an even stronger foundation for our belief in the maintenance of perpetual peace between nations? For the real bulwark of peace was not the League but the international working-class movement, and was not Germany, with its massive trade union and social democratic organisations, the strongest representative of that movement?

In saying this, of course, we were expressing our feelings just as much about our own country as about her defeated enemy. To sympathise with Germany was a mark of our violent revulsion against the Great War and its consequences, and against the generation which had helped to make it and to conduct it to victory. Germany was for us at the opposite extreme from everything we disliked in the land of our fathers; Germany, indeed, had done her best to kill our fathers, and we were not ungrateful to her for her efforts and sympathised with her failure, and to adhere to her cause and her culture was for many of us the most effective and the easiest protest we could make against the England of Mr Stanley Baldwin, Lord Birkenhead, and Sir William Joynson-Hicks.*

For politics were only a part of our infatuation with Germany. Weimar also represented to us all those experiments, in literature, in the theatre, in music, in education, and not least in sexual morals, which we would have liked to attempt in our own country but were so patently impossible in face of the massive and infuriating stupidity of the British middle classes. Was it not typical that our own *Beggar's Opera*, which as produced by Sir Nigel Playfair and Lovat Frazer* was nothing more than a pretty and insipid operetta, should under German skies become the cynical and subversive farce of Brecht's *Dreigroschenoper*?

We received reports of these experiments, not only through the Press, through German films, through books, but by word of mouth. Ever since the inflation young Englishmen had visited Germany in greater and greater numbers, and they returned to us in Oxford with wonderful travellers' tales of this land of freedom and, even better, licence; where one could be on the right side, the proletarian side, in politics, and at the same time take advantage of the fact that social disapproval had ceased to exist; where morals had been discarded as a bourgeois prejudice; where sex was permitted, indeed encouraged, to take any form it chose, however eccentric; where night-club tables were decorated with phalli made of marzipan; where Mr Issyvoo* was having a perfectly delightful time living in a slum in the Hallesches Tor; what more could a young man need to satisfy his heart's desire?

II

It may well seem to others, in the light of what happened later, that only a lunatic could have been quite so foolish as I was in those days; yet what I have written is by no means an exaggerated account of what I thought and felt about Germany at that time. I was very much a creature of fashion; I found the attraction of Germany irresistible; and so, in my first year at Oxford, I determined that in the summer vacation* I too must make the pilgrimage to Weimar and to Wedding, see the whores and the queens and the lesbians on the Kurfürsten-damm, observe the violence and confusion of German politics at first hand, so that I might have at least some idea of what politics might be like if they were properly conducted; I too must tramp in the Black Forest with the *Wandervögel*,* and breathe the inexpressibly sweet air of a society in decay. And indeed I succeeded in my objective of going to Germany; I should have felt terribly ashamed of myself if I hadn't; but somehow, as so often happened to me in those days, things turned out entirely differently from what I had intended.

Perhaps the reason was that I, unlike most of my friends, had no money for foreign travel; I used to wonder bitterly why I could not win scholarships to maintain myself in some *Nachtlokal** in Berlin instead of in the Wykehamist respectability of New College. How much more I should learn, I used to sigh. If I was to reach Germany in the summer I had to have a job, and so I answered an advertisement for a tutor to teach a German boy who wished to learn English. The advertisement gave no name nor address but simply invited applications and for a few weeks after I had replied I wondered happily what my destination would be if I were lucky enough to get the job. Would it be Berlin? I thought. Would I meet Mr Issyvoo and savour the delights of Hallesches Tor? Or Hamburg, which was highly recommended by the more extreme hedonists among my friends? And whom would I live with? Social-Democrats? Communists? Poets, musicians, sculptors, painters? It seemed to me at that time that the entire population of Germany consisted of left-wing politicians or artists of some kind.

The reply to my application put an end to all these speculations. I had indeed been successful; somehow I had never doubted it; for how else could I get to Germany that summer? But somehow my pupil's address had never figured in any of my day-dreams; there was something about it which even to me, infatuated though I was, looked somewhat barbarous and repellent: *Boguslavitz, bei Breslau, Schlesien.*★

This was not at all what I had anticipated; and the name of my employer was equally disconcerting: Herr Baron Franz von Reichendorf. It seemed to me impossible that out of the eighty million people in Germany I should have picked on a Silesian baron to spend my long vacation with. The name itself had sinister overtones. I had associated war, for the Germans, with a desperate struggle against odds which in the end proved overwhelming, with defeat, disaster, starvation, and revolution; and somehow this had made the Germans sympathetic. The name Reichendorf had none of these associations; the only holder of it of whom I knew had indeed been killed, but he had been killed in his glory as a famous German air-ace in the Great War.★ He had been a part of everything in Germany against which Weimar was a protest. There was nothing about him which was either pitiful or defeated; his name had the sound of something formidable, a *nasty* ring, almost, of heroism. I hardly dared say it myself as I set out for Germany, but I had a horrid feeling within me that once again I was going to find myself, as so often before and after, *in the wrong set.*

III

These feelings did not become quite clear to me until I found myself in the train from Berlin to Breslau. Until then my preconceived picture of Germany had not been seriously damaged. Cologne especially, with its great clean glass-vaulted station, had delighted me; here was *Modernismus*, here was *Baukunst*,★ here was Social Democracy at work! I thought with contempt, mingled with pity, of poor dingy old Liverpool Street, from which I had set off to Harwich the day before. From Cologne to Berlin the train had been crowded, and from the carriage window I caught sight of new buildings, factories, offices, villas, in steel and glass and concrete; I had an impression of a universal coming-and-going, of large numbers of people catching and leaving trains on purposes which, I was sure, were connected with politics, art, or literature. After all, what else was Weimar for?

In Berlin, I only had time to cross to the *Ostbahnhof*; with a pang of the heart, I had to leave Wedding, Alexanderplatz, the Kurfürsten-damm unvisited. It was like passing through Rome without seeing the Sistine Chapel. And as the train left the *Ostbahnhof* I became aware that a strange, almost sinister emptiness had descended upon it. There were no more comings and goings on urgent and exciting business; I sat alone in my compartment and when I walked up and down the corridor I saw that the other compartments were deserted also. And as the train rolled through the dusk, across a plain which seemed as sombre, monotonous, and featureless as the dusk itself, it suddenly seemed to me that I had still as far to go as when I had landed at The Hook that morning. I felt as if I had already crossed Germany once that day; could it be that there was another Germany to cross before I reached my journey's end? As darkness fell, I stared out of the carriage windows and on the bare platforms of deserted stations I saw strange incomprehensible names that seemed more Slav than German. I felt suddenly and acutely that if this were indeed still Germany, it had nothing to do with anything I had known or thought about Germany until now.

Journeys make us abnormally sensitive to impressions; landscapes acquire a significance which they do not usually have; we find hidden meanings everywhere. When night finally blotted out the views from the carriage window, it seemed to me that the train racing into the darkness had no reason to stop or even falter until it reached the shores of Asia. What occasion could there ever be to halt in that everlasting plain which repeated itself for mile after mile like a sad, meaningless refrain. I felt slightly frightened, perhaps because I was tired at the end of the long day; but also because, alone in my brightly lit compart-ment, I felt as if I were travelling through some immense solitude. I told myself that such feelings were absurd; after all, Breslau was not Kamchatka,* and thousands of very ordinary travellers must take precisely that same route from Berlin to Breslau every day. It was only, I said, that I was rather cold, that I had been travelling for a long time, that I was tired; that, after all, I *was* a very long way from Oxford and even further from my home in Wales. It was no good; whatever I said I could not shake off my impression of a landscape that stretched around me for thousands of miles, flat, grey and mournful, of the darkness outside that was not the familiar comforting darkness of home but was foreign, alien, and somehow hostile. It even *smelled* different.

To restore my spirits I went to the restaurant car where I ate a large and heavy German dinner, and treated myself to a bottle of wine and drank too much German brandy. I said to myself that here I was, at eleven o'clock at night, in a *Mitropa* car, alone, in the middle of Europe, that if I wanted to I could go on as far as Warsaw, or even farther, that there was no one who could prevent me from doing exactly what I liked, and that therefore I ought to be very happy; but I could not reassure myself, my melancholy only deepened. When I returned to my compartment I fell asleep, and when I awoke at Breslau I was still so dazed with sleep and drink that I hardly had sense enough to get out. When I did so, I stood for a few moments alone on the platform until a man in a peaked cap and a leather coat came up to me and said that the Herr Baron was waiting for me at the hotel and he was to take me to him.

He took my bags and led me to the car, an ancient open Adler, and drove me through the empty streets to the hotel. There, waiting for me, were Herr Baron and his son Fritz, who bowed and spoke to me in very broken English to which I replied in even more broken German, and they said that I must be very tired after my long journey, and that they hoped I would be very happy at Boguslavitz, and that Fritz had a horse for me to ride; I suddenly felt that these were very kind people, and they insisted on my drinking some coffee and a great deal of brandy. It seemed to me that they said they were hoping to shoot some wild cats on the way home, but I felt that this was too improbable to be true and that I must have misunderstood them.

I was really too tired to take in much of what they said or where I was. In that room, in that hotel, five years later, Heines, Gauleiter of Silesia,* sprawled back in his chair and took pot-shots with his revolver at the portrait of the Führer hanging on the wall; but when I read about this in the newspapers I could remember nothing about the room or the hotel. I could only remember kind voices and the smell of cigars and brandy. When finally we went to the car I fell asleep immediately, and when I awoke we were driving slowly through a dark forest. The rough track in front of us was brilliantly lit by the Adler's headlamps. The Baron was standing in the front of the car beside the chauffeur, silhouetted against the light like a cardboard figure. He had a gun in his hand. As I watched, a large black cat leaped out of the forest across the track. The Baron raised his gun and fired down the track. The cat gave one convulsive jump and then seemed to disintegrate completely. I could not be quite sure whether I was awake or still dreaming, and in a moment I had fallen asleep again.

IV

When I awoke the next morning I saw something I had never seen
before in my life. It moved me as the first sight of the sea must move
those who have never seen it before. I had slept in a plainly furnished
room above the stables; it was probably meant for a groom or a stable-
boy, and it was as bright and polished as a horse's harness. A wooden
verandah ran round the stables at the level of my room, and I stepped
out on to it through the french windows. As I stood there in my
pyjamas, to north and south and east I could see nothing but mile after
mile of golden corn that stretched away to the horizon as far as the eye
could see; only in the very farthest south, hardly to be seen, there was a
faint blue shadow of mountains.

At first sight, I could hardly credit the reality of this great golden
ocean of corn that lapped me round on every side. It seemed so vast,
boundless, drawing the eye on and on as if there was no limit at which
it could stop. I suddenly remembered, and for the first time understood, a statement I had read somewhere; Germany has no frontiers.
And later, when the first shock of surprise was over and I became
accustomed to the presence of this single immense cornfield that filled
the world to its farthest horizons, I began to feel for the landscape an
emotion that seemed as vast and boundless as itself. When I stood on
my verandah and looked out, like the captain of a ship from his bridge,
I felt as if I were cradled and rocked on the great golden bosom of the
corn, as if I floated in some element that would both cherish and feed
me. And sometimes, as if in response, the surface of the corn would
move, and the corn stalks gently incline their heads, as the clouds
passing over cast a shifting shadow upon them. In the brazen heat a
little breeze sprang up and rippled the heads of the corn for mile after
mile until the impulse seemed to expend itself at last on some far off
and invisible shore.

Fritz and I would get up every morning before dawn, while it was
still cold and dark, and ride to the racecourse outside Breslau, five
miles away. He had a powerful bay mare which he was preparing for
the races at Halle later in the summer; I rode beside him on a little
cossack pony that was convinced it could do everything, whether jump
or gallop, at least as well as the mare could do. In the hour before
dawn, the cornfields were dun-coloured and sighed softly as the dawn
wind passed over them; and as we rode, and as his English and my
German began to improve, Fritz and I discussed the matters which
filled his head and his heart and which to me seemed strange beyond
belief.

He was seventeen, with a lean sunburned horseman's face and thick blond hair that perpetually fell in a heavy lock across his cheek; and I was twenty* and therefore looked down on him from the heights of an intellectual superiority which made me dismiss his ideas as childish imaginings. All the more so, because I quickly found that they were in all respects at variance with mine, and indeed seemed to reflect a world which bore no relation to any I had ever known.

Fritz thought a great deal about the Great War, but in a way which was quite alien to me, who shared the fashionable view among my contemporaries that the war had been a culpable aberration of our fathers, which had best be forgotten as soon as possible. For Fritz the war, or rather its result, was a personal affront, and he fought all its battles over again in his mind as if by thinking he could change Germany's defeat into victory. One day he puzzled me considerably by talking about Germany's naval victory at Skagerrak, and it took me a long time before I could identify this as the Battle of Jutland, which I (and I had assumed everyone else) knew to have been won by the Royal Navy. But when I tried to explain his error to him, as kindly as I could, I found to my distress that he knew so much about the battle, its strategy and tactics, the weight of guns employed, the details of ships sunk, that I was in no kind of position to refute him.

I found also that in discussion with Fritz it was difficult to preserve my feelings of sympathy with the defeated Germans. His attitude was quite simply that the Germans had not been defeated at all; they had won the war, but somehow the result had been wrongly recorded. He was like a boxer who knows that he knocked out his opponent in the third round but finds to his amazement and indignation that the verdict has been given against him on points. His conviction that the German army had won the war brought an added element of confusion into my ideas about Germany, which were already confused enough.

It is quite easy, and does not require any large degree of imagination, to sympathise with an enemy who has been totally defeated and disarmed. It is much less easy when the enemy regards himself as the rightful victor, who has been cheated of the spoils of his victory by some monstrous perversion of history. And it is even less easy when the enemy thinks, as Fritz did, that his first duty in life is to ensure that the error should be corrected at the first possible moment.

Fritz's passionate belief that, in the name of historical justice, there must be a radical revision of Germany's status in the world was all the more confusing because it was enriched by literary and romantic associations which at that time conveyed little or nothing to me. It was strange to find a boy, whom I found extremely likeable and attractive, in love with ideas which seemed to me harsh and repellent and, very often, ugly. At Oxford I had been brought up to admire Proust and James Joyce and Virginia Woolf and Lytton Strachey; we went in for a combination of cynicism in regard to the feelings of those who did not agree with us, and extreme sensitiveness in regard to our own: *Only connect* we said in Mr Forster's famous words,* but we were very careful and exclusive about whom we connected with. Now Fritz introduced me to writers whose names even, in some cases, were utterly strange to me and whose ideas were even stranger.

Some of these writers, like Nietzsche, of whom then I knew nothing, carried with them an air of faded nineteenth-century romanticism; how was I to know that this was also the air of a world which was yet to come? And what was I to make of the great English writer, Houston Stewart Chamberlain? Fritz was profoundly shocked by my ignorance when I had to confess that I had never even heard of him, but forgave it as a typical example of British philistinism, and kindly gave me a copy of *Die Grundlagen des neunzehnten Jahrhunderts** to read. And novel and disconcerting as these writers were, they were all the more so because, for Fritz, they spoke with a voice that was also the voice of Hölderlin, and Stefan George, and Rilke – and also of Moeller van den Bruck* and Josef Goebbels. For me these writers, as I came to know them, seemed so disparate, both in content and in quality, that it was impossible to accept that they were part of a single literary tradition; the ideas of some of them, certainly, seemed to reach such a pitch of lunacy and brutality that it was impossible to take them seriously. But for Fritz they were all profoundly and equally serious; to him they all spoke a secret wisdom which provided him with an answer to life. And through him, indeed, I came to admire and love Hölderlin and Nietzsche, George and Rilke, but I could never understand how it was that to him they could mean such utterly different things from what they meant to me.

Fritz was a charming companion and friend, and I was puzzled that I should find him none the less so even though most of his ideas and beliefs were to me both fantastic and repellent. I solved this contradiction for myself by dismissing them as the imaginings of a half-educated schoolboy, and for this reason I never came to suspect that, in various forms, they were shared by thousands of young men and women all over Germany. It seemed to me that no one could seriously believe in such a farrago of nonsense, and what is more, such brutal and barbarous nonsense; coming from Oxford, I was firmly convinced that the irrational is the unreal. And so I did not take Fritz's ideas about politics and literature seriously; any more, for instance, than I took him seriously when he talked to me with rapture about his hero, the ex-Crown Prince Wilhelm, and more particularly about the beauty of his Hohenzollern profile, in which one could see, said Fritz, all the courage and virtue of his race.

Riding along beside him, on the dusty Silesian roads, I dismissed this as yet another of Fritz's absurd fantasies; and indeed it was no odder than many of the ideas which formed the staple of our conversation at Boguslavitz. When we reached home, the rest of the family would be having breakfast on the verandah which ran across the plain stone front of the house. On the table were bowls of boiled eggs, a crock of fresh butter, black bread, smoked ham, and innumerable varieties of cold sausage. The sun was already hot overhead, and the long grass of the overgrown lawn looked cool and green in the shade of the pine-trees surrounding the tennis court. The Baron was finishing his enormous breakfast and threw scraps of sausage to the dachs-hunds; under the admiring eyes of his two plump and sturdy daughters, and of his wife, who was small and gentle and came from the Rhineland and was half French, he discoursed eloquently and violently on the political events of the day.

V

The Baron was *Reichstagsabgeordneter*⋆ for Lower Silesia. He was a devoted and conscientious member of the German Nationalist party, though he never ceased complaining because his parliamentary duties took him away to Berlin from the affairs of his estate. During the first few days of my stay at Boguslavitz I seized eagerly upon the opportun-ity of discussing German politics with him, but I soon came to realise that, however hard we tried to understand one another, we were divided by an abyss which no amount of effort could bridge, so profound indeed that the words of our discussions seemed to reverber-ate meaninglessly in its depths.

I had felt in honour bound to explain to the Baron, at the start of our acquaintance, that I was a socialist, and it was quite obviously completely incredible to the Baron that any Englishman could hold such political views. *Kommt nicht in Frage,*⋆ he would say curtly, and proceed with the discussion on his unshakeable assumption that, like himself, I was an old-fashioned country gentleman. It did not help when I explained that I was not an Englishman but a Welshman; that was all the same to the Baron. No one could have been more acutely sensitive to racial and social differences between his own countrymen, but the British Isles he regarded as inhabited by one single homogeneous race whose individual members were all, without exception, gentlemen, and being gentlemen could not possibly be socialists. It followed for the Baron that when I said I was a socialist either I could not be telling the truth or I did not know the meaning of the word. On the whole, I think, he favoured the latter solution, but in any case I soon realised that he regarded my political ideas in exactly the same light as I regarded Fritz's, that is to say, as childish fantasies which no one could possibly take seriously. This solved the matter very satisfactorily for the Baron, who was very fond of me, and having dismissed my politics as a form of infantile disease he proceeded to lavish upon me all the affection which he invariably showed to children and to animals.

His kindness indeed went so far that he tried to explain to me what kind of people socialists really were and why therefore I could not possibly be one. In the first place, they were all Jews, and there were no Jews in England, or at least English Jews were not really Jews at all; the only real Jews came from over there, he said, waving his hand vaguely in the direction of Poland and the Ukraine. Moreover, socialists were men who were ready at any moment to betray their country. Indeed, they had betrayed Germany, the German army, and the Kaiser. Further, their sexual habits were disgusting and obscene, they did not love God or their country, and they knew nothing about agriculture. And as his catalogue of sins continued, his bright little eyes would shine affectionately at me and he laid his hand upon my shoulder as if to say that I must now surely see how impossible it was for me to believe I was a socialist.

In the early days of my stay at Boguslavitz, I used to reply to this kind of appeal by reaffirming my socialist beliefs and by trying to expose the absurdity of the Baron's own views. In particular, I used to attack the Baron's own party, the *Deutschnationalen*, and its leader Hugenberg,* the Beaverbrook of Germany, as the representatives of aggressive German capitalism and nationalism. But it had no effect: Fritz, the Baron, and I were caught up in a kind of chain reaction of misunderstanding. The Baron regarded me as a child, and I regarded Fritz as a child, and both Fritz and I, in our different ways, regarded the Baron as a child, a kind of foundling left on our doorstep from an age which had entirely vanished. Our misunderstandings, indeed, were so comic that for the first time an element of scepticism began to creep into my dogmatic political outlook. I began to wonder whether perhaps all political conflicts were not based upon similar misunderstandings and a universal inability to take any point of view seriously except one's own. But comic as the situation was, it was also, in a sense, tragic. Because in misunderstanding Fritz and the Baron I was in fact misunderstanding all the ideas which later were to coalesce and provoke the most profoundly revolutionary movement of the twentieth century.

In any case, it was futile for me to discuss politics with the Baron because he obstinately refused to accommodate himself to my preconceived political categories. When I denounced Hugenberg, the Baron heartily agreed with me and broke into far more violent denunciations. For the Baron, I discovered, belonged to a faction of the party which had followed Graf Westarp,* 'a good old man,' said the Baron, when he had been driven out of the leadership by Hugenberg; and if my attacks on Hugenberg were violent in the sense that they abounded in the stereotyped terms of abuse which in those days the Left used against the Right, the Baron's were far more impressive and effective because expressed in good earthy obscenities, straight from the sty and the stall. Even so, they did not exhaust his indignation. They left him red-faced and furious, yet somehow still smiling, as if pleased because our common hatred of Hugenberg showed that in the end our ideas and feelings were the same. 'We must put an end to all that,' he said, pointing in the direction of Berlin, as if he and I together were entrusted with the historic task of cleaning out the Augean stables of German parliamentary democracy.

I was even more surprised by the Baron's reaction to my attacks on the senile President of the Reich, Field-Marshal von Hindenburg. For after all, I thought, to whom could the Baron give his loyalty and admiration if not to the Field-Marshal and ex-Supreme Commander of the German armies which the Baron, like Fritz, believed to have never been defeated. The Baron totally ignored any reasons I had for criticising the Reichspresident, but he warmly welcomed any condemnation of him. 'What a man!' he cried. 'What a President! A traitor to his country! A field-marshal who broke his oath and drove out his Kaiser. What a difference from that poor Ludendorff!* You don't have men like that in England.' Tears came into his eyes at the thought of the Kaiser. He seized my hand and shook it warmly, and so once again, to my intense irritation, I found myself drawn into the Baron's political embrace. Indeed on this occasion he was so moved that before the loving eyes of his family he flung his arms around me and from that day on had no shadow of doubt but that we were the firmest of political allies.

VI

Because of this, but also because the Baron was a man of warm and
impulsive affections, he insisted thenceforth on making me share all his
pursuits and pleasures. Most of Fritz's time was taken up with his
horses; his thin figure, in very elegant white breeches and black riding-
boots, was always to be seen in the stables, where he spent hours with
his groom endlessly discussing his chances of winning in the races at
Halle. At first he had tried to involve me in these discussions; but the
groom was a wizened little old Englishman from Swindon, who in
spite of forty years spent in Germany promptly recognised me for what
I was, a would-be intellectual from Oxford, and refused to speak a
word about such mysteries in my presence. As for my duties as a tutor,
one hour's English lesson a day on the verandah after breakfast seemed
to be all that was expected of me; for the rest of the time I was at the
Baron's disposal.

Boguslavitz was one of the largest estates in Silesia; it was also one of
the most modern and the most highly mechanised, for however
reactionary his political views, the Baron's farming methods were
extremely advanced. Each day the Baron inspected some part of his
estate, or one of his enterprises, taking me with him. With a patience,
an absorbing interest, a quite inexhaustible and insatiable curiosity,
which sometimes wearied me to the point of exhaustion, he examined
crops, farms, machinery, houses, schools, accounts, woodlands, newborn babies, newly married wives, horses, pigs, granaries, and, most
frequently of all, his estate railway that carried his crops down to the
junction on the boundary of the estate. We talked to managers, bailiffs,
tenants, labourers, engineers, tractor men, gamekeepers, carpenters,
schoolmasters, children, and to each as if our lives depended on
obtaining the last and minutest detail of their activities. But when at
last the end of the day came, and the heat of the sun began to die, and
as it seemed to me we had inspected every particular ear of corn on all
the Baron's thousands of acres, a happy smile would come across his
face, he would take my arm and lead me to the decrepit Adler, and we
would drive at an appalling speed to one of his forests to shoot deer.

In the cool of the evening, with the same endless patience and
cunning which he showed in administering his estates, the Baron
stalked the deer for hours, and I clumsily tried to follow his movements. And once again the Baron should have been disappointed in
me, or at least should have begun to revise his idea of the British
people as a race composed exclusively of sporting gentlemen. For I am,
and always have been, violently gun-shy and have a profound

repugnance to shooting anything, even human beings. But after my
first stalk with the Baron, I realised there was no need for me to be
nervous. After hours of patient pursuit, while the forest green grew
darker and darker, and in the cool damp undergrowth each fern and
leaf seemed to have its own sweet particular scent, the Baron at last
had the stag's head between his sights; for a moment his bright eyes
stared into the stag's great wild ones, and then the Baron lowered his
rifle and muttered apologetically: *Die sind aber so schön.** Then we
walked together through the forest to his forester's little hut where he
and I and the forester drank beer in great quantities, and he and the
forester, who had been his batman during the war, talked of Lange-
marck and Verdun, and with great gusto and pleasure of their blood-
thirsty experiences as *Ostkämpfer* in the Balticum* after the war and in
the Polish insurrection in Upper Silesia in 1921. And it was there in
the hut that I first heard the names, until then unknown to me, of
Maercker, and Schlageter, and Salomon, of Erhardt, *der Kapitän*, and
Kern and Fischer and von Pfeffer, who to the Baron were heroes,
saints, and martyrs, though in fact they were the most depraved,
because the most idealistic, of assassins and murderers.*

In such strange pursuits I spent most of my time at Boguslavitz.
They were only interrupted when the Baron had to leave for Berlin to
attend the Reichstag, and from these visits he would return in a fury of
rage and disgust with all politicians. In his absence I rode with Fritz, I
played tennis with his sisters, we paid visits to the Reichswehr garrison
in Breslau, where Prittwitzes and Nostitzes, Schwerins and Moltkes
and Haases flirted in an extraordinarily stiff and old-fashioned way
with the Reichendorf girls, and where one night Fritz and I became
outrageously drunk under the portrait of Frederick the Great which
hung on the wall of their mess.

And now the end of my visit began to approach. Fritz's training
schedule was almost complete, and soon the entire family were to
move to Halle in order to watch him ride his race. The Baron, however,
was very anxious that during their absence I should spend a few weeks
with a friend of theirs who had a large estate on the Baltic and who, he
said, would be delighted to have me to stay and tutor his grand-
children. This was an East Prussian gentleman named Oldenburg-
Januschau and I had what I thought at the time the extreme good sense
to refuse. For one thing, even the name of Oldenburg-Januschau
frightened me; and moreover, if the Baron and his family could quite
reasonably be regarded as somewhat conservative in their outlook and
habits, even by their own description it seemed as if Herr von
Oldenburg-Januschau's way of life had as yet hardly advanced as far as

the feudal stage of civilisation. But I had already begun to feel that from any serious point of view I had completely wasted my time in Germany. I had seen none of all the many things I wanted to see; of all the progressive, revolutionary, subversive movements I had hoped to study I had found not a trace; for all I had learned of Marxism and Social Democracy in action I might just as well have been at the court of the Great Elector as at Boguslavitz. I felt that to visit Herr Oldenburg-Januschau on the Cimmerian shores of East Prussia, among his lakes and forests, his wolves and bears and wild cats, would take me even further than I was already from the realities of modern Germany; and after all, what had I come to Germany for, except to study reality?

So I refused the invitation which the Baron extended to me on his friend's behalf, even though I could hardly resist the simplicity and sincerity of his assurance: 'Oldenburg-Januschau is a real Prussian. There aren't many like him left. You would like him.' I told the Baron that it was really time for me to return home and devote myself to my vacation reading, of Bradley and G. E. Moore, of Hume, Locke, and Berkeley, whose ideas seemed somehow strangely thin and insubstantial in the great corn-laden immensities of the Silesian plain. It seemed to me then that, for once, I had made a serious and responsible decision; but like all the serious and responsible decisions I ever came to in my youth, I greatly regret it. If I had gone to Herr Oldenburg-Januschau's I might have made a little further progress in my peculiar and unwilling initiation into German life and politics. Indeed, if I had eyes to see, which seems improbable, I might have learned a great deal about some of the most practical realities of German political life. For Herr Oldenburg-Januschau had some very business-like views about the duties which the state owes to its patrons. He was a great friend of Oskar von Hindenburg, the President's son, and together they had promoted the purchase of the estate which had been presented to the President by his admirers. And I suppose it was at just about the time of my proposed visit to him, that he was engaged in the wholesale plundering of the *Osthilfe* funds* which he regarded as a reasonable *quid pro quo*, and which helped to destroy the government of Herr Brüning, and thus to inaugurate the triumph of the National Socialists. Today I would give much to know what kind of conversation went on in Herr Oldenburg-Januschau's house that summer.

My refusal of his suggestion depressed the Baron; he had hoped that after visiting Herr Oldenburg-Januschau I would rejoin them at Boguslavitz. He seemed genuinely upset at the idea that I must leave, but he recovered his spirits when he came to the conclusion that, since

I would not change my mind, some very special farewell party must be arranged for me. For a few days he was unable to decide what form it should take; his sunburned forehead, above the straight fine Prussian nose, was furrowed with his effort to devise something that would really be good enough for me. Then one morning he cried out happily: 'We'll go to see Felix!', and I could see from the faces of the family that at last the Baron had found the perfect solution to his problem. '*Grossartig!*'* cried Fritz; the others smiled with delight at the mere idea of the pleasure the Baron was going to procure for me.

Felix it appeared was the Baron's cousin, Graf Felix Waldstein, who owned an estate some distance away from Boguslavitz. He was, the Baron assured me, a perfectly delightful person, though recently he had become something of a recluse because of the disasters and evils which had come upon Germany as a result of her defeat. He had handed over the management of his estate to a bailiff, and lived alone as an *Einsiedler*, or pioneer, in a cabin he had built for himself in one of his own forests, where he devoted himself to ornithology and botany and only at rare intervals encountered any of his fellow men. But in the depths of his retirement he retained one distinction which seemed to me quite fabulously improbable; he held the European record for duck-shooting. And in spite of having abjured a world in which a German Kaiser had been forced to abdicate, it appeared that Graf Felix still occasionally welcomed a visit from relatives and friends. 'He will like to see you,' the Baron said confidently, as if his description of his cousin showed quite clearly how much we had in common.

'*Sofort anrufen!*'* shouted the Baron to Fritz. He was so struck by the brilliance of his idea that he was in a fever to leave at once. It was typical of him that he should have chosen this expedition as his last particular parting gift to me. Though he knew how incompetent I was with a gun, how badly I rode, he could not disabuse himself of the idea that somewhere inside me was concealed an English country gentleman, who spent his days in hunting, shooting, and fishing and in the evenings retired to his library to drink port and read Houston Stewart Chamberlain.

But the Baron had to restrain his impatience. It appeared that Graf Felix, in his wilderness, was engaged in writing a philosophical treatise on the psyche of flowers, birds, and plants, and that his train of thought was so absorbing at the moment that it could not be interrupted; he would welcome a visit, in particular because of *the Englishman*, but he would not be free to receive us until the very day before I was due to leave for England. This information, reported by Fritz after a telephone conversation with Graf Felix, provoked a flood of speculation among the ladies of Boguslavitz; they could not quite believe that it was philosophy which was occupying him in the depths of his forest. 'If only he would marry,' they sighed. 'He is so handsome.' But the Baron swept all this aside as womanly chatter. It seemed to him quite natural that the holder of the European record for duck-shooting should be preoccupied with philosophy, and he ordained that we should leave Boguslavitz on the appointed day, taking my luggage with us, and that after visiting Felix we should drive direct to the station at Breslau in time to catch my train.

VII

So early one morning, the Baron, Fritz, and I set out in the Adler and drove wildly and dangerously to Graf Felix's estate about a hundred miles away. The Baron and Fritz stood up as we drove, their guns at the ready to annihilate any cats that crossed our path. I forget what our bag was that day, but they shot several. I was fascinated by the way in which the animals seemed to disintegrate completely on the impact of the shot. At one moment the dark sleek body of the cat filled a given area of space; at the next, there was nothing there. But these isolated acts of slaughter were as nothing compared with the holocaust of game that took place on our arrival. Graf Felix had so far transcended his misanthropy, and surmounted his philosophical difficulties, that he had invited a few other friends to join us. They seemed to have driven immense distances in order to enjoy the privilege and the pleasure of meeting Graf Felix, but once having arrived they seemed intent on blazing away with their guns until every form of animal life in Silesia had been destroyed.

The sound of their guns deafened and confused me. I have a memory now only of a group of tall, slender men, long-headed, long-nosed, who all seemed to be of the same physical type, dressed in belted jackets with fur collars and in heavy boots, which seemed some-how to emphasise the military air with which they carried themselves. They moved stiffly, like soldiers. They spoke in hard, clipped Prussian accents, and their very sentences seemed to aim at the same ideal of style as Stendhal's, a style that should be *soldatesque*.★ Their long, narrow heads, with the prominent bones, suggested some fine animal which is both finely bred and savage, and for once I almost began to understand Fritz's extravagant rhapsodies about what he called 'the Hohenzollern type'. They were immensely polite to me and I had the distinct sensation that on the slightest provocation they would have cut my throat or shot me in the back.

I remember also how damp and quiet it was in the forest and on the fringe of the marshes in the evening, and again in the dawn, with the cold mist circling round our ankles and in the east the first flush of dawn beginning to climb into the sky. Waiting there, among the reeds on the edge of the marsh, for the guns to fire and momentarily destroy the silence until it as suddenly returned again, I watched the slender figures of my companions and had an acute melancholy sense of the vast monotonous distances surrounding us and the huge sky which over-reached us. I say melancholy, not only because of the mysterious silence of the forest, the cold, bleak breeze that blew across the marsh, but because I and my companions seemed pitifully small and impotent amid their immensities. I felt as if I were in the company of the disinherited, of men who had lost everything and would waste their own lives and the lives of a million others in the attempt to recover what had never really belonged to them.

In part this feeling may have been an effect of the conversation in Graf Felix's cabin the previous night. When night had fallen, we had eaten a vast cold supper washed down with wine and beer and schnapps; I received the impression that Graf Felix's solitude was not quite as complete as it seemed. His cabin was built of logs, on a pattern familiar to Germans from the novels of Karl May;* it had one long room which served as sitting-room and dining room, a study filled with his specimens and books, and two small bedrooms. After supper we sat in his study and drank huge quantities of brandy and schnapps. The room filled with cigar smoke. I was tired after the long day in the open air, drowsy with food and drink, indeed I suppose half tipsy. I sank into a kind of torpor in which I was only partly conscious of the conversation that went on around me until late into the night, indeed until it was almost dawn, and time to take to the fields and the forest once again.

I heard the Baron repeat his denunciations of the politicians in Berlin, and his familiar refrain: *we must put an end to all that.* I heard Graf Felix, melancholy and yet passionate, deliver a long soliloquy, which I only half understood, on the necessity for Germany to return to a more simple and primitive way of life, to live as the plants and animals do, by nature and by instinct, which apparently implied that the working classes should recognise a hierarchical order and a principle of authority in the organisation of society. Apparently, also, the secret and mysterious life of nature, to which Germany should revert, required a periodical blood-letting in the state.

Such thoughts were too deep for me, especially because, for the others, who enthusiastically agreed with them, they seemed to lead to extremely practical conclusions; as for instance, that the salvation of Germany was dependent upon a thorough liquidation of all the existing political parties and a restoration of the Prussian virtues of probity, self-sacrifice, and military efficiency. The programme they proclaimed seemed to me both confused and impractical; certainly it never occurred to me that one day it would be put into practice, though with a brutality which I am sure my companions of that evening would have found distasteful.

As the evening wore on, politics gave way to reminiscences, of the war, of the *Stosstrupps* and the Argonne, of the *Freikorps* and the Balticum,* episodes in history that had played no part in our Oxford studies of the war and its aftermath; but to these men they represented some ideal of soldierly violence which had been betrayed and degraded by Weimar. And from this they went on to telling soldiers' stories and singing soldiers' songs, tears in their eyes as they recalled one act of violence after another; until in my eyes, tired and confused as I was, they began to take on the air of drunken conspirators, plotting some revenge of unimaginable savagery which would satisfy all their feelings of hatred, bitterness, and humiliation. But by now their faces seemed so blurred and vague, their voices so distant, the cigar smoke hung so heavily in the cramped book-lined little room, the words they uttered seemed so improbably sinister, that I felt as if I had entered a world of fantasy and dream, that nothing I heard that evening could possibly have any relevance to the world to which I would wake in the morning. I seemed to be in one of those nightmares which never reach the ultimate revelation of evil because even as one horror opens on to another, one can still say to oneself reassuringly: 'It's all right; it's only a dream.'

And indeed when I awoke in the morning, and as we walked in the forest, and as we drove back to Breslau, I could not believe that my memories of the previous night were anything but the products of an over-excited imagination, that the improbable scraps of conversation which recurred to me, the sudden glimpse of a violent gesture seen through a haze of cigar smoke, had any basis in fact. I must have been drunk, I thought, I must have fallen asleep, I must have been dreaming; they could not really have said such things. So that when at last, on Breslau station, the Baron finally embraced me with tears in his eyes and I boarded the train for Berlin, my most vivid memory of my visit to Silesia was of something which, as it seemed to me, had never really happened at all.

VIII

How could I have known that I would never see any of them again? That their dreams of revenge would be realised in a form that exceeded their most violent imaginings, and that in the realisation they would suffer even worse humiliations than those on which they brooded so intensely? In today's paper I read that the large estates in Silesia, having been broken up after the war, then communised, are now being broken up again, because the peasants are refusing to work the land; it gives me a shock to think that one of these estates is Boguslavitz, and I wonder what has happened to the Baron's estate railway, of which he was so proud, and whether the corn still stretches away as far as the eye can see. In the same way it gives me a shock to look beside me at the photograph of the Baron which I still possess, at the short straight nose and high cheekbones and the firm and smiling mouth under the little grey moustache; and I wonder at precisely what moment, and under what circumstances, he and his family succumbed to the disaster which overcame them. I only know that under the National Socialists, the Baron, still clinging to the principles of that 'good old gentleman' Graf Westarp, was confined to his estate; but though he survived the displeasure of the National Socialists, he did not survive their defeat. And I wonder if he was fortunate enough to die or be killed, or whether in some Asiatic prison-camp he still lives to discourse on the virtues of being a Prussian.

I never went back to Boguslavitz. And when I returned to Oxford in the autumn for the Michaelmas term I did not boast about my experiences in Germany. My friends who also returned from Germany after the vacation came back with far more interesting stories. They had been to the Rhineland and to Munich and to Hamburg and Berlin and Bayreuth; they had been to the theatre, had met artists and writers, had had love affairs and attended political demonstrations; and all they had seen and done had given them an even greater enthusiasm for the progress of social democracy and for the free air and freer culture of Germany. Who could doubt, on such evidence, that Germany was approaching a crisis in her affairs that would gloriously inaugurate the revolution? All this seems difficult to believe now. To us it seemed obvious; and under such conditions what possible import-ance or significance could I or anyone else attach to Boguslavitz, or to the Reichendorfs, who seemed in retrospect both dull and slightly absurd? How could anyone believe that those ridiculous political fantasies, compounded of Nietzsche and Houston Stewart Chamber-lain, were to have far more effect on the future of Germany than the complicated and refined theoretical structure elaborated by Marxists and Socialists?

I certainly did not believe it; I gladly and passionately believed the opposite. Like many others whose education had been almost exclusively literary, I had a wonderful faculty for ignoring what lay under my nose and clinging to purely verbal constructions for which I possessed no empirical evidence whatever. I lived in a glorious state of euphoria in which facts were only valuable when they proved what one wanted to believe. It never occurred to me that at Boguslavitz, in the Baron and in Fritz, in Graf Felix and his friends, I had been introduced to a type of political thinking which was going to determine my own life as well as theirs, that the conspiracy which had seemed so dreamlike and unreal in Graf Felix's log cabin was in fact a real conspiracy which had its roots throughout Germany; that it was Weimar which was the dream. It was only later, when Weimar had been liquidated in shameful defeat and disaster, that I began to think again about my visit to Boguslavitz and wonder whether there I had not stumbled across a secret which might help to explain some of the events which followed Weimar's collapse.

Scenes of Military Life

I

When I joined the Territorial Army, in the spring of 1939,* it seemed to me one of the most unlikely acts I could ever commit, like climbing Everest or joining a leper colony; but it also had for me the kind of attraction, criminal and seductive, which the *acte gratuit* had for Lafcadio in *Les Caves du Vatican.** As for my friends, it was the criminal nature of the act which struck them most strongly; its seductiveness they did not understand.

Yet I suppose that thousands of young men joined the Territorial Army at just the same time for just the same reasons as I did. It seemed to them, as it seemed to me, that war with Germany was now inevitable and that, this being so, they had no choice except to prepare for it, however unwillingly. Some of these new recruits had voted, six years earlier, for the Oxford Union resolution, 'That this House will in no circumstances fight for its King and Country', and the change in their convictions in the meantime was a measure of the effect which Hitler had made on an entire generation. But it would be wrong to suppose, as some have supposed, that the change implied a conversion from frivolity, irresponsibility and decadence to a recovery of faith in the virtues of patriotism, conformity and self-sacrifice. It was not as if we had woken one morning and made the surprising discovery that Wystan Auden was wrong and Quintin Hogg was right. The last thing that young men lacked in 1933, despite or perhaps because of their many follies and illusions, was faith; if anything was lacking, it was grace. But faith they had in superabundance; they had faith in everything, in international cooperation, in the League of Nations, in the inevitable triumph of the working class, in the supremacy of reason, and in a great many other things which now seem to be too silly even to be worth remembering. How different those young men seem from the young Socialist intellectual of today, who gives as his reasons for voting Labour the two motives which until now have always provided the best apology for reaction; habit and self-interest.

This superabundance of faith was accompanied by incorrigible optimism; we had no doubts at all when our leading political theorist, Mr Richard Crossman, announced from New College that the huge increase in the National Socialist vote in the Reichstag elections was a sign of the Party's impending decline and of the imminent victory of the KPD (*Kommunistische Partei Deutschlands*). How could we have any doubts? Mr Crossman had only recently returned from Berlin, like a Moslem pilgrim from Mecca, and there he had talked to Willi Münzenberg himself, as Moses did to God on Mount Sinai. Who were we to doubt so authentic a revelation, especially as it sounded so silly? *Credo quia impossibile*★ was as easy to us as to Tertullian.

Innocent faith, unbounded optimism, uninhibited by fact and least of all by common sense, were the distinguishing marks of the young men who voted for the Oxford resolution, however hard they tried to conceal them under a somewhat childish cynicism, which they could never maintain for long. The trouble was that these young men, who made every possible effort to dissociate themselves from the society in which they were so comfortably ensconced, were happy, in a way which I think has not been possible for young men since that time or in other places. However much they might attack and denounce the society and the conventions which their elders had made for them, they could not prevent happiness and pleasure from breaking in, and this now fixes them irrevocably in the absurdity of the past, like the young men one sees, in flannels and caps and blazers, in early photographs of college rowing clubs.

But it was for the last time, I think, that this particular kind of absurdity was possible. Since that time, absurdity itself has become a kind of religion and has long lost any association with pleasure or happiness. Six years later, when the same young men, now slightly older, enlisted in the Territorial Army and in the eyes of conservative fathers atoned for sins both of commission and omission, it was not with faith or with optimism but with a kind of dumb acceptance of the fact that in Germany, in Austria, in Spain, in Czechoslovakia, and in England also, all reason for faith and optimism had been destroyed. They found themselves now in the position which once they would have despised more than any other; the position of those who, having lost so much, and being by no means sure what they were fighting for, at length have no alternative except to fight. And in the next few years they were to suffer yet another transformation, because though war in no way terminated but only intensified all the problems they had themselves so signally failed to solve, yet even war has its own strange satisfactions, so that looking back from the end of the war these once reluctant soldiers would have entirely failed to recognise the young men they once were:

> Not much remains, twelve winters later, of the hater
> Of purgatorial pains.★

II

In those days of 1939, my friends and I still believed that underlying all political phenomena was a substratum of reality which we called, according to our mood, 'the Working Class' or 'the masses' or 'the proletariat'. This belief was a curious hybrid of Marxism crossed with Oxford idealism, of the Communist Manifesto translated into terms of T. H. Green, Joachim,* and H. W. B. Joseph. If one happened to come from Cambridge instead of Oxford, historical materialism was similarly modified to accommodate G. E. Moore's doctrine of the absolute value of personal relationships. Perhaps even then we were aware of our own muddle-headedness; we felt like Plato's man in the cave, our backs were turned to reality but we believed that we could reconstruct it from its flickering shadows on the wall. The words 'working class', 'the masses', 'the proletariat' were illuminated for us by the light of the Idea. I do not think that anyone attaches any serious meaning to these words any more, except as historical curiosities, but for us they had a powerful emotional force and they inspired the kind of hope and confidence which anyone feels who firmly believes he has in his possession the key to all the mysteries of existence. To possess that key and join the British Army was as if one had the key to the vaults of the Bank of England and gave it away to the nearest beggar.

It is quite clear now that our hope and our confidence were the result of an act of faith and not, as we believed, of reason; they rested on the evidence of things unseen, and the more brutally they were contradicted by facts the more tenaciously and dogmatically we clung to them. But any faith so dearly held has to be paid for; it was a corollary that we should never do anything, in thought, word or deed, which conflicted with the interest of 'the masses' who were the sacred cow of our esoteric religion. War was the state of affairs by which the masses had most to lose and least to gain, and it followed that anyone who contributed to it was in a state of mortal sin. Of course, as in the case of other religious dogmas, there were circumstances which might mitigate one's depravity or even translate it into virtue; there were some wars, like the Spanish Civil War, which conferred merit on those who took part in them, so long as they were on the right side. But there were no possible circumstances which could palliate the sin of fighting in a British Army under a Conservative Government; this was like going to battle for the Devil himself.

Or rather for two devils, who though apparently on different sides, conspired and cooperated to plunge us all into sin. During the years from 1937 to 1939 many men were troubled by bad dreams, and these dreams were haunted by two nightmare figures, Adolf Hitler and Neville Chamberlain. In dreams they appeared as blood brothers, mirror images, *doppelgänger* who could not exist without each other. Shabby and sinister, they seemed like two figures out of one of those old-fashioned melodramas which are revived in order to make people laugh; but instead they made men's flesh creep. Or again they seemed, in bowler hats and umbrellas, in brown shirts and jack boots, like evil projections out of *Anima Mundi*,★ in which men's worst imaginings had taken physical shape. All this may seem exaggerated now, hysterical even, and certainly the facts do not confirm the almost mystical kinship, as of *âmes damnées*,★ which people like myself were inclined to attribute to Chamberlain and Hitler; but without understanding such feelings it is impossible to understand the guilt one felt in joining an army which was, after all, in the service of a government of which Chamberlain was the head. I found it difficult not to agree with my friends when they pointed out my inconsistencies to me, and if I resisted their arguments I felt that it was only through a kind of obdurate persistency in evil-doing which made my errors all the worse. As I walked every Wednesday evening to the Drill Hall where my regiment held its parades, to cheer myself up I whistled the tune of a children's hymn I had learned in the Sunday school in Wales:★

> 'Rwyf innau'n filwr bychan
> Yn dysgu trin y cledd
> I ymladd dros fy Arglwydd
> Yn ffyddlon hyd fy medd.

> I am a little soldier
> Who learns to draw the sword
> To battle for my Saviour
> Till death brings my reward.

III

The Drill Hall where the new recruits paraded once a week was a long high building whose roof was supported on naked iron girders; on the concrete floor stood the two eighteen-pounder guns which were used for gun drill. The Drill Hall was in the heart of Bloomsbury,★ but a very different Bloomsbury from any I had ever known before; it was difficult to believe that if one had thrown a stone from its front door one would probably have hit Virginia Woolf. We spent most of our parades in idleness, boredom, and gossip, because the flood of new recruits who had enlisted that spring had reduced the regiment to utter disorganisation; it was impossible to carry out any kind of training except the most elementary form of foot drill, which we executed under the direction of Sergeant Bulford, whose orders were accompanied by those monotonous and repetitive obscenities which are an essential part of speech in the grammar of command in the lower ranks of the Army. Apart from this, the most that the harassed adjutant could achieve was to give us all a rank, a name and a number on his nominal roll.

So after our foot drill we stood and listened to Sergeant Bulford's stories of the regiment's exploits in the past. They appeared to consist chiefly of glorious and gigantic orgies of drunkenness at its annual training camp in the summer. Sergeant Bulford assured us that until we had undergone this experience, a kind of initiation ceremony, it seemed, into military life, we could hardly be considered as members of the regiment, certainly not as soldiers, and he himself would regard us simply as a 'gang of f— babies'. But even Sergeant Bulford was not always available to instruct us, and then we simply stood and gossiped, and where the army had failed to organise us the English social system asserted itself and divided us, in the drill hall as outside, into more or less mutually exclusive groups.

The regiment drew its recruits from the City and from the East End of London, which was as if they came from two entirely different nations, which did not speak each other's language. On the one hand, there were the respectable young men from the City, in neat suits and trilby hats, who worked in banks and insurance firms, in finance houses and solicitors' offices, who had quiet homes in the suburbs where they lived with their parents and were members of tennis clubs and had steady girl friends whom one day in the far distant future they hoped to marry. They talked of cricket and football, of flannel dances and tennis hops, and altogether they gave the impression of well organised, well washed lives that nothing short of war could ever disturb. They had come into the regiment as into a social club and were somewhat shocked by the crude obscenities of Sergeant Bulford. And on the other hand, there were the native inhabitants of the East End, casual labourers, barrow boys, dock workers, bell founders, for whom home was simply the place where they slept at night and who carried with them an indescribable air of good-natured anarchism. On parade nights they invaded Bloomsbury like a savage tribe, bringing with them their own strange customs and taboos and speaking in an incomprehensible language that was compounded of cockney dialect, rhyming slang, back slang, and Yiddish. They were soon on good terms with the prostitutes who lived in the blocks of cheap flats nearby and when parades were over they spent their money, when they had any, which was not always, drinking with them in the neighbouring pubs.

Between these two groups there was no communication; language alone was an almost unsurmountable barrier, for to the young man from a suburban grammar school who worked at Lloyd's the dialect of his neighbour in Aldgate might just as well have been Choctaw* as English, but language only concealed even deeper barriers of thought and feeling and custom and convention. By agreement they constituted two entirely separate societies, and in a kind of No-Man's-Land between them wandered a few social misfits like myself who belonged to neither. There was, for instance, Foxy Barker, who by origin belonged to the East End and was the son of a costermonger. He had a master passion, which overrode all his other instincts, to live a life of elegance and sophistication, and by titanic efforts of self-education he had cured himself of his East End dialect, hardly ever relapsed into rhyming slang, and had secured a job as an assistant in a small but rather smart hatter's and haberdasher's in Jermyn Street. His private trouble was that he had a head of wild red hair which he unsuccessfully tried to keep in order by the use of various kinds of hair cream, as it clashed so violently with the air of smooth and fashionable sophistication which he aimed to achieve.

There was also Whitey. I have forgotten his other name, nor can I ever remember knowing or hearing anyone addressing him by it. I suppose that somewhere his surname must have been entered on a nominal roll, so that he might receive his pay, but he had no need of it for any other purpose because he had as it were contracted out of the normal machinery of social life. He was simply Whitey, about five foot eleven inches in height, about twelve stone in weight, with deep chest and barrel shoulders, a narrow waist, and powerful muscular legs. He moved, when he wanted to, which was not always because he was lazy and lethargic by nature, with surprising grace and lightness and he was in fact a boxer who had been fighting for small sums of money in the East End since the age of sixteen. But in the later stages of his career he had lost control of his reflexes and had been fearfully beaten-up; his nose was broken, there was a deep scar over one eye, and he was deaf in one ear, which was permanently swollen. He showed all the symptoms of being punch drunk, and his processes of thought were confused and incoherent to a degree which gave them a kind of wild poetry. Both by nature, I think, and as a result of his experiences in the ring, he was quite incapable of understanding any kind of discipline and his only reaction to authority was to try and circumvent it. His mental reactions were so slow, that he quickly became the butt and buffoon of the unit, but he enjoyed one very solid form of respect. All the jokes about him were made behind his back, or in terms he did not understand, because no one dared to mock him to his face; he could have quite easily fought and beaten anyone in the unit with one hand. Yet it is doubtful if he would have done so, even if he had understood the jokes, because he was in all things gentle, kind and generous.

Foxy Barker and Whitey were to become my two great friends in the regiment; they did not care greatly for each other but for some reason both seemed to think I was in need of care and protection. I found it difficult to reconcile their characters with my theoretical notions of what 'the masses' were like, or ought to be like if they were to fulfil the part assigned to them in my political ideology. I am afraid that in our relations with each other we must have displayed what Bertolt Brecht describes as 'the fake, bad collectivity (the "gang")' as opposed to 'the historically timely, genuine social collectivity of the workers'.* Certainly I could not feel that there was anything historically timely or genuinely social in our friendship; any friendship with Whitey very quickly put an end to that sort of thing.

IV

It was on the evening of our medical inspection that I first noticed Whitey. We paraded and stripped in the Drill Hall, and waited shivering to present ourselves to the medical officer; under the naked lights of the electric light bulbs hanging from the iron girders of the roof the naked bodies of my companions, caught in ungainly poses, looked like anatomical studies for the figures of the archers in Pollaiuolo's Martyrdom of St Sebastian.* Yet even nakedness did not obliterate, it even emphasised, social distinctions. One set of bodies were smooth, fresh, pink, well nourished, as if games had provided the only hardships they had ever had to endure. The others were wiry and powerful, but they bore the marks of illness, of industrial accidents, of underfeeding and showed those muscular distortions which come of prolonged physical labour. But among them all Whitey's body stood out by a kind of perfection and nobility; one forgot the battered nose, the cauliflower ear, the gap-toothed smile, and saw only how solidly the round neck was set on the wide shoulders, and noticed that the long powerful legs gave an impression at once of lightness and of stability.

But it was not only by our bodies that we betrayed our origins and the way life had treated us; our behaviour also betrayed us. The genteel youths from the City took off their clothes without reluctance and without self-consciousness; as they stripped and folded their clothes, they provoked memories of school changing rooms and hot showers after games of football. It was as if the medical inspection was still a kind of game. But for the others undressing in public was a matter of shame and embarrassment, and they had also that aversion of the poor to parting with their clothes, as if once lost they could never be replaced. As we waited for our names to be called, they stood as if on guard beside their clothing, shrank from the light, and averted their eyes from each other's nakedness. But Whitey was not embarrassed. He stripped as if he were once more going into the ring, flexing his muscles, ducking and weaving and executing a little dancing jig on the balls of his toes to loosen up before the fight. I asked him as we waited if he were going to fight any more, but he shook his head and a look of sadness came over his ravaged face. He explained that in his last fight he had been so badly beaten that his licence had been taken away and it was not likely to be renewed; in any case, no manager would handle him any more.

'You look fit enough,' I said.

'It's my 'ead,' he said. 'It's the 'ead that matters. I got no 'ead any more.'

He said this sadly, but without resentment, as if he had misplaced something which he had once valued, and as we talked he continued to execute his little jig step and make sharp quick nods and ducks of his head and shrugs of his shoulders as if avoiding invisible blows. I wondered if he suffered from any kind of permanent disability which might make him unfit for military service, but when we went up together to be examined, one look at him was sufficient to satisfy the medical officer. I had to help him complete the form we were required to fill up on that occasion; he entered his occupation as 'Professional Boxer'. He was quite unreasonably grateful for my help and after the examination we drank some beer in the pub around the corner from the Drill Hall. He told me that he was working as a casual labourer in the docks and that this suited him very well because he liked to be 'on his own'; in more regular employment, I gathered, employers tended to behave as if they owned you. As I went home, I wondered how Whitey fitted into the concept of 'the masses'; I decided that, technically, he must belong to the *lumpenproletariat* but at the same time he seemed to possess a kind of virtue which Marx had not attributed to that class.

V

When we went to our practice camp in the summer, we travelled by special train which left Paddington soon after eleven o'clock at night. I felt uneasy in my service dress and huge issue boots, as if I were travelling under false pretences; but the booking clerk did not look up when I handed in my warrant, and when I went to the buffet for a drink the girl behind the bar gave me a bold and inviting scrutiny, as if any soldier had only to ask her and she would cheerfully be his. And the other Territorials crowded into the buffet equally accepted me as one of them. No one looked at me as if I were an imposter, and I began to understand that a private's uniform confers an anonymity which is itself a kind of freedom.

We were all solidly packed together in the buffet, a homogeneous, undifferentiated mass of khaki that bent and swayed as men pressed forward to buy their last drinks before the bar closed. Cigarette smoke hung thick and blue in the air, beer slopped on the floor, there was a warm unpleasant smell of unwashed bodies and stiff, newly issued khaki. I could not see anyone from my own regiment; territorial units from all over London were travelling to their training camps that night and Paddington looked as if it had suffered a military occupation. A month later it would be quite normal to see every railway station packed with troops moving to unknown destinations but at that moment we were still at peace, there were even some who still believed that we might remain at peace, and there was something sinister in the way in which Paddington had lost its everyday look as a result of this invasion by the military.

In the end it was time to go, and to catch our trains, to Tidworth, to Okehampton, to Bulford, and other grim military establishments whose names until then had been almost unknown to me. We travelled to these uncouth destinations in reserved military trains, which slowly clanked and rumbled through the night, halting interminably at wayside stations that seemed to have no name and then painfully resuming their journey into the darkness.

I found myself in a compartment with eight other gunners from our regiment; they were strangers to me because they belonged to one of the field batteries which had their parades on a different evening from the new recruits. They made room for me in the compartment but otherwise took no notice of me and settled down to playing solo, which they did throughout the long night, to an endless commentary of unintelligible cockney phrases and compulsive obscenities. It occurred to me, with a sinking of the heart, that for fourteen days I was not likely to hear any other form of human speech. It did not occur to me, strangely enough, that it might be for very much longer; at that moment fourteen days seemed an eternity.

The carriage was feebly lit and the blinds were drawn on the ghostly countryside through which we crawled; soon the atmosphere became thick and murky with cigarette smoke, we enjoyed a kind of stuffy, airless intimacy as of cattle crowded together in a truck. The light of the two electric bulbs threw a feeble glow on the heads of the card players, as they bent over the blanket stretched across their knees and monotonously shuffled and dealt the cards in a rhythm which lulled me into an uneasy sleep, through which there ran like a river the repetitive obscenities of their filthy and meaningless chatter; and when they faded away in dreams I would awake with a start as the train ground to yet another halt, to find the card players crouched as ever over their mysterious game, fixed, immobile in the weird chiaroscuro of the carriage, like figures in a painting by Rembrandt. Suddenly waking to such a scene, one found it hard to know what was dream and what was reality.

VI

The camp stood on an exposed bare upland, which on one side sloped down to a broad valley and the little town through which the river ran; on the other, it rose to the low hills where the firing ranges were. We arrived at dawn and in the cool grey light detrained and marched from the station to the camp. After the long journey in the crowded carriage, the broken snatches of sleep, the strangely vivid glimpses of the card players huddled over their cards, it was a relief to breathe the fresh morning air, to stretch one's legs and watch the grey-green downs emerging from the mist as we marched through the country lanes. As we marched we sang 'Home on the Range' and 'Down Mexico Way', and our spirits rose as the road climbed steadily towards the camp. After dawn a few faint gleams of crimson, like veins of blood, streaked the sky in the east, but soon the mist rolled down on us and we were marching through a heavy drenching downpour that hardly ceased again for the whole fourteen days which we spent in camp.

Indeed, when we arrived it was to find that the rain, which had been falling ceaselessly during the previous three weeks, had already transformed the camp into an expanse of thick and heavy mud, which was to be the dominating element in our lives for the next fortnight. It crept into our tents and into our kit, it clung to our clothes and to our limbs, it seemed to cramp and clog our movements and even our thoughts, while the rain which continued to pour from the grey and sullen skies seemed to deny any hope that we should ever be free of it. And the rain put an end to the programme of firing practices which it was intended that the regiment should carry out during the training camp; only once did we see the long line of guns and ammunition lorries crawling slowly like a snake up the road which wound over the hills to the firing ranges. Time passed, for most of the regiment, in unbroken idleness, as they stood aimlessly talking under the leaden skies or lay on their palliasses in the damp fuggy warmth, as of some tropical greenhouse, of their tents, striving hopelessly to contend with the boredom that, like the mud, threatened at every moment to overwhelm them completely.

Whitey, however, refused to be discouraged by such conditions. I had marched up from the station with him and when, on our arrival, we found that no food had been prepared for us, we dumped our kitbags in a tent and while the rest of the regiment waited disconsolately at the door of the tin hut which served as a canteen, I followed Whitey on a reconnaissance of the camp in search of food. The cookhouse was in the rear of the canteen, and when Whitey had explained the situation to the cook, who was a Cockney like himself and spoke the same incomprehensible language, we were quickly given bacon sandwiches and slivers of hot sweet tea. In the meantime the rest of the regiment waited patiently in the rain. This was the first time I had observed Whitey in process of making himself comfortable and even then it began to be borne in upon me that, despite the confusion which seemed so often to reign in his mind, he was in fact a person of considerable resource and initiative, where his own ends were concerned. He had three clear, simple, and consistent objects in life; somewhere to sleep at night, enough food, and the greatest possible degree of freedom from any form of interference. Anything else muddled and confused him, but these three objects he pursued with the single-minded determination of a bloodhound on the trail of its quarry.

I had never before met anyone whose life was concentrated on such limited objectives, and it was some time before I realised that Whitey displayed such a passion of cunning and ingenuity in his pursuit of them because in fact he had very rarely enjoyed them. He came, I gathered, from a family of eleven children and in the hovel in the East End where they lived it was not often that there was a bed, or even space, for Whitey to live. His mother was Irish and his father, like himself an ex-prize fighter, was a casual labourer, and I gathered that the economic doctrine on which the household was run was that up to the age of fourteen children had a right to be fed and clothed but after that must look out for themselves. Whitey had been doing this, with varying success, for seven years, but he regarded himself as having been continually thwarted in his efforts by the attentions of various busybodies, social workers, charitable organisations, probation officers, the police, who regarded him as in need of care and protection.

'Never leave you alone, they don't,' he would repeat resentfully, and with these words dismissed for ever all efforts to remedy the precariousness of his existence. For him they represented the enemy; today one might have said that he was against the establishment, only in his case the establishment represented the whole of society except those like himself who had voluntarily contracted out of it. His firm and settled purpose in life was to outwit organised society and this gave a kind of consistency to his actions that otherwise would have been hard to detect. It brought a brightness into his rolling eye, the light of intelligence into his confused and disordered brain, a succession of victories and triumphs into a life that would otherwise have seemed to consist entirely of defeats.

Such an attitude was something new to me. I had known many people who wished to overturn, or reform, the existing order of society; but they were all people who wished to substitute some other kind of organisation in its place, perhaps fairer, perhaps juster, perhaps merely more efficient. I had not known anyone who, like Whitey, regarded any form of society as necessarily hostile. And what made it alarming was that Whitey seemed to take it for granted, without any words being spoken, that I shared his feelings. Of course, there was no reason to believe that he was right in his assumption; but what made him even imagine that I was one of his own kind?

As we stood in the cookhouse, surrounded by dixies of tea, huge cauldrons of porridge, grease-covered pots and pans, I might have realised that here Whitey would at once recognise one of those unlikely Paradises which from time to time met all his demands on life. But he showed no sign of recognition that heaven lay about us. He looked, if anything, stupider than ever, his expression became dull and listless, as if veiling his intentions from an unwary opponent; his eye displayed no gleam of intelligence.

'What's the grub like here, mate?' he said to the cook, a dried-up little man in a filthy apron, who in a leisurely, contemplative way was supervising the mysterious messes that boiled and bubbled in his pans.

'— awful,' said the cook, with a note of pride, as if he could absolutely guarantee the complete accuracy of his words.

'Get any help in here?' said Whitey. There was a wary look in his eye now; one guessed he might be approaching some exceptionally delicate topic.

'Cookhouse fatigues,' said the cook briefly.

'Volunteers?' said Whitey hopefully.

'No bloody volunteers for this — job,' said the cook, staggering under the weight of a huge dixie of tinned tomatoes. 'Listen to the bastards!' The regiment, still waiting in the rain, were beating on their tin plates with their knives and forks and rhythmically chanting: 'We want grub! We want grub!'

'Let them — well wait,' said the cook. 'Who do they — well think they are?'

Whitey relapsed into thoughtful silence while we finished our sandwiches and our tea. I began to feel sleepy. It was deliciously warm in the cookhouse; a languorous feeling of fatigue began to steal over me. The cook, now aided by two helpers who seemed even more wizened than himself, began to carry the dixies over to a bench below the serving hatch.

'Let's get out of this,' said Whitey. 'We'll get some more grub in there.'

But the bacon sandwiches had been enough for me, my hunger was appeased, and while Whitey went round to join the end of the queue that had formed on the other side of the service hatch, I retired to my tent where I slept until I was awoken by Whitey in time for our first parade.

VII

'That's the place for us, Taffy,' Whitey had said to me as we left the cookhouse. I realised, with a certain sense of alarm, that I was now included in his plans for the future; he seemed to take it for granted that in me he had found one of his own kind. Only he also seemed to take it for granted that I was not as expert as he was in the risks, the precautions, the war of all against all, which he accepted as a necessary part of his own existence, and now, apparently, of mine also. When we went to bed that night, twelve of us ranged concentrically around the pole of the bell tent, he watched me in silence as I undressed and put away my money and my watch under the folded shirt and tunic that were to serve as my pillow. He waited until I was under my blankets, then knelt down beside me and whispered in my ear.

'Hand them things over,' he said.

I did not understand what he meant.

'The ticker,' he whispered impatiently; 'and the dough. They'll be gone by the morning if you leave them there.' I felt outraged by such suspicions of our companions; I even had some suspicions of Whitey himself. But I obeyed him and handed over my possessions, which Whitey placed in the pocket of a canvas belt which he wore around his waist at night. Our companions watched this ceremony in silence. In the morning Whitey handed my possessions back to me, and thereafter every evening I repeated the process of depositing them with Whitey for safe keeping. And I was glad that I had done so, for I was never troubled by the series of petty thefts that continued through all our period in camp.

But at the time it seemed as if I had handed over more than my property to Whitey; it seemed as if I had given over myself into his keeping and that henceforward my military career was to follow the lines laid down by him. I do not know by what means Whitey achieved his object, or why he had included me in his plans, but after that first day I found that he and I were assigned to permanent cookhouse fatigues for the rest of our training period. Perhaps the army had already realised that Whitey was never likely to make an efficient soldier, and I acquired a kind of guilt by association; perhaps it was simply one of the accidents which so often decide one's fate in the army; perhaps it was an effect of the general disorganisation which prevailed in the regiment after our arrival in camp. Whatever the reason, for the next fortnight my duties, and Whitey's, were confined to assisting the cook. Others came and went in the cookhouse, but Whitey and I, like a pair of aged butlers, sat day after day on our bench beside the huge cookhouse range, peeling potatoes, cleaning vegetables, washing dixies, chopping meat with a monstrous weapon that was more like a halberd than an axe, scrubbing the cookhouse floor, or performing any of the other menial tasks of the kitchen.

At first I felt a certain resentment at such employment; I foolishly thought that even the army might make better use of my services. I began to remember my friends' warnings that in joining the army I was simply wasting whatever abilities I might possess. But Whitey soon persuaded me that this was to take a false view of our situation; the point was not whether our talents, such as they were, were being misapplied, but what advantages we were obtaining from our position. I very soon realised that these were considerable; certainly they satisfied Whitey's minimum demands on life. In the first place, we had the pick of the food, both in quantity and quality, in the cookhouse; tinned bacon, tinned tomatoes, tinned pilchards in tomato sauce, all the greatest delicacies of a soldier's life, were available to us in abundance and we were probably the two best fed men in the camp. Secondly, during the day at least we had a roof over our heads, even though it was corrugated iron, when everyone else had only canvas, and this was no small advantage, when the rain continued to pour from the leaden skies and rising seas of mud threatened to engulf the entire camp. As parade after parade was cancelled, the soldiers stood about disconsolately, their groundsheets wrapped about them like ponchos, or crowded into the little Salvation Army hut which was the only recreation room the camp provided or sat in their sodden tents playing endless games of solo. Meanwhile Whitey and I were warm and dry in the cookhouse, happily absorbed in our domestic duties, with supplies of hot tea always on hand and only the whims and sudden furies of the cook to disturb our peace.

Most of all, as Whitey did not cease to impress on me, in the cookhouse *they* could not get at us. *They* were the officers, who did not trouble to inspect the cookhouse, because it was part of the permanent establishment of the camp; on cookhouse fatigues we were beyond their jurisdiction and for all we saw of them, or they of us, we might not have been under their authority at all. For Whitey this was Paradise indeed; we spent our days in the stifling, stinking, blissful obscurity of the cookhouse, and since we were actually paid for attendance at camp, in the evenings Whitey could afford to accompany me on the long walk through the rain to the town, where every night the entire regiment invaded all its public houses and drank huge quantities of beer, ate fish and chips and lay in muddy fields with the rustic tarts who had flocked to the town for this annual military orgy.

These nightly debauches were in fact the real purpose of the camp; I began to realise why the heroic feats of drinking had figured so largely in Sergeant Bulford's legendary history of the regiment's past. It did not matter that the regiment was hopelessly badly trained, organised or equipped for any military operation. It did not matter that the training camp was, for the purpose of acquiring military efficiency, an enormous waste of time and effort and money. What did matter, it seemed, was that recruits to the Territorial Army should be broken as quickly and thoroughly as possible into the habits of military life; that they should learn to accept boredom, monotony, inefficiency and waste as the fundamental conditions of life in the army; and that they should also learn to regard themselves as amply compensated for learning such lessons by the opportunity to drink themselves silly whenever the occasion offered and their means afforded. It was like being blooded for the hunt; it was the way to acquire *morale*.*

No army ever received a more inadequate education for war or for peace; war itself had to eradicate its results, which were disastrous.

They were all the more disastrous because the kind of training, or lack of training, which was offered to the other ranks was only a crude reflection of what was enjoyed by their officers; Caliban gazed at Caliban in the mirror of the parade ground. The orgies which we enjoyed every evening in the pub, amid that indescribable smell of stale beer, vomit, and urine which clings to the kind of establishment we patronised, our officers enjoyed equally in the privacy of their mess; only there they were enlivened by that particular kind of horseplay which seems to be the privilege of all classes except the lowest in England. As the regiment stumbled drunkenly back to camp through the darkness and the rain, bawling those verses which begin

> As he walked up the pathway
> To the baronial hall,
> 'Gor blimey,' said the butler . . .

their voices would mingle with the voices of their officers roaring the same song from their lighted mess to the accompaniment of the noise of broken glass and falling furniture.

From this aspect of military life, as from so many others, I was preserved by Whitey. In the isolation of the cookhouse we were cut off from both the pains and pleasures of the camp, and when we met our comrades in the crowded pubs of the town, it was as strangers from another world. So usually Whitey and I drank alone, and alone we walked back to camp past the groups of staggering soldiers who stumbled in the hedges and collapsed into the ditches under the effects of the beer they had drunk. We were more like camp followers than soldiers; we existed on the fringes of the regiment, like those vagrants who attached themselves to Elizabethan armies for the sake of the pickings which can always be found in the train of war.

Fourteen days is not long to learn entirely new habits, but during that time I found myself beginning to imitate all Whitey's reactions to any situation which threatened the privileged world he had created for us. If in the distance I saw an officer or an NCO I automatically took the nearest available cover. If anyone in authority, even the cook, whose authority was the only one we recognised, addressed a question to me, I either took refuge in silence, as if the question was far too difficult for me to understand, or replied smartly and blankly, 'Don't know, sir'; one could be sure that irritation at one's stupidity would overcome any desire to secure an answer. I learned also that there were great advantages in maintaining as slovenly an appearance as possible; one thereby joined that special class of untouchables of which, in the army as elsewhere, nothing is either asked or expected. Unshaven, unwashed, collarless, in grease-stained denims and a filthy overall lent me by the cook, I very rapidly cultivated such an unprepossessing appearance that even Whitey was struck with admiration. 'Gawd, you look — *terrible,* Taffy,' he said, in a voice as of a master whose pupil has excelled him. Very soon I did not have to make any effort in order to escape attention; people were only too glad to avoid noticing me.

All these were lessons that were to serve me well later, during the long years of war. I owed them all to Whitey. Under his tuition, the fortnight of camp passed rapidly and pleasantly, most of all because in my degraded position in the cookhouse I tasted a kind of freedom which was completely new to me. It was the freedom of being utterly and completely without any kind of responsibility whatever, even the kind of responsibility which one is sometimes told one owes to oneself. When I returned to London from camp I felt as if I had been initiated into a mystery, whose meaning I could not entirely understand, and that it was Whitey who had showed it to me; I was very near to regarding him as a kind of saint. It seemed to me that I had been through a very valuable experience, from which there was much to learn, if only I had time to learn it. Strangely enough, it did not occur to me that very soon I might have all the time in the world to do so. When at the end of camp, I returned to my flat in Ebury Street and flung my uniform into the corner of my bedroom, it was with the wholly irrational thought, in which there was immense relief, that I should not need it again for another year; it seemed impossible that within a few days I should be back again in the world which Whitey had invented for me.

VIII

In those days I lived in a flat which consisted of the top floor and the attic of a little house in Ebury Street; the rest of the house was occupied by my landlord* and his wife, a charming couple whose married life offered the most perfect example of domestic bliss I have ever known. He had been a regular soldier, and with his fierce little ginger moustache and slightly bloodshot eyes he had carried with him into civilian life the manners and habits he had acquired in the Brigade of Guards. Being accustomed to regard him as a relic of a war which had long ago passed into history, I was now startled to find that he was returning to duty as adjutant at his regimental depot. His wife seemed to find no reason for surprise in this sudden metamorphosis; she seemed to expect that at the depot her Charley, whom she adored, would continue to show the same kindness, good humour, and lazy indifferent charm as in their cosy little nest in Ebury Street. It was as if, for the duration of war, the Welsh Guards were going to live under Charley's loving eye in some slightly enlarged and militarised version of their own little drawing-room, with its vases of flowers and silver-framed photographs of Charley on the piano, its warm fire in the pretty Victorian grate, and the tea laid out on the silver tray waiting for Charley to return from his afternoon at the club.

Perhaps, though it seems unlikely, Charley may have carried with him into the Welsh Guards that air of charming domesticity by which he was surrounded at home; but there was very little sign of it in the barracks of the 90th Field Regiment on the night when the Territorial Army was mobilised. The regiment at full strength consisted of about eight hundred men and the arrangements for mobilisation had proved too much for its primitive administrative structure. A happy air of confusion, excitement and improvisation reigned in the Drill Hall; I reported to Sergeant Bulford, struggling amid obscenities with the nominal rolls lying on the trestle table before him, and having dumped my kitbag in a corner of the Drill Hall waited until some kind of order should emerge from the confusion. But I had already learned enough from Whitey to know that it is always a dangerous thing to wait for anything in the army; it can only end to one's disadvantage. So in the crowd of khaki-clad figures I walked unnoticed out of the Drill Hall, passed the sentry at the entrance who gave me a friendly and understanding smile, and walked round the corner of the street to the nearest pub. Here it was evident that others had come to the same conclusion as myself, for the pub was crowded to suffocation with gunners in uniform spending what seemed likely at that moment to be their last few hours of freedom.

The air of the bar was dense with cigarette smoke; soldiers pressed and jostled against each other as they passed to and fro with their drinks; and from this khaki-clad mass came a hum, as of bees, of excited cockney voices discussing what the immediate future of the regiment was likely to be. The theories put forward were many and various; none seemed more unlikely than any other at that moment, at which all things were possible. We were to be shipped immediately to France; we were to move for training to Salisbury Plain; we were to be converted into an anti-aircraft regiment. The authority quoted in each case was Sergeant Bulford, who now from time to time began to make momentary appearances in the bar, harassed but confident, to drink a hasty glass of beer before returning to his duties in Handel Street. The only dependable item of information, however, which he left behind him was that affairs in the Drill Hall were a 'f—ing shambles' and that there was no point whatever in reporting there again until after the pubs had closed. In any question affecting the care and welfare of the troops, which he took to be exclusively a matter of beer, Sergeant Bulford rarely made a mistake.

So we remained happily to drink and discuss each sensational rumour as it came in to the pub from every kind of unreliable source, including the women who had now joined us from the neighbouring streets, delighted that war should bring such a throng of new customers and confident that, if even this first evening of mobilisation were such a success, things could only improve when once the blood-shed had really begun. I found myself in conversation with a red-haired full-bosomed slatternly girl who indicated tactfully that she lived very near the Drill Hall and that since her husband had already been called up in another unit there was no reason why she should not be entirely at the service of the 90th Field Regiment, as if this were a duty imposed on her by her patriotism, which was local rather than national. She was young and, in a slovenly way, rather pretty and she was also rather drunk. I had known girls like her in Germany, especially in Berlin, but never before in England and I was fascinated to find that already the army, in one evening, was separating me from my ordinary way of life as effectively as if I had travelled abroad. After a day of such changes I was quite happy to get drunk with her, and in the crowded smoke-filled bar her crown of red hair seemed to shine as if it symbolised all the sanctity and romance which I attributed to the *working class*, the *proletariat*, the *masses*; only here all their mystery had assumed a richly feminine form.

I had turned away from her for a minute in order to fill our glasses at the bar when suddenly a hand emerged from the crowd and dragged me firmly aside.

'You keep off of her, mate; she's no good for you,' a voice said. I was myself slightly drunk by now, and had some difficulty in making out the connection between the hand and the voice; I wanted to protest against this uncalled-for interference with my liberty and also against the affront to my new friend, when I suddenly realised that the hand belonged to Whitey. I ought to have guessed at once from its huge ham-like shape, its swollen knuckles, as it lay upon my sleeve.

'You leave her alone; she's no good,' he repeated, and somehow, despite my protests, he gently, irresistibly, impelled me away from her to the far corner of the bar until her red hair had vanished completely among the mass of soldiers who surrounded her.

So this virgin of the slums was lost to me, and I to her, perhaps fortunately, and until closing time I listened to Whitey's expostulations at my folly in succumbing to such squalid charms and to his precise, explicit warnings of the dangers involved in such behaviour. I was irritated by his assumption that I was not fit to look after myself, yet I could hardly protest because I knew he was right; but how could I explain to him that this evening, as it seemed to me, the normal rules of prudence had been suspended and nothing would ever be as it had been before? And indeed it seemed to me, as we drank our beer and struggled to keep our places at the bar against the waves of soldiers and women which ebbed and flowed in and out of the pub, its doors flung wide open and the pavement outside equally crowded with soldiers drinking and children waiting in the warm August evening for their fathers and mothers, that these few hours irretrievably divided my life until then from another in which everything was new and strange and nothing I had learned up till now was ever likely to be of use to me again.

Dis alter visum;* things did not look that way to Whitey. He was confident that the manœuvres, shifts, stratagems, subterfuges which had carried him through twenty-one years in Whitechapel would serve him just as well in the army, and that he would survive war as he had survived the ring, though slightly battered in the process. 'Stick to me, mate,' he repeated; 'we'll be all right,' and indeed he had already begun to make plans for his future, in which I seemed to be included. He had established, from sources of his own, that the regiment's first move was not to France or to Salisbury Plain or anywhere else so far afield, but to the West India Dock, where without guns or any other equipment we were to play our part in defeating the air raids which were expected at any moment. His information proved to be correct; indeed it appeared that two of the regiment's batteries and most of its officers were already there. Perhaps this explained why the functions of command at the Drill Hall seemed to have devolved upon Sergeant Bulford.

For Whitey, the move to the Docks was as if he had been ordered to protect his own front doorstep. 'We'll have our feet under the table down there, mate,' he repeated, and outlined for me the delights and comforts we might expect to find there, speaking as if a tour of duty in the East End would be like a holiday in the South of France. I felt as if I were talking to a native of some warmer climate than ours, still tanned by its sunshine and still faintly redolent of its warm breezes and its spicy airs. And my spirits and my confidence rose still higher when at last closing time came and amid drunken cries from the women we returned to the Drill Hall, to find that in its now uncontrollable confusion Whitey had cleared a secluded corner amid the piles of stores and equipment in the basement, where we could unroll our blankets and lie down to sleep under the electric light bulbs dimly revealing the steel girders and cast iron pillars which supported the concrete ceiling. 'This is a bit of all right,' said Whitey, surveying this gloomy catacomb with satisfaction; it was like being buried alive. But he was visibly upset when he saw my pyjamas and bedroom slippers, as if he doubted even his powers to protect someone who was sunk so deeply in self-indulgence and he insisted on repeating the ritual of taking my money and my watch into his safe keeping. I tried to resist; it did not seem to me that I could go through the war under the care of this ex-pugilist who had constituted himself my nanny. But I was too tired to argue. I felt sure that Whitey understood far better than I did the rules of this strange new game in which I had become involved. So I fell asleep, but not before noticing that Whitey's simple preparation for the night consisted in taking off his boots, his tunic, and his collar and tie.

IX

In the morning, as if matters had suddenly become serious, we were issued with rifles; but since most of us did not know how to use them, and we were not issued with ammunition, our new possessions also added to the sense of make-believe, of dressing up as for a charade, which affected all our activities in those early days when war had still not yet begun. We felt like actors waiting in the wings, costumed, made up, and ready for the moment when the curtain would rise; but we were also very conscious that we had not read the play and no one had given us any parts to learn. Also our rifles added considerably to the difficulties of our new life. We spent a good deal of time in recovering them when stolen or lost, and in cleaning and polishing them for Sergeant Bulford's inspection. I felt like a mother with a newly-born and unwanted baby, who suddenly finds her life, so carefree before, determined by its needs and wants, and all her pleasures, her frivolities, her social life, constantly interfered with by a nagging anxiety about what the baby might be doing. I tried to explain my feelings to Sergeant Bulford, but he was not sympathetic.

'A rifle's a soldier's best friend,' he said sententiously. He had a number of phrases of that kind, which for him summed up the art of war. As for me, I could hardly disagree, for I had a great respect for his military knowledge and experience; compared with me, he was, after all, a kind of Clausewitz.* But at the same time I could not help feeling that this new friend I had acquired was one of those who, however deeply one is attached to them, never cease to involve one in trouble, are always absent when most wanted, and never fail to make the greatest demands on one at the most inconvenient moments.

Thus armed, however, we were now ready for action, and that morning we were transported in hired lorries, for we had none of our own, down to the docks. It was only then that for the first time I tasted to the full that sweet sense of total irresponsibility which compensates for so many of the miseries of military life. For here was I, with a dozen others, dressed in a ridiculous uniform and clutching a useless rifle, squatting in an open truck which exposed us to the wondering eyes of civilians as they gravely went about their work, driving I hardly knew where for purposes I did not need to understand; surely no situation could be more absurd or, strangely, more pleasurable? I thought rather sadly of how seriously, with what searchings of conscience, I decided to join the Territorial Army; I remembered my friends' warnings that I should only succeed in making myself ridiculous and realised how right they had been; once again, it seemed, as so often before, I had disqualified myself from the respectable company of serious persons who can rightfully expect that their opinions and their actions should carry some weight in the world. I reflected almost with horror that, on the eve of war, which would totally destroy and revolutionise the world as I had known it until now, I was actually enjoying myself.

This brought a moment's depression; what I could not have expected was that it should be immediately swept away again by a wave of elation and joy, of sheer inexplicable pleasure at bumping and rattling down Holborn as we drove through the sunny air. Our feelings have no conscience, and our hearts and our senses do not behave as they ought to, and life would be intolerable if they did, as perhaps it is intolerable for those, if there are any, who never know moments of such keen joy in circumstances which could not possibly justify it. No wonder, I thought, as we drove now through the City, that my companions lying in the truck beside me, shouting at the bowler-hatted, black-suited passers-by, waving and whistling at the girls, should behave as if they were on some outing to Southend or Brighton, as if they did not have a care in the world. The truth was, at that moment they did not have a care in the world, and nor did I, all the cares were on someone else's shoulders and there was nothing we could do about them; for the moment we were, inexplicably, free.

'This is a bit of all right,' said Whitey, taking the cigarette I offered him. We had reached a kind of agreement, unspoken but thoroughly understood, that he would take my cigarettes and I would take his protection. 'We'll be all right down 'ere, Taffy,' he repeated. 'I know my way about down 'ere.' It was like being taken to his home by a friend.

X

But Whitey did not have much opportunity to show me round his home. When we arrived at the West India Dock, we found the greater part of the regiment in occupation of a huge abandoned warehouse alongside the waterfront, and already in discharge of their military duties. These were to provide guards at a large number of key points in the dock area, in spells of two hours on and two hours off by day and by night; what we were guarding and against what, and what action we should take in what circumstances, were matters which were not revealed to us, but with a cheerful fatalism we stood to our posts, prepared, or unprepared, to meet air attack, civil disturbance, sabotage, espionage, looting, foreign invasion, arson, or any of the other dangers which rapidly flying rumour asserted to be imminent. But reality refused to correspond with rumour and remained profoundly peaceful and calm in the docks, with a kind of tranquillity that would have been hard to find elsewhere at the time, except in similar oases of peace of the kind which the army so quickly makes for itself, on gunsites, in camps, in training areas, isolated from a world where all the conventions of ordinary living were already beginning to crumble as war approached. Elsewhere men and women were trying to make up their minds for themselves about how to meet the revolution which war was bringing into their lives, homes were being broken up, wives were learning to live without husbands, children were being evacuated to the country and with their arrival thousands of middle-class families were beginning to realise, for the first time, what a mass of poverty, dirt, ignorance, and disease lay hidden by the grimy but respectable façades of the towns and cities of Britain. But from this we were all insulated by the protecting wall which the army raises round its soldiers, like children who are not fit to face the harsh realities of ordinary life. Our peaceful, water-bound world consisted of the dock area, to which we were strictly confined and from which everyone else was as strictly excluded unless they had urgent and necessary business. We received no newspapers and no letters, largely I think because no one knew where we were, and we knew nothing of what went on outside the dock gates, except from official announcements on the wireless, to which nobody listened. I began to be aware, for the first time, that for most men and women the kind of news that comes from Downing Street and the Foreign Office, from Printing House Square and Kemsley House, from all established centres of power and influence, is of no interest whatever and is received with the same indifference as if it were transmitted in an unintelligible code from Mars, or from some satellite in which our rulers are whirled, like conditioned dogs, in interstellar space.

In the docks the profound calm was broken only by the rumblings and rattlings of military trucks bringing in rations, stores and equipment. In this lull between peace and war shipping was for a moment at a standstill; as we stood on guard or looked out of the broken windows of our warehouse we could see the ships lying idle in their forest of masts and derricks and cranes that spread its leafless branches against a sky of the purest blue. How paradoxical it seemed that, at this terrible moment, when war was no more than a few hours off, we should enjoy a sense of profound peace; that the hours of guard duty, recurring monotonously every two hours, should be an opportunity for meditation as untroubled as a saint's. It was as if one had suddenly become totally and completely anonymous, without name or character, stripped of everything which previously had been important to one; and how curious it was that, with all one's previous existence suddenly wiped away, like colours cleaned from a canvas, the change should be felt not as loss but as gain.*

Since there were no guard-rooms or rest-rooms in the huge dirty warrens of our warehouse, we spent all our hours off duty in our sleeping quarters on the second storey, where we could read or write letters or join in that meandering aimless stream of conversation which was the delight of my companions, a river that wandered over an endless plain and never reached the sea. There were fifty or sixty of us packed into the empty store-room, lying on blankets on the bare rotting boards, our kit at the head of our beds, and so closely lodged that at night one could feel the warmth of the body that lay next to one. I was lucky, because on arrival Whitey had secured sleeping space for us in the corner of the room, immediately under one of the long low windows from which one could overlook the docks and the ships; and beside me lay Foxy Barker, who with his ceaseless aspiration towards bourgeois standards of decency, cleanliness, and order insisted that our corner of the warehouse, our blankets, and our kit and our equipment, should be as neat and as spick and span as the little haberdasher's shop in Jermyn Street in which he was so proud of working.

Whitey and I accepted Foxy's fussy supervision with some grumbling, for Whitey, like myself, was by nature lazy and untidy; but we knew that it would have given Foxy deep spiritual distress if in his own domestic corner of the warehouse, among his friends, he had been forced to live in the same slovenliness and disorder, a kind of military Bohemia which would have suited Whitey and me well enough, against which his whole peacetime life had been a protest. Foxy liked things to be *nice*; it was a ruling passion, a neurosis, to which Whitey and I unwillingly submitted. But though he might bully us, he could do nothing about our sleeping quarters. We had moved in, it seemed, at a moment's notice and there had been no time to clean the filth and grime of years which encrusted the walls and the floor. There was no glass in the windows, and the smoke and soot and the thick heavy fog of the docks drifted in and gave to every surface a kind of greasy patina which gradually seemed to spread to our own bodies and to all our possessions.

At night, indeed, our sleeping quarters took on a positively macabre and sinister aspect which seemed more proper to a doss-house than a military billet; when one awoke in the darkness it was as if suddenly one had entered the world of a Marmeladoff.* There was the heavy stale odour of human bodies, the thick and suffocating atmosphere of human bodies pressed closely together like a litter of animals. One felt it difficult to breathe; in the darkness, that hung close and heavy around one like a blanket, one heard the snores and groans, the whimpers, cries, sighs, the sudden intake of breath, the uneasy tossing to and fro of men sunk in heavy sleep and dreams; and this intricate web of sound, like the stirring of bats, was broken only by the echoes of steel-shod boots ringing down the long corridors of the warehouse as men returned from guard duty. And sometimes these echoes seemed to become thunderous on the wooden staircase and floors as men came back from the single pub that lay within the dock gates and was not out of bounds to us; stupid and fuddled with beer, they stumbled clumsily over the sleeping bodies or sprawled helplessly across them, and sometimes, drunk, in sudden desperation relieved themselves as they stood. One awoke in the darkness to see the shadow of a soldier swaying above one and peeing quietly on one's bed. And to the human noises, that in the night sounded so inhuman, were added the soft scufflings of the great rats that infested the warehouse, and now seemed to multiply on the scraps of food and refuse that began to litter the building, becoming bolder each day as they became used to our presence, so that waking one night I was aware of a light pressure on my chest and opening my eyes stared directly into the blazing little red eyes of a gigantic rat which held me for a moment in its wicked gaze before scampering off across the floor.

From such nights, during which one awoke time and again in sudden panic at the absolute impossibility of recovering one's own identity in such totally strange surroundings, one rose to try feebly to wash and shave in the water of the single tap that ran along a galvanised iron trough standing on wooden trestles outside the warehouse. This had to provide for the ablutions of the entire regiment, and under such circumstances it was not easy to keep clean; even Foxy Barker almost gave way to despair, though he still tried desperately to cling to his ideal of a gentleman, spotless and untouched by the grime and mire of a dirty world, which he had formed for himself somewhere down in Blackfriars. As for myself and Whitey and others untouched by such ideals, we soon ceased to struggle and rapidly became a mockery and parody of what a soldier is supposed to look like. So it was not surprising that the adjutant, dismayed by the utter demoralisation which gradually infected us all, should have been astonished and shocked when one day he received a letter from the War Office informing him that I had been nominated for a commission in the Welsh Guards and that arrangements should be made to transfer me to the next officers' training course at the Royal Military College, Sandhurst. The adjutant was a regular soldier and it offended his instincts that the Welsh Guards should resort to recruiting its officers from the untrained rabble, more like *francs-tireurs** than soldiers, which formed the rank and file of the 90th Field Regiment. But curiosity overcame his amazement and indignation so far that he could not restrain himself from dispatching an orderly to identify the gunner whom the Welsh Guards had so eccentrically claimed as their own, with an order that I should report to him immediately in his office. It was as if he wished to see with his own eyes how low the army had sunk.

I had been on guard duty the night before and when the adjutant's order reached me was asleep on my blankets, so that when I had hurriedly dressed and presented myself before him, unwashed, unshaven, and hardly awake, I was certainly very far from anything that corresponded to his ideal picture of a soldier. From my point of view, the interview was no less disturbing; it was indeed the first time in my military career that I had spoken directly to an officer. Until then, I had successfully followed Whitey's guiding principle that officers were persons to be avoided at all costs. At that time, also, I had not yet learned how to salute; such refinements had not yet proved necessary in the 90th Field Regiment; so that the adjutant's horrified look as he gazed at me standing at what I conceived to be attention was no doubt fully justified. He looked indeed as if he could not credit what he saw before him, as if I was some kind of spectre conjured up to make his hair stand on end. To reassure himself he referred to the War Office letter lying upon his desk.

'Gunner Rees, M. G. 976504?' he asked, incredulously.

'Yes, sir,' I said.

'This letter states that you have been nominated for a commission in the Welsh Guards. Is that so?'

This was the first time I knew that Charley, my charming landlord in Ebury Street, had any intentions with regard to my military future; how indeed could I have heard of them, in my happy isolation in the West India Dock. The information was as astounding to me as it had been to the adjutant.

'Don't know, sir.' I was able to answer the adjutant in the formula which Whitey and I accepted as the perfect reply, safe, non-committal and conveying just the right degree of stupidity, to any question addressed to us by anyone of higher rank. It rose automatically to my lips; it also happened to be true. A spasm of despair crossed the adjutant's face; he was a good man and a good soldier, and it was the future of the army he was thinking of.

'Well, that's what the War Office says,' he said. Suddenly he looked at me like a dog, hopefully, helplessly, as if I might help him to understand what was happening.

'Yes, sir,' I said. The dog-like look in his eyes was suddenly blotted out. He looked down at his papers and then at me. I was at that moment dressed in a suit of grimy dungarees, which was the only working uniform I possessed, and a greasy side cap perched cockily on the side of my head; the sight of me did not reassure him.

'This means you're going to be an *officer*,' he said. 'Do you think there's been a mistake?' He looked at me hopefully.

'Don't know, sir.' Hope vanished again.

'Well, we may have more details later. I thought I'd better have a look at you.' He looked at me now as if, having seen me, he wished that he had not. 'You can dismiss.'

'Yes, sir.' I saluted as well as I could, executed the kind of double-shuffle which served me as a right turn, and left the room at a quick march which was like a run.

Behind my back, as I closed the door, delighted that this dangerous interview with the higher ranks was over, I head the adjutant cry furiously, as if in pain: 'Good God, what's happened to the Brigade!'

XI

Soon after this I was given forty-eight hours' leave and spent it at my college in Oxford.* But I found myself ill-at-ease; it was difficult to believe that my colleagues belonged to the same species as Whitey and Foxy Barker, or that the language which they used so intelligently, with such refinement and elaboration, to give clarity and wit to their opinions, was the same language which was used so differently, and for such different purposes, in the warehouse in the West India Dock. I felt almost ashamed to admit to myself; it was like deliberately choosing the worse instead of the better; but in the candle-lit common room, as the port circulated, I began to feel a kind of home-sickness for the 90th Field Regiment.

I was almost glad when the weekend was over; and on my return, as I walked along the dockside to our abominable warehouse, I felt intensely eager and curious to know what had happened to the regiment in my absence, as if my absence could somehow have made a difference. But my curiosity was not unjustified, because in the interval an 'advanced' and a 'rear' headquarters had been formed, and Whitey and Foxy and a few others of what were referred to as the 'odds and sods' had been sent back to Handel Street. Since I unmistakably belonged to the 'odds and sods', it was clearly my duty to join them, though it was difficult to find anyone who could tell me what to do. For since the adjutant had received his astonishing message from the War Office, the habit had grown up of treating me as more-or-less supernumerary to establishment, a bird-of-passage who would soon be migrating to a warmer clime. From the regiment's point of view it was clearly a waste of time to devote any attention to my military training; and so I was left at anybody's, or nobody's, disposal, useful only as an extra hand in the cookhouse, or for sanitary duties, or any other odd jobs that might be going. I did not object to this, because it gave me a quite unparalleled degree of freedom so long as I could keep myself out of sight or notice of anyone in authority.

I decided therefore that an additional night's absence was very unlikely to attract attention and after collecting my kit and saying goodbye to a few friends made my way to my flat in Ebury Street where I spent a luxurious night before reporting to Handel Street the following morning. My guess had been quite correct; no one had noticed that I had overstayed my leave by twenty-four hours. I had the strong impression, indeed, that if I had totally disappeared no one would have noticed. On the other hand, in Handel Street there was work to do. The Drill Hall was being put into an attitude of defence, and the first task of rear headquarters was to give it protection against air attack. So under the curious eyes of civilians walking about on their ordinary business, and to the jeers, whistles, and catcalls of the tarts in the flats across the way, we spent several days furiously filling and carrying sandbags until our defences satisfied even the adjutant's meticulous eye, for he now spent his days between the docks and Handel Street, where he worked at the order of march for a mysterious move to a secret destination which was the subject of a thousand rumours.

Sandbagging was a long, monotonous, and to me, though not to Whitey, a physically exhausting occupation; to Foxy it was simply a profound social affront. During breaks in our labour I almost automatically fell asleep, wherever I happened to be, and when I awoke resumed work in a kind of trance that was more like sleep than waking. I was discovered in such a state of somnambulism one day by a rich friend who had heard that I was stationed in Handel Street and had driven down on an errand of mercy, determined to put an end to what he took to be the waste of my talents and to have me transferred to some kind of civilian employment in which they might be more properly used. My visitor, in his large and gleaming car, which in itself proclaimed his importance to the war effort, caused a sensation in Handel Street, and this was rapidly converted into enthusiasm as his driver began to unload huge supplies of chocolates, cigarettes, and boiled sweets which were handed down to me through the railings as we toiled among our sandbags in the area below; we might have stood as subjects for a Grosz cartoon of Capital standing above on its heap of gold, bestowing alms upon the proletariat sweating at his feet.

It was not difficult, in the atmosphere of *laissez-faire, laissez-aller,*★ which prevailed in Handel Street, to persuade Sergeant Bulford that I had urgent and important business to discuss with my friend, especially since he would share in the largesse being handed down from the car. So I was given permission to accompany him for a cup of tea in a cheap café nearby. My friend gazed with horror and dismay at such squalid surroundings, and with even greater dismay at me, a ghost in filthy denims, grey from head to foot with the dust of our sandbags. He clearly considered that I had fallen into some bottomless social abyss from which it was his duty to rescue me; my condition was genuinely and profoundly shocking to him and he was determined to use all his influence to set it right. How could I explain to him that I was profoundly happy in my abyss and that I only wished to stay there for as long as I might be allowed? I hardly knew myself how this could be so. I could only say that I did not want him to use any efforts on my behalf, that he was unduly distressed by what seemed to him the discomforts of my condition, which after all I was sharing with thousands of others, and thank him for his cornucopia of gifts which would transform Handel Street into a land of Cockaigne* for many days to come. He shook his head sadly, as if I had taken leave of my senses, and when at last he climbed into his car and waved goodbye it was with the look of a man who sees a drowning friend refuse the rope that is flung to him as the waves close over his head for the last time.

But I was far from drowning, for life in Handel Street at that moment seemed like an island of peace and tranquillity in an ocean of war. Apart from filling and piling sandbags, our duties were few and simple. Twice a day, at seven o'clock and eight o'clock in the morning, a party of eight men were despatched by lorry to a small eating-house in the Commercial Road to pick up the rations for the main body of the regiment still on duty in the docks. The food was already cooked, in a small, filthy, suffocatingly hot underground kitchen, presided over by a huge Negro cook and his Chinese assistant, both stripped to the waist; sweat poured off the Negro's glistening ebony body as he bent over the pots and pans in which the food was prepared. Dismounting from our lorry, we plunged down the outside steps to the basement and into the steam and stench of this Hell's kitchen and in a moment began to sweat as profusely as the cook, though without the advantage of his nakedness. Under his direction, enlivened by grinning teeth and rolling eyes, the Chinaman ladled the boiling food, porridge, soup, stew or bacon awash in fat, into huge metal containers. They were almost too heavy for two men to lift and dangerous because it was difficult to carry them up the steps and load them on the lorry without spilling their contents and getting burnt or scalded. For the brief period while this operation continued, we felt like those sinners whom one sees roasting and burning in Hell in a picture by Breughel, with the Negro and the Chinaman as its presiding devils. When it left the eating house the food was burning hot; by the time we reached the docks it was cold and greasy, and a large part of it had spilled and congealed on the floor of the lorry as we bumped and rattled along. It seemed a curious way of feeding a military unit; one wondered how our officers had ever made the acquaintance of that squalid eating house, which apart from us seemed to be patronised only by Lascar seamen. And did the adjutant himself, shining and spruce in his uniform, plunge into the steam heat of the kitchen to strike a bargain with the gigantic cook?

Yet despite the horrors and perils of the descent into that infernal kitchen, everyone enjoyed and looked forward to the journeys from

Handel Street to the docks. The weather was beautifully fine and we shouted and sang like schoolboys on holiday as we rattled through the city, as if the simple act of becoming a soldier had banished all cares and responsibilities, and we had nothing to do except enjoy the fine fresh feeling of the golden autumn air, the pleasure of being alive made all the more acute because, as we seriously believed then, we might very soon be dead. And back in Handel Street, when our daily quota of sandbags had been filled and piled, our lives continued to move in this atmosphere of careless freedom. We ate our meals in a little workman's eating house, very different from that horrific establishment in the Commercial Road, which was under contract to supply us with breakfast and lunch; we shared it with the workmen of the neighbourhood and soon we came to feel as if we were among its old and well-established customers, with our favourite places, our *Stammtisch*,* and remnants of the *Daily Mirror* to read if we did not care for the conversation. In the evenings, unless we were on guard duty, it was easy to obtain a pass, and Whitey and Foxy and I would spend our time walking around the neighbourhood of Handel Street, drinking quietly in the pubs or sitting in Lyons' Corner House at the bottom of Tottenham Court Road, or very occasionally going as far as Piccadilly Circus, where Foxy introduced us to the establishments which he patronised in the days of his splendour and gentility in Jermyn Street.

What a different London I saw with them from the London I had known before! It was a London which was essentially a collection of villages, in which every man had his established place and status, and no one minded what they were so long as they did not interfere with his own. It was a London of small working men's pubs in unfrequented side streets, of eating houses and cabmen's shelters commended by word of mouth, of quiet, respectable and well conducted brothels, tolerated by the police because of the strictness and decorum with which they were run. It was a London in which gossip was not concerned with great events or public personalities of any kind, but with the domestic gossip of the local street corner, as if in the great city a thousand tiny hamlets were huddled together and hidden away in the darkness of alleys and side streets. And since soldiers in uniform are nowhere strangers, and Whitey and Foxy were native speakers of the esoteric language in which Londoners reveal their identity to each other, it was easy for the three of us to walk into each of these little worlds without provoking hostility or suspicion, only I had to be careful to speak as little and as quietly as possible for fear of embarrassing my two friends.

Very different again was the London I saw when occasionally Sergeant Bulford invited me to accompany him on an evening out; for he was unaccountably impressed by the news that sooner or later I was to be transferred to Sandhurst and felt it his duty to introduce me to higher circles of society than I could enter through the ranks. Sergeant Bulford, five foot four inches tall and about three foot six inches wide, with a square jaw and toothless grin and narrow forehead, and his fair hair cropped close in a style which would now be taken to be American, was a veteran of the First World War and twenty-one years' service in the Territorial Army, and his manners and habits and language were those of the British Army as it had been in the Peninsular War; he made it unnecessary to read Fortescue* and certainly he was closer in mind and spirit to Sir John Moore's riflemen than to the soldiers of the British Army of today. When Sergeant Bulford went out for the evening he went for one purpose and one purpose only: to get drunk, and it was his view that if I were ever to make good as an officer, which he doubted, I ought to learn to take my pleasures in higher social circles than Whitey's and Foxy's. What he liked when he went out was bright lights, strong liquor, excitement; with Whitey and Foxy I drank beer, with Sergeant Bulford I drank whisky, far too much of it.

We began our drinking in The Horseshoe in the Tottenham Court Road, then worked our way down to Shaftesbury Avenue, where Sergeant Bulford liked to talk to the tarts, take them into a pub for a drink, and occasionally vanish altogether in company with one of them. He was by trade a compositor, and in peacetime had earned very good money; it was all I could afford to drink with him on equal terms, but I could not have followed him in his sexual adventures, even if I had wanted to, though sometimes in an expansive and generous mood he would offer to share a tart with me. But his tastes were not mine; and in any case what he really wanted of the women he picked up was conversation, company, friendliness, gossip, and an opportunity to satisfy his devouring curiosity about their lives and about their clients. Fornication was only a brief mechanical interlude in a relationship that was essentially social. Sometimes I sat and waited for him in a pub while he performed this ritual act; when after a surprisingly short absence he returned, it was not to boast of his sexual adventures but to tell me some new and fascinating social fact he had discovered in the course of them; for it seemed that Sergeant Bulford went rambling on even at the summit of pleasure.

He liked to end our pub-crawl, after closing time, at Lyons' Corner House at Charing Cross, where he could listen to a band and continue my instruction in the habits and customs of the Brigade, of which he gave me an account that might have come from the pages of Ouida,* though with the addition of a few curious items of information derived from his conversations in Shaftesbury Avenue. His only reason for envying me was that my commission would give me the chance of verifying his information; but he could not really credit the apotheosis that lay ahead of me, and from time to time he shook his head sadly at my complete inadequacy for the part in which the War Office had so mysteriously cast me. Indeed, he felt it his duty to tell me that I could never pass muster in the glittering world of the Brigade and that if I had any ambitions to be an officer I should ask to be commissioned in the 90th Field Regiment itself. He even promised to use his influence on my behalf; and when I said that it was most unlikely he would be successful, as in the regiment I seemed to be assigned in perpetuity to cookhouse and sanitary fatigues, he promised to secure my transfer to a gun crew in one of the field batteries, which was the only position in the regiment any self-respecting man would consent to fill. But I said that I was perfectly happy where I was and in any case had no desire to be an officer, which made Sergeant Bulford shake his head more sadly than ever and prophesy that I would never come to any good in the army; an early and inglorious death was the best he could foresee for me.

By this time we were both drunk, though Sergeant Bulford showed little sign of it, unless by his maudlin and increasingly melancholy reflections on my future in the army if I did not show some soldierly ambition; in my drunkenness his squat, immensely powerful figure began to take on a queer resemblance to that of my tutor at Oxford, warning me of what failure lay ahead unless I applied myself seriously to work. But Sergeant Bulford was not willing that the evening should end as yet. It was time for me to return to the Drill Hall; there was no such need for Sergeant Bulford, who had leave to sleep at home, which was close by. So swaying slightly, and held firmly upright by the elbow, I accompanied him from the Corner House to a kind of night club off the Strand, which seemed to cater entirely for the needs of non-commissioned officers and the more prosperous, and more extravagant kind of working man. It was not like any other night club I had ever known, for in my experience, the working class generally likes to take its quiet pleasures in pubs and to go to bed at closing time. The customers, who were entirely male, did not bring their girls or their women with them because almost their only object in being there seemed to be to talk to each other and get drunk; but there were a few women belonging to the establishment, older, coarser, and more battered, and with a greater wealth of bosom and stouter legs than their sisters in smarter clubs; one felt that they might have spent their days at a fairground before their evening's work. There was no dancing and no floor show; and there was no band, but there was a piano, to which we sang bawdy choruses and from time to time one of the women would get up and give a performance, half-dance, half-patter, half-song, which was comic, lewd and macabre in a way that would not have been permitted in Mayfair. There were also two small rooms opening off the bar in which one could, if one wished, indulge for low stakes in curious games of chance of a startlingly obscene nature. Yet the atmosphere was strangely innocent and respectable; it was as if pleasure had lost all its vice by being stripped of all its charm.

Here Sergeant Bulford and I continued to drink huge draughts of whisky, until he fell into the hands or the arms of a middle-aged lady with brightly peroxided hair and a vast exposed bosom which seemed to be suffused with a permanent blush, and I was left to stumble home to the Drill Hall, where in an effort to enter by the basement door, which I knew was unguarded and hoped was unlocked, I climbed over the railings and fell into the area below and immediately sank into a drunken sleep; and there I happily remained until the morning when I succeeded in creeping into the basement before my absence had been noticed. Whitey was very disapproving when I told him how I had spent my evening.

'You didn't ought to go to them places, Taffy,' he said. 'They're only out to skin you.'

'But I was with Sergeant Bulford,' I protested.

''E's no better 'imself,' said Whitey, who felt there was a kind of treachery in my associating with a sergeant. He knew of course of my approaching transfer; but I had not discussed it with him, as it was so obviously distasteful to him, and, in any case, in those days it seemed such a very long time before anything was likely to happen and so very improbable that any War Office order would ever have any effect in the ranks of the 90th Field Regiment.

After such evenings it was an extraordinary contrast to find oneself on guard duty in the silence and tranquillity of the long moonlight hours of that first autumn of the war. Every night, as if to mock all our fears and expectations, the moon shone with untroubled splendour out of a cloudless, starlit sky and drenched the empty streets around the Drill Hall with a flood of cold and brilliant light. In those night hours there was no traffic, no sound except one's own footsteps ringing on the pavement and only if one stopped to listen could one catch a low distant murmur as of the heart of London beating while the city slept. Under the flawless night sky, in the light of the moon which blazed with an icy radiance so brilliant that it dazzled one like the sun at noon, the flats and lodging houses of the shabby street stood out with absolute clarity, every detail of their surface, every roughness and unevenness of every brick, exposed by the moonlight with a meticulous and uncanny realism. Throughout that month the moon, cold, splendid, and indifferent, continued to pour out its torrent of light over the city. It seemed impossible that this could be the beginning of a war. In the night hours of guard duty the city seemed to enjoy a greater peace, a more untroubled beauty, than any it had ever known. It was as if the moonlight had bewitched us all.

XII

All this time the adjutant had been hard at work on his movement order, and at last, by the devious ways of rumour, our future was made known to us. The halcyon days of Handel Street were to come to an end, the field batteries were to be withdrawn from the docks and advanced and rear headquarters were to be reunited. But we were not to move very far, and our destination disappointed those, like Sergeant Bulford, who cherished romantic dreams of being sent to France; we were to go no further than Forest Row, in Sussex, where the regiment was to undergo an intensive course of training.

Forest Row is a dormitory of the Stock Exchange; our regimental headquarters was established, and we ourselves, as its hewers of wood and drawers of water, were quartered in the mansion of some City gentleman who in peacetime had happily commuted between London and Haywards Heath. The only difference which the move made to Whitey and myself was that it was now no longer so easy to escape the eye of authority; the regimental office was established in the City gentleman's ornate drawing-room, the adjutant was continuously on the alert for evidence of idleness or inefficiency, there were some who even swore that they had seen our commanding officer. Foxy, who was always clean and smart and well turned out, apart from being literate, that is, could read and write, was now enrolled as a clerk in the office; this satisfied his profoundest dreams as it brought him into daily contact with officers and gave him the opportunity to study their manners, speech, dress, as a model which he could follow himself. His dreams satisfied, he became even nicer than before, so nice indeed that he even forgot to be ashamed of Whitey and me, who were really not fit companions for him. Gentle, red-haired, pink-faced, with a touch of acne which was the source of great distress to him, he found it difficult to understand that we did not wish to better ourselves, as he did, and neither Whitey nor I could explain that we were happy as we were, as long as no one interfered with us; it seemed too absurd a hope to cherish in the army. Foxy was later killed as a warrant officer in Burma, a glad and willing victim of a system which he did not understand because he so profoundly admired it. He would have said that the war, though it killed him in the jungle, had given him more opportunities than any he had had before, even in Jermyn Street.

Foxy and Whitey and I, with four others, slept closely cramped together on the floor of an attic which presumably had been once a maid's bedroom in our stockbroker's establishment. Foxy's position as a clerk in the adjutant's office was valuable to us because, at night, in that small stuffy room under the rafters, when the light was out, he could tell us all the gossip of that post of command; the state of the adjutant's temper, which was scrutinised as closely as sailors study a barometer, to see whether fine weather was ahead, how Sergeant Bulford was getting on in his new rank of battery sergeant-major of one of the field batteries, the prospects of leave, the adverse report which had been made on Lieutenant Jackson, who was not likely to be with us long. He was able to give us the name of our commanding officer, whom Whitey and I had never seen and hoped fervently that we should never see.

For Whitey and I had now found our level, or, as Lord Montgomery likes to say, our ceiling, in the military hierarchy. We were once again in the cookhouse, where we cleaned and washed and scrubbed and scoured in blissful innocence that war could impose any worse duties than these. The only difficulty was that I could not get myself permanently assigned to the cookhouse, as Whitey now was; it was assumed that sooner or later I should have to go off to Sandhurst, and in the meanwhile, I was always being detailed from the cookhouse and Whitey and given other fatigues which there was no one else to perform. Most commonly I was detached for latrine duties; I learned what extraordinary documents, papers, letters, diaries, people abandon with their excrement, as if twice a day they died to a part of themselves. For a fortnight I was a waiter in the sergeants' mess, while their regular waiter was on compassionate leave, and was fascinated to see how closely the complicated totems and taboos which regulated their eating and drinking resembled, in their general pattern and intention, those of my college of All Souls at Oxford; I wished that the Manciple were with me so that we might compare notes. And in cleaning out baths and lavatories used every day by about forty or fifty men I learned what peculiar and eccentric habits individuals may practise when alone.

My experience in the sergeants' mess, the cookhouse, the latrines, convinced me that I had now settled down, happy but slightly bewildered with the wealth of new knowledge which flooded in upon me daily, at the very lowest level of the military and social scale, and there seemed to be no reason why I should ever leave it, as it seemed to me most unlikely that any more would be heard of my having to go to Sandhurst. And if by any extraordinary chance I should be sent there, it seemed to me certain that I should immediately be sent back again; there really could be no place for me there. In any case I had no desire to go; it seemed to me that, by the good fortune of war, I had been given the chance of living an entirely new life, and I had no wish to return to anything that resembled the old one, in which one had a name as well as a number, and it was assumed that one had a personality of one's own, involving rights and responsibilities and complicated because permanent relationships, and there were other people who cooked one's food and cleaned one's lavatories for one. The army had relieved me of all these burdens; I had no wish for them to be imposed on me again. In my latrines I had a peculiar sense of freedom of a kind I had never had before and I wanted to go on enjoying it as long as I could.

I had another reason for not wishing to leave Forest Row. For since we had left London a change had come over Whitey. Perhaps the genteel landscape of Forest Row, neither town nor country but a collection of desirable residences each isolated in its impeccably kept garden, like a house agent's vision of Paradise, was too violent a change from his native land of the Commercial Road; among the mock-Tudor mansions he longed to hear, not the birds, but the cockney songs of home. The trees, flowers, gardens, the monotonous, insistent green of the English countryside irritated and depressed him; and most of all he missed those thousands of people among whom he could lose himself in the streets of the East End. At Forest Row he felt exposed, naked to the eye of authority; according to Foxy, our spy in the enemy camp, Whitey's name had even been put forward for a course in butchering. I could not help feeling that there might be certain risks involved in arming Whitey with choppers, axes, cleavers and butcher's knives; but all that made Whitey uneasy was the idea that others were taking an interest in his future. He had never been very talkative; now he became more and more silent, and he no longer assumed, as he once had, that it was his duty to protect me against the hazards of military life. Sometimes it was almost as if he looked to me for protection, or at least comfort, and while I busied myself happily with my sanitary duties, which required some ingenuity as I was not issued with any equipment for carrying them out and had become interested in the mysteries of Vim and Izal and Harpic and the relative merits of different kinds of scrubbing brush, Whitey sat taciturn and moody as he peeled potatoes in the cookhouse, making no response either to the abuse or the jeers of the cook, who behind his back commonly referred to him as 'that f—ing deaf-and-dumb cockney bastard'. And when in the evening we walked down to the village pub, Whitey no longer entertained me with stories of the wonders and delights of the East End but sat morosely over his beer and only occasionally broke out into gloomy speculations about what fresh miseries our superiors were contriving for us. In our happy days at the Drill Hall he had been temperate and even abstemious in his drinking; now as he grew more silent he drank more and sometimes got drunk so that we had difficulty in getting him home. Occasionally he became violent and then one realised what immense reserves of physical strength remained in his boxer's body.

Foxy, indeed, whose passion was for respectability, did not care for Whitey in his new character; perhaps he had only tolerated him until now for my sake. But now he began to make new friends in the office, who had the same sharpness and gentility as himself, and soon Whitey and I found ourselves reduced to our own company during our evenings in the pub. And this was embarrassing, because just about that time I achieved a certain degree of popularity in the regiment by displaying a talent, long forgotten, for rugby football. Administration had by now so far advanced that it was even possible to organise recreations for the other ranks. We had a regimental rugby team, in which officers and other ranks played together, and on Saturday afternoons travelled by truck to play against local sides and in the evening enjoyed their hospitality, which involved officers and men drinking huge quantities of beer.

This was a considerable step up from the latrines; but for Whitey it constituted a form of fraternisation with the enemy. To him, not without reason, rugby football was a kid's game, played only by schoolboys and gentlemen, and those who were silly enough to want to imitate them. It was no good trying to explain to him that this was not so in Wales, because for him the only true proletarian customs and habits were those of the East End; anything else was an affectation of the rich and powerful. We almost quarrelled as a result of Whitey's jeers, so far as it was possible to quarrel with Whitey, whose only method of expressing disagreement was silence, but this time the silence was longer and more stubborn than ever before. It was lucky for me that I twisted my ankle while playing and was able to pretend that the injury was worse than it really was, so that I had an excuse for not playing any more; otherwise I think that my friendship with Whitey would not have survived the strain to which I had foolishly exposed it.

Yet the damage was done; a shadow had fallen on our relations. He could no longer trust me never to join the side of those whom he thought of vaguely and confusedly as the enemy. The seeds of treachery had been sown. The serene, untroubled days of our first acquaintance were over; and perhaps this was only a sign of the change which gradually, almost unnoticeably, had come over the regiment. It was becoming, perhaps had already become, an efficient military unit. Twenty-five-pounders had replaced our old-fashioned practice guns; we had received our full complement of motor vehicles; every man had his full issue of clothing and personal equipment. Administration, staffed by bright young clerks like Foxy, who was now a bombardier, had began to function smoothly and predictably; the old air of confusion and improvisation had disappeared from our headquarters. Even our officers were being sent on courses, from which some never returned, where they were forced to acquire at least an elementary knowledge of their duties. It was as if the regiment had passed through the transition from a pastoral to an industrial society and there was no place left in the new age for the primitive methods of self-preservation by which Whitey and I had learned to live. It was almost as if one day we might go to war.

Yet Whitey still took my watch from me every night before I went to sleep and occasionally he still warned me against the dangers of attracting the attention of anyone in any kind of authority; but it was no longer really necessary, under the new dispensation I was more at home than he was. He was still convinced that man's first and only duty was to look after himself, but he had begun to doubt whether I shared his conviction any more. It was as I was handing over my watch to him one night, while he stood astride his blankets in his long woollen issue underpants that made him look like a prize-fighter from the days of John L. Sullivan or Gentleman Jim Corbett, that Foxy warned us of the great event which was to mark as it were the regiment's coming of age and prove that we were no longer a guerrilla horde, a kind of cockney *maquis*,* living on the land and armed with whatever equipment we could lay our hands on. We were now a fully mobilised and equipped unit in the military forces of the Crown; and to prove it we were to be inspected by a general. Who the general was, or what kind of general, Foxy could not tell us; even his privileged position did not give him access to such mysteries. Nor were Whitey and I interested; the notion of a General-Officer-Commanding was to us so hazy, so completely out of our sphere, that it could hardly occur to us that such personages had names of their own, or that there would be differences of rank among them, as among the Gods on Olympus. It was only later, long after I had left the 90th Field Regiment that I was able to identify this particular divinity as the General Officer Commanding London District.

Foxy's information seemed to add to Whitey's depression and irritation. It was as if he personally was the sole object of the general's inspection, and as the days went by, as billets, equipment, weapons, uniforms were cleaned and scrubbed and polished and blancoed to bring them to a condition which would not offend the general's sensitive eye, Whitey began to exhibit symptoms of persecution mania. New standards of cleanliness and hygiene were being demanded in the cookhouse, and even the adjutant suddenly began to be interested in dirty saucepans and greasy stewpots. 'Like a f—ing Ideal 'Omes Exhibition,' said the cook contemptuously; but Whitey continued to be absent whenever an officer made his rounds and mysteriously disappeared altogether during his hours off duty.

'They're not going to get me, Taffy,' he said to me one evening, a few days before the inspection. 'We ought to keep out of this, you and me.' He spoke as if he and I had criminal records, and could not afford to expose ourselves unnecessarily. But during the next few days he did not mention the inspection again; indeed I hardly saw him, his absences from the cookhouse seemed to become longer and longer and off duty he was nowhere to be found. At night, when we laid out our blankets on the attic floor, he hardly spoke and the expression on his scarred and beaten face was one of intense and painful thought; the eyelid that drooped slightly over his left eye had developed a disconcerting twitch, so that it seemed as if he were continually winking at one.

The days that autumn were windless, golden; it seemed as if each day was not long enough to contain the sunshine which overflowed it. Leaves began to fall and lay where they fell at the foot of the trees. In the early morning, as I made my way to the latrines which were my special responsibility, cobwebs of frost lay on the grass and melted quickly in the sun. And as the leaves fell, and the sunshine grew thinner and paler, as if its warmth were slowly draining away, Whitey became more and more depressed, uncommunicative, even incalculable, as now he seemed disposed to quarrel with anyone, even me, on the slightest pretext. Yet when at last the morning of the inspection came, he seemed suddenly to have recovered all his cheerfulness. Once again, as he handed back my watch in the morning, he greeted me with his battered smile and for the moment at least his eyelid seemed to have stopped twitching.

'You stick to me today, Taffy,' he said. 'I got something to show you.'

'The general's coming,' I said. He seemed so cheerful that for a moment I thought he had forgotten the inspection.

''E's not going to f—ing inspect me,' he said, with all his old happy confidence that he could always escape notice if he wanted to.

I wondered how he was going to do it. Headquarter battery, with the exception of those on necessary fatigues, was to be paraded for the general at ten o'clock. With almost obsessive pains I had satisfied myself that my latrines were fit for any general, though I doubted whether they were really worthy of his notice, not knowing then, as I came to know later, that generals have a neurotic interest in such matters; after breakfast I visited them again and then made my way to the cookhouse, where the cook had been issued with a new chef's outfit for the occasion. He was utterly transformed from the grease-stained scullion I had hitherto known; white-aproned, immaculate, he had even washed and shaved and among his shining pots and pans was as unrecognisable as his own cookhouse, where none of its customary filth remained. Only his temper had not changed; as I entered he was screaming abuse at Whitey.

'You get out of 'ere,' he shouted. 'You make yourself f—ing scarce, or I'll 'ave you on a f—ing charge.'

His rage was perhaps understandable, as Whitey had made no effort to clean himself up, and unshaven and unwashed, in his normal working outfit of filthy denims, he completely destroyed the illusion of spotless cleanliness which for that day reigned in the cookhouse.

'Sw'elp me God,' screamed the cook. 'I'll cut your f—ing throat if you don't get out of 'ere,' and snatched up a butcher's knife, burnished and sharpened, that lay upon the table.

'Let's get out of this, Taffy,' said Whitey. He seized me by the arm and under a hail of obscenities from the cook we left the cookhouse as rapidly as possible. 'This way,' said Whitey. Obediently I followed him through the kitchen garden, already falling into disorder and decay, to the little wood that stretched in a semicircle round our headquarters. As the cook's screams died away in the distance, we entered the wood where the morning sunshine fell in golden bars between the trunks of the trees. Suddenly it seemed as if we had entered a region of absolute peace. In the heart of the wood the silence was broken only by the sound of our footsteps as we trod the dry leaves that were spread between the trees. I had never explored the wood before; it was as if unknown to any of us an enchanted forest lay on the very edge of our headquarter area. Whitey seemed to know exactly where he was going as he led me confidently forward. Suddenly he stopped at a break in the trees, and I saw that he had brought me to a little grassy clearing. It stretched away from us in a gentle slope, totally enclosed by trees, and in this little space the sunshine on the grass seemed to lie as thick and yellow as butter.

In the middle of the clearing, beneath a bank which partly sheltered it from any wind, stood a tall metal incinerator, alight and glowing, and I realised that Whitey had brought me to the headquarters' rubbish dump where the waste from the cookhouse was disposed of. But someone had taken the trouble to preserve the charm of the little clearing; there was no litter around the incinerator and the refuse that remained for disposal had been neatly piled under the trees on the edge of the wood and enclosed by rough pieces of timber. When we came up to the incinerator I saw that beside it stood a small brazier made out of an old bucket standing on a pair of bricks, and in the side of the bank someone had dug a small recess in which stood a battered kettle, two enamel mugs, and some bottles filled with milk and with water. Whitey waved his hand at the brazier, the incinerator, the little clearing in its ring of trees with a proprietary air and smiled at me as if they were some delightful surprise he had prepared entirely for my benefit.

'I been coming 'ere a lot,' he said. I began to understand where he had spent all his long absences and whose hands had tried to protect the peace and seclusion of this little hollow in the trees.

'They won't find us 'ere,' he said. 'Nobody'll go looking for us 'ere.' And indeed it seemed inconceivable that his little hide-out could be of any military interest to anyone, or that even the most painstaking inspection could bring it to the general's notice. Secret, secluded, the little clearing seemed to live a life of its own, into which anything so brutal as the army had never penetrated; there was only the incinerator to give any evidence of its presence.

'We'll 'ave some char,' said Whitey, and from his little larder, like an animal's burrow, he produced his tea things. 'Won 'em from the cook'ouse,' said Whitey. 'I been collecting them.' We collected twigs from the wood to fill the brazier and when the kettle had boiled we lay under the bank and drank our tea, while the sun poured down on us out of a sky of palest November blue. The incinerator gave warmth to the pale sunshine. We lay relaxed and luxurious on the grass, and the warmth and the great blaze of sunshine and the trees clustered so closely around us wrapped us round in a great cocoon of idleness and peace.

'It's nice 'ere, Taffy,' Whitey said. 'They'll never catch us 'ere.' We laughed as we thought of the general on the rounds of his inspection;

no one was likely to notice our absence, or if it were noticed it was likely to be welcomed, for Whitey and I were certainly nothing which the regiment might be proud of.

We lay silent on the grass; a bird alighted on a tree and rustled the dry leaves on its branches. I think we must have slept, or at least I did, for when I awoke the sun was higher and warmer and Whitey was squatting on his haunches beside the brazier, where the kettle was boiling.

'This is the life, Taffy,' he said. 'Just you and me and none of them bastards to worry us.'

I stood up to take my mug of tea from him, and at that moment we heard footsteps treading the fallen leaves in the wood. Into the little clearing, resplendent, Jove-like, red-cheeked, red-tabbed, in breeches and boots, came the general and behind him came the adjutant, the general's ADC, and a fiery little officer who looked harassed and angry. Being bare-headed, Whitey and I were unable to salute, but I put down my cup of tea and we stood to attention as well as we could. The fiery little officer's eyes flashed wickedly; he glared angrily at the adjutant; no one spoke. I could feel Whitey tremble as we stood side by side; for a moment I almost feared that, hunted out of his lair, he might suddenly attack the general.

'What's this?' said the general, raising his stick and pointing at Whitey and me and the incinerator. He looked cleaner than any man I had ever seen, as if every inch of him had been scrubbed and polished for years; his face had a curious tan, like old wood.

'Refuse disposal squad, sir,' said the adjutant promptly.

'Very nice,' said the general. 'Very nice indeed.' He looked at the ground around the incinerator, at the sky, at the trees, at Whitey and me. 'No litter; very well kept. Always tell a good unit by its refuse disposal.'

The fiery little man, in whom at last I had recognised our commanding officer, stared at him in amazement; the adjutant looked astonished but pleased, as if compliments had been scarce that day. The general gazed again at our kettle on the brazier, at the grass, at the sky that was as blue as his eyes.

'Brewing up, eh?' he said, addressing himself, to our astonishment, to Whitey and me. 'Shouldn't mind a cup of tea myself,' he said to the adjutant. 'It's a nice place here. But I suppose I'd better be pushing on.' He turned away, almost, it seemed, with regret; as they left we heard him say to the commanding officer: 'Very good show, colonel; you may be a bit behind in training, but you get full marks for hygiene.'

While they were still in sight Whitey and I did not dare to move or speak; in the sunshine we stood rigidly side by side until they had disappeared into the wood and we looked at each other in amazement at the first words of approval we had earned since we joined the army. Then we lay down again in the grass to enjoy the long golden hours that lay before us. For once we felt that we had deserved them.

XIII

That day is almost my last clear memory of Whitey. The regiment continued with its training, and I with my sanitary duties, but not long after, to the adjutant's astonishment and my own, the order came through for me to attend the first officers' training course to be held at Sandhurst after Christmas.* I was given leave at Christmas before reporting at the Royal Military College, where I found myself in the hands of violent and efficient drill sergeants from the Brigade of Guards, headed by a famous or notorious regimental sergeant-major who boasted, in tones that proved their own assertion, of the loudest voice in the British Army.* At Sandhurst officer cadets were addressed as 'Sir'; how often the square echoed with that brassy voice screaming at some cowering candidate for a commission: 'If you don't call me Sir, Sir, I shan't call you Sir, Sir!' Absurdity and ferocity went hand in hand at Sandhurst; I missed the cockney gaiety of the 90th Field Regiment. I did not hear from Whitey, nor did I expect to hear from him, being, as he said, not much of a hand at a letter. It was many months later that I was told by a gunner from the 90th Field Regiment, whom I met by accident in London, that after I had left Whitey's persecution mania had become almost psychopathic. For some reason his fantasies had concentrated themselves on the savage terrier-like little figure of the commanding officer; perhaps his hatred had been conceived that day when he and the general had broken into our seclusion in the little hollow in the woods. One day Whitey had taken a shot with his rifle at the commanding officer as he left his headquarters in his car; he hit the car but missed the colonel. For this last assertion of his independence he was sentenced to several months' detention in the military prison at Aldershot; in the meantime the regiment had moved again and Whitey had never returned after he had been to the Glasshouse. I do not like to think of what may have happened to him in that terrible place, and I do not think that anyone has ever missed him except myself.

A Day at the Seaside*

I

At the beginning of 1942 I was posted to London as a GSO 2 (Intelligence) at GHQ Home Forces.* I was happy to return to London and for several months I enjoyed a pleasant and extremely unwarlike life, disturbed only by an elaborate battle exercise in which, long after the danger of invasion had passed, Home Forces for the last time pushed the German invaders into the sea. Thereafter even GHQ Home Forces reluctantly put away its plans for resisting invasion and turned its mind to other problems.

Henry Yorke* had offered me a room in his house in Rutland Gate, where I lived in great ease and comfort. My only regret was that I hardly ever saw Henry, who was on night duty in the London Fire Brigade. We played a game of Box and Cox with one another; he came in when I went out. On fine spring mornings I walked happily down Knightsbridge past the barracks where my brother was stationed at that time,* and as I passed he would wave at me from his window and we shouted greetings to one another across the street. It was as if in returning to London in the middle of war I had returned to the bosom of family and friendship; and since there was now no conceivable enemy for GHQ to fight, there were also no intelligence functions for it to perform, and my duties as GSO 2 (I) were reduced to those which are politely described in the intelligence manuals as 'circulation and collation'. There seemed to be no reason in the world why I should not enjoy whatever pleasures London had to offer, and indeed, at the heart of a great Empire at war and still faced with the prospect of defeat, I lived the most peaceful and comfortable of lives.

But like most such interludes in the army, in which one was continually being required to play some new part, each more unlikely than the previous one, this could not last for long. My immediate superior at GHQ was an intelligent, sensitive, and conscientious regular soldier, who interfered very little in my discharge of my flimsy duties; beyond and above him was a BGS (Intelligence) with whom I had even less contact, as he spent most of his time visiting units and formations which GHQ had under command. There, to selected audiences and before a map of the world, he delivered vast surveys of global strategy, which made one admire him for his soldier's determination to do his duty in spite of the boredom which his 'appreciations' inspired both in himself and his audience.

I was therefore surprised when one day the brigadier summoned me to his presence; I might even have been alarmed, except that my duties were so perfunctory that I felt confident even I could not be accused of neglecting them. But when I entered the brigadier's room, with its large-scale maps beautifully marked with little coloured flags showing the latest position on every conceivable front, I was even more surprised by the air of embarrassment with which he addressed me. He was essentially a kindly man; those huge movements of opposing armies which he described so often in his lectures would have horrified him if he had seen them with his own eyes; and it was easy to guess that the cause of his embarrassment could only be that he had something unpleasant to say to me. But when, after asking me if I was happy at GHQ Home Forces, and even going so far as to compliment me on my work, he came to the point, it was nothing worse than to tell me that I was to be transferred to HQ South-Eastern Command.* I could see no cause for his uneasiness in this; it seemed to me yet another of those wartime transfers which one accepted as inevitable in the army. I was only sorry because it would remove me from my pleasant life in London.

'Of course,' said the brigadier, 'this means, you'll be on General Montgomery's staff,' and under his beautiful white eyebrows he shot me a sympathetic look as if he were sentencing me to immediate execution. The name of Montgomery meant no more to me than that of any other general; I had never heard it before and I saw no reason why it should ever mean any more to me than it did then. The brigadier seemed surprised that the name should evoke so little response in me.

'He's a bit of a terror, you know,' he said. 'Very keen on physical fitness, and all that. Makes all his staff officers do a five-mile run once a week.' He spoke as if it were an affront to the human race and gave a little shiver of distaste. To me it seemed merely eccentric, but no worse, and I had always imagined that all generals, like schoolmasters, had their own particular eccentricities.

'Monty wants to get rid of his present G 2 (I),' said the brigadier. 'Says he's no good and he won't be satisfied till he gets somebody good to replace him.' The brigadier looked at me nervously, as if he might have offended me. 'So we're sending him you,' he went on brightly. 'But you'd better be on your toes, or he'll have you back here in no time and then there'll be hell to pay. He'll be up here himself before you know.' He spoke as if this were to be avoided at all costs. I had the feeling that I had been selected, for no very good reason, for a specially dangerous mission, with the particular objective of protecting

GHQ Home Forces from this unknown but mysteriously terrifying general.

'So I want you to do your best,' said the brigadier; 'we're expecting a lot of you.' There was a note of pleading in his voice now, and I began to feel a little of his own alarm. At the same time I felt a certain curiosity about this general whose name provoked such fear.

'Of course,' said the brigadier, 'there's nothing wrong with Monty really. He's just a bit mad and he likes showing off. And he's always causing trouble. But I think you'll get on with him.' He gave me a long intent look as if I had mysterious powers which would ensure my survival where many better men would go under. I wished I knew what they were.

'Well, good luck,' said the brigadier despondently. 'But don't say I didn't warn you. Keep your eye out for Monty. He really is a terror.'

II

After a few weeks at South-Eastern Command I began to understand a little of what the brigadier had meant. If in London the name of Montgomery inspired the kind of fear one has for an enemy whose mere existence is vaguely menacing but who is at least some distance away, at Reigate his presence was immediate and awful. Every Wednesday afternoon a straggling line of staff officers, including the most exalted and the most elderly, stumbled across the hills and commons and golf courses of Reigate. It was said that some officers had never returned from these cross-country runs, but as they were, in pullovers and shorts, had made their way to the local station and taken the next train to London to ask for a new posting. Mysterious slogans, menacing even in their absurdity, appeared on notice boards at units and formations and headquarter offices: 'Do you wake up full of ZING? If not, why not?' ADCs spoke glumly of the rigours and austerities of the general's mess; no drinks and bed at nine o'clock. Orders were issued, signed B. L. Montgomery, that henceforward South-Eastern Command should be known as South-Eastern Army and he himself as the Army Commander. And every day new rumours would circulate about his latest eccentricities. There was the long-range gun on the Channel coast which the Army Commander in-spected. He was informed by the subaltern in command of the crew that the gun could only be fired on the direct command of the War Office. 'Fire it,' said the Army Commander.

'No,' said the subaltern.

'Fire it,' said the Army Commander. '*My* Army, *my* gun. Fire it.'

The gun was fired, with what effects were not known; but its detonation reverberated through our headquarters.

All this was a part of a calculated effort by the Army Commander to inspire his South-Eastern Army with those feelings of aggression so highly valued by generals and psychoanalysts; in some of his staff at least it created feelings that were close to panic, and at his headquarters an atmosphere that was near to farce. At that time the name of the Army Commander, however awful in Whitehall, had not earned the fame which belonged to it later; soldiers who cared for the dignity of their profession were often scandalised by the pretensions of the GOC-in-C, South-Eastern Army, while those who suffered from them directly, like his staff and his formation commanders, sometimes wondered, with a mixture of alarm and scepticism, whether they were playing a part in war or *opéra bouffe*.* Sometimes, in Reigate, one had the feeling that the Army Commander might at any moment lead his army directly across the Channel in a personal campaign to liberate Europe.

As for me, however, despite my brigadier's forebodings, I found it no more difficult to avoid Monty's notice than any other general's under whom I had served; the only difference was that at least I knew this general's name, but I felt confident he did not know mine. A GSO 2 (Intelligence) at a large headquarters is a very modest and subordinate person who does not warrant the attention of an Army Commander; to my great relief I had no direct contact with him, indeed I never even saw him, and I felt sure that as long as I dutifully ran my five miles every week there was no danger of my doing so. It was pleasant to listen to the innumerable stories that were told about him in the Mess, to discuss whether he was a charlatan or, as some said, an exceedingly able soldier; one might even dimly feel an odd kind of pride at being commanded by so notable an eccentric; but I had no fear at all, and certainly no wish, that we should ever meet face to face. It was therefore alarming and disturbing in the extreme when one evening an ADC appeared in the bar of our Mess and informed me that after dinner, at 8.15, I was to report personally to the Army Commander; it was even worse because the ADC was quite unable, or unwilling, to tell me why the Army Commander wished to see me. I was stunned and dismayed, searched my conscience and assured myself that I had faithfully performed my weekly run, that I woke up full of ZING, and that I could think of no sin either of omission or commission that could possibly warrant the Army Commander's attention. I rapidly drank several large whiskies until I reflected that this was the very worst way to prepare for my interview, and unsuccessfully implored the ADC for a little further enlightenment; he only smiled rather maliciously, said, 'He's not so bad as all that, you know,' and then gracefully left me to my fears and doubts. At dinner I did not enjoy my companions' commiseration, either assumed or sincere, nor their congratulations on my close relations with the Army Commander. All I could think of was that uneasy look on my brigadier's face at GHQ Home Forces and his words: 'Look out for Monty. He's a real terror.' When I left the Mess, it was with the feeling that very soon I should be telling the brigadier how right he was.

III

The Army Commander occupied a comfortable villa on the hill over-looking Reigate. When I arrived, the ADC showed me into a large dark study and told me the Army Commander was in the garden and would be with me in a moment. Through the open french windows I could see a small, rather unimpressive figure walking on the lawn, head slightly bent and hands clasped behind its back. I prayed desperately that, at this last moment, some final devastating cataclysm might rescue me from what lay before me; a bomb, I thought, perhaps even now some German dive-bomber is about to swoop on the house and blow the Army Commander to pieces. But the evening sky was clear, no friendly drone of enemy aircraft was to be heard, and in a moment, when he had received his ADC's message, the little figure turned and came into the study.

One saw a narrow foxy face, long-nosed, sharp and intelligent and tenacious, with very bright and clear blue eyes, and a small, light, spare body. The effect was not at all imposing, except for his eyes and an indefinable look in his face of extreme cleverness and sagacity, like a very alert Parson Jack Russell terrier. But what was impressive was an air he had of extraordinary quietness and calm, as if nothing in the world could disturb his peace of mind. He spoke in a quiet voice and his manner, though incisive, was quiet also; one had the feeling that with him everything was in order, like a good housewife whose domestic arrangements are always ready for any conceivable emer-gency. And to my surprise, after experience of many senior officers, though none so exalted as him, he was extremely polite, so that one almost forgot his rank, and this could have been dangerous, except that not for one moment could one forget that one was in the presence of a very remarkable person.

That air of calm and peace which he carried with him was so strong that after a moment my panic and alarm began to die away; it was something which one felt to be almost incongruous in a soldier. He made me sit in a window seat with my back to the garden, so that my face was in shadow and the evening light streamed in on his and I had the opportunity to see how very finely it was moulded, with the kind of fineness one sees in some animals that are very highly bred and trained for the particular purpose they have to fulfil. And as one talked to him, one was aware all the time of the stillness and quietness that reigned all around him, in the study itself, in the entire household, in the garden outside, as if even the birds were under a spell of silence; it was a kind of stillness one would associate more easily with an interview with a priest than a general.★ And indeed our conversation itself had something of the same character; it was very one-sided and I had to speak nearly all the time, as it took the form of a long, precise, patient interrogation about my previous career, both in civil life and in the army. It was not revealed to me what the point of his questions was, and as I answered them I was surprised because the Army Commander listened to what I had to say as if it were worth listening to; only at rare intervals did he interrupt, to say, 'Very good,' or 'I don't think much of that.' I was to learn later that this gift of listening without interruption to subordinate and very junior officers is one of the rarest one can meet with in generals, who on the whole only listen to what they like to hear and is pleasant to them in the hearing; and not very much is.

We must have talked in this way for about three-quarters of an hour, and during this time there was not a single interruption from outside, either from staff officers, or orderlies, or ADCs or from the telephone, and again I was slightly surprised, because after all Army Commanders are very busy men, yet for three-quarters of an hour Monty seemed to have no concern in the world except me. When the time was over he looked at his watch (bedtime, I thought, remembering the rumours of his sleeping habits), suddenly said, 'Well, that's all,' and then, with the politeness which had great charm for a very nervous officer, 'Thank you very much.' One might almost have thought I had conferred a favour on him.

If I had been alarmed before my interview, after it was over alarm had given way to confusion and bewilderment. I could discover no reason whatever for the Army Commander's interest in my military career and qualifications; was it simply another of his eccentricities that he liked to spend his time interrogating his staff officers about themselves, like a schoolmaster with his prefects? But what bewildered me even more was the complete contrast I had found between the Army Commander in person and the 'Monty' who was the subject of so much rumour and criticism. In the small polite man who had listened so attentively to my report on myself I could see no sign of the disagreeable and pretentious exhibitionist who was the subject of so much rumour and gossip or anything to justify his reputation as a 'terror'. The only things that were alarming about him were the sharp bright gleam of intelligence in his eye and his extraordinary air of utter and complete self-confidence, as of one who accepts his own worth as axiomatic, like a fact of nature. Perhaps that is what soldiers mean by a terror, I thought; in the meanwhile I decided, as I walked down the hill to my billet, to dismiss my interview with him as one of those odd and rather enjoyable incidents which sometimes brought an element of mystery and charm into life in the army. Certainly, I thought, one would always be glad to meet such a remarkable man as the Army Commander; he was clearly, as engineers say, 'one off'; but I saw no reason whatever why I should ever meet him again. I should remember him; but why should he remember me?

IV

But I was wrong. In the Intelligence room the next morning, the smiling ADC, that elegant young man who suffered so much by the Army Commander's puritanism, which deprived him of all the privileges normally attached to his appointment, once more appeared, like a messenger from the Gods, to inform me that after dinner that evening I was again to report to his master. For a moment I was almost irritated with him and thought he must be deceiving me; things were getting beyond a joke. But he solemnly assured me that there was no deceit, though once again he had to confess that he had no idea what I was wanted for. I thought I almost detected a note of chagrin in his voice, because he was normally our best source of information about the Army Commander and rather enjoyed his position as an accredited go-between; but on this occasion even he could not, or would not, tell me anything.

So once again, puzzled but not quite so alarmed, I presented myself at the villa and again, found the Army Commander walking in his garden, head slightly bowed, hands clasped behind his back, in that attitude of profound and peaceful meditation which seemed so incongruous with thoughts of war. Again he sat me in the window seat, but this time it was he who did the talking and not me. In his clear, precise voice, which even when he was making a statement sounded as if he were giving an order, he told me that the Chiefs of Staff had decided, for reasons best known to themselves (and here he indicated that the reasons were no concern of ours and did not necessarily have his approval) that the time had come to make a large-scale landing on the coast of France. He, General Montgomery, had been made responsible for the operation, and he had selected the 2 Canadian Division, which was under his command, to carry it out. The divisional commander, he observed in parenthesis, was not much good but he had a first-class GSO 1 (Ops) who could be trusted to do most of the work: 'He's a card, that fellow,' he said, smiling rather grimly.* It was rather disturbing when he smiled, there was always a touch of malice in it.

The operation, he went on, would be directed against Dieppe, which offered suitable beaches, was within range of fighter cover, and was a town of sufficient size and importance to make it an appropriate place for a large-scale demonstration in force. It would involve an opposed landing against a heavily defended position, would be preceded by an extremely heavy air attack by night bombers, and would be supported by Churchill tanks which would be transported across the Channel by tank landing craft. The object of the operation would be to occupy Dieppe, hold it for about twelve hours, and withdraw the assault force in good order at the end of the operation. The planning of the operation would be carried out by Combined Operations Headquarters. 'That's Admiral Mountbatten's show. Yes, Admiral Mountbatten; Admiral Mountbatten.' He had a queer trick of repeating certain words, phrases, names, as if they carried a special weight of significance; it was a trick that could be used to convey malice, derision, contempt, admiration, respect, and it was left to one to guess which was intended. But sometimes it could also express simple and almost naïve self-satisfaction, as when he said: 'They've made me responsible for the operation. Yes, me; (pause) *me*.'

All this he told me in cool, level tones, adding that the operation was a matter of the greatest possible importance and secrecy and I would not discuss it with anyone at his headquarters or with anyone else unless I was specifically authorised to. That seemed natural enough; what I could not understand was why he should be discussing it with me. It was certainly not to have the benefit of any comments I might make on the operation, and I made none; nor could I see what possible part I might have to play in it. I almost felt that at the end of his simple recital of interesting facts the Army Commander would once again say, as before, 'Well, that's all. Thank you very much,' and once again I would go away puzzled and bewildered by what seemed to have become, on the part of the Army Commander, an almost obsessive desire for the pleasure of my company. Instead he said, with a cheerful air of complicity: 'Well, that's the plan. Now you know as much as I do.' And strangely enough I felt that I did, though this did not answer my unspoken question why I should be chosen to receive such confidences. But the Army Commander went on to say that since he was formally responsible for the operation, it would be necessary for him to be kept informed of the progress of planning and training, of any needs or difficulties that might arise, or any decision taken that might require his approval. He had therefore decided to attach me as his personal representative to Admiral Mountbatten's headquarters and I was to report to him as and when I thought necessary. He would be at my disposal whenever I wished to see him or to speak to him, but I was not to bother him with any unnecessary detail. I could be assured of his full support in anything I did. I was to ask his A branch for anything I needed. I would leave for London in the morning, and a car would be at my disposal whenever I needed it for travelling between London and Reigate. I would come and see him again as soon as I thought it necessary.

I listened to these remarkable instructions in considerable confusion of mind and felt sure there were a great many questions I should ask before attempting to carry them out. But the Army Commander seemed to feel that he had solved what was essentially a very simple problem to his entire satisfaction and before I had time even to formulate the questions I ought to ask, our interview had been terminated, as before, with the words, 'Well, that's all. Thank you very much.' He went to bed, in his usual tranquillity of mind, and I returned to my billet wondering feverishly how I could possibly carry out this mission for which, as I knew, I was far from well equipped.

V

The following night I slept on the floor of one of the planning offices at Combined Operations Headquarters, 'Admiral Mountbatten's show'. I had been issued with a security pass labelled Operation Rutter, and had met the members of the Combined Operations staff who had been assigned to the planning of the operation, and also Lt.-Col. Churchill Mann, GSO 1 (Ops), 2 Canadian Division. And after that we had set to work, and under Colonel Mann's direction the work had gone on until two o'clock in the morning. 'He's a card, that fellow,' I thought, and the Army Commander had not exaggerated. Lt.-Col. Mann was a

pure pyknic type,* small-headed, with sleek black hair and the long
legs of a cavalryman; before the war he had been one of the finest
horsemen in North America. He was a brilliant staff officer, but what
was more exceptional was that his mind had a wild and incalculable
originality, and his contempt for normal military codes and conventions was extreme. He immediately disposed of all my doubts about
how I was to carry out my mission by assuming at once that I was a
working member of his own staff; that is why, on my first day at
Combined Operations Headquarters, I found myself still at work at
half-past two in the morning. The assumption was in fact an eminently
reasonable one, both from his point of view and from mine. On the one
hand, for reasons of security he was the only staff officer of 2 Canadian
Division who had as yet been initiated into the secret of Operation
Rutter, and my assistance at Combined Operations Headquarters was
very welcome to him, especially since he had the gift of making one
work both hard and well. On the other hand, the only way in which I
could learn to understand the planning of Rutter was to take an active
part in it myself; I was thus saved from the awkward and invidious
position of being the personal representative of the Army Commander
with nothing else to do but represent him. And since Lt.-Col. Mann
was punctilious in telling me of anything which he thought the Army
Commander should know, we soon found a basis of co-operation by
which I did some of his work for him and he did all of mine for me.
From my point of view, it was an admirable arrangement.

But there were difficulties. Admiral Mountbatten's headquarters was
at that time bursting with young soldiers, sailors, and airmen who had
not only been elaborately trained in the technique of combined operations but had both planned them and carried them out in person; all of
them had taken part in raids in which the roles of soldiers, sailors, and
airmen were almost indistinguishable. They all talked learnedly about
tides and wind and moon and weather, of navigation by sea and air, of
beach gradients and landing craft (T&P) and many other matters of
which the ordinary soldier was completely innocent, and for purposes
of planning they had evolved an esoteric jargon of their own which had
nothing in common with the conventional language of any of the three
separate services. To join this fish-flesh-fowl company was to find
oneself almost literally at sea or up in the air; one felt oneself hopelessly earthbound, a clumsy and an ignorant landlubber, irretrievably a
pongo,* enjoying none of that freedom of all the elements which the
others by now took for granted, as if they had been born not only with
arms and legs but with wings and scales and fins and webbed feet. And
the difficulty was not only, or primarily, a matter of feeling; the fact was

that these officers possessed a body of detailed technical knowledge of which one was oneself completely ignorant.

The GSO 1 (Ops), 2 Canadian Division, who was essentially a horseman and a soldier, not a mythical beast who moved by land, air, and sea at once, knew as little of all this as I did; but his attitude was that what any officer of any service could do he could do as well or better. He set himself to master the mysteries of combined operations with the enthusiasm and assiduity of a scholar to whom entirely new fields of research have been opened, and I had no choice except to follow him as well as I could. Fortunately, in one respect our labours were made easier. The knowledge and skills assembled at Combined Operations Headquarters were derived on the whole from experience of innumerable small raids, sometimes successful, sometimes disastrous, made by very small groups of highly trained men against carefully selected objectives which were not an integral part of the fortress-wall of Europe. No one had as yet considered the problem of deliberately landing in divisional strength in the face of the enemy in one of his most heavily defended areas; the difference was so great that problems of quantity for once really did change into problems of quality and were so transformed that all the wisdom and experience of Combined Operations Headquarters was not much more helpful than the ignorance of persons like me. Faced with this problem, we were all amateurs. In particular, no one had experience of landing heavy tanks on open beaches in the face of the enemy. I went down to Selsey Bill with a member of the naval planning staff to try out a Churchill tank on a shelving beach under conditions rather more difficult than we might expect to find at Dieppe. The monster passed the test, but there was no sea wall at the top of the beach as there was at Dieppe, nor any of the guns in concrete pill boxes which the tank would have to face when it lumbered ashore during the assault.

For the next few weeks, such problems occupied me completely and obsessively; I dreamed about them at night, even the geological composition and consistency of the shingle on the beach at Dieppe were of absorbing interest, since there might be variations in it where it might not carry the weight of our tanks. Only occasionally did it strike me, with horror, that the only reason why I had developed such an obsession with every detail of the topography of this charming little town was that we intended to capture and destroy it. As we advanced in our planning, the idea that Dieppe existed simply and solely to provide an objective for Operation Rutter overshadowed any other reason it might have for existence, and all the more because the difficulties of the operation seemed to increase with every step we took in arriving at a plan to which all three services could agree. And apart from the differences of inter-service planning, changes had to be made in the original outline plan which heavily increased the odds against the success of the operation.

The original intention of the plan approved by the Chiefs of Staff had been that the bombing of Dieppe during the hours of darkness preceding the landing should be so devastating in its effect that any opposition would be merely nominal. This was an integral and essential element in the plan, which had been originally conceived of as a large-scale exercise which would both raise morale and provide us, without great loss, with the answers to some of the technical problems which had to be solved before we could undertake the invasion of Europe. Now there came the day when at a planning conference Admiral Mountbatten, handsome and breezy, like Brighton at its best, announced that Mr Churchill had decided that, for political reasons, it would be inexpedient to undertake the bombing of Dieppe.*

It was not for soldiers to question such a decision; and it was even welcome, both on grounds of humanity and because it meant that Dieppe would escape obliteration; but in effect it knocked the bottom out of Rutter. Yet no one drew the logical conclusion that Rutter was no longer feasible as a serious operation of war; henceforward it could only be an expensive and murderous laboratory experiment designed to arrive at certain results which might well have been achieved less expensively, certainly in blood, by other means. But even if anyone had drawn such a conclusion, it would have been almost impossible to resist Admiral Mountbatten's inspiring confidence that unexpected obstacles of this kind were precisely what Combined Operations Headquarters existed to overcome, by some commando-raid of the imagination which would gaily overleap them. This charm was so great that it would have been shameful not to respond to it.* Indeed, we responded so well that we were not dismayed even when we learned that the landing would not have the fire support, as we had originally hoped, of two or three old battleships, as the Admiralty were not willing to risk them in the Channel, or indeed anywhere else, as they were not fit to take part in any modern naval action. So little by little the support by sea and air on which the success of the operation depended was gradually taken away from it, but almost without anyone noticing, and without seriously discussing whether it ought now to be cancelled; so much so that I believe that the operation would have proceeded even if the troops had been asked to land with no better weapons than their bare hands and fists; in the event, they had very little more.

Indeed, from another point of view, it hardly mattered whether Rutter succeeded or failed as a purely military operation. For it appeared that to the RAF its principal objective was to force the Luftwaffe into the air and to give battle over the Channel. We were assured that a landing in France on the scale of Rutter would compel the Luftwaffe to react violently; if it did so, the RAF was confident of winning a decisive victory in the air, which would change the whole position over France and elsewhere to our advantage. To capture and hold Dieppe for a limited period could therefore be regarded merely as a subsidiary and minor objective. Thus the military forces employed in the operation were not only guinea pigs. They were also bait.* What did it matter if the bait was devoured whole, so long as the fish, or rather the Luftwaffe, was properly hooked?

VI

Combined Operations Headquarters lived in an atmosphere of continuous improvisation, of meetings and conferences hurriedly called and as hurriedly cancelled, of brilliant and unorthodox ideas adopted with enthusiasm and abandoned when found to be impracticable; floating gun batteries mounted on artificial ice floes were by no means the wildest of such chimeras. In such an atmosphere of sustained drama and crisis, I did whatever I could to assist Lt.-Col. Mann and at the same time to collect the kind of information which I felt the Army Commander would require of me. Apart from representing him at Combined Operations Headquarters, I had also to play the same part at GHQ Home Forces, where I had to approach the Commander-in-Chief with requests for the allocation of additional resources to 2 Canadian Division. At GHQ Home Forces, at its higher levels, something of the same air of tension and strain prevailed as at Combined Operations Headquarters, though uncoloured by those flashes of inventive genius which made one think that, if politics is the art of the possible, war is that of the impossible, or certainly the improbable. At GHQ Home Forces, staff officers at the higher level always seemed to be overworked, harassed, pressed for time and as a result irritable; they were apt to regard my requests as unreasonable and an additional cause for irritation. When an appointment was made with the Commander-in-Chief, there was always a long wait while he dispatched business that always was urgent and pressing, yet protracted, and when finally I saw him, it was difficult to explain my requests in face of his criticisms of Rutter, for which he appeared to hold me largely responsible. It was during these interviews that I formed the theory that generals, as a class, suffered from some profound neurosis which made them subject to sudden and irrational gusts of anger and irritation which could only be appeased by the smell of battle. In battle, their inflamed nerves were calmed, they became cool and resourceful, rational and calculating; except of course for those whose nervous disorders had gone so far that even battle could not appease them. In the case of the Commander-in-Chief, however, I knew that his brusque manner, that seemed to combine rudeness and bad temper, were the result of the almost continuous pain in which he lived as a result of an old wound suffered in the First World War.* But I began to understand a little why Monty liked to have about him men who were physically well and whose nerves were relaxed by the sedative of physical exercise.

And indeed how different things seemed when at regular intervals I went down to Reigate to report to the Army Commander. It was never difficult to see him; when an appointment was made, he was always punctually available, and he always gave the impression that he had nothing in the world to do except the business which was in hand. There were never any papers on his desk, there were never any interruptions; one almost had the feeling that here was an idle man, and that but for one's own visit he would have been at a loss to fill up his time. Most remarkable of all, to myself, was that he actually listened to what I said, gravely and politely, though very often I felt it was not worth listening to; and when he made any comments, or issued any instructions, one felt that they had already been considered, calmly and dispassionately, in the cool of the evening, in the garden, when he had given himself just the right amount of time required for reflection. I began to think that the difference between him and the other commanders I had come to know was that he actually *thought*, in the same sense that a scientist or a scholar thinks. His subject matter happened to be war, but the mental processes, of definition and analysis, of coming to conclusions on demonstrable evidence, were the same. This was, however, only true when he was thinking about war; on any other subject he could be as silly as anyone else. But when he was thinking about war, which he did with wonderful lucidity and concentration, he seemed to me to come as near as any could to exemplifying the dictum of my old tutor, H. W. B. Joseph, that the will is reason acting. I had never found this very convincing, but the Army Commander seemed to give sense to it.*

Perhaps it was an awareness of this particular difference between himself and other commanders that sometimes stimulated him to make personal comments, which nearly always took the same form. When I once remarked that, in the confusion and excitement that ruled at Combined Operations Headquarters, it was sometimes difficult to discover what decisions had really been finally and irrevocably taken, he said reflectively: 'Yes, Admiral —, Admiral —. A very gallant sailor. A very gallant sailor. Had three ships sunk under him. *Three* ships sunk under him. (Pause). Doesn't know how to fight a battle.'* Or of another general, exceedingly brave, exceedingly competent, with the charm and panache of a Renaissance *condottiere*, he said: 'General —? Yes. General —. A very brave man. Killed three men with his bare hands. The man's a brigand. Doesn't know how to wage war.'

Such remarks sometimes seemed malicious, but they were said with an amused, tolerant, and confident air which deprived them of their malice, as if the Army Commander was simply stating an objective difference which he knew to exist between himself and other commanders. *Waging war, fighting a battle*, had for him no emotional connotations, or if they had he tried to exclude them altogether from his mind; they were phrases which represented problems to be solved, and the primary difficulty to be overcome was that of reducing the imponderable elements involved in *waging war, fighting a battle*, to factors which could be measured, weighed, calculated. Once that was done there was simply the problem of thinking correctly so as to arrive at the proper conclusion. The Army Commander had a mind of classical directness and lucidity; when he talked of problems of war they seemed to assume an almost elementary simplicity, but this was only because of the strictness of the analysis which had been applied to them. And if he seemed malicious in his comments on others, whose *style* he disliked, as a painter might find the style of other painters corrupt, or insincere, or, above all, not painter-like, he could also be generous in praise of those in whose methods he saw something of what he aimed at himself. In later years, after he had won the victory of Alamein and had become famous, I often remembered his comment on General Alexander: 'The only man, yes, the *only* man, under whom any admiral, general, or air marshal would gladly serve in a subordinate position.'

When I reported to him at Reigate, I usually saw him at what seemed to be his favourite time for such meetings, in the evening after dinner. Sometimes I could not get there until later; then, if it were not too late, he would receive me in bed, looking exceedingly clean, like a schoolboy after his bath, in his flannelette pyjamas, his Bible open beside him on his night table, himself propped up on his pillows, his foxy face alert as ever, showing no trace of tiredness. I had the feeling that the moment I had gone the eyelids would close like a shutter and he would immediately be asleep. When he was awake, he was thinking, clearly, rationally, lucidly; when he was asleep, he really slept. I felt sure there were no dreams. And why should there be? After all, there was nothing, no, nothing, to worry about.

VII

At last, after weeks in which we worked late into the night on the military plans for Rutter, and by day sat in conference trying to reconcile the conflicting demands of land, sea, and air, the combined plan was agreed and approved and we prepared to move to the Isle of Wight where 2 Canadian Division was to undergo intensive training for the operation. The demands made on the division were heavy; in addition to achieving the degree of physical fitness and of skill in the use of their own weapons which the operation would demand, they had also, in a few weeks, to learn and practise the techniques of an assault landing and of disembarking heavy tanks on open beaches. They had also to acclimatise themselves to sea sickness. Worst of all, they had to overcome the fact that they had never been in action before; as far as they could, they had to try and lose their innocence, and prepare to be initiated into war under the worst conceivable conditions. No training could achieve this; being fresh and untried, they looked forward to the operation with enthusiasm, with pride that they should have been chosen to carry it out, with a complete and naïve confidence in success. The rank and file of the division, if not its officers, were probably as good material for making fighting men as could be found anywhere in the world. They were tough and adapt-able, by the standard of British troops they were well educated, they were accustomed to hard lives in the open air and were also mech-anically skilled, and by temperament it was natural to them to use their own initiative and to act independently. Above all, they had a positive desire, which perhaps only fresh troops who have never seen the horrors of war really possess, to prove themselves in action and win glory for themselves, their division and their country; for the Canad-ians had the naïve and unsophisticated patriotism of citizens of a new country with its future still to make which is not to be found among British troops. Also all these men were volunteers and not conscripts.

Divisional Headquarters established itself in a block of flats at Cowes; the Naval Force Commander raised his flag in the Royal Yacht Squadron; and the divisional staff set to work to produce the operation orders, to which I contributed the paragraphs and appendices concerned with intelligence. In doing so, I came to know Dieppe better than any town I have ever known or lived in, down to the last pebble on its shingly beach. For reasons of security we were unable to carry out adequate air reconnaissance; for much of our knowledge of the topography of the town and the beaches we had to depend on picture postcards and family snapshots which we collected from every available source. How strange it seemed sometimes, as one studied some old-fashioned photograph showing a French family taking its luncheon on the beach, the little boys in sailor suits and straw hats, as in some illustration of a scene from Proust, that the reason why this particular photograph was of particular interest was that it showed with extreme clarity the gradient of the beach at the exact point where our tanks would disembark. Yet even so our patient researches were not sufficient for their purpose. We knew, for instance, that the cliffs surrounding the old harbour of Dieppe were honeycombed with caves that had long been used for human habitation; we had descriptions of them, we had photographs. Yet we did not draw the obvious deduction that the Germans would stuff the caves with machine guns which would enfilade our troops with a murderous fire that could neither be silenced nor neutralised. Nor, in the event, did this matter much; within our resources, there was nothing that could be done about those machine guns.

During this period of training, the division was sealed off on the island. The troops were not allowed to reveal their location, and so far as possible the troops and the staff were cut off from all communication with the mainland. But the division had left a small rear headquarters behind at its previous location, where officially the division was still stationed. There an intelligent young officer, speculating why the division had suddenly disappeared into the blue, correctly inferred that it must be going to undertake some special operation of great secrecy and importance. Bored at his empty headquarters, he studied the coastline of France, calculated the range of fighter cover, examined suitable beaches, and came triumphantly and correctly to the conclusion that there was about to be a raid on Dieppe. He announced his discovery to a large number of friends and acquaintances in London and elsewhere. The officer could hardly be blamed for being intelligent, or even for indiscretion, because he had been told none of the plans for Rutter; I had the unpleasant task of informing him that, since he had been quite right in his deduction, he was now by far too dangerous a person to be left at liberty and would have to be detained in some suitable, and I hoped comfortable place until the operation was over. He was appalled by his error of having guessed correctly, and drawing his revolver from his holster asked whether he could atone for his guilt in any other way than by using it upon himself. I had not anticipated such melodrama and hastened to assure him that he had been guilty of nothing except of being too intelligent. As I left him, an enormous young officer in a kilt from a Canadian-Scottish regiment, he was still gazing at his revolver with the puzzled look of one who had never realised before that it might be dangerous to be too clever. It had taken the whole of the Chiefs of Staff's organisation and of Combined Operations Headquarters several months to decide on Dieppe as the objective of Rutter; it had taken him, alone, about a week.

Such odd duties took me away from the island, where Lt.-Col. Mann and his staff worked at all hours of day and night at the elaborate and intricate movement orders required to transport the division across the Channel and land it at Dieppe. Overworked and harassed by now, they were like old astrologers who anxiously studied all the phases of the moon in order to discover the most favourable auspices for the operation. While they laboured, I continued to report to the Army Commander in Reigate and to Combined Operations Headquarters in London, crossing on the ferry from Southampton and always glad when I was back on the island. One evening I was too late to cross; there was an air raid on Southampton that night and I lay in my bedroom at the Dolphin and wondered if the raid was directed at the mass of shipping and assault craft collected in the Solent; for as the date of the operation grew nearer it began to seem more and more likely that the Germans might have received information of our intentions. During those weeks it seemed as if the island might be the last that I and many others might see of England, and all the more beautiful because of that. A large part of its population had been evacuated; houses, offices, yachtsmen's villas stood empty, there were no sails on Southampton Water. On the beach at Osborne our tanks damaged Queen Victoria's pretty little bathing hut and we had to make profuse apologies for this offence given to history, without being able to explain why Osborne should suddenly have been invaded by our unwieldy Churchills. I visited Tennyson's house at Farringford, and thought of Swinburne bathing in the cold Channel and Gosse collecting his marine specimens in the rock pools that in his day blossomed like gardens. It seemed sad and pathetic that such a world should have given way to our tanks and our LCTs and LCPs and LCAs;* for the moment at least the island, empty and deserted, seemed to belong to us, which meant to Canada. Transatlantic accents, Anglo-Saxon and French, were heard in the country lanes that were covered with wild roses, and roses bloomed in the overgrown gardens of neat little villas and cottages; the island seemed to float like some enchanted Tennysonian rose garden in the waves of the Channel.

But as the island seemed more beautiful, the operation seemed riskier and harder. For all the efforts made in training and preparing the troops, it was difficult to believe that they would be ready in time; and in any case no amount of training could really equip inexperienced troops for an action which combined, in the short space of twelve hours, two of the most difficult operations of war; an assault landing against prepared positions and a withdrawal and embarkation by sea in the face of the enemy. Trained as they were, at the peak of physical fitness, longing for the weeks of preparation and make-believe exercises to be over so that at last they might face the reality of battle, the very inexperience of the troops and the staff inspired them with a fatal self-confidence, a supreme conviction that the navy had only to put them ashore in the correct place and the battle was won. They knew it would be hard; they did not know it was impossible. This conviction persisted even after the large-scale exercise which was carried out in Studland Bay, where the division on landing fell into an indescribable confusion, which was in itself sufficient to throw doubt on the feasibility of the operation, even though there was no enemy present to turn confusion into bloodshed and slaughter. We sailed back to Cowes by destroyer, lying on deck stripped to the waist under a blue and cloudless sky; all of us suffered from the same fatal lack of imagination which prevented us from translating the depressing lessons of the rehearsal into the murderous consequences they would have in battle. In any case, what possible good could imagination do in such circumstances? The date of the operation was now fixed; the decision had been made. Lying on our backs in the blazing sun, we enjoyed the few hours of idleness as we steamed down the Channel and like an amateur dramatic company assured ourselves that everything would be all right on the night.

The Army Commander came down to watch the exercise, noted severely, impartially, the mistakes that were made, emphasised the need for further training. The Divisional Commander, who was as rough and ready as Monty was fine and calculating, commented that no doubt General Montgomery was an admirable trainer of troops but perhaps he was getting a little old to lead them into battle; what was required, he seemed to imply, for the test of war was someone of the same coarse fibre as himself. Knowing nothing of war myself, except from books, training manuals, exercises, courses, I even thought he might be right, though I was offended by such a criticism of the Army Commander, for whom my feelings at that time did not fall far short of idolatry. But I was surprised, when I visited him next in Reigate, that the Army Commander should be so little perturbed about the risks of the operation. It was, he implied, an operation which had been decided on by the Chiefs of Staff, not by himself, and for reasons with which he was not concerned. He was responsible for mounting the operation and for allocating the troops and equipment for it, and he did not refuse any requests the division made for anything that was lacking or fail to support such requests when they had to go to a higher level. But the planning of the operation had not been in his hands; its execution equally was not in his hands but in those of the Military, Naval, and Air Force Commanders. There was nothing he could do to affect the result, and it would therefore have been a waste of time and effort for him to worry about it. Being supremely logical where questions of command were concerned, he did not worry. I almost wished that he would, and suspected that behind his calm lay a wish that the formal responsibility for the operation had not fallen on him; all the more so perhaps because the Canadian Commander-in-Chief, General Mc-Naughton, had protested vigorously that, since Canadian troops were involved, the responsibility should properly be his. Somehow Monty gave me the impression that he would not mind if it were.

And in the end, so it was. Training had come to an end; and the troops had been drilled in every detail of the plan, from the assault to the withdrawal. The last sentences of the operation order had been written and approved and the bulky document distributed throughout the division. But even at this last moment odd and bizarre excrescences added themselves to the plan. In my capacity as odd job man I received instructions, I was not quite clear from whom, that I would be issued with huge numbers of forged French notes in large denominations which would be distributed to a small party of Sudeten-German socialists in British uniforms who were to be attached to the operation in order to carry out some suicidal mission. The notes were delivered to me by a sergeant of no known regiment in a sealed parcel under the clock at Victoria Station. I gave no receipt for them nor was ever asked for any account of them. The mission was extremely secret and its purpose not revealed to me. Back on the island, I located the suicide party who spoke no language except their own dialect of German. Room had to be found for them in the boats; they were an embarrassing responsibility. I was unable to distribute all my enormous funds because some members of the party were missing and I had no means of locating them. So I kept those thousands of francs, and I had them in my possession until long after the war, when I finally destroyed them; nor did I ever know what happened to those bewildered

Sudeten-Germans, fighting their own private war in a hopeless cause; I imagine that they disappeared without trace on the beaches of Dieppe and that their names, like those mysterious francs, never appeared in any official record. But somewhere in the loading tables for Rutter will be found the last-minute addition of a party of twelve men to be included in the assault.

So at last all was ready. I paid my last visit to the quiet house in Reigate, for the last time heard the words: 'Well, that's all. Thank you very much,' and returned to the rose-bound island on the evening before the assault force was due to sail. But that night there was a gale, and in the morning it was announced that the operation would be postponed. Time and tide only allowed us three days on which the operation was feasible; the bad weather continued for the next forty-eight hours and on the third day postponement was no longer possible; Rutter was cancelled. Sadly we repaired to the little pub on the shore where unlimited supplies of Dimple Haig whisky were still available, and sadly, like schoolboys cheated of a cricket match by rain, we lamented the bad luck that had frustrated all our weeks of effort. Then we returned, to our billets and packed our kit and drove back to Combined Operations Headquarters to tidy up all the loose ends left over after the cancellation of Operation Rutter.

VIII

Winding up Rutter, collecting and arranging papers, assembling material for a report, took several days which were overcast with the sense of anticlimax; it was as if one were documenting a piece of history that had never taken place. Combined Operations Head-quarters seemed drab and dusty and bureaucratic after the island and the gusty days on the beaches and the sea watching the troops practising their boat drill. We all felt depressed and frustrated at the thought of so much effort gone for nothing; and then, like a little ripple on a sluggish sea, the rumour began to grow that the cancellation of Rutter was not final, and that the operation would take place in a month's time,* when moon and tide would once again be in a favourable conjunction. At first it seemed hard to credit the suggestion; it had been difficult enough to guard against security leakages during the period when the troops had already been isolated on the island. It seemed quite impossible to go on doing so any longer. But for once rumour was true, and finally it was announced at a conference that Jubilee, as the operation was now to be called, would take place, weather permitting, in a month's time; but at the same time I was told that responsibility for the operation had been transferred from General Montgomery to General McNaughton, and almost immediately I received a telephone call from Reigate instructing me to return at once, as the Army Commander had no further need of a personal representative at Combined Operations Headquarters.

It was quite obviously true, but I felt reluctant to surrender the freedom which the Army Commander had allowed me while I represented him; despite his puritanism, and his strong instinct for economy, he had not even objected when I said that when in London I proposed to live at the Mayfair Hotel, though he strongly disapproved of it. All he had said was: 'A bit swish, isn't it?' I had enjoyed all the novel and sometimes surprising tasks that had been given me; it was sad to decline from the position of personal representative of the Army Commander, armed with his authority and the threat of his displeasure if I were not treated with due respect, to the humdrum duties of a GSO 2 (I) in a non-operational command. My friends, as they had become, in 2 Canadian Division, protested against my being taken away from them, greatly exaggerating any services or help I had been able to give them; but the Army Commander, as always, saw no reason to change his mind. He had no further part in the operation; it would have been illogical if any officer of his did either.

So I returned sadly to Reigate and for the next three weeks tried to avoid embarrassing questions about what I had been doing during my absence from headquarters, and wondered how the preparations for Jubilee were proceeding. Having been occupied to the point of obsession with the operation for so long, it seemed to me astonishing that no one was aware that it was even contemplated. It seemed to me even more astonishing that on the island about ten thousand men were waiting amid the roses and the sea without anyone knowing what they were waiting for. And indeed as the weeks went by I myself began to doubt whether all those complicated and elaborate plans had ever had any real existence; those agitated conferences at Combined Headquarters, the angry pain-ridden Commander-in-Chief, Monty lying in bed with his Bible beside him, the crimson roses of the island, all seemed part of an improbable dream created in the feverish imagination of Combined Operations Headquarters and I could not really believe that at any time now the assault force would sail from Cowes to make the crossing to Dieppe.

Yet it was not a dream. One morning I was summoned to the BGS (Ops) and told that a request had been received from combined Operations Headquarters that I should report there the following day and that the Army Commander had given his consent for me to go. As a reward, it seemed, for services rendered, I was to be allowed to accompany the assault force as an observer. If I could take no part in the operation, I was at least going to be allowed to watch it.

The next day I lunched at my club in London.* In the library I picked up a new biography of Sickert and all through luncheon I gazed unbelievingly at a series of illustrations of his paintings of Dieppe, hardly able to credit that in less than twelve hours I should be looking at the same scenes myself. And for a moment, looking at those pictures, I suddenly felt a violent sense of nausea and disgust at the business of war and of nostalgia for the days of peace when a town like Dieppe could achieve immortality as the object of a painter's vision; now it seemed to enjoy only an abstract existence as the objective of Operation Jubilee. When at last the car came to pick me up, it was almost with shame that I thought of why it was taking me down to Portsmouth.

I travelled down with a distinguished American war correspondent who severely criticised what he knew about the operation and grumbled at the inadequacy of the arrangements made for the Press. This seemed to be for him the criterion by which he judged any military operation;* but in addition he had a profound and jeering lack of confidence in any action carried out by limeys, a term which for him included Canadians as well as Englishmen. His criticisms seemed to leave a sour taste in his own mouth as well as mine and he washed them down with large draughts of whisky from a pocket flask. He was loud-mouthed, arrogant, and overbearing, and frankly contemptuous of any attempt by the British to play at soldiers; I did not like him and refused his offer to share his whisky. I was glad when at last we reached Portsmouth, where we were to go aboard HMS *Garth,* one of six Hunt class destroyers which had been allocated to Jubilee. Indeed they were all that were left of the heavy naval bombardment for which we had once hoped; and their four-inch guns, firing at land targets, were quite ineffective against German shore defences.

Garth's task was to cover the flank of the assault force during the sea crossing, and later to engage, and if possible silence or neutralise, one of the gun batteries which we knew to be located on the high cliffs on the eastern side of Dieppe. On our arrival her commander, narrow-jawed, taciturn, tight-lipped, greeted us politely enough but without enthusiasm, as if he did not like the idea of carrying passengers aboard his ship. It was still light when we reached Portsmouth; I went below to the wardroom, where the steward served us with drinks and sandwiches. The war correspondent had become sulkier than ever when he realised that he was not likely to receive any great marks of respect from the commander; he relieved his feelings by criticising *Garth*'s cramped accommodation and comparing her unfavourably with the newest American destroyers. I asked the steward whether he was looking forward to the next day and learned that in action he served in one of the anti-aircraft crews and hoped he might help to bring down a German aeroplane. He spoke rather as one who had been unexpectedly invited to a day's shooting and was hoping he might add to the bag.

I was glad to accept the commander's offer of the hospitality of his quarters and in his narrow little cabin I lay down and slept until the throbbing of the ship's engines and the unaccustomed motion of the ship woke me and I realised we were under way. In the harsh light of the cabin's electric bulb I found it difficult at first to remember where I was, or why I was there; it was hard to grasp that at last Operation Jubilee had really begun. At that moment I remembered being told that a destroyer is so thin-skinned that a revolver shot will pierce its armour; it seemed strange that men should be exposed to so many dangers in so frail a vessel, as if they were to venture to sea in an egg-shell; for the first time I even began to have some slight qualms about my personal safety, and I wondered what the men of the assault force were thinking at that moment.

I had slept for several hours; night had fallen; still confused with sleep, I was not prepared, when I went on deck, for the sudden impression of travelling blindly at great speed into a darkness that was filled with the noise of wind and water. *Garth*, like a hunting dog, was making great sweeps on the flanks of the assault force, casting to right and left in the darkness as if at any moment she might smell out an enemy and pick it up in her teeth and worry it to death. Perhaps what surprised me most was that in this darkness, cold and wet with spray as we curved through the pale and shadowy waters, we seemed to be entirely alone. On our maps and charts of the operation the assault force, each ship and craft carefully shown in position, had seemed a solid and compact body, as if we were going to cross the Channel in a pack, shoulder to shoulder and side by side, almost without room to move; here on *Garth* nothing was to be seen of the ships of the assault force, there was only a grey waste of waters surrounding us, and in the darkness the destroyer rushing forward seemed like some highly strung neurotic animal that had broken away from the herd. This impression of panic and hysteria came from the shivering and trembling of the destroyer as its engines raced at top speed; she seemed to shudder through her whole frame as she hit each successive wave; I felt ashamed of such imaginings when I went up to the bridge where I found the commander and his first officer standing calm and silent as if what seemed to me such an extraordinary display of power and energy were simply a matter of routine.

I stood beside them on the bridge listening to the uninterrupted series of orders that flowed from the commander's thin precise lips. The first officer told me that their only worry was whether at first light they would be able to take up their proper position and identify exactly the gun position on the cliff which they were to engage. I said that, after studying so many maps for so long, I thought I ought to know the coastline like the palm of my hand and felt sure we could not make a mistake; he looked at me for a moment in surprise at the idea of assistance coming from such an unlikely source. Then he said that the gun position was a difficult target; objects on land were so much more difficult to hit because they stood still. I wanted to enquire into this mystery of naval gunnery, but at that moment, away in the east, we suddenly saw a flicker of light in the sky, crimson, deep yellow, violet, followed by what seemed to be the sound of gunfire. There was something sinister, because so unexpected, about that streak of colour in the distance; it had no part in our plan or our timetable, at this moment the assault force should still be steaming under cover of darkness and silence. It was as if chance had suddenly decided to interfere in our careful calculations and throw us all into doubt and confusion. Wondering, we continued to gaze at that unsteady burst of colour in the night sky; I had a sudden sickening feeling that somehow, somewhere, disaster lay ahead of the operation. *Garth* took another bound into the darkness as if intent on hunting out the cause of our confusion, but our orders were to protect the flank of the convoy and sweep the Channel to the west of it; we turned our backs on the flickering lights in the east until, as mysteriously as they had begun, they died away. But they left us with a feeling that already something had gone wrong; could it be that the Germans were aware of our approach? We only learned later that a coastal convoy, taking advantage of darkness to steal up the Channel, had cut across the convoy and bewildered and confused at the sudden appearance of so large a force had fired distress signals and attempted to engage with what armament it possessed. Their paths had crossed in the darkness and the assault force had continued on its course, but the hand of chance had already interfered in our plans and this accidental meeting in the darkness had almost certainly destroyed any element of surprise the operation may have had.

Garth continued to make her wide sweeps to the flank of the assault force, until at last, almost imperceptibly, the night sky began to pale and in the shadowy light before dawn we saw the ships of the assault force dimly outlined to the east. *Garth* had completed her first task of search and protection and now we turned towards the convoy to engage the gun position on the cliff. But already, as night passed into day and darkness lifted, the fog of confusion began to fall upon the scene so that it was impossible to recognise any sign of those carefully planned and calculated movements which were so meticulously coordinated in the operation orders. And indeed our own attention was now completely absorbed by the successive waves of enemy aircraft that dived out of the sky over the assault force, while overhead our own fighters had opened the air battle which it was one of the objectives of Jubilee to provoke. Like angry bees they buzzed and swarmed in the sky, while below them the enemy pressed home their low-level attacks on the ships of the fleet. As they screamed over our heads, their bombs fell slowly downwards, turning in the air like beer bottles, so slowly that one could count the seconds as they fell, and it seemed impossible that they should not hit one. Each wave of aircraft was greeted with a furious outburst of anti-aircraft fire directed at anything which came into range; the fleet defended itself like a man desperately trying to brush away a swarm of wasps and in its indiscriminate fire some of our own aircraft were shot down.

After the silence and darkness of the night, when the only sounds had been the throbbing and shuddering of *Garth*'s engines, and the hissing and slapping of the waves against her sides, this sudden outburst of furious activity was bewildering. One hardly knew where to look, at the tiny assault craft, loaded with men, as they dashed towards the shore, at the aircraft shrieking down at one out of the sky, at the line of smoke at the water's edge where the assault craft hit the beaches, at those tiny objects like beer bottles dropping slowly towards one so that one felt one could almost catch them in one's outstretched hands. Everything was in furious and angry movement, as if time had been foreshortened and compressed so that each second contained the multitudinous events of a lifetime. Out of the sky one of our own aircraft suddenly dived precipitously down and plunged into the sea. *Garth* broke off her course to search for the pilot. The wreckage floated on the water in an inextricable tangle of wires and broken struts, the tip of a wing showing above the waves like a shark's fin. Not far away a dark round object bobbed on the waves like a football and coming up to it we saw, with a sudden feeling of sickness, that it was the pilot's head, its black hair wet and sleek as a seal's, neatly severed at the neck.

Now *Garth* herself was hit by one of the bombs that fell so lazily out of the sky. The fragments of the bomb ricocheted madly round the deck. Beside me was a tall fair-haired young artillery officer, assigned to *Garth* as a ship-to-shore gunnery officer. He turned to me with a look of surprise on his young serious face, a look so intense that at first I could not understand what had so profoundly startled him. Then slowly he tumbled to the deck and I saw that his leg had been cut off above the knee by a flying fragment. He lay on the deck, still staring up at me with that intent profoundly serious look of surprise and as I knelt down beside him he clutched my hand in his as if at that moment some kind of human reassurance was of far more importance than any first aid I could give him. He had played no part in the action nor was there any conceivable part he could have played; the units ashore with whom he was in radio communication had been destroyed on the beaches and it did not matter that he was no longer there to answer requests for fire support that never came.

By now the beaches were strewn with the wreckage of assault craft lying broken-backed on the high water line; heavy Churchill tanks, like monsters that had waddled slowly and clumsily out of the sea, were stuck hopelessly in the shingle. Some had reached the sea wall of the promenade but had been unable to climb it and sat back on their haunches exposed to the point-blank fire of the beach defences. But it was only in momentary glimpses that one could see what was happening on shore; over sea and land drifted a curtain of smoke, broken by flashes of gunfire, but even as much as one could see through the smoke was enough to show that the troops had failed to clear the beaches, that the tanks had not penetrated into the town, and that the men on the beaches were exposed to a murderous fire that poured in on them from every side.

But *Garth* was steaming away from the beaches parallel with the cliffs where she had located and engaged her target, and the gun on shore and the destroyer at sea were now joined in a private battle of their own. Calm and unmoved on the bridge, the commander continued to issue his series of rapid, precise, thin-lipped orders. *Garth*'s tactics were simple. We dashed along the shore and when opposite the gun position fired broadside with all our four-inch guns. At the same time the gun on the cliff replied, bracketing us with one shot over us, one short of us, and one accurately on the target. At that moment, *Garth* dived behind the blanket of smoke which she had raised as soon as her salvo had been fired; then we raced behind our protective smoke screen to reappear again and release our broadside at the gun position on the cliff. Each time that we did so, the gun replied with greater accuracy; the manœuvre became monotonous and repetitive, and each time harder on the nerves, especially after we had been hit twice, the second time with considerable casualties and damage. Indeed, the second time we were hit I thought, and wished, that *Garth* would break off the action. But the commander imperturbably repeated the same orders; once again we emerged from our smoke screen to carry out the same manœuvre. The petty officer on the bridge looked at me, shrugged his shoulders, raised his eyebrows, like a nanny in charge of an obstinate child; under his breath he muttered, 'The old bastard's going in again.' It was spoken in a tone in which wonder, tolerance, and admiration were all equally combined.

Nothing now could be seen of the battle on the beaches. Other ships like ours were making smoke to protect themselves against attack. By now, according to plan, Dieppe should have been captured; there should have been the noise of demolitions as each unit destroyed its particular objectives. And they should have been regrouping to hold the town against counter-attack and to carry out the orderly withdrawal which formed the closing phase of the operation. Nothing of this was to be seen or heard; at this late hour the Divisional Commander in the Headquarter ship was despatching his last floating reserve, the Royal Marine Commando, to the beaches in a hopeless attempt to drive the assault home. It seemed a waste of life to do so when the landing had so clearly failed; but however wasteful it was, it would have required a very strong man to call off the operation before all his resources had been engaged, and the Divisional Commander did not have that kind of strength.

But this was the last effort he could make to influence a battle which from the start had not been under his control. The Headquarter ship, on which it had been originally intended that I should sail, had at no point been able to maintain proper communications with the troops on shore. There had been no opportunity of applying the doctrine of flexibility so dear to the Staff College, *always reinforce strength, never reinforce weakness*. It was simply a question of using what reserves one had, if one were to use them at all, at precisely that point of the battle where there was least hope of success, and the Divisional Commander went on doing so until he had nothing left to use. And after that, there was nothing else he could do, for better or for worse. All there was left to do was to call off the operation. And now there could be no question of an orderly withdrawal according to plan; it was simply a question of rescuing anyone who could make his escape from the beaches.

In the meanwhile, *Garth* had become incapable of playing any useful part in the operation. We had watched our sister ship *Berkeley*, another Hunt class destroyer, so badly hit that she had had to be sunk by the torpedoes of our own fleet; now we ourselves were badly damaged and

our ammunition was exhausted. We received the order to withdraw
from the operation, pick up as many survivors as we could and return
to Portsmouth; by now the assault craft, still under heavy fire and air
attack, were being ordered to the beaches to take off as many men as
they could. Once again they made their run in; fire poured upon them
from the land and from the sky; but the men they brought back were
not the same men as they had landed in the dawn. The men we took
aboard *Garth* looked as if they had learned some terrible lesson that
was still too vivid to them for them to express it clearly either to
themselves or to anyone else; but that was because they had learned it
so thoroughly. 'Never glad confident morning again!';* many were
badly wounded, all were suffering from shock and exhaustion. They
had the grey, lifeless faces of men whose vitality had been drained out
of them; each of them could have modelled a death mask. They were
bitter and resentful at having been flung into a battle far more horrible
than anything for which they had been prepared, and as they came
aboard one heard the oaths and blasphemies, the cursings and revil-
ings, with which men speak of leaders by whom they feel that they have
been betrayed and deceived. I thought that this is what a beaten army
looks like, for no army is beaten until it has lost faith and confidence in
those who command it. These men had, at that moment, and it would
be a long time before they recovered them again.

We took wounded and survivors on board until we could take no
more. *Garth*'s crew at least, though some of them were dead, had no
cause for bitterness; they had acquitted themselves well and if they had
not succeeded in silencing their target, at least they had completely
engaged its fire throughout the action. And if some of them thought
that their commander had persisted in his attacks beyond the limits
compatible with a decent and sober sense of self-preservation, this was
something that provoked a not unwilling sense of admiration and even
a certain degree of pride, now that it was all over, that they had shared
the risks with him. Now they showed the tenderness and gentleness of
men who recognise that others are in a worse case than their own,
soothing the hysterical with words like women's, comforting the
exhausted with cups of hot sweet tea, carrying the badly wounded with
infinite care down to the emergency hospital which had been hastily
prepared below deck. For a time pity took the upper hand of the
curious emotion, compounded of affection and contempt, which the
Navy feels for *the poor bloody pongos*. Plans for Jubilee had not provided
for withdrawal under such conditions as these; elaborate as they were,
they had not taken complete failure into account. The wounded lay
stretched out side by side on bunks and stretchers and hastily

improvised beds, none of them wholly conscious, mumbling words of shock and pain, their faces drained of blood and each with a look in his eyes of dumb surprise, as if each had a question to ask which no one could answer. The ship's medical officer tried desperately to improvise arrangements for blood transfusion which were far beyond his resources; and while we tried to help him to do so, *Garth* turned her back on the curtain of flame and smoke that hung over the beaches of Dieppe and the remnants of the assault force. For us, at least, Jubilee was over.

Victory

I

Bad Oenhausen is a little German spa set in gently rolling hills on the edge of the North German plain; to the south lies the Teutoberger Wald, where the German tribes once won their greatest victory over the West.* Around Bad Oenhausen are other little resorts where the German middle classes take their modest holidays. They all have a kursaal, and a park, where the band plays in the evenings, and small family hotels and innumerable lodging houses, and they cater for German families for whom the first condition of pleasure is that it should be respectable. They all have an indescribably smug and stuffy air, as if here, in spite of war and revolution and the terrible convulsion which produced National Socialism, the atmosphere, dull and heavy and oppressive, of the *Wilhelminischezeit** had never for one moment been disturbed. It was easy, at the end of the war, to believe the frequent protestations of the local citizens that they had never been aware of the atrocities of the National Socialist regime and that Belsen or Sachsenhausen were no more to them than places of correction where bad men were properly punished for offences against German propriety and decency. If these people had seen Jews being butchered before their noses they would somehow have succeeded in not noticing, and would later have sworn in all sincerity that they did not know that Jewish blood was red.

In May 1945 the tides of war had swept past Bad Oenhausen, and it escaped defeat just as it had escaped all the effects of bombing during the war. Its streets were undamaged; there were no gaping holes in the roofs of its pretentious little villas; walking in the park one found it hard to understand why the band was not still playing to stout Germans drinking beer and smoking cigars. And in the great plain beyond the town, the countryside was already beginning to carry its rich burden of crops; in the farmyards the huge barns with their red roofs and their black and white timber-and-plaster walls would soon be full. The village streets were filled with blonde, healthy, beautiful children, their flaxen hair burned almost white by the sun; on Sundays the farmers and their wives still walked to church along the dusty country lanes, the men in black frock coats and top hats and the women in their traditional stiff black dresses and elaborate white starched caps.* It was hard to believe that the Kaiser was not still on the throne or that Bismarck was dead.

Since Bad Oenhausen and its surroundings were undamaged, indeed almost untouched, by war and since it could offer all the accommodation intended for its holiday-makers, it made an admirable headquarters for the British element of the Control Commission for Germany which was now to take up the task of governing the British Zone of occupation.* At least, it would have been admirable, if local conditions had not been in such complete contrast with those which prevailed almost everywhere else in Germany, so that a certain air of unreality infected all the labours of the Commission. It was rather as if the Germans, having conquered Britain, had decided to govern it from Llandrindod Wells. And now the war was over, the local citizens began to feel, if not the sufferings, at least the inconvenience they had been spared while it continued, and for the first time were forced to defend themselves against the enemy, in the form of their new rulers. It was the oddest confrontation of antagonists that could be imagined. On the one hand were the worthy tradesmen and lodging-house keepers of Bad Oenhausen, bewildered that their obscure little town had been selected as a seat of government and wildly protesting that they had done nothing to deserve this, as they had never sympathised with Hitler and that each one of them had at one time or another risked their lives by helping a Jew; and on the other were the officers and other ranks of the Control Commission, most of them amateur soldiers suddenly transformed into equally amateur administrators, determined to secure for themselves the best available quarters and living conditions. Thus in the narrow streets of Bad Oenhausen the great issues of war and peace, victory and defeat, justice and injustice, became reduced to a series of petty little campaigns to capture or defend a lodging or a bed, and one might see a British officer of field rank, struggling but triumphant, borne down by the weight of a magnificent mattress he had succeeded in requisitioning for his own use and had removed with his own hands.

Inspecting a house which I wished to requisition for a batman and driver, I was implored by the family, father, mother, and grown-up daughter, to leave them in occupation, and it was hard to resist their appeals, because once dispossessed of their house they were not likely to find another. Besides, they spoke with a kind of wheedling sincerity which, though distasteful, was almost convincing; they had never been National Socialists, they had helped the Jews, they had suffered for their convictions. In feeling at least they were as British and freedom-loving as myself, and surely it would be one of the crowning injustices of a war which had been unjust from start to finish if precisely such people as themselves should be the first to suffer at the hands of their liberators. All this was said with an eloquence and conviction to which I could not fail to respond; and in any case the shabby little house, with its smell of cheap cigars, and the spectacle of the two elderly Germans and their daughter prostrating themselves in their appeal to my mercy, combined to inspire me with a sense of distaste which made me want to get away as quickly as possible.

Curiosity alone made me ask to see the only room in the house which had not been shown to me. They told me it was empty; it was never used; it was locked; they had lost the key. It was impossible to misinterpret the looks of guilt and alarm which showed in their faces. I wondered what possible skeleton this innocent family could be hiding, and wild and melodramatic ideas began to fly into my head, for indeed one never knew what kind of desperate fugitive one might expect to discover in any German household at that time. I persisted in my request and threatened to have the door broken in unless it were opened; at length, reluctantly, they found the key and the door was opened to reveal a bare room, with damp and peeling wallpaper, containing as its single article of furniture an ancient rocking chair in which sat a very old man, thin and frail, collarless and unshaven, and in his watery grey eyes the feeble light of senility. 'It's only grandfather,' said the daughter. 'You needn't take any notice of him.'

There was something rather horrible in the sight of that feeble-minded old man locked in that empty room, where the stale smell of cigars seemed stronger than ever, and my curiosity subsided as quickly as it had been aroused. But grandfather was staring at my uniform, with a sudden look of cunning tinged with humility which showed that even he knew what was expected of him. With a quick, subservient glance at my companions, he raised himself painfully on his old legs, raised his hand in the National Socialist salute, and like an obedient child repeating a lesson quavered proudly: 'Heil Hitler!' 'He doesn't understand,' said the father; 'he's feeble-minded, he doesn't know what he's saying.' It was only too clear that he did not; yet I could not help wondering how many years of threats and beatings and cajolery it had taken to teach that feeble-minded old man the trick of which he was so proud, too old a dog now to learn the new tricks which would please his new masters. And it was difficult to forget the look, of fear and yet of effrontery, which the old man's ridiculous gesture had called to the faces of his family.

II

We selected as the residence of the Political Adviser to the Commander-in-Chief, to whose staff I was attached as senior intelligence officer,* the glass and concrete villa belonging to a leading business man of Lübbecke, a little town a few miles away from Bad Oenhausen. On our arrival its owner had chosen to disappear, but his wife was still in occupation and when I called on her to inform her that her house would be requisitioned, she kept me waiting for a short time before appearing in a flowered silk dressing-gown, apologising profusely for the delay, as she had been taking her afternoon rest. She was a faded blonde who seemed very confident of her attraction, and she appeared to be under the impression that I was paying her a social call, and immediately summoned a servant to bring me whisky, as the most proper drink for a British officer. Perhaps she found my visit perfectly natural, as during the war she had entertained large numbers of the dignitaries of the Party and the *Wehrmacht*, and now, under the new regime, it was only proper that the occupation authorities should wish to pay their respects to the leading hostess of this little provincial town. She was extremely gracious to me as the Political Adviser's representative; lying back in an art nouveau chair, sipping her whisky, her long legs crossed under her dressing-gown, she seemed to hint at unnameable pleasures we might enjoy together. In everything she said there was the implication that the miseries and sufferings of war and of defeat could have nothing to do with people like herself, and that under the British occupation she would continue to enjoy the same privileges as under National Socialism. I tried to disabuse her of her illusions, without success, and when I informed her that she must vacate her house within three days, she was at first incredulous, then surprised, and finally outraged, transformed before my eyes from a provincial woman of fashion into a screaming termagant who heaped abuse on me and asserted that I was exceeding my authority, as she felt sure that the Political Adviser was an *English gentleman*, a *sporting man*, who understood the principles of *fair play*, and finally threatened to report me to the Commander-in-Chief himself.

It was difficult to persuade her that this was not likely to have much effect or that Field-Marshal Montgomery had more important work to do than listen to her complaints; she felt that she knew how to deal with Field-Marshals, and it was only when I informed her that if she resisted the requisition order she would immediately be placed under arrest that she began to take me seriously. Her fury gave way to pleading; her dressing-gown fell away to reveal a naked shoulder and swelling breast; it seemed that there was nothing she would not do to please me; I began to see myself in the ridiculous role of the brutal soldier softened by the charms of a captive and helpless woman.

The position was all the more absurd because she took it for granted that it was the beauty and luxury of her home which had excited the cupidity of the conquerors. The truth was that her house was the only one in the little town that was large enough to accommodate the Political Adviser and his staff; but it was also a classical monument to the kind of bad taste that flourished under the National Socialists, in which new and old were mingled without any discrimination and architect and interior decorator had worked harmoniously together with an unerring eye for whatever was most vulgar and ostentatious. Its architecture was modern and advanced and contrived only to look gimcrack. India rubber plants in pots stood in plate glass windows that stretched from floor to ceiling. Chairs that were both hideous and uncomfortable were arranged about low glass-topped tables that hurt one's shins when one sat down; on the walls, in heavy black frames, hung large landscapes of German woodland scenery. It had a dim, dark, pretentious library, with very few books except a selection of those heavily bound, pseudo-scientific works of pornography which seem an essential part of the furniture of any educated German business man's house. No house could have been less agreeable to the tastes of the Political Adviser, who was the simplest and least ostentatious of men and at home lived in a modest little suburban villa called Tree Tops; every detail of its design and its furnishing reflected with almost scientific accuracy the corruption of its mistress, and even when at length she had departed, her spirit still remained to haunt us in the folds of her damask curtains and the shining surfaces of her parquet floors.

His new surroundings, so different from the dingy splendours of the Foreign Office, could not fail to make the Political Adviser uneasy; his rapid birdlike glances recoiled with distaste from every object offered to his view, and their very grotesqueness only increased the air of unreality which pervaded our life at Lübbecke. It seemed as if he were asking himself what on earth he was doing in this chamber of horrors and what possible service he could perform in this provincial little backwater, still enjoying a smug prosperity while the rest of Germany was in ruins. He became more and more impatient to move to Berlin, where the Four Powers composing the Commission were to exercise their joint control of Germany. In the meantime, he decided that he could endure Lübbecke and his horrible mansion no longer, and that it was his duty to acquaint himself with conditions in the British Zone of occupation; to my alarm I was instructed to prepare an itinerary for his tour and accompany him on his journey.

III

A week later we set off on our tour* in the large black Humber limousine which had been provided for the Political Adviser until his Rolls-Royce arrived from England. The Political Adviser had once played a sinister role in my political mythology as that obscure Foreign Office official, Mr William Strang, who had been despatched by Mr Chamberlain to Moscow to obstruct any possibility of an Anglo-Soviet military agreement. I had assumed that he would correspond with the unattractive part for which I had cast him in history; now I found him in every way a surprising contrast to my idea of what a British diplomat should be like. The son of a farmer and educated at a grammar school and University College, London, he was entirely free of those mannerisms of speech and behaviour which are acquired at a public school and the older universities; he was modest and shy and diffident, irked by the grandeur imposed on him by his ambassadorial rank, and had a touching faith in my capacity as a soldier to overcome any difficulties which might meet us on our journey. But with his shyness and diffidence went an immense capacity for work, and he corrected the drafts of messages and dispatches with a meticulousness that was very near to pedantry. Indeed, in all things he gave the impression of a scholar rather than of a man of affairs and to me, after five years in the army, where even scholars very quickly began to impersonate men of action, this was immensely refreshing.

Soon after we had begun our journey, the Political Adviser confessed to me that in all his long years of service in the Foreign Office this was the first time he had been posted abroad; he found it difficult to adjust himself to the privileges and perquisites that belonged to him as His Britannic Majesty's representative in Germany, and was the despair of his personal assistant, a smart young artillery officer whom I had recommended to him, who was continually thinking of new and ingenious ways to increase his master's comfort, prestige, and dignity. But for all his modesty and charm, which made him such a wonderful change from generals, who do not practise these virtues much, the Political Adviser could be harsh with any display of inefficiency and I could not help wondering how I was going to survive ten days of conducting him across a Germany whose road system had been almost totally destroyed; after five years as a soldier my powers of map reading were still elementary and my natural sense of direction has always been almost non-existent.

My lack of confidence in my capacity as a guide alarmed me all the more because our driver, Tamplin, who made up the third of our party, had a single and fixed idea of his own functions; it was simply to drive as fast and as far as possible in whatever direction chance or necessity might dictate. The consciousness that he was in control of our splendid new Humber, with the Political Adviser's flag flying proudly on the bonnet, was enough to exaggerate this idea to the point of mania; wherever the roads permitted we shot through the ruins of Germany like a bullet, and wherever they did not, he simply took the nearest turning which would allow us to continue our headlong career. I vainly tried to follow Tamplin's erratic course on the map, while from time to time the Political Adviser, who was a nervous man, gently enquired whether it would not be possible for Tamplin to moderate his speed a little. But Tamplin was a soldier, and the Political Adviser had a great respect for soldiers; he was hardly capable of distinguishing their rank, they were all heroes to him, and he could hardly bring himself to give Tamplin a direct order, but treated him rather as if he were a foreign power who had to be handled with the greatest tact and discretion. As for Tamplin, he took the view that he now belonged not to the RASC, but to the *Corps Diplomatique*; he was in the personal service of the Political Adviser, and flew his flag on his car, and if his master did not wish to give Tamplin orders, it was certainly not for a mere lieutenant-colonel like me to do so.

Thus we were delivered into the hands of our furious charioteer, yet despite the dangers and deviations of Tamplin's driving, we had not been long on our way when the Political Adviser shyly volunteered that he was enjoying himself. His life had been spent at desks in the Foreign Office, which gradually grew more and more imposing as he advanced in his profession; to be whirled like this through Germany, even with Tamplin at the wheel, gave him the thrill of a schoolboy who has escaped his lessons and he almost seemed to wonder whether those arduous years in the Foreign Office had not been too great a sacrifice of the pleasures of life. When I had prevailed upon Tamplin to stop for lunch, I unpacked the hamper of food and wine which had been provided for us and we sat down to eat and drink in a rich green meadow, under the shade of a tree, on the banks of a smooth and clear stream. It was wonderfully quiet and peaceful, and difficult to think of the problems of Germany; as he raised his glass of hock to his lips the Political Adviser rather wistfully murmured: 'Do you know, I've never done anything like this in my life.' For a moment, it was almost as if we were partners in a particularly enjoyable form of crime.

IV

But we were driving towards the Ruhr; we were soon out of the un-ravaged countryside and evidence began to collect of the consequences of war and defeat. I began to understand the man who said that war may be hell but defeat is worse. For in most of Germany at that time, and certainly in its industrial areas, it seemed true to say that even the most elementary conditions of civilised life had ceased to exist. Wher-ever the war had been, it had remorselessly ground to pieces the whole structure of organised society and all we could see around us was the ruin and rubble that remained. Even Tamplin's headlong progress was halted by broken bridges whose arches and girders projected crazily into the sky and by roads that were a continuous series of potholes and craters; our journey became slow and erratic wandering along whatever highways and byways still remained open to us, like lost travellers painfully exploring some landscape of the moon. And all around us, at every turn, was the same monotonous repetitive vista of gap-toothed buildings, houses brutally torn apart, endless miles of fallen and broken masonry, and a few bent and solitary figures scratching in the ruins for anything that might be useful to them in the struggle to survive. It was a landscape as mournful and fantastic as those Piranesi drew of the ruins of ancient Rome, in which a few tiny human figures are dwarfed and overshadowed by the colossal fragments of a ruined world.*

As we penetrated deeper into this scene of devastation, which had once formed the greatest industrial complex in Europe, moving slowly forward as if through some dense jungle of shattered stone and brick and steel, rain began to fall, the sad grey drizzle of a world that had come to an end. When we entered Düsseldorf on a Sunday afternoon, it was pouring from a leaden sky, the colour of dead ashes, and in this downpour the ruined empty streets had the mournfulness and melancholy of some tragic funeral dirge, as if we had come to attend a burial ceremony. But we were the only mourners, for the streets were totally deserted; in this dead city there was nothing any longer to support life, neither food nor water nor shelter nor heating and everyone who could leave had already left; only the rats still scuffled in the rubble. We drove to the offices of the commander of the local Military Government detachment, who occupied the only building in the town which seemed to be relatively undamaged; that is to say, it had a roof and its walls were still standing and its broken windows had been repaired, though it was as grimy and cheerless as the ruins themselves. As we walked down the passage we crunched underfoot the little piles of broken plaster that had been shaken from the walls.

We found the local commander at work among a litter of papers in his naked ground floor office; from his window he had a view, through the rain, of the ruins which constituted his empire. He was a lieutenant-colonel who only a short time ago had commanded a battalion which was enthusiastically engaged in completing the final downfall of Germany; now, with equal enthusiasm, he was doing what he could to mitigate the effects of her defeat. The breast of his tunic was covered with ribbons and in all the miles around him of dirt and devastation, he was the only object that was spruce and clean and shining. By one of those magical transformations, like a scene in pantomime, which occur in war, he now found himself the administrator and absolute ruler of an area containing over one million human beings who had suddenly been deprived of the means of existence. He might just as well have been dropped from the skies in the middle of tropical Africa and told to get on with the job of governing some primitive tribe living on the edge of starvation.

Indeed, he would have been better off, for there at least he would have found some form of tribal organisation through which he could have given his commands. But the tribal organisation of the Germans had vanished overnight; the whole complex interlocking structure of State and Party and local government had been swallowed up in defeat and with it had disappeared all the men responsible for working it. So far as local administration was concerned, the lieutenant-colonel might just as well have been operating in the desert, and to a more rational man the task in hand would have seemed so grotesque and futile as to be not worth attempting; but he was not a rational man, particularly because he seemed quite unaware of the irony of his endeavours to succour a people whom a short time ago he had been doing his best to destroy. When the Political Adviser suggested that there might be dangers in adopting so wholeheartedly the cause of our defeated enemies, he asked rather angrily whether it was the intention that they should be left to starve, or in winter to freeze, to death. He was not concerned with the preoccupations of political advisers; his only, his obsessive interest in life, it seemed, at that moment was the baffling problem of how, without transport, he could bring enough coal into the city to allow the Germans to get to work again; for without work they could not live. Until that moment I had not really understood that without fuel and transport it is impossible for men to exist in cities.

But the lieutenant-colonel also had another obsession as well as coal, without which the Germans, or what he sometimes referred to as 'my people', would also lack all the other means of subsistence. Kafka says somewhere that the worst horror of war is that it dissolves all the established rules and conventions of life; after a few weeks of trying to control its results, the local commander in Düsseldorf would have agreed with him. For his area, like other areas of Germany, was at that moment overrun by thousands of foreign workers, Frenchmen, Poles, Czechs, Russians, who had been the slaves of the Reich and now, suddenly released and at liberty, were determined both to keep themselves alive and take their revenge by plundering its corpse. At night the countryside was alive with bands of what were politely called 'displaced persons', who with considerable reason felt themselves entitled to pillage, plunder, rape, and murder with impunity; for what crimes could they possibly commit worse than the crimes which had been committed against them, and who more than they had the right to act on Bacon's dictum that revenge is a kind of primitive justice?* The lieutenant-colonel found himself faced with moral problems of a kind he had never envisaged; he had solved them on the simple principle that of all evils the complete absence of any form of law and order is the worst, worse even than the lack of the means of subsistence, and that his first task was to re-establish them, even though individual justice might be compromised in the process. When the lieutenant-colonel talked about coal and food, he talked like a Marxist; *Erst kommt das Fressen, dann kommt die Moral.** When he talked about morality, he made one think that perhaps, after all, it is not merely a consequence of material conditions.

It was fascinating to listen, in that dingy office, while the rain poured down outside, to the representative of Military Government explaining his problems, with a passion and eloquence which were certainly not native to him; they were the product of the appalling situation in which he found himself. He was like a man who finds himself lost in a dark and impenetrable forest and is determined, if necessary, to hack his way through the undergrowth with his own hands; but now he looked to the Political Adviser as one who might throw some light into the darkness which surrounded him and give him some help in his task. But the Political Adviser was essentially an honest man. He had the sense to know that in our absurd ivory tower in Lübbecke we knew far less about these matters than the local commander himself did, and that in his place he could do no better than he was doing. So he contented himself with saying that he would report the condition of affairs to London, and that he thought this might make some difference to those politicians who, following in the footsteps of Mr Morgenthau* and Mr Noel Coward, still thought that the fundamental problem in Germany was how to be beastly enough to the Germans;* and to this the lieutenant-colonel answered simply that if there were such people who had office or influence, they should come and do the job themselves and not leave it to British soldiers.

It was with a certain feeling of shame that finally we left him in his office to address himself to what at that moment seemed a hopeless task, with an enthusiasm which did him so much honour; while we drove off gropingly in the darkness to find our way to the luxuries and comforts of a Corps Headquarters, where the Political Adviser was received with the lavish hospitality befitting his rank but so repugnant to his taste. The Corps Commander, silvery haired, with an aquiline face and a manner which a tragic actor might have envied, was giving a very good imitation of a Renaissance prince enjoying the pleasures of his latest conquest, and was anxious to show that in him the exuberance of victory was refined by the discrimination of taste. Certainly in his freshly furnished and furbished *Schloss*, from which all traces of war had been effaced, or in its green and peaceful park, it became almost impossible to believe in the dark picture painted for us in Düsseldorf, of a population not merely ruined but abandoned and betrayed and a country devastated and denuded and systematically pillaged by bands of brigands who would have been affronted by the mere suggestion that Germans could have any rights against themselves; indeed, we might well have thought the local commander guilty of sentimentality or exaggeration if we had not heard the same account at every post we visited in the course of our journey.

But indeed as we continued on our journey it seemed to acquire something of the unreality of a fairy tale, of a journey through a country which had fallen under a sinister enchantment, like that journey of Manawydan and Pryderi in the third book of the *Mabinogion*, through a land in which 'where they used to see the flocks and the herds and the dwellings, not a thing could they see: neither house nor beast nor smoke nor fire nor man nor dwelling, but the houses of the court empty, desolate, uninhabited, without man, without beast within them'. Over large areas the country had precisely this air of abandonment; 'not a soul could they see. In mead-cellar and in kitchen there was nothing but desolation.'

Only where it might have been least expected, and in its least expected forms, did life seem to continue. In a huge hangar abandoned by the *Luftwaffe* we visited a vast camp of men, women, and children who had been transported to the factories of the Ruhr when the Germans occupied the Ukraine. By night many of them joined those bands of bandits and marauders who roamed and pillaged the countryside; by day also they went into the woods and fields and lanes, but the only plunder they brought back with them were green branches plucked from the trees and flowers picked in the fields, with which, under the immensely high girders of the hangar roof, they wove for themselves green and leafy little huts and cubicles in which each family made a home of its own. Entering the hangar, one suddenly had the impression of being in some huge green conservatory, as at a flower show at Chelsea or Shrewsbury, filled with the hundreds of little green-leaved huts into the foliage of which their inhabitants had also woven the fresh flowers they had picked that day, and under their arched roofs their tenants lay or squatted while their food cooked in whatever served them as a family pot; for these citizens of the Soviet Union, conscripted into National Socialist Germany, treasured above all their individual family life and stubbornly refused to share in any form of community feeding. Rations had to be distributed each day to each family, who then cooked their own meals in whatever way pleased them best.

Walking among them was like visiting some huge gypsy encampment set down in the heart of Europe in the improbable setting of that abandoned hangar; it made one feel that the war had transformed Germany, and indeed the whole of Europe, into a vast transit camp, in which all permanent relationships had been dissolved and men and women tried desperately to improvise the best substitute for them which conditions would allow. It was as if all that remained to these people were their little huts of boughs and branches which reminded them of a home and homeland which had been destroyed. And we saw these same people, or their brothers and sisters, once again later on our journey, when driving along a dusty road alongside a railway track we overtook one of the few trains that were to be seen in Germany at that time. It dragged slowly and painfully along, overloaded by its weight of passengers, who crammed every compartment to overflowing, stood on the running board clutching the window frames, lay on the roof strumming their balalaikas and singing their Ukrainian songs, which rang so strangely across the German fields. They had wreathed the engine and carriages with the same green branches out of which they made their huts in the hangar, and when the train jolted to a stop they flung themselves from the carriages and from the roof into the fields to collect fresh flowers and foliage. These people had been liberated from one dictatorship, which had collapsed, and were travelling across Europe to return to another, which still survived. In the interval they were free, nomads wandering across Europe without home or habitation. Thousands of others were in the same condition, moving from west to east or from east to west. We seemed to be in the world of Saint-John Perse's *Anabasis*,* as if the age of the *Völkerwanderung** had returned.

V

When we returned to Lübbecke, the Political Adviser asked me for a report on our journey, as it might be useful to him in preparing the despatch he proposed to write for the Foreign Office. I had not been prepared for this, but with a forethought very unusual for me I had kept a diary of our journey in which I had recorded anything that might be of interest. I showed the diary to the Political Adviser and to my astonishment he, who was normally so meticulous and pernickety about every word and comma of a draft, included it as it stood as a supplement to his despatch and I had the pleasure of seeing it printed and circulated on Foreign Office green paper;* it was certainly the first time anything I had written had had such a distinguished and restricted circulation since I had written examination papers at All Souls.

But by the time it was printed, we had without regret left the grotesque villa at Lübbecke for Berlin, where the joint Secretariat of the Four Power Commission had now begun its labours. The Political Adviser was established in a large mansion in the Grunewald belonging to a merchant banker; compared with our gimcrack palace in Lübbecke it was solid, dignified, and respectable, and his personal assistant strained all his ingenuity to ensure that it should even be luxurious as well. I made haste to verify that its library contained the same essential pornographic works as the library in Lübbecke.

Rather than live in the mess which had been established for the Political Department, I found a little house where I could live by myself. In Berlin the same frenzied search for objects of art, luxury, or comfort continued as had taken place at Bad Oenhausen; returning to my house one day, I was surprised to find an extremely distinguished civilian member of the Commission on his knees in my sitting-room examining the markings of a Persian carpet. Being of very much higher rank than myself, he seemed to think it natural that the carpet should belong to him rather than to me, and he seemed extremely surprised at my view that it did not belong to me at all but to my German landlords. He was a very rich British industrialist and informed me, with the full weight of his authority, that it would never do to pamper the Germans in this way. But I, or rather my landlords, kept the carpet.

But at last, with infinite relief, I began to see the time coming nearer, when after the interminable years of the war, I should be demobilised and civilian life would bring to an end the series of military masquerades which war had imposed on me. And indeed it had by now become exceedingly clear that any further use I might have in Germany had come to an end. In Berlin I had been given as an assistant a quite exceptionally intelligent and efficient staff officer,* who was to succeed me when I left, and it seemed quite clear to me, as well as to everyone else, that there was no reason whatever why he should not take over my duties at once. So while he began, with immense enthusiasm and conscientiousness, to lay the basis for a properly organised intelligence system, I searched the German papers which had begun to appear for such odd items of scandal or sensation as contrived to pass the censorship. One of the oddest, perhaps, reported a performance of Schiller's *Der Parasit* in the newly opened theatre in the American sector of Berlin. The play ends with the well known words: 'Justice! You only see that on the stage', which had been received with a passionate outburst of applause by an audience of Berliners indignant at what they took to be the injustices committed by the occupying powers. A distinguished American writer visiting Berlin had been deeply affronted by this insult to the dignity of the armies of liberation; he protested to the American authorities and in the name of liberty and democracy the performance of *Der Parasit* was forbidden.

Apart from searching for such ironic *faits-divers** of the occupation, I walked about the ruins of Berlin, attended the market where outside the Reichstag building, now shattered like an eggshell, Russian soldiers of all ranks prosecuted their endless and insatiable search for wrist-watches, whose beauty and delicious tick-tock amazed and delighted them, beyond any thought of their possible utility. I executed a raid on the remains of the abandoned Japanese Embassy, where I secured for our Mess what I was informed was the last remaining grand piano in Berlin, and in the evenings visited the first shabby and squalid night-clubs that had begun to open. How different they were from those I remembered, for now they were patronised almost exclusively by Germans occupied in black market deals, tarts of the new generation who had managed to survive the war with some faint traces of attraction still left, and Russian officers; the members of the other occupying forces still observed, in public at least, the absurd order against 'fraternisation' with the Germans, and German night-clubs were out of bounds. With the Russians I drank horrifying amounts of vodka, bad whisky, and Steinheger, and entered into endless conversations that lasted into the early hours of the morning and were not in the least hampered because they knew not a word of English or I a word of Russian. They seemed to be infinitely friendly and warm-hearted, and behaved to me rather as if one came from a world in which one could never have been exposed to the kind of dangers, risks, and hazards which were normal in their own life. In our bouts of drinking, I should certainly have become involved with the exceedingly dubious German ladies who had attached themselves, like camp followers, to these Russian officers and lived off the leavings of the thick wads of notes which they scattered broadcast like propaganda leaflets; but the Russians, by furious headshakings, waving of fists, conveyed to me that I should not have anything to do with them. *Bad women,* they said gravely, shaking their cropped heads, *bad women, nekulturny** who all had venereal disease. They seemed to think this was a danger which the Russian Army could take in its stride but that it was not right that the effete British should be exposed to it. *Bolshoi Narod!** they shouted, waving their glasses, *Bolshoi Narod,* as if in love and war their greatness was equally impregnable.

The women on the other hand dragged me aside and volubly whispered their complaints against the Russians' brutal and unhygienic habits; it was hard to know which they condemned most, and they had the natural and unaffected German assumption (it was the only natural and unaffected thing about them) of superiority to the Slavs as *Untermenschen* and *Unmenschen.** In spite of all this, Russians and Germans seemed to have established a remarkably good practical understanding of each other, like totally alien species of animals who have settled down in the same cage together. I was grateful to the Russians for their curiously protective feeling that this ménage was not for me, particularly after I had accompanied one of their German ladies home one night and found that, convinced of the superior civilisation of the West, she proposed to enter into an affair with me, on a commercial basis, which was to be conducted, in the presence of her baby daughter, in a room on the third floor of a bombed building which entirely lacked an outside wall.

This kind of embarrassment was very different from any I met with in my relations with the Russians, who were only embarrassing because of their overpowering friendliness when drunk. It was difficult to persuade them at any time not to shower upon me their medals or their money, both of which they seemed to possess in great abundance; I felt that I cut a poor and niggardly figure beside them, but this did not prevent them, in moments of extreme drunkenness, from pressing me in a bearlike hug to their barrel chests, made uncomfortable by decorations, and roaring those meaningless Anglo-Russian phrases which they seemed to regard as the seal of our friendship: '*Bolshoi Narod!* My boy! My boy!'

VI

My investigations into the primitive night life of Berlin were brought to an end when I was informed that it was imperative that the Political Adviser should be able to offer adequate hospitality to his guests and visitors and that this must be of a sufficiently high standard to compete with, if not surpass, the French, American, and Russian generals and marshals who were now established in Berlin and had all the loot of conquered Europe to draw upon. For this purpose he would require, though he himself was blissfully unaware of it, a well-stocked cellar, and though suitable supplies would in time be forthcoming from the Foreign Office, for the moment it was bare. There was no drinkable wine in Berlin, except in the possession of the generals or in the black market, so it was suggested that I might like to make a visit to France and to the Rhineland to procure whatever stocks I might be able to lay my hands on. I do not know whether this proposal was intended as a reward for five long years in which I had done the best I could to impersonate a soldier, or whether it arose simply because I was so obviously at a loose end now that my military service was so nearly over; in either case it was extremely welcome to me because, in spite of the curious diversions to be found in the evening, life in Berlin had begun to exercise a profoundly depressing effect upon me.

Wherever I walked, I saw, behind the long avenues of shattered façades and mountains of rubble which were all that was left of the city, the faces of friends now dead with whom I had once been intensely happy there. I visited my old rooms off the Kurfürstendamm and found the house gutted and abandoned, except for a senile incoherent old crone living in the cellar, in whom I could not recognise my prosperous and garrulous Jewish landlady; and she could give me no news of my German teacher and her family who had lived on the floor above me, except that, like everyone else, they had disappeared in the collapse of Germany. But perhaps even more than the fate which had overtaken my friends, it was the daily and continual acquaintance with the physical landscape of destruction that oppressed me. One walked through streets which once, for me, had been alive and enchanted with every kind of childish hope and illusion; now they showed nothing but the endless perspective of ruin and devastation, grey and mournful and empty except for the human chains of shabby and tired women passing from hand to hand the broken bricks of what had once been their homes. In the hot August sunshine, a kind of golden haze formed by the dust which rose from the mountains of debris overhung the city; and the heat brought out the sweet and sickly smell of the corpses still buried under the ruins and gave every street the stench of putrescence and decay.

And in my own little house, in its neat garden, I could see that however many were dead there were others for whom life was only another form of dying. The wife and daughter of its owner, who had been seized by the Russians and had disappeared without a name into some prison camp, now occupied the basement and attended to my needs; they thought themselves lucky to do so because they had been ordered to evacuate the house and I had only with difficulty obtained permission for them to remain. Both the women were prematurely old; mother and daughter, with twenty years between them, they might have been of the same age and there was no distinction between the sickly waxen pallor of their faces, the dirty white of their withered hair or the slightly crazed look in their eyes. All that kept them alive was the daughter's baby, still too young to walk, which lay day after day in its cot in the shade of the trees in the garden, perfectly still, perfectly silent, never uttering a cry either of pain or of pleasure. There was something uncanny in its silence; each day and all day the two women waited for some sign that it was still human. The whites of its eyes had lost that delicate misty blue which only babies' eyes have; they seemed to have been infected, like the eyes of a person suffering from jaundice, with the sickly yellow of its wizened face. Its stomach was distended and enlarged, and in the summer heat lay swollen under the tattered night-shirt which seemed to be its only garment.

Motionless, like one of those tiny effigies which one sometimes sees on family tombs in country churches, it lay unsmiling for day after day, while the two women watched over it in anxious silence, brushing away the flies which settled on its face. I gave them whatever I could out of my rations and sent for dried milk from England; they received these gifts without thanks, as if they were their right, and with only a slight softening of the crazy look which had been left with them by months of bombing. They fed the baby with the milk I gave them, and sucked the chocolate so that they might smear it on its lips, but it could neither eat nor digest and each day it became yellower and yellower, more shrivelled and monkeylike, as it lay under the trees in the garden without a sound to break its unnatural silence.

The sight of these two women bent anxiously over the dying baby's cot, never speaking to one another, but watching with a fixed intent bright stare as if they knew that every moment might be the last one in which they might see it alive, began to oppress my days and haunt my dreams at night. It seemed futile and ironical beyond all measure that for me five years of war should end with that scene in the garden where the two bomb-crazy women and their baby presented so perfect an image of what victory really means.

VII

So I was glad when the higher necessities of diplomacy gave me a reason for leaving Berlin, and I gladly undertook the task of stocking the Political Adviser's wine cellar. It seemed an odd mission with which to end my military career, but after all it was no odder and a good deal more enjoyable than many others I had performed in the course of the war. But it soon became obvious that my task, delightful as it was, was not quite so easy as it sounded. There was, for instance, the question not merely of buying the wine but of bringing it to Berlin, over a thousand miles of ravaged Europe in which hardly a road or a bridge remained intact and any vehicle travelling alone ran the risk of being pillaged and plundered. It seemed hardly likely that a valuable cargo of wine, which commanded a prohibitive price on the black markets of Europe, would survive the hazards of such a journey without some form of protection. So it seemed necessary to organise the expedition on a military basis, and this was slightly difficult as the Political Adviser was a civilian with neither troops nor military transport under his command. But by intrigue and persuasion, and the unauthorised use of the Political Adviser's name, I succeeded in borrowing, first, a five-ton lorry, second, a machine gun, and third, a magnificent corporal and a private of the Scots Guards, who were to act as drivers and bodyguard. Thus equipped, and with a draft on Paris for what seemed a gigantic amount in French francs, together with adequate supplies of food and drink, it seemed to me that I was once again on a war footing and ready to travel as an independent unit wherever the lure of wine might carry me.

Indeed, I was not at all sure where the search might take me, for in Berlin our information about the wine situation in liberated Europe was both scanty and undependable. Stocks of wine had disappeared, had been hidden, had been looted and plundered by the Germans and by the Allies alike; the new wines were undrinkable though the Americans were said to be very fond of Algerian red wine hotted up with medical alcohol; no one could tell me anything about hock or moselle. Our French colleagues in Berlin were secretive and unhelpful, as they had the greatest difficulty in supplying their own needs, though they did volunteer the information that the finest French wine had all been captured, by a masterpiece of strategy, by General de Lattre de

Tassigny in his advance from the south of France and it was very unlikely I should get any from that source. The only assistance in my mission I obtained from diplomatic sources was a personal letter to Prince Chimay in Rheims, with a request that he would let me have the best champagne he had available. But in fact, though it comforted me on setting out, it proved to be unnecessary, for at Trier, in the French Zone of occupation, I fell in with the headquarters staff of a French division who entertained me to a magnificent banquet and on learning the object of my journey, confessed that they were in possession of what was probably the finest store of champagne in Europe. It had been looted by the Germans from France for the use of the *Ober-kommando der Wehrmacht** and had fallen into the hands of the French again when they occupied Trier. The divisional staff drank it for breakfast, lunch and dinner, they almost bathed in it, and were quite willing to supply my relatively modest demands. So I had no need of my letter to Prince Chimay.

But the expedition was not in every way as fortunate as this. Every main road between Berlin and Paris was cratered and in some places still mined; every bridge was blown; and where the roads were passable they were crowded with military traffic. We bumped and crawled across Europe at a snail's pace; we were forced into long detours that took us hundreds of miles off our direct route; we ran out of petrol and slept in the lorry, mounting guard with our machine gun on our steadily mounting stock of wine. We resisted capture and arrest by a company of Algerian Chasseurs, who took us for black marketeers in disguise, and when they discovered their mistake, entertained us to a banquet in their Mess, where life resembled that of some African outpost magically transferred to Europe.

In the Rhineland I sat in little vineyards overlooking the Rhine trying to persuade their proprietors that the inferior wines they sold so easily and profitably to the Americans would not do for the Political Adviser, who would have been surprised by the delicacy and subtlety of taste with which I credited him. They were surly and unresponsive, and took the view that what was good enough for the Americans was certainly good enough for the British. I was only successful at last because I discovered the first honest German I had met since the war ended, who freely admitted that he had been, and remained, a Nazi and would not, if he could help it, dispose of anything but his worst wines to the occupying forces. I was so astonished by so sincere a declaration of hostility that we entered into a passionate and heated political discussion. We sat on his little stone terrace in the sunshine, the vineyard and the Rhine beneath us, and as our argument became more and more heated, he descended at more and more frequent intervals to his cellar, returning with a bottle of hock that each time became more mellow and golden. Evening descended on the Rhine, that to me in the sunset seemed itself to bloom like hock, and at last my host conducted me down the stone steps to his cellar; at a little iron gate he took a key from his pocket and said, 'Now I'll really show you what I've got.' Indeed it was a treasure, preserved intact throughout the war, fit not for Political Advisers, but for princes, and since by this time political passion and drunkenness had combined, however improbably, to make us friends he allowed me to take away with me as much as I asked for. When I returned to Berlin some of my purchases came under severe criticism. The champagne was admitted to be excellent; my red wine was no better than mediocre; but the hock was noble, beyond criticism, and the envy of Berlin.

In Paris I discovered that NAAFI had a monopoly of purchasing wine for British use and it was exercised with a severity and efficiency which neither persuasion nor bribery could circumvent. So I obtained an authority to buy from the senior officer in charge of purchasing and spent several happy and slightly bewildering days testing and buying claret and burgundy in the wine markets at les Halles. During this period I lost my bodyguard and my driver. Our lorry and its cargo were safely under lock and key in a transport depot, and the two guardsmen had asked if they could arrange their own accommodation in Paris, as they had friends there. I wondered who their friends could be and it was with some astonishment that a few days later I saw them outside Maxim's, seated in the back of an enormous new American car which was the property, I learned later, of one of the richest men in Paris to whom they had been of great service during the early days of the liberation; and thereafter I continued to see them emerging, in all the incomparable splendour of a guardsman, from the smartest bars and restaurants in Paris, which were far beyond the means of any British officer, who had to be satisfied with the officers' club.

But by now my purchases were completed, and my funds were exhausted; otherwise, it seemed to me that I might well have continued for ever our strange journey through liberated Europe. With some difficulty I succeeded in tracing my two guardsmen, who reported for duty as spruce as ever, though slightly exhausted by their experiences amongst the newly made millionaires of Paris. And then, our lorry loaded to the full with champagne, hock, moselle, burgundy and claret, we began our interminable journey back to Berlin and faced again the endless hold-ups in streams of military traffic on the dusty cratered roads. And once again we had a view, from the seat of our lorry, of ravaged Europe where everyone seemed to be endlessly and continuously on the move, though transport was practically unobtainable, and entire populations crossed and recrossed each other, as they tried to return to homes that no longer existed, or to leave homes that had been destroyed for anywhere in the world where conditions might conceivably be better and could not possibly be worse. It was fortunate that we had renewed our stocks of food in Paris; our lorry was suffering from the wear and tear of its long journey on execrable roads and repeatedly broke down, so that our return journey was even longer than our setting out. We limped into villages that seemed to be totally abandoned, the windows shuttered, the shops closed, where it was impossible to find food or drink or a bed for the night or any facilities for repairing our crippled lorry. The roads that led into Germany ran through a devastated area from which life had withdrawn through sheer lack of anything that could give it sustenance. I had the uncanny feeling that for months I had been wandering in a kind of universal No-Man's-Land and had seen an entire civilisation wither away before my eyes. And as we slowly travelled those endless monotonous miles of ruin and destruction I felt again the sense of nausea and sickness which had made me so glad to leave Berlin, and began to wonder if on my return I should see again those two women crouched over their yellowing dying baby, smell again Berlin's summer smell of the corpses rotting under the rubble, and see the rats which crept out, sleek, shining and well fed, from the ruins which lined the road from my house to the offices of the Control Commission. And when at night we camped beside the road, machine gun mounted against possible marauders, I dreamed vague frightening dreams of the death of a society and woke with the sour taste of victory in my mouth.

The Great Good Place*

I hope that Henry James would not have minded my using the title of his story for this account of my experience in the hospital at Ascot. It is a long time since I read the story, but what I remember most vividly is how its hero, sick, neurotic, and exhausted, wakes up in the coolness and peace of the strange institution, a combination of nursing home, monastery, and club, in which he recovers his sanity and health.* Something of that description colours my memories of the orthopaedic hospital at Ascot, though perhaps I was in even worse shape than Henry James's hero when I arrived at my place of healing, and perhaps, in spite of the feelings of profound gratitude which both *The Great Good Place* and the hospital inspired, there cannot really be much in common between an establishment run by the National Health Service and the place of physical and spiritual therapy so beautifully invented by The Master.

I too was sick and neurotic and exhausted; but there was also something very much more definite the matter with me when I woke up in hospital. I had had concussion, my head and face were badly injured, and I had a compound fracture of the tibia and fibula. I had in fact been run over,* and for a few days had been very nearly dead, but of this, when I awoke, I was not aware, and could not have said what had happened to me, or where I was now, or what my personal relationship was with the curiously mangled body which I seemed so provisionally to inhabit. Above all, I could not understand what the strange object was which, encased in plaster to the thigh, hung in a kind of cat's cradle suspended from an elaborate. iron structure attached to my bed. Of my whole life I had at that moment only a single memory, of lying in an unknown place, at the bottom of the profoundest well of darkness, through which showed from time to time, pale, shadowy, nameless, the faces of strangers calling to me in unintelligible words from an immense distance. I was conscious, as of a definite verifiable fact existing somewhere outside me in that intense blackness, of pain, dull, heavy, and all-pervading, yet not *my* pain but as it were a quality of the darkness, that bore down upon me, embraced me, enfolded me, a great weight that pressed closer and closer upon me until at the terrifying moment when it threatened to enter into me, become apart of me, *become mine*, the darkness roared down on me and swept me away.

I remembered also waking for a moment to a sense of movement, as of the sea, and being told that I was being taken from one hospital to another, before once again the darkness overwhelmed me. I was frightened; I knew that somewhere in a universe that had become completely strange and alien to me there was always the pain that threatened to become mine, not now heavy and dull and dark, but sharp and vivid and shrill, flame-coloured, a high-pitched singing excruciating note like those notes so high in the scale that they are intolerable to the human ear. I felt like a dog that can hear sounds that no man can or should hear. But there was always the blessed darkness that swept over me and engulfed me before it was too late and the pain entered into me and made me its own.

But gradually, like the ocean, the darkness receded and for longer and longer periods left the shores of consciousness exposed. I emerged from its depths like a swimmer exhausted from too long immersion in its waters; I lay outstretched on the sands, amazed that I was still alive, and with eyes that seemed to have been washed clear of all past knowledge in the gulfs and abysses where I had so nearly drowned. Then slowly I began to perceive, remember, distinguish and identify the shapes and objects of the world to which I had returned.

II

The most immediate, as it was the most striking, of these objects was the strange iron contraption which enclosed my bed. It was a curiously primitive arrangement of uprights and cross-bars clumsily bolted together and supporting a network of ropes and weights and pulleys; the general effect, as I looked up at it from my bed, was strangely reminiscent of the superstructure of a ship. Into the intricacies of this construction protruded a long white heavy object which I finally came to recognise as my own leg, which had grown a protective carapace of plaster of Paris. There it hung or floated in air, seeming to have no connection with the rest of my body; it seemed to belong rather to the absurd scaffolding that had grown up around it. Even more surprising was that this useless limb did not hurt, and was no longer a cause of pain, and seemed capable of no sensation whatsoever. Yet something told me that it was not altogether dead and this seemed even more probable when I discovered, to my intense joy and delight, that I could move the naked toes which emerged from the plaster. I could not, however, quite understand how this miracle was performed, for I had no confidence that any of my limbs or any part of my body could or would respond to any demands I might make upon them. Indeed, it seemed to me rather that my body was *not mine*, was no longer part of me nor I of it; we were like two strangers, by some accident bound up with each other yet with no means of communication, and I had the clear and precise consciousness of dwelling within this body as within a shell, which was rather a surface presented to me by the external world than any part of myself.

This feeling was infinitely pleasant and delightful, as if a great burden had been lifted from me and no further effort or exertion could ever again be required of me; as if, indeed, now that I and my body were no longer one, I could now look forward to being free in a sense which I had never known before. Yet when, to express my joy, I murmured to myself the words, *I am at last free*, there mingled with my joy a feeling of intense grief, as if the bondage from which I was now released had once been the source of innumerable pleasures which I would never know again, as if I had said goodbye to an old and dearly loved friend from whom I had parted for ever. And though my joy persisted, the grief of the parting was terrible; it seemed to me then that the pain and terror of the darkness from which I had only just emerged must have been simply the tearing and ripping of every nerve and sinew which had bound me to my body and now could never be renewed, that I had seen the horrors that lie on the other side of the doors of death and by a miracle had been allowed to return.

Yet despite the strange amalgam of pain and joy that arose out of my new relationship with my body, the stubborn fact remained that I could wriggle my toes. There could be no doubt about it. In response to an impulse which I could control, they moved, willingly, even eagerly, and there seemed also to be no doubt that they did this as and when I wished and for no other reason; and this seemed to be assurance that, whatever I might think or feel now, my old relationship with my body, so familiar, so intimate, so well loved, would one day be restored. This seemed to me then of immense importance; but what was curious was that, as I grew better, it was not only I who attached importance to the absurd fact that my toes would move when I wanted them to. To my surprise, this seemed important to everyone, for the first question which surgeons, doctors, sisters, nurses, even patients used to ask me was: *How are your toes?* And in reply I would say, *Very well, thank you*, as if we were talking about a friend or a relation, and if they seemed to doubt me, I would wriggle my toes until a look of satisfaction came over their faces and they would smile and congratulate me before moving on to the next bed.

It seemed to me surprising that they should ignore the other results of my accident, the fractured leg, the stitches in my face and head, the appalling headaches that suddenly descended upon me, and confine their interest entirely to the condition of my toes; and though I knew how important this was, yet it seemed to be immensely perceptive of others to understand what possibilities of pain and grief were involved for me. And I continued to be surprised, for I am profoundly bored by medical questions, whether they concern others or myself, and this made me something of an oddity in the hospital where for everyone medical questions were the most fascinating and absorbing subject in the world and even the most illiterate and uneducated of the patients would talk learnedly of the more obscure anatomical details. So that it was some time before I finally enquired why everyone should be so interested in my toes, and then I was told that if I could not move them it meant that the nerves were severed and it would be even more unlikely than it was at present that I should recover the use of my leg. This seemed quite an adequate explanation for the curiosity and concern of others; I did not need to tell them that for me, for a short time, the fact that I could wriggle my toes seemed to be the only evidence I had that one day, if I wished (and of this I was by no means sure) I might resume that old familiar relationship between my body and myself which had been so roughly severed on the night of my accident.

III

In the early morning, before the ward was awake, or the night staff had paid us their last visit, I stared through the long, plate-glass windows which occupied the whole of the far wall of the ward. I was not interested in the hospital beds that were ranged against the windows, or in the patients who lay in them in the awkward and unnatural postures which their injuries dictated. This was the first morning since my accident on which I was aware of the external world beyond the surface and extremities of my body, and I had no interest whatever in the human beings it might contain or in any of their pains or troubles or diseases; my only interest was in the extraordinary beauty of the world outside the windows.

It was the moment before dawn. A veil of mist and darkness still clung to the forms of the trees in the garden outside, but gradually it lifted and the first faint light of dawn broke palely over the garden. As if I were seeing them for the first time, I watched the leaves and branches of the trees grow distinct against the morning sky. A ragged line of neglected rose bushes ran across the unkempt grass of the lawn and where it ended the trees formed a semicircle which cut off the rest of the world from my sight. I could not even guess what lay beyond the trees; for me the grassy space they enclosed, so cool and damp and green after the horrors and torments of the darkness in which I had wandered for I did not know how long, was the whole of the universe. I wanted only to watch, with wonder and amazement, as the pale and tender light of morning gently stripped the veils of darkness from the garden, and I should have liked to delay each moment of the dawn's advance because each fresh moment seemed so wonderful. And it seemed to me also as if I were a part of the miracle that was taking place in the garden outside, and that as the pale morning light restored their colours to the trees and the grasses and the flowers, it laid its finger on me also and gently summoned me back to life.

So I lay there for hours, watching the slow advance of day across the garden, hardly aware of the routine of the ward, submitting occasionally to be fed or washed, but as soon as these interruptions were over returning to my intense contemplation of the green and leafy space outside the windows, and so completely did I become a part of it that when from time to time I fell asleep it was as if the trees stretched their long green fingers into the ward and took me up and enfolded me until I woke refreshed by the cool touch of their leaves. Yet each time that I awoke there was a moment of panic that the rough neglected garden would have disappeared and that what would meet me again would be the return of darkness, and something that would be worse than darkness, the pain and horror and terrible distress for which the darkness itself was only a cloak and a concealment. But each time the moment passed, and I found myself once again absorbed in watching the minute changes that were taking place in the scene outside the window.

A leaf trembled, a blade of grass stirred. A shadow moved on the rose bushes. Light fell on the glossy plumage of a bird so that it glowed with an infinitely mysterious richness of colour. And above, the clouds were so high and the blue between them so infinitely distant! It seemed to me that what was happening, in the garden, in myself, was so extraordinary that nothing like it had ever happened before, that nothing mattered except what was taking place minute by minute before my eyes, that so long as the garden was there nothing would ever matter again.

IV

Yet though by day the garden completely absorbed me, nightmare was always ready to return, bringing with it not only terror and panic but something crudely and coarsely comic that only intensified its horrors. When darkness fell the garden would be blotted out and I would become aware of the two long rows of beds ranged on either side of the ward. I lay in an emergency bed next to the swing doors which gave access to our wing of the hospital. Beyond them, and at right angles to them, another pair of doors led to another ward which was occupied by patients suffering from tuberculosis of the bone. From time to time they would open and nurses would pass in and out, and I would catch a glimpse of a long row of beds which for some reason were covered with the thick red blankets which in our ward were only used when a patient was to be taken down to the operating room. These red coverlets lent the other ward a sinister aspect, as if it were never free of the tinge and taint of blood, which at night seemed to invade our ward also. At 9.30 the lights above our beds were turned out, and from then throughout the night the only illumination came from the night lights which hung in metal bowls from the centre of the ceiling. They had a dim rosy glow, thrown upward on the ceiling, which gave an infernal tinge to the half-darkness in which we lay, as if the ward were an ante-room to Hell.

Perhaps it was natural that when I awoke in the middle of the night, I utterly failed to recognise where I was; the contrast was too great with the green shades of the garden which so utterly absorbed me during the day. I tried desperately to remember where I could be and how I had come to be there, and when I failed, panic, which was never far away at that time, began to overcome me.

The scene was all the more strange to me because, by some oversight, the communicating doors with the next ward had been left open that night, so that from where I lay I could see a long vista of crimson stretching the whole length of the ward, which, as it seemed to me, I had never seen before. In the rosy glow reflected from the ceiling that long stretch of crimson seemed to have the quality of plush and something of the sordid splendour of a scene in a novel by Balzac. I suddenly realised, with complete conviction, but without any under-standing why it should be so, that I was looking into some deserted bar or night-club; that length of dark red plush was the covering of the seat which ran the whole length of the room. And I realised also, with alarm, that I must have got so drunk that I could not remember where I was or who had brought me there. But even for a night-club the atmosphere was strangely sinister and oppressive. All was silent, the revellers had departed; and from what position was I looking into that deserted establishment, with its air of sordid splendour and the empty bottles and glasses littering the bar which I *knew* stretched the length of the other wall of the room that was out of my sight?

I desperately tried to discover where I myself could be, and it was with an unaccountable sense of horror that I found I was in bed, at the head of a long double row of beds in which bodies lay outstretched, silent and unmoving in the baleful pink glow of the night lights over-head. I realised at once that I must be in some other part of the night-club, as it seemed to me in an upper room, half brothel and half doss-house, of extraordinary squalor and dreariness (no red plush here!) where I and my companions in sin were sleeping off, or even at that moment indulging in, who knew what unnameable orgies. For the atmosphere of vice and crime and the prevailing tinge of blood were as thick and heavy here as in that nineteenth-century interior of the night-club of which I had had so terrifying a glimpse. With rising panic I thought, *I must get out of here*, it was impossible I should remain a moment longer, or I should be faced with terrible exposure and shame. So with a great effort I tried to get out of bed, but only to find with even greater horror and panic that my left leg was trapped in some extraordinary apparatus that seemed to be partly an instrument of torture and partly a mechanical device of incredible clumsiness designed for some completely futile purpose. I struggled to free myself with the violent yet feeble efforts of a fly caught in a spider's web, and only then realised with what maniacal ingenuity my leg had been entangled in the intricacies of the grotesque machine. It did not occur to me that there could be anything wrong with my leg; and with yet another flash of insight into my horrible situation, I knew without doubt that what had happened was that my friends and companions in the debauchery of the night before had devised this monstrous practical joke to trap me in this terrible room where so many victims of such degrading vices lay stretched out beside each other.

I must get out of here, I repeated to myself, and saw at once that in order to do so I should have to take to pieces the monstrous engine in which my leg was trapped. I eased myself painfully in bed, at the same time wondering why I should be so weak, and began to unscrew the bolts and nuts which held the iron frame together. It shook and jangled as I attacked it and the noise awakened one of the profligates in a neighbouring bed. I heard him call out: 'Is there anything the matter?' and turning my head could see him standing in a nightshirt beside his bed.

'Can I help you?' he said politely. His voice was certainly kind, but I was by this time intensely suspicious and to my nightmare-distorted eyes he presented a figure which only confirmed the dangers of the predicament into which I had fallen. He wore a flannel nightshirt of an off-white colour, the kind of garment which seemed to me in my distress appropriate to a house of charity or ill-fame, and in the rosy darkness of the ward his eyes were huge purple shadows, he seemed unshaven and unclean, a dipsomaniac, a drug addict, perhaps, sleeping off some protracted bout of debauchery. He was in fact, as I learned later, a mild and sympathetic little man who was in hospital to have his hammer toes straightened.

'You keep out of this,' I said fiercely. 'You get back to bed. I'm getting out.'

He looked surprised but obediently went back to bed and I returned to my task of dismantling the scaffolding in which I was entangled. A cross-bar collapsed upon the bed as I succeeded in detaching it from the upright; my injured leg in its case of white plaster lay encumbered in the tangle of ropes and pulleys that collapsed with it; another iron tube fell with a clang as I proceeded feverishly with my work and the whole elaborate structure began to disintegrate. With infinite difficulty, and disregarding the shafts of pain and the queer clicking sensation of fractured bones grinding against each other, I freed my leg from the wreckage which littered the bed. It still did not occur to me that my leg was damaged, or that I might not be able to use it once I had extricated it from the extraordinary jumble which now lay on the bed.

At last I was free and was about to make my escape when suddenly a night nurse approached and stared at me in horror. 'Whatever are you doing? Get back to bed at once, you *naughty* boy,' she cried, in that tone of maternal indignation which nurses commonly adopt with fractious patients. But when she saw the extraordinary collection of objects which lay in disorder on my bed, her indignation gave way to helplessness. Giggling slightly, she retreated from the ward and in a moment returned with the night sister, a plump and exceedingly pretty girl who began to laugh uncontrollably when she saw me lying back in bed exhausted, like Samson with the pillars of the Temple in ruin around him. Nightmare and hysteria vanished in the face of her laughter, her pink cheeks, her enormous blue eyes. Suddenly I knew exactly where I was. I was in hospital, I had been run over, my leg was broken. The night-club, the brothel, the dipsomaniacs and drug addicts seemed to disappear in a moment, as if they had never existed, as the night sister and the nurse, giggling and scolding, tried unskilfully to restore my leg into its hanging cradle. 'You are a one, and no mistake,' the night sister said. 'You might have broken your leg all over again.' She had a high-coloured, rosy face and black curls that escaped from under her stiff, white cap.

'I wanted to get out,' I mumbled, ashamed now of the trouble I had caused, and almost mesmerised by her preternaturally large blue eyes. She was quite extraordinarily pretty.

'It will be months before *you* get out,' she said, giggling. 'You won't get away from me so easily.' She made up my bed and smoothed the pillows. 'Would you like some tea?' she said.

I thanked her, and when she brought the tea I drank it and wondered desperately what on earth my nightmare had been about.

'Now you be a good boy and go to sleep,' the night sister said. She bent down over me to take my tea cup. 'You know, you remind me of someone. Do you know who?'

'No,' I said.

'James Dean,' she said, and left me to sleep.

V

My nightmare remained with me for a long time and every evening when the night lights were turned on, the ward recaptured for a moment the sinister glare in which it had been bathed. But from that night I began, as they say, to get better; or at least I was no longer afraid of relapsing into the darkness from which I had returned. And equally I was no longer so completely obsessed by the garden outside the windows and I began, slowly and reluctantly at first, for I found that the effort tired me, to take some notice of my immediate sur-roundings and of my fellow patients.

Perhaps the nursing staff also realised that some change had taken place in my condition. For the next day, the male nurse who was in charge of the day staff came to me and asked me how I felt. He was an extraordinarily efficient person who was always immaculately spruce in a freshly-pressed white linen uniform. He looked like a doll who every day had been newly unpacked from its box. I told him I felt better.

'It's time we cleaned you up a bit,' he said. 'You look terrible. You're beginning to frighten the visitors.'

It was a shock to me to realise that I had an appearance of my own or that anyone could possibly be interested in what I looked like; after my accident, I had come to feel that my body existed for no other purpose than that surgeons or nurses should practise their skill and science upon it, like the corpses which Burke and Hare sold to the anatomy school in Edinburgh, or the dummies which nurses use in order to practise the seventeen different methods of making a bed. Perhaps the nurse, who was always addressed by the mysterious hierarchical title of *Staff*, noticed my surprise or may even have taken it for refusal, for he simply held up to my face a hand mirror which until now he had held behind his back.

'Have a good look,' he said, with a kind of grim cheerfulness, as if I might well be surprised but nothing could surprise him. And indeed what I saw was the face of a particularly unprepossessing stranger, a rough customer who might have been badly mauled in a street fight. My face was a network of deep scars from which the blood had not yet been removed, and the week-old growth of stubble which covered it sprouted from an ugly mass of wounds and scabs. Other scars, red and raw where the stitches had been put in, ran across my skull, and one eye was hardly visible in an enormous bruise of deepest purple and violet and inky black; even the eyelids were scarred, and pitted with the tiny grains of gravel and dirt that clung to my flesh like nutmeg to a nutmeg grater.

'It's not very nice,' I said.

'You're damn right it's not nice,' Staff said. 'After all, we've got to look at you.'

So with infinite care and patience he shaved the minute portions of my face that were unscarred, tried to brush my hair over the bald patches where the stitches showed, and washed away the crust of blood around the wounds. When he had finished, I felt as immaculate as he was, like a member of the German General Staff: *immer bereit, immer rasiert.** I was indeed no beauty but somehow I felt, and perhaps others felt too, that I had now been officially recognised among the living. Nurses began to stop and talk to me as they went on their rounds; walking patients came to my bedside and told me all the innumerable details of their illnesses and operations; I even began to understand the almost military differences of rank between the various grades of the hospital hierarchy, the godlike respect due to a doctor or surgeon, and the immense gulf which separates him from any member of the nursing staff, from the matron herself down to the giggling young nurses who, fresh from school, gleaming and gay in their stiffly-starched uniform, performed the most sordid and menial tasks with an incomparable air of sweetness and humility. At the very bottom of the hierarchy, the rank and file of this extraordinary army devoted to the common purpose of healing and being healed, came the patients themselves, all crippled, all neurotically obsessed with their own ailments but all so convinced, in their own particular case, of the immense importance of getting well, that they submitted without a murmur to the most painful or the most humiliating treatment.

'Angels, that's what they are,' said a voice, 'little angels wivout wings.' It was a patient in a neighbouring bed; he was talking about the nurses, and was protesting because someone had uttered some slight criticism of them. I could not see him very well, because he lay on the far side of my immediate neighbour on my left, who sat in an upright position with his body totally enclosed in plaster. He had a face which, under a crown of thick, white hair, had a look of great calm and serenity, as of one who had satisfied all his earthly desires. He was, I learned later, a murderer from Broadmoor, who over fifty years ago had thrown his wife out of a top-storey window and had been detained at Her Majesty's pleasure ever since. A warden from Broadmoor, half-nurse, half-guard, sat at the foot of his bed by day and night; there were three of them, and they took eight-hour shifts in keeping watch over this helpless old man who was in no better condition to escape than a newborn baby. He seemed, however, quite oblivious to the presence of his guards, whom he ignored completely; above the neck of his plaster, his face had a look of intense and radiant happiness, as if fifty long years had not been enough to exhaust the ecstasy of that beautiful moment when his wife had disappeared out of the window.

Opposite to him lay a man who was recovering from an operation to his knee-cap. He had the ruddy face of a young farmer, but in fact he was a topiarist who would talk for hours, to anyone who would listen, about the delights of his profession and the great houses whose yews and hedges he clipped and shaped. Every morning, in the long hours of waiting before the day nurses brought our breakfast, he greeted the day with his favourite song, *To be a farmer's boy*, which he sang in a fine light tenor voice to the great pleasure of us all and repeated cries of *encore*. And at first, before I had made the acquaintance of any of my other companions, I used to think how wildly improbable it was that my two neighbours should be something so completely untypical of the British welfare state, as it is supposed to exist today, as a murderer and a topiarist. It seemed to be an offence against all statistical laws that I should lie beside such a pair; and all the more so perhaps because both of them seemed to share a profound happiness which showed itself as much in the topiarist's voice when, like a bird, he burst into his early morning song, as in the almost imperceptible smile on the murderer's face as he meditated on his great act of fifty years ago. I began to feel that, if these were my companions, there must be something equally strange, equally unlikely, about myself, that it was not mere chance which had thrown us together but some careful though mysterious method of selection which had brought us together on the basis of some common though improbable quality, as if all three of us were albinos or spoke Volapuk.*

I was somewhat reassured when, as days went by, I began to know some of the other inhabitants of the ward and found that not all of them were quite so exceptional in their tastes or their vocation. It was a rapidly changing society; broken bones healed; the maimed got up and walked; new faces came and went; so that every day it was possible to make new acquaintances who restored my belief that the pattern of English life could not be quite so eccentric as it had at first seemed. There was Fred, for instance, an ex-sailor turned postman, who explained to me how sadly conditions had deteriorated in the post office since the days when he had first worn its uniform. It seemed that a misguided zeal for economy and efficiency had infected that institution, and he spoke of the happiness of an earlier period as if he were talking of the days of Trollope. 'I'd rather be back in the Navy,' he said bitterly. 'At least you knew where you were.' He was also deeply occupied by the problems of bringing up children, of whom he had many: 'Devils when they're young, and a heartbreak when they're older,' was his view.

There was also Mr Emilio Pinza, by profession a head waiter, who startled and impressed the ward on his first arrival by depositing one hundred pound notes with the charge nurse, and thereafter behaved towards him much as an old and valued client might behave towards his banker. At first there was considerable speculation about the sources of Mr Pinza's immense wealth. It soon appeared, however, that they were connected with the Turf. Mr Pinza's betting operations were considerable, and in hospital he conducted them through a kind of underground which existed to serve the patients' illicit needs; he financed them by drawing upon the charge nurse for such sums as he might require from time to time.

Every morning and evening Mr Pinza studied the racing news with profound concentration; at midday he laid his bets; in the afternoon, when the results were known, he entered an account of the day's operations in a little black book which he kept under his pillow. From time to time he deposited further large sums with the charge nurse; after a few weeks it seemed to us that Mr Pinza's fortune must be colossal. He explained to me that indeed he hoped to make his stay in hospital a protracted and a profitable one, as it gave him the proper leisure and freedom from distraction which are required if one is to make any kind of success of following the horses, a serious occupation which was hardly compatible with the frivolity and self-indulgence of earning one's living. 'Six months in 'ere,' said Mr Pinza, 'and I ought to make a tidy packet. And then,' he added dreamily, 'I think a little 'oliday in the Isle of Wight.'

There there was Mr Shenfield, whose task in life was to drive the directors of an enormous firm of building contractors about their business, which Mr Shenfield regarded as very largely his own. He was greatly preoccupied with the two new schools which the firm was erecting in Hertfordshire, with the difficulties involved in the contract they had undertaken for a new aerodrome, with the even greater difficulties of the negotiations regarding the construction of a new dam in Africa. These matters frankly worried Mr Shenfield; but what worried him even more were the personal troubles between Mr Willy and Mr Tom, and their continual dissensions at board meetings. He hardly knew how the firm could continue unless the directors could discuss such matters with him as he drove them around in the firm's Rolls-Royce. Mr Shenfield worried so much about these things that it was seriously hampering his recovery. Mr Shenfield also had a wife and several children. This was known, though he never mentioned them, because they came to see him on visiting days; and when they came it was clear, from the careworn expression on the faces of all of them, down to the smallest, a little girl hardly out of her perambulator, that the frightful responsibility of the firm's huge operations lay heavy upon them all.

Above all, there was Ginger, a builder's labourer who lived on a caravan site near the hospital. He had two exquisite fair-haired baby daughters of almost angelic beauty who came to visit him with their mother and gazed at this practically illiterate young man with enormous blue eyes which showed a love and adoration that a god might have been glad to inspire. Ginger's trouble was that he was a walking patient who was no longer confined to his bed. Having no intellectual resources of any kind, such as horseracing, or playing cards, or listening to the radio, he could find no other use for his time or his abounding energy, his huge fund of high spirits, than to make himself useful to others. He made the early morning tea which he brought round on a trolley almost as soon as dawn had broken; he boiled the breakfast eggs with which patients were allowed to supply themselves if they wished; he helped the nurses to make the beds; indeed, he was as useful to them as to the patients and, in the end, became a kind of supernumerary nurse himself. In the afternoon, when the walking patients were allowed to leave the hospital grounds for two hours, he ran errands for the other patients, bought cigarettes, posted letters, collected laundry, or did anything else that anyone was kind enough to think of asking him to do. For Mr Pinza he undertook telephone calls to his bookmaker too confidential to be trusted to the underground. All these services Ginger performed as if he were receiving and not giving a kindness; with inimitable good manners he made one realise how good it was of one to make use of him. After a time it was not difficult to understand the adoration that shone in the huge blue eyes of his daughters, who were as beautiful as he was good.

VI

And there were many others, who all displayed before me what were, from their own point of view, the richness and variety of their individual lives. For of one thing I became convinced during my long stay in hospital; that for all men their own lives are a matter of inexhaustible interest, incomparable jewels which, however cheap or dull they may appear to others, are for themselves beyond all price. Each man looks upon himself with the infinite loving kindness of God; each man is a Christ in his own behaviour to himself.

The patients would talk to me from the neighbouring beds, or as they walked to and fro from the ward to the dayroom, and after a few polite and formal enquiries about my leg ('How are your toes?'), would begin to tell me about their own ailments, with that wealth of medical detail which never ceased to astound me. And from their illnesses they progressed to their work, their amusements, their wives, girlfriends, children, habits, prejudices, hopes, pleasures, troubles, all that immense ramification of interests and feelings that goes to make a human being.

Perhaps if I had been in any other condition, I would not have listened; perhaps it was the shock of my accident that left me so passive and receptive, so entirely without feelings or interests of my own, that just as the mere contemplation of the garden outside absorbed me so completely that my whole being seemed to dissolve in its embrace, so these individual human beings who were displayed before me, like the trees and flowers of the garden, had a strangeness and mystery which attached to every detail of their lives, however trivial they might have seemed at any other time. How Ginger acquired his dog, what Mr Shenfield said to Mr Willy after his last row with Mr Tom, Mr Pinza's plans for a great *coup* during Ascot week, the strange behaviour of the scar on Mr Langley's leg which would not cease from, as he expressed it, 'weeping', all these things and many others seemed to me profoundly interesting and significant and I should never have ceased to listen to them, except that I found at the end of the day that such a torrent of personal experiences, springing from so many sources, left me exhausted, as if, in the course of the day, I had lived twenty men's lives as well as my own.

Sometimes I wondered why it was that each man seemed so willing to display, as it were, so much of his life and sometimes of his deepest and most intimate feelings, like someone offering a tray of precious jewels for sale. But then I realised that the hospital itself was a kind of forcing-house for such revelations. In ordinary life we are so occupied with the pursuit, not alas! of anything so idealistic as pleasure, but of immediate practical objectives, and these objectives are so often mutually incompatible, that we can spare little time for the lives of other people, or even, in the more serious sense, for our own, so deeply are we absorbed in the affairs of the moment. But in hospital, so far as we had any practical interests at all, we had only one, and it was one which we all shared, and moreover it was one we could do very little about; it was quite simply the interest of getting well, and this was something which in no way depended on our efforts or our own wills, but was largely a matter which had to be left to Nature herself, and the army of doctors, surgeons, and nurses who had entered her service.

So perhaps understanding, or receptiveness, grew out of our freedom from the practical egotisms which dominate our ordinary life (though not from that other and deeper egotism which makes every man a kind of miracle to himself). But in my own case there was another factor at work which perhaps was hardly less important. The public ward of a hospital makes an incomparable observation post for anyone who is interested in his fellow men, and most of all because it is organised on principles which tend to abolish all those differences of class, income, and education which in ordinary life raise such impenetrable barriers between the citizens of this country.

It must be accepted that, in this country at least, an educated man is an object of intense suspicion to the majority of his fellow countrymen, that is to say, unless he is merely an object of mockery or complete indifference; and those who believe that by their personal qualities they can overcome this barrier for the most part only deceive themselves. But in hospital that barrier tends to disappear, in the first place because no particular reason or explanation is required for one's presence, on terms of absolute equality, at that particular time and place; the reason, after all, is only too obvious. And in the second place, that very reason, which in every case is illness or disability of some kind, in itself creates a ground of sympathy with one's fellow-sufferers who, after all, are all there for exactly the same reason as oneself.

So that, for me at least, it was an enormous pleasure to find that my fellow patients appeared to take me for granted, certainly to a greater extent than I took them for granted, for their habits and their behaviour never ceased to be a source of wonder and astonishment to me; and in this, perhaps, they showed better manners than I did. Yet in one respect at least I always remained at a disadvantage; for I found once again, as I had found years ago when I served in the ranks in the army, that among the many varieties of spoken English in use in the ward, there were several, quite literally, I could not understand at all.

This was not perhaps surprising in the case of Mr Pinza; after fifty years in England his language was that of some remote and isolated rural area thickly overlaid with Italian overtones, and even this was less of an obstacle than the system of free association, amounting to unbridled licence, which appeared to govern his train of thought. But even in conversation with those who had been born and bred in this country, and whose minds appeared to work in a manner which was recognisably rational, I was frequently at a loss to attach any meaning whatever to the sounds which they uttered. It was embarrassing to listen to an account of some complicated family incident, or of the latest operation performed by Mr —, the surgeon, and at the end be unable to offer any comment whatever, because one had not understood a word of what had been said. Or at least it would have been embarrassing if any comment had been expected, but I soon learned that to listen was in itself sufficient, and after a time established a modest but recognised position for myself as one who could always be depended upon to listen sympathetically but from whom not much could be expected in the way of intelligent discussion. It is quite untrue that education broadens the mind; it makes the arts and the sciences more accessible, but in England at least it cuts off communication with a large part of the human race.

VII

I now had two interests which were quite sufficient to occupy all my waking hours. There was the garden, which at any hour from dawn to dark never ceased to fill me with wonder and delight; and on the other hand there was the endless panorama of human life that unfolded before me in the ward.

Why was it that each of the young nurses who came to my bedside every night to give me my sleeping pills seemed so absolutely and uniquely different from every other, so that it almost seemed as if they wore their stiff crisp uniforms in an effort to reassure me that they had this at least in common and did not each of them constitute some special race or species with no other member except herself? Even the way in which each one of them handed me the little medicine glass in which lay two small orange pills, with their assurance of sleep, was so entirely different that it seemed to proclaim the uniqueness of her being. Was it perhaps that, as one lay there, grotesque and hideous and helpless, an object merely of mercy and healing, all power of the will was suspended and that, the will suspended, one sees people as they really are? Such questions, seeking abstract answers to abstract questions, did not bother me; it was the fact alone that enthralled me, the simple indefensible assurance that spoke in every gesture of every body, in every tone of every voice, in every single action of every single person with whom I came into contact. Four times a day one of the nurses toured the ward with a little rubber-wheeled trolley covered with bottles of spirit, lotions, a bowl of water, boxes of powder, and washed and anointed one as a precaution against bed sores; with eyes closed, and not a word spoken, I could tell which nurse it was whose fingers rubbed and washed my body, as if by touch alone I knew the uniqueness of her fingerprints.

This conviction of the single and unique existence of every living person was at first so overwhelming that it could not have occurred to me that these extraordinary beings with whom the ward was filled could have any qualities or habits in common; they seemed to me to have completely monadic existences and that anything that was in any way common to them all, as for instance that, divine substances as they were, they still ate their meals at the same time or had physical needs which were satisfied in the same way, seemed to be a result merely of laws and rules that were imposed from outside as the very condition of life in the hospital. Yet after a time I began to recognise that after all they did have some things in common, similar tastes, similar likes and dislikes, similar reactions in similar circumstances. What surprised me, when at last I had made this astonishing discovery, was how different these common qualities were from anything I might have expected.

It was true, for instance, that a particular song which at that time was popular had an almost hypnotic effect on every single person in the ward, including the nurses. It was called *Magic Moments,* and was probably one of the most banal sequences of notes and words that has ever been contrived. There was rarely a moment from the first to the last of the day when someone was not singing, whistling, humming, or merely shouting this terrible composition. During certain radio pro-grammes, such, for instance, as *Housewives' Choice,* one of the patients would be ordered to stand by at one of the earphone sets which were attached to each bed; if by any chance (and the odds were fairly high) that song were to be announced, he would shout peremptorily '*Magic Moments!*' and patients and nurses alike would seize a pair of earphones and immediately achieve the condition of mindless ecstasy which the song appeared to induce:

> Magic moments, mem'ries we've been sharing,
> Magic moments, when two hearts are caring,
> Time can't erase the mem'ry of
> These magic moments filled with love.

As it soon became patent that I was either immune or allergic to this particular drug, as it might be to penicillin or aureomycin, one nurse always ran to my bed in order to have the privilege of having both earphones of the set to herself, instead of having to share them, as the other nurses did, with one of the patients. How touching it was to watch the nurses' pretty heads pressed close to those of the patients, so often old and grey and careworn, as they listened side by side to Mr Perry Como, who was the acknowledged *gran maestro* of all those who interpreted *Magic Moments*. There was another song which almost competed with it in public favour; it was called *Lollipop, Lollipop*, and appeared to have no other words and practically no music.* Nor were they necessary, because the mere repetition of the two words, *Lollipop, Lollipop*, uttered compulsively from time to time, appeared to be sufficient to appease the nerves and the needs of all who were under their charm.

Music of this kind supplied a running accompaniment to everything that was said and done in the ward; it appeared to have a far greater power over the minds and feelings of patients and nurses than either the written or the spoken word. Indeed, though many patients complained of the long hours of inactivity and boredom, very few resorted to books for distraction. Newspapers were delivered morning and evening and were eagerly seized upon; but to judge from the sudden outburst of conversation which they always stimulated, they were read for no other reason than to study the racing news and results; the vast circulation of the daily press in this country must depend to an overwhelming degree on horse-racing.

The racing news, however, was read with minute and concentrated attention, and afterwards discussed with a wealth of knowledge and reference, a scrupulous respect for fact, that would have been worthy of a learned society discussing the minutiae of a classical text; we were all mandarins in our respect for the scholarship of the Turf. So far as I could discover, there was no other subject whatever that in any degree commanded so much general interest and attention. It was true that once a week everyone completed his entry for the pools and that every Saturday night everyone checked his coupon against the results; but this was done quickly and cursorily, though accurately, as if it were some routine duty that every self-respecting person had to perform. Moreover, it seemed to be fully recognised that this was an activity whose results were completely governed by the inscrutable laws of chance, and therefore not worth serious study. It was only racing that inspired the arduous and protracted concentration of men who know they are at grips with a subject to which knowledge is the only key. And if in this field Mr Pinza was regarded as the master of those who know, the Virgil of the racing world, it was only because we all recognised that for long years he had devoted to the subject the long unrewarded hours, the ardent and unremitting labour, which all true learning requires. He was the Scaliger of the Turf.*

Apart from racing all other distractions were of minor account. There was no television set in our section of the hospital, either in the sick-ward or in the day-room, where the walking patients spent their day, from seven in the morning until eight at night. What surprised me, who had been led to believe that television has become the opium of the people, was that no single person ever complained of the lack of it, or talked of what programmes he might have been watching if he had been at home, or what his favourite programmes were, or his favourite television stars, or what are called 'personalities'. For us, Mr Gilbert Harding, Lady Lewisham, Lord Boothby, and all the rest of the illustrious obscure might just as well have never existed; only occasionally a nurse would say wistfully that she wished she could hear Mr Perry Como sing *Magic Moments* on the television.

In the same way, I never heard anyone discuss any politician, or political party, or political event; so far as we were concerned, neither government nor opposition seemed to exist, and it is worth recording, as a matter of observed fact, that during a total of three months in hospital I never heard any of the subjects, with one exception, of either the leaders or the headlines in a newspaper mentioned in conversation; the exception was the disaster that overcame Manchester United at Munich. I never heard the name of Mr Macmillan or Mr Gaitskell; so far as my fellow patients were concerned the government and political system of Great Britain had no existence; nor had its literature, nor its drama, nor its music, unless one counts *Magic Moments*; the *only* name I ever heard mentioned, both on the radio or in the press *and* in the conversation of the patients, was that of Lady Docker.*

In the day-room the patients played, interminably, at billiards, snooker, and cards. Yet with so much of the world excluded, as it seemed, from their interest, they never lacked for subjects to talk about. There was, of course, racing; there were their own ailments and operations; there was, strangely enough, an intense interest in the birds that appeared in great variety in the garden outside, of which the favourite was a lone, plump cock pheasant which from time to time dropped heavily into the grass; there was an endless exchange of personal reminiscences of every sort and kind; there were no dirty stories. After long hours of listening to conversation of this kind I came to the conclusion that the overwhelming interest of my fellow patients was in the personal life, adventures, and especially disasters, of individual human beings, known not at second-hand, as from literature or from the press, but from the direct experience of daily life.

VIII

In the earliest days of my stay in hospital, when I only recovered consciousness at rare and brief intervals, which usually seemed to occur, for some reason, at night, I became aware of a figure which occupied a bed almost opposite to mine and next to the glass partition which divided the day-room from the ward. It did not lie, but squatted on its bed in the rosy glow of the night light immediately overhead, and seemed, so far as I could tell, to be writing feverishly with concentrated haste, as if what it was writing were of immense importance and there was little time to finish it. I could not see very clearly; in the half-darkness everything was ghostly, vague, indistinct. But before I lapsed into sleep again, I had an impression of a head bowed in profile, like a late and decadent Greek coin, and of black curly hair that fell in profusion almost to the line of the eyebrows.

On the following days, this figure became familiar to me and acquired a name and a personality, and at first it was to me a source of irritation and annoyance. It was the figure of a young man of eighteen or nineteen, and he had only to open his mouth for one to know that he was a Scotsman; his name was Jock McGregor. The first impression he made, by the light of day, was one of perpetual and incessant movement, and it was this that annoyed me, because it continuously broke into the kind of trance in which I lived at that time. His leg had been cut off between the knee and the ankle, but this seemed to stimulate rather than to hamper his incessant physical activity. He had a pair of steel elbow crutches on which he moved with incredible speed and agility, swinging through the air on his one good leg, as if he were an acrobat rather than a cripple. But even without their aid he was equally mobile, as he then proceeded in a series of gigantic hops that carried him headlong from one end of the ward to the other, like an atom whose intervening positions cannot be calculated. Even his amputated leg was not useless to him; he used it as if, instead of being crippled, he had been given an additional limb. His favourite trick was to stand at the billiard table on his good leg and play billiards with the amputated one. He reminded me of a wonderful Negro dancer I had seen in my youth, called Peg Leg Bates, who on one good leg and one wooden one executed the most complicated and painful steps to the music of a Negro jazz band.

When I came to know him, I learned that Jock had been in and out of the hospital, at very short intervals, for a period of four years. Even before that, he had injured his foot by treading on a nail while walking barefoot on the sands of the Clyde, where he had been born. From that time, his life had been a series of extremely skilful, difficult, and wholly unsuccessful operations which had culminated in the amputation of his now useless foot and ankle. I never heard him complain of what he had suffered, and it did not seem to occur to him that he was now in any way handicapped; and indeed in this he was perhaps right, for by comparison with most of us in the ward, and perhaps indeed with most men, he was a miracle of physical energy. He had an extraordinary vitality that buzzed and hummed within him like a powerful electric dynamo; he also had an extraordinary physical beauty that seemed as it were the reflection and expression of the energy by which he was possessed. He had a small, beautifully proportioned body that was marred only by the round, smooth, ugly stump of his amputated leg; his thick, black curly hair grew low over his forehead, above a short, straight nose and a mouth that was astonishingly mobile and ex- pressive. His eyelashes were the envy of all the nurses, with whom he was a favourite; sometimes one would ask him jokingly if she could borrow them for the dance that night. An animal, one would have said; but like most animals that are domesticated, as he was domesticated in hospital, his natural instincts were overlaid by neuroses that almost made him human.

When I first came to know him, he had been waiting for a month for the artificial foot which was to replace his own, and he talked endlessly of what he was going to do when it came; though indeed it seemed to me that it could not possibly make him any more active than he was already. Most of all he talked of how he would be able to play football again, of which he was very fond, but he accepted that now he might have to play in goal instead of at inside-right. There was really no reason why, during this period of waiting, he should have stayed in hospital at all; he was physically perfectly capable of making his way about in the outside world. But gradually I learned that he stayed because he had nowhere else to go. His mother was dead; his father, a steelworker in the North of England, had married again and since that time neither he nor his new wife had taken any interest in his son. Without bitterness Jock told me that during his four years in hospital he had never received a visit or a letter from his father or his step-mother, nor did this seem to surprise him in any way; how he lived during the brief intervals when he had been discharged from hospital I could never quite discover, though he spoke vaguely of friends and I learned that immediately before his leg had been amputated he had worked as a builder's labourer and had without difficulty earned sixteen or seventeen pounds a week.

The truth was that the hospital had become his home; he had no other. The only regret he appeared to have in life was that, because of lack of education, he could never become a surgeon. He had acquired an astonishingly accurate knowledge of everything to do with his own operations and those of every other patient in the ward, borrowed medical books from the house doctors, and pestered them for permission to be present at the operations in the operating theatre; and yet it was clear that, for all his knowledge, his ambition to be a surgeon meant chiefly to him that he would never have to leave the only home he knew. When I asked him what in fact he proposed to do when he did leave hospital, he said that he would enter a government training establishment where he could live in a hostel and train to become an aircraft fitter.

Alas, I could not think that he would be well fitted for such an apprenticeship. For just as he had come to regard the hospital as his home, so the hospital after so many years seemed to regard him as its child, and a particularly privileged one, for he broke all its rules with complete impunity. Every night, when everyone else was either asleep or trying vainly to sleep, he squatted on his bed, the stump of his amputated leg protruding from his pyjamas, and wrote interminably until the early hours of the morning. I wondered at first what immense work he was engaged upon; later I learned that these were letters to a nurse whom he was in love with and who worked in another section of the hospital. I gathered indeed that during his long stay in hospital he had made love to most of the nurses; many of them treated him with the detached affection with which ex-wives treat their former husbands. Each morning the product of his night's labours was sealed in an envelope and handed to one of the departing night nurses for delivery to its recipient; when the day nurses came on duty, one of them would hand over an equally bulky envelope to him. This immense correspondence, conducted from one ward to another, had been in progress for several months, and was a matter of intense interest to all the nurses. I often wondered what he could find to write at such length each night; once he produced for me from his suitcase the whole series of his correspondent's letters, neatly docketed, filed, and indexed. How I wanted to read them! but when I asked what she wrote to him each day, he only murmured mysteriously: *You could make a novel out of these.*

No one disturbed him at his nightly task, though for everyone else the rule of rest and sleep after lights out was strictly enforced; it was as if the staff and the patients alike realised that in his case the enforcement of discipline would be intolerable. They seemed to recognise instinctively in him a principle of anarchy which was as much deserving of respect as any other principle by which a man, or a boy, may live; and yet no one else seemed to take advantage of the freedom which he abused unscrupulously. Having written through the night, when the day staff arrived to serve breakfast at some appallingly early hour he would be fast asleep and continued to sleep throughout the morning until he felt hungry enough to wake up and help himself, amid giggles and scuffles, to some food in the little pantry where the nurses made cups of tea for themselves throughout the day.

The time came when at last his surgical boot was ready, and having been driven over to the neighbouring town to have it fitted by the makers, he at length returned triumphantly with it to the hospital. It was an elaborate and ugly contraption of composition attached to a steel and leather gaiter which fitted over the amputated stump of his leg, and he proudly demonstrated to us how skilfully it was made. Yet it soon became evident that it didn't assist those nimble and agile movements with which he flashed through the ward with the aid of his crutches, or those immense, birdlike hops by which he seemed to take off from the ground altogether. Crippled, he had been swifter and more active than an athlete; now he dragged his new foot behind him and limped awkwardly as the stiff new leather rubbed and chafed at his amputated flesh. He had seemed like a great bird that flew through the ward, but now he was truly a cripple, as awkward and earthbound as any of us. Yet he did not cease to declare that now he was whole again, even though the horrible boot soon rubbed his flesh into ugly and painful sores.

He now revealed that writing was not his only accomplishment. During the afternoon hours, when walking patients were allowed to leave the hospital grounds, he would drag himself painfully for miles over the heath near by and return sweating with pain but still asserting triumphantly that his new limb was as good if not better than the old one had been. On his return from these walks he would show me his sketch book in which he had drawn views of the landscape around the heath. They were immensely detailed, drawn with a meticulous accuracy that recorded every tiny detail of tree and field and flower, so that they never in any sense composed a picture yet expressed with surprising vividness and freshness the love which he had expended on them. He took immense pains with them, working on them after he had returned from his walks, but when I complimented him on them, he merely complained that however hard he worked at them they always missed the only really important thing he had seen on his walk, though what this one thing was he never told me.

I used to wonder how this extraordinary creature would be able to adapt himself again to the world outside the walls of our hospital, for he had become so much a part of it that it hardly seemed he could exist outside it. And indeed when I asked him about his life on his brief excursions out of hospital, it seemed to have been very largely a matter of liquor, love, and fights. He was exceedingly fond of the whisky of his native land, and when I succeeded in smuggling a bottle into the hospital, we used to drink surreptitiously together when the others were asleep. And with his physical energy and good looks it was impossible that he should not always be involved with women, and equally impossible that outside hospital he should meet with the same long-suffering patience and affection which he met with there. When I asked him where he was going when he left, he spoke again of his training establishment, but without conviction, as if he knew he would not really be able to endure it. Also it seemed that anyhow he would not enter it for a month and in the meanwhile he had nowhere to go. He spoke enthusiastically of being at liberty again, of being able to do exactly what he wanted, yet there was in his voice an uncertain note, as if he suspected that outside the hospital only loneliness and disaster lay before him.

Yet at last the time came for him to leave, and by a coincidence it was on the same day on which I was myself discharged. I talked to him while he waited to catch the bus which passed the gates at the end of the hospital drive. He was wearing a cheap and worn blue suit, with a check cap on that wonderful dark-featured head, and when he walked the dreadful surgical boot seemed to drag painfully and heavily on the ground. And at last he went, promising to write to me though I knew that he would not, and now when I have almost forgotten the hospital I wonder what has happened to him and what extraordinary and disastrous adventures he has met with outside its protecting walls.

❧

A Chapter of Accidents

❧

One

I

I was born on November 29th, 1909, at Aberystwyth in Cardigan-shire, in the early hours of Monday morning, while my father was away on a preaching engagement which had taken him from home for the weekend. This only happened twelve times a year, and it was thought particularly unfortunate for my mother and myself that I should have been born in my father's absence, as if he could have eased the pains of it both for her and for me.

He was a very intelligent and able man, with a force of character which enabled him to have his own way in most things on which his mind was set. With his natural endowments, he would have achieved success in any walk of life he might have chosen. Originally this was to have been the law, and for this he would have been admirably adapted, intellectually and temperamentally; he was by nature just and fair-minded, and his mind would have been at home in its complexities without being led away into abstractions, because he was essentially practical and commonsense in his judgements. He also had a gift for eloquence and persuasiveness which would have served him well before any jury or court of law.

I have no doubt that, if he had followed his original choice, he would have achieved great distinction even in so fiercely competitive a profession, all the more so, perhaps, because to his other gifts he added the essential arts of the politician. He understood the motives which influence men and assemblies and how to manipulate them, he was patient, persistent and flexible in pursuing his own objectives and was always ready for the compromise which would carry a majority with it. His enemies, of whom he had some, would have said that he was a trimmer, but whether this was so or not, it is not often a vice or a virtue which stands in the way of success.

Such qualities eminently fitted my father for that world of politics and the bar to which, in the days when he was young, lack of means was no disqualification. Many young men had started life with worse prospects and fewer abilities than he and had achieved the most eminent positions in the state and at the bar. Some of them I met when I grew up; it never occurred to me that they were superior to my father in either intellectual or practical ability.

But while he was still a boy at the City of London school, something happened to my father which changed the whole course of his life, and therefore, I suppose, my own; or rather, perhaps, it would be true to say that my own existence was merely a subsidiary effect of this intervention of providence. At the age of sixteen my father, like Paul on the road to Damascus, received a call from God, so direct, personal and compelling as to leave no doubt of its authenticity. It was a voice which banished from his mind all thought of worldly ambition and commanded him thenceforward to devote his life to the ministry of the church.

Such a call was of course at that time much less rare than it is now. In those days God often spoke to ambitious young men and changed their lives in a twinkling of an eye, and perhaps it was even less surprising that he should do so to my father than to other young men. For in the middle of the East End of London,* with its lurid combination of vice and violence, of squalor and destitution, he had been brought up in a strictly religious and devotional atmosphere, in which the voice of God was heard as frequently and continuously as a television announcer's today, and it is therefore in no way surprising that when He spoke personally to my father, He should have found a willing and obedient listener.

In one respect, however, His message might be thought to be unusual. When He spoke, though it was within the sound of Bow Bells, it was not in English, or even Cockney, but in Welsh. For in the heart of the East End, my grandfather and my grandmother preserved in almost artificial purity the manners and customs, the religious observances, above all the language of the remote Cardiganshire hills from which they both came. They lived there as Negroes or Pakistanis might today, and in their loyalty to an almost primitive way of life they were strengthened and confirmed by frequent and regular attendance, both on Sunday and weekdays, at the Welsh Methodist chapel which stood within walking distance of their home.

Both my grandfather and my grandmother came of a long line of tenant farmers* on the Cardiganshire estate of the Pryses of Gogerddan, whose mansion near Aberystwyth was said to be the oldest inhabited house in Wales. The Pryses administered their estates in the traditionally feckless manner of the Welsh landowner, but they had one distinction which marked them out from most of their class and excluded them from the hatred which the Welsh peasant and farmer felt for most landowners. In politics they were liberal, and indeed the family finances had never recovered from the large expenditure incurred during the nineteenth century in maintaining the liberal interest in Cardiganshire. In a country where every man was a politician, and every working man a liberal, this identity of political interest gave the Pryses a closer hold on the affection of their tenants than was common in Wales in those days. My father used to tell me the story of relations of his from Pembrokeshire, tenants of the Cawdor estate, who had been evicted from their farm because of their refusal to vote in the conservative interest. They had taken to the road, carrying their belongings with them, and made their way to Cardiganshire to appeal in their distress to my great-uncle. Putting on his Sunday suit and hat, he had interceded on their behalf with Sir Pryse at Gogerddan, who had granted them the lease of one of his farms, partly to spite the Cawdors and partly to reward their fidelity to the good old cause.

But if the Pryses shared the political convictions of their tenants, they looked upon their estates, which extended to over thirty thousand acres of wild hill country, primarily as a means of maintaining the riotous and almost feudal way of life to which they were accustomed, and any measures of improvement were strictly a matter for their tenants, who in any case had little to spare for them out of the meagre income derived from the few sheep and cattle their barren fields would support. Nor, so far as money was concerned, was the landlord much better off. He suffered from a chronic shortage of cash as great as his tenants', and in my grandfather's time, when debts were pressing or the call of pleasure insistent, Sir Pryse would ride out from Gogerddan on a tour of his estates offering reductions in rent to any tenants who happened to have any ready money in the house.

Under such conditions neither tenant nor landlord prospered, so it was natural that my grandfather, being a younger son, should, when he married, obey the iron economic laws which were already depopu-lating the Welsh countryside and set out for London to make his fortune like many other young Welshmen of the time. His prospects should have been bright. In Wales, Cardiganshire men have an unenvi-able reputation for thrift, meanness, hypocrisy, money-grubbing and business ability; a 'Cardi' is the Aberdonian of Wales, but these qualities had passed my grandfather by, and he was altogether too generous and open-hearted a person to be much of a success in business.

He was not, however, without resources. He had acquired the skill of a stonemason, and my father used to point out to me with pride the roof of the old St Thomas's hospital, which my grandfather had helped to build. His earnings as a stonemason were supplemented by the proceeds of a small dairy which my grandmother managed, for together with their language and their religion they had brought with them to London their traditional attachment to the cattle which had provided them with a living for so many centuries; so that, in the East

End, they formed as it were a little pastoral enclosure, where the Bible was always on the table and the cows lowed to be milked in the byre at the back of the shop and occasionally, for their health, were driven out for a blow on Hackney Marshes.

I do not know what commercial ambitions my grandparents cherished when they came to London. Whatever they were, they were not absurd, because, at the end of the last century, the dairy business, like the drapery business, provided many Welsh families with the basis of substantial fortunes. But my grandfather, like his children, and their children after them, lacked commercial sense; he was deficient in that feeling for money which is only given to those who think it more important than anything else, and he was far more interested in his duties as a deacon of the chapel, in the intense political struggles of the period and not least in the varied and turbulent life of the East End streets, than in his business. My grandmother was left very largely to run it herself, and while she did so with moderate competence, she also was too much a child of the country and the chapel to serve Mammon with the exclusive devotion he demands from those on whom he confers large rewards.

Moreover, my grandparents in their own family lacked the support which is very often the reason for the growth of a small into a large business. They were fortunate in having two clever and gifted sons but neither to them nor to their parents did it occur that their future should be devoted to the milk business. My father, when as a boy he accompanied my grandfather in his milk float on his early morning round through the empty streets of the City, was less intent on assisting him than on studying his Greek and Latin texts in preparation for school, while his younger brother had already formed the ambition of becoming a doctor.* For both, in their circumstances, the careers they had in mind required a considerable concentration of effort and left them little time to assist in the promoting of my grandfather's business. Nor, indeed, would my grandparents have had it otherwise.

But if my grandparents did not make their fortune, and if their dairy business languished until finally, after my grandfather's death, it died of inanition, it at least provided them with a modest living, threatened neither by poverty nor affluence, sufficient to maintain the standards of independence and respectability which they had brought with them from Wales, and to give them the freedom to pursue those religious and intellectual interests which were also a part of their inheritance. In such matters, at least, they might be said to have prospered; and since my grandfather had a countryman's hospitable nature, as his sons grew up his little house in Hannibal Road became a natural centre for their friends, for young Welsh people whom they knew through the chapel, relations from Wales on a visit to London, medical students from Guy's Hospital whom my uncle brought home, a place of high spirits and eager discussion whose attraction was increased, for young men, by the presence of my father's unmarried younger sister.

Certainly it was a home and a place which offered my father much wider opportunities, in particular as regards schooling, than he would have known on an upland farm; and though in fact he was to spend the greater part of his life in Wales, retracing the steps which had led his parents away from it, it was London that he thought of as his home. He felt that he had been a native of no mean city, and this saved him from the parochialism and provincialism of his native Wales. He remembered that as a boy he had seen the great Mr Gladstone himself addressing an East End crowd from a brewer's dray, an image that remained vividly impressed on his mind, and this gave him a kind of standard by which he judged men and events in later life.

Most of all, I think, London left him with memories of a kind of happiness, wider, freer, more open to the gales of the world, than he was to know again. No doubt this was partly because, for him, London was bathed in the magic of childhood and youth, and when he died, not long ago, at the age of ninety-six it was to those days that his mind recurred. As his mind wandered in the delirium of his last illness, he told me of the thrill of horror that had passed through the East End at the news of the arrest of the murderer Wainwright,* with whom my grandfather was slightly acquainted, an imposing figure in frock coat and silk hat, wearing a gold watch and chain, greatly respected in the neighbourhood of the Mile End Road; and of how, when the next morning he walked hand-in-hand with my grandfather through the streets to school, while people gathered on street corners to discuss the sensational news, he felt as if he were walking through a city in which everything was possible, a kind of English Baghdad in which there was no need to be Haroun-el-Rashid to enjoy every conceivable adventure. Dying, it was not of the green fields, the hills and streams of his native country that he babbled but of Stepney Green and the Mile End Road and the East India Docks, as if in those unsalubrious districts there lay buried, like a crock of gold, all the dreams and ambitions he had cherished when he was a boy.

II

It was a natural corollary of my father's decision to preach the gospel that he should enter the ministry of the Presbyterian, or Calvinistic

Methodist, Church of Wales, of which the chapel at Jewin which his family attended was a constituent member. The Calvinistic Methodist church was the old, the most respectable and the most prosperous of the many Nonconformist denominations which flourished in Wales. It derived both its theology, which was Augustinian, and its elaborate system of church government, from the rule established by Calvin in Geneva, and to this extremely conservative institution, which in Wales represented what we would now call the Establishment, my father for some sixty-five years devoted all his energies and talents. The very name by which the Calvinistic Methodist connexion was familiarly known, *Yr Hen Gorff*, 'The Old Body', shows how far, with the passage of years, it had departed from the spirit of revolt against the established church in which it had its origins.

It was equally natural that, to prepare himself for the ministry,* he should return to his native Cardiganshire. For, by a curious succession of historical accidents, there had recently been founded in the remote little seaside town of Aberystwyth the University College of Wales, and side by side with it stood the theological college maintained by the Calvinistic Methodist connexion. The university college had been founded, by public subscription, which was largely made up of the pennies of the Welsh poor, to provide young Welshmen and women with an opportunity for higher education which had hitherto been totally lacking in Wales; it was in many ways the crowning achievement of over a century of agitation to improve the education standards of the Welsh people. It had the advantage of being cheap and was therefore within my grandparents' limited means; many a country boy arrived at the college laden with a sack of potatoes and a side of bacon which would provide his principal means of subsistence during the coming term.

Having returned to Cardiganshire, it was almost inevitable that my father should repeat a step which all his forefathers had taken before him; that is to say, he fell in love and chose for his future wife, and my mother, the daughter of a small tenant farmer in the same narrow valley in which his parents had been born.* It is likely that if he had searched the whole of the world for a wife he could not have made a more fortunate choice.

As for me, I have often wondered at the chance or fatality by which the blood that runs through my veins has been drawn, so far as I know for centuries, from so unmixed a source; and wonder also, sometimes with dismay, what the genetic effects might be of so rarified an heredity. Pharaohs of Egypt could hardly have intermarried more closely than my forebears. This sense of coming from a peculiar people was heightened when as a child I was taken by my father to see the great Professor Fleure,* who then held the chair of anthropology at the university. The professor was interested in the shape of my skull, and after close examination and much measurement of frontal lobes and occipital cavities, finally and triumphantly announced, as if I had been some invention or discovery of his own, that it displayed every characteristic of the purest Celto-Iberian stock and none of any other. In England, in later years, I have sometimes felt myself an exile; but so pure a descent almost makes one an exile anywhere, outside an area of about twenty miles square which is almost uninhabited except for one's own relations.

My father, as he confirmed to me later, was too preoccupied with his love for my mother, and also by his interest in radical politics, to devote himself wholeheartedly to his studies at Aberystwyth. He left with a second class degree in classics and then, as a candidate for the ministry, proceeded to Mansfield College, Oxford, where he took a first class in Theology, one of the earliest Nonconformists to take an Oxford degree, as the disabilities imposed on them had only been removed by the abolition of the Test Acts as recently as 1878.* To have a degree of any kind was something of a rarity in Wales at that time, and, among a people as passionately devoted to education as the Welsh, was a sure passport to public esteem and respect; to have a first class Oxford degree was rather like being elevated to a peerage in a country of philistines like England.

Thus it was again natural and inevitable that, after a brief stay in Pwllheli,* in Caernarvonshire, my father should have been summoned to undertake the ministry of *Y Tabernacl*, 'The Tabernacle', in Aberystwyth, which was then one of the largest and most prosperous chapels in the gift of the Calvinistic Methodist connexion, and it was thus that I came to be born in Aberystwyth and to spend my childhood there. I have described elsewhere something of what such a childhood was like, and perhaps it is sufficient to say here that for me they were years of intense happiness. They had all the warmth and security of the womb, only they were also coloured by the green waves and waters of Cardigan Bay, the grey stones of the little town huddled between the sea and the hills, and the streams that poured down in silvery waterfalls and cascades to form the estuary on which the harbour was built. Concealed mysteriously in the depths of Cardigan Bay were the battlements and turrets of the Cantref Gwaelod,* the lost land of Cockaigne submerged beneath the waves when the drunken Seithenyn omitted to lock its sea gates. Still, on a clear day, the sound of its bells could be heard across the bay, so that one might imagine all the wealth and wonder of that mythical kingdom preserved in its water world beneath the sea.

For a child it was a kind of paradise, drenched in the waters of streams and rivers that might have flowed through Eden. Not far away was the eighteenth-century Gothic mansion which Thomas Johnes had built for himself amid the woods of Hafod and the garden which his little daughter had made for herself beside the waterfall which plunges through them. Coleridge, making an excursion on horseback from Nether Stowey, had once appeared on the skyline overlooking the house and its grounds; surveying as if in a dream its towers and minarets, and the stream cascading beside its water garden, he had absorbed the images which one day were to reappear to him:*

> In Xanadu did Kubla Khan
> A stately pleasure-dome decree
> Where Alph, the sacred river, ran
> Through caverns measureless to man
> Down to a sunless sea.

For me the lines have always echoed, as in a sea shell, the music of my childhood; but there were even greater wonders there than in Xanadu. For in the same enchanted circle, beside* the ruined monastery of Strata Florida, at Nanteos, the valley of the Nightingale, stood the house which contained the most fabulous and legendary of all treasures, that had given birth to the Matter of Britain: the Holy Grail itself brought there on his miraculous wanderings by Joseph of Arimathea, to become the inspiration of all the poets of Europe and still, in my childhood and even fifty years later, the object of a cult that extended throughout the world. How strange I found it, when I came to read *The Waste Land* and T. S. Eliot's learned references to Miss Jessie Weston,* to feel that those myths which had so stimulated his imagination and scholarship, the Grail itself, the Lance and the Wound, the Fisher King, were all part of a world which in my childhood had been as familiar and tangible as the pots and pans in my mother's kitchen.

These were stories which my father told me, but though they enchanted a child's imagination, they lay far apart from my father's interests, which were essentially practical; he lived by works rather than faith. In his years at Aberystwyth his intelligence, his administrative ability, his gift for oratory, made him one to whom, in a small closely knit community, people naturally look for leadership; they earned him the respect, admiration and affection of all who knew him and at a relatively early age gave him an authority unusual in a society in which the principle of gerontocracy was sacrosanct. In the way of life he had chosen, or which had chosen him, the path before him lay smooth and untroubled, and there was no reason why he should not have continued in it with the same happiness as he had begun. All the more so, perhaps, because in the lives of people who, like him, have dedicated themselves to religion, there is a mysterious, irrational element, an X-factor, which removes them from the arena in which worldly success or failure is important.

My father, indeed, had plenty to occupy him; the pastoral care of a large flock, the affairs of the Calvinistic Methodist church, with its elaborate system of ecclesiastical government, the composition of scholarly biblical commentaries, preaching twice on Sunday both in his own and other chapels, where his services were in large demand, the responsibilities of a large and growing family; all this provided an active and interesting life, and I have no doubt that, if left to himself, he would have continued in this course for the rest of his days.

But we are not left to live our own lives and to this rule my father was no exception. The first interference in his orderly, almost pre-destined course came from an entirely unexpected quarter. In 1921, as a result of the death of the sitting member, a by-election took place in Cardiganshire. Normally, this would have been an event of no more than local interest. Cardiganshire was a stronghold of liberalism, and it was unthinkable that it should be represented in Parliament by anyone but a liberal. But who, in 1921, represented liberalism? The Liberal party led by Herbert Asquith, the true inheritor of the pure Gladston-ian tradition in which my father believed, had been annihilated in the general election of 1918 and reduced to a remnant of twenty-seven members in Parliament, and Asquith himself and all its leaders had been defeated. The party had been broken by the devious machina-tions of the great Welsh statesman and demagogue, Lloyd George, the man who had won the war and now stood at the head of the coalition government, in which one hundred and twenty-seven coalition liberals were outnumbered by three hundred coalition unionists; all alike owed their election to the coupons certifying their loyalty to himself which Lloyd George had issued at the height of his triumph in 1918 as a means of ensuring the return of his government.

In the eyes of many Welshmen, among whom my father would normally have been included, Lloyd George, himself a Welshman and a liberal, was a traitor to the cause with which Wales had hitherto identified its political fortunes, the architect of its defeat and the prisoner of reactionary and imperialist forces which Wales could never look to for any benefits; he had made *il gran rifiuto** and deserved to be consigned to the deepest circle which Hell preserves for treacherous politicians. Besides, for the religious, like my father, moral as well as political considerations were involved; for like everyone else he was aware of the well-substantiated rumours of the Goat's sexual promiscuity, and indeed was well acquainted with a lady who happened to be one of his mistresses at the time. How could a minister of the Gospel, who was also a liberal, hold up such a man to the admiration of his flock?

And now Lloyd George's government, bedevilled by intractable problems of unemployment and industrial unrest, and by its leader's adventures in foreign policy, was tottering to its fall, and Wales prepared to rejoice in it. It had already lost three by-elections in succession, and a further defeat in Cardiganshire might prove a final contribution to the great man's ruin. For a moment the eyes of the world were on Cardiganshire; for Lloyd George was no ordinary politician, he was a world statesman of towering genius and when such a man falls, the world holds its breath. Representatives of the national and the international press descended like a flock of migrating birds on Aberystwyth, drink flowed in the hotels and public houses, and both the Asquithian 'Wee-Free' Liberals* and the Lloyd George Liberals organized their forces to consummate or avert the ruin of the Goat. Never since the Midlothian campaign had so tiny an electorate been treated to such a feast of Liberal oratory, and there was not a man or woman in the county who was not made aware that on their votes depended the fate of the nation and of the Liberal party.

My father was by nature and tradition intensely interested in politics, and he was as involved as anyone else in the issues which were so inappropriately fought out in Cardiganshire. But he was a politician in more senses than one, and instinct told him that, in his case, the path of wisdom lay in standing aloof from the violent passions provoked by the election. For they were so fierce and so deep that parent was divided against parent, family against family, tribe against tribe; to all the national reasons for bitterness and acrimony were added all the local and personal motives for mutual hatred that exist in a small rural community. The flames of politics were fed by personal and family feuds, by rumour, gossip, malice and slander, until, as the election approached, one might have thought there was not a man in the county who would not gladly have slit his neighbour's throat if it would have had any effect on the result of the poll.

To a person of my father's temperament, essentially reasonable and judicious, not easily given to emotion unless it was a calculated emotion, unsympathetic to the irrational furies of warring Welshmen, with something in him of Asquith's own spirit of compromise and procrastination, a man who liked to weigh his words and the consequences of his actions, it would have been natural to stand aside from the conflict that had broken out in Cardiganshire and try to moderate passions and reconcile personal animosities so that when at length all was over the belligerents might live together once again in concord and amity. All the more so because the conflict was nowhere more violent than in the bosom of his own congregation, in which, indeed, religious feeling only seemed to give added fury to political differences. In such a situation, pastoral duty required that he should act as a moderator and try to ensure, so far as he could, that the love of Christ should rise superior even to hatred of Lloyd George.

Providence, however, denied him so congenial a role, for which he was so well fitted. The Asquithian candidate in the election was an ageing lawyer from South Wales, who had already represented the party in Parliament but had been one of the victims of the massacre of Liberal members in the 1918 election. He had served the party, and Wales, well, and enjoyed the affectionate regard and esteem of his countrymen, of whom only the most bigoted took it amiss that on occasions he was known to over-indulge in alcoholic liquor.

The candidate of the Lloyd George Liberals, on the other hand, was a young barrister who had scarcely begun his legal career and was as yet without any claims upon the feelings either of the local electors or of the party at large. He was also the son of a prosperous solicitor in Aberystwyth, who could be depended on to contribute generously to party funds and the expenses of the election, and was a pillar of my father's chapel, its largest single benefactor, and a close personal friend of my father's.

In so closely fought an election, the respect and influence enjoyed by my father in Cardiganshire were factors of not inconsiderable importance. Many would follow where he led, and it was natural that his support was solicited by both parties, and that the Lloyd George candidate's father should press the claims of friendship and gratitude on his son's behalf. Against his instincts, personal, political and pastoral, and with many doubts about the wisdom of his decision, my father yielded to his appeal. What is more, having committed himself to the support of the coalition candidate, he flung himself into the electoral battle with an enthusiasm and effectiveness which surprised even his admirers, shocked others and convinced many that his talents were worthy of some larger arena than Cardiganshire and Calvinistic Methodism. After all, he was a very able man. Like a good advocate, having accepted his brief he made the best of it. He spoke at meetings throughout the county. He could be passionate, eloquent, persuasive, scornful, witty, as the occasion demanded, and was particularly skilful in finding the effective reply to hecklers. When the Asquithians dismissed his candidate contemptuously, because of his youth and inexperience, as a 'spring chicken', he delighted his rural audience by replying that he would himself prefer a young bird to an old boiling fowl; it was generally held that he had the best of the exchange, and his candidate's youth ceased to be an election issue.

I say 'his' candidate because, even though he doubted the wisdom of his own choice, my father made the cause of Lloyd George and the coalition his own, and while the election campaign lasted he devoted to it all his energies. And if the result proved to be, by the narrowest of majorities, a triumph for the government, it could be and was said that he was largely responsible; in so hard fought a struggle, the formidable qualities he had displayed might well have reversed the result if they had been exerted on the other side.*

But alas! victory brought him very little satisfaction, because the consequences he had feared inevitably followed. There were some who regarded him, like Lloyd George himself, as a traitor to Liberalism, in Wales then a cause hardly less sacred than that of religion itself. Others said that he, in preferring the worse to the better cause, had put expediency before principle; this criticism came mainly from those who in their own lives would never have dreamed of taking any other course. Some thought that he had been overborne by the influence exerted by Lloyd George and the coalition; some hinted that his motive had been personal ambition and that he had been bribed by who knows what promises of future advancement. What made things worse, in the eyes of his critics, was that his intervention in the election had been so effective. The Welsh admire a victor, but his success always stimulates their secret resentment, and it is the defeated Cato who really wins their hearts.

Worst of all, for my father, such feelings divided even his own congregation and as their shepherd he never again possessed that unchallenged moral and pastoral authority which had previously been his. He had plunged into the muddied waters of politics and had not come out of them unstained; he had shown himself to be, not the servant of truth but a man like other men, with the same passions and weaknesses, a brawler in the market place; his aura had been diminished and in Cardiganshire it would never again have the brightness it once had. Though with time the bitter feelings inspired by the election passed away, for my father things would never be quite the same again.

What made it worse for him was his own feeling that, as he confessed to me many years later, he had allowed personal considerations to get the better of what he himself knew to be right.

III

Thus, for my father, the by-election of 1921 cast a certain shadow over his life at Aberystwyth. But another influence also contrived to disturb it and helped to persuade him that after all it would not be right to spend the rest of his days there, as he might otherwise so easily have done. This disturbing influence was, oddly enough, my mother, who though devoted above all to my father's interests and happiness, was also critical enough to feel that life at Aberystwyth made altogether too few demands on him to be entirely for his benefit.

For despite the many claims it made on him, they were not really large enough to place any strain on his abilities, which were quite sufficient for the successful discharge of all his duties without any undue exertion. He was, my mother felt, in danger of becoming too easily satisfied with the part he played in life, and perhaps in this she was right, for there was in my father, as in myself, a certain strain of lethargy, perhaps even of laziness, which made him immune to the kind of inducements which might have appealed to a more ambitious man.

My mother, on the other hand, was compact of energy and activity, and her tiny figure, her large dark eyes, concealed a restless spirit which was never content unless engaged in some occupation, in the home or in the chapel, which taxed all her strength. She was the image of *das ewig Weibliche** which leads men on to larger enterprises than they would have conceived of themselves and provides, by its dissatisfaction with things as they are, a compulsion towards things as they might be.

She had received, at a small boarding school at Towyn, a few miles up the coast from Aberystwyth, a rather better education than most of the farmers' daughters of the class to which she belonged, and a quick mind and an instinctive intellectual curiosity ensured that she made the best use of what she had learned. She was well equipped for the multifarious duties that devolve upon a minister's wife, presiding at the sewing class and the mothers' meeting, teaching in the Sunday school, taking care of the poor and needy, visiting the sick, organizing tea parties, outings, treats, festivals; to all this was added the care of her husband and children and her domestic duties, in which she was assisted by a country girl of a simplicity which was a constant anxiety to my mother because of the temptations offered by what was, in contrast with Martha's native surroundings, the almost metropolitan sophistication of Aberystwyth, whose lights, though dim enough, were almost dazzling compared with the Stygian darkness of night on the mountains. Martha's evenings out were always a period of anxiety for my mother. Who could tell what moral perils she might encounter in the streets and alleys of the town? And indeed her fears were not groundless, for Martha, though slightly slatternly in appearance, was lavish of heart and body and repeatedly found herself pregnant. Except for recurrent and unexplained absences, this seemed to have no effect on her immutable status as maid-of-all-work to the household.

For misfortune, even if combined with immorality, had an irresistible attraction for my mother. She loved all those whom the world has rejected: tramps, gypsies, beggars, lame dogs of every kind, both human and animal, and she loved the needy and the helpless, in particular babies and small children, and it is for this heart overflowing with charity that I most remember her; perhaps because, as the youngest of her children, I was so often its object.

One might have thought that her life, with all its cares and duties, was quite sufficient to absorb all her energies. And so perhaps for herself it was. But she did not think a small Welsh town gave sufficient scope to my father's abilities and for my brother and myself she cherished the hope of wider educational opportunities than Aberystwyth had to offer. On one of the rare holidays which she and my father were ever able to take together, they had spent a fortnight in Oxford, where my father had shown her the scenes which had meant so much to him in his youth. What she had enjoyed most of all there was to sit and read with him in the gardens of New College. This had appeared to her the most delectable spot in Oxford, perhaps in the whole world and, as my father told me after her death, she had then and there decided that, however unlikely it might seem given our circumstances, I too should sit one day in the same place, not as a visitor, but as of right as an undergraduate of the college.

It was very unlikely that her ambition for me would ever be realised, and it was certainly one of which I, at that time, was entirely unaware. But certainly one of the conditions of achieving it was that I should be given some rather better schooling than was available at Aberystwyth; for we were then still in the days when, for the poorer classes, opportunities of going to Oxford were rare and were the object of the most intense competition.

Thus when the chance came for us to leave Aberystwyth for Cardiff, the after-effects of the great by-election combined with my mother's ambitions to induce my father to accept it, somewhat reluctantly I think on his own behalf, because of the change it would involve in his way of life, but with a sense that he was doing no more than his duty. For his move to Cardiff was again a response to a call from God, as his original return to Wales had been. And in Cardiff there was an excellent boys' grammar school, and to my mother this presented a valuable stepping stone towards realizing the hopes she had formed for her children.

Fortunately the school agreed to waive, in the case of both my brother and myself, the payment of fees, which, small as they were, would have been an additional strain on my father's purse. And so, in the summer of 1922, when I was twelve, my father shepherded us down to Cardiff, like mountain sheep moving down from the hills. It was to be many years before I saw Aberystwyth again, and when I did so it was with very different eyes.

IV

My family's move to Cardiff* brought about an almost total transformation in the way I had lived until then. To some extent this was true for all my family, but less so, I think, than in my own case, because they were older and had some experience of the world outside Aberystwyth, which for me was still the only world there was. My elder sister was ten years older than I. She had already taken a degree at Aberystwyth, and shortly after we moved took up a teaching post in Barry.* My younger sister was looking forward to getting married shortly, and her eyes were exclusively directed towards Briton Ferry, where her future husband, also an ex-student of Aberystwyth, was attempting to learn his way in the steel industry.*

As for my brother, Cardiff was for him only a brief staging post, at which to matriculate before returning to Aberystwyth, where the university at that time possessed an excellent law school; for he was to be a barrister, as my father had once intended to be, and was already single-mindedly determined to begin his legal studies as quickly as possible. He was a clever boy, and it was normal at that time for Aberystwyth's best law students to proceed to Cambridge after taking their degree.*

But for me Cardiff was to be the place in which I spent the whole of my adolescence, as different from childhood as Cardiff itself was from Aberystwyth, and perhaps I associate it with unhappiness both because of the confusion and turbulence of such a phase in one's life and because our migration seemed to bring an end to the warmth and security of the close-knit family life we had hitherto enjoyed. It seemed to me that my brother and sisters had grown up and had already entered, or stood at the threshold of, the world of men and women of which I knew nothing, while I was left behind in some grey and mournful limbo of my own, from which all the familiar landmarks of the past had been obliterated. And I think that, in a curious way, my parents had something of the same feeling, with their children growing up and away from them and their own lives so greatly changed from what they had known before.

For my mother especially, who was essentially a country girl, the city of Cardiff always remained as faceless, anonymous and characterless as it was to me; and to her, as to me, the change from the rural atmosphere of Aberystwyth, which was hardly more than a large seaside village, to the great city which Cardiff was by comparison, was a change from community to loneliness. Indeed, the change made itself felt even in our house, for in my later years in Cardiff, when I lived alone with my father and mother for most of the year, it seemed as if the house were empty and deserted, as if we inhabited some melancholy solitude together.*

Indeed, everything seemed to contribute to this sense of loss, and for my parents at least it was hard to see what had been gained. The call which had taken my father to Cardiff was an invitation to become the head of what was known as the Forward Movement. This was essentially a missionary enterprise, founded at the end of the nineteenth century, only it was a mission carried out, not among the dark skins which were familiar to us from photographs in reports on Methodist missionary activities in India, but among the heathen of the South Wales coalfield. For the immigrants who poured into the South Wales valleys during the nineteenth century, both from the rest of Wales and from England, formed a very different society from the traditional Welsh rural community on which the Presbyterian Church of Wales was founded. They had either never known the Welsh language or had quickly lost it, and with the language they also lost the religious practices with which it was so intimately bound up. The life of the valleys was savage and turbulent, unblessed by the means of grace, and when the miners emerged out of their underground kingdom into the light of day, they came to the surface like troglodytes out of their caves, not to attend chapel or Sunday school, but to drink and fight, and if they sang hymns it was not to praise God but to celebrate the victory or mourn the defeat of their football teams.

In the eighteenth century, religion had been one of the means by which the Welsh people had been lifted up out of the dark abyss of ignorance, apathy and superstition. The immense growth of population in the South Wales valleys, the birth of a new, raw industrial society, with all the evils that attended it, in the eyes of the Methodist church threatened Wales with a new paganism, a relapse into heathen ways, and called for a new missionary effort to bring the light of religion into the darkness of the pits. The Forward Movement was an attempt to preach the gospel by methods more suited to the passionate temperament of the miners than the staid and respected rituals of the established faith, which from their point of view were irredeemably 'square' and middle class. Visions of hell fire and of being washed by the blood of the Lamb from the sins which clung to him like the coal dust he carried with him out of the pits, were what the miner needed if he were to turn to God, and the God to whom he turned had to speak directly to him in words he could understand, not in the subtle theological terms of the Welsh Calvinists or through a ministry which had become as sacerdotal as a bench of bishops. He wanted words that were tinged with the colour of fire and brimstone and promised him that, if only he would turn to God, he would be led to meet his Saviour like a bride prepared for the bridegroom.

It was with such words as these that the Forward Movement had been intended to call the miners to Jesus and to such a mission as this that my father now found himself summoned. My father, though his religious faith was the most important element in his life and he could not have lived without it, was essentially a rational man and for him religion was a part of the life of reason; it came to him in the terms of a theologian and not of an Elmer Gantry, and just as he was a liberal in politics so he was a liberal in theology,* for whom religion and reason were nothing without the other. He distrusted enthusiasm as much as any eighteenth-century cleric and he had a respect for the opinions and beliefs of others, an instinctive delicacy in his dealings with them, which inhibited him from capturing their souls by violence. I never knew him to press his own beliefs on me or to try to influence me in my opinions, though gradually they became so different from his own that he could hardly fail to regard them as heretical and even blasphemous; though I was never quite sure whether this restraint was due to the fact that I was a hopelessly lost soul or in God's eyes so immutably one of the elect that it didn't matter what I thought.

He found it difficult to speak the language in which it was thought appropriate to save the souls of the miners, though easy to find his own way to their affection and respect. But there was also a quite different obstacle to the task of winning the miner for God. For by the time my father moved to Cardiff, conditions in South Wales had changed since the Forward Movement had been founded nearly fifty years before. For if, then, religion could have been said to be the only force that thought the miner's soul worth saving, forty years later there was an alternative means of redemption, in the form of socialism, and it was not to the chapel or the mission hall that the miner looked for salvation but to the Labour party and to the local lodge of the South Wales Miner's Federation; while the place of the devil in his cosmology had been usurped by Mr Evans Williams, the chairman of the South Wales Coal Owners' Association.

A man may well turn to God if it's a question of saving his own soul, but personal salvation does not seem an urgent matter if his wife and children are starving. During the long years of the great depression which weighed upon South Wales after the First World War, it might well have seemed to the miners that God had abandoned them in their valleys, and if they were to be saved at all, it would only be by their own efforts; it was not surprising that the evangelical seeds sown by the Forward Movement fell increasingly on barren ground and that the congregations of its mission halls dwindled as conditions in the coalfield deteriorated. It was not in Jesus but in Mr A. J. Cook* that the miners hoped to find a saviour; though in the agony of the miners' strike that followed the General Strike of 1926, he hardly proved to be any more effective.

Until that time, indeed, I was hardly aware of the circumstances under which my father laboured to bring the light of the Gospel into the valleys. What I felt more personally and directly were the changes which had taken place in our own domestic life. I had been used to have my father as a continuing presence in the house, where, unless absent on pastoral visits, he worked in his study on his sermons and his commentaries or on the business of the chapel or the Methodist connexion; one had to lower one's voice or moderate the turmoil of one's games so as not to disturb him and one was always aware that there, in his first-floor study, slightly awesome but always reassuring, he was at work on the mysterious business to which God had called him.

But now he left the house every morning like any business man for his office in the centre of Cardiff, from which he administered the affairs of the fifty or so mission halls which were under his care, or travelled up and down the valleys to visit them. Somehow this diminished him in my eyes; he might have been any company director engaged on the humdrum routine of administration and had lost that essentially personal and individual status of a priest who mediates directly between God and man. And on Sundays it was no longer from his own pulpit that he preached, to his own congregation, every member of which he knew as well as his own family, so that his voice was the voice of a father to them as well as to us, but to strangers in some grim mission hall in a bleak mining village, so that at home his place was empty at table and there was no one to occupy his armchair in which he sat by the fireside to read.

My mother especially missed his presence, day by day and almost minute by minute, for they had lived in much closer and continuous contact than most married couples; and almost as much she missed the cares and duties which she had shared with my father in his ministry to a flock of which she was as much the shepherdess as he the shepherd. It was equally a break with everything she had known till then that the language she heard in the streets was no longer Welsh but English, for the Welsh language was dying in South Wales and even God now spoke in a strange tongue on Sundays. For we also now attended, not the chapel which had hardly been more than an extension of our own home, but one of my father's mission halls in Cardiff and the language of the Forward Movement was English, for the Welsh language was no longer a medium in which to carry the word of God to the masses. The evangelist in South Wales had to preach in English if he was to be understood, just as a missionary in a strange land must use the language of the heathen if he is to touch their hearts.

My mother's life had become lonelier and emptier and perhaps it was because of this as much as for any physical reason that suddenly she, who had always been so active and occupied, seemed to become weaker and frailer; and she had begun to suffer from the heart disease which a few years later was to kill her. She had never seemed old to me, though I was the last born of her children; her love of everything that was young had seemed to make her so herself, and it had never occurred to me that life could continue without her. Now, for the first time, though still with disbelief, I began to realize that one day, in some unimaginable future, it might be possible that she should be taken away from me.

V

I was too young, or too selfish, to understand the changes involved for my parents by moving to Cardiff; or perhaps I was at first too much taken up in my own sense of deprivation, and when that passed too preoccupied by new interests, to notice what was happening to others. For to me at first the loss of my childhood world, so tiny and circumscribed, yet somehow open to all the seas and skies of the world, was a shock that was almost traumatic. I felt as if I had been cast out of paradise, and with a sense not of loss only but of guilt, as if somehow it was my own fault. Most of all I missed a certain quality of perception which, in my childhood, had seemed to make everything at once familiar and magical and now, under the shock of removal to the city, seemed to wither away like some fabulous plant that would only blossom in its native soil.

For my first, yet enduring impression was of the unrelieved ugliness of the city, of it long grey streets and the monotonously repeated vistas of identical terrace houses, the muddy complexion of its stones and the hideously flaring red and orange of its bricks that inflicted themselves on one's sight like a wound. They affected one's eyes like some painful ailment, as if they had been rubbed sore by seeing. To me this world which man had built for himself seemed utterly inhuman, hostile to all the innumerable responses of the nerves and the senses, while the natural world which pressed so closely upon one in Aberystwyth had been so perfectly attuned to every infinitesimal impulse that it seemed to fit one like a glove.

I had never been to a city of any size before and its wastes of brick and mortar weighed upon me with a dull sense of oppression that was like a physical pain. It was years before I realized that even city landscapes can have their own beauty and certainly there was little of this to be seen in Cardiff. Walking or cycling to school through the long grey tunnel of Mackintosh Place in which every grey little house faithfully reproduced the hideousness of its neighbour,* or down the tramlines of the City Road where neither the shops nor the objects offered for sale in them had any quality or virtue except the grimmest utility, I would feel a sense of leaden hopelessness, as if these streets stretched on into infinity and there would never be any escape from them, mathematically parallel lines projecting the city and its inhabitants in an endless future of which every moment was nothing but the exact and senseless repetition of what came before and after it. Sometimes I could hardly believe that the sea, blue, smiling, and welcoming, was not awaiting round the corner and it was with a sense of doom, as of a condemned man, that I realized there lay before me only another monotonous perspective of the no-man's-land of the city.

In those first years in Cardiff I began to feel, for the first time, that destructive sense of depression which reduced the whole of life to a uniform monochrome and transforms every impulse to thought or action into the meaningless reflex of a mechanical puppet. It is a sense which has frequently recurred to me in later years; for those who feel it, it is so acute that it eats like acid into the texture of life, so that it falls away from one in shreds and tatters, like some threadbare garment which has worn so thin that it can no longer hold together. And whether or not it was the fact of our removal that induced my depression at that time, or whether it had its roots in deeper causes, it is true that for a year or two I underwent some mysterious form of sea-change, some hidden revolution in the depths of the self, which coloured all my experiences and made them so dark, confused, and fragmentary that they hardly seemed to be mine at all.

We cannot truly see what is happening in the darkest recesses of the self, nor can memory accurately reproduce what is so fitfully and partially perceived. Perhaps it would be better simply to say that for a time I felt totally disorientated in the new world we had entered, stumbling about in it awkwardly and childishly as if my limbs were no longer under my own control and my feet no longer knew where they were carrying me.

For at first it was a world of strangers, and the boys I met in my new school seemed to me so different from those I had known before that they hardly seemed to belong to the same race. And indeed to a large extent they did not, because Cardiff is as much an English as a Welsh city, a mongrel border town in which the Welsh strain has been so diluted as to produce a far more variegated social pattern than I was accustomed to. But to me at least the boys in my school were alike in that they were all different from me, and in particular in being, or appearing, infinitely more mature and sophisticated, with the sharper wits and quicker intelligence of the town dweller, and the adaptability that came of living in a more complicated social structure than Cardiganshire had to offer. They laughed at my country accent, and even more at the curious garments my mother had constructed for me from a cast-off suit of one of my uncles, with trousers that hung well below the knee to allow for growth and a high buttoned jacket that might have been fashionable today but then had more than a touch of the grotesque. I had been proud of the suit when I first wore it, because the material was excellent and it had been tailored by mother's own hands, but now I quickly and shamefully realized that in the town it made me an object of ridicule and mockery.

So perhaps it was not surprising that for some time I found it difficult to adapt myself to my new school. My brother, who had a better character and a more single-minded purpose than I, appeared to escape such difficulties and continued to achieve the same excellent academic results as ever; I on the other hand failed lamentably. In Aberystwyth I had been thought a bright boy,* as became the son of my father; but in Cardiff I tended towards the bottom of my form with such consistency that my mother's ambitions for me seemed to be more absurd than ever. Indeed, even she began to lose faith, and when, at the end of my second year in the High School, I returned home with a report which was more than usually unsatisfactory, and my brother with one which was, by contrast, of almost dazzling achievement, my mother burst into tears and confessed that she could not see what was to become of me. 'If you go on like this,' she said amid her tears, 'you'll never be anything better than a bank clerk.'

A bank clerk! It was a curious threat, for in those days when any form of employment was hard to come by in South Wales, to be a bank clerk might seem to promise an enviable future to almost any boy, secure, relatively well paid by our modest standards, and with the assurance of an eminently respectable social status. Yet my mother was right, and to me her words were words of doom; for to me as to my mother they signified a life of dull-minded devotion to commerce and the worship of Mammon, unilluminated by any higher interest, and neither she nor I thought that was a life worth living. As for me, I had already formed a quite different conception of what my life was to be, though if my mother had known of it she might have been no less dismayed than by the future with which she had threatened me. For I had already decided that by some means or other I would become a writer, though how this was to be achieved I could not guess, nor had I any reason for thinking that I possessed any of the talents it would require. In my eyes, there could be nothing more incompatible with a writer's life than the to me infinitely dreary calculations of profit and loss which I supposed to be the exclusive occupation of a banker.

But however vague my ideas of how I was to satisfy my literary ambitions, or even, indeed, of what it really means to be a writer, they were already sufficiently clear to make me face the choice which presents itself to every young Welshman with the same heritage and upbringing as myself; it was the choice of whether to write in English or Welsh, either of which, at the time, would still have been possible to me. Nor was this simply a choice between two languages, entailing no further consequences. For every language has its own particular genius, and the language which one writes and speaks also very largely dictates what one thinks and what one feels. There are things that can be said in Welsh that cannot be said in English, just as there are things which can be said in English that cannot be said in Welsh, and in choosing a language one is not only choosing a vocabulary and a syntax but what one can say with them. Otherwise, the problem of translation would not remain the almost insoluble one that it is.

Today I feel surprised that, given my attachment to the scenes and language of my childhood, I should have made the choice so easily, almost without thinking, as if, for me at least, no choice was really necessary. Indeed, I can distinctly remember the moment when I made it. When I was fifteen, my Welsh master in school,* himself a minor poet in his own language, asked me what I wished to be when I grew up. I answered that I wished to be a writer. 'In Welsh or in English?' he asked; and went on to explain that a writer in English, which is a universal language, must expect to meet the most intense competition, which only the most talented could hope to survive, while in Wales, which has no professional writers and all are amateurs, the field was narrowly confined, and given any talent at all I could hardly fail to make some name for myself.

The advice was well meant, and I have no doubt that my Welsh master may well have been in the right; certainly he had my best interests at heart. But it was an unfortunate argument to use to a boy, and it was all the less attractive in the mouth of a patriotic Welshman. I have no doubt that, in a sense, and without knowing it, I turned my back upon Wales at that moment and since then I have had no reason to regret it. For literature then was already becoming for me something that is more important than nationality, a means of release from a way of life that had begun to seem cramped and constrained, and the key to some wider world than Wales had to offer. It was as if, in choosing the language of my childhood, I should have chosen to remain a child for ever, and this is something Welshmen often do. As for me, I felt that in leaving Cardiganshire I had left the happiness of childhood behind and, even if I wished, could not have it again. The trouble was, I suppose, that I wanted to grow up and felt that I could not do it in Welsh.*

It was not ambition that made me want to be a writer, nor any belief in my literary talents, for this I have always lacked. It was the thought that outside there lay a wider world in which there were larger issues at stake than those which obsessed us in the narrow circle in which I had been brought up, where everything seemed certain and predictable and one might live and die without encountering more than a very few of the infinite varieties of human experience. It wasn't that one wanted to compete with others; one wanted to compete with oneself and see what one was capable of, like a gambler who will never leave the table until he has lost everything.

It is difficult now to unravel the labyrinthine workings of a boy's mind, partly because at the time one was largely unaware of one's motives and even now they have hardly become more clear. But somehow I date to this period, somewhere between my fifteenth and sixteenth year, a kind of awakening out of the mood of depression, compounded of nostalgia and apathy, into which I was thrown by my parents' move to Cardiff.

It helped to save me, at a time when I myself doubted whether I was worth saving, that my mother proved to be right in her instinct that, educationally at least, our migration to Cardiff would prove to be for my good. The High School at Cardiff, at the time when I attended it, between 1922 and 1928, was indeed an excellent one, so good indeed that for me it still represents the ideal of what a school should be, and I still sometimes wonder at my good fortune in attending it. In the classics, in mathematics, in history and in English we were taught by men of quite exceptional ability and qualifications; my history master later held a university chair and became a Welsh historian of the greatest distinction.*

I have often wondered since why men of such high intellectual capacity should have been content to devote themselves to the ungrateful task of teaching a somewhat rough and unruly set of boys. Partly, I suppose, it was because at the time schoolmastering as a profession provided a security and, especially in Wales, a social status which, alas, it no longer does, and a salary envied by many at a time and place where unemployment was a constant threat. But it was also because those men felt a genuine compulsion to impart their know-ledge and their own high intellectual standards to their pupils, and this gave to their teaching a kind of urgency and passion which made education both an inspiration and a pleasure.

Most of all they were marvellously responsive to any sign of talent or ability and were wonderfully generous in the pains they took to foster it. They talked to one as if one were as adult and intelligent as they were; they answered one's questions and discussed the answers as if everything they said was only a basis for further questions; they lent one books and encouraged one's own interests; somehow one felt that the distinction between master and pupil ceased to have any import-ance compared with what was shared between them.

In all this we were the beneficiaries; and all the more because the school combined with its high standard of teaching an admirable freedom in matters of discipline, and for me, who was apt to resent any form of restraint, this was particularly fortunate. The headmaster,* who looked rather more like a Prussian officer of the old school than a teacher, was himself only a moderate scholar, though he had a passion for the classics; but he had something which is even more valuable than scholarship in a schoolmaster, which was a deep and sincere respect for the individuality of every boy in his care, whether clever or stupid, docile or rebellious. There was little attempt at what is known as 'character forming' and, outside their work, boys were left to become very much what they wanted to be. For the headmaster and his staff had grasped the essential truth that the larger part of life lies outside the walls of a school, and especially a day school like ours, and consciously or unconsciously they drew the conclusion that they could best serve their pupils by concentrating on the one function they were in a position to discharge most effectively; that is to say, the task of inculcating the highest intellectual standards which their pupils were capable of absorbing and of providing them with the basis of knowledge which they would require if they were to achieve either success or pleasure in life.

And curiously enough, by doing so they achieved, though by indirection, a far greater moral influence than if they had consciously attempted to shape and form that most elusive and amorphous of all natural phenomena, the character of an adolescent boy. For the process of learning, at any stage above the most elementary, has a moral value of its own, in which respect for truth is the greatest ingredient, and even boys are capable of absorbing it when properly taught; it is a kind of uncovenanted grace which is added to the other advantages and pleasures of learning. And perhaps something of this civilizing influence did make itself felt in the school. We were on the whole a rough lot, mostly of the lower middle class, and most of us were passionately addicted to rugby football, which is not the most civilizing of pastimes; but there was very little of the cruelty or brutal-ity, physical or mental, to which boys sometimes subject each other, or are subjected to by their teachers. If this was so, it was largely because of the staff, who were themselves humane and civilized men and were too interested in their teaching to have time to waste on the kind of petty persecution which sometimes goes by the name of discipline.

I do not know what kind of verdict would be passed on the school if it were judged by modern educational standards. I imagine it might be said that it was too insistent on formal academic instruction, that it took things like examinations very seriously and prided itself on its academic record; yet in fact the education it gave was surprisingly wide and varied, and opened a boy's eyes to much broader intellectual vistas than the ordinary curriculum normally provides. Even today I am still surprised that our history master should have thought it worth while to include in his course a class in Plato's *Republic*, which was in fact an excellent introduction to philosophy; or that our English master should take me to his home to show me his excellent library and especially his fine editions of Blake and Donne, and by doing so inspire a lifelong devotion to both poets. He had once been a minor poet himself but was now a bibliophile and he did not care for the turn which modern poetry was taking; but when I, having found *The Waste Land* on the shelves of the Cardiff Public Library, announced my admiration of T. S. Eliot, he asked me to his home to explain to himself and a friend what were then still the mysteries of that poem. I do not know that I, a schoolboy with even less knowledge of life than of literature, made much of my job of exposition; but I do know that, in my youthful and incoherent enthusiasm, I was listened to with as much interest and respect as if I had been Mr Eliot himself, and that at the end of a long evening's discussion of what the poem meant and of what it portended in the development of English poetry, I had learned far more than either of my sympathetic listeners.

Under such circumstances, learning becomes a pleasure and certainly it was largely due to the kind of education I received at school that after a time I began to struggle out of the mood of bewilderment and incomprehension induced by our moving to Cardiff, and that the acute sense of having lost the world of my childhood gradually diminished and gave way to the hope that perhaps, somewhere, life might again have to offer the same infinite possibilities which surrounded me as a child. Most boys, I think, in the process of growing up, suffer the same sense of transition from one world to another and it is only accident which decides with what particular places or experiences it is identified, and accident also which decides with what degree of pain or difficulty the transition is made, or indeed whether it is made at all. For there are some unfortunate ones for whom the attachments of childhood are never overcome, and some for whom the pain and confusion of its passing never wholly cease, so that they remain for ever irretrievably fixed in a past which has never been transcended.

As for me, I was lucky, so much so indeed that for many years, until experience taught me otherwise, I was accustomed to think of myself as a favoured child of fortune. I was lucky in finding people who gave me a hand across the bridge which, poised so precariously above an abyss of doubts, confusions and uncertainties, leads from childhood to manhood. It was not only they who made the difference; but they helped as it were to dispel the mist which fogged my sight, so that at moments one might at least catch a glimpse of what the future might be. Certainly, so far as education was concerned, their encouragement was so far effective that my academic performance after a time began to inspire a hope that my mother's ambitions for me were not, after all, quite so absurd as they had once seemed. From about my sixteenth year, it began to be taken for granted that I should sit for a scholarship to Oxford, and preferably, because of the pleasure the gardens had once given my mother, to New College.

The trouble was that so simple and, as it seemed, so obvious a choice, did not altogether recommend itself to me. It would be difficult to explain my reluctance to follow my parents' and my schoolmasters' choice, because partly at least they coincided with my own. Perhaps it was simply that they were my parents and schoolmasters and therefore in my eyes incapacitated by age and experience from giving any advice which could have any possible relevance to me. I realized, of course, that they wished to do their best for me and that it was my own good they had at heart; but after all, who were they to know what was best for anyone as peculiar as myself. By peculiar I did not mean anything that was in any way flattering to me. It was only that I recognized in myself, however obscurely, something which would make it impossible for me to live or want to live as they did.

It was part of the trouble that I really knew nothing about what either Oxford or Cambridge was like, and the little that I did know did not altogether recommend them to me. There were a few older boys from the school who had already preceded me there, for though in those days it was difficult and rare for any secondary school children to attend either of the older universities, there was one sure way to secure both admission and the necessary financial resources. This was rugby football. It is a peculiar reflection of both the economic and the educational environment of the time that football could protect a poor boy against his disadvantages in either respect. It could open a way to Oxford or Cambridge because of the immense importance which its colleges, and the English ruling class of which they were the cradle, still attached to playing football, and there was always some form of financial assistance available to anyone who played rugby football well enough to be a potential blue or international.

In the same way, he was protected against the threat of unemployment, which was a very real one in the valleys, because he could always turn professional and go to the Northern League. Wakefield and Balliol were equally open to a boy who was moderately good at his work and a very good scrum half. In later years I knew a miner's son who having both won a scholarship and been offered a contract by Huddersfield, was tempted to choose the latter because it would allow him to contribute to the support of his family, of which the father and his three brothers were all unemployed. In fact, he chose the scholarship and eventually became a professor but ever after felt he had taken the selfish course.

None of the boys from my school who went up to the ancient universities on the strength of their athletic promise was stupid; they were above rather than below the standards required for admission in those days. But what they were in the first place was superb footballers, and when they returned to Cardiff in the vacations they had adopted all the physical and mental attributes of the typical university athlete of the time, the hearty bonhomie, the Philistine outlook, the public school slang. They had become almost a caricature of the type; in their Oxford bags, their tweed caps, their scarves and blazers, they appeared to us who were still at school as some kind of athletic *jeunesse dorée*⋆ and it seemed to me that if this was all the university could do for them, it could not do very much for me.

On the other hand, I had seen some of the almost tragic cases produced by the then fierce competition for the few scholarships available to those who had no ability to kick a football; clever and poor boys, inspired by ambition, who had set their hearts on proceeding to the older universities but had never quite succeeded in amassing the financial means to do so, and so had stayed on in school year after year to repeat the same dreary cycle of scholarship examinations which, even if sheer persistence eventually brought them success, had already broken their hearts and their spirits. There seemed to me something both cruel and pathetic in such endeavours and they did nothing to encourage me to enrol in what was fundamentally a harsh and inequitable system. For I was already a socialist, or thought myself one, and in 1926 had already had my first view of industrial and civil strife, when the stalwart members of the Glamorgan constabulary had stood shoulder to shoulder against the sullen crowds in the streets of Cardiff and mounted police had charged them in St John's Square. Nor had my affection for either Oxford or Cambridge been increased by the sports-jacketed undergraduates who had descended upon us to assist in maintaining the public services and in breaking the threat to their way of life represented by miners who, up in the valleys, had emerged from their underground kingdom to claim a share of the wealth which had been so generously bestowed upon these oafish and arrogant youths.

Oxford seemed to me the very heart of the English class system, of what we had not yet learned to call the Establishment, and, as such, to be entirely alien to the romantic dreams which had begun to haunt my imagination. For Oxford, in my prejudiced view, not merely represented the opposite of what I felt to be the just and natural order of things; what was even worse, it seemed to me the enemy of those affections of the heart and those flights of the mind which are both the source and the material of art.

For it was such matters that, by the time I was in the sixth form, had begun to fill my mind and take the place of what had hitherto been an obsession with rugby football. And once again my own instincts and inclinations were encouraged by the atmosphere which prevailed in my school. It was one of the headmaster's firm beliefs that by the time they entered the sixth form boys were in danger of having a surfeit of formal instruction, and of working to the demands of a rigid curriculum, and that the time had come for them to find out for themselves where their real interests lay. So that for a year we were left very much to ourselves, to do what we liked or even to do nothing at all, following no particular curriculum and with the easiest possible schedule of prescribed work. It was the principle of the Sabbatical year applied to schoolboys, and it seemed to work with the greatest possible success. Nothing could have been more unlike the pressure exerted today on an aspiring schoolboy, the grim insistence on specialization and all its attendant evils, the *ewige Wiederkehr*⋆ of the examination system, and for myself I still remain grateful for that year of idleness and freedom suddenly granted one in the middle of the long process of education.

I say idleness and freedom because that was how it appeared to me. It would be truer to say that for a year nothing was asked of one which one did not choose for oneself. My brother used the same year to take the London Matriculation examination, instead of the normal Higher School Certificate, because it allowed him to go to the university a year earlier than usual. I used it to indulge what has become an almost obsessive passion for literature and in trying to penetrate its secrets for myself. My English master's fine editions had already introduced me to Blake, who has remained one of the abiding interests of my life, and through reading Edwin J. Ellis's *The Real Blake* and his and Yeats's commentary on Blake's mystical works, I came to read Yeats's own poetry. When a boy is started on a course of reading like this, there is no knowing where it may lead him; it is an addiction as powerful and compulsive as drugs. In my own case, Yeats led me on to read Arthur Symons,⋆ to struggle, with the aid of my schoolboy French and pocket dictionary, to make sense of the French symbolist poets and to try to find some meaning in Yeats's combination of Celtic mythology and cabbalistic lore. I placed roses under my pillow at night so that I might dream of the Secret Rose,⋆ which is the rose of all the world, and believed that, if only I concentrated enough, I would hear the shields and spears clashing in the Valley of the Black Pig.⋆

Such ideas make a heady draught for a boy of sixteen and they drove me into ways which were no doubt absurd but which I have never regretted. For I was possessed by a state of exaltation which made me believe that in such books I might, with sufficient effort on my part, seize hold of the key to the secrets of the universe; they were not only literature to me, they were the deepest manifestations of life itself. The chief source on which this exaltation fed was nothing more esoteric than the open shelves of the Cardiff Public Library, where as if drawn by some invisible thread, like that one which led Theseus to the Minotaur, each book seemed to direct me to another so that I became engulfed in some strange universe of discourse, infinitely remote yet infinitely real, whose secret paths and tortuous ways were only revealed to the adept.

On Saturday nights in winter, after playing football for the school in the afternoon, I would walk through Cardiff's streets, crowded with miners come down from the valleys to watch the match at Cardiff Arms Park and their wives enjoying the city's sights, and through the market near St John's Church where under their garish lights the stalls displayed the hot meat pies and black puddings and laver bread which were then the delicacies of the poor. The lights, the crowds, the drunks lurching out of the pubs, the girls waiting to be picked up made of Cardiff something entirely different from its drab every day; it was like walking on to the stage of a theatre in which everything has suddenly become much larger and brighter than life. I was already bemused and dazzled when I entered the cool mock-Gothic spaces of the library, but what lay within was no less enthralling than the scenes outside, and for a moment, in the entrance hall, I paused, almost dizzily poised between the real world and that other one which lay embalmed within the covers of the thousands of books that filled the library's shelves.

Yet to me in those days there was no real distinction between the two, and my experience of the world was so small that I saw the people in the street with the same eyes with which I absorbed the treasures that lay on the printed page. Chance alone first made me lay my hand on *The Waste Land*, and this led me to *The Sacred Wood*, and *The Sacred Wood* to the Elizabethan dramatists, and they in turn to the metaphysical poets. One day my hand fell on a book that was strange to me, *Centuries of Meditation*, by Thomas Traherne, and on the first page where I opened it I read: 'The corn was orient and immortal wheat, which never should be reaped, nor was ever sown. I thought it had stood from everlasting to everlasting. The dust and stones of the street were as precious as gold. The gates were at first the end of the world, the green trees when I saw them first through one of the gates transported and ravished me; their sweetness and unusual beauty made my heart to leap, and almost mad with ecstasy, they were such strange and wonderful things. The men! O what venerable and reverend creatures did the aged seem! Immortal cherubims! And young men glittering and sparkling Angels, and maids strange seraphic pieces of life and beauty! Boys and girls tumbling in the street, and playing, were moving jewels. I knew not that they were born or should die. But all things abided eternally as they were in their proper places. Eternity was manifest in the light of the day, and something infinite behind everything appeared: which talked with my expectation and moved my desire.'

How can one explain why this should have struck one with the force of a revelation, not by its beauty only, but as an expression of objective truth, which applied as much to the streets outside the library as to anywhere else in the world. I added it, like some jewel of infinite worth, to the personal treasury I had amassed out of my reading, a kind of Aladdin's cave in which was piled a jumbled and heterogeneous hoard of ideas not only from Blake and Yeats and the French symbolists and Eliot, but also from *The Golden Bough*★ and Sir John Rhŷs's *Celtic Pantheon*,★ which was on my father's bookshelves at home and, even more incongruously, Wyndham Lewis's *Time and Western Man*. For in those days everything seemed to lead on to everything else, and in these universal lines of communication I felt as if I had discovered some secret wisdom which enabled me to interpret the world as it really is, if we only had the eyes to see it; and as I walked home from the library, weighed down by a pile of books bound together by a leather strap (for I had impounded all my family's library tickets) the streets of Cardiff, gaudily lit in the centre and gradually growing dark and deserted as one penetrated into the suburbs, were not populated by men and women or built of bricks and mortar but had become a theatre for figures and images out of the *Spiritus Mundi*,★ which reveals itself through that secret system of correspondences which only the initiated can decipher.

The mysterious workings of chance led to another discovery. One of the few social centres for the ordinary citizens of Cardiff, except, of course, for public houses, was the café attached to the Capitol Cinema where people in search of some distraction from the grim tedium of lower middle class provincial life could sit and drink coffee, and eat egg and chips, amid what seemed then the grandiose surroundings of this recently built super cinema. There my brother one night had fallen into conversation with a stranger, a slight dark thin man, with the high complexion of the tubercular but with a gaiety and vivacity which were enhanced by his Dublin accent. His name was Nagle,★ and he was an actor from the Abbey Theatre, forced into his retirement by his complaint and living in Cardiff because its air was said to be good for it, though it would be hard to say what recuperative powers he drew from the coal black waters of the river Taff, flowing between its muddy banks past the particularly sordid actors' lodgings which he occupied on its embankment; unless, perhaps, the river reminded him of the Liffey.

My brother struck up an acquaintance with him, and before he left Cardiff for the university, introduced me to him, believing, rightly, that he would appeal to my literary tastes. For his conversation was full of reminiscences of the Abbey Theatre, of Moore and Gogarty and Synge, in whose plays he had appeared. He had even seen and heard and known Yeats himself, which for me was as if he had met Blake, and had lived in Paris and had acted on tour in the United States.

Nagle was the first person I had ever known for whom literature did not come out of books but out of life, and this seemed to give another dimension to the dreams and fantasies that filled my mind, as if, poor and ill as he was, his mere existence seemed to endow them with flesh and blood. But he opened my mind to vistas and possibilities to which until then my only access had been through books, and he spoke of writing and writers as if they were not something alien and exotic but as natural and familiar as the air one breathed, and for that I owe him a debt which I was never able to repay, because soon after I left school his condition deteriorated and he died in a sanatorium to which he had been removed high up on the Brecon Beacons.

His large and general claim upon my gratitude included one obligation which was particularly heavy. One evening, as we sat over our coffee cups in the café, he placed upon the table a thick volume covered in brown paper so that I could not read its title. I instinctively reached out to take it but he placed his hand over it, as if he could scarcely bear to let it out of his possession.

'What is it?' I asked.

'It's a book,' he said.

'I can see that,' I said rather rudely; 'but why so much fuss about it?'

'It's by the greatest writer now alive,' he said, and opening it showed me the title page: *Ulysses*, by James Joyce.

It was a copy of the first edition printed by Sylvia Beach in Paris. In those days, *Ulysses* was still banned by the Home Office, copies of it were difficult to obtain for most people, and except in the very smallest circles it had not yet established itself as the masterpiece which it is. As for me, for all my reading I had never heard of it, and regarded with some scepticism what I took to be Nagle's extravagant claims for the author, who, he explained, was a Dubliner like himself; it was as if I had claimed that one of our obscure neighbours in Roath Park was a great writer. But he lent me the book, and for a few weeks I was plunged into a world, a city and a language that were not like anything I had ever known before. I do not know that I understood even a tenth of what I read, but somehow, through the kind of empathy which enables the young, in their reading, to penetrate the secret of what they do not understand, the book became a part of me, and Buck Mulligan beside the snot green sea, and Mr Bloom and Stephen Daedalus the kind of friends who remain beside one throughout one's life.

I even took the book to school with me to read in my spare time, and being discovered doing so by the headmaster was beaten for introducing pornography into the school; even his tolerance did not extend to *Ulysses*. It was the second of the only two times I was ever beaten at school. My father, on the other hand, after looking through the book one day when I had left it lying in his study, merely said: 'There seems to be a lot of obscenity in this book,' and handed it back to me with distaste indeed, but with no further attempt to interfere with my choice of literature.

VI

The truth is, I think, that during much of my last years in Cardiff I was on a trip quite as delirious and hallucinatory as any recommended by Dr Timothy Leary, only its motive power was provided by literature and not by drugs. But there are cases in which the one can be quite as powerful as the other. The breathtaking flights into the unknown, the precipitous plunge into mysterious caverns of the imagination, were as dizzying as any psychedelic addict's; one's eyes were dazzled, one's ears roared with the boom of undiscovered oceans, the world was a storehouse of cryptic messages which only awaited one's attention to unlock their meaning. It was as if one monitored the communication system of an invisible universe, infinitely distant and yet so close that one had only to lift a hand to touch it, and at times so vividly and intensely seen, heard, felt, smelled that the senses became confounded and bemused.

To me this world to which I could give no name was at times so real and palpable that it blotted out my everyday experiences, the people who surrounded me seemed no more than tenuous ghosts and I myself had no more individual existence than a tree or a stone. One could quite truthfully say, in modern jargon, that I was both disorientated and alienated; every day

News from a foreign country came,
As if my treasures and my joys lay there*

carrying such a wealth of meaning and significance that I could not conceive of any other country worth living in; nor could I understand how its claims could be reconciled with any kind of conformity with the rules which govern our ordinary lives.

Yet these rules exist. The time came when at length I had to decide what I was to do with myself, and it was becoming increasingly evident that, short of something totally impossible to foresee, Oxford was the fate or the doom that lay in wait for me. Feebly, spasmodically, I tried to resist. To me it seemed that no life was worth living which did not allow one access to the voices which seemed to speak to me from some invisible sphere, yet even I was not so stupid as to believe that these voices were of a kind to carry me very far on the road to academic success. I forced my father, much against his will, to write to Edward Garnett,* with whom he had been friends at the City of London School, to ask his help in placing me as an apprentice to a printer in London, for it seemed to me that in such work one might find the kind of freedom which I wanted and after all, hadn't Blake been a printer? It was with dismay that I read Garnett's very sensible reply that this might mean committing myself to a very hazardous and precarious existence, and that anyone who had any chance of going to Oxford would be very foolish not to make the most of it.

It was not the reply I had hoped for, though indeed I hardly knew myself what I wanted, but short of running away altogether, which for a moment I contemplated, I could see no way of escape. So, reluctantly, I fell in with the wishes of my parents and schoolmasters, and amid my other preoccupations began to study seriously for a scholarship to Oxford. It was also necessary, in order to accumulate sufficient funds, to win a state scholarship, of which at the time there were twelve for the whole of Wales, and awarded strictly by competition on the marks obtained in the Higher School Certificate examination.

I was determined, however, that if I was to sit for a scholarship to Oxford, it should not be in English. It seemed to me that the kind of pleasures I derived from language and from literature could only wither under the dead hand of academic study; what had scholarship to do with the visions and revelations I found in Blake or Donne or Traherne? It seemed to me that literature was far too serious a matter for scholars, who were of necessity divorced from that life of sensation from which literature springs, and I recited to myself Yeats's lines:*

> They'll cough in the ink to the world's end;
> Wear out the carpet with their shoes
> Earning respect; have no strange friend;
> If they have sinned nobody knows.
> Lord, what would they say
> Should their Catullus walk that way!

Literature and scholarship seemed to me worlds apart and I could not conceive that the one could be a fit subject for the other. So instead of English I chose history as the subject in which I should specialize; the decision was all the easier because of my respect and admiration for the intellectual standards demanded by my history master.* If I could satisfy him, I felt, I could satisfy any examiner; it would also be a delight to study under him, because, himself the son of a village black-smith in North Wales and a passionate Welshman, he was also a man of unusually wide and varied culture and the least provincial or parochial of men in his vision of what the study of history entailed.

And so indeed it proved. For my last two years at school I followed the course he plotted for me, which included, in addition to English history, the history of medieval Europe and of the French Revolution. Under his tuition, I found history as absorbing and enthralling as anything to be found in literature, and indeed they seemed to be only two different ways of apprehending a single reality; for what was it, after all, to study history but to plunge into that great ocean of the past which laps us round at every moment of our waking and dreaming lives? Or so at least it seemed to me at that time, and I delighted to try and discover in the saints and mystics of the Middle Ages, and in the cathedrals which are their greatest creations, the same vision of reality which I found in poets and artists. The cathedrals indeed seemed to me like vast epics written in stone, great forests of images and dreams drawn from the most secret and sacred recesses of the human heart, through the tracery of whose interlacing branches one caught glimpses of the same heaven and the same hell which are the provinces of all art. And when I passed from the middle ages to the French Revolution, how else could I think of Danton bellowing his courage and his despair in his gigantic bull's voice except as yet another of those titanic figures out of *Spiritus Mundi*, as heroic as Achilles or Cuchulain, and perhaps even more because the powers and forces with which he wrestled, like Jacob with the angels, were so much closer to those with which men wrestle in our own time?

I have no doubt there was much that was merely fanciful in my attitude to history and the ideas and images which I imported into it. Now, I cannot help thinking that they tended to bemuse and bewilder me rather than to throw any light on the subject. I do not think that a boy who tries to interpret history according to a system of correspond-ences borrowed from Baudelaire or a belief in the literal truth of Blake's prophetic books is ever likely to achieve a high degree of objective truth, and I do not think that I ever came very near to understanding the past *wie es eigentlich gewesen war* – as it actually existed.* But I do know that the curious, even absurd, hotchpotch of ideas by which I tried to decode the past made of it to me something which was genuinely my own, and of use and value to me in my own life, a living and not a dead thing, which was shot through and through with my own dreams and imaginings; and this at least had the advantage of making the past so fascinating that by the way and almost by accident I absorbed a good deal of knowledge, for even I could not make bricks without any straw at all. When many years later I read Nietzsche's essay *Vom Nützen und Nachteil der Historie für das Leben* (*Of the Uses and Disadvantages of History in Life*), I felt grateful that for a time at least it had been the usefulness, in Nietzsche's sense, of history which had been most apparent to me; and perhaps that is an experience which once gained can never be wholly lost. But today I cannot help wondering what kind of stuff it was that, writing in feverish haste and with hardly a pause for thought, I poured out in my examination papers at Oxford and can only wonder at the ability of my examiners to make head or tail of it.

During my last year at school I worked extremely hard, especially in the long winter evenings when I sat bent over my books at the table in our parlour while my mother and father read in silence in their armchairs on either side of the fireplace. The crimson tablecloth on which my books were piled, the glowing light of the fire, fed by the best Welsh coal, the dark mahogany furniture and the Victorian prints on the walls, the scratching of my pen on the paper, the absolute and unbroken silence, induced in me a feeling that time had come to a stop and that we three were preserved for ever in an immobility which change could never threaten. And I was happy that it should be so, for the quiet room with its shadows in the corner where the lamplight never penetrated was transformed into a kind of enchanted cave peopled by all the spirits called up from the past by my books, which I read as if they were works of necromancy that could endow me with magical powers. If I pause for a moment and looked up from my reading, the sense of being encapsuled in some timeless moment, of total and absolute insulation against everything that existed outside those four walls, was so intense that I seemed to float free of my body and to look down on the room as if it were one of those Dutch interiors in which every worn and familiar object, and the faces of those who sit among them, are illuminated by an internal light, a warmth, a glow, a splendour that came from some world which is beyond the world of change.

This was in winter. In summer I worked alone in my bedroom and on golden evenings before the sun had finally set would allow myself the pleasure of walking through the gardens of the public park nearby to hire a boat and row for an hour on the shallow waters of its artificial lake. The park would be crowded with the citizens of Cardiff taking the evening air, tradespeople and their wives, courting couples, children bouncing balls and trundling hoops on the concrete paths between the symmetrically ordered flower beds, and the presence of so many others in a world which for me had become intensely solitary, the contrast with the dreams that filled my mind, momentarily bewildered and confused me, and yet this world of flesh and blood was as mysterious and alluring as anything the imagination had to offer. One evening I had been reading the *Lyrical Ballads,* and it seemed to me that it did not need the genius of a Wordsworth to infuse the light of poetry into the sober and somewhat drab reality of our municipal park, for it was not a light which we imagined or contrived for ourselves, as by some trick of stage production, but was as much a part of these men and women, these trees and flowers, these stretches of freshly watered grass in the yellowing evening sunshine as it had been of Adam and Eve as they walked in the garden of Eden.

The lake stretched beyond the gardens, and in the cool and mysterious shadows of the trees on the two small islands at its further end I let the boat float among the ducks that dabbled in its waters. One section of the lake was enclosed to form a bathing pool, where on warm evenings I used to swim and watch the slender long-legged bodies of the girls who swooped like swallows from the diving board and flashed like fish through the waters. To me they seemed like creatures out of mythology, nymphs, naiads, ondines, water sprites, and when sometimes I summoned up my courage to make their acquaintance I was tongue-tied with shyness and embarrassment and could find no words to express the confused desire which consumed me. I envied the boldness and brash confidence of my schoolfellows who, when darkness began to fall, would accompany the girls up the hill to the woods above the lake and next day regale the form with boasts of their sexual achievements. Only rarely did I overcome my shyness sufficiently to emulate their example, and then, lying in the grass beside a girl whose dark hair still wet from bathing hung down her back like a mermaid's, made clumsy attempts at love-making which only her more experienced hands, limbs, body, guided to success. But the memory of those girlish bodies – limbs that entwined one like seaweed, the smell as of fresh milk that exuded from their skin – haunted my dreams and blurred my vision as I sat bent over my books and they also had to be included in my vision of the world, in which almost everything else had been derived from literature and not from life.

VII

At length, in the Christmas vacation of 1927, the day arrived when I travelled up to Oxford to take the scholarship examination. I had only once passed beyond the borders of Wales, on a Saturday afternoon coach trip to play football against the Crypt School at Gloucester, and when we passed through the Severn Tunnel it was truly a foreign country that I entered. It was something of a comfort that I was not alone on this voyage of discovery. My companion was a school friend who had the advantage of being a superlative football player, and was therefore assured of some sort of scholarship at Brasenose, which in those days was more like an athletic association than a seat of learning. I had no such advantage and my chances of success at New College were decidedly slimmer. Indeed, they seemed to me non-existent when, after three days of writing examination papers in New College Hall, I waited in the Warden's lodgings with the other candidates until my turn came to be interviewed.

They seemed to me, as in fact they really were, of another race from myself, or indeed from anyone else I had ever known. Their voices were different, their clothes were different, their manners were different, and to me they even seemed to look different. They all came from public schools, and some of them had been at school together; they had brothers, cousins, friends already at the university, they knew each other's sisters, and for them Oxford was simply the natural and inevitable sequel to school and not the realization of an impossible ambition. They were in no way awestruck or abashed, as I was, by the Gothic ambience of the long gallery in which we waited outside the Warden's study. They felt at ease and at home there, and as they waited they lounged gracefully around and gossiped to each other in a manner which seemed to me the height of elegance and sophistication. It struck me forcibly at that moment that they were made for Oxford, in a way which I was not, and Oxford was made for them, and I could see no reason why Oxford, or New College, should go so far out of their normal course as to bestow a scholarship on me, especially as I was still not quite sure whether I wanted one. But though I was not sure what I wanted, I was also combative and competitive and did not at all like the idea that, with all their advantages, these people seemed certain to succeed where I seemed equally bound to fail.

It was not that I thought them cleverer, or more intelligent, or better educated than myself. Some hidden source of self-confidence or vanity told me that they were not.★ It was simply that in the long medieval gallery, with the portraits of past Wardens hanging on the wall, they moved as naturally as fish in water while I hardly dared to speak for fear of attracting attention to my uncouthness, to my Welsh voice, to my ill-fitting suit, my lack of any of the social accomplishments which sat so easily on them. It was really all quite simple; they were at home and I was not.

I felt strangely naked and vulnerable when I entered the Warden's study and found the Warden and some of the Fellows seated in a semi-circle which I faced from a chair beside the fire.★ What comforted me, though it came almost as a shock because I had entirely failed to fore-see it, was the tone of kindness and friendliness in which all their questions were directed at me, the politeness of the interest with which they listened to my answers, the air of ease and urbanity, of gentle consideration, with which the interview was conducted, and in those few moments the seeds of an abiding affection for Oxford were im-planted in my heart. It was less like an interview than a form of seduction.

There was a charm in it which conquered me, so that when at length the interview was over and I made my way home from New College to my room in St Aldate's, for the first time I felt a real regret that perhaps I might never see Oxford again. I had felt, for a moment, a sense that Oxford might have much to teach me, in matters not only of learning but of living. When I left the next morning to stay for the weekend in London with my grandmother, I felt that if I had failed I should be the loser in more senses than one. So that when the following day I received a telegram informing me that I had been awarded an open scholarship, I was not only gratified by the sense of having achieved something that was not easy. I felt also, with a certain stirring of excitement, that I was on the verge of making new discoveries and that, whether I wished it or not, a new and different world was opening out before me.

Two

I

M y childhood and youth, and the slightly odd person they had made of me, were perhaps not the best sort of preparation for Oxford as it was when I first proceeded there at the age of eighteen in the autumn of 1928. For in those days Oxford was still very much of a closed society, with its own traditions, even its own morality, all of which were as strange and alien to me as if I had suddenly found myself in Timbuctoo or Kamchatka.

This is not to say that Oxford at the time was a completely homogeneous and monolithic society, with which I alone was out of step. Like all societies, it had its own internal divisions and distinctions into the interstices of which a stranger might settle himself with a reasonable amount of comfort. They were not, as they were to become later, political divisions, because politics had not yet assumed that dominating part in the life of the university which it was to play in the thirties. Nor was there the slightest sign, at that time, of the general revolt of the young against the old, of the taught against the teacher, which has become a characteristic feature of the universities today. In this respect, both dons and undergraduates lived in a kind of age of innocence, in which neither had as yet discovered that they hated each other.

Undergraduates indeed were, by modern standards of student revolt, a singularly amenable and submissive lot. This was largely due to the fact that for most of them Oxford presented a blissful liberation from the restrictions imposed on them at their public schools. If the yoke of the university, and of the colleges, would seem intolerably heavy to the undergraduate of today, it was then easily borne because it was so much lighter than what had gone before. Youthful revolt was directed, not against the university, but against the public school system; quite a large library could have been collected of adolescent novels in which, from *The Loom of Youth*★ onwards, their authors described the tortures and sufferings imposed on them at school, as if they had escaped from some premature form of concentration or labour camp. To read them, one would have thought that the entire middle class had in its youth been the victim of an organized system of educational terrorism. The scars, however, had not penetrated very deep, and in no way prevented the victims, while licking their wounds, from enjoying the liberties and pleasures they were now offered; rather, they only added a keener and sharper flavour to them.

Politics, in the form in which they have manifested themselves both in the 1930s and 1960s, have so transformed the Oxford which I first knew that today I hardly find it recognizable. The greatest change they have introduced is the assumption that the university is no longer a preparation for adult life, an interlude in which the undergraduate, half boy, half man, is not yet fully grown, but is already a part of the adult world, with the same intensely practical concerns and interests, among which is the inescapable duty of changing it for the better.

In this sense, it could be said that Oxford, in 1928, was still in the pre-industrial stage of its history, enjoying the last golden glow of a kind of pastoral civilization which had endured, in some respects unchanged, since the Middle Ages; this was true even of its physical environment, because the name Morris did not yet fully spell out the doom which the internal combustion engine would bring upon the city and the university. Perhaps this lack of adaptation was Oxford's condemnation; but it did not make it any less enjoyable. Of course, even then, there were little enclaves in the university in which politics reared their ugly head. There was, for instance, the Oxford Union, a kind of school debating society for budding professional politicians, but no one except a very small minority of its members took its proceedings very seriously, and certainly no one would have dreamed of attributing to them the kind of importance they assumed when, only a few years later,* the Union with typical frivolity carried its famous resolution 'That this House will under no circumstances fight for its King and Country'. And there was already at Oxford, and particularly at New College, a group of admirably serious and dedicated young men who many years later, after many vicissitudes, would provide the Labour party with an entirely new leadership and stamp it with their own peculiar form of Wykehamist socialism.

But they also were exceptional, both in their intelligence and the seriousness with which they prepared themselves for the life of politics. They already exuded an air of professionalism and puritanism which was somehow out-of-tune with the fin-de-siècle atmosphere of the end of the twenties. It was perhaps a sign of my own frivolity that, though I thought of myself as a socialist, I found their ideas altogether too humdrum and dreary to fit into my Utopian dreams of revolution.* Equally, perhaps, there was something in their public-school version of socialism which offended against instincts which were rooted in my origins. Somehow it was tainted by the charitable, and estimable, motive of 'doing something for the poor'. I felt that I was one of the poor myself, and was not at all sure I wanted them to do something for me.

Politics was not yet a cause of contention. Nor was age. The university was still by modern standards very small and a college was hardly more than a large family. Married dons were the exception and not the rule, their strictly academic duties relatively very light and there were few distractions to turn their minds away from Oxford. Dons and undergraduates lived in an intimacy which is no longer possible and by knowing each other overcame the barriers of age and learned a mutual affection which today has largely disappeared from university life.

The most obvious division within the university when I first arrived there was between the Hearties and the Aesthetes. The Hearty saw himself as representing virility as opposed to decadence, the Aesthete was the self-conscious champion of culture against barbarism. Hearties went in for beer and games, club scarves and blazers, fast cars and motor cycles, picking up girls on Saturday night in the Carfax assembly rooms, and throwing Quintin Hogg into Mercury, the pool that adorns Tom Quad at Christ Church. Aesthetes were dedicated to poetry and the arts, they were, or affected to be, homosexual, spent their holidays in Germany and came back with stories of the wonderful decadence of the Weimar Republic; in dress and appearance they reflected, at long range and modified to suit English tastes, the image of the dandy created by Baudelaire. Hearties and Aesthetes alike boasted representative types who displayed the characteristic features of the species in their most extreme form; on the one hand the oafish rowing man whose greatest pleasure was the wrecking of some studious and inoffensive undergraduate's room after a bump supper,* on the other some exotic immigrant like the Queen of Peru, a South American male tart who, amid surroundings of Second Empire Parisian splendour, held court in rooms somewhere off Beaumont Street.

Between these two camps there raged an undeclared war; they represented as it were the two poles towards which undergraduate life gravitated. They were divided by a kind of plain or marsh, neutral ground in which the majority of undergraduates had their being, uncommitted to either side but each responding in his particular way to the pull exerted by the one or the other. There were poets who, though by every other sign they were to be recognized as Aesthetes, were as devoted to beer and football as any Hearty; there were athletes who, off the track or river, were as intellectual in their tastes as any aesthete. And there were many who simply took the pleasures Oxford had to offer as they came, without bothering too much about what they implied, content, and more than content, to spend their three years there as if they formed one long summer afternoon.

In this no-man's-land which was the abode of the average under-graduate, I managed to create a particular limbo of my own. Inclination and temperament led me towards the aesthetes, whose taste for literature and the arts I shared; but at the same time I remained fond, as I had been at school, of playing games* and this made me something of an eccentric in their ranks.

But if, in the company of friends, I often had the sense of being not wholly accepted, or acceptable, I felt it even more strongly with regard to Oxford life in general. For the divisions and distinctions within the university, of which that between the Hearty and the Aesthete was only the most obvious, were only superficial as compared with the social uniformity which Oxford presented to a stranger like myself. For Oxford was then still an almost exclusive monopoly of what Keynes somewhere calls 'the great capitalist class' and its breeding ground, the public schools. Interlopers from the state educational system formed so small a minority that we made scarcely any impression upon the system as a whole, which could afford to tolerate, even welcome, our presence because we represented no kind of threat to its cohesiveness. New College, particularly, represented a special case of this general condition. It owed its existence to the same founder as Winchester College, William of Wykeham, and an unbroken historical connection between the two institutions, together with a generous provision of closed scholarships, made it a special preserve of Wykehamists. They gave the college a particular sub-culture of its own, and an historian of manners would have been fascinated to observe how precisely they conformed, after so many centuries, though in modern dress as it were, to the pattern of piety, respect for scholarship, and dedication to the service of Church and State, which had been the idea of the founder.

Of such sub-cultures there was an almost bewildering variety at Oxford, flourishing not only in particular colleges but in every kind of undergraduate club, association and society, and, even more perhaps, in purely ephemeral and transitory groups of friends bound together by nothing more than common tastes and interests, which might vary from bird-watching to seventeenth-century music. It was for me one of the particular charms of the place that one might stumble across such mini-cultures in the most unlikely corners. I used to sally out from my room in New College like a traveller following the course of an unexplored river, never knowing what strange flora and fauna, what exotic tribes and customs, one might encounter on its banks.

One of the oddest, perhaps, of such societies, which I came across rather late in my university life, was a group of three undergraduates who shared rooms together far off in Wellington Square. They rarely ventured out except to attend lectures and tutorials, and their rooms themselves had the grim and cheerless austerity of a monastic cell. No pictures adorned their walls, and their bookshelves displayed only a few works of the most rigorous scholarship; the very air in them seemed to breathe abstraction. There they shared together a life devoted entirely to a peculiarly refined and rigorous process of self-examination, like medieval flagellants chastising themselves and each other with the whips of logical analysis. No intellectual peccadillo was so trivial that it escaped each other's condemnation; no social distraction so innocent that it did not provoke a frown of disapproval, almost of disgust; no sign of frivolity, intellectual or moral, that did not represent a fall from grace. Their only concession to self-indulgence was, so far as I knew, a cup of cocoa at bedtime as they listened to a Bach concerto. When, fascinated by the penances they imposed on each other, I used to visit them, I used to be greeted with a chilly and disapproving silence, and felt like some butterfly which has violated the privacy of an anchorite's cell; but the strangest thing about it all was that they were, all three of them, blissfully happy.

At a different extreme, there were those for whom Oxford provided an opportunity for almost total idleness and dissipation, though even these sometimes assumed eccentric forms. A friend whom I had not known as an undergraduate later confessed to me that his life at Oxford had followed a rigidly determined pattern, which never varied from day to day. At eleven o'clock in the morning he was woken by his scout with an orange and a glass of brandy, which formed his breakfast. He then shaved, bathed and dressed, and strolled to the Carlton Club where he lunched, each day, on a grilled steak and a bottle of claret. The afternoon was spent in a cinema, and from five to six he played billiards with the professional at the university billiards club. Returning to college, he made ready for the evening, which was spent in dining with friends and consuming large quantities of alcohol. By twelve he was back in college, and retired to bed; and at eleven the following morning his scout appeared with an orange and a glass of brandy, and the daily routine was repeated. After two years he felt that he had learned everything Oxford had to teach him and, without regret and without a degree, left the university to prepare for the serious business of life by going to work in a factory in Birmingham. This case history of idleness, however, concealed a talent which later made its subject a very distinguished novelist, Henry Green.

Not many undergraduates, of course, devised quite so bizarre a programme for spending their time at Oxford, though I have no doubt that if one looked into the darker corners of some of the more obscure colleges one would have found recluses who were enjoying themselves in an equally eccentric fashion. Indeed it was precisely the charm of Oxford at the time that, within the not very demanding limits of college and university discipline, it allowed young men to spend their time exactly as they pleased, with the least possible interference of any kind of authority, and encouraged them to indulge their tastes, whether frivolous or serious, with a liberty which few societies have ever permitted their members.

There is a story of the great German classical scholar, Wiliamowitz-Moellendorf, that once, on a visit to Oxford, he was taken to the top of Magdalen Tower on a summer's afternoon and from there looked down at the streets and buildings spread out beneath him. The town was still then much as Gerard Manley Hopkins described it in 'Duns Scotus's Oxford'.

> Towery city and branchy between towers;
> Cuckoo-echoing, bell-swarmèd, lark-charmèd, rook-racked,
>   river-rounded;

and on an afternoon in May its streets were filled with undergraduates in white flannels or rowing kit making their way to the river or the cricket field or the tennis court. And the great scholar averted his eyes from the scene and scornfully spat out the words: *Eine Luststadt!* (A pleasure resort!)

A pleasure resort! It certainly was to me; yet I do not know that, in the end, the grim austerities of Prussian scholarship have served the cause of learning, or of civilization, better than the more humane traditions of Oxford. I have no doubt that, in my own time, there were people who were as committed to the most exacting forms of scholarship, and spent their days, and their nights, as laboriously as even Wiliamowitz could have wished. But even in them it was love not duty or discipline which drove them to their labours, and the harsh demands of scholarship were sweetened and mellowed by Oxford's air of freedom and toleration, by acceptance of the Rabelaisian doctrine of *Do What Thou Wilt is the Whole of the Law;** most of all perhaps by acceptance of Mark Pattison's belief that the final end and object of scholarship is not a book, but a man.*

As for the rest of us, learning, if it was of any interest, was only one among the many other pleasures Oxford had to offer. Some managed to get on very happily without any learning at all. I myself did not totally succumb to Oxford's particularly seductive form of hedonism;

but if there was anything which I took away with me from Oxford it was the belief that learning is a kind of pleasure and pleasure a kind of learning, even if it is only the pleasure of learning about oneself. On the whole it is a belief which is conducive to happiness, though perhaps it is not a very good guide to the sterner realities of life. But it always seemed then that there would be plenty of time for them later.

In this respect Oxford, when I first arrived there, was not perhaps the best of preparations for a future which was to turn out far uglier than anyone might have reasonably expected. It was still bathed in a kind of golden glow, as of a setting sun, which allowed a certain class of young Englishman a kind of happiness which I do not think has been possible for him since. For the end for the twenties was perhaps the last time the English ruling classes, and their children who were my contemporaries and friends, could look forward with any confidence to the continuation of the kind of world on which their privileges and their prosperity depended. That confidence had already been severely shaken by the First World War and its immediate aftermath in Europe of revolution, the fall of dynasties, the collapse of ancient empires; the wisest perhaps already knew that there could be no real recovery from so great a disaster, but if so this was a wisdom which was reserved only for the few. Since 1924 the world had enjoyed an unprecedented economic boom, and stable political conditions had been re-established; and Britain also had shared in the general restoration of confidence which this inspired, the revival of hope, the sense that after all total disaster had been averted and that the world could look forward to a new era of peace and prosperity in which Britain would still play a dominant if slightly diminished part.

It seemed as if the lights which had been extinguished in 1924 had gone up again. Europe, which Hermann Hesse had seen in 1920 as 'on the way to chaos, staggering drunkenly in holy madness on the edge of the abyss, singing like Dimitri Karamazov in drunkenness and ecstasy',* had been restored to financial and political stability. The United States was enjoying an economic boom so prodigious that every country in the world felt its effects. The Covenant of the League of Nations and the Pact of Locarno guaranteed the world, and particularly Europe, against a renewal of the aggressive and bellicose policies which had provoked the tragedy of 1914. In such conditions, even the Kellogg–Briand Pact* outlawing war in perpetuity did not read like a fairy story, and the preparations for the World Disarmament Conference seemed to promise that the entire world would beat its swords into ploughshares; was not even Krupp doing so already at Essen?

No doubt the happy expectations inspired by so astonishing a recovery from the depths of disaster were largely based on illusion, but in 1928 it would have taken a wise man to realize it, and undergraduates are not, on the whole, very wise, nor were their teachers any wiser. Their fathers' recovery of assurance and confidence, the general feeling that all Britain now needed was a policy of enlightened apathy, was reflected in the sons by a sense that the world was their oyster, and the only difficulty was what particular breed of oyster to select. Some chose learning, some chose art, some chose self-indulgence, some chose games; some even chose rebellion against their fathers and everything they represented, but with a subconscious assurance that this also was only another kind of game and nothing very serious would happen as a result. And whatever the choice there was an underlying assumption that what mattered was to choose for oneself, and that the sum of individual choices could only contribute to the greatest happiness of all.

Of course, for the undergraduate, there were limitations to the liberty which he enjoyed, but they were easy to bear because they were the price of his privileges. In this respect Oxford was more like a club than a modern university, and despite the still almost medieval domestic arrangements of the colleges, the undergraduate lived in considerable comfort, which in some respects at least amounted to luxury. With his own bedroom and sitting room, which at any moment could be totally sealed off from the outside world by the simple expedient of 'sporting his oak',* he enjoyed an enviable degree of privacy. The services of his scout relieved him of all domestic cares and responsibilities. The precise degree of luxury with which he surrounded himself was a function of his, or rather his father's, income; if it were large enough, he could afford to indulge every taste, from lavish hospitality to keeping polo ponies. But the basic luxury was the independence and privacy which every undergraduate enjoyed, the sense of being able to live and breathe in a space of his own and of freedom from interference with what he chose to do with his own time. There was, of course, the risk of being sent down if he wasted it too conspicuously; but this, after all, was very much a matter of his own choice.

To me at least these were luxuries indeed. By the standards of most of my contemporaries I was poor, but a state scholarship, a college scholarship, and a scholarship from the city of Cardiff provided me with a total income of £250 a year, which to me was wealth.* It was sufficient to cover my basic needs, largely supplied by the college, and enabled me to buy as many books as I wanted, clothe myself, and indulge in whatever minor pleasures, though none of the major extravagances, that I chose. There was even the special pleasure of never needing to have any money in one's pocket, for cash was quite unnecessary when everything was to be had on credit. My own debts, after three years at Oxford, amounted to £70, which were promptly paid for by my father, without question, reproach or hesitation.

Thus, on arrival at Oxford, I suddenly enjoyed the illusion of total financial independence and for me this was one of the uncovenanted graces of being an undergraduate. It was an illusion which, once acquired, I never wholly lost, even when any justification for it had disappeared, and in later life this led me into many mistakes. For of course we never really are independent, whatever we may think or feel, and perhaps it is best if we come to realize this at an early age. But this was a thought which, if it had occurred to me, I should certainly have rejected with scorn and contempt. My newly acquired freedom seemed to me absolute and the only urgent problem, if one could call it such, was what one was going to do with it.

Such an attitude seems all the more curious to me now because I believed myself to be a socialist and a Marxist, a worshipper at the shrine of what was sometimes familiarly referred to as the MCH; the Materialist Conception of History. For me this was an important article of faith; but somehow I felt that, though it applied to everyone else, it did not apply to me. This, however, was only one of the many contradictions which I had no difficulty in accepting at that time. After all, were not contradictions an essential part of the dialectic?

Perhaps it was the inscrutable working of the dialectic, or merely something contrary in my own nature which ensured that, though aware of my own good fortune, I was more often than not miserable at Oxford. I was lonely, and felt the need of my parents and home. I missed the intimate, fire-lit domesticity of our sitting room at night, the silence which reigned when we sat together in the long winter evenings; I missed the city streets and the girls in the park and the feeling that, even when one was alone, the city and its people and the dark valleys groping like outstretched fingers into the coalfield, were packed close around one, dense, mysterious, yet familiar. For in Oxford I was a stranger, and remained one. The city played no part in one's life; girls rarely penetrated it; my rooms, high up in Gilbert Scott's New Buildings, or, later, in the garden quadrangle, seemed bare and austere compared with home, and El Greco reproductions I had hung on their walls sometimes seemed to throw a lurid and sinister glare on their emptiness.

Dining in Hall, under the high oak roof that multiplied the din of the dinner tables, I would listen to the conversation around me, and the English middle-class voices sometimes seemed to be the voices of foreigners, speaking an alien tongue; or rather it was I who was the alien, surrounded by people of whose manners and customs I knew nothing. For it was not only differences of language, voice, accent, which divided us; tricks of phrase and turns of speech revealed the gulf between two nations and two cultures.*

'Do you know the Angleseys?' an aristocratic and very beautiful young man* said to me one evening as we were drinking sherry in the buttery; sherry was the staple drink of the day and sometimes we seemed to drown in butts of it, like the Duke of Clarence in malmsey.

'The Angleseys?' I said. 'There's only one of them.' He was as puzzled by my reply as I was by his question, and it was some time before I learned that the name of a place could also be the name of a person or a family. And when I did, it was with something of the same sense of poetic discovery with which Proust learned that names which for him conveyed the blood-shot mysteries of the Dark Ages were also the titles of living people. The Angleseys, I felt, must have all the gentle charm and beauty, the legendary fertility, as of heaped-up corn, of the island from which they took their name.

Such misunderstandings showed what a rich and varied field of exploration Oxford offered, and after a time they were enough to tempt me out of my nineteenth-century Gothic tower in New College. There was of course more familiar ground for me to frequent. I could, for instance, have sought the company of compatriots, including some of my schoolfellows, who were at Oxford at that time. They were most concentrated in Jesus, *Coleg yr Iesu*, a kind of Patagonian colony in the Turl, where they cultivated the Welsh language and the nostalgia which the Welsh call *hiraeth*, and in general lived the life of exiles for whom Oxford was only a form of foreign posting before they returned again to their native land. But I had no wish to join this kind of Welsh old-colonial society. If Oxford were to be of any value at all, I felt, it would only be if it offered a wider and more varied world than Wales. Otherwise I might just as well, perhaps better, have stayed at home. What was the point of the pains of parting if they brought me nothing new?

Fortunately, curiosity alone was enough to drive me abroad, and gradually I began to make friends, at first in my own college, and later elsewhere, both with undergraduates and with dons,* who in those days were willing to devote what now seems an almost inordinate amount of their time and their affection to undergraduates. To me, these new friendships had something of the pleasure and excitement of foreign travel; I felt as if I were conducting a kind of miniature Grand Tour of English society, as reflected in the microcosm of Oxford. But sometimes, equally, I saw myself as a spy, dispatched on some desperate mission abroad, whose successes depended above all on disguising his identity by a process of protective coloration and on the thoroughness with which he adopted the manners and customs of the country to which he had been assigned.

In such a role, I was to some extent protected against such exposure, because I was at that time extremely, perhaps, for my own good, excessively impressionable, quick to adopt all the imitative devices which are necessary for survival in an alien environment, and equally quick to discard anything which might reveal how little I was at home in it. I exploited such gift, or faults, to the full, so that much of my time was spent in an elaborate exercise in simulation. I do not know how successful it was, and I dare say that it was a good deal less successful than I imagined. But there was a certain pleasure in the performance, even though it imposed a considerable strain, which revealed itself in frequent attacks of the depression which has afflicted me all my life and made me often a difficult companion, most of all to myself.

Such a temperament provided a very precarious basis for my social life at Oxford, which became increasingly a matter of friendships, of parties, of drinking rather more than was good for me, of 'nights spent in arguments and ignorant good will'* and of generally neglecting my work. Fortunately, terms at Oxford were admirably short, so that it was never necessary to maintain any disguise for more than eight weeks. When they were over, and the vacation came, I could return home as to a refuge where no disguises were necessary. This happy arrangement also helped to solve the problem of how to combine my exploration of English life, as represented by Oxford, with the necessary amount of work required to satisfy the demands of the curriculum. My scholarships were quite sufficient to cover my needs during term but left little over for the vacations; they were periods of financial stringency in which I made up for the extravagances of term by strict economy at home. Thus gradually term came to represent to me the season of pleasure, the vacation a period of penance in which I laboured to make up for my idleness at Oxford. It was curious reversal of the academic calendar, but on the whole the arrangement worked very well. Perhaps it explains why my memories of Oxford are coloured with the idea of frivolity and self-indulgence; the world's work, and mine, took place elsewhere.

During term I hardly worked at all, apart from producing a weekly essay for my tutor, and never succeeded in completing a single course of lectures, partly because most of them did not seem to be worth attending, partly because I learned better and faster from books; but mostly because regular attendance would have seriously interfered with my other preoccupations. I made friends, and these were the greatest benefit Oxford conferred on me. I read a great deal, but this was a confirmed addiction before I ever arrived at Oxford. I discovered Proust, who became an obsession to me, and I tended to view my own flibbertigibbet existence through his spectacles and to see in my acquaintances a Baron de Charlus, a Bloch, a Cottard. I also learned some German and acquired a taste for German literature which has remained with me through life, long after Germany had ceased to be fashionable and at times when Germany herself seemed to deny all the values on which her literature is founded. Despite bouts of depression I enjoyed myself excessively, so that my undergraduate days have retained in memory a special colour and a special flavour, as if drenched in some special ichor that was only distilled at that time and at that place.

But all this, alas! had nothing to do with my academic work. In my first year I had changed my school from History to Modern Greats, in the mistaken belief that philosophy, politics and economics provided the key to the secrets of real life, but they were singularly reluctant to yield them up to me. My new studies never acquired for me the charm which history had once had and I was delighted when, walking in Christ Church meadow, a friend, A. J. Ayer, triumphantly announced to me that he had solved all the problems of philosophy which would shortly, therefore, become a dead subject. But to me it only remained a difficult and intractable one, and distaste only accentuated my idleness. It became sufficiently noticeable to provoke warnings from my tutors and even from my friends that unless I mended my ways I was unlikely to obtain the kind of degree expected or hoped of me as a scholar of the college. The college chaplain,* a distinguished theologian to whom my father had commended me, was particularly distressed. 'He is *far* too great a social success!' he wailed, in his high nasal voice that always sounded as if he were intoning the lesson in chapel; 'he will *never* get a First!' I think his distress was increased because he regarded me as in some sense in his pastoral care. In my third year we lived on the same staircase in the garden quad and he was continually finding pretexts for entering my rooms. Starting out of my chair from a drunken slumber on a winter's afternoon, I found his slightly simian countenance bent over me, his hands on my biceps as he shook me out of sleep. 'You must be eee-mensely strong!' he intoned as I struggled to my feet.

By contrast with such absurd scenes, home and vacations came to represent long hours of study, by which one paid for what one had enjoyed. My friends went away on glamorous foreign travels, to Germany, to France, to Italy; I remained, somewhat enviously, at home, to settle down once again at the sitting-room table, where on the maroon tablecloth medieval saints and mystics had been replaced by Locke and Berkeley and Hume and Kant, with whom I wrestled in growing dismay as I realized that I had no talent for philosophy. And this division, not of labour, but between labour at home and pleasure at Oxford, accentuated for me the sense of living a double life. However much one enjoyed being at Oxford, one never felt that one properly belonged there and would always remain in some sense an interloper; while at home, labouring at neglected studies, one always felt that there was a part of me, idle and pleasure-loving, which had been left behind in Oxford, a frivolous ghost haunting the garden at New College, waiting for the beginning of term to be brought back to life again. It was not altogether an unpleasant feeling.

II

The first invitation I received at Oxford was to play bridge with a Wykehamist scholar who lived on the next staircase to me in New College. I had no business to accept the invitation, as I hardly knew how to play bridge; also I guessed that I should have to play for money, and had visions of incurring losses beyond my means. Both my fears were proved correct. Nevertheless I accepted; I had spent nearly every evening alone since my arrival at Oxford, and it had begun to seem to me that my stay there was to be spent in a kind of solitary confinement.

The three undergraduates with whom I played bridge that evening became my firm friends during my three years at New College, and I spent many similar evenings playing bridge with them. I never became a good bridge player and I always lost more money than I could afford, but I do not regard those evenings as wasted, because they afforded an opportunity of observing the English character at its most typical and characteristic. Indeed, my three bridge-playing friends were in many ways so typical of the class from which Oxford was then almost exclusively recruited, that perhaps I could not describe it better than in terms of my meetings with them on that first, and on many subsequent occasions.

Bridge is a game that very quickly exposes a player's temperamental virtues and vices and my three companions that first evening were no different in this respect than any other three card players chosen at random. These three, however, were not chosen at random, for they were all three the carefully selected products of a social system which bred to type as truly and carefully as any scientifically managed racing stud. This is not to say that it suppressed individual variations. Rather, they were encouraged, but only so long as they did not interfere with the preservation of the species. But by some mysterious social process, akin to the bio-chemistry of genetic inheritance, individual variations were so modified and transmuted that in the end it was the characteristics not of the individual but of the type that were dominant.

My three companions were all scholars of the college, and all came from the very best public schools. I do not know what motive had encouraged that first invitation. Perhaps it was curiosity, as in some curious breed of animal they had never previously encountered; or perhaps they had simply taken pity on my isolation, because there was a genuine kindness in their welcome, which, however, took the form of taking it for granted that we were all exactly like each other. Very early in the evening, I realized that they had so much in common in the way of social background, education, mutual friends and shared experiences that they were able to talk in a kind of conversational shorthand, in which a large part of their meaning was unspoken and suppressed; they were like the tips of three icebergs projecting from a vast ocean in which the greater part of them was submerged. Later, I learned to recognize this as a characteristic of a certain class of Englishman, who, because he plays, or played, a dominant part in English society, is often taken by the foreigner to be the type of the Englishman as such and judged alternatively to be mysterious, rude or arrogant. Yet it is not mystery, or rudeness or arrogance which dictates his behaviour; it is a rather topsy-turvy kind of politeness, which assumes that whatever is known to themselves is known equally to all and has no need of explanation.

Indeed to me the conversation that evening was, by reason of the density of its implications and unspoken assumptions, almost unintelligible. A large part of it centred on comparisons of their experiences at school; my knowledge of public-school life was confined to the novels of Talbot Baines Reed and the adventures of Billy Bunter,* but Greyfriars seemed to provide no kind of model by which to judge their gossip about Winchester or Eton.

Equally mysterious, and disconcerting to me, was the assurance and confidence with which they faced the present and the future; the element of chance, of the unexpected, seemed to have been eliminated from both. One intended to enter the Civil Service, and preferably the Treasury, and it did not occur to him or to anyone else that a good classical degree might not be the best possible qualification for such a career. Why should it? For nearly a hundred years it had been taken for granted that the classics provided the best possible preparation for administering the nation's financial affairs and there was no reason for thinking that this would be any less true in the future than in the past.

A second had chosen the Sudan service; the sands of the desert had for him the glamour and romance of empire, and if he had any doubt about the future it was merely whether he would get a blue at hockey, because the colonial service regarded some form of athletic distinction as an advantage in governing coloured peoples. He had not considered the possibility that, within his own lifetime, there might no longer be an Empire to govern. With boyish enthusiasm he saw himself in the Sudan following Gordon and Kitchener across the desert to bring civilization to the Fuzzy-Wuzzies. A third was interested in becoming, by way of the bar, a Conservative politician, and proposed to devote much of his time to the activities of the Oxford Union. As for me, I had not the slightest idea of what I intended to do or be, and indeed it seemed to me very possible that no one would ever be likely to give me any kind of useful employment. After all, back in Wales there were thousands of better men than I to whom life offered no prospect except the bread line and the dole.

All three of my friends that evening were well-educated, intelligent and able. They had been well-taught at school and what they under-stood they understood very well; what they did not understand in-cluded almost everything which would change the world in their lifetime. They took it for granted that, with a moderate degree of application, the highest offices in the state, the law, administration or business were theirs for the asking, except that business still had something of its old, ugly, connotation of *trade* and was not really a proper occupation for a gentleman. The strange thing was that, so far as they themselves were concerned, their assumptions proved to be correct. Despite economic collapse, wars, revolutions, nothing did in fact happen to them to frustrate their hopes and ambitions, and the careers they proposed for themselves were in fact the careers they successfully followed for most of their lives.

They were, I later realized, a very representative cross-section of John Maynard Keynes's 'great capitalist class' which in the nineteenth century had made Britain, and to a large extent the world, what they were, and at that moment it appeared that it would continue to do so for the foreseeable future.* It is true that, by birth, temperament and inclination my three bridge-playing friends were conservatives. But in other rooms in New College, or elsewhere in Oxford that night, there were other young men who were socialists, and who shared the unconscious assumption that by some in-built providence which worked in favour of the products of Oxford and Cambridge they too belonged to the governing class; curiously enough, some thirty-five years later they also proved to be right. Political differences between undergraduates might be large, even sometimes violent; but in their underlying belief that the world was theirs for the asking, they were alike as eggs from the same basket.

To me, however, it would have seemed incredible at that time that so bland a certainty about the future would in fact turn out to be justified. The particular version of socialism which I professed was an extremely confused and incoherent one. So far as ideas went it was largely derived from Marx, William Morris and George Bernard Shaw; emotionally it was deeply coloured by a kind of naïve industrial populism, based upon an intense admiration for the South Wales miners and an acute sense of what seemed to me the injustices which they suffered in their lives and in their work. If I had been asked what I wanted or hoped for, and if I had answered truthfully, I think I would have said that it was a world governed by the South Wales Miners' Federation.* My new friends' expectations from life, based upon the prescriptive right to power and privilege of the class to which they belonged, were an offence to everything I believed, which was roughly that some day soon everything would be made anew and that in this glorious apocalypse I too might find a place amongst those who on the appointed day would arise as if transfigured from the dead. For I had an incurable habit of thinking in images and if anything this grew upon me at Oxford, because as an undergraduate I discovered a love of painting and in particular of the Italian and German primitives which I had been able to see in the Ashmolean and, on my rare visits to London, in the National Gallery. Admiration for Proust had made me read Ruskin, and after him, Berenson and Burckhardt. Visual images further confused my intellectual processes, if such they could be called. Revolution presented itself to me as in some *quattrocento* vision in the Biblical imagery which I had learned in the chapel,* in the shape of men and women who, out of great tribulation, and from the pits and valleys of Wales, had come to History's great seat of judgement. *Die Weltgeschichte ist das Weltgericht!** I could not think that the verdict could now be long postponed nor that it would be given in favour of those who, from Oxford, looked forward so confidently to the future.

Of course, I would not have confessed, even to myself, that my socialism was so coloured by such childishly apocalyptic dreams, as if it were made up out of those coloured lithographs which illustrated the text of our Welsh Bibles. I regarded myself as a strictly rational being, whose political beliefs were based on science and hard fact and might even have formed a proper subject for an essay for my tutor. But in reality they were the product of a part of me I did not understand, and hardly cared to enquire into, and this being so, in argument or debate they left me with feelings of irritation and frustration, as if the real meaning of what I wished to say escaped me, and always would escape me, however hard I might try to put it into words.

No such doubts or frustrations, I think, afflicted my bridge-playing companions and indeed, to the eye of a stranger and newcomer, one of their most striking characteristics was a certain complacency, as if even so early in life they already knew exactly who and what they were and what they would become and saw no reason to be dissatisfied with the knowledge. For me, this conferred an air of mystery on them which was almost certainly a product of my own imagination. I saw them like fishes moving slowly and sedately within a transparent tank, lazily stirring its weeds and grasses with their fins and staring out through its glass walls with eyes that were blind to everything except what went on within. Later, as I came to know them better, I used sometimes to feel a sense of anger that nothing had ever happened, nothing perhaps might ever happen, in spite of all my hopes, to ruffle their assurance; but even at that first meeting I also felt a sense of disappointment because I knew I could never share with them any of the ideas and feelings which had so occupied my mind in my later years at school.

There seemed to be lacking in them some principle of the imagination which was all that I valued at the time, and which somehow I wished to see translated into reality. They had seen a great deal more of the world than I had, and, to judge by their conversation, the future seemed to offer them wider opportunities than were open to me; yet somehow I felt assured that whatever happened to them, however unexpected or surprising it might be, it would lose all of its particular essence by being translated into the forms and categories by which their minds were circumscribed.

This seemed all the more likely because I could see no evidence that their ideas had ever ventured beyond the limits approved by their parents and their schoolmasters. When I had the opportunity to wander round the room and look at its books and pictures and ornaments it was quickly clear that one could not expect to find anything that would not have satisfied the conventional taste of twenty-five years earlier; some Greek and Latin texts, *A Shropshire Lad*, school groups, photographs of Mummy and Daddy. There was nothing to suggest that in the interval there had been a revolution in ideas and in tastes, nor indeed was there any reflection of it in their conversation, which, apart from the formal jargon of the bridge table, consisted chiefly of gossip about people I didn't know, reminiscences of school which I did not understand, and accounts of holidays abroad in places where I had never been.

Yet despite my disappointment, I could not deny to myself that I had found the evening agreeable. It was a relief from loneliness, all the more acceptable because of the genuine friendliness of my new acquaintances' welcome, their general assumption that my being there at all made me of their own kind. If they talked of matters of which I knew nothing, it was not in order to exclude me but because they took it for granted that they were as familiar to me as to themselves. Otherwise, what was I doing at Oxford at all?

I should not have found it at all easy to answer that question myself. It was rather as if I had joined a club without realizing what I was doing. But fortunately the question never seemed to arise because, as time passed, I found myself too preoccupied with the distractions Oxford offered to wonder whether, as far as I was concerned, they served any good purpose. Indeed, the initial disappointment I had suffered did not last. Later, I made friends who shared my own interests, and widened and deepened them, and in this sense at least Oxford did not disappoint me. They varied as widely in temperament and intelligence and character as people do anywhere else; but what gave them, for me, an added fascination was that they also, in all their variety, displayed so clearly the marks of the English ruling class from which they all sprang; indeed, their individual differences seemed only to emphasize its almost infinite ramifications and complications. A youthful, rebellious left-wing poet, at odds with every social and sexual convention, nevertheless did not fail to display, in all his personal dealings, the native shrewdness and powers of calculation of the Jewish banking dynasty from which his money derived. An embryo musician,* who neglected all his studies to devote himself to Schoenberg and Webern, and to passionate homosexual affairs, still had about him the faintly clerical air of the cathedral close in which his parents and grandparents had lived. Indeed the extravagances, personal and intellectual, in which so many of my friends indulged were in some respects simply a kind of holiday, an interval between childhood and manhood, before they reverted for ever to the social or hereditary type to which at heart they belonged. Bertrand Russell once defined a gentleman as someone whose great-grandparents had £1,000 a year. In this sense, all my friends at Oxford were gentlemen, and they bore the marks of it inescapably, just as I did not.

'You never know what anyone's really like until you've met his brother,' someone once said to me; he meant that, in most cases, differences of personality are superficial compared with the underlying similarities which are the product of social and family environment. And in this sense my friends and acquaintances at Oxford could truly be said to have belonged to one large family, which, however many and varied its branches, impressed upon all its members certain distinguishing marks which they all shared, just as every Spanish Hapsburg shared an hereditary tendency to haemophilia. For the same reason, there operated in them a certain principle of exclusiveness towards all who, whether by descent or adoption, did not share the same tribal affinities. The little world of Oxford, though within its own limits it offered the most generous opportunities for the development of the individual, nevertheless excluded far more than it embraced.

As time went by, I began to feel a kind of dissatisfaction because, just as Oxford had once seemed to offer a wider world than Wales, so it began to seem that beyond its walls there lay even larger possibilities, which might indeed be a jungle as compared with its cultivated garden, but where nothing survived except at the cost of a struggle against which Oxford offered all too adequate a protection. My dissatisfaction was muted because of the generosity with which Oxford opened its arms to me. It was not the individual which she excluded but only the social and intellectual forms which were not compatible with her own assumptions. From one point of view it was a closed city; but from another it was an open-ended one, in the sense that anyone might enter it who had the means and the wish to, and Oxford made his entry easy, with all the grace of a bountiful mother who, already endowed with plenty of children of her own, is always happy and willing to adopt more. The Oxford of my day was certainly the creation, in many ways a beautiful one, of a highly of a highly developed class system; but it was also a gate which was open to anyone who had the necessary entrance ticket.

It was also the corridor by which the ticket holders might pass, on favourable terms, into the adult world for which Oxford was a preparation. They would become civil servants, judges, politicians, bankers, soldiers, dons, doctors, scientists, schoolmasters; they were officer cadets in the great army of legislators, administrators and executives required to rule Britain and its empire, which still covered a third of the world's surface. There was even room in the system for writers and artists, and some of my friends, and those I liked the best, had already decided that this was to be theirs; they did so with an assurance which amazed me that for them also society would provide. Nor did those who, out of natural idealism, had formed the hope, and the intention, of changing, even overturning, society, feel excluded from its benefits;

somehow they assumed that society itself would provide them with the means of achieving its own reform, and that the labyrinth of the British constitution had its own signposts which would lead them to the minotaur they wished to slay.

There was another confidence which my contemporaries shared. It was the confidence that the adult world which they were soon to enter would essentially reproduce the pattern of relationships which they had learned at Oxford, and that among them the personal connections they had formed at Oxford would continue to play an important part. Society would continue to bring them together, their paths in life would continue to cross, and this in itself would be part of the machinery through which society would exercise its functions. It was a justified assumption because Oxford foreshadowed the adult world as an embryo foreshadows the grown man; all the elements were there which would later be operative in the society which my contemporaries would administer together. Of course, not all expectations would be fulfilled. Some would rise higher than others, and it was a popular after-dinner pastime to compose lists of those most likely to succeed; the laws of probability made it statistically certain that many of those at Oxford then were bound to succeed greatly and it was only a question of picking out whom the wheel of fortune would carry highest.* Others would falter by the wayside, some would sink into decent obscurity. But somehow it was always assumed that all would continue to exist on the same terms of easy familiarity as they had learned at Oxford, that the channels of communication established there would always remain open, that friendships once founded would never quite fail, and that the fine web of relationships of which Oxford was the centre would always permit even them some degree of influence on the society of which they were the privileged class.

I do not know whether it was simply my origins and upbringing, or something else in me, which prevented me from making the same confident assumption about my own future. Perhaps it was the latter, because in the case of my brother I could see no reason why, having proceeded from Aberystwyth to Cambridge, he should not continue his progress to an assured place in the English Establishment. There was a sense in which I loved Oxford; but it was more like a passing infatuation than a lifetime's affection. With the best will in the world, I could not see myself at home in the world to which Oxford was the natural entry; the trouble was that I could not see myself at home in any other either. On the whole, it seemed to me that chance, luck, Providence or misfortune had led me to Oxford, without much collaboration from me, and that I should do better to trust whatever

mysterious power had been at work than to interfere with its operations by any initiative of my own.

Such a view was all the more persuasive because the will, it seemed,
was a faculty in which I was almost totally deficient. It showed itself, at
most, only in a stubborn determination to have my own way in anything
that concerned my own pleasure, but it was apparently incapable of
implementing any coherent or consistent plan for the future. It may
have been some vestigial remains of my father's Augustinian theology
which so convinced me that no deliberate purpose of mine would have
any effect on what happened to me; I looked on myself as the child of
some inscrutable power compounded of grace and chance, a ball on
some cosmic roulette wheel on which the same number never turned
up twice. Sometimes I had the curious sensation that the most I could
do was to bet on where it would fall next, without any power of
affecting the result. Nor was I particularly anxious to, though some
rudimentary sense of self-preservation warned me that I should be
making some kind of preparation for the future. My own expectations
varied with whether at any particular moment euphoria or depression
was in the ascendant. In moments of elation, which were many, I felt I
could not do better than to trust in the luck which had carried me to
Oxford; in moods of gloom, which were no less frequent, I felt that
whatever turn the wheel of fortune should take next, it could only be for
the worse; in either case, I felt, there was nothing I could do about it.

Thus I felt that my existence at Oxford was a strictly provisional and
transitional one, in the sense especially that neither Oxford nor the
society which had produced it could provide any settled habitation for
me. This was an all-pervading sense, that applied to every aspect of life
at Oxford; but it was accentuated by one particular aspect which more
than anything else distinguished it from anything with which I had
hitherto been familiar.

There were very many things which at that time made Oxford a very
different place from the world outside its walls; ease, comfort, freedom
from material pressures, intellectual opportunities, friendship, access
to almost any of the pleasures which most satisfied one's tastes. These
were genuine privileges, even luxuries, and one was lucky to enjoy
them; one would have been ungrateful indeed if one did not. But it had
one distinctive feature which, for me at least, almost cancelled all its
other advantages. For Oxford was at that time, in a way it has long
ceased to be, an almost exclusively male society, from which the *ewig
Weibliche* was totally absent, both in the spirit and the flesh, and this
made life there even more abnormal, one might even say unnatural,
than it would otherwise have been. Women of course did physically

exist there, both in the town and, on its dim outskirts, in the women's colleges, but in the life of the university they exerted little or no influence; so far as most undergraduates were concerned they might just as well not have existed.*

This was not so much through force of circumstances, but as a matter of choice. Women undergraduates were indeed few in number at that time, but it was not so much their number, or lack of them, which counted. It was that they were second-class citizens in the hierarchy of the university, whose activities, whether serious or frivolous, were organized entirely for the satisfaction of masculine tastes; except, that is to say, of that one taste which in most men, particularly young men, is one of the most dominant and powerful.

In Oxford, on the other hand, it seemed to be almost entirely in abeyance, as if, for most undergraduates, normal biological laws had been for the time being suspended. In this sense, Oxford was for them merely a continuation of the conditions under which they had lived at their public schools, where, willy nilly, their emotional and sexual instincts could find no personal objects of satisfaction except in each other. For most of them, by the time they came to Oxford, this had come to seem the natural condition of human life and it was natural that at university they should, like well-conditioned animals, persevere in the habits and the attitudes to which they had been trained at school. Nor, on the whole, was there anyone to teach them otherwise. Universities are not designed to be schools of sexual therapy; and in any case dons, for the most part, were then precisely those who as adults remained happy with the same range of emotional satisfactions that they had known as schoolboys and undergraduates.

It might be said that most undergraduates, and their elders, at Oxford in those days lived in a state of sexual infantilism. It pervaded the entire life of the university, giving it a peculiar colour and flavour of its own, which accentuated even further the differences between life within and without its walls; it was as if some thousands of young men lived under conditions which, in one important respect at least, approximated to those of the nursery. What was more remarkable was that to most of them this was quite imperceptible, as if, in such matters, they were colour blind or their taste buds had not developed. To them, the notion that men should live without women was perfectly natural; to some, even, it was the only acceptable way of life. It was the idea that women are an essential and indispensable part of a man's existence which struck them as abnormal and bizarre; indeed, as an undergraduate, I was sometimes rebuked for deliberate eccentricity or gross exaggeration when I ventured to assert such a proposition, which to me was self-evident.

Yet men, especially young men, do not deprive themselves of the company of women without undergoing a modification of their whole nature, often in ways so subtle and pervasive that they themselves are hardly aware of it; in particular, their capacity for feeling and emotion is turned upon each other and not, as they would be otherwise in the great majority of cases, towards members of the opposite sex. I do not mean by this that men without women necessarily become homosexual in the direct and simple sense of that word, nor that most under-graduates in my time were homosexual in that sense, though a large number were and almost aggressively so;* perhaps indeed it was they who had the best of it. I mean rather that under such conditions what men love and admire most is formed in the male image and not its opposite, that their ideas, their affections, even their intimations of good and evil are exclusively expressed in the masculine gender, and that it is in the man, that is to say themselves, that they find their deepest aspirations realized. For them, the Fall was an event that only happened to Eve; only she was expelled, and Adam was left to enjoy the garden alone with the serpent.

Some such version of the Biblical legend might have served very well as a description of Oxford in my time. Oxford, with its towers and spires, its cupolas and pinnacles, its river-bounded meadows and elm-tree walks, its ancient stones that crumbled and flaked beneath one's fingers, might very well have served in those days as an image of Paradise, but it was a paradise which was men's exclusive preserve. It followed that their pleasures and passions were directed towards each other, and this gave what might well have seemed to others an exaggerated intensity to the experiences which they shared together. Perhaps this helps to explain the kind of golden haze which envelops, or once enveloped, many people's reminiscences of Oxford, as a kind of land of lost content in which, given the peculiar nature of their education, they did what came most naturally to them. It was what came after that seemed a fall from grace.

In some cases, of course, this attitude took an overtly sexual form, and they were the more conspicuous because they included some of the most gifted of my contemporaries, both among undergraduates and dons. For many, homosexuality was simply a fashion; to the committed homosexual is was a creed and a cult, with its own rituals which were hidden from the profane. It was also a standard which could be brandished bravely in the great war between the Hearties and the Aesthetes, it was the flag of culture as opposed to philistinism, and it was also a symbol of that intense cultivation of personal relations in which Oxford placed so much faith. Moreover, it was a flag of rebellion; to be homosexual was at once the easiest and most flagrant way of affronting the moral values of Bird's Custard Island and for many it served the same purpose as drug addiction today.

But such standard-bearers of the cause of homosexuality, precursors of the hippies and dropouts of today, were, like them, very much in a minority. What was characteristic of the Oxford scene was the prevalence, even in those who were least aware of it, of an attitude of mind and heart which took it for granted that the deepest emotional satisfactions were only to be found in a masculine society, and that any others could never be anything better than second-rate; it was an attitude which not only conditioned their behaviour at Oxford, their relations with each other, their ideas of what is best and worst in the world, but continued to do so long after they had gone down and had become the most respectable of citizens and fathers of families. Whether such an attitude is properly to be called homosexual I do not know; but it was an attitude which profoundly affected an entire generation of middle-class Englishmen of the governing class, and even today has not entirely vanished.

It was all the more striking to me because, as I thought, I could trace a clear relationship between this underlying prejudice in favour of the male, which was characteristic of the most normal undergraduate, and the more overt and ostentatious manifestations of homosexuality. These, in the more extreme cases, sometimes took the form of affectations in dress which clearly proclaimed their wearer's sexual loyalties, or in a particular manner or gesture, gait and physical comportment whose significance was no less unmistakeable. Sometimes they combined to create creatures who paraded through the streets of Oxford like brightly plumaged birds of paradise, attracting the attention of all by their flamboyant costume, their high-pitched cries, their quick, elusive movements. But these after all were only the outward and visible signs of an inward emotional commitment which was shared by Oxford society as a whole, even though the great majority of undergraduates would never have dreamed of indulging in such extravagances. It was a commitment which in Oxford's sister university of Cambridge had, under the influence of a long and distinguished line of teachers and moralists achieved the status of philosophy, explicitly in the writings of G. E. Moore and implicitly in the novels of E. M. Forster, and more especially in Forster's famous pronouncement: 'Only connect.'* It could be said that those two words, so seductive in their simplicity, so misleading in their ambiguity, had more influence in shaping the emotional attitudes of the English governing class between the two world wars than any other single phrase in the English language.

Oxford at the end of the twenties had no such great names to give moral authority to its predilection for the male over the female principle, or its belief that intense personal relations between persons of the same sex embody one of the highest moral values. Compared with Cambridge, Oxford was intellectually indolent in its approach to such matters; practice, not philosophy, was what it was interested in. But the two universities were bound together by an elaborate network of relationships, historical, institutional and personal; both drew their undergraduates from the same social class; and both sent them out to rule England and its empire imprinted with the belief that life would never have anything better to offer than the kind of relationships they had enjoyed with each other at the university.

I do not know whether such an education so narrowly based upon class and the domination of the male worked for their own good or, later, for the good of the country and the empire which to all intents and purposes they governed and administered up to the end of the Second World War. The history of England between the wars suggests that on the whole it did not. But I certainly derived far too much pleasure from the company of my friends at Oxford to wish that they should have been otherwise than what they were, or that education had made them different. But they came at the end of a long historical and intellectual tradition, itself the product of very exceptional social conditions, which at that moment was very rapidly running into the sands. It was not, I think, on the whole a good thing that young men designed and destined to form the executive and governing class of a great country should have received their higher education at institutions which were a combination of a monastery and a nursery. In this particular respect, Oxford, and Cambridge also, at the end of the 1920s had advanced very little beyond the Middle Ages. Its products were still, as then, in essence clerks whose future lay in supplying church and state with the staff required to operate their administrative machines; and in effect they still, as then, subscribed to the rule of celibacy which applied to the medieval clerk. Only that rule no longer derived its authority from the love of God, but, rather, from the kind of love which David had for Jonathan, a love surpassing the love of women; and to that kind of affection, in all its many variations, they attached an importance and value which were as near absolute as anything could be.

As for me, my instincts rebelled against such a system of values, even though I might accidentally profit by it, and I felt that in such a society there was not likely to be much of a place for me. It was not that I regarded it with horror or aversion. It was simply that I believed it rested on false intellectual and emotional foundations, and somehow this seemed to involve yet another division between my friends and myself. Public schools were bad enough; it was even worse if they were to provide the standards for adult life. I felt reinforced in my instinctive feeling that Oxford was not for me nor I for Oxford.

III

I am aware that what I have written applies almost entirely to an Oxford which no longer exists, and that the Oxford of today bears little or no resemblance to Oxford as it was then, any more than I do to the young man I was as an undergraduate; both might be said to have died together. So far as Oxford is concerned, much of the change was due to the great expansion of the university which took place after the Second World War, and not less to social and industrial changes which have totally destroyed that sense of intimacy and privacy which was once an essential part of Oxford's charm, just as they have totally transformed the character of its academic population. But the change had begun even before I myself ceased to be an undergraduate, and the Oxford of the 1930s was already not the place that I had known when I first went there in 1928.

The distinguishing mark of Oxford when I first knew it was a kind of enlightened pursuit of pleasure. This gave Oxford a certain air of frivolity and gaiety which was in itself highly agreeable; but it was also compatible, in those for whom ideas were the greatest of all diversions, with a genuine devotion to learning for its own sake. Indeed, I am not sure that true learning, so opposed to what is today called research, can flourish in any other kind of air. This particular combination of frivolity with the pursuit of knowledge was something in which young men, according to their capacity, were very privileged to share, because it was unlikely that they would ever come across it again anywhere else; it had something of that *douceur de vie* which Talleyrand ascribed to the *ancien régime* before the French Revolution. It was the product of the late last flowering of an empire which was already in decay, but was still strong enough and wealthy enough to support a class which was largely immune to the pressure of material care and could afford to devote itself to pursuits which from one point of view were an extreme form of conspicuous waste but from another were essential to a humane and liberal education. Its existence was made possible by the vast wealth accumulated by Britain in over a century of triumphant material progress; the hoard had been appreciably diminished by the

First World War, but it was still very large and still sufficient to maintain Oxford as a kind of seminary/nursery/playground for its privileged youth. Not many of them, at that time, made the direct connection between their privileges and what went on beyond the walls of Oxford; most of them took it for granted that this was as things were and as they would continue to be and, this being so, why should they not continue with the cultivation of their own personal tastes which, consciously in some cases, unconsciously in others, was their main preoccupation at Oxford?

But already, while I was an undergraduate, the first warning shadows, like the first touches of evening, fell across the scene. The first, perhaps, in the spring of 1929, was the collapse of the consider-able financial empire created by the great embezzler Clarence Hatry.* This, though it shook the City of London and some have attributed to it a considerable influence on the great slump that was to follow, made no great impression on Oxford; but it had considerable repercussions among the class which provided Oxford with its recruits, and at least two of my acquaintances disappeared before their time as a result. Of far greater significance, in the Michaelmas term 1929, at the beginning of my second year at Oxford, and shortly before my twentieth birthday, was the great stock exchange collapse on Wall Street, which, with its consequences, was to affect the lives of an entire generation, in ways which would have been unthinkable only a year before. At first it went unnoticed, even by those who, like myself, were supposed to be interested in economics; my economics tutor, in reply to my enquiries, assured me that it was a purely superficial stock exchange phenom-enon, that would have no effect except the healthy one of shaking out the lunatic fringe of the great Wall Street boom. But in fact it was the beginning of the great economic depression of the thirties, which convulsed the capitalist world and led to the triumph of Hitler in Germany and finally to the Second World War.

In such a world there was no room for Oxford as I had first known it. Increasingly, the eyes and minds of undergraduates were directed to events that were taking place beyond her walls, and particularly in Germany, where the Weimar Republic, the home of so many avant-garde experiments in the arts and in morals, was entering its death throes. As the depression deepened, and capitalism seemed helpless either to remedy it or to alleviate the sufferings it inflicted, it trans-formed Adolf Hitler from an *opéra bouffe** Bavarian politician into a world figure of nightmare proportions, and his triumph in Germany was the prelude to a series of political disasters that followed one another with the inevitability of a Greek tragedy. This tragedy was enacted against a background which was occupied by a vast, grey army of workless men, whose existence seemed both to threaten the capitalist system and to make a mockery of it as a method of satisfying human needs. Some of their bitterness and frustration spilled over even into Oxford, when the long shabby columns of the hunger marchers shuffled into the city, to be fed in soup kitchens and put to rest in whatever shelter could be found for them. For many undergraduates, it was the first time that they had ever seen a hungry man with their own eyes.

It is to the credit of undergraduates of a younger generation than mine that, as economic and political conditions deteriorated, they became increasingly concerned with the world outside Oxford and with efforts to avert the catastrophes which lay ahead. In this they followed a humane and generous instinct. It was not from any sense of self-preservation that they flung themselves into political agitation and debate, because they did not really feel that they were themselves directly threatened; it was rather out of sympathy with the victims of the economic depression and the rise of fascism, which made it impossible for the young and generous in spirit to ignore the ugly realities of the world outside. But such feelings put an end, perhaps rightly, to the kind of society which had existed in Oxford during the 1920s. Love of the arts, sexual experiment, personal relationships, delight in the many-coloured surface of life, seemed a poor and inhuman response to the sufferings of millions of men and women. Pleasure gave way to politics; aesthetes and homosexuals suddenly turned revolutionaries, political agitation took the place of dinner parties and conversation gave way to polemics. Voices grew shrill, and the masses took the place of the individual as the object of reverence and respect; undergraduates awoke to the fact that even in Britain there were three million men and their families who were near the starvation line and that there actually existed in the world, especially in Germany, bad men possessed by an evil will which could not be constrained except by force. Moral and political indignation persuaded them that the time had come to change the world instead of enjoying it. In the eyes of many undergraduates, Oxford, so encumbered with the remains of a past which had given birth to the horrors of the present, had suddenly ceased to be a pleasure garden and become an ivory tower, whose only function was to provide an escape from the catastrophes of the 'real' world.

In Cambridge, this revulsion against the comforts, amenities, and intellectual delights of the academic *hortus conclusus*★ was even more violent than at Oxford, just as its analysis of its system of values had been more refined. There, some of the brightest and best of their generation, like Guy Burgess or Kim Philby, totally committed themselves to forms of political action which in fact were even worse than the evils they were intended to avert, with results which, many years later, were to astonish the world. Oxford, on the whole, did not go as far as this; even in her conversion to politics there remained, for most of the converts, a certain residue of dilettantism, of worldly wisdom, which forbade total sacrifice or martyrdom. But even at Oxford political commitment, however muddle-headed or even farcical it sometimes was, went far enough to destroy the university as I first knew it. The left-wing political generation of the 1930s may not have had much success in their efforts to change the world; but they certainly transformed Oxford out of all recognition.

IV

When at length the time came for me to go down from Oxford, it found me in a mood compounded of gloom and relief; gloom, because I had no idea of what was going to happen to me, and felt a certain apprehension that it might not be very pleasant, certainly nothing like so pleasant as the three years I had just passed; relief, because I had begun to feel that the time for those particular pleasures was over, and that beyond Oxford events were taking place which somehow made them look trivial and unimportant.

On the last day of term, when the college was already deserted, I walked with a friend round New College gardens. His future was decided, and after the vacation he was proceeding to Paris to study for the entrance examination for the diplomatic service. The evening was grey and chilly, with that air of damp and melancholy which seems to settle in Oxford at almost any season of the year. A cold wind ruffled the branches of the trees; it seemed as if autumn had already come. My final examinations were over and I had the sense of having performed very indifferently; twinges of conscience for so many wasted hours, guilt at having disappointed my parents' expectations, afflicted me intermittently like an infected tooth. My own prospects seemed unbelievably bleak and depressing, and those last hours in the garden had a dull note of finality because, however the future might turn out, I was quite sure that it was not likely to bring me back to Oxford. I felt as if I were looking at it all for the last time: the green lawns, the city walls that enclosed the garden, the tree-grown mound on which King Charles had mounted his cannon to bombard Cromwell's army, the little Norman tower of St Peter's-in-the-East where Walter Pater lay buried; I was quite sure that I should not see any of it again.

Of course, I was quite wrong, as my expectations of the future have always proved to be; manic-depressive types suffer such regular alternations of mood that the fears or hopes they form in one stage of the cycle are never, for good or bad, realized in the next one. When the results of my final examinations appeared, I was surprised and pleased to find that I had after all been given a First, though candid friends also informed me that it had been a very close thing. My philosophy tutor* ended his letter of congratulation enigmatically with the words: 'So I hope you have learned a lesson; and the *Right Lesson!*' I was not at all sure what the Right Lesson might be, but the letter effectively disposed of any satisfaction I might have felt at the result. It was quite clear that it was not merit, it was luck, that had been at work.

That summer my mother died,* as if, having sent me to Oxford and received the news of my success, there was nothing more for her to do. It was the worst single thing that has ever happened to me, and it left me dazed and bewildered, as if it were totally beyond my apprehension. Its effect was all the worse because at night, in the neighbouring bedroom, I could hear my father crying out her name in his sleep.

Unless one is a singularly pure character, grief, especially when compounded with guilt, confuses all one's reactions; one does not know how to respond to a situation for which one had deliberately contrived not to prepare oneself. My mother's death, that summer, deprived me of any power to make a rational decision about the future. Without my mother, indeed, the future seemed to be a concept that had no meaning. I simply took what came along, which happened to be an offer of a senior scholarship at New College, which would make it possible for me to return to Oxford for another year to read history. I accepted it rather in the spirit of a doomed man who sees no alternative to execution, for my other scholarships had now come to an end, and I did not really see how I was to survive a year at Oxford on an income of £120 a year. But there seemed nothing else to do, so that having in June said farewell Oxford for ever, I found myself back there once again some three months later, looking for rooms in which to spend the coming academic year.

Once again chance took a hand. My history tutor during my last year was a Fellow of All Souls; meeting me in the street as I pursued my searches, he took me to lunch at the college and suggested I should sit for its fellowship examination, which was to take place shortly.* There did not seem much point in doing so, but he was encouraging and persuasive; in any case, as he said, I had nothing to lose, and even to fail the examination is a kind of distinction of its own. So I followed his suggestion, went through the somewhat bewildering series of trials which All Souls imposes on candidates for its prize fellowships, and on All Souls' Day, November 2, while I was lunching with some friends in my rooms, I was astounded to be waited upon by a servant from All Souls and informed that I had been elected to a fellowship* and would be expected, in my new-found capacity, to dine in the college that night. So it seemed as if Oxford had not yet done with me. There were some children playing the street outside my windows. I collected all the money I had in my rooms or could borrow from my guests and in an expansive gesture of gratitude scattered it from the window and watched the children as they tried to catch the coins as they fell or chased them along the pavement and the gutters.

V

In those days a prize fellowship at All Souls was regarded as one of the greatest gifts Oxford had to bestow, and a sure guarantee of success in whatever career one chose to adopt. When I was elected, the college included among its forty members one archbishop, one bishop, an ex-Viceroy of India, several cabinet ministers, the two brightest luminaries of the English bar, and the editor of *The Times** (an office which had become almost hereditary in the college). I was not the first product of the state system of education to be elected to the college, but I was certainly the first Welsh one, and in Wales itself my election was regarded as a matter for national self-congratulation.* It was a matter of grief to me that my mother was not alive to know it; she would have regarded it as the culmination of all the ambitions she had cherished for me, but it was some compensation that it was a considerable source of pride to my father.

On the other hand, perhaps perversely, to me my election was, and remained, a source of guilt; partly because I thought I detected in it once again the hand of chance or luck, and also because I felt it identified me with a way of life which was opposed to everything which I desired. For I too had succumbed to the wave of radical political feeling which was beginning to sweep through the universities. It confirmed me in the socialist ideas which I had cherished since my schooldays, and now, as the depression deepened, and its consequences became increasingly evident, it began to seem as if any day the hour of revolution might be at hand. The year was 1931, which Arnold Toynbee called the *Annus Terribilis*, when government after government was falling under the impact of the depression; the walls of the capitalist Jericho seemed to be crumbling before one's very eyes.

It seemed absurd, at such a moment, to find oneself safely and comfortably installed at the very heart of the Establishment, all the more so because this meant, in my case, occupying in his absence the rooms of Sir John Simon, then Secretary of State for Foreign Affairs. I used to go through his wardrobe and finger, and sometimes even wear in cold weather, the excellent thick striped flannel shirts in which it abounded. My condition was even worse, it seemed to me, because the college welcomed one, as a junior fellow on such easy and generous terms that they really left one nothing to rebel against; there was only the conviction that the college, with its narrow Hawksmoor towers, its Wren sundial, its beautiful view of the dome of the Radcliffe Camera poised like a marvellous bubble outside its gates, represented the kingdom of this world which was about to be punished for its sins, and which, in any case, it was the duty of any good Calvinist or socialist to reject.

The emoluments of a prize fellow were then £300 a year, with free rooms and a free dinner, and if one chose to drink, as I did, one did so at ludicrously cheap rates which were heavily subsidized by the college. To me this was a fortune, and despite my socialism, it only slightly marred my enjoyment of it that an unemployed family in South Wales lived on 30/- a week. But it was not only the material comforts which were felt as a source of potential corruption. The college was a very small community, of whose members only a very few were at any moment in residence. There were no undergraduates to disturb the *luxe, calme et volupté** of the fellows; one lived as if in some retired country house, its peace only broken by the dim hum of traffic in the High, and sometimes, at night, walking its corridors and staircase while the college slept and outside the moonlight turned to silver the leaden dome of the Radcliffe, one could imagine that one was its sole proprietor and only the dead surrounded one.

It was all the more pleasant because the house was supplied with every facility for the pursuit of learning, even if no one very much bothered whether one made use of them; and because one lived on the easiest and most comfortable terms with its other residents. All of them were older than myself, most of them very much older, and some were men of great distinction and achievement; but all had the gift of treating one as if one were their equal, and a bishop or a cabinet minister listened to one with the same patience and attention as if one were a bishop or cabinet minister oneself. All Souls indeed repeated in an even more concentrated form the same lesson I had learned at New

College; that once accepted by the ruling class there are none of their privileges which they will not willingly and gladly share with you. The only difficulty was that I could not accept myself in such company.

Otherwise, life was very agreeable and to me all the more so because, for two years at least, a prize fellowship seemed to entail practically no duties whatsoever. For those two years, out of the seven for which one was initially elected, it was assumed that one was still continuing a course of initiation into an adult life which had not yet really begun. After all, once a fellow one's future was in some sense assured, there was no need to hurry, there was time to make mistakes and to pursue false scents; the serious business of life could be postponed for a few years longer. In the meantime, as the youngest and most junior fellow, it was my duty to prepare the salad before dinner, and in common room after dinner, as Mister Screw, to decant the port.

Some of this was explained to me when, the morning after my election, and having celebrated it by drinking rather too much the night before, I waited upon the Warden of All Souls in his study.* He might have been taken as a model for a scholar and a gentleman of the old school, to whom all mundane cares were both alien and distasteful, but he was in fact an eminently practical, if slightly idle, man of affairs. A moderate classical scholar, for a time a moderately successful barrister, a moderately good administrator whose motto was above all *pas trop de zèle*,* he was admirably suited to his position and it to him, all the more so because the long Oxford vacations allowed him to spend a large part of his time on his estates in Shropshire; he had the fresh pink cheeks of a country squire who spends many hours in the open air without exposing himself to its harsher elements. I was not sure whether I could not also detect a hint of something slightly sly, almost shifty, in his faded blue eyes.

To me that morning he was kindness itself. He enquired politely about my schooling and my career as an undergraduate, and when I had told him everything I thought it proper for him to know, he surprised me by saying: 'You must have worked very hard.'

My tutor's complaint, it had seemed to me, was precisely that I had not worked very hard, and I was inclined to agree with him; all the same, I was touched by the Warden's perception that perhaps, after all, there had been a good deal of effort involved.

'It's not easy to take the fellowship examination straight after your schools,' he went on. 'What are you thinking of doing now?'

I said that I had very little idea. I had intended to take the history school in my additional year at Oxford, but now that seemed rather pointless.

'I should think a rest would be good for you,' he said kindly.

It had not occurred to me that this was what I needed, but somehow it was pleasant to be told that it was.

'Go abroad perhaps. Look at some pictures. Go to the opera.' The last words were spoken almost wistfully, as if they represented some almost unattainable peak of happiness. I suddenly began to feel that the Warden was a man after my own heart. If there was anything I wanted it was to be away from Oxford and from academic life, to be 'abroad', which seemed to have not so much a geographical as a spiritual connotation. I said that I wanted to go to Vienna and to Berlin, to improve my German and also of course to enjoy those delights which the Warden held out to me as if they were his to dispose of; but also, though I did not mention this, because I thought that in Germany and Austria revolutionary events were at hand.

'A very good idea,' the Warden said heartily. 'Only of course you'll have to pernoctate.' This meant that the statutes of the college required that a prize fellow had to spend a given number of nights in college during an academic year. It was not a heavy burden; if I spent three months in Oxford I could go away for at least a year.

We drank a glass of sherry before we left. It was a cold November day and my head was aching, yet the sun seemed to be shining brightly, as if some totally new prospect of the future had suddenly been revealed to me. And somehow, both on that day and in later years, it seemed to me that Oxford would never again mean to me what it had meant before.

Three

I

In fact, I did not go abroad until later than I expected.* Life was very pleasant at All Souls, and I thought I had better prepare myself for the task I projected for myself in Germany, which was to write a biography of the great politician and demagogue, friend of Marx and Engels, and founder of the German Social Democratic party, Ferdinand Lassalle. I regarded the prospect with some apprehension; I felt that the walls of the academic prison house were beginning to close around me and yet struggled only feebly to escape them. All that could come later, I thought.

It was at the beginning of the summer term of 1932 that I first met a visiting Cambridge undergraduate called Guy Burgess.* He was staying for the weekend with Maurice Bowra, who was then Dean of Wadham and, during my undergraduate life, had probably influenced me more than anyone else at Oxford. I had heard of Guy before, because he had the reputation of being the most brilliant undergraduate of his day at Cambridge, and I looked forward to his visit with some interest.

We met at a dinner party given by Felix Frankfurter who was then a visiting professor at Oxford, and Guy and I immediately made great friends. Indeed, he did not belie his reputation. He was than a scholar of Trinity, and it was thought that he had a brilliant academic future in front of him. That evening he talked a good deal about painting and to me it seemed that what he said was both original and sensitive, and, for one so young, to show an unusually wide knowledge of the object. His conversation had more charm because he was very good looking in a boyish, athletic, very English way; it seemed incongruous that almost everything he said made it quite clear that he was a homosexual and a communist.

After dinner, though it was late, we walked back to All Souls together, and I took him into the deserted smoking room, where we drank whisky together for a long time. At first he made tentative amorous advances, but quickly and cheerfully desisted when he discovered that I was as heterosexual as he was the opposite; he would have done the same to any young man, because sex to him was both a compulsion and a game which it was almost a duty to practise. He went on to talk about painting, and its relation to the Marxist interpretation of history, and about the busmen's strike which he was helping to organize in Cambridge; it seemed to me that there was something deeply original, something which was, as it were, his very own, in everything he had to say.* It was not that the matters he talked about were unusual; by 1932 they had become topics of almost incessant discussion by the intellectual-homosexual-aesthetic-communist young man who was rapidly establishing himself as the classical, and fashionable, type of progressive undergraduate.

To such a young man, Marxism and communism were something to be argued about, debated, elucidated, defended; it was something which lay outside the bounds of his experience, and remained an opinion or a faith to be held with a greater or less degree of conviction. For Guy it was simply a way of looking at the world which seemed as natural to him as the way he breathed. It was a kind of category of thought, like the Kantian categories of time and space, which was fundamental to the way in which he perceived and apprehended the world. This was something which I never met among Guy's, or my, English contemporaries who, during the 1930s, adopted communism as an intellectual creed; somehow there always remained in them an assimilated residuum of their liberal upbringing which was in conflict with the faith they professed. In Guy such a conflict seemed to have been entirely resolved; in this respect at least he never changed through all the years I knew him, so that, whatever the vagaries of his conduct or his professions, I somehow took it for granted that fundamentally he always remained a communist, even if, for reasons of his own, he chose to deny it. Marxism had entered so deeply into him that he simply could not think in any other way. This is a characteristic which I came later to recognize in professional communists whom I met in Germany and Austria, but never, so far as I am aware, in any English ones.

During his weekend visit Guy and I liked each other well enough to make tentative plans to visit the Soviet Union during the summer vacation. For some reason these came to nothing as far as I was concerned, and Guy took as his companion a young undergraduate from Balliol, who was also both communist and homosexual.* He gave me a vivid account of Guy lying dead drunk in the Park of Rest and Culture in Moscow; otherwise I could not discover much of what went on. Guy described to me a long discussion he had had with Nikolai Bukharin, ex-secretary of the Comintern, ex-editor of *Pravda* and later to be executed by Stalin, and treated me to a long and brilliant disquisition on the pictures in the Hermitage. Otherwise I never knew him to talk about his experiences in the Soviet Union, and I do not think they ever affected his beliefs one way or another. It was as if his communism formed a closed intellectual system which had nothing to do with what actually went on in the socialist fatherland. If one had pointed out to him that at the moment of his visit the Soviet Union was recovering from a profound economic crisis and was now entering a period of violent political reaction, he would have regarded it as being, even if true, irrelevant.

Side by side with his political activities, Guy conducted a very active, very promiscuous and somewhat squalid sexual life. He was gross and even brutal in his treatment of his lovers, but his sexual behaviour also had a generous aspect. He was very attractive to his own sex and had none of the kind of inhibitions which were then common to young men of his age, class and education. He regarded sex as a useful machine for the manufacture of pleasure, and perhaps for this reason was very successful in satisfying his appetites. In this he was unlike his friends at Cambridge, who were nearly all homosexual but a good deal more timid than Guy, a good deal more frustrated, and a good deal less successful in their sexual adventures, which on the whole were coloured by sentimental and emotional overtones which to Guy were simply absurd. At one time or another he went to bed with most of these friends, as he did with anyone who was willing and was not positively repulsive, and in doing so he released them from many of their frustrations and inhibitions. He was a kind of public schoolboy's guide to the mysteries of sex, and he fulfilled his function almost with a sense of public service. Such affairs did not last for long; but Guy had the faculty of retaining the affection of those he went to bed with, and also, in some curious way, of maintaining a kind of permanent domination over them. This was strengthened because, long after the affair was over, he continued to assist his friends in their sexual lives, which were often troubled and unsatisfactory, to listen to their emotional difficulties and when necessary find suitable partners for them. To such people he was a combination of father confessor and pimp, and the number of people who were under an obligation to him for the kind of services which the confessor and pimp can supply must have been very large indeed.

I learned all this from Guy himself, who spoke of such activities with a kind of amused candour, from which any sense of shame was entirely lacking; no doubt he thought that such frankness was more likely to provoke my interest than my disapproval. Indeed, he seemed to take a delight in offering one, as if for inspection, the psychological puzzles in which his character abounded. One could not help wondering whether the services he performed for his friends were genuinely given, as they themselves believed, out of altruism, or whether they were the result of some conscious or unconscious wish to dominate. The second alternative seemed the more likely; he saw himself sometimes as a kind of Figaro figure, ever resourceful in the service of others in order to manipulate them to his own ends.

Such a possibility only occurred to me many years after I first met him, when the contradictions in his character and behaviour seemed to have become so acute as to be insoluble. While I was still an undergraduate I had driven over to Cambridge with a young don, for whom the main object of the visit had been to visit Guy, with whom he was at the time in love. When, long after, I reminded Guy of the incident he laughed and said he remembered it very well, and then added: 'And indeed I still have his letters.' I thought perhaps he was boasting; but after a search through the incredible disorder of his rooms he produced a neat little bundle of letters labelled with the name of the enamoured don.

I had known already that Guy never destroyed a letter but had simply put this down as yet another among the many oddities in his character. But that he deliberately preserved them and that somewhere there might exist an enormous accumulation of letters, neatly filed and docketed, from his former lovers had never occurred to me. Certainly it was not affection which had prompted the preservation of this particular bundle of letters; but what other motive could there be? I must confess that for a moment I contemplated with a kind of horrified fascination the power which such a collection might confer upon its possessor and of the jeopardy in which they might conceivably place those who had written them. But then, as so often with Guy, I put the idea aside as far-fetched and exaggerated; the trouble was, I thought, that he stimulated my imagination too much. It was only a kind of magpie instinct which prevented him from destroying even the most trivial piece of correspondence.

II

After that summer, in which I saw Guy frequently, I went abroad, and on my return went to work in Manchester as a leader writer on the *Manchester Guardian.** For the next two years I saw little or nothing of Guy, but I heard of him from friends we had in common and it seemed that the bright confident morning of his undergraduate days had begun to fade. In particular, he had failed to fulfil the promise of a brilliant academic career, or indeed of any particular kind of career at all. In his third year at Cambridge he had suffered a severe nervous breakdown and had taken an aegrotat degree; nevertheless, he returned to Cambridge with the intention of submitting a thesis for a fellowship at Trinity. At this point he was still an open and active member of the Communist party; shortly afterwards, however, in circumstances of great publicity, even scandal, so far as the confined world of Cambridge was concerned, he quarrelled ostentatiously with his communist friends and even his more liberal-minded ones, and left Cambridge for London.

The effects of Guy's rupture with the Communist party reflected very clearly the peculiar condition of the English intellectual Establishment. To be a communist, with the declared intention of subverting and destroying the fabric of existing society was to occupy a respectable, and respected position; the difference between a communist and a liberal was merely one of those differences of opinion which arise between the best of friends and which both find mutually stimulating. The underlying assumption was that both shared the same humane and enlightened purpose, and that only questions of method were at issue; so that when, for instance, Stephen Spender wrote a book called *Forward from Liberalism*,* it was regarded as perfectly natural that the forward movement should be in the direction of communism. Indeed, the communist in certain respects commanded the admiration, and almost the envy, of the liberal, because he was willing to risk more in the cause to which the liberal was committed; it was almost as if, by a curious inversion of Marxism, the communist in England had come to represent the most advanced and militant section, not of the proletariat, but of the liberal and progressive middle class. And in fact this is in most cases what he did represent, and perhaps this was the final reason for the failure and eventual disruption of the entire left-wing intellectual movement of the 1930s.

To apostasize from communism, on the other hand, was not merely to reject the cause of the proletarian revolution; it was to reject also the progressive purposes which the liberal shared with the communist and which he felt, rather vaguely, that the proletariat might one day help him to realize. And somehow it also besmirched the image which the communist had succeeded in imposing on his liberal collaborators as a man of superior moral integrity, as the fighter who is always in the front line, unhampered by the bourgeois inhibitions and reservations by which the liberal was afflicted.

Thus it was felt that when Guy reneged on communism he did not merely betray his own cause; he disgraced the whole of liberal England and he was ostracized not merely by his comrades in the Party but by most of his friends outside it. He was a man who had fallen from grace, and to some people this was welcome because they felt that he was, in any case, graceless. Various explanations were offered for his conduct, and in the atmosphere of moral indignation which it inspired, not many of them were to his credit. Some said that Guy's sexual life had become so promiscuous as to become a scandal and an offence to the Party which, after all, had long ago abandoned the ideas of sexual morality preached by Lunarcharsky and Madame Kollontai.* Communists said that Guy was, after all, a product of Eton and Trinity, and very conscious of it, spent his leisure hours in the company of the gilded intellectuals of Trinity and King's, and of writers, artists and bourgeois intellectuals, and had failed to bridge the abyss which divided him from the proletariat. He had simply fallen a victim to the seductions of capitalism, and this view seemed to gain in probability when it was rumoured that on leaving Cambridge he had become some kind of a political adviser to the House of Rothschild.* This particular rumour seemed on the face of it improbable, indeed so bizarre that it introduced into Guy's career an element of farce which was to become increasingly prominent as the years went by.

Guy himself, it was reported, said that he had discovered fundamental errors not so much in the theory as in the practice of communism. The Marxist analysis remained true, but it had been misapplied and the Communist party had become a reactionary movement. The progressive forces were in fact on the extreme Right; he had in fact become, so it was said, some strange new kind of Marxist fascist.

I myself had no opportunity to test the truth of these reports. They came to me from afar, and simply made me feel that Guy had suffered some inexplicable change which had transformed him into an entirely different person from the one I knew. In any case, I was not greatly interested. In 1933, convinced once more that everything that was important in the world was taking place outside England, I had left the *Manchester Guardian* and gone abroad, first to Vienna and then to Berlin, where I had every opportunity of watching the progressive forces of the Right in action.* I played at conspiracy with the decimated and demoralized remnants of the German Communist and Social-Democratic parties and talked to storm troopers who were already envisaging a 'second revolution' against Hitler; they gave the impression of a country in which all the progressive forces had been ground ruthlessly to pieces under an iron heel. When, on my return to England, I met Guy by accident in St James's Square I was not in a very receptive frame of mind to listen to a lecture on his new combination of Marxism and fascism. Nevertheless, I accompanied him to a pub near by and I asked him to explain what it was that had so changed his political views. I told him that I thought they were abominable and that he reminded me of those instant converts to fascism in Germany, the *Märzhasen*,* who had jumped on Hitler's bandwagon and earned even the contempt of Dr Goebbels.

I was offensive; I was aggressive; I wanted to quarrel. But he took my rudeness calmly and said that communist colonial policy, especially in regard to India, had convinced him of the incompetence and futility of the Party and the Comintern. Their policy was aimed at revolution and the immediate withdrawal of the British from India; yet the objective interest of the Indian masses required that the British should remain until they had completed their historic tasks there. Only then would revolution become a possibility; the only alternative was that India should fall to pieces and relapse into feudalism. But if communist policy was directed at revolution in India, and to a British withdrawal as a necessary preliminary to it, so also was the policy of the British Labour party, though on different and doctrinaire grounds of national self-determination; so also, though on different grounds, was that of the large majority of the Conservative party, which no longer had the courage to undertake responsibility for India; 'Men like Irwin,' Guy said with contempt; 'they're *always* in favour of surrender, on principle, in any circumstances. They don't believe anything's worth fighting for except the Church of England.' Guy's contempt for Lord Irwin continued when he became Lord Halifax. Years later he quoted to me with approval a comment on him which he attributed to Churchill: 'Halifax has only one principle—grovel, grovel, grovel . . . !'

The only people, said Guy, who really believed in holding India, and had the will to do so, was the Right of the Conservative party, led by Mr Churchill; but the Right was too weak to achieve anything in Britain, where neither the working classes nor the middle classes had any conception of imperial interests which, at the existing stage of capitalist development, were identical with the interests of the colonial peoples. Their only hope of success was in alliance with the extreme Right in Europe, as represented by the German National Socialists and the Italian Fascists, who had no objection to a strengthening of British rule in India so long as they were given a free hand in Europe and the opportunity to expand eastward against the Soviet Union. 'But surely that would mean war?' I said, rather stupidly; in those days, we always said it would mean war whenever we objected to any particular policy.

One must imagine two young men, in the year 1935, sitting in a pub off Pall Mall, drinking, by this time, double whiskies and gravely discussing the fate of the British Empire. It was an absurd enough position, but at the time it was being repeated, in all its absurdity, in some form or other wherever two young men of our particular type of intelligence or folly happened to meet; politics obsessed us as sex and drugs obsess the young today, and sent us on hallucinatory trips like those produced by LSD. I am sure that anyone reading this today will find it very hard to take Guy's arguments seriously; even at the time I did not, and by now I know, as I did not then, that they were invented in order to provide an intellectual defence for a change in his way of life which he had made for quite other and more practical reasons.

Yet considered in themselves they had a kind of mad logic which carried a certain degree of conviction, or could at least be imagined to carry a certain degree of conviction to anyone who was accustomed to Marxist methods of argument and analysis. They were a kind of Marxism-in-the-Looking Glass. And they also carried, in respect to India, overtones of the kind of argument which the Mensheviks had directed against the Bolsheviks in respect to Russia, and more sinister overtones of the arguments by which the German communists had convinced themselves that their greatest enemy was Social Democracy. It was as if Guy, like a deep-sea diver, had plunged into the great ocean of communist dialectics and come up with weapons which would enable him to demonstrate the precise opposite of what he had previously believed and now professed to deny. To me it was a slightly bewildering operation, and yet it had a certain fascination, which was all the greater because his argument was adorned with long disquisitions on the historical role of the British in India, and on the significance of Mr Baldwin and Lord Halifax as traitors who were destined to lead the British Empire to destruction.

The truth is that Guy, in his sober moments, had a power of historical generalization which is one of the rarest intellectual faculties, and which gave conversation with him on political subjects a unique charm and fascination. It was a power which was, I think, completely native and instinctive to him. It might have made him a great historian; instead it made him a communist. He saw historical events as following rational and intelligible principles and as developing according to general laws, and when he talked about politics he demonstrated these laws and principles in action. Somehow this seemed to endow politics with a gravity and dignity which they do not possess when they are regarded merely as a more or less fortuitous series of conflicts between individual wills and ambitions.

My philosophy tutor at Oxford used to tell me that the will is reason acting. It is an absurd definition and not for a moment did I believe it to be true, yet often when arguing with him I had the feeling that it would be far better, for myself and everyone else, if it were. Talking about politics with Guy had something of the same effect on me. He would have said that history was a rational process which we can understand if we wish to and he had the gift of demonstrating this process at work in different historical periods, in different historical events, in certain works of art. I was never able absolutely to believe that these demonstrations, however fascinating, were true; they seemed so often to lead to conclusions which required one to ignore or deny what was going on beneath one's nose. But when I listened to Guy I always felt how much better it would be if his view of history were true than if it were not, and how much more interesting and satisfactory life would be if one knew it was the product of reason and not of chance, whether benevolent or malevolent; how much better one would oneself be if one were oneself a product of reason!

Perhaps Guy's powers of generalization were never more effective than on that day when he was trying to persuade me, for reasons which were thoroughly disreputable and unscrupulous, to accept conclusions in which he did not himself believe. He was so far successful that my bad temper began to vanish, my liking of him began to revive, and I found myself quite willing to listen to his account of what he had been doing to put his conclusions to practical effect. He had become, it seemed, secretary to a member of Parliament who was so far to the right of the Conservative party that it was quite reasonable to call him a fascist.* He also shared Guy's sexual tastes, and Guy's duties combined those of giving political advice and assisting him to satisfy his emotional needs. They had, it appeared, recently made a visit to the Rhineland, where a Hitlerjugend camp had fulfilled their ideals both of politics and of love.

Guy talked about his employer with a kind of genial contempt; he was once again playing his Figaro role of the servant who is really the master, and in describing their Rhineland visit he knew just how to introduce that element of farce which made it absurd rather than distasteful. When he wished, and when he thought it worthwhile, he had an acute insight into people's character and knew exactly how to pander to them; he knew that the best way to please me was to make me laugh, and that day, as we consumed further whiskies, he certainly succeeded. His account of his Rhineland visit, and its extension to the Danube and Budapest, became an immense comic epic, a kind of Nibelungenlied turned into farce; its hero, sailing like Siegfried down the Rhine, was Guy's employer, his head bemused by the servant's elaborately sophisticated defence of fascism and by romantic illusions about German youth which reflected his own more primitive political ideas. Their journey down the Rhine and Danube was interrupted by strange characters who popped up as if from nowhere, like the

Anglican Archdeacon much interested in the affairs of the Orthodox Church, whom Guy claimed to have rescued from a particularly scandalous predicament in Vienna. The story was like one of those eighteenth-century picaresque novels in which one is conducted scene by scene through the criminal world, only in this case that underworld was exclusively homosexual and thereby seemed to acquire a specifically modern flavour.

Was it all, or any of it true? There were incidents, dates, events, persons which seemed to verify it; yet its general character was that of a work of imagination rather than a record of fact. Guy's master undoubtedly existed, and he was certainly an MP, with the tastes which Guy ascribed to him and made use of for his own purposes; whether the Archdeacon ever did, or whether he suffered the absurd mishaps which Guy described, I never knew, and yet in later years I was to hear Guy talk of him to others as if there could be no doubt of his existence* and the scandalous incidents of his pastoral visit to Budapest were a matter of historical record.

I suppose that, on this occasion, Guy succeeded in amusing me so much that I no longer condemned him quite so wholeheartedly for his conversion to fascism. And I was fascinated by the vivid glimpse he gave me of a homosexual European half-world which I knew would be forever closed to me, even if, as I seriously doubted, it had any existence outside Guy's imagination. And yet, amused as I was by our meeting, I nevertheless had no desire to see him any more; dimly and obscurely I felt that something had happened to him which henceforth made any kind of frankness or sincerity between us impossible. If I had been asked what that feeling was based on I should not have been able to say. I should probably have said that it was due to his political volte-face. But at the back of my mind there was the sense that the element of farce in Guy's life had become completely uncontrollable, and that it represented something which was false within, just as some malignant growth may be the symptom of an obscure and profound disturbance of a person's metabolism.

III

In fact, I did not see him again for about a year, which for me was a particularly unhappy one.* For a large part of it I was out of a job. I had resigned the research fellowship I had been given at All Souls and rarely went to the college. I had quarrelled with the girl I was supposed to be going to marry and this mean quarrelling with the friends we had in common. For some months I worked on *The Times*, which was not a very satisfactory experience for either of us. Altogether, I felt a failure and tried to keep out of the way of my former friends; in any case, I was too hard up to keep up with their standard of life. I was in fact very lonely and miserable.

But one day I decided to visit the college again, and in the queue at Paddington station found myself standing next to Guy. He was looking remarkably fresh and spruce; his smile, his curly hair, were as boyish and engaging as ever. He told me he was going to visit some friends in the country, a painter who was married to a particularly beautiful and gifted woman; I envied his gift for acquiring talented and interesting friends and thought how much I should like to be doing just what he was doing. We parted on the platform; I spent a rather unhappy weekend at Oxford and on Monday returned to the flat which I had taken in Ebury Street.

I was surprised when, that evening, I entered a pub on the corner of the street and found Guy standing at the bar. I was also pleased, because I spent so many evenings alone at that time that I dreaded the prospect of yet another one; I was all the more pleased because Guy was once again the charming and amusing companion he had been when I first met him.

He talked about his weekend in the country and what wonderful people his hosts were, especially the wife who, by his account, possessed every beauty, every virtue and every talent which are possible in a woman. 'You really ought to get to know her,' he said. 'She's just the girl for you. After all, you're not homosexual; she's rather wasted on me.' It was just as if he was making me an offer of her; he was in his Figaro role of the go-between, who is all things to all men, and always has something in hand to satisfy every need. I thought rather sadly that there wasn't much in me at that moment which could possibly interest such an exceptional woman; and at the same time I thought how very characteristic it was of Guy to attribute to his friends every possible virtue and charm.

I asked him about his political views, and for a moment he seemed slightly embarrassed, but then he cheerfully refused to discuss the subject, rather like a schoolboy who had committed some peccadillo of which he felt ashamed. But he had given up his post as secretary to the member of Parliament ('He really was *too* absurd') and was now, it seems, acting as a correspondent for various newspapers, though what they were I did not discover. His work took him abroad a great deal; he spoke vaguely of trips to Paris, and as always he seemed to have plenty of money. It appeared also that he had made up the quarrels with his

Cambridge friends which had followed his defection from the Communist party. He spoke much, and with profound, almost exaggerated, admiration of some of them who, even though they might not be communists, had still more not been fascists and had deplored Guy's invention of a Marxist version of fascism. It even seemed that he had abandoned it himself.

I spent a very agreeable and interesting evening with him. We drank a great deal, and I was pleased to discover that he lived just round the corner from me in Chester Square. From then on I saw him constantly, and certainly a week hardly ever passed without our meeting. It was indeed only as a result of such repeated meetings that it was borne in upon me what a fantastic pattern his life followed. The trouble was that as one became aware of the pattern, so also one became used to it, and therefore took it for granted. But when one thinks of it in retrospect, and therefore sees it whole, one finds it hard to believe that such a person as Guy ever existed; it is as if he were some gigantic hoax that life had played on one. It is true, of course, that with hindsight many of the bizarre twists and turns in the pattern of his life become intelligible, in a way that they were not then. The curious thing is that the easier it becomes to understand certain details of the pattern which puzzled one then, the more extraordinary the pattern itself becomes.

How well I remember, for instance, walking round to his flat one fine Sunday morning in summer. It was decorated in red, white, and blue, a colour scheme which he claimed was the only one which any reasonable man could ever live with; white walls, blue curtains, red carpet. But this patriotic décor was completely submerged in the indescribable debris and confusion of the party which had evidently taken place the night before. Guy himself was in bed, in his blue sheets beneath his red counterpane, which was littered with the Sunday newspapers. On one side of his bed stood a pile of books, including *Middlemarch*, which he must have been reading for the twentieth time, *Martin Chuzzlewit*, Lady Gwendolen Cecil's *Life of Lord Salisbury*, Morley's *Gladstone*, and John Dos Passos's *Manhattan Transfer*. These were all favourite books of his, which he read and re-read continuously, and always with the gift of discovering something new in them at each re-reading.

On the other side of the bed stood two bottles of red wine, a glass, and a very large, very heavy iron saucepan filled to the brim with a kind of thick, grey gruel, compounded of porridge, kippers, bacon, garlic, onion and anything else that may have been lying about in his kitchen. This unappetizing mess he had cooked for himself the previous day, and on it he proposed to subsist until Monday morning. As he pointed out, it was economical, sustaining, and entirely eliminated the problem of cooking for the entire weekend; as for intellectual nourishment, what more could one require than the Sunday newspapers, including the *News of the World*, and the books that were piled up beside him?

So there, for a blissful twenty-four hours, he would lie, at intervals eating his gruel and drinking his wine, while around him moved the ghosts of Lord Salisbury and Mr Pecksniff and Lulu Harcourt.* I sat beside him on his bed and we drank one of his bottles of wine while he explained to me precisely why Lord Salisbury had come to back the wrong horse in his foreign policy, and why Mr Pecksniff tells us everything we need to know about Victorian morality; and then I left him and as the day drew on, and the sunshine faded, I felt a slight shiver at the thought of him in his flat high above the square, happy, at peace, with his gruel and his ghosts, as if he were a very particular kind of lunatic in a very particular lunatic asylum of his own.

At about this time my own life took a slight turn for the better, as in 1935 I was made assistant editor of the *Spectator*, for which I was paid £500 a year for three days' work a week and was paid, in addition, for reviewing any books I chose.* This was a considerable improvement in my affairs, and I also fell in love with a girl* with whom all that summer, I was very happy. She had a sharp, almost microscopic, painter's eye and was continually making me see things which otherwise I would have missed, so that when one was with her, in the park, in the streets, in the Zoo, one always came home with a collection of *choses vues*,* like the hard brightly coloured objects which a magpie picks up for his nest. Her own flat was rather like just such a nest, filled with odd pieces of bric-à-brac that had taken her fancy, with paintings and drawings given her by her friends and cut-outs from magazines, and her own bright sharp eye and high clear voice had something which reminded one of a bird. It was with her, one Sunday, that I went down to Southampton Water to spend a day on a friend's yacht and there met Donald Maclean, a young man whom I did not like and thought rather superior, and whom I was only interested in because Guy had talked about him with admiration and had claimed to have gone to bed with him at Cambridge.

I think I would have been totally happy that year, if it had not been for the shadow of politics which fell increasingly heavily upon anyone who took any interest in such subjects. I had enough money, my job left me a good deal of leisure, I was in love, and I was writing a novel. But also the Germans had occupied the Rhineland, in Germany the concentration camps were full, in 1936 the Spanish Civil War began and several friends of mine joined the International Brigade and some were killed. Very often in the evenings I would visit Guy's flat or he would come to mine and we would drink a bottle of Irish whiskey and we would discuss for hours what was happening in Europe.

In such discussions I became aware that Guy's political opinions had undergone yet another transformation. He no longer talked of the natural alliance between British conservatives and German fascists. He was now, as I was, for the Republic in Spain, he was for the Franco-Soviet pact, he was for the Popular Front. And yet the arguments he used for such policies had nothing to do with those which came so easily to me and others like me, which were based primarily on instinct and emotion, even though we might try to give them a show of reason.* Guy's arguments had nothing to do with emotion. They were based on complicated and somewhat cynical analyses of power relationships in Europe, only now they seemed to lead him to very different conclusions from those he had previously arrived at. And he seemed positively to dislike and despise the liberal and humanitarian instincts which led others to the same conclusions as himself.

But since we were now in agreement, had formed as it were a personal Popular Front of our own, it made friendship firmer, even though I sometimes suspected that we made an odd pair of allies and that somehow there was a profound misunderstanding involved in our agreement. When I, for instance, became indignant about the German dive-bombing attacks on defenceless peasants in Spain he would reply coldly that such things were inevitable in a war, and, if it were worth fighting at all, such disasters must be taken for granted; nothing was gained by becoming emotional about them. And when George Orwell and others returned from Spain with somewhat disconcerting reports of the behaviour of the Spanish Republic's Russian allies, he dismissed them as the sob-stories of sentimentalists who willed the end without willing the means and were in effect sabotaging the Republican cause. He was an awkward person to have in agreement with one; so often it turned out that one had agreed about something quite different from what one had intended.

Usually we were alone when we met. I was greatly taken up with my girl, and he with his own sexual adventures, but on occasions when we were both free we made a habit of spending the evening together. Sometimes, however, though much more rarely, he would ask me round to his flat when he had friends there, and at such times it used to strike me forcefully what a very strange collection were gathered in one room together.* There was, for instance, a grossly obese Central European whom I never knew by any other name than Ignatz, who was said to have been a colleague of Béla Kun's in Budapest and to be a correspondent of *Imprekorr*, the journal of the Comintern. There was a clever young English historian, who had a kind of pupil-and-master relationship with Guy, from whom he imbibed the principles of the economic interpretation of history. There was a working-class ex-chorus boy called Jimmy, who for a time lived with Guy in his flat as a kind of servant-valet and was later handed round among his friends. There was a mysterious Englishman who conducted some kind of sales agency in the Balkans and came to visit Guy whenever he was in England. There was an anti-Nazi diplomat from the German Embassy. There was a peculiarly detestable Frenchman, named Pfeiffer, who seemed to me to smell of every kind of corruption and later, to my astonishment, suddenly emerged from what I had assumed to be an indecent obscurity as *Chef du Cabinet* to the Prime Minister of France, Edouard Daladier. There was Kim Philby, a young Cambridge friend of Guy's, of whom he always spoke in terms of admiration so excessive that I found it difficult to understand on what objective virtues it was based.

Any or all of these, or others who added even greater oddity to the company, might be found at Guy's flat. I used to wonder what common quality held them, or rather us, together, for after all I was among them. It could have been said, perhaps, that all were to some degree infected by Marxism, which is a particularly insidious drug to which many unlikely people become addicts. But this was only true about some of them; it was certainly not true, for instance, about the historian,[*] who was by nature and instinct a scholar, even a pedant, and it was even less true about Jimmy and the horrible Pfeiffer, to whom nothing was important except boys and money. It might be said also that the bond was homosexual; but to this again there were exceptions, including myself. In this respect I often felt that I was a fish out of water and indeed that Guy's other friends slightly resented his friendship with so normal a person as myself; the *petit noyau* which Guy had gathered around him had, I felt, certain inner secrets from which I was excluded, and I was not particularly anxious to be initiated into them.

The truth was, I think, that the only real link between the members of Guy's little group was the personality of Guy himself, just as Mme Verdurin's was of her own *petit noyau*.[*] Yet it was not easy to explain his domination over them. Ignatz, for instance, was not an easy person to influence; he was tough, and cynical, and experienced in a much rougher world than most of us had ever seen. And Pfeiffer was the kind of man who would not normally respond to anything except the grossest kind of appeal to self-interest. But none of those men could quite resist the spell which Guy cast on them. It was based partly on genuine intellectual qualities, on his gift for producing original ideas which in his presence seemed extraordinarily fruitful and illuminating but in his absence seemed to wither and fade; they required the force of his personality to make them come alive. Partly it was based on his talent for adapting his own interests to the varying tastes of his friends; for talking about boys to Pfeiffer, about the underworld of politics to Ignatz, about the seventeenth century to the historian, about Dickens to me. But added to all this was the gift of extravagant flattery. Guy seemed to have learned at an early age what most people only accept after long experience; that the thicker flattery is laid on the more palatable it is, for after all, when the recipient has made every reduction from it on the score that it is flattery, there is still left over a substratum of what he can regard as the irreducible truth.

It used to amuse me to observe Guy's power of manipulating his friends, and it was clear to me that on the whole they were chosen precisely because they were willing victims of it. Nor was there any reason to be anything more than amused by it, as by yet another addition to the general spectacle of the human comedy. It would have been absurd that there could be anything serious in the influence of one who was so obviously an anomaly in the social system, so compulsive a drunkard, so completely promiscuous in his sexual life, whose fingernails were so neurotically bitten and filthy, and whose ordinary behaviour was so outrageously and childishly designed to *épater les bourgeois*.* One might as well have taken Mme Verdurin seriously. Yet even so, it was, to me at least, an interesting fact that Guy's influence on his friends was never relaxed; secretly, persistently, it was always there, whether they acknowledged it or not.

And indeed he was the most persistent person in achieving his own ends that I have ever known. If one went to the cinema with him and wanted to see Greta Garbo, while Guy wanted to see the Marx Brothers (and he invariably did want to see the Marx Brothers), it was always the Marx Brothers whom one saw. If one went for a drive in his car, and wanted to go to the country while he wanted to go to the seaside, somehow one always found oneself at the seaside. If one wanted to drink white wine and he wanted to drink red (and he always did want to drink red), it was always red wine that one drank. He was persistent as a child is persistent, who always knows it will have its own way if it is willing to behave badly enough; and Guy always was willing to behave badly enough. And in this persistence there lay a formidable power of the will, which, because of the general disorder and absurdity of his personal life, for the most part went unnoticed.

IV

At about this time, I wrote a long review in the *Spectator* of a rather emotional and sentimental book about the condition of the depressed areas;* it made the rather simple point that the depressed areas were not an isolated phenomenon but were a result of historical conditions which could not be changed except by concerted political action. I thought it was a good review, but Guy praised it in terms which even I thought exaggerated, as if I had suddenly written a masterpiece; he analysed it at great length, showed me that it contained ideas of a scope and interest which I had never suspected, and generally made me feel that I was a writer of great originality and power. This was unusual, because normally Guy regarded my writing simply as a harmless hobby, or a useful means of earning my living, but not possibly of any wider interest.

One evening, when we were sitting in my flat, with as usual a bottle of John Jameson's whiskey on the table between us, he once again began talking about my review, in the same terms of exaggerated respect. Dimly I felt I was being made a fool of, and also that praise of such a kind quite obliterated any real merits the review might have had. Slightly irritated, I said to him: 'I do think it was a good review, but all the same I don't quite see that it was everything you say it was.'

Guy paused for a moment and said: 'It shows that you have the heart of the matter in you.' There was a note of solemnity in his voice which surprised me, and besides, I could not attach any meaning at all to his words. The heart of what matter?

'What on earth do you mean?' I said. A strangely detached expression came over his face, as if for the moment I did not exist and his eyes were turned inwards upon some secret known only to himself.

There is in Sainte-Beuve's *Port-Royal* a description of how M. de Saint-Cyran, before giving spiritual direction to a penitent, fell into a profound silence, as if he were waiting for some inner voice to tell him what to say. He must have looked very much as Guy looked to me at that moment. Abstracted, his eyes oddly empty and expressionless, he looked as if he were considering some immensely important decision, with a seriousness and gravity which were so unusual in him that I began to feel uneasy; it was as if I were seeing an entirely different Guy from the one I had known.

Then suddenly the life returned to Guy's eyes and he said, with the same serious expression: 'There's something I ought to tell you.'

I almost felt relieved. I though I was going to hear some confession about his personal life or perhaps some more than usually scandalous misdemeanour, though I could not quite see what this could have to do with what had gone before.

'What is it?' I said.

'I want to tell you,' he said slowly, 'that I am a Comintern agent and have been ever since I came down from Cambridge.'

I was so surprised that for a moment the words seemed to convey nothing at all to me, and I had to recover myself while I tried to realize their significance. I saw that Guy was watching me with a steady, intent gaze, which after a moment gave place to a look of – what was it? I found it difficult to say, because it so strangely combined expectation and apprehension.

Then I recovered myself sufficiently to say: 'It's not true.'

'Why not?' said Guy. Suddenly he seemed brisk and alert.

'I just don't believe you.'

'Why not?' he said again. 'Why else do you think I've behaved as I have since I left Cambridge? Why should I have left Cambridge at all? Why should I have left the Party and pretended to become a fascist? I hope you didn't believe all that ridiculous rigmarole about India and the conservatives and the Nazis; but I had to invent something to say. They told me that before going underground I must break off all connection with the party as publicly and dramatically as possible, and with anyone connected with it, and try to start a new career of some kind. So I did it. And all that nonsense worked. Do you know, there were some people who not only thought I believed in it myself, but actually thought that it was true. There is really no limit to how stupid people can be.'

'But why are you telling me this?' I said. 'What has it got to do with me?'

He gave me a long look, at once challenging and appraising, then said: 'I want you to work with me, to help me.'

'How can I help you? There's nothing I can do for you.'

'Never mind that. You can leave that to us. The question is, will you do it?'

'I don't know,' I said. 'What could I possibly do to help you?'

'The first thing you'll have to learn is not to ask questions,' he said. 'If you're willing to help, you can leave it to me to tell you what to do.'

'Does anyone else know about this?' I asked.

He was silent for a moment and subjected me again to a long scrutinizing gaze, as if he were trying to come to a decision.

'A few,' he said. 'You don't know most of them, and there's every reason why you shouldn't know. But I'll give you one name, so long as you don't ask for any more.'

I don't suppose he could have named a person who could have

carried more weight with me.* He was someone whom I both liked and respected greatly, and with whom I would gladly have joined in any enterprise. Nor was I alone in my admiration; there was no one I knew who did not praise his intelligence, his uprightness, his integrity. Indeed, he quite conspicuously possessed all those virtues which Guy did not; all they had in common, except friendship, was that both were homosexuals. But it now appeared that they were both also Comintern agents.

'But you must never speak to him about it,' Guy said. I was so surprised and bewildered that he seemed to be speaking as if from some great distance. 'I shouldn't really have mentioned his name to you. It's essential, in this kind of work, that as few people as possible should know who is involved. You must promise never to mention the subject to him.'

So I promised,* and after that Guy did not speak again that evening either about his work or about the part which he appeared to assume that I would play in it. But he did talk at great length of the anguish it had cost him to break with the Communist party and his friends at Cambridge, of how much he had wished to continue working for a fellowship, of what it had meant to him to be despised and denounced by those whom he liked and admired most and how much he envied those open communists who were not condemned to a life of conceal-ment and subterfuge. His account of the sacrifice he had made for his convictions seemed to me both sincere and painful, and it also seemed to me that perhaps the strain of it might do much to explain the extraordinary aberrations and excesses of his private life.

When I awoke the next morning, my first thought was to remember our conversation of the previous evening, and, as if the day then breaking was a very special one after which nothing would be the same again, I tried to acclimatize myself to the extraordinary fact that a friend of mine was an agent of the Comintern. It is perhaps not necessary to explain that the fact did not shock me; in any case, it would take too long, as it would entail writing the history of an entire generation, and also describing once again the appalling political tragedy of the thirties. I was indeed not shocked;* rather, Guy's revelation seemed to provide a genuine and solid basis for my liking and admiration for him, as one who had in the most real sense sacrificed his personal life for what he believed in and, unlike myself, who was merely a political dilettante, had committed himself seriously, professionally, and totally to the tasks of politics, however painful, even repellent, they might be.

The only trouble was that, with Guy about, I could not quite believe it. For after all, what evidence did I have for it except Guy's word, which was notoriously untrustworthy and unreliable. And if it were true that the strain of life as a Comintern agent, the necessity for concealment, for lies, for pretences, might provide an explanation of the tension under which he lived, revealing itself in such orgiastic excesses of drink and sex, might it not equally be true that the story was a fabrication, a mere dream-release and wish-fulfilment of a kind to which he was in any case addicted?

It was hard to see Guy as a hero; easy to see him as a *fantaisiste*. For if his story were true, why should he after all reveal this highly compromising piece of knowledge to me, who as far as I could see could be of no possible help to him and for whom he appeared to have, for the moment at least, no useful employment? Might not Guy's story be one more of his elaborate manœuvres for exercising power over his friends, in this particular case me, for whom it had precisely the romantic quality to which I was most vulnerable? In all Guy's comments on history and politics, illuminating though they often were, or in his accounts of his own adventures, there was a myth-making element which belonged to art rather than sober empirical fact; did not this have precisely the same quality? Did it not provoke in one precisely that willing suspension of disbelief which would endow Guy, in my eyes, with all the romantic virtues of a revolutionary and conspirator, while he himself suffered none of their penalties?

There was of course that one person whose name Guy had revealed to me under so strict an oath of secrecy, who could put all my doubts at rest. But if it were true, as Guy said, that conspiratorial principles demanded that members of an espionage network should have no direct contact with each other, why had he revealed the name to me at all, for under the circumstances it was entirely unnecessary? Except, of course, Guy realized that no other name would have more effect on me in establishing his *bona fides*, as it were, as a Comintern agent.

When I thought about Guy's confession, I felt as if I were trying to solve one of those Chinese puzzles in which one box opens only to reveal another, and not one finally gives up its secret. And just as one box leads one on to open another, so curiosity drove me on to examine one possibility after another, because, never having accepted any statement of Guy's as the plain and unqualified truth, I could not now simply take his word for it that he was what he said he was. The whole thing was too preposterous, and Guy was too preposterous also. Yet somehow, at the same time, I also believed he had been telling the truth.

V

And now it was 1937, and events in Europe began to move very fast towards the disaster which had threatened for so long. That summer I attended a conference of the Writers' International in Paris.* The Writers' International was one of the many front organizations which proliferated from the mind of Willi Münzenberg* as a means of prosecuting the war against fascism, and though it included writers of every variety of political opinion, it was dominated by communists. I was therefore very surprised when Guy said that he would like to come to Paris with me. Why should a Comintern agent, who had advertised so loudly his breach with communism, associate himself in any way with an openly left-wing organization, which he himself must have known to be a communist front; more especially because the conference took place under circumstances of considerable publicity.

But one of Guy's most striking characteristics was a devouring curiosity. He really did not like to think that anything was ever happening anywhere in which he was not in some way involved. And he always like to think, or pretend, that behind every public event that was reported in the news there was a private and usually disreputable story of which he alone knew the secret. It was as if, in reality or in his own imagination, he was always searching for the human vices and weaknesses which might explain any public event and which he might one day have an opportunity to exploit. The Writers' International, which oddly enough had a social as well as a political cachet, attracted him as a candle attracts a moth.

Guy attended several meetings of the conference with me and was extremely outspoken in his contempt for most of the writers who attended it; his contempt extended both to their literary talents and to their political activities, which he regarded as those of well-meaning but muddle-headed amateurs, and in his comments on them there was always the slightly sinister implication that if, in their flirtations with communism, they really understood what they were doing, they would very quickly think better of it.

The only writer at the conference whom he wholeheartedly admired was Theodore Dreiser, then an old man, white-haired, tall and shambling, with the appearance of a middle-western farmer. He addressed the conference at immense length, and unlike most of the speakers, who devoted themselves chiefly to denouncing the evils of National Socialism, or the wickedness of non-intervention in Spain, or appeals for consolidation of the Popular Front against fascism (subjects indeed on which few of them were qualified to speak),

Dreiser confined himself to a dispassionate and yet extremely moving account of the growth of American capitalism as he had known it during his lifetime, and of the society which had given birth to *Sister Carrie, An American Tragedy* and *The Titan*. His address, delivered in his slow, ponderous, American voice, that seemed to reproduce the leaden rhythms of his own prose, plainly bored his audience, because indeed it seemed to have little relevance to the immediate problems of Europe and little of that impassioned revolutionary oratory which came so easily to most of the speakers. It was typical of Guy that it should have inspired him to raptures, for the capitalist system was what passionately interested him, what he understood, what indeed in a strange way he admired. He had for it the same *Hassliebe*★ as Dreiser had. It was not for love of a new Utopian world that he had become a communist; it was because he thought that capitalism was at the end of its tether and could no longer fulfil its historic mission. He felt that it had betrayed him; in Dreiser's attack on American capitalism, through which there breathed a deep nostalgia for an America that had vanished long ago, he saw the counterpart of his own rejection of British capitalism which could no longer serve the interests of the British people and could no longer shoulder the burdens of Empire. His hatred of capitalism was not that of the idealist who condemns it for its sins; it was that of a disappointed and embittered imperialist who rejects it because of its failures. Perhaps for that reason it was all the more profound.

It was equally typical of him that, because first Britain, then the United States, had led the world in the development of capitalism, he regarded them as the only countries which in the long run were of any importance. He had an instinctive dislike, even contempt, for other than Anglo-Saxon countries. He did not speak their languages or read their literature and he regarded their politics as childish; in this respect he combined all the prejudices of an American WASP and an English country gentleman, and was as provincial, as insular, in a sense as patriotic, as a reactionary colonel.

This became evident when one evening he and I dined in the Bois de Boulogne with Dreiser and Louis Aragon. Aragon was brilliant, cultivated, socially *chic*, as only a French communist intellectual can be. He had been converted to communism by way of surrealism, and he looked on communism as the natural heir of all the avant-garde movements in which he had played a part. Fundamentally, he was less interested in changing the world than in shocking it. No one could have been less like him than the slightly uncouth, slow-moving, slow-speaking Dreiser, who beneath his Marxism remained an un-reconstructed

Middle Western populist. Both he and Guy were irritated by the intellectual acrobatics which Aragon performed for our benefit. Like two Anglo-Saxon puritans they regarded him as frivolous and affected and superficial; they thought him too clever by half. Their revenge came when he mistakenly entered on a disquisition on English literature, in which his taste was no more sure than that of any other Frenchman. Then they flung themselves upon him with great Anglo-Saxon swings and uppercuts which he as nimbly avoided, until at length he was borne down by the sheer weight of their attack and Guy was given the opportunity to launch into his favourite dissertation on George Eliot as the greatest of English novelists, which was new to them though far from new to me; yet in its way it was so good that I was always glad to listen to it again.

But what, I thought, is a Comintern agent doing in this *galère*,* delivering Marxist literary lectures at the top of his voice to two well-known communist writers, from whom he differed only in his greater fidelity to the party line? What had been the point of the elaborate cover he had built up for himself, at so much personal sacrifice, if he could abandon it all so lightheartedly? The puzzle seemed to me all the greater the next morning when Guy went gaily off to see the ineffable Pfeiffer, now Daladier's *homme de confiance*.* I was tired of the unending stream of eloquence and rhetoric that flowed through the conference hall and had taken the day off. I waited for him in a bistro near the Arc de Triomphe, and when he returned from his meeting he was bubbling over with gaiety and enthusiasm and excitement, as if a few hours' talk with that truly disgusting man were the most delightful experience in the world. It began to seem to me that there was no end to the contradictions in Guy's character, as if I were in contact with an acute case of schizophrenia.

That morning he told me a good deal of backstage political gossip, punctuated by a considerable amount of sexual scandal, and went into some detail about Pfeiffer's secret relations, on Daladier's behalf, with the French Right, together with some hair-raising stories about Pfeiffer's activities as an important officer of the French Boy Scout movement. Some of his stories amused me greatly; but their general effect was to depress me, as they would have depressed anyone who had faith in France as an ally against fascism, for the kind of world they reflected was one whose rottenness had become irremediable. They certainly gave a better picture of the French internal situation at the time than anything which could have been found in the British press, which still regarded France as Britain's strongest and most trustworthy ally; and Guy's confident prediction that in a crisis France would not fulfil her obligations proved to be perfectly accurate. But none of his information could in any way be described as secret; it was the kind of information which was accessible to any persistent and inquisitive enquirer who would take the trouble to cultivate some of the more seedy and disreputable characters on the French political scene. This was a part which Guy was singularly well equipped to play, and Pfeiffer was undoubtedly a valuable source. I myself assumed that Guy was exploiting him in his self-confessed rôle as an agent; yet I had to admit to myself that he might just as well have been doing so for some obscure personal motive of his own, or even simply to satisfy his insatiable curiosity.

When we returned home, I did indeed ask him how he disposed of whatever information he obtained. He was annoyed by my question, but he finally said that he made contact with a Russian at regular intervals in a café in the East End.* Apart from this, I do not think that he ever again offered any information about his activities as an agent. I formed the impression that if in fact they existed, he regretted having revealed them to me, or that, if they did not, he was annoyed with himself for having made them up.

Perhaps, I thought, it had all been a dream. Perhaps we had been drunk. Perhaps it had been a misunderstanding. And indeed at this time Guy's life seemed to have acquired a certain degree of stability and respectability, so far as such words ever could apply to him, which somehow seemed to make it more unlikely than ever that he was in fact what he had professed to be, an agent of the Comintern. He continued to drink to excess, he still picked up boys at every opportunity, I still used to meet in his flat those oddly ambiguous characters who seemed to live on the criminal fringes of European society. But somehow a certain tension seemed to have disappeared from his life. He had taken a job in the Talks Department of the BBC which he enjoyed very much, and had been given charge of a programme called *The Week in Westminster* which brought him into contact with a great many Members of Parliament who spoke on his programme. This was the kind of thing which Guy liked; I was told both by members of the BBC staff and by Members of Parliament who had talked for him that he did his job very well; so well indeed that to his great amusement he became much sought after, and much wined and dined, by ambitious Members of Parliament anxious to make a name for themselves on his programme. He had an intuitive grasp of the possibilities of broadcasting, and a natural gift for the spoken, as opposed to the written word. He took infinite trouble with his performers' scripts, which were often either dull or incoherent; he was fertile in suggesting ideas to people who often had no ideas of their own, and he could make them sound, on the air, natural, easy and unaffected when by nature they were pompous, or dogmatic or shy.

The truth was that he was genuinely interested in what he was doing, and whenever he was interested in anything he did it well. And it was natural that, in doing so, he should have gained the affection of those who appeared on his programme. They appreciated the trouble that he took, and were gratified when their talks were a success. Radio, not television, was then the way to becoming a 'personality' and I have heard several Members of Parliament who later rose to high office say that they were grateful to Guy and owed to the talks they had given for him their first real start in public life. I have no doubt that some of them, under his influence, found themselves expressing ideas which they had never previously dreamed that they possessed. But at least they were interesting ideas, and people listened to them. On the whole it could be said that for the first time in his life Guy was performing a useful function and performing it very well.

Yet from time to time incidents occurred for which on the whole I could offer no explanation except that he continued to play his professed part as a secret agent. The time of Munich was approaching, and Konrad Henlein, the leader of the Sudeten Deutsch National Socialists in Czechoslovakia, paid a visit to London to establish relations with British political figures who rightly or wrongly he thought might prove useful to his cause. He stayed at the Goring Hotel, and to my surprise I learned that the boy Jimmy whom I used to meet in Guy's flat had managed to establish himself as the telephone operator at the hotel and at the end of each day delivered to Guy a record of the calls made by and to Henlein, and of the telephone conversations that had taken place. Guy told me of this coup with a kind of schoolboy glee, and yet with the implication that this was part of his espionage activities. I did not question the implication, and yet could not help wondering whether it was not yet another example of his almost megalomaniac compulsion to meddle in matters that were none of his business. And there were hurried and mysterious visits to Paris, and bundles of banknotes which one suddenly caught sight of stuffed away in his indescribably untidy cupboards, and a general air of conspiratorial activity which had the flavour more of a spy story in a children's magazine than what I imagined to be the sober and discreet methods of an efficient espionage network. The trouble was that I simply could not take Guy seriously in the character of a spy.

Meanwhile, Munich itself occurred; and throughout the crisis Guy, on the basis of what he claimed to be direct information from Pfeiffer, maintained an absolute assurance that there was no conceivable possibility of war, that under no imaginable circumstances would France fight while Daladier was in power, that the British Government was well aware of this, and that consequently we had not the slightest intention of fighting either. In the circumstances of the time, when people were confused, frightened, despairing, Guy's calm assumption of knowledge irritated me considerably and I was perhaps even more irritated when he, and Pfeiffer, proved to be right.

Throughout 1938 and 1939, as war became more and more certain, he maintained this calm assurance, as if he possessed some secret source of information which would prove him right when everyone else was wrong. My own feelings, however, had led me, in 1939, to join the 90th Field Regiment, a Territorial unit stationed in Bloomsbury, conveniently near my office at the *Spectator*. After all, I had spent a large part of the previous two years in trying to persuade people, so far as I could, that it was imperative to resist the advance of National Socialism, by fighting if necessary, and since the time seemed to have come when we would finally have to, I thought I ought to accept the consequences. Guy of course, like most of my friends, regarded this as simply a foolish and romantic gesture, perhaps even worse, for to many it seemed an act of treachery to fight for any government as detestable as Mr Chamberlain's, and all that it represented. To me it seemed that the time for such refinements was over.

Guy thought me even worse than foolish and romantic, he thought me ludicrous, when in the summer, dressed in my absurd and ill-fitting uniform, ammunition boots clamped to my feet like lead, I went off with my regiment to camp. Ludicrous indeed I felt, because I feel sure that no one was less well fitted to adopt the profession of arms than I was. And indeed the embrace which the army offered me, submerged for a fortnight in the mud of an artillery camp in the West Country, our guns crawling painfully every day to the mist-veiled hills above, was hardly a warm one. I began to feel very foolish indeed, especially since Guy had gone happily off for a month of sunshine in the South of France. Why, I thought with irritation, did he somehow always manage to get the best of all worlds, and why should I be shivering in the rain and mist of Okehampton while he was hogging it at Antibes? Somehow, there seemed to be no justice in it.

When I returned to my flat in Ebury Street, I stripped off my horrible uniform and flung it into the corner of the room. For one entirely irrational moment, I had the acute pleasure of feeling that at least I should not need it again for another year. But in the next days there came the announcement of the Soviet–German Non-Aggression Pact, and it was clear that war could not be postponed for much longer. The next day, in the evening, Guy appeared in my flat, having driven back from Antibes the moment he heard the news, left his car at Calais, and crossed over by the night boat. His car was one of the possessions which he valued most in the world, but on this occasion he appeared to have abandoned it without a thought. He was in a state of considerable excitement and exhaustion; but I thought I also noticed something about him which I had never seen before. He was frightened.*

He seemed strained and apprehensive in his behaviour towards me, and this was something new in our relations. I imagine he already knew what my feelings would be, and when I denounced the treachery of the Soviet Union and said that the Russians had now made war inevitable, he merely shrugged his shoulders and said calmly that after Munich the Soviet Union was perfectly justified in putting its own security first and indeed that if they had not done so they would have betrayed the interests of the working class both in the Soviet Union and throughout the world. I said that neither he nor the Soviets really understood what Hitler was like, and that one might as well entrust the interests of the working class to a rattlesnake as to him. But he was clearly not interested in my opinions and he spoke wearily, almost absent-mindedly, as if he had already discounted this particular argument and wished to get it over as quickly as possible. And indeed it was only when it had come to an inconclusive end, and my indignation had half subsided, that his interest began to revive and the same look of anxiety which I had already observed returned to his face.

'And what do you intend to do?' he said.

'To do? I don't suppose I've any choice. I'll be called up.'

'And what about me?' he said. 'And the Comintern?'

'I never want to have anything to do with the Comintern for the rest of my life,' I said. 'Or with you, if you really are one of their agents.'

'The best thing to do would be to forget the whole thing,' he said.

'I'll only be too glad to forget about it,' I said. 'After all, it doesn't seem to have any importance now.'

'And never mention it again,' he said eagerly. 'The best thing to do would be to put it out of our minds entirely. As if it had never happened.'

'I'll never mention it,' I said. 'I want to forget about it.'

'That's splendid,' he said, with obvious relief. 'It's exactly what I feel. Now let's go and have a drink.'*

That was the last drink I had with Guy before the war began. We drank a great deal, as if we both knew that we were drinking the old world out. A few days later I had picked up my uniform from the corner of the room where I had flung it, had rejoined my regiment and found myself in the East India Dock where, unarmed ourselves, we had the slightly absurd task of maintaining order in case of civil disturbance. For the first six months of the war I lived in such a state of complete physical exhaustion that, even if I wanted to, I could not have devoted any thought to such questions as whether Guy was or was not a spy, or, if he was, whether it was now of any importance at all. All I thought about was such problems as whether one could avoid fatigues in order to snatch a few moments' sleep, or how it was humanly possible to get oneself shaved before presenting oneself on parade by 6 o'clock in the morning. The kind of problem presented by Guy was far too complicated for me to solve or even to contemplate.

VI

War changes all things, materially and morally, and we ourselves change with them. As a private soldier I quite quickly became accustomed to living and behaving in ways which were unlike anything I had ever experienced before, and, not without effort, adapted myself to the code so admirably and succinctly expressed by Brecht: *Erst kommt das Fressen: dann kommt die Moral.** Under the shock of the German–Soviet pact, and its consequence, the war, I had ceased to be a theoretical Marxist, because there was quite obviously something wrong with a doctrine which could lead to, and justify, such results; but I was not far from becoming an unconscious Marxist instead.

War not only changes things; it changes them continuously, as if one found oneself on an endless moving staircase. No sooner had I adjusted myself to life as a gunner than, in the spring of 1940,* I was transferred to an Officer Cadet Training Unit at Sandhurst where I struggled to master even more esoteric mysteries of the military life; I found it even harder to be an officer than a private. By the summer I was commanding an infantry platoon in the Royal Welch Fusiliers, a regiment which seemed hardly to have changed at all since Robert Graves described it in *Goodbye To All That* and David Jones in *In Parenthesis*. In the interval I managed to write an article for *Horizon*, in reply to an editorial by Cyril Connolly in which he claimed that the only possible attitude for a writer to adopt towards the war was to take as little notice of it as possible; this seemed to me like advising writers to ignore the most profound and all-embracing reality of their time.* Guy wrote to tell me that he had liked the article and envied me being a soldier. For the life of me I could not see why he should, nor why he should not be one himself if he wanted to. But at that time in England there was still a feeling that for an intellectual to be a soldier was in some way beneath his dignity and a waste of his talents. To enter the civil service, the Office of Information, the BBC, was in some way or another to serve one's country usefully and intelligently, without lending oneself to the more brutal arts of war; but there was something immoral and absurd about being a soldier.

By the end of that year of, for me as for so many others, violent and abrupt transformations of one's personal life I was married, a state I had never hitherto contemplated entering, to a girl I hardly knew and who was hardly out of school;* she would not even have known what one was talking about if one had mentioned the word 'Comintern' to her. When I wrote to tell Guy that I was getting married, he replied in a long, affectionate and almost paternal letter about the dangers which both I and my wife were about to incur. I was, he gently but firmly pointed out, an extremely unstable, volatile and undependable character, fickle, changeable, and much addicted to women, who had hitherto shown few signs of being able to support himself, let alone a wife or a family; I was egotistic and pleasure-loving; he could not envisage me as a faithful husband and he hoped I had not deceived my wife into thinking otherwise; in general, it was extremely unwise of me to think of getting married at all and even more foolish and rash of my wife to marry me. In spite of this, he said, if I were really determined to take such a desperate step, he was delighted if I were happy and hoped that we should all three meet at the first possible opportunity.

I showed the letter to my wife, who cried a little, but was quickly reassured when I told her that Guy was only doing, as he thought, his best, by trying to pluck me out of marriage like a brand from the burning; no doubt he thought it would be in both our interests. Even so I could see that she thought it a very odd letter from a very odd person, and suddenly I had a very sharp sense of how very strange a creature Guy must seem when seen through the eyes of someone who had not become as inured to his eccentricities as I had.

His letter, however, also informed me that the opportunity of meeting was not likely to arise soon, as he was leaving England almost immediately for the United States, en route via the Pacific and Vladivostok for the Soviet Union, where he was to join our Embassy staff in Moscow. He told me no more about his mission, nor could I conceive of what possible use he could be in the Soviet Union; I almost felt that he must be indulging his gift for fantasy again, and also had a momentary twinge of apprehension, as of an old toothache, that the fortunes of war should be taking him to Moscow. But in neither case was I seriously worried. War teaches us to accept fantasy as fact, and especially in the first year of the war when everything rigorously followed the rule that it is always the unexpected that happens.

Yet something went wrong with Guy's mission. In a few weeks he was back in England, and when I next met him, in the spring of 1941, he would make no reply to my questions about what happened other than to be even more evasive than usual.* Nor would he offer any explanation of a brief paragraph I had read in a newspaper stating that he had been arrested for drunken driving in the Mall and describing him as 'a War Office official'. The drunken driving he admitted; as to the War Office, he fell impressively silent and said he could tell me nothing because matters of the highest security were involved. Somehow I began to feel that the war and Guy were on a converging course towards a point at which the distinction between fantasy and reality totally disappeared.

In fact, however, I did not see him much during the war; I was occupied with too many other things. But I visited him when on leave in London, and used to talk to him about the war and politics and literature, and envy him because he always seemed to be so much better informed than I was. He now lived in a large and very comfortable flat which he shared with a friend who for the duration of the war had abandoned scholarship to become an officer in MI5. The flat was also shared by two girls who were employed as secretaries in Whitehall. One was timid, gentle and genteel. The other had as keen an appetite for pleasure as Guy himself. He used to refer to her as 'Semiramis'* and was half envious, half censorious, of her capacity for enjoying herself. This oddly assorted collection of tenants sometimes gave the flat the air of a rather high-class disorderly house, in which one could not distinguish between the staff, the management and the clients.

On the one hand Semiramis entertained a stream of visitors, including one who, having once entered, 'hung up his hat' as Guy said and proved impossible to dislodge.* All appeared to be employed in jobs of varying importance, some of the highest, at various ministries; some were communists or ex-communists; all were a fount of gossip about the progress of the war, and the political machine responsible for conducting it, which sometimes amused me, sometimes startled me, and sometimes convinced me that I could not possibly be fighting the same war as themselves.

On the other hand Guy brought home a series of boys, young men, soldiers, sailors, airmen, whom he had picked up among the thousands who thronged the streets of London at that time; for war, as Proust noticed, provokes an almost tropical flowering of sexual activity behind the lines which is the counterpart of the work of carnage which takes place at the front. The effects was that to spend an evening at Guy's flat was rather like watching a French farce which has been injected with all the elements of a political drama. Bedroom doors opened and shut; strange faces appeared and disappeared down the stairs where they passed some new visitor on his way up; civil servants, politicians, visitors to London, friends and colleagues of Guy's, popped in and out of bed and then continued some absorbing discussion of political intrigue, the progress of the war and the future possibilities of the peace.*

I watched this absorbing and animated scene most frequently during 1944, when I had been posted to London to the planning of staff of 21 Army Group. I was at that time almost totally immersed in all the details of the invasion; I thought of nothing but beach gradients, underwater obstacles, tables of moon and tide and weather, figures of reinforcements, subversive activity, army-air support, and all the other factors which had to be fitted in precisely to the framework of that immense operation.* The work of the planning staff, which for reasons of security was restricted to a minimum, was hard, the hours were long, and an evening at Guy's flat was like some fantastic entertainment devised specifically to take one's mind off one's labours, though I doubt very much if Field Marshal Montgomery would have greatly approved it. Watching, as if in a theatre, the extraordinary spectacle of life as lived by Guy, I felt rather like some tired business man who had taken an evening off to visit a strip-tease club.

And yet, an insidious doubt would occasionally creep into my mind. Most of my time in the army had been spent in military intelligence of one kind or another. It is a peculiar, and frequently underrated, branch of war which induces, in its best practitioners, an almost animal sensitivity to the risks which it involves, not to themselves, but to others. A good military intelligence officer will be continually aware that, by any error or failure on his part, he will be directly responsible for the deaths of many men, in numbers which may vary from those of a platoon to those of an army. In this he is both at an advantage and a disadvantage compared with others engaged in different forms of intelligence operations. In military intelligence you at least know, usually fairly quickly, whether the intelligence you have collected and disseminated has been correct or not; the evidence is before you in the shape of bodies spreadeagled on beaches or on wire, or, quite simply, mangled beyond recognition. I myself, by 1944, had been offered such objective verification; unfortunately for others, it was evidence of my own errors.*

The advantage of the military intelligence officer is that his work, like a scientist's, is subject to empirical proof; his disadvantage, that where he is proved to have been wrong, the evidence is provided by the tortured flesh of men who have been unnecessarily sacrificed, and thus places on his conscience a burden which is hard to bear. In other kinds of intelligence operations, such objective evidence of success or failure is rarely available; one rarely knows whether things have gone well or badly, and indeed one hardly even knows how one would distinguish between the two. On the other hand, this being so, one need never feel that one is directly responsible for whatever results, if any, have been achieved.

I am afraid that the lessons I thought I had learned from my experiences as a military intelligence officer proved useless when I tried to apply them to the case of Guy, simply because the principle of objective verification did not seem to apply. From time to time I used to wonder whether he had been telling me the truth when he said that he was a Comintern agent, and sometimes it even occurred to me that, if indeed he had been telling me the truth, and if he were continuing his activities, the flat made an admirable operational base, simply because its exaggerated element of farce would prevent anyone from ever taking it seriously as such. But however much I searched my mind, I could never get any further than totally unverifiable suspicion and speculation, and these, I think rightly, I dismissed.

Certainly Guy himself never directly gave me any reason for thinking that he was anything else than what at the moment he pretended he was, a rather eccentric member of the British intellectual ruling class, who was using the war to advance his own career. Sometimes I used to remember that once, and it seemed already so very long ago, he had asked me to help him in his work as an agent, and it used to amuse me to think that at that moment I happened to be in possession of what I suppose was one of the most valuable, the most important and best kept secrets of the war; this is to say, the exact date, time and place of the invasion of Normandy, the precise naval, military and air force order of battle involved, and the fact that we had misled Stalin about the date at which we intended to launch the operation.

Sometimes, indeed, despite the various *fêtes galantes** which were offered for one's amusement, I used to be irritated almost beyond endurance by the conversation in Guy's disorderly ménage. For those who frequented it, including Guy, were all unconditional partisans of the Soviet Union and completely accepted the scepticism of the Russians, and of the Communist party, with regard to our intention to invade Europe. I used to find it difficult to sit silent while Guy or some visitor asserted on the highest possible authority that the invasion would never take place and that we would never enter Europe until the Russians had rendered any effective resistance impossible.

At length, one day in Spring 1944, I was entrusted with the task of taking the final draft of the operation orders for Overlord to each commander-in-chief in turn for his signature. It seemed part of the absurdity that attended any military duty I ever performed that it did not occur to me to take an official car but, with the operation orders in my briefcase, walked out of our headquarters in St Paul's and took a taxi. Each commander-in-chief predictably behaved in character. My own, on the authority of his Chief-of-Staff, had already appended his signature. The Naval Commander, Admiral Ramsay, knowing exactly what the Royal Navy had to do and how he proposed to do it, politely asked me where to sign and added his name. The Air Commander, Air Marshal Leigh Mallory, examined every sentence of the long docu-ment with the minuteness of a scholar and pedant, and to each of them suggested last-minute alterations of phrasing, of style, of punctuation. I had to say that at this moment, after eighteen months of preparation, when at last, in accordance with an infinitely complicated timetable, the men, the ships, the planes were ready to move to their battle stations, no further changes were possible, and somewhat surlily, slowly, painfully, he wrote his name. It was a long and tiring morning, and as I sat in my taxi as we drove from one headquarters to another I could not help wondering what the effect would have been on Guy if I had suddenly ordered it to his flat and placed Overlord in his hands. Would he then, perhaps, have told me what he was up to?

Yet in fact I had by this time dismissed any real suspicions of Guy, even if they sometimes recurred to me as an interesting hypothesis. There were several reasons for this. The first was that even if, before the war, his communist convictions had been strong enough to drive him into the Comintern's espionage network, there was no reason to think that he had not abandoned his underground activities once the war had begun; in this, he would have merely been following the example of so many British communists after the signature of the German–Soviet pact. Secondly, he now took no trouble whatever to conceal his sympathies for the Soviet Union, and this seemed to me a reason for thinking that, whatever else he might be, he was no longer a communist agent. Thirdly, there was the presence in Guy's flat, on terms of the most intimate friendship, of an extremely important member of the security services.* I had every reason to believe in his integrity and his intelligence, and at that time he certainly knew more about Guy than I did. He was in a far better position to know about Guy than I was, and if he saw no reason to worry, why should I?

There was yet another reason. Despite the disorder and confusion of Guy's life in war-time London, Guy's career seemed once again to have taken a turn for the better. After his mysterious attachment to the War Office, he had returned to the BBC and from there he had been transferred to the News Department of the Foreign Office. This was a post for which he was admirably adapted. He liked the feeling of having an inside knowledge of British foreign policy and the considerations out of which it emerged. He liked expounding that policy to others, and employing all his ingenuity in showing that British policy was rational and coherent and corresponded to long-term historical interests. He liked and understood journalists, and sympathized with, because he shared, their passion for news, and he enjoyed being on intimate terms with them and exchanging with them that kind of backstage political gossip which was the breath of life to him. All this made him very good at his job, he was evidently very happy in it, and this again made me feel that there was no underlying conflict in his life, such as there would have been if in fact he were pretending to be something quite different from what he was. And once again, if the Foreign Office had no doubts about him, why should I?

Four

I

When I returned to England from Germany after the war, I had to enter seriously on the business of married life. I now had two small children* and before I returned my wife had succeeded in finding a pretty little doll's house in St John's Wood which, with its garden and its little pillared portico, was as agreeable a place to live in as one could have hoped to discover in bomb-shattered London. And now, perhaps because I was so happily settled in, I began to see more of Guy than at any other period of my life. He liked the domestic atmosphere of my house; he became very fond of my wife and was devoted to the two children and was an affectionate and generous godfather to the elder of them. He used to compare me to the head of that contented little petit-bourgeois family which made Flaubert exclaim, when he visited them: *Ils sont dans le vrai!** I was not sure that I deserved the compliment, or wholly appreciated it, but to Guy it evidently meant something which was sincerely felt.

Indeed, at this time I began to feel that perhaps some real change had taken place in him. One sign of it was that he had almost entirely ceased to discuss politics with me, almost indeed as if there was no longer anything to discuss. Perhaps this may have been because of the way politics had developed in Britain after the war. The objective of the great anti-Fascist crusade of the 1930s had now been achieved, though in a way, and under circumstances, which no one had foreseen; it almost seemed to have been won in spite, and not because, of the crusaders. But certainly the victory had removed the prime motive for that intense concentration on political issues which had dominated intellectual life in the years before war. Moreover, the victory of the Labour Party in the election of 1945, and the introduction of the welfare state, had satisfied a large part of the ambitions of the Left and held out the hope of even greater satisfaction; for the intellectual Left there was, for the moment at least, no great cause to fight for.

Guy at least professed to be happy and pleased with Labour's victory, and at the News Department he expounded and justified very ably the ideas and policies which animated the Labour government. After the war indeed, I can remember only three political events which seemed to stimulate him to undertake those long, elaborate and fundamentally hostile analyses of British policy in which he indulged so often before the war. The first was the civil war in Greece, where he was violently opposed to Anglo-American intervention. If one ventured to defend it on the ground that it was the only alternative to a communist dictatorship in Greece, he would sink into a gloomy silence which put an end to any argument. The second event which greatly excited him was the Alger Hiss case in America,* to which his reaction was in some ways very odd. From the very first, when the evidence against Hiss was very thin, he professed a firm conviction of his guilt. At dinner in our house one evening a lawyer suggested that in an English court of law Hiss could never have been found guilty. He said that the proceedings against Hiss were a travesty of justice and that he was the victim of a form of persecution which was directed at every manifestation of liberal and progressive thought in the United Sates. Guy agreed that such a campaign of persecution was in progress. It was, he said, a delayed reaction against Roosevelt and the New Deal and marked the rise of American fascism in the disguise of anti-communism. But he dismissed the legal arguments against Hiss's conviction as mere pedantry; they showed, he said, how far all lawyers, and especially English ones, lacked any sense of political realities. Hiss was certainly guilty; he was precisely the kind of person who was capable of carrying out the systematic programme of espionage of which Whittaker Chambers, so improbably as it seemed, had accused him; and only a communist could be capable of such a feat. But the implication of what Guy said was that it was Hiss, not Chambers, who deserved our admiration; and indeed he repeated with great relish all those unsavoury rumours which were being used to discredit Chambers in the United States at that time.

The Hiss case fascinated Guy; he saw it as a battle of good and evil in which all the good was on the side of Hiss and all the evil on the side of Chambers. The case fascinated me also;* only I saw it in precisely the opposite terms from Guy, for by that time I had come to regard communism, or rather, the Soviet Union in the age of Stalin, as no less an evil, and perhaps an even greater danger, than the Germany of Adolf Hitler. Our divergence of feeling and opinion about Hiss reflected a deeper disagreement which made any form of political discussion increasingly difficult.

The third political event which inspired Guy to eloquence and even passion was the British withdrawal from India, which he denounced as a cowardly betrayal of the Indian masses; he pointed to the partition of India, and the bloodshed by which it was accompanied, as proof that British had surrendered her historic mission to maintain the peace and unity of the Indian subcontinent. In such outbursts, there were curious echoes of arguments he had developed during that episode in his life when he had been a supporter of Anglo-German understanding.

Apart from those subjects, Guy refused to discuss politics with me; one reason for this was, as it seemed to me, that it had become impossible to talk about politics at all without discussing, in one context or another, the subjects of communism and the Soviet Union, and Guy was resolutely determined to avoid discussion of either of those matters. If I pressed him on the subject, he simply drank more and faster of whatever he happened to be drinking at the moment, and eventually sank into a kind of morose and alcoholic torpor, hardly speaking a word and, as it seemed, hardly capable of taking in whatever it was one was saying to him.

Such moods became all the more frequent as Guy became more addicted to other forms of drugs, as well as alcohol. He was now perpetually taking sedatives to calm his nerves, and immediately followed them with stimulants in order to counteract their effect; and since he always did everything to excess, he munched whatever tablets he had on hand much as a child will munch its way through a bag of dolly-mixtures until the supply has given out. Combined with a large and steady intake of alcohol, this consumption of drugs, narcotics, sedatives, stimulants, barbiturates, sleeping pills, or *anything*, it seemed, so long as it would modify whatever he happened to be feeling at any particular moment, produced an extraordinary and incalculable alteration of mood, so that one could not possibly tell what condition he would be in from one moment to the next. On the whole, however, it was fair to assume that sooner or later he would lapse into one of those moods of morose silence to which he was more and more frequently liable. And while one could hardly help deploring the extra-ordinary regime to which he subjected himself, it was also difficult not to be astonished at the equally extraordinary physical vitality which enabled him to survive it. Anyone else, one felt, would have been dead long ago; Guy seemed to suffer no ill effects, except for the recurrent states of silence and profound depression by which he was overcome; one felt sometimes that he was made of some special light alloy, immune to metal fatigue, which was resistant to the normal physical processes of human life.

Those who, like myself, were fond of him, and they were many, would from time to time discuss his moods of depression and wonder whether there was anything that could be done about them or him. The most charitable explanation of them was that, for whatever reason, he was profoundly unhappy and that alcohol and drugs provided him with a kind of oblivion in which he found relief; but this was not a very satisfactory answer, because it only led one to ask why precisely he should be unhappy. There was of course the fact of his being irretrievably homosexual; but certainly Guy was the last person in the world to regard this as a reason for unhappiness.

In my own mind, from time to time, I used to consider two other possible explanations. One was, of course, that he had been telling the truth when, long ago, he had claimed to be a communist agent. It was possible therefore that in the past he had been a spy, and that he continued to be a spy; and that the strain and effort of playing such a part was gradually, slowly but irresistibly proving too much for him.* What made one reject such a possibility was, in the first place, the inherent improbability that anyone whom one had known so well for so long was playing such a part; and secondly, that, apart from that one evening before the war, Guy had never in the slightest way betrayed himself. If the hypothesis were true, it argued a degree of self-control, and a depth of dissimulation, which would be quite extraordinary in anyone, but in Guy seemed entirely out of the question.

There was, however, an alternative possibility which seemed at least equally plausible. This was that Guy may indeed have been a Comintern agent for a short time but had later abandoned his allegiance to communism and was now genuinely trying a create a place for himself in society as it exists in the Western world. But we know very well that such breaks with the past are not accomplished easily; on the ex-communist they inflict profound psychological scars, and painful mental and spiritual lesions, which, in many cases, prevent him from successfully accomplishing the transition from one world to another. Was it not reasonable to suppose that this would be quite sufficient to account for the distressing condition of mind into which Guy had lapsed?

II

So I concluded that, whether or not Guy had once been a spy, he no longer was one. On the whole this seemed to involve far fewer impossibilities than any other view; perhaps I ought to add that it involved the fewest difficulties for myself. It also seemed more likely to be true because at this time Guy, in spite of the extraordinary aberrations in his personal life and behaviour, seemed again to be making what might be called a success of his career, however modestly and even eccentrically. Given his behaviour, one could not quite understand how this could be so; and yet on the whole the facts seemed to show that it was. In 1944 he had transferred from the BBC to the Foreign Office as a temporary press officer; in 1947 he had succeeded in getting himself established, and had become personal secretary to the Minister of State, Hector McNeil.* This was a good deal nearer to the heart of the establishment than Guy had previously penetrated, and it even seemed possible that he might now, with a little good luck, be on the verge of a successful career in the foreign service.

McNeil was not only Guy's superior but a personal friend. He had spoken on Guy's radio programme and the two of them had liked each other, and McNeil had considerable respect for Guy's political judgement, his fertility in ideas, and his gift for analysing concrete political situations. Indeed, he listened to Guy's views with a deference which often seemed as if it were Guy who was his superior, rather than the other way round; McNeil felt that Guy had a valuable contribution to make in the foreign service and he tried to foster and advance him in his diplomatic career with almost paternal care. The truth was that McNeil was a very nice man, and Guy had managed to find the way into his affections.

Yet I often used to wonder how any Minister could possibly tolerate Guy as a subordinate. He was quite incredibly disorderly and irregular in his habits; he had very little of a civil servant's capacity for expressing himself clearly and briefly on paper; and one imagined that some at least of his personal idiosyncrasies could not fail to be irritating, and even offensive, in a well-regulated office. He was, for instance, inordinately fond of garlic, and was as impregnated by its aroma as a French peasant. He ate it not, like most people, as a herb or a seasoning, but as a vegetable or fruit; he kept knobs of it in his pockets or in his desk and from time to time gobbled a few of them like apples. He told me one day, with triumph and amusement, that a departmental minute had been circulated to the following effect: 'Mr Burgess will in future refrain from eating garlic during office hours.' He laughed; I laughed; who could have helped laughing? The minute had just that air of farce which Guy always succeeded in introducing into the most solemn proceedings. But I never noticed that the supplies, or the smell, of garlic ever became any the less.

There was indeed a general air of good-natured disorganization and disorder in the secretaries' room in the Minister of State's office in those days, which to myself, who had a certain awe of the Foreign Office, made it a very surprising, interesting and rather attractive place; certainly it had the charm of being entirely untainted by that air of industry, sobriety and decorum which I have always associated with HM diplomatic service When I used to call on Guy there, I would normally find him and his colleague, the Private Secretary,* facing each other across an enormous desk littered with an assortment of official papers and a large selection of the daily press, of which Guy was a devoted and assiduous student. There would also be a few volumes from the London Library, a few sketches and caricatures which Guy had tossed off in the course of the day (it was one of his talents that he drew extremely well) and a few sets of humorous verse composed by his colleague.

The room had that particular uncared for and dilapidated atmosphere which it is the genius of the British civil service and British Railways to create wherever they penetrate, but to this Guy and his colleague had added a few touches of their own; that is to say, there seemed to be even more overflowing ashtrays, burned-out matches and empty cups of tea than usual, while a few gnawed knobs of garlic, as if mice had been at them, added a bizarre and original element to the disorder. The bare and austere neatness of the normal civil servant's desk had entirely disappeared under a luxurious profusion of papers, documents, files, memoranda that looked as if the entire Foreign Office archives had overflowed into the room. Messengers entered, looked vainly for in- and out-trays under the deluge of paper, and dropped their files and messages wherever Guy indicated with a negligent wave of the hand. Either he or his colleague would pick up one or two of them, marked URGENT, glance at them for a moment with a look of distaste, and as hurriedly restore them to their appointed place among the debris.

In this scene of disorder, Guy and his colleague would sit and discuss the events of the day, or, rather more often, of the night before, for the Private Secretary was, in his own way, as addicted to the *chasse au bonheur** as the Personal Secretary, though his tastes were more normal. Conversation in the secretaries' room was very largely devoted to whatever pleasures they had enjoyed the night before, either together or apart, and to reporting whatever material for gossip or scandal they had picked up in the course of it. Not the Chanceries of the world, but the night clubs and brothels, the pubs and cafés of London, were the objects of their interest and discussion, which from time to time would be interrupted by a buzz from the adjoining room where sat the Minister of State, occupied, I used to imagine, in vainly trying to restore order to the chaos created in his affairs by his two assistants. The peremptory summons would normally be greeted by some such words as:

'Oh Lord, there's Hector again.'

'What on earth can HE want?'

'I can't think.'

'Perhaps you'd better go in, Guy.'

'Oh no! He can't possibly want *me*. I've been in *twice* already today. You go. It's your turn.'

After that there would be silence, while they waited to see if the Minister would ring again. If he did not, it would be agreed that he could not really want anything at all, and that it really was too bad of him to disturb them to no purpose.

All this was a reflection of Guy's basic attitude that established institutions were created for his own convenience and use; he regarded them with a mixture of contempt, indulgence and amusement as if fundamentally they were playthings which only children could take seriously. One evening I called on him to borrow a book he had promised to lend me. This was Kinsey's report on *Sexual Behavior in the Human Male,** which was as yet unobtainable in England but which Guy had been sent from the United States. When I called, he told me there was such a press of would-be borrowers in the Foreign Office that he had been forced to hide it.

'I'll have to go and get it,' he said. 'Come with me.'

I followed him out of the room and down the dusty corridors of the Foreign Office. 'I wish they'd have Kinsey in here,' he said. 'He'd find some pretty queer evidence about the human male.' We came to what was evidently a very important room indeed, so that even Guy stood abashed for a moment on its threshold. Then he said:

'It's all right. He's not here,' opened the door into a vast room which seemed to be all faded crimson and brocade, with heavy, rather shabby curtains and a carpet that had seen better days. Yet it had a kind of dilapidated grandeur, and I felt alarmed.

'Where are we?' I said. 'Whose room is this?'

'It's the Foreign Secretary's. I thought you'd like to see it. Don't you love it? I do.'

'For God's sake,' I said, 'let's get out. I've no business to be in here.'

'Oh, it's all right,' Guy said, 'Ernie's away. Besides, I've got to get Kinsey for you.'

At one end of the room there was a bookcase filled with what appeared to be reference books. Guy fumbled among them for a moment, then withdrew his hand holding the Kinsey Report.

'There you are,' he said, offering it to me.

'What on earth is it doing here?' I said.

'O, I keep it here,' he said. 'Everyone's trying to get hold of it, and I had to hide it somewhere safe. No one would think of looking for it here and if Ernie found it he wouldn't know what it was about. It couldn't be safer.'

Then he showed me a portrait of Lord Salisbury and once again repeated his favourite story that, on his death bed, Lord Salisbury had said he had backed the wrong horse in failing to come to an agreement with Russia. I have never known the origin of this story, and was never quite sure whether Guy had found it in Lady Gwendolen Cecil or whether he had invented it. But Guy always repeated it as if it came from some sacred text to which only he possessed the key. Perhaps the reason was that it seemed to bestow the authority of Lord Salisbury, for whom he had a veneration verging on idolatry, on the policy of friendship and alliance with the Soviet Union, of which he had become a passionate and persuasive advocate.

III

Despite his drink and his drugs, his sudden surrenders to despondency and silence, there were still periods in Guy's life when gaiety predominated, and at such times he was always charming; only such moods became increasingly rarer, and they were almost entirely a matter of private and not the public life. He had moved into a flat in Bond Street, which he had redecorated in his favourite colour scheme of red-white-and-blue and furnished with those particular articles of furniture which were essential to his scheme of life. First, an enormous double bed with an elaborate Italian ornamental head of stripped oak. Then a gramophone, on which he could interminably play to himself his favourite records. They made a curious collection in which *The Marriage of Figaro* easily came first, but was followed by a song from a pre-war musical by Beverley Nichols:*

> I've got a little white room
> With a window by the sea

and, more recently, by a song of Peter Lind Hayes:*

> Tin roof leaks and the chimney leans,
> There's a hole in the seat of my old blue jeans,
> I've ate the last of the pork and beans;
> Life gets tedious, don't it.

It would require an elaborate analysis of Guy's intellectual and emotional processes to show why such works had a common appeal to him; after the war his musical resources had been increased by a small and battered harmonium which he had rescued from a bombed house during the blitz and had carried half way across London on his back. In the evenings, when the noise of the Bond Street traffic had died down, he would seat himself at this precious acquisition and pick out pieces of Mozart and Handel to himself with one finger. After this came his books, a curiously mixed collection of Victorian and American novels, British nineteenth-century history, and a large number of books on Marxism and communism. Lastly, there was a model of a fully rigged frigate in full sail enclosed in a glass bottle, a symbol of his enduring love and admiration of the British Navy.

In these surroundings he could contrive to be happy. Apart from his inordinate consumption of drink and cigarettes, he made very few demands on life, and even his drinking varied and he never drank when he was alone, so that for considerable periods he was comparatively temperate. His only extravagance was motor cars, for which he had a passion which was both aesthetic and historical. He had an exhaustive knowledge of every make and model since the first days of motoring, and would relate each variation in design to the particular historical circumstances in which it had taken place; for the T-model Ford, and for Henry Ford himself, he had an almost religious veneration. They represented for him one of the supreme achievements, and one of the supreme creative geniuses, of an age of social and technical revolution to which political revolution was the natural sequel.

He had an equal and similar passion for the Reform Club, of which he was a devoted member. It had, after all, been built at a period which was for him the culmination of English history, and its architecture, its furniture (and indeed even some of its members) belonged to an age in which, in his eyes, society had been everything that it should be, that is to say, technically and politically progressive and expansive. He was in this sense one of the most old-fashioned of British patriots and, more than anything, it was the sense that Britain had ceased to play the part of a dominant and progressive world power that turned him against her, as if his love had been rejected. Indeed in the days when he still used to discuss communism with me I used sometimes to have the disconcerting feeling that he looked upon the Soviet Union as a kind of reincarnation of Victorian England, only with the irritating difference that it was inhabited by foreigners who did not speak English. And indeed, from this point of view, it was perhaps not altogether inappropriate that he should have ended his life in Moscow, for there he might still have found shabby remnants of vanished splendour, rags and tatters of a vanished imperial age which might almost have made him feel that he was back in the Reform Club ordering one of those immense beakers of port which to the waiters were known as 'a double Burgess'.

From Bond Street to the Foreign Office; from the Foreign Office to the Reform Club; from the Reform Club to a pub, or a party or a night club; occasional forays into smart society, because he liked to be friends with the great; Guy's life had begun to follow a routine in which even alcoholic or sexual indulgence fitted into a pattern of almost monotonous regularity. It might even seem, at moments, that Guy was growing respectable. He dropped hints that he was thinking of getting married, and once at least he professed to have decided on a bride, though I think that the lady in question would have been surprised and perhaps alarmed to know that she had been selected as Guy's intended victim. There were times also when he spoke of giving up the Foreign Office and finding some other career for himself; for a period he flirted with the idea of becoming the motoring correspondent of *Country Life*. I even began to feel that his interest in politics which, whatever side he professed to be on, had always been intense and even obsessive, had perhaps begun to die altogether, and that now he wished, however hopelessly, to settle down as an ordinary, one can hardly say respectable, but at least politically neutral member of society.

One day I said to him that he seemed to me to have lost his interest in politics. He said nothing. For some reason this annoyed and irritated me. I had always felt that Guy's political interests, whether misdirected or not, were the most important part of him, and that if they died, the most valuable part of him would die with them; it was as if by abandoning them he was betraying himself.

I said I assumed that he had long ago abandoned his activities as an agent, and asked how in fact they had finally come to an end. Again he made no reply, and when I persisted he first said he refused to discuss the matter with me and then relapsed into sullen silence. This irritated me even more, and even alarmed me; his silence seemed to suggest that in fact Guy really had been a spy and might even continue to be one. I felt that somehow I must at last put an end to the doubts and suspicions which had troubled me for so many years. I was provoked into saying, untruthfully, that I had written a record of our conversation on the subject before the war, and in particular of his declaration to me that he was a Comintern agent, and that for my own protection I had deposited a sealed copy of it with my lawyer.

To my surprise, this startled Guy out of his silence; indeed he showed every symptom of extreme agitation, asked angrily why on earth I had done anything so foolish, begged me to destroy the document and said that if it were ever made public it would not only put an end to his career at the Foreign Office but prevent him from following any other. Indeed, his agitation was so great that I had difficulty in calming him; and I was so disconcerted by the storm my harmless fiction had caused that it did not even occur to me that Guy's alarm was somewhat exaggerated if, as he professed, he was only concerned about his diplomatic career.

When I thought over the incident later, it left me with a sense of uneasiness and disquiet; it seemed to me that somehow Guy's reaction had been out of character and had been quite different from anything I would have expected. There had been real and genuine fear in his face and for a moment it had been as if I was looking at a person I had never seen before. I had not succeeded in putting an end to my suspicions; rather, they had been strengthened to a point at which one conclusion seemed to be unavoidable.

Given Guy's character and behaviour as I had known them before the war, it had been quite reasonable to assume that he had been boasting or romancing when he claimed to be a Comintern agent; it was quite impossible to go on doing so when the mere idea that his statement was on record should throw him into such extreme agitation. If the claim had been invention there was no reason whatever why he should be frightened, for I, certainly, had no evidence whatever to show that it was true. I could only conclude that he had been telling me the truth, that he now greatly regretted telling me, and that at the time he really had been what he claimed to be, an agent of the Comintern. The only question that remained was, had he ever ceased to be one?

IV

The certainty that one of one's greatest friends has been, and may still be, a spy is a considerable shock, even though one has considered such a possibility for a long time. Suspicion is a long way from certainty and when one's affections are concerned one is always inclined to give its object the benefit of the doubt. Certainty, even if it is only subjective, no longer leaves room for such a possibility. Moreover, it leaves one with a very unpleasant problem on one's hands; what, if anything, is one going to do about it?

Merely to ask that question was to be made acutely conscious of the change that had taken place in one's political beliefs since the end of the war. Before 1939, if like thousands of young men one was passionately opposed to the policies of the British Government, and believed that they could only end in war, one was as likely to admire as condemn anyone who had enlisted as an agent of the Comintern; especially because in those days the Comintern still enjoyed a prestige which did not necessarily attach to the Soviet Union. After the Soviet–German pact it became difficult, if not impossible, for anyone except a committed and convinced communist to maintain such an attitude, and after the war it became even more impossible to do so with each year that passed. Even so, it was still difficult to condemn anyone for having held and acted upon political convictions which one had in fact shared; in Guy's case, it seemed to me, it was only possible to condemn his behaviour if, in the very changed circumstances of 1945 and after, he had persisted in underground activities which might have been excusable, and even praiseworthy, during the period of the Spanish Civil War and of Munich.

It was with some relief that I came to the conclusion that this was very unlikely. During the war, Guy had lived on close and intimate terms with people who had occupied extremely responsible positions in the British security services; they were in fact the people who had known him best during that period, and certainly far better than I had. It seemed to me inconceivable that such people were not in a far better position to judge Guy's activities during the war and after than I was. If there was anything in those activities of which the security services should be informed, they were the very people best placed to know. It seemed to me therefore that if anything needed to be done, it had almost certainly been done already; and if nothing had been done, it was not necessary to do anything.

Indeed, on reflection, it seemed to me that the whole pattern of Guy's life after the war confirmed the correctness of this conclusion. As I have said, his career at the Foreign Office, if not brilliant, was at least more successful than might have been expected, and this seemed to show that, if there was anything against him, it was not anything which his superiors took very seriously; certainly nothing so serious as a suspicion that he might constitute a security risk.

There were other aspects of his life which seemed to confirm that his career as a spy had ceased long ago. One of his most striking personal characteristics was his devotion to a small number of friends who had remained his friends through all the vicissitudes of his life. Now, by a curious chain of historical events, some of these had risen to posts of great authority in the security services, and it was precisely these whose company Guy frequented most, with whom he lived on the most intimate and friendly terms, and who were in the best position to know everything about him. Indeed, when I met him in their company, as I sometimes did, he showed so much knowledge of their works that it was clear he was on the most confidential terms with them, and they with him. Frequently, they spoke in a kind of professional shorthand which was completely unintelligible to me.

I think in particular of one small group of people who played a particularly important part in Guy's social life. Guy used to meet them regularly every Monday evening for the particular purpose of attending the music-hall at the Chelsea Palace in the King's Road; it became part of the repetitive pattern of his life that every Monday evening was religiously set aside for this little social excursion, for which the party was always the same; two women, Guy, a high official of MI5 and another of MI6. Even to me, who knew them well, they always used to seem a strangely constituted quartet.* There was something *queer* about them, not in a homosexual sense, but in the sense which applies to members of the security services when they are off duty. At the same time, Guy's relations with them reassured me, because I could not believe that Guy could be on such peculiarly close terms with these particular individuals if there was any justification at all for the occasional qualms of doubt and uneasiness which seized me in respect to him. Indeed, in such circumstances, to have any doubts at all about him seemed to open up such appalling prospects that it seemed best to suppress them. It seemed safer, wiser, and less presumptuous to assume that since both the Foreign Office and the security services were perfectly happy about Guy's *bona fides* there was no reason for anyone else to question them.

Indeed, during this period Guy's relations with the security services seemed to become increasingly intimate and confidential. Of course, the very existence of a secret service was for Guy a challenge, almost an affront, to his curiosity. He had always been possessed by a devouring interest in affairs that were none of his business; he liked the *coulisses* of politics,* and for a Marxist he was curiously inclined to accept the conspiratorial theory of history. He liked to know, or pretend to know, what no one else knew, he liked to surprise one with information about matters that were no concern of his, derived from sources which he could not, or would not, reveal; the trouble was that one could never be sure whether the ultimate source was not his own imagination. Yet, even so, it is certain that, during the period after the war, both in London and later in Washington, Guy amassed a large body of information about the working of the security services and about their officers. It would be easy to exaggerate the amount of strictly political information available to him; a minor Foreign Office official does not have access to many state secrets. But it would be difficult to exaggerate the value to an enemy, or a potential enemy, of the knowledge which he had acquired about the machinery and methods of the security services, their organization, and the names and positions of those who worked in them. It is the kind of information which a rival security service values most, because it is the hardest to obtain, so that as a potential defector Guy's value was very high indeed.

It was yet another symptom of the astonishing and schizophrenic contradictions in his character that he could not keep even this kind of knowledge to himself, and in 1949 his lack of discretion nearly proved fatal to him. He had been for a holiday to North Africa, visiting Gibraltar *en route*, and leaving behind him wherever he went a record of drinking bouts and brawls which would have done credit to a Dimitri Karamazov. He had also at each stage in his travels insisted on visiting the local representatives of MI6 and on discussing their characters, habits, opinions and professional inadequacies with anyone who chose to listen to him in any bar in which he happened to be drinking. In addition, he had personally applied himself to the task of trying to persuade MI6's slightly startled representatives of the errors of British foreign policy in general and the follies of MI6 in particular. His journey through the Maghreb became a kind of wild Odyssey of indiscretions, and it is not surprising that such behaviour on the part of a member of HM Foreign Office should have created some consternation. Not unnaturally, it was reported to London, so that for a moment it seemed that his diplomatic career would come to an abrupt end, and indeed he himself spoke as if he had no alternative but to resign or be dismissed.

On occasions when he was in trouble Guy would often consult me; he did so in spirit of mingled contrition and amusement, and never failed to recount each disaster as if it were simply one more incident, in the gigantic farce of his life, so that it seemed as if it were not so much he as the Comic Muse herself who was responsible. On this occasion he had prepared, for the benefit of the Foreign Office, a memorandum explaining and defending his conduct, which he showed me and asked for my advice. It was not a very impressive document; it was long drawn out, tedious, and extremely detailed and by entering into very complicated and elaborate explanations of incidents which were quite obviously indefensible only seemed to magnify their importance. I felt at the end of it that it made Guy's case even worse than it was at the beginning. So I advised him to reduce the memorandum to the shortest possible compass and to say as little as possible about any of the particular charges against him, reserving the right to ask for a board of enquiry if he were threatened with anything more serious than a reprimand.* The manœuvre seemed to work very well and having been in due course severely reprimanded Guy happily and only slightly chastened resumed his diplomatic career.

This incident had the effect of weakening even further any suspicion that still lingered in my mind that Guy might still be an enemy agent. For whatever view one might have held about the efficiency of the NKVD,* it seemed quite impossible that any responsible intelligence agency could possibly employ anyone capable of such behaviour; there was in it a kind of infantilism which made one doubt whether he was really capable of serious work. It seemed to imply that by now Guy's irresponsibility had become completely out of control, and indeed at the time there were even grounds for thinking that perhaps some process of mental degeneration was taking place. A short time before he had suffered a severe concussion, as a result of having been pushed down the stairs during a drunken evening spent at *Le Bœuf sur le Toit** in the company of his amiable colleague, the Private Secretary to the Minister of State, and its effects upon him had been alarming. He suffered from severe headaches, his dependence on drugs increased. He obtained his supplies through a boy friend, whose sister was a vet and prescribed for Guy the same dosage as for a horse. Drugs, combined with alcohol made him more or less insensible for considerable periods in which, when he was not silent and morose, his speech was rambling and incoherent. The holiday in North Africa had been intended partly as a rest cure, even though it turned out to be something quite different.

Yet, even so, my doubts were not set entirely at rest. His conduct in Tangier might indeed have been a purely temporary aberration, due to his concussion; it did not necessarily mean that he was no longer capable of carrying out his duties, whatever they might be. As for the argument that no serious organization would contemplate employing him in his mental condition at that time, I could not help reflecting that the Foreign Office seemed quite content to, despite his misdemeanours. So that really one was no further than before.

Later, the Foreign Office in a White Paper said of Guy's behaviour that 'while on holiday abroad (he) had been guilty of indiscreet talk about secret matters of which he had official knowledge'. This was misleading in several ways. It implied that this was an isolated incident in Guy's life, whereas his behaviour in North Africa was in no significant way different from his behaviour in London, where his indiscretions were equally flagrant. The only difference was that in North Africa people had been surprised by them. The White Paper equally implied that his indiscretions related to matters with which he was officially concerned; in fact, they related to matters with which he had no reason whatever to be concerned and were breaches of information which he had acquired only as a result of his compulsive curiosity, his devouring interest in everything affecting the security services, his obstinate refusal to accept that, in his case, there were any matters which could be regarded as secrets. To him, the very word *secret* was a call to battle, a challenge which he never failed to accept. He hunted out secrets like a hound after truffles.

V

Alas! Guy's African holiday, even though he escaped its severest consequences, was the beginning of the end, or perhaps the end in itself, of what had been, comparatively speaking, a stable and successful period in Guy's career of public service. Under the protective wing of Hector McNeil, who never wavered in his devotion to Guy, he had been to some extent sheltered from the buffetings of fortune, and indeed McNeil showed an almost pathetic paternal interest in his welfare. In 1950, however, McNeil became Secretary of State for Scotland, and his successor as Secretary of State, Mr Kenneth Younger, perhaps understandably did not take over his two extraordinary secretaries. The Private Secretary was posted to Moscow, the Personal Secretary to the Foreign Office's Far Eastern Department.*

The transfer did not improve Guy's position. As secretary to the Minister of State, he had exercised a certain amount of personal influence on the Minister himself, and Guy had taken every advantage of his position. As a Third Secretary in the Far Eastern Department he was merely a very junior and humble member of the diplomatic hierarchy, and his position seemed all the humbler because of his age; at thirty-eight he must have been one of the most elderly Third Secretaries there has ever been. Nevertheless, he made the most of what opportunities the Far Eastern Department offered, more especially as a propagandist for the People's Republic of China; it could even be said that he made himself useful.

His interest in China was an old one, which had begun as far back as the days when he was a communist in Cambridge; he was a particular admirer of the Indian revolutionary, M. N. Roy, who from 1926 to 1927 had been the Comintern's representative in China. Guy had the kind of mind which is extremely tenacious of the knowledge and ideas acquired in youth; in some respects, indeed, he might be said to have never advanced beyond them, but he was extremely able and ingenious in adapting them to changed circumstances. In the Far Eastern Department he made himself useful by producing reasonable, comprehensive and historically based arguments in defence of the British policy of recognizing the Communist government of China, and was adept at expounding and interpreting the Chinese Revolution in terms which career diplomats could understand. In those days, professional theorists of the Chinese Revolution were hard to find, more especially if their theories appeared to coincide with British interests; so much so that when, in the summer of 1949, the Foreign Office held a weekend summer school at Oxford it was Guy who was chosen to lecture Britain's representatives, who included members both of MI5 and MI6, on *Red China*. And no doubt it was because of his renewed interest in the Chinese Revolution, in explaining which Marxist arguments could be so ingeniously used to justify British recognition of the People's Republic, that Guy's virulent anti-Americanism became increasingly acute as the months went by; for after all it was the United States which was the greatest obstacle to the adoption of the kind of policy towards China which in Guy's view Britain should in her own interests adopt.*

Guy's genuine interest and belief in the Chinese Revolution were sufficient to keep him happy in the Far Eastern Department; he always came nearest to happiness when his mind was being actively and usefully employed. Unfortunately, he had friends, and particularly Hector McNeil, who were interested in advancing his diplomatic career. During the whole of his service in the Foreign Office, he had been stationed in London; if he were to achieve promotion, it was clear that sooner or later he would have to undertake a tour of duty abroad, and that his appointment in the Far Eastern Department could only be an interlude before he emerged as an accredited representative of Her Majesty's Government on some foreign mission. Guy, however, did not respond to such projects at all sympathetically. For one thing, he was far too fond of London, of his Bond Street flat, of his friends, of the Reform Club; he was far too settled in his own peculiar ways to want to live abroad for any length of time. He regarded England, and London, as the only place in which a reasonable man could want to live; he was as convinced as Dr Johnson that there was nowhere else which could compare with them as a means to happiness, pleasure or interest. *Abroad* was for him a place which had only two functions: to provide material for political theories and diplomatic negotiations, and opportunities for holidays on which one could behave with even less restraint than at home.

He protested energetically that he had no wish whatever to be posted abroad; that he had no desire for promotion and that if he had an ambition it was to return to the News Department, in which he felt that his particular abilities could be most usefully employed; in fact, that he objected strongly to leaving London, even though this might mean that he never rose above the very subordinate position which he then occupied.

His protests were in vain. His well wishers, and the Foreign Office, decided that a move could no longer be postponed and that Guy should be posted to our Embassy in Washington. This particular decision was, from every conceivable point of view, a calamity. Even if there were any possibility that Guy could be groomed for a normal diplomatic career, for which foreign service was essential, there was certainly no foreign mission for which he was more unsuited than Washington. During the year he had spent in the Far Eastern Department he had become increasingly and aggressively anti-American and made no secret of his belief that the United States was an urgent menace to peace and was dominated by forces which were determined to lead her, and Great Britain, unless she succeeded in disassociating herself, into war against the Soviet Union. No one who knew Guy could believe that, in Washington, he was likely to disguise such beliefs in order to spare the susceptibilities of Americans; and given also that he was unlikely to make any change in his personal behaviour, it was impossible to contemplate his posting to Washington except with dismay. Sending him to Washington was as appropriate an appointment as if the Americans had sent us Senator Joseph McCarthy as their Ambassador.

Guy had no illusions about his suitability for the post, and if he could possibly have managed to stay in London he would have. We discussed it all one evening shortly before he was due to leave and he did not conceal his gloom at the prospect before him. Nothing I could say would relieve his depression; he spoke of resigning from the Foreign Office, and I could not really understand why he didn't, because I could not see that it held any future for him. Somehow one could not imagine him devoting a lifetime to writing inter-departmental minutes or attending Embassy cocktail parties. But then one could not really see that there was anything which held a future for him.

The prospect seemed all the darker because in the preceding months, for the first time since I had known him, he seemed to have been short of money. It was one of the oddest aspects of his character that, despite all his irresponsibility, his apparent lack of any kind of self-control, his gift, which amounted to genius, for involving himself in disaster, in some respects he was extremely punctilious; he never missed an appointment, he was never late, and until shortly before he left for Washington he always lived within his income and never ran into debt. But now he had borrowed quite a large sum from an affluent friend of mine and I knew that he had also borrowed money elsewhere. I was surprised and puzzled by this, because it was so marked a change in a pattern of behaviour that had persisted for so long, and because I could see no change in his circumstances to account for it.

But much as he disliked the thought of Washington, he had a kind of toughness and resiliency which made him respond to adversity and made one feel that he would surmount this as he had surmounted so many other reverses. He had survived so many setbacks, so many crises, so many appalling incidents that one almost felt that the ordinary rules of human life did not apply to him and that whatever happened to him he would always emerge unscathed.

And he did not leave without suitably celebrating or mourning his departure by giving a party in his flat. I went with an eager sense of curiosity, because Guy very rarely gave parties; when he drank, he liked to drink with at most a few friends, and preferably one, because his friends were so curiously ill-assorted that they did not combine easily; and besides he was apt to tell them so many conflicting stories about himself that if they met there was always the danger that he might be found out. I was curious to see what Guy's friends looked like when they were all collected together and I could not help feeling that we might make a very strange company. But even I was not quite prepared for the curious collection of humanity which had gathered to say goodbye to him.* Some were so respectable, like the Secretary of State for Scotland and his successor at the Foreign Office, that they could be regarded as the most authentic pillars of the Establishment; there were others, like three distinguished members of the security services, whose whole lives were devoted to guarding against any attempt to undermine the Establishment either from within or from without. There was a distinguished and homosexual writer of impeccable social origins. There was a member of the German Embassy, also homosexual, who before the war had actively plotted against Hitler and now lives in the German Democratic Republic. There were two women who seemed to be even more out of place than anyone else. There was Jimmy, who so long ago listened in to telephone calls and now lived in Guy's flat and acted as his general factotum. There were two very tough working-class young men, who had very obviously been picked up off the street either that very evening or not very long before. And the party proceeded as such parties normally do; the Establishment figures gradually departed, drink flowed faster, one of the young men hit another over the head with a bottle, another left with the distinguished writer who woke up in the morning to find his flat stripped of all its valuables.

As the evening wore on, as it were to a predestined conclusion, I could not help wondering what we all thought we were doing there and what a very odd collection we were. The only connection between us was Guy; it might almost have been a malicious joke on his part to bring us all together. And indeed, if one analysed each member of the party's particular relation to Guy, we presented a very strange commentary on English society at that moment. Some of them were friends he had known since they were undergraduates together, and some had been fellow members of his in the Communist party. Some were his professional colleagues in the Foreign Office. Some were there simply to minister to his and each other's physical pleasures; some were spies and hunters of spies; some were present merely because at some time or other they had succumbed to Guy's personality. The elaborate web of inter-relationships which had brought them together included strands which were political, social, personal, erotic, even criminal, enough indeed to supply the material for a whole society. And in some odd way this society was the same society which I had first come to know at Oxford, only with the years it had suffered a mutation which had profoundly changed its character. I remember thinking that the oddest thing of all about the party was that no one seemed to think there was anything odd about it at all.

VI

Under these distinguished auspices Guy departed to America and perhaps the United States never received a stranger guest. It so happened that soon after he left, I and my family moved from London to the country,* and the move, combined with Guy's departure, seemed to make a very definite break in my life. Certainly Guy's absence left a distinct void in it, but at the same time it made life a good deal easier. One was no longer liable to be rung up late at night and asked whether he might come round for a drink, or to have him for lunch and find him still with you at breakfast. Most of all, with Guy in America, the entire problem of Guy, like some overhanging shadow, was removed and one did not have to think about it any longer.

At infrequent intervals I heard from him, one letter an emotional outpouring because the village in which I lived happened to be the one in which his mother and father had spent their honeymoon; others of which the common theme was the increasingly virulent quality of his anti-Americanism. For Senator Joe McCarthy's anti-communist crusade was now in full swing, and Guy had come to the conclusion that he was both the most powerful and the most representative politician in the United States, and that the future of America was in his hands. What aroused Guy almost to hysteria was Senator McCarthy's identification of communism with homosexuality in the United States, and especially in the State Department. 'Things have reached such a pitch', he wrote, 'that two members of the State Department daren't dine together in public for fear of being called homosexuals and therefore Communists.' It was no use replying that McCarthyism in America was the symptom of a hysteria which would not last for long and that his own reaction to McCarthyism was also an hysterical symptom. This only earned me the stern reproof that I knew nothing about American politics and indeed seemed to have become incapable of understanding politics at all; and he repeated his conviction that McCarthy was the most powerful politician in America who would inevitably and deliberately lead or drive her into a nuclear war.

It was during Guy's absence in America that a slightly bizarre incident brought me once again into contact with Donald Maclean. He was now, after recovering from a nervous breakdown, head of the American Department at the Foreign Office, and his appointment had coincided with Guy's departure for America. I had not seen him for about fifteen years, had heard Guy and a few other friends mention his name once or twice, but otherwise had never had any reason even to think of him. Very soon after his appointment my wife and I and two friends went very late one evening to the Gargoyle Club, which at that time was a favourite resort of intellectuals. Maclean was already there and was very drunk; I would not even have recognized him if I had not been told who he was. To my astonishment he lurched over to my table, addressed me by name, and then said in an extremely aggressive and menacing voice, 'I know all about you. You used to be one of us, but you ratted.'*

I thought for a moment he was going to assault me, as by now he was leaning over the table towards me; at the critical moment, however, drunkenness betrayed him, his legs crumpled beneath him, and he sank slowly to his knees. There he stayed, his hands clutching the edge of the table, his large white face suspended like a moon at about the level of my chest, and from this absurd position he proceeded to direct an incoherent stream of abuse at me, which continued until after a few more moments of denunciation he rose unsteadily to his feet and stumbled away.

My first reaction to this ridiculous scene was rage and irritation, but one of my friends who knew Maclean explained patiently that he was very drunk and frequently was very drunk and that in such a condition he was not really responsible for his actions and therefore I should take no notice. So we left the Gargoyle for another nightclub; as we left I could not help wondering whether my contacts with the Foreign Office were at all typical and thought how splendidly Maclean would have fitted into the late Minister of State's office, if only he could have made room for one more lunatic among his secretaries.

The idea made me laugh and my annoyance passed, but when I thought about the incident again I was puzzled. What could Maclean have meant by: *You used to be one of us, but you ratted?* It could only mean, it seemed to me, that he thought that I had once been a communist, as he had been, and was no longer. But I hardly knew Maclean, had not seen him for fifteen years, and there was no reason why he should be any more interested in my political ideas than those of hundreds of young men who had gone through the same process. And why the slightly sinister: *I know all about you*, as if he shared some secret about me which was unknown to the rest of the world? This could not have any reference to my political opinions which, after all, had never been concealed from anyone.

A dreadful suspicion began to dawn upon me that Maclean had been a collaborator of Guy's in his espionage activities and that Guy had told him he had enlisted me also.* So far as I could see there could be no other explanation which was at all possible, yet I shrank from accepting it because of the appalling consequences it entailed. It meant that Guy had been telling me the truth about himself; for surely he would not have troubled to tell the same lie to two people, and in particular to Maclean, who by now held a very senior appointment in the Foreign Office? It also meant that Guy had been telling me the truth when he said that there were others associated with him in his work, though he had not mentioned Maclean's name.

But two spies in the Foreign Office? It seemed preposterous. But there were even worse conclusions to be drawn. If Guy was a spy, what was I to make of the fact that several of his most intimate friends held important posts in the intelligence service? Was I to assume that he had told them what he told me? It seemed hardly credible. Or was I to assume that he had not? In which case I had also to assume that, as a spy, Guy had successfully deceived them, even though some of them knew him a great deal better than I did; or at least, so I had always believed.

At that time, in 1950, one was a little less ignorant about the Soviet espionage system than one had been in the 1930s. After all, there had been the Hiss case, there had been a number of well-documented books on the subject, there had been the Canadian spy trial which had led to the conviction of Alan Nunn May,* who had himself been a friend of Guy's and Maclean's at Cambridge. Even so, I found it impossible to accept the terrible implications of Maclean's drunken outburst, if it meant what I took it to mean. So once again I looked for another explanation. The only one I could find was that, as members of the Communist party while at Cambridge, both Guy and Maclean had been enlisted by the Comintern into their espionage organization. For some time they had acted as Comintern agents; later however they had severed their connections with whatever organization they had worked for, though retaining their communist beliefs, and with time had gradually become more outspoken about them, for the very reason that it was no longer so necessary to conceal them. And holding such beliefs, as I no longer did since the German–Soviet pact and the outbreak of the war, they might well regard me as a political renegade who had deserted to the forces of capitalism and reaction.

It was not an entirely satisfactory explanation, but it had a greater plausibility and credibility than the alternative; certainly it was the only one I could find which allowed me to avoid the conclusion that Guy and Maclean were members of an espionage network which had penetrated the Foreign Office and possibly our intelligence services. As such, with some relief, I accepted it. Guy was, after all, my friend; and besides, I had no ambition to be the British Whittaker Chambers, and even if I had, I had nothing like the mass of evidence which Chambers had at his disposal. I had, at the most, a suspicion, which might prove to be entirely without foundation.

VII

For some time after this, I did not hear from Guy or write to him, and so I did not tell him of my curious encounter with Maclean in the Gargoyle. But from other sources I gathered that things were not going well for him. Visitors to America who had met him in Washington had complained to the Foreign Office about his violent anti-Americanism, and when I finally received a letter from him, which was indeed a scream of rage against American policy, it was clear from his own account that he was not in very good odour at the Embassy. This did not, however, appear to trouble him much; the approval of his superiors was not something by which Guy ever set great store. Moreover, life in Washington was made pleasant for him because he was living with an old Cambridge friend, Kim Philby, who, under the

cover of a second secretary at the Embassy, was the representative of
MI6 in the United States. My heart bled for Guy's host and even more
for his host's wife. I thought of the cigarette ends stuffed down the
backs of sofas, the scorched eiderdowns, the iron-willed determination
to have garlic in every dish, including porridge and Christmas pud-
ding, the endless drinking, the terrible trail of havoc which Guy left
behind him everywhere. Yet I knew his misdemeanours would be
readily forgiven, for Guy had a devotion to his friends which inspired
an equal and answering devotion, and strangely enough he never quite
strained it beyond breaking point; though the strain, admittedly, was
often very great indeed.

Somehow I had a feeling, however, that Guy's stay in Washington
would not be unduly prolonged; I felt that he could not live his kind of
life anywhere except in England, where people had become so
accustomed to his conduct and behaviour that they took them for
granted and almost ceased to notice how very odd they were. In
England he was like some bizarre feature of the landscape, like The
Needles or Stonehenge, which local inhabitants have long ceased to
notice unless their attention is directed to them; strangers and
foreigners did not find it so easy to overlook his eccentricities which,
even for an Englishman, were outrageous. So I was not surprised
when, in the spring of 1951, I received a letter from Guy saying that he
had once again become involved in one of those unfortunate incidents
which were so frequent in his experience. By his own account, he had
been driving south from Washington to deliver a lecture at a military
academy; I believe the subject was once again *Red China*. On the way,
he gave a lift to a young man. The journey was a long one and Guy
drove far and, as always very fast; beginning to feel tired, he asked the
young man to take the wheel for a time. He then fell asleep and woke
to find that the young man had been arrested for speeding; feeling that
he himself was responsible, Guy produced his passport and pleaded
diplomatic immunity, which had considerably annoyed the Governor
of Virginia, who had made the most energetic protests to the Embassy
against Guy's behaviour. The Embassy, understandably, was equally
annoyed.

The story had the silent characteristics of most of Guy's stories
about himself, that is to say, it covered most of the facts, in particular
the fact that he was in trouble once again, while contriving to show
that on the whole they were to his credit. Nor was I surprised to
receive a further letter saying that he was really in disgrace and was
being sent home;* he was arriving at Southampton on May 7th and
would like to come immediately and stay with me in the country. He

added that he would probably have to resign or be dismissed from the foreign service, but that this did not greatly worry him as he already had another job in view which he would like to discuss with me.

I must confess that I looked forward to his arrival with considerable interest, but also with some trepidation. I had been ill and had been told to stay in the country to rest and recuperate, and somehow visits from Guy did not conduce to rest and recuperation. Besides, after nearly a year's absence, one could not foresee what kind of condition he would arrive in. When he did arrive, however, after a night in London, and with his luggage still unpacked, we were all most agreeably surprised. America, despite his troubles, seemed to have been good for him. He looked young and well and was in much better shape physically than when he had left England. He did not munch pills continually, and even drank only in moderation. He was delighted to see my children and had brought them some very handsome and expensive presents from New York. And perhaps because of the higher standards of personal appearance required in the United States, he looked much *cleaner* than when he left, as if the Americans had put him through a special dry-cleaning machine for visiting diplomats. His suit was freshly pressed, his handkerchief was clean, even his fingernails were almost clean; so far as such improbable words could ever be applied to Guy, he was spick-and-span. He was gay and charming and delightful as I had not remembered him for many years, and very excited about our house and appreciative of what we had done with it; he gave us long, scurrilous and extremely amusing accounts of life in Washington, and especially in the Embassy, and we were all delighted to find him in such good order and humour.

But it was also evident that he was labouring under a tremendous sense of excitement, as if he were under intense internal pressures. Soon he began to launch into a fierce indictment of America and American policy and the menace of McCarthyism, the imminence of war and the total inability of our Washington Embassy and the Foreign Office to comprehend the catastrophe with which we were all faced. He had with him a briefcase which he never left out of his sight and said that he had some papers which he wanted to show me; 'but first of all', he said, 'I must show you this', and with an air of good-natured triumph produced a personal letter of thanks from Mr Anthony Eden (as he was then) for the extremely interesting tour of Washington on which Guy had conducted him on his recent visit to the United States.* I had a sudden vision of Guy and the Foreign Secretary standing on the steps of Grant's tomb while Guy analysed in great detail the economic conditions in the United States which had made a hero out of a whiskey-drinking ex-regular officer who had been a failure in civilian life; and why this precise concatenation had led to the strategy and victory of Vicksburg, followed I was sure by a convincing demonstration that just as the economic situation of the United States in 1860 had determined the triumph of Grant, so in 1950 it required the triumph of Senator McCarthy. Did Mr Eden enjoy the lecture? Did he even listen? It would have been hard to say; but his letter was very polite and Guy was almost childishly proud of it.

When he had carefully restored it to his pocket, he opened his briefcase and produced a long draft despatch, as from the Embassy in Washington to the Foreign Office. It was an able analysis of the elements in the American political situation, both long term and short term, which in Guy's opinion constituted an immense danger to peace; but it was unbalanced in the sense that it took no account whatever of any counteracting factors. Guy said with some bitterness that his ambassador, Sir Oliver Franks, had refused to forward the despatch to London, that this was the culmination of a series of reverses he had suffered in trying to make his views effective in Washington, and that these rather than his personal misdemeanours were the reason for his being sent home in disgrace. In all this there was not the slightest awareness that a Third Secretary* is not expected to have independent political views and certainly cannot hope that, even if they are brilliant, they are likely to have the official endorsement of his Ambassador. I suddenly had the slightly queasy feeling that I was talking to a lunatic. I had never had quite the same feeling about Guy before, in spite of all the monstrosities of his behaviour. He had always had an extremely sharp insight into the workings of the English social and bureaucratic system. Now he seemed to be throwing all this away, for some purpose which I found myself totally incapable of understanding.

It did not make things any clearer to me when Guy proceeded to say, with the new kind of excitement and agitation which were something quite different from anything I had ever known about him before, that he was not content to leave matters as they were, and that he intended to show his rejected despatch to those people he knew, both within and outside the Foreign Office, who were in any kind of position to influence British foreign policy. I asked him who in particular he meant, and he said that in the first place he would show it to the head of the Far Eastern Department and also to the ex-Minister of State for Foreign Affairs, Kenneth Younger. These, he said, were honest and intelligent men who would understand what he was talking about.

I told him that he was wasting his time and his energy and that, though much of his rejected despatch was a true account of the political situation in the Untied States, it was not nearly objective enough to persuade people who presumably had other and perhaps better sources of information to change their minds. I was quite suddenly appalled by realizing how extraordinarily abstract, and for that reason unrealistic, Guy's views about politics were. My comment for a moment depressed him, but that evening nothing could really affect his good humour and his happiness at being back in England. For a moment they gave me a sad and acute feeling of what a marvellous human being he might have been under better and happier circumstances.

To all my criticisms of his draft he replied, with a kind of cheerful stoicism, that I didn't really understand about politics, or the enormous issues that were at stake, and that there was not much point in discussing them with me. We went on to gossip about Washington and what had happened in England during his absence; he remained cheerful and charming, yet I had the sense that his mind was not really on what we were saying and that the inner tension within him was only awaiting a more sympathetic audience to express itself more completely.

It was a very beautiful spring evening. After dinner we walked down to the river and went to the village pub where we drank beer and Guy told me about his plans for the future. He said he had been suspended from duty and it was extremely unlikely that he would be reinstated. Yet he was extremely optimistic about himself, because through the influence of an old Etonian friend he had received the offer of an appointment as diplomatic correspondent to a leading national news-paper.* He seemed to look forward to the job with pleasure and anti-cipation, though with some twinges of conscience because, as he said, the paper's conservative views were not exactly his own. I tried to reassure him by saying that there was no reason why a correspondent should share his paper's political views,* and said that after so many years of working for bureaucratic organizations like the BBC and the Foreign Office it would be good for him to enjoy the relatively independent life of a journalist; and after all, if what he wanted to do was to bring about a change in British foreign policy, he couldn't do better than to start in his own paper. He laughed, and said I might be right, but I had a feeling that he wasn't really listening to me and that his mind was elsewhere. As we walked home from the pub he said very seriously that he was very sorry about my illness, hoped I would soon get better, and that it wasn't really fair to bother me with his own personal problems at such a time; it would be better, he said, if we avoided political discussions because by now our views obviously lay so far apart that it would only lead to argument. I suddenly had the feeling that in some sense he was counting me out and writing me off as a person who could be of any help to him, and that he had decided it would be a waste of time, or worse, to talk to me about many of the things he wished to discuss. In some kind of way it was like coming to the end of a long journey.

In the morning he got up very early and went down to the river and then came back and played for a long time with the children. Since my wife and I were still in bed, he asked the cook to give him his breakfast and later she said what a charming guest he had been and how beautifully he had played with the children, and the children said what fun it had been to have him to stay and when would he come again. When at length I managed to get up, we went up together on the train to London. In the train he gossiped and chattered placidly and amiably and again I had the impression that, despite his obsessions about American foreign policy, he was physically and mentally in much better condition than before he went to Washington. In London we went into a pub and arranged that he should come and spend the following weekend with me; he seemed almost childishly pleased at the prospect of doing so. While we were in the pub a friend of mine came in who also knew Guy and we gossiped for a few moments and then Guy left. I watched Guy's broad-shouldered figure, bent slightly forward like a bear's, and with a bear's heavy gait, as he went through the swing doors of the pub. It was the last time I ever saw him. When he had gone, my friend remarked how much better Guy was in looks and appearance since he had been in Washington, and how much good America seemed to have done him.

'So clean! So *spruce!*' he kept on muttering in surprise.

VIII

Oddly enough, as the weekend approached, I felt that I did not want to hear any more of Guy's anti-American ravings; they annoyed and depressed me, and yet they seemed the only thing that really engaged his interest or feeling. Since there was really no hurry to see him again, and there would be plenty of further opportunities, I thought it might perhaps be just as well to postpone his visit; there were times when a visit from Guy could seem oppressive and exhausting, as if his shadow blacked out everything else. I telephoned him and asked if he would mind my putting him off. He cheerfully assented and said he would come to see me again soon. I asked him what he had done about his memorandum, and he said that the only person he had as yet shown it to was Donald Maclean. I was surprised, because Maclean had not been mentioned among those to whom he had intended to show it. He also said that he was pursuing negotiations about his appointment as a diplomatic correspondent and was going to dine with his prospective editor the following week. There was nothing in his voice or manner during the conversation to indicate that he was in any way disturbed or distressed; rather, he seemed more than usually cheerful and happy.

So I did not see him at the weekend of the following week, and if I thought of him at all it was to assume that he was actually engaged in trying to reorganize his life. Later, I received accounts of his behaviour from friends of his which I found very difficult to reconcile with the impression I had formed of him. It appeared that he had relapsed into drinking heavily and taking large quantities of drugs and pills of various descriptions. Also a young American, whom Guy had picked up on the boat coming back from America, had suddenly made an appearance and had apparently inspired a series of emotional storms and crises in which both Guy and some of his friends were involved.

On the Thursday night, May 24th, of that week I went to All Souls. I had become Estates Bursar of the college and the time had come for me to prepare my terminal report on the college's finances to its stated general meeting. On the Saturday morning my wife telephoned me, and asked whether Guy had come to Oxford to see me. I was surprised. Why should he have? So I said no, and asked what made her think he might have come. She said she had received a telephone call from Jimmy, the young man who shared Guy's flat, and that he was evidently in a great state of agitation. It appeared that Guy had not returned to the flat on Friday night and that Jimmy seemed to be extremely alarmed by his absence. He had said that Guy had never before done such a thing without letting him know, though, as my wife said, Guy had in fact often enough spent a night with us without telling anyone. She said that Jimmy seemed rather hysterical about the whole matter without very much reason, and I agreed with her; hysteria had come to seem to me an almost inevitable function of all homosexual relationships. There were, after all, all kinds of reasons which would account for Guy's absence from home for one night; he might have got drunk and ended up in a variety of unlikely places, or he might simply have stayed the night in a friend's flat as he had so often done with us.

Yet my wife also seemed slightly distressed and puzzled. She said that on Friday morning Guy had telephoned her, and that they had had a long conversation, only it had been so incoherent and so little of it had made any sense to her that she had assumed he was either drunk or under the influence of drugs and had not really paid much attention to what he was saying. I told her not to be worried, that Jimmy was almost certainly being hysterical, and that really the world had become a very strange place if a person like Guy couldn't spend a night away from home without causing a panic. Yet I am not sure that even at that moment some slight premonition of disaster did not cross my mind; all the same, I assumed that Guy had simply been on a spree or bender of some kind and thought no more about the matter until I returned home on Sunday evening. I began to become seriously alarmed when my wife recounted to me the substance of her telephone conversation with Guy the previous Friday.

He had telephoned her from the Reform Club, and it was her he wished to talk to, not to me. The conversation had lasted about twenty minutes and my wife said it was difficult to give a coherent account of it because Guy had sounded so strange that she really hardly understood what he was saying. Among other things, he had said that he was about to do something which would surprise and shock many people but he was sure it was the right thing to do. My wife, trying to attach some meaning to these mysterious words, thought he was talking about his prospective job as a diplomatic correspondent and meant that some people would think it dishonest of him to join a paper whose political views were so much at variance with his own. But she did not take such qualms of conscience very seriously and uttered the kind of soothing words one uses to drunkards or babies, and said there really was no reason for him to be so distressed. Guy had gone on to say that he would not see me for some time and that this was really for the best, because we no longer saw eye to eye politically; he realized that I was ill and if we met we were bound to disagree and this would only distress me. But I would understand what he was going to do, and indeed was the only one of his friends who would; he repeated this several times with great insistence and then repeated that we should not see each other for some time, perhaps a very long time. By now my wife had resigned herself to a conversation which seemed to her entirely incomprehensible, and confined herself to uttering appropriate words as Guy continued incoherently to repeat that he knew he was doing the right thing and that I would understand.

I should add here that I had never told my wife, or indeed anyone else except one other person,* of my conversation with Guy before the war in which he had said he was a Comintern agent; even though I had so often wondered and speculated about it, I had regarded it as a thing of the past which was better forgotten. So it is not surprising that she could not have made much sense out of Guy's message. And from her account of it, it was not easy for me to make out very clearly what Guy meant. But at least I made this out: that the message was a warning of some kind, and also a farewell. I was not sure what the warning was, but at least it meant that Guy was going away and that this involved some action which might be regarded as sensational even for Guy. I did not by any means think quite so consecutively, but having got so far I suddenly had an absolutely sure and certain, if irrational, intuition that Guy had gone to the Soviet Union.

I may say that in the weeks and months that followed I was never quite so certain of this again; but for a moment the confusion created by all the inconsistencies and aberrations of Guy's behaviour seemed to disappear, and the explanation seemed to be crystal clear. So much so that to my wife's utter bewilderment, and almost without thinking, I said: 'He's gone to Moscow.' Yet even as I spoke the words I felt how wildly improbable and fantastic they would sound to anyone else, and I had only to look at my wife's face to see that this was so. Indeed, when once we began to discuss Guy's absence and to consider all the other and far more plausible reasons why Guy should have gone away for a few days, the more improbable my initial conjecture became.

Yet, after so many years of doubt and speculation, I felt that this time it really was not for me to decide what was the truth of the matter, even though anything I did was likely to involve me in ridicule or perhaps worse. If I was right about what Guy had done, then it seemed to me that even the claims of friendship did not allow me to be silent any more, because the consequences of his action might be in innumerable ways disastrous. I had no choice, I felt, except to inform the proper authorities of Guy's absence, and of what I thought to be the reason for it, even though I didn't much look forward to the polite incredulity with which my story was likely to be received. I explained to my wife what I thought I should do and my reasons for doing it, and even then felt how very odd my explanation sounded, even to a sympathetic listener. It seemed to come out of a past that had vanished, and conjured up a present and a future that bore no relation to our own lives.

It was now late on Sunday night and I telephoned to a friend,* who was also a friend of Guy's and a member of MI6, and told him that Guy had apparently vanished into the blue and that I thought MI5 ought to be told. When he asked why, I said I thought Guy might have defected to the Soviet Union. He was, naturally enough, incredulous, but I was insistent that something should be done and he promised, somewhat reluctantly, that he would inform MI5 of what I said. The next day I received a message from him saying that he had done so and that MI5 would be getting in touch with me.

On Sunday evening, however, I also told another friend of Guy's,★ who had served in MI5 during the war, and still preserved close connections with it, of what I had done. He was greatly distressed, and said he would like to see me. On Monday★ he came down to my house in the country, and on an almost ideally beautiful English summer day, we sat beside the river and I gave him my reason for thinking that Guy had gone to the Soviet Union; his violent anti-Americanism, his certainty that America was about to involve us all in a Third World War, most of all the fact that he may have been and perhaps still was a Soviet agent.

He pointed out, very convincingly as it seemed to me, that these were really not very good reasons for denouncing Guy to MI5. His anti-Americanism was an attitude which was shared by many liberal-minded people and if this alone were sufficient reason to drive him to the Soviet Union, Moscow at the moment would be besieged by defectors seeking asylum. On the other hand, my belief that he might be a Soviet agent rested simply on one single remark made by him years ago and apparently never repeated to anyone else; in any case, Guy's public professions of anti-Americanism were hardly what one would expect from a professional Soviet agent. Most of all he pointed out that Guy was after all one of my, as of his, oldest friends and to make the kind of allegations I apparently proposed to make about him was not, to say the least, the act of a friend.

He was the Cambridge liberal conscience at its very best, reasonable, sensible, and firm in the faith that personal relationships are the highest of all human values. He reminded me of E. M. Forster's famous statement★ that if he had to choose between betraying his country or betraying his friend, he hoped he would have the courage to betray his country. I said that in the appalling political circumstances under which we lived, to betray one's country might mean betraying innumerable other friends and it might also mean betraying one's wife and one's family. I said Forster's antithesis was a false one. One's country was not some abstract conception which it might be relatively easy to sacrifice for the sake of an individual; it was itself made up of a dense network of individual and social relationships in which loyalty to one particular person formed only a single strand. In that case, he said, I was being rather irrational because after all Guy had told me he was a spy a very long time ago and I had not thought it necessary to tell anyone. I said that perhaps I was a very irrational person; but until then I had not really been convinced that Guy had been telling the truth. Now I was, and I was tired of the deceit he had practised over so many years and was only anxious to get rid of all my doubts and suspicions and speculations and pass them on to those whose business it was to say what they were worth.

He pointed out, with some force, that they were not likely to think them worth much; he even gently hinted, out of his own experience, that they might even wonder what on earth I was up to in coming to them with so curious a story. I could not help wondering if this would have been his own reaction when he was a member of MI5 himself and for a moment I had a sense of how profoundly English he was; but I repeated that I now felt that the only thing I could do was to tell the security authorities what I thought I knew as fully and precisely as I could and leave to them what use, if any, they might wish to make of it. At least it would not be my problem any more.

And so we left. He did not disguise his disapproval of what I was going to do. I spent the night in some misery and marvelled at the wonderful web of trickery and deceit Guy had woven around himself and wondered even now if I was not being foolish in believing a single word he had ever said. And yet, despite all this, and despite my conversation of that afternoon, I somehow recovered something of my conviction of the previous evening that Guy had, for whatever reason, gone to the Soviet Union, and rather irrationally this somehow cheered me up and I went to sleep.

Cheerfulness, however, did not last for long. I felt both alarmed and despondent when the next day I went up to London and made my way to MI5.* I could not help reflecting on the process of events which, since my Oxford days, had finally brought me to the extraordinary position of laying information to the security authorities against one of my best friends, and on the almost total transformation in society, and perhaps in myself, this implied. It was as if somewhere along the line continuity had been broken and something new and strange had emerged, so that I hardly knew myself or the world I lived in.

At MI5 I was taken into the presence of an officer whom I had known during the war and who had also known Guy well.* For a moment this made things seem easier; it was as if it was all in the family. But it also made me feel even more foolish and the whole affair more improbable; this was not the kind of thing that happened between friends. I felt as if, from afar, Guy was exercising his gift of introducing the element of farce into everything he did, however serious or even disastrous it might be.

But this sense quickly passed when, after a few questions, I began my story and I became aware of the intense seriousness with which it was listened to. I had expected surprise or even incredulity rather than this atmosphere of concentrated, even strained attention. After all, it was a very improbable story; all I really had to say was that Guy had been absent for four days and that from this I had deduced that he had gone to Moscow.

And here this particular story really ends, for what I had to tell them at MI5 was the same story that I have told here. But when I had finished, feeling, as one always does under such circumstances, that what I had to say sounded extraordinarily thin and unconvincing, there was a long silence. Then the officer, who was the head of the department concerned, gave me a curious look; I shall never be quite certain what it meant. After a moment he said, in a detached and matter-of-fact voice:

'Of course, you knew that Guy did not go alone?'

It was certainly the last question I had expected and for a moment I was too bewildered to reply. Then I said, rather foolishly:

'You mean that Guy really has gone?'

'Yes.'

'And that someone else has gone too?'

'Yes.'

'Who is it?' I said.

'Donald Maclean. They went together.'

Then I realized with a terrible sinking of the heart that everything I had thought about Guy was true; but that matters were even worse than I thought. They seemed even worse when I emerged from the office and in the street saw the headlines in the evening papers announcing that two British diplomats had vanished into thin air.

Five

It might be thought that Guy's disappearing act would have confirmed all the suspicions I had ever had about him. In fact, it did not do so, and indeed it was surrounded by so much mystery that it merely raised a multitude of further questions. After his initial flight from England, and landing in France, all trace of Guy, and of Maclean, had been lost, and despite all the investigations that were set on foot, there was not the slightest clue to their whereabouts, or to why Guy in particular had taken so desperate a step. Maclean's case was different. He had every reason for flight; but, except for old friendship, there was no reason to connect Guy's case with his, and, after the event, there were so many different accounts of Guy's behaviour after his return from Washington that one could quite reasonably believe that he had acted on impulse rather than deliberate design. Had Maclean appealed to Guy in his trouble and had Guy merely assisted him to leave England, with the intention of returning himself later?* He had telephoned to W. H. Auden in Ischia; had he, for reasons of his own intended to visit him and take a Mediterranean holiday? Was there any reason to believe that he and Maclean were still together, or would remain together, or that their joint disappearance had been anything except a coincidence? Everything seemed to point to the fact that Guy's decision to leave had been taken on the spur of the moment; was it conceivable that, in the short time left to him, he could have so quickly and efficiently made all the plans and arrangements required to carry them across the Channel without leaving behind any clue to their destination?

Today, when so much more is known about their disappearance, and the part which Kim Philby played in it, and Guy himself is dead in Moscow, it is difficult to believe that one could ever have had any doubts about the answer to such questions. But at the time I was certainly not alone in doing so. The police, the security services, the press of all Europe scoured the continent in an effort to identify the whereabouts of the missing diplomats; who was I to be sure of what had happened, when so many other were not? It is not an easy thing to accept that one of one's oldest friends is a spy, even if he once told you that he was; in Guy's case I felt justified, for friendship's sake, in allowing him the benefit of every doubt so long as it was still possible to believe in his innocence, though perhaps innocence is not quite the right word. It would have been hard at any time to think of Guy as innocent. All one hoped for was that it would not be necessary to think the worst of him. I preferred to regard his disappearance as an unsolved mystery; sometimes I used to repeat to myself Browning's lines:*

> What's become of Waring
> Since he gave us all the slip,
> Chose land-travel or seafaring,
> Boots and chest, or staff and scrip,
> Rather than pace up and down
> Any longer London-Town?

Indeed it was perhaps not inappropriate to apply the poem to Guy. There was a real affinity between him and the poem's original inspiration, the swashbuckling, vainglorious biographer of Byron and Shelley who entranced all his literary friends with his tales of derring-do in outlandish parts of the world and his hints of dark and un-speakable mysteries in his life. Only what Trelawny related as legend, Guy turned into farce.

Guy's disappearance also had other, more direct consequences which were rather different from anything I might have expected. I had made my statement to MI5 in the belief, or the hope, that having once unburdened my conscience, I might dismiss him and his affairs from my mind. It was like Guy that by a characteristic oversight he should have made so easy an escape impossible; one might almost have thought he had done it on purpose.

His telephone call to my wife, on the morning of his disappearance, had been made from the Reform Club. It was a long and expensive call and Guy had forgotten to pay for it; but it had been easy for the club to trace, and the amount owing in Guy's name, together with the time and date of the call and my telephone number in the country, had been posted on the members' notice board at the entrance of the club. And there the notice remained until it was found by some enterprising journalist, who promptly and accurately deduced that this long personal call was the last Guy was known to have made before leaving the country. Surely it must contain some clue to the mystery of his disappearance?

The results, for me, and even more for my wife, who had actually received the call, were disastrous. My identity, my address in the country, and my telephone number were soon known to the Press of the entire country, whose representatives descended upon my house at Sonning as if some notorious criminal, or his accomplices, were in hiding there. Their cars packed my drive; the doorbell and telephone rang incessantly; they took photographs of my wife, myself, and my children from every conceivable angle. They camped in the village and besieged the local pubs and pursued their enquiries in all the village shops; they pressed chocolates and half crowns on my children in their search for information about Guy, and my children were only too happy to exercise their imagination on satisfying their curiosity. My wife's slightly incoherent account of her even more incoherent conversation with Guy only convinced the Press that there was something to conceal; indeed, even we had to admit that it didn't sound very convincing. Photographed as *Mother of Four Knew Burgess*, she became a regular feature of the daily papers, which somehow succeeded in importing an indefinable air of kinkiness into the relationship. Some members of the Press simply took this for granted; one who by some means penetrated into the house introduced himself with the words: 'It's all right to talk to me, Mrs Rees. I'm bi-sexual myself.'

This form of persecution lasted for several weeks. It seemed as if pandemonium had suddenly descended on our lives, and we learned to live with journalists as one does with bugs in the walls; it was impossible to drive them out. For the Cold War was raging; the 'Case of the Missing Diplomats' had become a world-wide sensation, threatening our national security, and we found ourselves at the centre of it. Each day new stories appeared in the Press, and each day, like modern Scarlet Pimpernels, Guy and Maclean, together or apart, were reported to have been seen in different parts of Europe. They had been seen in Paris, they had been seen in Monte Carlo, they had been seen in Berlin, they had been seen in Prague; once, to my dismay, I was rung up in the middle of the night to be told that Guy had been seen leaving Reading station, presumably on his way to visit me at Sonning. Amid considerable publicity, and at great expense, the *Daily Express* hired the redoubtable Colonel Pinto, 'the greatest spy hunter in the world', to conduct a search for the missing pair that would take him throughout the length and breadth of Europe without discovering a trace of them. Each item of news, or what purported to be news, provoked a fresh barrage of telephone calls or visits by reporters to ask what one thought about it; for the most remarkable feature of the case was that there was really no news at all, and any kind of comment, or even a refusal to comment was eagerly seized on as a means of stimulating and appeasing public curiosity.

It was clear that I was not going to be allowed to forget Guy very easily, however much I might wish to; he had become a kind of permanent shadow who never left my side. Sometimes I even had hallucinations in which I suddenly glimpsed his tall, slightly hunched figure, disappearing round the corner of the street. Even when, after some months, the appetite for news of press and public began to die of starvation, some stray item of gossip or rumour would revive it, and once again the telephone would ring, reporters would present themselves at the door, and the great machine of publicity lumber into action. For the truth was that the case of the missing diplomats had all the elements of one of those stories of crime and detection in which public interest never really dies, and it had an uncanny capacity for keeping itself alive. It had treachery and deceit, it had politics, it had espionage, it had sex, of an off-beat kind, it had the flavour of high society which people mistakenly associate with diplomatic circles, and it had, almost to excess, those touches of the eccentric and bizarre which have been compulsory in all detective stories since Sherlock Holmes first made them possible. What writer could create a hero, or a villain, whose favourite food was, like Guy's, a dried fish which, in the heart of London, he hung out of his window on a piece of string and occasionally hauled in, in order to cut himself a slice and satisfy his hunger?

Most of all, perhaps, it had as its heart and centre a profound psychological puzzle, which was how it could be that two young Englishmen, both of them gifted and intelligent, and of the most irreproachable social background and upbringing, should suddenly, for whatever motive, abandon everything to which their privileged position entitled them and take off into the blue. One would be hard enough to explain, but *two* of them? It made of the case not only a puzzle which, until the truth was known, provided an almost unlimited field for speculation, but, vaguely, a kind of threat; it made people feel that in a society in which such things were possible, anything was possible, and there was nothing one could be sure of, as if everywhere unseen abysses yawned beneath one's feet. The missing diplomats (how strange it was to think of Guy in the image of a diplomat!) not only evoked the kind of curiosity which makes one want to know the end of a detective story; it made people uneasy until they knew the answer.

For the time being, however, there was no answer to be had, and the story remained a mystery. But it was not only a mystery in itself, it suggested other possible mysteries. For if one assumed that Guy and Maclean had been enemy agents, was it likely or possible that they had worked in total isolation, without collaborators or accomplices; if there had been two of them, would there not also have been more? As months went by, it became evident that at least one possible accomplice existed in the person of the mysterious Third Man, who was believed to have given warning that Maclean was to be taken in for interrogation and so had provoked his, and Guy's, flight; but it had been authoritatively announced in Parliament that this hypothetical figure was not Kim Philby, Guy's friend and late host in Washington, who had indeed come under suspicion but after a rigorous enquiry by the security service had been totally exonerated.

What else could one do but accept such a verdict, delivered on such impeccable authority? Yet the whole of my association with Guy, together with the fact of his flight, had by now left me with an incurable disposition to doubt and suspect all impeccable authorities. If I had, for so many years, dismissed his own assertion that he was, or had been a spy, it was precisely because so many of Guy's friends and intimates had been in a position to verify his credentials and had presumably found no reason to doubt them; if their judgement was not to be trusted, whose could be? Who was I, who had so much less information at my command, to think that mine was any better? To do so seemed both presumptuous and to conjure up such a miasma of doubt and suspicion that one could put one's trust in no one.

Such mysteries, I decided, were not for me to solve; it would be impossible to live at all if one felt that at the very heart of the country's security system there lay some fatal flaw which constantly exposed it to error and disaster. It would be as if some explorer, having accidentally stumbled on some country's most secret shrine, had discovered that its altar was made of papier maché and its priests were a gang of devil worshippers – or perhaps merely grinning imbeciles. The whole thing was too absurd.

So at least I argued to myself; and in any case why should I worry if the altar was hollow, so long as I did not worship it myself? Espionage and counter-espionage were at best some kind of absurd game to which no rational person could attach any serious significance. Yet in fact, at some irrational level, all the circumstances of Guy's disappearance had left me with a sense that somewhere something was appallingly wrong and that if only I tried hard enough and thought deeply enough I should be able to find the clue to what it was.

In part this was an effect of the reception I had been given by MI5. When I first told them that I believed Guy had gone to Moscow, it was largely out of a sense of desperation and urgency. Guy had hardly been two days gone, and I had felt that it was still not too late to prevent a calamity, even that, if only the means and resources were available, I myself could follow his trail and might possibly prevail on him to return. At least, I felt that if anyone could so I could, if the opportunity were made available.

Perhaps this was too much to expect; responsible organizations do not take action on the intuitions of some uninformed outsider or respond to a slightly hysterical message out of the blue. What puzzled me then, and continued to puzzle me later was that, as far as Guy was concerned, my message must have been the first intimation they received that, as far as he was concerned, anything was amiss; could it really be that I alone, among all those who had known him, and some even better than I, was the only one who had ever had suspicions of him or any knowledge that threw doubt on his reliability? It seemed to me impossible that this could be so, and of course in fact it was not so; only unfortunately those who, like Kim Philby, had shared that knowledge were precisely those who had most interest in concealing it.

There was a further aspect of MI5's behaviour which made me feel uneasy. I had always felt that if at any time prior to Guy's disappearance I had told MI5 what I thought I knew about Guy, my story would have been received with polite scepticism, even incredulity, as the product of an overheated imagination stimulated by reading too much about Soviet espionage. But now that I had done so, and at the very moment of Guy's disappearance, it must surely have seemed to them something more than a coincidence; why, after so many years of silence, should a person like myself, with no professional interest in the case, suddenly volunteer information which certainly did no credit to one of my best friends and not very much to myself? The questions they put to me at my interview, indeed their very manner of asking them, made an oddly ambivalent impression; I seemed to detect in them a note of – what was it? – of something very nearly approaching moral disapproval, as if I had acted in a manner unbecoming a gentleman, combined with a hardly concealed disbelief in my motives for offering information at precisely the moment when it was too late. It would have been too much to say that they treated me as if I myself were an object of suspicion;* it was simply that they conveyed the impression that, from their point of view, there was something very peculiar about the whole performance.

I had been taken aback by their manner; somehow it was not what I had expected. It was almost as if they resented my intervention and I were an added embarrassment in a situation which was already embarrassing enough. On the other hand, it hardly seemed to matter what they thought of me. I had told them all I knew, and what use, if any, they made of the information was no concern of mine. And yet, just as they seemed suspicious of me, so I in turn was not without suspicion of them. I felt as if I had intruded into some complicated game they were playing and had made some unorthodox move which interfered with its smooth progress; their reaction, I felt, was to remove the intruder as painlessly as possible and reduce the effect of his intervention to a minimum.

Beneath all this was another consideration which made me feel vaguely uneasy. It had become clear that Maclean, at least, had certainly been engaged in espionage; and whatever doubts one might have had about what part Guy had played in his operations, there was no doubt that he had been willing to assist Maclean to escape the consequences of being found out. I myself felt sure that their behaviour had its origins in the days when many years ago they had been communists together in Cambridge; the most natural assumption to make was that at that time they had both been recruited into the Soviet espionage system.

All this seemed plain; but if this were so, then it also seemed highly unlikely that Guy and Maclean were the only ones among their contemporaries at Cambridge to have been recruited. The Hiss case had shown that in America in the 1930s large numbers of young intellectuals had been enlisted into the Soviet espionage system: they had been, *mutatis mutandis*,* of the same class and social background as Guy and Maclean, and they had had considerable success in penetrating the United States government; in this sense at least there was a basis of fact to the extravagances and demagoguery of Senator McCarthy's wild accusations. Was it likely that in Britain the Soviet Union would have been satisfied with some lesser objective and have been content with the recruitment of two young men of whom, at the moment, it would have been impossible to say whether they would have been of any future use? It seemed highly probable that if Guy and Maclean had been recruited as spies, so had others, and that, if they had vanished, others remained. But who? I had the uneasy feeling that the likeliest place to look was in the ranks of the security services themselves.*

There seemed to be only one other conclusion to draw. If one assumed that Maclean's value had been in the high-level political information to which he had access, then Guy's would have consisted in the extremely varied and comprehensive knowledge he had acquired, largely as a result of personal relationships, of the British security services. Of the two types of information, I had no doubt which would have been considered of most value by the Soviet espionage system; nor which was likely to have the most practical, and the most deplorable results.

Political or diplomatic information, however secret, is very rarely of great value; certainly of no greater value than the information available to any enterprising, pertinacious and intelligent journalist. Moreover, it is very rarely reliable, in the sense that it can be acted upon, because it is concerned with questions of policy, and policy is always subject to change and also to conflicting interpretations. In the great game of espionage, the information which is most highly valued is that which enables one to identify the players on the opposite side; that is to say, the members of the enemy espionage system.* In the same way, the highest degree of secrecy attaches to identity of the members of one's own team. That is why espionage is for the most part a self-defeating activity, in which the two opposing sides fight a fierce fratricidal battle behind closed doors with the ultimate objective of wiping the other side out. Any information which confers an advantage in the battle is of the very highest value; moreover, since it refers to individual human beings, it has the technical advantage of being concrete, detailed, and subject to verification; it can even be subjected to experiment. Moreover, it can be acted upon in the most direct and practical manner; that is to say, it can be used to destroy the reputation, credit, honour, and in critical cases even the lives of one's opponents. I had no doubt that Guy was admirably equipped to supply this particular kind of information; and also that it was information which could have the most disastrous results for the individuals whom it concerned.

But it was also true that his main source of such information was the friends and acquaintances he cultivated so assiduously in the British intelligence services; and that among them were several who had been contemporaries of his at Cambridge, that is to say, that they belonged to precisely those intellectual and radical circles to which Guy and Maclean had themselves. Given that Guy was a spy, the question for any alert intelligence officer to ask at this point was whether his sources of information were conscious or unconscious; whether they had merely been indiscreet or insecure in their conversations with him, or whether they, or some of them, had collaborated with him in the common task of penetrating the British intelligence services.

Why did I feel that our security services were incapable of seriously addressing such a question to themselves? I should have found it very difficult to give any very rational or convincing explanation, even to myself. It was simply the sense that the members of our intelligence services were, in so many cases, so closely bound together by ties of origin, upbringing, education and class that they were effectively inhibited from facing the possibility that there were traitors in their midst. Of course, in the case of Maclean, and possibly of Guy, it had already been shown that there were persons of their own kind who were capable of such treachery; but this in itself was so unnatural and monstrous that it could only constitute a unique case, never again to be repeated.

Our security services, in fact, seemed to me a microcosm of that 'great capitalist class', now in the process of intellectual disintegration, whose structure and organization, modes of behaviour and thought, I had found so alien when I first went to Oxford. In those days I had devoted much time and thought to studying them; they had fascinated me as the discovery of some hitherto unknown animal species might fascinate a zoologist. I had wondered at how easily they accepted the assumption that they were destined to form as it were 'the committee of management' of the country of which they were the most privileged citizens, believing indeed that their very privileges, not merely of wealth or birth, but of intellect and ability, gave them the right to be so. And in a sense they had been right; but even then, now nearly a quarter of a century ago, I had felt that there was a kind of worm at the heart of the glossy apple, ruddy and rounded to perfection, which they held out to one for one's admiration. The worm, I had thought, had been the inordinate and predominant importance which they had ascribed to personal relationships, organized into a philosophical and ethical system, and even into a system of government. In *Principia Ethica* G. E. Moore had appeared to give an absolute value to such an attitude; but Moore had been misunderstood, and even Moore, it seemed to me, had never done more than erect his personal intuitions into a philosophy. However deeply we may feel the value of personal relationships it is impossible to abstract and divorce them from other, impersonal factors in our lives both material and spiritual, which are of equal or of even greater importance, and indeed if we do so we may deprive personal relations themselves of the roots which give them their real life and vitality.

The exaggerated, indeed, supreme importance ascribed to personal relationships in Cambridge, as at Oxford, at the end of the 1920s, could be interpreted as the mark of a society which was becoming increasingly incapable of mastering, whether in theory or practice, the problems of the real world, and in this sense it reflected the decline of a great intellectual tradition, of which G. E. Moore himself was one of the inheritors. The decline may have been due in large part to the terrible blood-letting which the British governing class had suffered in the First Word War; a sharp awareness of this decline played a major part in the complex of reasons which drove Guy and many of his contemporaries into the arms of communism. They were inspired, not so much by sympathy with the suffering of the working class at a time of capitalist crisis, as by an awareness that their own class, 'the great capitalist class', could no longer find a remedy for them. Of the working class in fact they knew nothing and they worshipped it as an idol whose virtue and power they accepted on the evidence of things unseen. It was the defects and inadequacies of their own class which effected their conversion; in the Soviet Union and communism they saw a new world which they called in to restore the balance of the old.

No doubt their commitment to communism led some of them into ways which were infinitely more evil and destructive than those they had abandoned; but perhaps they were not mistaken in their perception of the declining vitality and intellectual power of the class to which they themselves belonged, even though their own conversion to communism might be only another manifestation of it. But at least they had achieved one particular insight which put them, as it were, one step ahead of those among their contemporaries who, while Guy and Maclean had become spies, had drifted, without particular conviction, into becoming counter-spies. These recruits to the British intelligence service, of whom Guy used sometimes to say that they had the characteristic vices and weaknesses of 'the failed intellectual', seemed to me to be fatally inhibited from solving the problems offered by Guy's and Maclean's defection by the intellectual and emotional assumptions of the class to which they belonged, and against which Guy and Maclean had revolted; by mistaken loyalties based on old friendships and intimacies, by failure to understand the inadequacy of their own attitudes and beliefs, by inability to accept that the motives which had operated in Guy's and Maclean's case might also operate in others. Perhaps indeed they might prefer that the problems might remain unsolved; for certainly the answer would reveal much about themselves as well as Guy and Maclean.

So I continued to feel that the task of unravelling the mystery of the missing diplomats was in ineffective hands; indeed, that some of those hands may have been engaged in the same kind of enterprises as Guy. I remained convinced that Guy and Maclean had not been alone in their activities, but that, for reasons which were deeply rooted in the English social system, it was unlikely that their collaborators would be discovered.

II

At the Christmas following his disappearance, I received a card, with an English postmark, from Guy. It merely sent his greetings and expressed the hope that some time we should meet again. It was at least evidence that he was still alive, though not of much else, but somehow the message did not affect me very deeply. Guy's flight had been the culmination of so many years of doubt and speculation, and had caused so much distress not only to my family and myself, but to a wide circle of his friends, that I no longer wished to see or hear any more of him. He had vanished out of my life, and when I thought of him it was rather as one thinks of a character in a novel or a play, who for some time has had the power to stir one's emotions and absorb one's interest but has no connection with the actual task of daily living.

Yet, perhaps, he still had the power of indirectly affecting my own behaviour. His disappearance, and the events which had led up to it, had somehow intensified my doubts and misgivings about the society in which I was now, it appeared, so firmly rooted. Perhaps this was because Guy, with all his eccentricities and deviations, had always seemed to me one of the most English of characters; indeed, one could not have conceived of him as being anything else than English. No doubt he was an exception, but he was also representative, an exception which proved the rule perhaps, only I could not quite make out what the rule was; unless it was that he was a part, and a significant part, of a society which, at this stage in its long history, had lost its way, and with it, the qualities which had once made it great. Perhaps his flight had only been the precursor of other flights, in different directions, which others would soon take in order to evade the realities of the world in which they were doomed to live.

There was a time, during the war, when England had seemed to recover the virtues of its past greatness. As a gunner in the ranks I had for the first time come into close, even bodily contact, with that great English working class which had so often been the object of Marxist theory and speculation; it had touched me to see in these dockers, labourers, clerks, drunkards, gamblers, from the East End of London the same qualities of the English as we know them in the works of Shakespeare, or Fielding, or Defoe, or Dickens; the same tolerance and forbearance, the same gifts of humour and imagination, combined with the residue of something which was almost barbarism yet gave them a kind of primitive power of endurance. Yet the war itself had proved to be one more stage in a long decline, and in post-war England there was little or no evidence that the decline could be averted or halted. There were of course objective reasons, historical, political and economic, why this should be so; but history is made by men and it seemed to me that the men who effectively ruled, governed and administered England after the war were not the men required to reverse its long decline into mediocrity.

> Get you the sons your fathers got
> And God will save the Queen.*

They were not the men their fathers were. They were in many ways more enlightened, more humane, more civilized, more progressive, but some mysterious inner core of adjustment to the world as it really is, and not as it seems or one wishes it to be, had been lost. It struck me, with an almost personal sense of involvement, that, grown to maturity, they were the men whom I had known some twenty years ago as undergraduates, and that having achieved the power and responsibility they had always assumed the right to expect, they were now unable to make effective use of them.

Perhaps Guy cast his shadow over such ideas. It had been one of his favourite themes to contrast the greatness of the Victorians, in politics, in industry, in literature, with the littleness of their descendants, and he would elaborate his theme by describing the fall of the British steel industry or the Royal Navy from their position of pre-eminence in the world, or by comparing George Eliot with E. M. Forster, or Dickens with D. H. Lawrence; nothing exemplified it better, to his mind, than the difference in sheer intellectual power between those eminent Victorians, Manning, Arnold, Newman, and their biographer, Lytton Strachey, who had chosen them as the victims of his wit and malice. It was a case, he thought, of a pigmy sneering at giants; and in that 'secret' society of the Apostles at Cambridge, of which he was a member, he saw the same decline from the greatness of the English past.

Perhaps such thoughts helped to intensify in me an uneasy sense of dissatisfaction with my own life, though on the surface at least there seemed to be little reason for it. My marriage, and my children, had brought me great happiness. I had ceased to be a journalist and had joined an old friend, Henry Yorke, as a director of his family engineering business. It was a change which I found eminently satisfactory, because after the war journalism had become less and less attractive to me, while engineering introduced me to an entirely new and unfamiliar world which I found unexpectedly fascinating.* My duties, which were far from arduous, were enlivened by day-to-day and almost minute-to-minute contact with Henry himself, who both as a writer and a person had something which was very near to genius, if genius means a completely individual view of life which reveals reality in an entirely new and unexpected light. To live side by side with him in the office was to see the world through a new and entirely different pair of eyes; in the course of the day he turned from Henry Yorke the businessman, much concerned with money and profit, to Henry Green the novelist, writing books between the intervals of negotiating contracts for brewing machinery and chemical plant, and he allowed me the same liberty in the use I made of my time.*

In addition, as Estates Bursar of All Souls,* I had been brought back into closer contact with the college, and with Oxford, than I had been for many years, though both had greatly changed from what they once were. Gone were the aesthetes and the hearties, and gone also the radicals and revolutionaries who had succeeded them; the immediate post-war generation of undergraduates was intensely serious and hardworking, far more responsible and mature than those of my own day and with no time for their kind of follies and eccentricities. Their studies came first, all the more so because the war had made England poor and economic pressures made the problem of a career very important to them. The dons also had changed; a much higher proportion were married, and the pleasures and cares of domestic life now occupied the place which had once been reserved for their pupils. The home, not the college, was now the centre of their lives, and that community in which both dons and undergraduates had played an equal part, of which not a trace remains today, was already beginning to break down.

But life at All Souls was agreeable and interesting to me at that time because of the presence of a group of young philosophers* to whom their subject was a matter of consuming interest; they pursued it with a passion which other men might have devoted to girls or horses. This was odd, because their particular kind of philosophy was arid and scholastic to the last degree and was almost exclusively concerned with linguistic and semantic problems. They argued about words, and more particularly those words of which, because they are a matter of common usage, everyone thinks he understands the meaning, with the same intensity as Browning's grammarian settled Hoti's business.* Under the influence of a remarkable man, J. L. Austin, himself once a Fellow of All Souls, who by moral rather than intellectual power ruled them as a stern schoolmaster rules unruly pupils, they pursued this philosophical game with almost religious devotion, and nothing could have been more curious than the fervour and piety with which they joined in his profound enquiries into the exact meaning, in a multitude of different contexts, of such words as 'is', 'if' and 'not'.

Their intellectual labours may have been arid but they themselves were not; on the contrary, they had the gaiety and lightheartedness of the single-minded. They were like young men who were engaged in a crusade, who felt that at last the mysteries of the universe were to be, if not solved, at least eliminated as the product of mere verbal confusions, and they applied themselves to this process of mental hygiene with the zeal of a highly efficient municipal cleansing department. Error, not truth, was their quarry, and they hunted it down relentlessly in every word or phrase one spoke; but like Austin himself, they brought to the chase a certain dry humour and wit which made it as much of a pastime as an intellectual exercise.

There was an absurdity about their entire enterprise, and their devotion to it, which gave it a certain eccentric charm, and to me at least made their company highly entertaining and stimulating. Their conversation enlivened my visits to the college to attend to its financial affairs, which was largely a matter of trying to reconcile our excessive income with an inadequate expenditure. For largely through the efforts of my predecessor, Geoffrey Faber, the college was rich. He had nursed its estates through the agricultural depression of the 1920s and 1930s, had undertaken large schemes of capital investment, built housing estates and roads, so that when I succeeded him they were in an extremely prosperous condition. There had been a time when no rent could be low enough to attract a tenant to some of the college's estates, and the college had to resort to direct farming; Whitsundoles, a farm in Romney Marsh, was a name that resounded mournfully at every college meeting because of the losses which had been incurred on it.

By 1951, when I succeeded Faber, the college estates had increased enormously in value, both because of the general prosperity of English agriculture and because of Faber's wise policies. One of the first problems which met me as Estates Bursar was how best to dispose of a sum of over £1,000,000, which had been received in compensation for the public acquisition of its lands in Edgware, a part of the college's original endowment by its founder, Archbishop Chichele. But colleges like All Souls, which have enjoyed a continuous existence since the Middle Ages, have a long communal memory which often proves stronger than the rational intentions of the living. They remember the bad times as well as the good, and tend to regard any increase in prosperity as purely fortuitous and accidental. When it was proposed that the college should seek a further increase in its wealth by investing its funds in equities, there was a sense that, for five hundred years, only the land had kept the college alive through all its varying fortunes. I could not help being impressed, as if by the voice of some ancient wisdom, by a remark of Lord Brand's, chairman of Lazard's and a director of the Bank of England, who was one of the college's shrewdest financial advisers: 'If there had been such a thing as equities in the Middle Ages,' he said scornfully, 'there wouldn't be a college in existence in Oxford today.' How astonishing it was, in the middle of the twentieth century, to hear one who was a master of all the mysteries of contemporary high finance, speak as if, so far as Oxford was concerned, what had been valid in the Middle Ages was still valid today! It was an assertion that, for a college, survival and continuity are more important than profit and that its primary duty is, like the land, to live for ever.

The land! When I first became Estates Bursar, it still constituted the main source of the college's wealth. In those days, the college estates consisted of some thirty thousand acres which extended as far as Yorkshire in the north, Kent in the south, Norfolk in the east and Shropshire in the west. I found the supervision of the estates, under the guidance and tuition of the college's extremely efficient agents, an absorbing and fascinating occupation.* Like Henry Yorke's engineering business, it brought me into contact with an aspect of England I had not known before; in this case the land, not as an object of beauty, or pleasure, or art, but as a means, and the most ancient means of all, by which men make their living. Sometimes, talking to the tenant of some bleak hill farm in Yorkshire, the wind from the moors whistling round my ears as I listened to his complaints, to his requests for a new milking parlour or some improvement to his house, I used to remember my grandfather's little farm in Wales and think it was certainly better to be the tenant of a wealthy Oxford college than to depend on the spend-thrift eccentricities of the Pryses of Plas Gogerddan. I could hardly believe that on the fat pastures of Romney Marsh an acre could carry eight of its ponderous Kentish sheep while one of our tender Welsh ones could hardly survive on eight acres of Plynlimon's sparse mountain grass. I used to recite to myself *The War Song of Dinas Fawr*:*

> The mountain sheep are sweeter,
> But the valley sheep are fatter;
> We therefore deemed it meeter
> To carry off the latter.

My wife and children; a pleasant house with a large garden on the Thames; a business that was in itself interesting and allowed me leisure to write what I wished; the academic life of All Souls, combined with the mundane realities of managing the college properties; all this was enough to provide me with an active and satisfactory life and should, I suppose, have been sufficient to keep me happy. And yet it was not. Somehow my life had taken a path I had not intended and chance had cast me in a part which I could not play with conviction. I seemed to have become a different person and I regretted the one I had been. I was not unhappy but I was vaguely dissatisfied and disorientated, as if forces beyond my control had set me on a course which I had not chosen for myself and from which henceforth there would be no deviation.

Such feelings, I am sure, were quite unjustified. In my case at least, the difficulties of living had never arisen out of pursuing too settled and regular a course, but rather out of failure to remain on any course at all except for the briefest periods. It was always the unexpected and not the expected that had happened; even my marriage had taken me by surprise; and winds, storms or soft and scented breezes had never come from the quarter in which one had looked for them. There was no reason for me to regret that, for the time being, life had treated me almost too kindly or to have felt that I was overburdened with security. All I had to do was to wait for the hand of chance to reveal itself once again, and in the meantime enjoy the good things which life had given me.

And indeed in a way chance did show its hand and in a way which could not have been more surprising; only this time it required my own collaboration to produce its effect, and this was disastrous. There is a particular class of people, to which I belong, which if offered a choice between two particular courses of action will almost invariably choose what is from their own point of view the wrong one, because they do not understand what they themselves are like and therefore mis-calculate the most important factor in the situation.

On this occasion chance showed its hand in the form of a letter from Aberystwyth asking me if I were willing to be considered for the appointment of Principal of the University College of Wales. If I had been wise, I would have recognized in the letter a most dangerous form of seduction; and if I had had any sense I would have realized that such letters, particularly if they come from Wales, are never quite what they seem and are usually the product of long hours of not entirely disinterested thought and deliberation.* I should have been warned, and I should have been even more on my guard if I had known that, though the letter did not come directly from him, its writing concealed the fine Welsh hand of Dr Thomas Jones, once Under-Secretary to the Cabinet, adviser to two Prime Ministers, now President of the University College and a kind of *éminence grise* in the management of the affairs of the Welsh people; for Dr Jones was a skilled manipulator of men and situations and nothing he did was ever as simple as it might seem.*

I did not, however, try to decipher the implications of the letter, because, on first reading, it simply appeared absurd. Why should anyone think that, after so many years of absence, I should return to that bleak little town in which I had been born and that now seemed as remote as the childhood I had spent there? It was like being asked to return to the nursery and play again with the toys which had been discarded since infancy, and all the more so since after leaving Wales I had thought of it as the land of a dying language and culture which could no longer satisfy anyone except the very young and the very old.

Yet the letter obscurely appealed to some confused instinct within me which told me that precisely now, after so many years, was perhaps the time when I should return. I was even inclined to flatter myself that perhaps my very absence might have given me something to offer, in the way of experience or knowledge which I should not have had if I had not lived away from Wales for so long. Had not Dr Jones himself entitled a book of his *The Native Never Returns*, because the native who does return is a different person from the one who left? Might it not be that he and the native who had never left his home might together achieve something different and better than either could have done in isolation? There was something stimulating, even exciting in the idea that there, in Aberystwyth, stood an institute of learning which had already played a large part in the life of the Welsh people and which now one might, with patience and persistence, help to play an even greater part. I was sufficiently persuaded of the value of university education, and especially the education of young Welshmen, to believe that this was something worth doing, and I thought that perhaps a university which genuinely fulfilled its function was perhaps of all things the one which my people most needed.

Such indeed had been the hope of the original founders of the university college, the first of its kind in Wales, at the end of the nineteenth century. It had been founded by private subscription and on the pennies of the poor, and had been intended to give the Welsh people educational and intellectual opportunities which had hitherto been denied them, to show them wider horizons than the confines of the farm or the coal-pit, and to enable them to play a larger part in the life of the world than had been open to them until then. Its founders had been inspired by a generous spirit; they had believed passionately in the native intelligence of the Welsh people and their capacity to achieve a wider and more self-critical culture than that of the mine, the chapel and the farm. They had dreamed of breeding a new race of Welshmen who, through the cultivation of the mind, might raise themselves and their people out of the slough of ignorance and poverty in which they had languished for centuries and out of which they had only recently begun to struggle. They had even hoped that the university might bring to Wales something of that sweetness and light which Matthew Arnold had believed was the quality which differentiated culture from barbarism.

It had been a noble dream, translated into reality in the face of immense difficulties and obstacles. If it had been only incompletely realized that only meant that there was still work to be done, and why should I not help to do it? Most of all, perhaps, I was tempted by the thought that it might depend very much on myself whether it was done; for after so many years in which, as it seemed to me, I had been a mere onlooker on life, never wholly committed to or engaged in any occupation I had adopted, was it not perhaps time that I should put my hand to something for which I myself would be responsible? I had been don, journalist, a traveller about Europe, soldier, businessman, bursar, and in each of these occupations it had seemed to me that I was only acting a part. I could have said with Rimbaud: *Je est un autre.** Was it not time to commit myself?

It was the temptation of action, on however modest a scale. But there were also other temptations. There was the feeling that in Wales, amid its hills and streams, my children* might enjoy the same kind of childhood as I had myself enjoyed, as if a lost paradise awaited them there, like the lost counties engulfed under the waters of Cardigan Bay, which only children could recover; I had never quite lost the belief that, whatever might be the case for grown men, Wales was the only country for children.

When I talked to my wife of such ideas, she was astounded and looked at me with that incredulous look, so familiar to me, which meant that she thought I had once again taken leave of my senses. For her, there could be no possible attraction in a voluntary migration to a small Welsh town, hardly more than a village, whose chief architectural features were a decrepit pier, twenty-two Nonconformist chapels, the vast Victorian Gothic hotel, a monument to the nineteenth-century railway boom, in which the University College of Wales had found its first home. Moreover, and partly because of me, she thought of the Welsh as of some primitive tribe which spoke an unintelligible language, practised savage rites and customs, and was in general shiftless, untrustworthy and hostile to strangers. To her, Aberystwyth represented a kind of Welsh ghetto, in which she would feel as much at home as in some Patagonian settlement full of naked savages.

When I showed her the letter, her first reaction was, like mine, that the proposal was of course totally absurd and not worth a second's thought. But women have more generous instincts than men and when, to her astonishment, she realized that the prospect of returning to Wales, for reasons she did not understand and certainly did not agree with, genuinely attracted me, she said, rather doubtfully, that of course if I knew what I wanted I must do as I wished. She acted out of the kind of generosity which in the end hurts oneself as well as others, and by self-sacrifice made it possible for me to persist in my folly.

I replied to the letter that I was willing to be considered for the appointment, though not if the college had any other candidate in view. In due course, after an interview with the college council in which I suddenly felt that perhaps my wife's view of my countrymen had a certain justification,* I found myself charged with the duties of Principal of the University College of Wales.

III

Accordingly, in the summer of 1953, we went into residence at Aberystwyth, in a charming little Welsh *plas*, or manor house, which stood on a hill which commanded a magnificent view of the entire sweep of Cardigan Bay down to the last glimpse of St David's Head in the south. I had known the house as a child, when I had been taken there by my mother and it was still the property of a typically feckless family of Welsh squires.* As is the normal fate of their class, they had fallen on evil days, and the Plas had only recently been acquired by the college, as a residence for its principal.

The house should have been, as it used to be, delightful, but it was not, and in this respect it seemed to typify the dead hand which a nascent Welsh Establishment had laid upon its own country and its own people. Its little park, that extended down the grassy slope of the hill on which it stood, was screened by a wide curtain of woods through which a mountain stream descended in a series of minuscule cascades. Buzzards hovered and swooped overhead; the woods were alive with red squirrels and in the mild climate of the Welsh coast the roses bloomed until Christmas.

But something had gone wrong. The modest grey stone of the house, that had once stood on the hill like an outcrop of the rock on which it was built, had been clad in a cement of so dazzling, so synthetic, a white that it seemed an affront to the green and grey of the landscape and of the sea that lapped the shore below. The sloping lawn outside the house had been geometrically dissected into botanical family beds, which gave it the appearance of a municipal park, and within, all the house's modest architectural features, its picture rails, pediments, cornices, wainscots had been ruthlessly stripped away in the process of renovation, so that each room presented the same blank repetitive surface to the eye. It was as if some mad geometrician had been at work, who had insisted that nothing should remain which would mar the mathematical perfection of straight lines and rectangles, and the result had been to achieve, in this old house where centuries had once left their mark, an almost Euclidean austerity which nothing could soften or domesticate. It made my wife cry; while I was slightly disconcerted to find that this ruthless work of reconstruction had been carried out regardless both of expense and of the strict building controls which were then in force; licences, it seemed, were a matter which did not affect the Principal.

This fine disregard for legality is something which comes very easily to the Welsh who, having endured an alien rule for so long, regard its laws as something which it is a duty to circumvent rather than obey. In the case of the Principal, especially, who in so small a community as Aberystwyth enjoyed an almost feudal pre-eminence, it was taken for granted that he was not subject to the petty restrictions imposed by an alien bureaucracy in Whitehall. I found such an attitude embarrassing; to my wife, with her English respect for the law, it seemed positively immoral, and all the more so because it was thought natural that she should benefit by it most of all. She spent much time and effort in trying to persuade tradespeople – coal merchants, butchers, grocers – that rationing applied to her just as much as anyone else. She did not have much success; they simply refused to believe that she meant what she said and she continued to be the unwilling beneficiary of a black market which worked in strict accordance with one's position in the social system.

My wife was all the more disconcerted, indeed positively alarmed, by such procedures because they were combined with an intense curiosity about our domestic and private lives. It was a genuine shock to her to discover that an elderly emeritus professor, and member of the college council, should make enquiries of our coal merchant about the size of our coal bill; I tried to explain that in a tribe, where the affairs of one are the affairs of all, there is no such thing as a private life, but she was apt to reply that this was all very well if one happened to be one of the tribe but it was not easy to bear if one were not. She had the native English sense that men and women are individuals who, within the limits of the law, should be allowed to pursue their own interests without interference by anyone else; she found herself among people for whom totem and taboo were superior not only to the law but to the individual.

There was material for high comedy in such a situation; my wife found herself in the position of a Daisy Miller,* a visitor from the New World, whose innocence cannot adapt itself to the unspoken assumptions and complicated rituals of an ancient folk culture. But the comedy was hard to appreciate because at its heart lay the hardly veiled hostility with which her new neighbours regarded the alien stranger who had come among them; an attitude expressed at its crudest and most direct by the local drunkard and ne'er-do-well who, lounging against the railings of the town clock in the mean little square at the top of the High Street, never failed to murmur *English Bitch!* beneath his breath whenever my wife should happen to pass. This was indeed extravagant enough to be comic; she found it more offensive when the more genteel and better-bred local ladies ostentatiously spoke Welsh whenever she was present, even though normally they would have spoken in English.

It was perhaps inevitable that, quite apart from racial and social differences, such antagonisms should arise, for she was everything that those around her were not. She was young and pretty and filled with gaiety and energy; love, laughter and work were what came most naturally to her. Aberystwyth was a town of the middle-aged and the old and its ladies were absorbed in the monotonous and repetitive social life of the town and the college, in which the pettiness of provincial life was combined with the acrimony of academic dissension. Gossip, morning coffee, tea parties at which dainty sandwiches and sugared cakes were handed round on lace doilies, academic and religious functions which were both equally impregnated with a Nonconformist gloom as thick as the sea fog which sometimes filled the streets of the town, were the only social diversions offered her. In such a society she was so much a fish out of water, a bird in a Methodist cage, that no basis for mutual understanding existed. She found her only natural allies among the students, who like her were young and eager for life and oppressed by the obsolescent orthodoxies of their elders, and to their affairs she devoted herself with admirable energy which only earned her further disapproval.

For in the social and academic hierarchy of Aberystwyth students occupied the lowest position. They were regarded as youthful and not strictly human barbarians, hobbledehoys from the mining valleys and the farms, whose only function was to accept with gratitude the instruction handed down to them from above. Little or no provision was made by the college for any form of social activity, except athletic, outside their studies. Their union consisted of cramped and dilapidated premises that would not have accommodated a tenth of their number and resembled a rather sleazy café in an industrial suburb. They were not permitted a bar, because the temptations of Demon Drink were still a spectre which haunted the mind of the college council;* as a result, those who fell victim to it haunted the slightly squalid public houses in which the town abounded. The weaker members of the staff, on the other hand, who were hardly more favoured in the way of amenities, tended to drift into the bars of the town's more respectable hotels.

The wonder was that despite the visible and tangible neglect from which the students suffered, there was an almost total absence of what would today be called 'student protest'. They accepted almost without question the rule of Primitive Methodism imposed on them by the college administration. The reason was that the college, for all its inadequacies, did provide a genuine escape from the cramped material and intellectual conditions of the homes from which most of them came and the opportunity to enter a wider world than most of their fathers had known. What was sad was that their elders and teachers, instead of encouraging their appetite for freedom, did their best to confine them within the boundaries of the same narrow ethical and religious code which they had themselves inherited.

In this respect, Aberystwyth was unique even among the four colleges which together made up the University of Wales; certainly it would have been impossible to imagine a similar situation at any other British university at that time. But Aberystwyth, by reason of its geographical isolation from any large centre of population, had in many ways remained a backwater whose sluggish waters had not been stirred by the currents of the main stream of contemporary life; idols and shibboleths which had long been destroyed elsewhere here still preserved their original power. For the students, however, they were rapidly losing their virtue, and in this twilight of Methodist gods they tried to create a community of their own from which new life might spring. They accepted the prejudices of their elders with an easy and good-humoured indifference, almost, indeed, indulgence. They were far more innocent and unsophisticated than their counterparts at any English university, and they accepted almost without question the gerontocracy which ruled the college to an even greater extent than it rules most university institutions. But they were young, they were hopeful, and they were, I think, more intelligent than their English counterparts. To any kind of interest or encouragement they responded with an alacrity which was touching and affecting; and the very isolation in which they lived at Aberystwyth fostered among them a community of spirit, a reliance on their own efforts in creating their own forms of social intercourse, a sense that if they did not do these things for themselves nobody else would, which were admirable. They were the only truly living and vigorous element in the college and were as good material as any university institution could hope to find; and in the years which my wife and I spent at Aberystwyth they formed the only justification for the hopes which I had conceived when I first went there.*

IV

This was over fifteen years ago and I have no doubt that in the interval things have changed very much for the better at Aberystwyth; it could hardly be possible that they should not. But when I arrived both the college and the town were in decay; they were like a house infected with dry rot which outwardly seems unchanged but is crumbling away within. So far as the college was concerned it was clear that many changes would have to be made, and some would have to be made quickly, which is never easy in any university; there had been an inter-regnum of a year since my predecessor had died, and many decisions had been postponed until a new principal had been appointed. There seemed to be skeletons in many cupboards, and they were only gradually revealed to me, sometimes with a certain *Schadenfreude* on the part of their curators at the thought that it was now my responsibility to dispose of them. At moments I had the impression that to dispose of skeletons was precisely what I had been called in for; only it was equally clear that there were many in the college, both on the staff and on the college council, to whom the skeletons were dear, like holy relics which should be treated with proper veneration. There were others who were equally determined that if any changes were to be made they should take a direction which conflicted sharply with all my ideas of what a university should be. Between them and myself the difference was in essence a very simple one, though in fact it showed itself in an extraordinarily wide variety of forms. I thought that a university could only have one single purpose, which is the pursuit of learning, either through teaching or research, and preferably through both; I equally thought an institution genuinely devoted to such a purpose could perform an invaluable service to Wales. But to others, who held their belief with a passionate intensity, learning was subsidiary, or should be, to the purpose of preserving Welsh culture and the Welsh language. At its simplest it was the difference between whether the college should be, or become, a university or a Welsh seminary.

I had been vaguely aware before arriving in Aberystwyth that there were some members of the college council who had strongly opposed my appointment, precisely on the ground that I did not have Welsh interests sufficiently at heart. Perhaps they were right, in the sense that I thought the interests of learning more important. I had not taken such opposition very seriously, though perhaps I should have when I was told by a friend at All Souls that he had been approached by a distinguished member of the council with an enquiry whether it was not true that I was a homosexual; the reason for the enquiry, it appeared, was my friendship with Guy, of which he had learned at the time of Guy's disappearance. Such a question seemed so absurd, to my friend as to myself, that I scarcely realized how deep a malice it concealed or to what lengths my opponents were willing to proceed.

I would have been wiser if I had understood that at Aberystwyth I was re-entering a society far more primitive than any which I had known for a very long time, in which nothing could be taken at its face value and everything had to be interpreted in terms of conflicts that were fought on some much lower level than the rational; it was something I had not encountered even in the lower depths of the army, though perhaps I should have reminded myself that in Germany I had seen how such forces can ruin and corrupt a great people. In the case of the college, I was exposed to the same atavistic instinct which wished to make of it an instrument shaped to achieve purely tribal ends and not an institution in which the light of reason might prevail. This instinct was all the stronger because the two forms in which Welsh tribal feeling had hitherto expressed itself most perfectly, language and religion, were in a process of rapid degeneration and decline. In my father's day a Methodist minister still commanded a greater prestige and respect than a professor; but now the minister preached to empty chapels while eager students clamoured for the privilege of listening to the professor; tribal feeling demanded that, religion failing, the professor should transmit the same ethical values as the minister had once preached. And my father had preached in Welsh, and now the Welsh language was also dying; tribal feeling demanded that in the university it should find a refuge in which it might arrest its decline and even recover a new strength. What was remarkable was that as Welsh culture lost its positive content, it expressed itself increasingly in an abstract nationalism in which fear and hatred played a larger part than love.

> An intellectual hatred is the worst,
> So let her think opinions are accursed.

says Yeats in his *A Prayer for my Daughter*. It was a prayer which I often felt like repeating at Aberystwyth.

Nationalism seemed to me necessarily hostile to the idea of a university, which unless wholly dedicated to the pursuit of knowledge, even when it threatens tribal idols, has lost its one single justification; without this, its functions are better performed by other institutions. Indeed, if the university were to be of any service to the Welsh people, and especially to the young students who had begun to win my affection, it could not do so by flattering their worst prejudices and their blindest instincts. I was prepared to say this publicly, and did so, and to apply it in the practical business of college administration; by doing so I earned the unremitting hostility of many of my Welsh colleagues, and it was all the fiercer because the support I found came in the main from English members of the staff, sad exiles in an alien land, for whom Welsh nationalism was an irritating irrelevance to the serious business of teaching and research.

It would perhaps be absurd to say that during the few years in which I remained at Aberystwyth the college became a battlefield between two diametrically opposed conceptions of what a university should be. To say so may seem to give too great an importance to what was happening in this obscure little corner of Cardiganshire. And yet the conflict made itself felt in almost every matter, important or trivial, which came up for discussion during my period as Principal. Inevitably, and primarily, of course, in the question of appointments; for which should come first in one's assessment of a candidate, his qualities as a scholar or as a Welshman? It made itself felt in the degree of liberty which should be permitted to students; for was the college really an institute of learning or a preceptor of Welsh morals? It affected the administration of the college's inadequate resources: should whatever there was to spare be devoted to departments which showed promise of making original contributions to learning, or to the provision of additional lecturers who would teach through the medium of Welsh? It even raised its head in the question of providing a community house for the academic staff; for if they had a house, would not its amenities include a bar, and would not a bar be in itself a betrayal of the Welsh Nonconformist ethic, and, even worse, would it not set a dangerous example to students? Most of all, the conflict entered into the question, none the less important because it could never be explicitly formulated, what kind of a person the Principal of the College should be? Should he be one who put the pursuit of knowledge above the preservation of the Welsh language, reason above Nonconformity, lowered his dignity by making friends with students and junior lecturers, was not greatly concerned with their morals as long as they did their work, and even helped to corrupt them by offering them a drink when he had invited them to his house?

In retrospect, I am sometimes amazed at, and ashamed of, the triviality of some of the issues which occupied so much of our time and thought at Aberystwyth, all given an unreal importance by the intrusion into the academic life of a principle of nationalism which was irrelevant to its proper purposes. It would be tedious, and certainly unedifying, to recount the number of occasions on which this permanent underlying issue made itself felt; but they gave to my few years as Principal of the college the character of a fierce and tenacious little war of attrition, enlivened by sudden sallies, patrol actions and commando raids, which both tried one's nerves and exhausted one's patience. It did not cause me the same kind of unhappiness which life at Aberystwyth caused my wife, because at least I had the satisfaction of thinking that I was trying to do something which was worth doing, while to her it seemed that both of us were wasting our lives; but certainly it made me wonder with increasing frequency whether this was the way in which I wished to live for ever.

My doubts were allayed because with time it began to seem that I and those who sympathized with my objects might even succeed in what we wished to do. Something of the gloom and stagnation which enveloped the college on my arrival began to lift. Something of the hierarchical stiffness which forbade professors to speak to senior lecturers, and senior lecturers to junior lecturers, and junior lecturers to students, and everyone to the Principal, was gradually relaxed. Skeletons became noticeably fewer in number. It sometimes became possible to discuss strictly academic subjects as if they were the real business of the college; it was even possible to relax or abolish some of the absurdly antiquated rules of discipline which were imposed on the students, and to persuade the college that young men and women of university age do not really benefit by being treated like school-children. Sometimes I began to feel that we were really behaving as a university should; and sometimes we were even able to laugh at ourselves. I even began to hope that from this small college by the sea, in its magnificent natural setting, so thrown upon its own resources by its isolation from any large centres of population, something might emerge which would be an original and unique contribution to the university system, not only of Wales, but of the entire country.

Certainly there were good reasons for such a hope; I felt that given a good many years of internecine warfare, of argument and persuasion, of innumerable committees in which, over and over again, nationalism and the Welsh language would continue to raise their King Charles's Heads,* the college might become a place in which the genuine academic virtues would flourish. For really there was no reason why they should not. The students were only too willing and eager to learn from anyone who showed them sympathy and understanding, and if on occasions they voiced their dissatisfaction, they usually had good reason, and were entirely without that kind of destructive malice which has infected student protest today. Malice indeed was almost a monopoly of the senior staff, who manifested it impartially to each other, to myself, and to the students. Even this, however, was on the decline; many of the issues which most frequently and most bitterly provoked dissent were so obviously related to the past, so much a matter of tribal memory, that it was possible to hope that with time they would lose their emotive power.

Thus I was not without reason for confidence. There remained, however, a stubborn body of opinion in the college which, as the defender of what was called 'the Welsh Way of Life', was unalterably hostile to the kind of policies I should have liked the college to adopt. Since I myself had described the Welsh way of life as that of a dying peasant culture which had its face resolutely turned to the past,* I offered an obvious target for their hostility, and I suppose that, from their point of view, they were right to see in me an enemy, though I found it difficult to believe that, most of all in a university, disagreements could be reduced to so personal a basis. It would have been difficult to define what they themselves meant by 'the Welsh Way of Life' because so many different elements entered into it. For some, it was a matter entirely of the Welsh language, and for this they were willing to sacrifice any other interest. To some its essential quality was religious and ethical, and for them the college was, or should be, a kind of advanced version of a Methodist Sunday school. To yet others, it was a question of nationalism and racialism, and for them the college was essentially an institution whose task was to train young men who would one day dedicate themselves to the cause of self-government for Wales. I found each of these aspects of the 'Welsh Way of Life' equally antipathetic, and indeed even slightly absurd, and perhaps this was fortunate for my opponents, because their beliefs were in many respects incompatible with each other and they found it difficult to make common cause, as the Welsh so frequently do; in me, at least, they found someone to whom they were all equally opposed.

I do not know what would have happened if I had remained in Wales. I myself have the firm conviction that time was on my side, that my critics were all, in one respect or another, the defenders of lost causes, and that neither language, nor religion, nor nationalism would in the end prevail. But time precisely was what was not given me, and of this I cannot, and would not, wish to complain, because the occasion of my leaving Aberystwyth, for a second time, was entirely of my own making.

V

Once again, I find it difficult to analyse the obscure, complex motives which determined one's behaviour, and more especially when it is of a kind that changes one's whole life; and perhaps one ought to be all the more suspicious of them if, to oneself though not to others, they seem to be to one's credit.

The prospect of remaining for long at Aberystwyth, perhaps for the rest of my life, was not one which attracted me greatly. Indeed, I had not been there long before I began once again to feel stifled by the stale and claustrophobic air of Wales, in which ideas wither and die, and no issue is ever of importance unless it has its roots deep in ancient memories; it was like the oppressive air of the little town huddled at the foot of the hills whose grey streets and mean conventicles seemed a fitting refuge for minds for which freedom was too dangerous an element into which to adventure. I told myself that I should not complain of this; after all I should have been forewarned and indeed had been repeatedly warned, by my brother, by my friends, that Wales was no place for me; if now I found my situation disagreeable I had only my own wilfulness to blame.

My dissatisfaction, however, was less important than my wife's unhappiness, which was intense. I was acutely aware that it was entirely due to me that she found herself an exile on this Celtic fringe of Britain, whose manners and customs were entirely foreign to her, its language unintelligible and its inhabitants hostile. Even the roses that bloomed at Christmas, the garden she had made for herself where everything grew in a wild profusion that was only accentuated by the grim austerity of the botanical beds, the little owl that perched at night on the edge of the path through the woods, did not comfort her; much as she loved her plants and flowers, they could not make up for the absence of recognizable human beings, which to her the Welsh were not.

Her unhappiness made for mine, though I am ashamed to say that my own behaviour at that particular time only increased her misery and loneliness. Perhaps, in the depths of my mind, or whatever it is that really determines one's actions, there was a sense that only some particularly flagrant act of folly could bring to an end a situation which was rapidly becoming intolerable; perhaps I was only obeying an instinct for self-destruction which my wife herself regarded as particularly Welsh. But if such motives entered into my behaviour I was unaware of them; strangely enough, I thought I was behaving rationally. However that may be, there was perhaps a kind of rough justice in the fact that provocation to action originated, certainly without any intention on his part, with Guy.

Since returning to Aberystwyth, I had not thought a great deal about him.* My life in Wales, from which either London or Oxford or Cambridge seemed at times infinitely remote, was so completely detached from everything, either serious or trivial, which had ever joined us together that at times I found it almost difficult to believe that he had ever existed. It was rather as if, living at the North Pole, one had tried to remember that once one had lived on the Equator. And if he had ever existed, it was by now at least doubtful whether he still did. In its White Paper* the government had said as little as it could about the mystery of his and Maclean's disappearance, in the hope, perhaps, that public interest in the case would die from lack of information; it had caused serious damage to Anglo-American relations and in the government's view the sooner it was forgotten the better. None of the enquiries indefatigably pursued by the Press had given the slightest clue to Guy's whereabouts, or indeed to whether he was still alive, though by then the most reasonable assumption was that both he and Maclean were in the Soviet Union.

If that were indeed the case, I myself felt that it were better if he were dead. For him, of all people, deprived of everything which he liked most, I could foresee nothing but a long-drawn-out disintegration in the Socialist Fatherland; the kind of adaptation required for an exile to make himself at home in a foreign country was beyond his powers. Yet somehow I knew perfectly well that he was alive; it was impossible that his grotesquely vivid nature should so abruptly have ceased to exist, even in the world of melodrama which he had chosen to enter. And equally I was convinced that if he were still alive, we had not heard the last of him, and that his disappearance would have further consequences.

For me, amid all my other preoccupations at Aberystwyth, he existed in a kind of limbo of the memory, a ghost on whom it was still possible to suspend judgement until one knew exactly how and why he had been removed from the land of the living. Despite all the trouble and distress he had caused to so many who had been his friends, I still retained my affection for him and continued to remember him as part of the world of my youth in which, strangely enough, I had been, despite all the terrible events which had led it to disaster, intensely happy. It seemed the best way to remember him; I had the feeling that if he were to reappear, the results might be exceedingly unpleasant. And so they were, and particularly for myself, though this was entirely my own fault.

On Saturday, February 11th, 1956, in the National Hotel in Moscow, Guy Burgess and Donald Maclean appeared before a hastily summoned Press conference, apparently in good health and spirits, handed out prepared statements and left. The statements left no doubt that they were indeed, and had been, communists and communist agents and that they had chosen to live in the Socialist Fatherland to which all their lives had been dedicated.

I find it difficult to account for the effect which their reappearance, and the public statements which accompanied it, made upon me. They were like some chilly official announcement that every suspicion I had ever had of Guy had been correct and that all the theories, excuses, explanations, which I had found or invented in order to exorcise them, had been merely self-deceptions practised in order to conceal the truth from myself. It seemed extraordinary to realize at last that Guy had in fact told me the truth, and that for nearly twenty years I had *known* that Guy was a Soviet agent but had been unable to acknowledge the fact; or had I, and merely evaded the issue?

The truth, at last, plain and unvarnished, was difficult to accept. Especially because, as a result, many people had suffered, some perhaps in ways I did not like to think of. It was equally difficult to accept that for all those years Guy, apart from his one single moment of self-revelation, had consciously and consistently betrayed all the affection which his friends had had for him, in spite of all the strains to which he had so often exposed it. I seemed to see Guy in a new light, as if someone in whom, for all his faults, one had recognized a kind of virtue, had been suddenly revealed in a character which belonged to a different mental and emotional world from oneself.

I do not know whether such feelings were justified. I suppose that it was still possible to make out a case for admiring Guy and what he had done; that is to say, as one who had committed himself so completely to a cause that he had not hesitated to sacrifice to it both himself and his friends. And indeed, in Guy's case, the extent of the sacrifice was so great that it might well inspire admiration. Unfortunately, in the years since the great Soviet state trials and the conclusion of the German–Soviet pact, I had come to look upon the cause for which the sacrifice had been made as no less ignoble than the methods which it used to promote its own ends; among which, by now, it was clear that one should include Guy's own activities.

It is perhaps not necessary to explain here the process of disillusion by which one comes to see a cause in which one has placed one's highest hopes as an embodiment of evil. Others have done it better than I can; the story of *The God That Failed** is one of the fundamental stories of my generation and it has been told in so many different versions during the last thirty years that my own version of it would add nothing to the others. It is perhaps enough to say that, far from seeing Guy as one who had sacrificed himself for higher ends, I saw him as one who had advanced an unworthy cause by equally unworthy means. Even more, he had become in my eyes one who had voluntarily engaged in the cruel and murderous operations of an organization which was directly responsible for the destruction of millions of people by death, torture, starvation and any other means which its ingenuity could devise to achieve that purpose. He was, no doubt, my friend; he was also a man with blood on his hands.

It might be said that I should have realized this before. The point was that I had not known it with certainty and that, in such a case, only certainty could justify one in passing judgement. On grounds of friendship I had for as long as possible made every reservation I could which would offer any explanation for Guy's conduct except the true one. In doing so, it seemed to me, I had to some extent made myself his accomplice; some of the blood had rubbed off on me.

Perhaps I was over-sensitive to feel in this way; but the guilt I felt in regard to Guy and my dealings with him was exacerbated by a more general sense of guilt which was inspired by the support and approval which, in the 1930s and even later, I had given to the Communist party of the Soviet Union. Indeed, in my attitude to the Soviet Union I had behaved in much the same way as I had to Guy; that is to say that, even after I had sufficient evidence to recognize it for what it was, I had continued to make every kind of reservation and excuse for its conduct, however evil its consequences might be.*

It would perhaps have been easy to forgive oneself on the grounds that one had been under the spell of an illusion to which thousands of others had also fallen a victim; one always finds it easy to forgive oneself. But in this case it was not merely a matter of forgiveness. It was also a matter, as it seemed to me, of trying to limit the amount of harm one had done, even if, in relation to the monstrous evils for which the Communist party had been responsible, one's own contribution to them had been so minute as to mean nothing, except perhaps to oneself. There are situations to which a moral calculus of this kind hardly seems relevant. I felt something of that wholly irrational sense which involuntarily recurred to Rubashov in Arthur Koestler's *Darkness at Noon* and which he expressed in the almost meaningless words: *I must pay.**

There is something absurd about such a comparison; and indeed I was sharply aware that my own feelings were absurd. Yet it seemed to me that there was something very simple I could do which might give some rational meaning to them; this was to tell the truth about my relations with Guy, and what one had learned as a result, as simply and truthfully as possible. At the time of his disappearance I felt that I had already discharged this responsibility by making my statement to MI5. Yet I was haunted by the suspicion that, for a variety of reasons, MI5 was inhibited from making any effective use of any information which I gave them; as later events showed, the suspicion was not unjustified. I remained convinced that Guy and Maclean had not operated alone, that others remained to continue their work, and that the likeliest place to look for them was in the security services themselves. In telling MI5 my story, was I not simply ensuring that it would fall into hands which had every interest in suppressing it?

Quis custodiet ipsos Custodes?★ If the security services themselves were not to be trusted, in whom could one securely place one's trust? I felt that I had become involved in a world of subterfuges and deceptions in which nothing was what it seemed; it was like one of those nightmares in which faces, masks, grinning images continually shift and dissolve to reveal yet other shapes behind them and there was also the sense that at the end of the nightmare's long corridors there lay the very real flesh and blood horrors for which Guy's masters were responsible, and through them reverberated the shrieks in the night of their victims.

These may seem strange thoughts to obsess the mind of the Principal of a small Welsh university college, safely removed from such horrors in the pastoral landscape of Cardiganshire. And no doubt, for a variety of reasons a certain element of the higher lunacy entered into them; this particular nightmare had, in a variety of forms, pursued me for so long, and with increasing intensity, that its subjective and objective aspects had become inextricably confused and I felt that only by some violent effort could I be rid of it.

There was, I thought, only one thing I could do, and that was to write down what I knew as accurately as I could, while taking into account all the doubts, hesitations, suspicions that had led me to behave as I had. I did not know that it would serve any very useful purpose, but at least it might help to put my own mind at rest. Yet there remained the conviction that the story of Guy and Maclean had not yet come to an end and that there were still developments to come which for some people might prove serious. If that were so, it seemed best that, so far as it was in my power, everyone concerned should be forewarned.

I did not think that my own account would do me very much credit. At best I would look foolish, perhaps absurd, and at worst tainted by my association with Guy. And to some, I knew, the mere act of committing to paper what I knew about him would be regarded as treacherous and dishonourable. I did not much look forward to such consequences but in the end, I thought, to tell the truth was the only alternative left to me. *Magna est veritas et praevalebit;** it was with some such naïve slogan in my mind that I sat down and rapidly wrote the account of my relations with Guy which, with only minor changes, forms the substance of the third and fourth sections of this book.*

There remained the question of what was to be done with the manuscript. I had not written it merely for the record; I wished it to be published, both as an account of the circumstances, so far as I knew them, which had led up to Guy's disappearance and as a kind of warning that his activities as a Soviet agent might be expected to have further consequences. I accordingly dispatched the manuscript to my literary agents, who were wise enough to warn me that publication might give rise to some scandal; when I replied that I was aware of this, but nevertheless wished to proceed, they arranged for publication, in five consecutive articles, in the *People*, a Sunday newspaper which felt that their material was sensational enough to appeal to its mass audience. The articles were to be based on the material contained in my manuscript but were to be written by a member of the *People's* staff, in a style which they felt would be more acceptable to their readers than my own, and would therefore appear anonymously. I had some doubts about the wisdom of this arrangement, but I felt that I was now committed to pursue the matter to the end whatever the consequences, and therefore gave my agreement.*

VI

My literary agent had certainly not exaggerated in saying that the appearance of the articles might have unfortunate consequences; they were indeed far worse than anything I had foreseen. In one respect, however, they achieved, in part at least, the object which I had intended; for among their earliest readers were MI5, who immediately dispatched two officers to Aberystwyth, with a request for a copy of my original manuscript; they read it with almost microscopic attention and interrogated me closely about every detail of its contents. Somehow they gave me the impression that, in the interval since Guy's and Maclean's disappearance, and perhaps as a result of it, there had been considerable changes in their organization and that, though my manuscript did not materially differ from my original statement to them, they were now prepared to pay rather more serious attention to what I had to say.

But it was not only MI5 who were interested in the articles, especially because their anonymity was not preserved for long, and a gossip columnist in the *Daily Telegraph* revealed that their author was the Principal of the University College of Wales. Even in the wider world the announcement created considerable interest; in Aberystwyth, and in the college, it had something of the effect of the bombardment of Fort Sumter in provoking the American Civil War. Nor perhaps was this surprising for the *People* had rewritten and edited my manuscript so as to achieve the most sensational possible effect. The result was such as to give my critics, both within and without the college, a scarcely hoped for opportunity to rid themselves of one whom they regarded as a renegade Welshman intent on destroying everything which they held most dear. It is almost impossible to dismiss the Principal of a college, once he has been duly appointed, except on grounds of flagrant immorality or neglect of duty, and even publishing articles in the sensational Sunday press could hardly be held to fall into either of these two categories. But it is possible, given sufficient determination and malice, to make life so unpleasant for him as to make his position untenable, and even, by innuendo and insinuation, to hint that his past has been stained by unnameable vices.

To this task my critics applied themselves with a vigour and virtuosity which were worthy of a better cause, and with such success that in Wales the affair of the articles quickly assumed the proportions of a national scandal, so grave indeed that I was politely informed by the President of the college,* a distinguished lawyer of impeccable virtue, a dull mind, and ardent Welsh patriotism, that he had no alternative but to ask for my resignation. He was, however, prepared to do a deal; that is to say, if I were to go quickly, quietly and without resistance, he was prepared to make my departure as easy for me as possible.

I was not, however, prepared to resign; it seemed to me that it would not be for the good of myself nor, in the long run, of the college, and I was reluctant to abandon my friends on the staff and on the council who were in sympathy with my ideas for reforming it. Nor indeed did I believe that my position as its Principal in any way precluded me from writing and publishing whatever I liked and in whatever manner I pleased. My refusal to resign required that less diplomatic means of attack should be adopted; at the next meeting of the college council, a resolution was proposed that a committee should be set up to enquire into my conduct in writing and publishing the articles. I opposed the resolution and it was defeated, and with a sense that a storm had subsided in a tea-cup, I left Aberystwyth with my wife and family to spend a holiday on the marvellous estuary of the Mawddach in North Wales.*

I should not have been deceived by so easy a victory, and within a few days I was summoned back to Aberystwyth, to attend an emergency meeting of the council, summoned by the President in response to a demand by twelve professors that a committee of enquiry be appointed.* When I returned the atmosphere of the little town was something between that of a fairground and a public execution; the streets were crowded with farmers in for market, newspaper placards announced the summoning of the council, and members of the Press and eager sightseers crowded the precincts of the college and the bars of its hotels and public houses.

On this occasion I did not feel I could resist the demand for an enquiry, but I repeated my belief that it could serve no purpose, as there could be no possible subject of investigation except the articles themselves, and as these had already been studied with microscopic attention by the entire population of Wales, I did not feel that the committee could add anything further to them. I was of course mistaken, as indeed I was at every stage of this strange little drama; in the course of it I came to realize, as I should have realized before, that common sense and practical judgement are qualities with which perhaps I am not conspicuously endowed.

The committee, when it was at length constituted, consisted of three gentlemen of impeccable social, professional and academic credentials;* they were all English, because it was felt that the passions of Welshmen were so deeply engaged that an impartial judgement could not be expected of them. It had not been easy to constitute the committee; a long list of eminent persons had to be approached before three could be found who were willing to undertake the disagreeable commission with which they were entrusted. Once appointed, however, the committee set about its task with a thoroughness and a zest which protracted their proceedings over a period of some eight months.* I and other members of the college staff were summoned to appear before them in London; my own interview consisted of a lengthy and unmistakably hostile cross-examination by the chairman, who appeared to consider that his terms of reference included any possible aspect of my public or private life which might be open to criticism.* A devout Anglican, he could not conceal his horror that Guy should have been a godfather to one of my two sons; in fact, Guy could not have been a kinder or more affectionate one. The Vice-Principal of the college,* a distinguished physicist who throughout my troubles behaved to me both as a friend and as the most loyal of colleagues, was handled with almost equal severity and subjected to an inquisition to show that, with my connivance, he had failed to maintain proper discipline among the students; for such a suggestion there was not the slightest evidence, except the exemplary tolerance and understanding with which he had administered the almost medieval rules of discipline which obtained in the college.

Having completed its enquiries in London, the committee proceeded to visit Aberystwyth, where it sat for three days taking evidence from anyone who wished to offer himself, or herself, as a witness. They were many, because the committee's procedure permitted every kind of allegation, however false or irrelevant, to be made about me; many strange bees escaped from many Welsh bonnets. A sympathetic member of the college council found it necessary to warn me that I was charged, among other things, with homosexuality, with hostility to Welsh nationalist aspirations, and with corrupting students by offering them a glass of sherry when they visited us; it was not clear which was the most serious of these charges.

It had by now become clear to me that the committee was conducting, not an enquiry, but a prosecution. This became even clearer when, in reply to my request that I should be told what offences I was charged with, and shown the evidence on which they were based, the committee refused on the grounds that this was not customary in an enquiry of a disciplinary nature. But the committee's attitude also revealed to me something which I had not hitherto understood, which was that by publishing the articles in the *People*, I had, at one stroke, simultaneously succeeded in giving offence not only to the Welsh, but also to the English Establishment. That the Welsh should be offended was perhaps not surprising; the articles had simply confirmed their feeling that I was not the man required to fill the honoured position of Principal of the University College of Wales, a national institution of which Wales was proud. To the English Establishment, however, the articles were a breach of the complicated moral code by which it is held together, and most of all of those personal loyalties to which it give an almost religious value. They were worse than a moral transgression; they were an act of bad taste, which tended to throw an unpleasant light on the *sacra arcana*★ of the English Establishment.

My sense that I had committed a double offence, against good taste and decent feeling, was confirmed by letters and protests which I began to receive soon after the first of the articles was published. The warden of an Oxford college,★ for whom I felt an affection which dated from my undergraduate days, wrote to suggest that I should plant a screen of Judas trees around the college athletic fields. A distinguished moral philosopher,★ also an old friend, was shocked, not by the content of the articles, but by the fact that they had appeared in so vulgar and sensational a paper as the *People*; in some more reputable journal, they might even have had some literary value. In the *People* they were unforgivable. Such a letter seemed to me to reveal an almost classical confusion of moral and aesthetic values, reducing both to triviality; moral indignation of such a kind seemed to spring from singularly impure sources. It was perhaps hardly worth more than the reaction of a literary lady with whom I was to dine in London who hurriedly cancelled the invitation on the ground that my presence would give offence to her other guests; I was no longer, as the Germans would say, *salonfähig.**

I was, it seemed, in disgrace not only with my Welsh critics but with my English friends, except however for some few, like Louis Mac-Neice, John Sparrow, R. C. Zaehner,* A. J. Ayer, F. W. Deakin, Douglas Young and David Footman,* who continued to show me the same affection as before; I record their names out of gratitude for the sympathy and understanding which they showed during the worst of my troubles. I even discovered new friends, both in England and in Wales, who encouraged me to believe that the disapproval provoked by the articles was purely ephemeral and that with time it would disappear and my tribulations would be over.

I found it difficult to believe that they were right. The articles had provoked such violent feelings that I felt they had destroyed any further usefulness I might have at Aberystwyth; Welshmen have the most tenacious of memories, especially for scandal, and I knew that for many years to come the articles would remain a cause of controversy both within the college and outside it. In any case, they had already provoked so many manifestations of malice and hostility, so many shabby manœuvres, so much rancour and gossip, that I knew I could never again make my home in Aberystwyth; my feeling was all the stronger because gossip spared my wife and children no more than myself. To my wife this was only another addition to the unhappiness she had felt almost as soon as she had taken up residence in Aberystwyth; to my children, however, it was something entirely new to find themselves, in the local schools which they then attended, the victims of the malice which their school-fellows had learned from their parents.*

As the months went by, and the committee continued its apparently interminable researches, I decided both that it was impossible, and that I did not wish, to continue as Principal of the college. It seemed to me clear, from the wholly partisan spirit in which the committee had pursued its enquiries, that I could expect nothing from its report which would be likely to make me change my mind, for it was indefatigable in investigating the slightest innuendo or insinuation that had been made against me. Whether it believed them or not, its procedure tended to give them an importance which they would otherwise have wholly lacked. The mere fact that presumably serious and intelligent men should think them worth listening to seemed to endow them with significance. That they should travel to Aberystwyth to ensure that not even the most trivial item of gossip should go unheard seemed in itself evidence of the importance they attached to it.

After these mountainous labours, their report emerged as a vicious little mouse.* They reviewed, without indicating their sources, the evidence that had been laid before them, and concluded that they could find no ground for criticism in it either of myself personally or of my conduct of the college's affairs; indeed, in this latter respect, they conceded somewhat reluctantly, that they had been conducted very well and to the benefit of the college. The articles, however, they condemned as a 'lewd document', a phrase so heavy with moral and legal implications that it was in itself sufficient to indicate their belief that I was not a proper person to be Principal of the college. They took an even worse view, however, of my own manuscript, on which the articles had originally been based. Their moral susceptibilities were offended both by the fact that I had written it and, almost worse, that my wife had typed it for me. The report implied that my wife had connived at some particularly distasteful form of literary obscenity.

The report was certainly not calculated to alter my decision to resign my appointment and immediately I received it I informed the college of my intention. My friends in the college pressed me to stay; the students, in particular, demonstrated in every way open to them their wish that I should remain. But a college, or a university, is essentially a community which depends on the mutual trust and confidence that exists between all its members and I was well aware that, by my own action, I had provoked far too much criticism and antagonism for good relations within the college to be easily restored. If I remained, it was inevitable that the college would divide into two bitterly hostile factions, and I was sure that such a situation was one in which neither the college nor I would prosper. The atmosphere of the college meeting at which I insisted that my resignation be received was in itself sufficient evidence of this; it was bitter and acrimonious and revived once again all the old animosities which had plagued the college since my arrival. It was perhaps some small satisfaction that the college refused to approve the committee's report but merely recorded its reception.

On the morning after the college meeting I left Aberystwyth, leaving my family behind. The future seemed bleak in the extreme. At the age of forty-seven, with a wife and five young children to support,* I found myself homeless, without visible means of subsistence, unemployed and, in any academic capacity, henceforth virtually unemployable. Even so, as I stood on the platform at Aberystwyth's grim little railway station, waiting for the train to carry me on the nine-hour journey to London, I could not repress a sense of happiness and liberation at this second escape from my birthplace.

A month later* I was run over by a Volkswagen mini-bus at Littlewick Green, on the road between Reading and Maidenhead, and, I suppose, came as near to death as it is possible without actually dying. I suffered multiple injuries and severe concussion, and for some time it was thought unlikely that I would recover. When, after several weeks, I regained consciousness it was like being born again, but into a world which was very different from anything I had ever known before.

A Winter in Berlin

I spent the winter of 1934 in Berlin. It was then, in intellectual circles, an unfashionable thing to do, because Hitler had already been in power for a year, and in that short time had totally destroyed the culture which had made Berlin as irresistibly attractive to enlightened young men, particularly English ones, as Rome is to Catholics or Mecca to Muslims. It had been a place of pilgrimage, with its own particular Holy Places, on the Alexanderplatz, in Wedding, on the Kurfürstendamm, but now the shrines were desecrated and abandoned, their high priests and their congregations scattered to the four winds, hunted, persecuted and traduced. The more fortunate of them sat in cafés, editorial offices, publishing houses, in Paris or Prague, or took ship to England or America; in their own country, they took refuge in attics and cellars or in remote hiding places in the provinces, and by their hundreds and thousands were hunted down and herded into prisons and concentration camps. It was the greatest intellectual diaspora since the fall of the Temple in Jerusalem.

In Berlin one felt as if the Germany of Weimar had never existed, or, as in some transformation scene in a pantomime, had totally disappeared overnight. A friend of mine, Werner von Trott, to whom I had been introduced by his brother Adam, walking with me on the sandy shores of the Wannsee kicked his foot into their thin soil and said contemptuously: *das ist ja Preuseen – auf den Sand gebaut*; that is Prussia – built upon sand. And indeed, in that winter of 1934, it was as if the whole structure of life had crumbled away in the capital of Prussia, and of Germany, and under the shock of disaster Berlin had become again what it had been before and would one day become again; a city of phantoms.

It had been the vulgar and ostentatious capital of the Hohenzollerns, and had seen their empire and their dynasty disappear without a trace in the ignominy of military defeat. It had been the capital of republican and democratic Germany and had seen that regime also collapse equally ignominiously under the assault of Hitler and his Storm Troops. And one day, many years later, I was to see the city almost totally destroyed by the fires which descended upon it from heaven as upon the cities of the plain. Of this, in 1934, I had no premonition, but already it seemed to me that Berlin was essentially a city in which everything was provisional and ephemeral, desperately balanced between disasters past and disasters yet to come; in 1934, it was still too early to say which would prove to be the worst.

In the meantime the city waited, in the new-found silence and order of streets which only a year before had reverberated with the clash of arms and threats of civil war. Yet even to those who welcomed the restoration of order there was something sinister in the silence of the streets, as if by straining one's ears one might hear the cries and screams of those who were being hunted to death like rats in a cellar. One entire section of the population, the Jews, which had made a particularly brilliant contribution to the life of Berlin, had been officially pronounced unclean, outside the law, extruded like excrement from the body politic, and lay defenceless at the mercy of anyone who chose to take advantage of its helplessness.

Not that such horrors pressed themselves upon the attention of even inquisitive observers. The total *Gleichschaltung** of the press and the radio had deprived the city of its eyes and ears, and its only source of information was rumour and gossip, or what the Nazis called *Greuelpropaganda*, atrocity mongering, which was itself a crime deserving the death sentence, or worse. Prudent men did not listen to it, for fear of being contaminated by it. Political differences were being settled, on terms that allowed of no mercy; at such times a good citizen is well advised to turn a deaf ear to screams in the night, and then it was all the more tempting to do so because of the peace and order, as of a mortuary, which ruled the streets. *Solitudinem faciunt pacem appellant.**

It was a peace which was welcome to many, perhaps even a majority of Germans, their powers of resistance drained and exhausted by the long terrible years of the depression and the violence of the political struggles which had torn to pieces the body of the Republic. If, in a quiet street at night, where one could once again walk in comfort and security, one were unlucky enough to meet a lorry load of Storm Troopers, revolvers and *Gummiknüppeln** at the ready, engaged on a *razzia** against some suspected enemy of the regime, or some Jew whose mere existence was an offence against German blood, it was best, whatever one's feeling, to hurry home and lock one's door, and hope or pretend that this was some isolated incident which should be left to be forgotten in the darkness and obscurity of the night.

The suppression of all organs of opposition had deprived the vast majority of Germans of any means of making an objective assessment of what was happening to themselves or to their country. No one who has never experienced it can quite understand the sense of helplessness and apathy which affects a people which is denied access to any source of information except that which is officially approved. And since, in politics as in other matters, people cannot live without believing something, they almost by default and often unconsciously begin to accept the official version of their situation, which, in Berlin at that time, was that of a Germany which had suddenly recovered its vitality and virility, and thereby had come to rediscover the old Prussian virtues of *Treue, Pflicht, Gehorsamkeit* (Loyalty, Duty and Obedience).

For myself, things were rather different. I was not, after all, a German and the old Prussian virtues had very little appeal to me. But what was more important, I had access to the foreign press and could read the admirable, though gruesome, accounts of the Nazi terror by Frederick Voigt* which were that winter appearing in the *Manchester Guardian*. Better still, perhaps, I could talk to some of the foreign correspondents who congregated every evening at their *Stammtisch* in the *Taverne* café, and hear by word of mouth the monstrosities they were aware of, even though, in most cases, their editors did not encourage them to report them. It was from the correspondents chiefly that one could discover what was happening in Berlin, and in particular the fate of men and women who for years had played a distinguished part in the cultural and political life of Germany and had now suddenly sunk into oblivion. For the most part it was a repetitive story, of exile, arrest, imprisonment, torture, murder; they had been swallowed up in an abyss too terrible to contemplate and I sometimes felt that, if one were to keep one's sanity, it was better not to think too much about such things.

Among those who listened with me to the talk at the *Taverne* were a few young Germans who, like me, found it the best way of learning what was happening to their country. They were not, as one might have expected, liberal or left-wing opponents of the regime; they were young men of conservative, even reactionary principles, and from the best military families, to whom Prussian virtues still meant something different from National Socialism, and perhaps their strongest feeling was a sense of shame, not unmixed with snobbery, that such a man as Hitler should exercise unlimited power over them; but they were also very brave and gay young men whose natural instincts were to enjoy life, and I found it very easy to make friends with them. How could I guess that one day, ten years later, on a battlefield in Normandy, I would pick up an English newspaper and find their names, von der Schulenberg, von Hase, von Prittwitz,* inscribed, *honoris causa*,* on the list of those who had been executed for their part in the attempted assassination of Hitler?* Such things were still far from our minds; bad as things were that winter, no one had any idea of how much worse they would become later.

For as yet it was still possible to hope, though not in the way of those who believed that murder and torture were juvenile excesses of a young and vigorous regime which, recognizing its errors, would quickly return to the paths of legality and respectability. The hope of those who opposed the regime was that the situation in Germany was still so precarious and uncertain that Hitler might find his position intolerable and become once again what he had so recently been, an obscure Bavarian politician, in no way qualified to govern a great and civilized country. In the last twenty years in Germany there had been so many changes and reversals of fortune, so many plots and counter-plots, so many threats of revolution and counter-revolution, and in the last months before the *Machtübernahme*⋆ the air had been so charged with uncertainty and speculation, with intrigue and counter-intrigue, that Germans had become used to thinking that anything might happen at any moment; in politics, the exception had become the rule.

When General von Blomberg had been hastily summoned to Berlin from the Disarmament Conference in Geneva, to become Minister of Defence in Hitler's newly formed government, he had been met at the station by two emissaries with conflicting orders. One, Major Ott, came from General von Schleicher and summoned him to the *Kriegs-ministerium*⋆ in the Bendlerstrasse; the other, Oskar von Hindenburg, ordered him to the Presidential Palace. Von Blomberg obeyed the latter, and had thus assured Hitler of the support of the Reichswehr; but what would have happened if he had gone to the Bendlerstrasse?⋆

When the fate of nations hangs upon such hazards a prudent man assumes that luck, chance, fortune, providence may undo what they have already done. In 1934 there were many Germans who, on prudential grounds alone, hesitated to commit themselves finally to Hitler, whose regime still had the marks of illegitimacy and instability. As for the imprudent who were willing to accept the appalling risk of active opposition to Hitler (and there were still some of them), it seemed impossible to believe that the German working class, in which they had for so many years placed their hope and their trust, had capitulated so completely and ignominiously. After all, might not the Communists be right in claiming that Hitler's triumph was the last convulsive effort of a capitalist system on the point of collapse, and that somewhere, even now, in secret, underground, in Moscow, in Berlin perhaps, the forces were organizing which would undertake the revolutionary seizure of power for which Hitler had prepared the way.

Others had less visionary, if no less deluded, reasons for indecision or for hope. Was not Hindenburg still alive? It was notorious that he detested Hitler, whom he regarded with ill-concealed contempt. Was not Papen, whom Hindenburg loved, still Vice-Chancellor and had he not set himself the task of bringing Hitler to heel and, ultimately, disposing of him? Papen had got rid of Brüning, he had got rid of

Schleicher, he had even, as in some dashing cavalry charge, got rid of the government of Prussia; was Hitler the man to withstand his subtleties and intrigues and treacheries? And even in his own ranks Hitler had his enemies. In that winter of 1934 the Storm Troops were dissatisfied, sullen, mutinous. They had not yet received the rewards they had earned by their sacrifices in fighting the Communists in the streets of Berlin. They might enjoy the freedom to revenge themselves on their enemies, but blood alone was not enough for men who looked for, and had fought for, something more solid than revenge, in the shape of jobs, appointments, salaries, recognized positions in society and the state. Was not Dr Goebbels grumbling that the Party had not put Hitler into power to satisfy the greed and ambition of the *Märzhasen*, the March Hares who in the previous year had rushed to join the party once its victory had been assured? It was said that Röhm had threatened to resign; and from Breslau came rumours that Heines, the convicted murderer and homosexual now elevated to be Gauleiter of Silesia, was on the point of open revolt. Gregor Strasser* was calling for a second revolution in which the Party would finally settle all its accounts with its enemies, left, right, and centre, and in particular with the timorous bourgeoisie which was now trying to rob it of the spoils of victory.

History is written when the consequences of men's actions are known, so that everything seems determined by what went before; but it is made by men who cannot foresee the results of what they do and can only guess at what they may be. In Berlin, in 1934, there was plenty of room for guessing, even though many of the guesses were wide of the mark. For Hitler, though Reich Chancellor, had not yet established that total domination over the German people which he was to achieve later, nor was he surrounded by that aura of victory which his spectacular triumphs were to bestow on him in years to come. Even a dictator, and even a Hitler, cannot destroy an entire culture and replace it with another in a space of nine months. Such things take time, even when they have brute force and unrestrained violence behind them; and as yet indeed Hitler did not even have a monopoly of force, for alongside the Party and the Storm Troops stood the Reichswehr, a military and political power in its own right, still relatively immune to the blandishments of National Socialism, and capable, if it so wished, of blowing Hitler and his entire regime to bits.

So gossip, rumour, speculation multiplied wherever men might meet without fear of Party fanatics and informers. For in that winter of 1934 there still remained two great imponderables and incalculables. No one knew what Hitler was thinking, and no one knew what the

Reichswehr was thinking, and so long as this remained so, no one could foretell the future. So the city waited, like an animal which feigns sleep yet is still alert to any sign of approaching change or danger. And as it waited it held its breath, because the only thing that seemed certain was that so precarious a situation could only provide a transition – but to what? Everywhere one heard the same phrases. *Dass kann doch nicht mehr länger dauern* (Things can't go on like this much longer). *Entweder oder* (One thing or another). For some people the alternative provided a hope when all hope seemed to be lost; for others, an added determination to carry Hitler's seizure of power to its logical conclusion.

And so Berlin waited. It was very cold. Flakes of snow fell slowly, heavily, congealing on the frozen waters of the Spree, and Schinkel's monuments of the dead past looked more than ever austere, aloof, withdrawn. Hungry Storm Troopers, still awaiting their awards, aimlessly tramped the streets. In the icy air there was a feeling strangely compounded of expectancy and fear. It was the air of a city waiting to see the Janus head of the future, without knowing which face of it would be revealed.

II

My own reasons for being in Berlin had nothing to do with the political situation. Indeed my instincts told me that Berlin was a city of the dead, and that only a political necrophilist could find it of any interest. And yet the city, though so utterly transformed from the one I had known before the *Machtübernahme*, retained a strange fascination for me; something made me feel that it was here, more than anywhere else in the world, that the shape of the future would be decided, and even though it might be distasteful, I wanted to see what it looked like.

Besides, I had work to do, which was to pursue my researches into the life and work of Ferdinand Lassalle, founder of the German Social Democratic Party, student of Heraclitus and prophet of the 'iron law of wages', of whom, under the terms of my fellowship at All Souls, I intended to write a biography. With the German Social Democratic Party proscribed and persecuted, neither the time nor the place were altogether propitious for such a task; but in the suburbs of Berlin lived the greatest living authority on the subject, the elderly Professor Hermann Oncken,* author of the standard biography of Lassalle and in the *Preussische Staatsbibliothek** was a wealth of material relating both to Lassalle himself and the early history of the party he had founded.

Did I hope to find there, in the character of Lassalle and the nature of the party which he had created in his own image, some explanation of the ruin and destruction which had fallen upon it? After so many years I cannot be sure, but what is certain is that as I walked to the *Staatsbibliothek* from my lodgings off the Kurfürstendamm, I felt the presence of Lassalle very close to me; after all he had walked these streets so often himself, dressed in the height of fashion, his head full of youthful dreams and ambitions, and impelled by a restless energy which had impressed everyone who knew him, even his bitter critic and rival, Karl Marx. I maintained with him an endless dialogue of question and answer, all directed at discovering the secret of his flamboyant personality, dandy, man of affairs, *coureur de femmes,*★ a frequenter of the salons of the rich, yet the most effective Socialist leader of his day, whose tragi-comic death in a duel was mourned by the entire working class of Germany; but where was the flaw, the error which had doomed his great political creation, the German Social Democratic Party, to destruction?

In answering such questions, I found Professor Oncken a dis-appointment; indeed, he thought it foolish even to ask them. He was the perfect type of meticulous German historian, arid and desiccated, to whom all facts were of equal value, because they could be verified. To him, history, *wie es eigentlich geschehen ist* (as it actually happened), was whatever was preserved in the documents, and nothing else, and he regarded me with disapproval as one who would evidently never satisfy his own austere standards; indeed, he regarded my entire enterprise as a kind of bold guerrilla raid into territory which he had long ago staked out as his own. As for any implication that there might be some relationship between Lassalle's achievement and the great drama that was now being played out in Berlin, he regarded such ideas as unworthy of the historian, all the more because he was terrified at any attempt to involve him in discussion of the current political situation in Berlin.

Oncken offered me neither encouragement nor inspiration, though I've no doubt the fault was as much mine as his. After reporting progress on my work, I used to leave his comfortable, shabby house, with its books and its neatly ordered garden, in a mood of profound depression; he seemed to deprive the past of any life or colour it ever had, and in his hands it became a shapeless mass of inert material whose only value or interest was that it gave the historian the opportunity to write a book about it. Outside his own subject, he was the complete German *Philister,*★ and the idea that the study of history might, as Nietzsche suggested, be of use or disadvantage to us in life, filled him with alarm and abhorrence. There were times when I thought that Professor Oncken, as a type of the German academic, was more worthy of study than Lassalle himself, and that, with all his faults and his virtues, he threw more light on the contemporary situation than anything one might learn from the history books. Perhaps the men who wrote them might, in the last analysis, be more interesting than what they wrote.

Initially, there were difficulties also in pursuing my studies at the *Staatsbibliothek*, for most of the books and documents I wished to consult were by now subject to censorship and withdrawn from the eyes of the general public; they had become a kind of political pornography, against which the German reader had to be protected. I was able to prove my reliability with impeccable references, including one, surprisingly enough, from Sir John Simon, then Foreign Secretary.* He was also a Fellow of All Souls and nothing was too much trouble for Sir John if he could help a member of the college, however junior and obscure. He was probably, at that time, one of the most hated members of the British establishment, but he was never anything but kind to me, though there was probably no subject in the world on which we agreed. He seemed an odd sort of friend for me to have; but the Nazi authorities very reasonably concluded that no friend of Sir John's could be a danger to the Third Reich and I was given the freedom of the library.

I found my work heavy going, though I dutifully spent the greater part of each day in the library; indeed, my days fell into a regular and arduous routine which would have become monotonous if it had not been for the peculiar effect which the air of Berlin has always had on me. It is an effect which is largely that of the Berlin climate, which is stimulating and invigorating, including a sense of physical wellbeing, which even the oppressive political and intellectual atmosphere of the new regime could not dispel. Berlin is a great industrial city and has all the sadness of an industrial city; yet one third of its municipal area consists of lakes, and one third is forest, and a considerable proportion is agricultural land, so that wherever one is in the city one is conscious of the proximity of water and forest and farmland. Even among slums and factories one feels as if the country were extending green fingers into the city, so that an agreeable sense of *rus in urbe** relieves the *Wilhelminisch** weight of the city's architecture. And perhaps, that winter, the air was even keener and sharper because of that curious sense of uncertainty and expectancy which overhung the city.

I needed any stimulation I could find as I wrestled with Lassalle's huge two-volume work on Heraclitus, which he had confidently expected to establish his fame as a philosopher. It turned Greek philosophy into an anticipation of Hegel and Heraclitus himself into an early master of the Hegelian dialectic. Lassalle himself took his book very seriously; it was to provide the philosophical basis for his political programme. But with him the dialectic remained a movement of ideas and not a materialistic one, as with Marx, who rightly saw in Lassalle a formidable political enemy; though admiring his energy and dynamism as a political leader, Marx dismissed him as a part adventurer, part charlatan, part demagogue, and in all this he was quite right, only he could not help envying him the capacity for playing a spectacular public role which he himself lacked.

Could it be that in the antipathy between Marx and Lassalle there lay the germ of that bitter conflict between the socialist and communist parties which had had such fatal effects in Germany and could its effects be seen even now as communists and socialists alike were hunted down in the streets and cellars of Berlin?

No one reads Lassalle's *Heraclitus* any more, but its spirit was the same spirit which had inspired Lassalle to action and Marx to contempt and derision, so that it was still possible that some spark of life still lingered in its turgid and contorted prose, and I struggled to think so, though not with great success. But the effort to do so occupied my mind as I walked home across Berlin from the library to the Kurfürstendamm and to my lodgings where every evening I took a German lesson from Frau Meyer, who occupied a flat above me in the same apartment building.

Frau Meyer taught me to speak German with an impeccable Prussian accent, so that German friends, on first acquaintance, were apt to ascribe to me some reactionary Junker background which was totally removed from my real origins. This gave rise to awkward misunderstandings; working-class friends regarded me as an alien in their midst, not because I was English* but because they suspected I was some kind of German, but from a Germany which represented everything they hated most. I found it difficult to point out this disadvantage of her teaching to Frau Meyer, and in any case she would not have understood me, as she had a fanatical devotion to the purity of the German tongue and was determined that any pupil of hers should only speak it as it was spoken in the best families.

This indeed had been her profession before, rather late in life, she married. Before the war she had been governess to the children of Herbert Asquith, then Prime Minister of England, and much of my lessons with her was devoted to her reminiscences of life in the Asquith family, of the Prime Minister's passion for bridge and his unfortunate tendency to drink too much brandy after dinner and of Margot Asquith's indiscretions and love of gossip. All this was said not with malice but with love, as if the Prime Minister and his wife were wayward children whom she had in her charge. Frau Meyer herself had at one moment made her own contribution to British political history. She had been loved and cherished by the Asquiths, who had continued to employ her after the outbreak of war in 1914, despite the public outcry which this provoked; with the result that the Prime Minister was accused of maintaining a German spy in Downing Street, through whom the German General Staff was fully informed of everything that went on in his household. Angry crowds collected in Downing Street, demanding the dismissal of the spy, whose presence at the very centre of power was felt as a danger and an affront to the whole nation, and in the end even Asquith, so aloof from the mob passions inspired by the war, had to yield to their demands and Frau Meyer was sent back to her native land.

It was not a change she welcomed. Tears came into her eyes when she spoke of England and the Asquiths, as if they formed some island of the blessed immune to the misfortunes of other peoples. And indeed life had not been good to her when she returned to Germany; her experience had been a kind of model of all those millions of German lives which now, suddenly, had coalesced to project upon the world the monstrous image of Hitler. From the amenities of Downing Street and the Barn,* she had returned to war, blockade and defeat, the fall of the monarchy, the revolution and the republic, the inflation, depression and now the triumph of National Socialism; a sequence of events which in the course of twenty years had destroyed all those certainties and hopes of happiness which Frau Meyer had known as a girl.

She found some protection against the violent vicissitudes of German life in marriage, but it was only a frail one. Herr Meyer was a small and not very successful businessman, who had just managed to keep his head above water during the depression, and now ran indefatigably about Berlin in pursuit of orders which always seemed to elude him and returned in the evening, pale, harassed and exhausted, to the flat in the Tauentzienstrasse.

Life had been too much for Herr Meyer; he was ready for anyone who would rescue him from it. Sometimes he would return when my lesson was still in progress and then, seated in the circle of light around the table, we would drink a glass of Rhine wine together while he recounted the events of the day to Frau Meyer. Normally he spoke in a tone of quiet resignation which perhaps concealed a profound despair; for many Germans it was the only rational attitude towards a world which had so often cheated their hopes. Listening to Herr Meyer, I sometimes used to think of Erich Kästner's Herr Schmidt* (Kurt Schmidt, *komplett*);

> *Er merkte, dass er nicht alleine stand.*
> *Und dass er doch allein stand, bei Gefahren.*
> *Und auf dem Globus, sah er, lag kein Land,*
> *in dem die Schmidts nicht in der Mehrzahl waren . . .*
>
> *9 Stunden stand Schmidt schwitzend im Betrieb.*
> *4 Stunden fuhr und ass er; müd und dumm.*
> *10 Stunden lag er, ohne Blick und stumm.*
> *Und in dem Stündchen, das ihm übrigbleib,*
> *bracht er sich um.*
>
> He noticed that he was not alone,
> Yet that he was alone when dangers threatened.
> And, the world over, he could see no country
> In which the Schmidts did not form the majority . . .
>
> 9 hours long, Schmidt stood sweating in the factory.
> 4 hours he travelled and ate, tired and stupefied.
> 10 hours he slept, sightless and dumb,
> And in the little hour that was left over,
> He cut his throat.

But even now Herr Meyer would report sometimes that business gave signs of looking up and that perhaps we could give credit for this to the new regime; it was only the most hesitant and tentative of suggestions, as if such a situation would be too good to be true. Herr Meyer had been disappointed too often to take anything on trust. It was the nearest Herr Meyer ever came to discussing politics, yet I had the feeling that even in him a National Socialist was struggling to be born. Nor did Frau Meyer dissent, though she was Jewish; for her the only real politics were English politics, the politics of gentlemen, and had ended with Asquith. And besides she had a German housewife's submissive instinct that, whatever a Margot Asquith might think or do, in Germany a wife left politics to her husband.

I should have liked to protest to the Meyers that, whatever whiff of prosperity Herr Meyer scented in the air, it would at best prove, in the long run, only a prelude to the yet greater disaster and, in the short run, would be bought at the cost of the misery and persecution of millions of others. But I felt both that any protests of mine would be unavailing against Herr Meyer's Stoic acceptance of things as they are, and somehow even that it would not be just to address them to him, so much at the mercy of all those forces which had pressed upon him in his lifetime, so impotent to offer any resistance to them or even to comprehend them, so much without choice in everything that had happened to him in his life. It was best to leave him with whatever hopes he might still cherish and Frau Meyer to her memories of London.

After I left Germany that year, I heard no more from the Meyers, and I sometimes wondered how life under National Socialism had treated them. When I returned to Berlin again, in May 1945, I revisited the Tauentzienstrasse but the house where Frau Meyer and I lived had, like most of the surrounding area, disappeared. I made enquiries about the Meyers and learned that they had continued to occupy their flat during the war, in increasing poverty and distress, and had finally perished in the cellars of the house during the mammoth air raids on Berlin in the winter of 1945.

III

The Meyers had a certain fascination for me, both because their life, in their sombre flat with its heavy German furniture, seemed so typical, in its quiet despair, of thousands of other German lives, and because it was in every way, except Frau Meyer's devotion to German literature, so utterly alien and detached from everything, including politics, which made Berlin interesting to me. Though we occupied the same house, and lived in the same city, we existed side by side like islands between which there are no means of communication. They had about them an air of loneliness and isolation, which I found slightly infectious, as if I might be condemned to live alone on my island, as they on theirs.

Not long after I arrived in Berlin, however, and my days had already settled into their regular routine, I received a telephone call from a friend of Adam von Trott's, who had written to him to say that I was in Berlin and that we might like to meet each other. I asked him to come for a drink in my lodgings and the next evening there was a ring at my door, and I found myself faced by a handsome young German, with blonde hair and a golden complexion, who bowed stiffly, extended his hand and said: 'Von Seebach.'

This was Hasso von Seebach,* who was to become a great friend. There was something disconcerting in his manner which made one think of the disinherited heir of a great estate, and in one sense this was not a wholly misleading impression. His father had been a general, and came of a long line of generals, but no one could have been less of a soldier or a militarist than Hasso, though I have no doubt that under different circumstances he would have shown the same traditional virtues as his ancestors. As it was, he had inherited nothing from them except his father's boots, thick heavy boots, of the very best leather, but better designed for a route march or a day's shooting than a stroll along the Kurfürstendamm. They were in fact the only footwear he possessed, because he had become almost entirely *déclassé* and proletarianized; both his parents were dead and whatever fortune they may have possessed had disappeared in the inflation. He rarely talked about his parents, but he once conjured up an entirely different Berlin for me when he told me, with a rare touch of nostalgia, that as a child one of the things he enjoyed most was watching the maid every morning polishing his father's sunburned close shaven skull till it shone like a billiard ball, as in his general's uniform he sat before his dressing room mirror making his morning *toilette*.

After his first call, we met twice or three times a week in the evenings after my German lesson was over, or at the weekends when we went for walks on the Wannsee or the Havel. But meeting places were a difficulty. Sometimes he would come to my house for a drink, but more often we would meet on a street corner and walk for miles around Berlin, long promenades on which he pointed out to me objects of architectural or historical interest, in the icy air and sometimes in the falling snow which made me understand why he treasured his father's boots and long to stop for refreshment at some warm welcoming pub or café, but Hasso would always refuse because any entertainment would have to be at my expense and he had no means of entertaining me in return. Quite simply, he had no money at all and he was too proud to accept what he could not return.

He lived not far from me, in Wilmersdorf, near the Sport Palast, where Dr Goebbels competed with six-day bicycle races for public attention. He rented a tiny single room in a working-class family's tenement flat, unfurnished except for his books and a narrow truckle bed. Sometimes, though rarely, I would call for him there and whenever I entered I would smell the stale, suffocating odour of poverty that filled the flat and hear the children crying and see the remains of their scanty meals on the table. The family were socialists and despite everything remained socialists, but with Hitler's triumph the whole of their social world, the union, the working men's club, the party newspaper, the sports club, the pension fund, had been destroyed, their friends were scattered and dispersed, and now they sat quietly at home and listened to the radio amid the smell of poverty.

Hasso took all his meals with them and paid them twelve marks a week for food and lodging. He never ate anywhere else and would never let me entertain him to dinner. His only source of income, I gathered, was a part-time job he had as a secretary or assistant to Frau Braun, the widow of Otto Braun, for twenty years Prime Minister of Prussia until Papen's soldiers dispersed the Prussian Diet at the point of the bayonet. I do not know what his exact functions were, but I gathered vaguely that they were to do with helping her to write her memoirs of her husband, which she hoped one day might be published abroad.

Hasso had for a time been a fellow student of Adam von Trott's at Heidelberg, and talked of him with a boundless admiration as one of the men who might one day lead Germany out of the morass into which she had fallen. It was the first time I realized how great a personal and political influence Adam exercised on Germans of his own generation or his power to make them follow where he led.* I had known him at Oxford and was greatly attached to him, but somehow, in England, it was difficult to take seriously his particular combination of socialism, German patriotism, Hegelian idealism and Protestant ethics. It seemed hard to believe that anyone who thought in so many and in such conflicting abstractions could ever make an effective politician, which is what Adam wanted to be. I should have remembered that what in England may seem abstractions can in Germany become the most formidable realities.

Now, talking to Hasso, I realized that Adam might indeed possess that one gift which is essential to all politicians, which is that of making people believe in them, and of capturing their loyalty and devotion. It is a gift which is indispensable even when it involves deceiving people. It was clear that Hasso, who was so modest and deprecating about any gifts of his own, was willing to give Adam all his trust and to follow wherever he led and if I were to believe him this was a feeling which had been shared by many of his fellow students at Heidelberg.

Hasso himself had embraced socialism, partly under Adam's influence and as a result seemed almost to welcome the proletarian way of life which had been forced on him. But his socialism was of a highly ambivalent kind; he was a socialist, not for political reasons, but out of a kind of general revulsion against the traditions of his class, and in particular that military tradition which had plunged Germany into the holocaust of the Great War and was now being reborn in an even more perverted and aggressive form in National Socialism. He belonged by nature and temperament to that Germany which had once liked to think of itself as *das Land von Dichter und Denker* – the land of poets and thinkers – and he regarded German history after 1848 as, quite simply, a mistake; in this he was a throwback to a Germany which had long ceased to exist. Indeed, like many Germans of his own class, from whose prejudices he was so admirably free, he regarded the German Reich as a misbegotten creation of Bismarck's, in which everything that was best in Germany had been lost. In his heart what he believed in was not the German Empire but the Kingdom of Prussia *von Gottes Gnaden** and in this he was even more reactionary than the most fanatical German nationalist.

The only thing, which for him, still made Germany worthwhile was her literature, to which he was as devoted as Frau Meyer herself. I often thought that I should introduce them to each other, but I do not think that their meeting would have been a success. Frau Meyer would have disliked in Hasso the combination of the aristocrat and the proletarian – so very different from Mr Asquith – while he would have found both her character and her way of life intolerably *petit bourgeois*. And even in literature they would have found little in common. Frau Meyer made me read Goethe and Schiller and Heine and Fontane; Hasso made me read Hölderlin and Büchner* and Schopenhauer and Nietzsche, and after them those poets, Rilke and George and Brecht who have lent such distinction to twentieth-century German literature. They were his constant companions, and they became mine as they joined us on our walks through the Berlin streets. He spoke of them with the enthusiasm of one to whom literature is not an ornament or a decoration of life but a part of living itself. From time to time, if he came for a drink with me in my rooms he would present me with one of the small cheap selections from the German classics, new and old, which were then published by the Deutsche Verlag. When I finally left Berlin, he came to see me off at the station, and, to occupy me on the long journey, gave me Nietzsche's *Vom Nützen und Nachteil der Historie für das Leben* (*The Advantages and Disadvantages of History as an Aid to Life*). I have the little book still and I wish that every university student and teacher were made to read it.

IV

It was through Hasso that I came to know the Bauers,* Peter and Lola, who kept a second-hand bookshop on the second floor of a large and dilapidated apartment house in Wilmersdorf. They also were Social Democrats and like other members of the party they now led a life of extreme seclusion and privacy, rarely venturing out and avoiding anything which might draw unnecessary attention to themselves. And like Hasso they were in financial straits, because their stock-in-trade consisted for the most part of socialist and Marxist literature and their customers had been drawn precisely from the two parties which were now the objects of persecution by the National Socialists. Fortunately, Peter Bauer also had a lucrative sideline in high-class pornography and for this, in Berlin, there is always a good market, whatever the political situation, and the affluent businessmen whom Peter Bauer supplied did not withdraw their custom merely because Hitler was in power; this side of his business may even have picked up a little. In particular, Peter continued to enjoy the patronage of his most important customer, Arnold von Borsig, a partner in the great industrial firm of Borsig AG, locomotive manufacturers and one of the pioneers of the industrial revolution in Germany. Borsig, large, genial, pleasure-loving and radically-minded, may even have increased his orders, partly to relieve the plight of the Bauers and partly, perhaps, to relieve a melancholy and boredom induced by the *Machtübernahme*, for Borsig was no supporter of Hitler's and one day was to become one of his victims.

If Bauer had been content to be a purveyor of pornography, to which he applied the same discriminating and erudite standards as to the rest of his business, he might even have prospered under the National Socialist regime, as a kind of *Hofjude**★* privileged to satisfy the corrupt tastes of the Nazi élite. But Bauer was not only a committed and active socialist, he was also a genuine Marxist scholar, a better one indeed than Oncken, and it was intolerable to him to live under conditions in which any public display of his ruling passion had become an offence against the state. He and his wife were already engaged in the devious and protracted negotiations required in order to take themselves and their stock-in-trade abroad. In this they were helped by Herr Borsig, a friend as well as a customer, with large and powerful connections abroad, but there were many difficulties to be overcome and in the meantime the Bauers waited for their hour of deliverance.

Despite their reduced circumstances, there was always a welcome for one at the Bauers. Apart from the books which lined the walls and covered the floors, their flat was bare and sparsely furnished and had that indefinable odour of cheap cigars and bad plumbing which is characteristic of the poorer quarters of Berlin. There was always a cup of coffee waiting, and Bauer himself ready to talk endlessly about the problems of socialism, past, present, and to come; in his hands they developed an almost metaphysical subtlety and refinement and I often felt that if he had not been a socialist he would have been a theologian. The spirits of Hegel and Marx were very present to us in that shabby booklined room, while Bauer's wife Lola, a young, slightly buxom

Jewess, busied herself with making coffee and offering one the small delicacies, of sausage, ham, cheese, which they could still afford. It struck me, in these conversations with Bauer, how little England had contributed to the theoretical controversies which so obsessed him; even in our socialism, it seemed, we remained too pragmatic and empirical to interest Bauer, and I wondered if for that very reason the British Labour Party still remained an effective political force while in Germany both the socialist and communist parties were in ruins.

From the academic point of view, however, I learned a great deal from my conversations with Bauer. He knew the whole range of socialist and Marxist literature far better than I ever would, and he taught me more than I could ever have achieved in my long hours at the *Staatsbibliothek*. Quite apart from the books he lent me, and the guidance he gave me in my reading, he introduced me to a type of thinking which is profoundly alien to English habits of mind, and yet is indispensable to the understanding of the international socialist movement. Professing to be scientific and materialistic, it is at the same time both dogmatic and sophistical, determined by certain *a priori* categories which are never subject to doubt; its greatest subtlety and ingenuity are devoted to adjusting and adapting the events of the real world to its preconceived views of what they ought to be, indeed must be if one can penetrate to their deeper reality. I was so much affected by this view of the world that it was many years before I could shake myself entirely free of it and when at length I did I was left with a peculiar feeling of helplessness, as if, in an intellectual sense, I had been suddenly thrust naked into the world.

Bauer also affected my life in a more immediate and practical way. He was intensely interested in Marx's early writings, to which, at that time, few people paid any attention, and which were hardly known, if at all, in England; he infected me with his own enthusiasm to such an extent that it gradually superseded my interest in Lassalle and I formed the intention of writing, not his biography, but an intellectual history of young Marx. When, however, on my return to England, I announced my plan at All Souls, the Warden took alarm.* Marx, and Marxism, were not then intellectually respectable at Oxford, even as a subject of scholarship. Had not Roy Harrod, in a series of lectures at Christ Church, destroyed any pretensions he may have had to be taken seriously either as an economist or a philosopher and would not everything that anyone required to know about him be shortly revealed in Isaiah Berlin's forthcoming little book on him in the Home University Library? The Warden felt that the college should not support so unorthodox a project; with the result that I resigned my research fellowship and abandoned the security of All Souls for the uncertainties of a wider and rougher world.

But Bauer's bookshop also offered other distractions from the true path of scholarship. From time to time, customers who clung to the true faith still presented themselves at his door in search of socialist literature. They could not yet accept that, for many years to come, socialism was, so far as Germany was concerned, a dead subject, and they still hoped that, in the sacred books which Dr Goebbels consigned to the flames but Bauer lovingly preserved in his flat, they might discover the secrets which would make their dreams come true. Sometimes such visitors were of an unexpected kind. One afternoon there was a ring at the bell. Bauer answered it and there was revealed in the doorway a burly young Storm Trooper, brown-shirted and top-booted and nervously fingering the revolver which hung in the holster at his side.

Bauer, by nature not the most courageous of men, shrank away in alarm. His wife and I looked desperately around the shelves loaded with the damning evidence which was quite enough to condemn Bauer, a Jew as well as a socialist, to the concentration camp. The Storm Trooper followed our gaze with wondering eyes; for a moment there was an appalled silence.

Yet there was something odd about the Storm Trooper; his manner was not, like that of his kind, brutal and aggressive but rather, despite his revolver, hesitant and diffident. Finally, he broke the silence by saying mildly: 'You're a bookseller.'

'Yes,' said Bauer.

'They say one can buy socialist literature here.'

'Well, yes,' said Bauer nervously; 'but they're only old books really. But I've got some very nice pornography.'

'Do you have Karl Marx? *Das Kapital*?' He spoke as if it were a new novel he had just heard of.

'Yes, I do have a copy,' said Bauer reluctantly.

'I'd like to buy one,' said the Storm Trooper firmly.

Now that we were able to inspect the appalling apparition more closely, we saw that it had a friendly and ingenuous air, there was something innocent and appealing about it, as if it had come, not to threaten, but to invite assistance.

'Why do you want it?' said Bauer suspiciously.

'Why, to read, of course,' said the Storm Trooper.

'To read?' said Bauer. 'It's heavy going, you know.'

'All the same,' said the Storm Trooper, 'I'd like to read it. The boys in the troop are always talking about it. Some of them used to be communists. They say there are lessons to be learned from it. Things are not going well, you know. The *Bonzen** are still on top and we've had nothing. There's got to be a change.' He had a look of determination in his eyes, like a stubborn child.

'All right,' said Bauer. 'I'll let you have a copy. But – be careful with it, you know.'

'Oh, I'll be careful,' said the Storm Trooper. 'You needn't worry. I won't give you away. Nice place you've got here.' He looked wistfully around at the bookshelves.

And so, at the cost of a few marks, the transaction was completed, and, with a soldierly *Heil Hitler* and Hitler salute, the Storm Trooper marched away. We stared at each other in silence. What could such a visit from across the abyss portend? Was the Storm Trooper to be trusted, or would he shortly return with reinforcements, to wreck the bookshop and take the Bauers off, perhaps myself also, to whatever fate they felt we deserved? Or was he really a harbinger of that second revolution, that final assault on the system and the bosses, which Dr Goebbels was demanding? We sat and talked until late in the evening, speaking in the sophistications of the dialectic, with something of the same ingenuous hope which had shone in the eyes of the Storm Trooper.

I wondered later what became of him. Whatever it was, he could be trusted. Nothing happened to the Bauers and eventually they were able to make their way to Paris, taking their books with them.

V

The Storm Trooper, of course, was an exceptional customer. Most of those who came to the Bauers represented the scattered remnants of the Social Democratic Party; like Bauer himself, or his wife, or myself for that matter, they still believed that politics was a rational process, and judged by this criterion the rule of the National Socialist Party, and Hitler himself, could only be regarded as a purely transitory triumph of the absurd and grotesque, as if History, in a capricious mood, had suddenly played a malicious trick on us. It was simply not possible that a great and civilized people could continue for long to be ruled by a gang of criminals and thugs led by a crazy and ignorant fanatic. We had not yet accustomed ourselves to accept that the rule of the absurd may be as powerful, or even more powerful, a factor in history as the rule of reason; but even I began to suspect uneasily that henceforward it was going to play an increasingly important part in our lives.

So the survivors of the German working-class movement, no longer members of a powerful organization but a few scattered and helpless individuals, searched feverishly for signs of Hitler's approaching end; the one thing certain was that he could not survive for long. When they could meet, they made optimistic plans for reviving and reconstructing the movement, which would, of course, take power when Hitler finally fell; most of all, they endlessly analysed all the mistakes which had led to their defeat and drew up blueprints for the future which would ensure that they would never again be repeated.

They could not realize or accept the magnitude or finality of their defeat, nor could they acknowledge that in Hitler there had appeared one of those demonic figures who never leave the stage of history before all their capacity for evil has worked itself out to the very end. To have done so would have been to feel despair even deeper than that which they already knew and for this History had not yet prepared them.

There was one such survivor who sometimes came to the Bauers with whom I made friends. He was a gaunt, intensely serious, under-nourished young man who, before the *Machtübernahme* had made a living as a freelance contributor to various socialist and trade union papers; now they had all been liquidated and so far as I knew he had no visible means of subsistence. Yet he had sufficient resources to spend all his days travelling, by bus, underground, S-Bahn and on foot, from one end of Berlin to another, in an effort to maintain contact with former comrades who remained loyal to their convictions and to keep alive in them the hopes by which he himself was inspired. He welcomed every item of rumour and gossip which pointed to the growing dissensions within the National Socialist Party, and in each, however trivial and unreliable, he found proof that the dialectic of history would not permit the continued triumph of Hitler. He was consumed by the conviction, as of a kind of original sin, that the German working class had lost its way because of the split between the communists and the social democrats and dreamed of a day when it would be healed and the working class, one, single and undivided, would re-emerge in glory to redeem a fallen world.

His dreams were not as unpractical as they may seem today; in his way he was a premature proponent of the Popular Front to which, later, all the hopes of the Left were attached; but in 1934 official communist doctrine still held that the immediate enemy was not Hitler but the social fascists, that is to say the Social Democratic Party. There was something both noble and pathetic about the efforts of this pale and starved young man to repair the sins and errors of socialism which won my admiration and, so far as that was admitted, affection, for he was far too much obsessed with his one-man struggle against evil to be concerned with personal relationships.

So far as I could I used to help him in his crusade. This took the form of running mysterious errands for him and delivering letters for him in scattered quarters of Berlin. He was by nature a conspirator, but a bad one; otherwise he would not have entrusted such tasks to me. Somehow, however, he and his friends had collected sufficient funds to install a small hand-press in a boat on the Wannsee, on which they printed pamphlets and broadsheets denouncing the Hitler regime, and trying, with their minimal resources, to counter the flood of propaganda poured out by the Nazis. I used to supply him, as material for his leaflets, with copies of the English newspapers, especially the *Manchester Guardian*, and such items of information as I picked up at the *Taverne*; for what he and his friends wanted most was to feel that there, in Berlin, they were not totally isolated in their struggle, that somewhere, in another world, there were forces at work which would come to their aid, that they were not alone in trying to fight Hitler but were encompassed by a cloud of witnesses to the significance of what they were trying to do. In all this they were of course quite wrong; no one knew of their existence or their efforts, much less came to their assistance.

There was a certain recklessness in my anonymous friend's activities which only increased my admiration for him. To me, they were romantic; to him, however, they were quite literally a matter of life and death.* He had none of the expertise or the techniques of the professional revolutionary; he saw his task as that of an evangelist, of keeping the Word alive, and how can the Word live unless it is spoken to all who wish to hear it? But he did not deceive himself about what was likely to happen to him if his activities were discovered, or the probability that they would be, and he faced this prospect with a selflessness in which there was something of the heroic. I do not know how many such men there were in Germany at that moment. For the most part they have long ago disappeared from history and have remained nameless. At the most they may have been reckoned in hundreds and all their efforts proved vain and futile. But failure is not the worst fate that can attend a politician, and in their failure such men did something to alleviate the shame of defeat.

Yet ironically enough it was precisely my excursions to visit these socialist survivors in the slums and back streets of Berlin, or in the shanty towns of the unemployed on the outskirts of the city, that in the end disabused me of any hope that Hitler's triumph might prove to be short-lived. They were working men, the Old Guard of the working-class movement, who despite everything clung, like Hasso's landlord, to their ancient faith. But they were few in number, and grew fewer every day, and they were so obviously lost and isolated among the mass of their fellow workers who, if not enthusiasts for National Socialism, were at least increasingly willing to give Hitler the benefit of the doubt and to accept any disadvantages that might accrue to them from his regime.

Those who actively opposed Hitler were not only a tiny minority; they were a defeated and dispirited minority, living, in the middle of industrial Berlin, like castaways on some desert island with only their hopes and their dreams to sustain them. It was impossible to believe that they would ever feel the touch of victory.

As the long winter drew on and gave way to spring, it became increasingly clear that, whatever happened to Hitler's regime, it would not fall as the result of any opposition from inside Germany itself, and with this realization I fell victim to a profound depression, as if for the first time I had really grasped the full horror of what had happened to Germany. The gossip and rumours of dissension within the ranks of Hitler's followers continued, but to me at least they no longer carried any message of hope, because when I considered the alternatives to Hitler, all I could see was a vision of grey-faced, poverty-stricken men who had lost all capacity for united action and whose only strength was their loyalty to something which perhaps had never been more than a dream.

For me, the air of Berlin began to grow oppressive with the sense of defeat and England began to beckon as temptingly as it did to Frau Meyer. Socialism, I thought, had died in Germany, as Kafka's hero K had died in *The Trial*, 'like a dog, as if the shame of it would outlive him'. If there were to be any salvation for Germany it would have to come from abroad; unlike Frau Meyer, there was no reason for me to remain in Germany when I could be elsewhere. I suddenly felt that I wished to see the last of that great sad city on the Spree, and one evening on an impulse I packed my bags, and next morning took the train for Paris, while Hasso waved goodbye from the platform.

I never saw my friends of that winter again but when I next returned to Berlin, in 1945, there were none of them left. In the years between I thought of them often, and always with affection, but the memory brought no happiness with it, as unconsciously I already thought of them as if they were dead.

Notes

~

Notes to *Introduction*

1 Eddie, in the *The Death of the Heart* (1938), is modelled largely on Rees.
2 Shiela Grant Duff, *The Parting of Ways: A Personal Account of the Thirties* (London, 1982), 41, mentions another novel begun after *The Summer Flood* but abandoned and torn up by Rees; 'I seized up the bits and have them still.'
3 An undated essay discovered among Rees's private papers, it was published in two parts in *Planet*, 111 (1995), 13–24, and 112 (1995), 29–39.
4 Besides this appreciation, Rees offered the dedication, 'For Margaret Morris *In Memoriam*': his mother-in-law, Peggy Morris, had recently died, aged sixty.
5 Published by Heron Books in 1970, this lavishly illustrated edition contained an outstanding introduction and afterword which Rees later adapted for his essay, '*Darkness at Noon* and "Grammatical Fiction"', in Harold Harris (ed.), *Astride Two Cultures: Arthur Koestler at 70* (London, 1975), 102–22. Rees most certainly had Koestler's novel in mind when writing *Where No Wounds Were*.
6 Rees had spoken of John McVicar in a May 1973 *Encounter* column which considered a newly published sociological study of the maximum security wing at Durham prison (we 'condemn men to a lifetime of imprisonment under conditions which make life itself unendurable').

Notes to *'Goronwy Rees: The Memoirist'*

1 Samuel Hynes, *The Auden Generation: Literature and Politics in England in the 1930s* (London, 1976), 322.
2 'Letter from a Soldier', *Horizon* (July 1940), 467–71.
3 The exchange took place in the *Sunday Times*, 5 June 1960, 33; other responses, by senior military officers, appeared on 12 and 19 June, 1960. In a *Sunday Times* review of the following year (12 March 1961, 32) Rees returned to Operation Jubilee. Bernard Fergusson's *The Watery Maze*, a mostly admirable account of Combined Operations, had 'the fundamental flaw of continuously and persistently underestimating the vital role played by air power'; the book failed even to mention that one of the main objectives of Jubilee was to defeat the Germans in the air, or that 'in this as in every other respect it conspicuously failed'.

4   'Arms and the Man', *New Statesman*, 16 April 1976, 508–9 (a review of Alun
      Chalfont, *Montgomery of Alamein*).

5   G.R., 'Two Faces of War', *Encounter* (November 1959), 68–70.

6   *Country Life*, 4 August 1960, 258.

7   See especially Jenny Rees, *Looking for Mr Nobody: The Secret Life of Goronwy
      Rees* (London, 1994), 266–79, Nigel West and Oleg Tsarev, *The Crown Jewels:
      The British Secrets at the Heart of the KGB Archives* (London, 1998), and
      Christopher Andrew and Vasili Mitrokhin, *The Mitrokhin Archive: The KGB in
      Europe and the West* (Harmondsworth, 1999). John Costello and Oleg Tsarev,
      Deadly Illusions (London, 1993), was the first study positively to name Rees as
      one of Burgess's recruits.

8   Yuri Modin, *My Five Cambridge Friends* (London, 1994), 94; Andrew and
      Mitrokhin give examples of information passed by Rees (code-named GROSS
      and FLIT), describing it as 'of slender importance'.

9   Quoted by West and Tsarev, *The Crown Jewels*, 143.

10   'It is now clear that Guy Burgess really wanted to kill Rees', write West and
      Tsarev; the promise of silence was not enough, since Rees, according to
      Burgess, was a 'hysterical and unbalanced person' who might at any time let
      slip his knowledge of Burgess's past political associations (*The Crown Jewels*,
      162).

11   Noël Annan, *Our Age: Portrait of a Generation* (London, 1990), 226.

12   Shiela Grant Duff, *The Parting of Ways: A Personal Account of the Thirties*
      (London, 1982), 109, 112.

13   The phrases here are taken from reports on Burgess, quoted by West and
      Tsarev, *The Crown Jewels*; Yuri Modin provides further KGB assessments of
      Burgess, as does Costello and Tsarev.

14   G.R., *TLS*, 23 December 1977, 1496 (a review of John Fisher, *Burgess and
      Maclean: A New Look at the Foreign Office Spies*).

15   Rees reviewed *The Road to Wigan Pier* in the *Spectator*, 12 March 1937, 480.

16   *TLS*, 23 December 1977, 1496.

17   'The World of Lytton Strachey', in Goronwy Rees, *Brief Encounters* (London,
      1974), 83.

18   West and Tsarev relate how Burgess himself reported in November 1948 that
      his excellent relations with Foreign Office colleagues owed much to the
      Etonian background he shared with them ('things of this kind have great
      importance').

19   'Beyond the Dyke', two BBC Wales broadcasts, June 1938, partly reprinted in
      Patrick Hannan (ed.), *Wales on the Wireless: A Broadcasting Anthology*
      (Llandysul, 1988), 6–7, 133–4.

20   'Have the Welsh a Future?', *Encounter* (March 1964), 7.

21   Ibid., 8.

22   'From a Welshman Abroad', *Bookman* (November 1934), 105.

23   'Back to the Boathouse', *TLS*, 29 April 1977, 505 (a review of Paul Ferris,
      Dylan Thomas, and Daniel Jones, *My Friend Dylan Thomas*).

24   G.R., 'Memories of New College, 1928–31', in John Buxton and Penry
      Williams (eds.), *New College, Oxford, 1379–1979* (Warden and Fellows of New
      College, 1979), 120–6.

25 E. L. Ellis, 'The Man of *The People*: Goronwy Rees and the Aberystwyth Episode', *New Welsh Review*, 29 (1995), 45.

26 G.R., 'In Defence of Welsh Nationalism', *Spectator*, 10 September 1937, 416–17.

27 The Willink Report is quoted in part in Jenny Rees, *Looking for Mr Nobody: The Secret Life of Goronwy Rees*, 193–9.

28 Her 'Goronwy – and Others: A Remembrance of England', *Partisan Review* (January 1996), 11–47, is a just and affectionate portrait of Rees, whom she first met in 1964.

29 Rees's lecture to a 1954 conference of extra-mural tutors at Aberystwyth was published in *Welsh Anvil / Yr Einion*, 7 (1955), 18–31.

30 West and Tsarev, *The Crown Jewels*, 186; Yuri Modin (*My Five Cambridge Friends*) provides much evidence in support of such a judgement.

31 'Keidrych: A Memoir', *Planet*, 104 (1994), 20.

32 His most extended post-Aberystwyth essay on Wales is 'Have the Welsh a Future?', *Encounter* (March 1964), 3–13; see also 'From Another Country', *New Statesman*, 24 February 1961, 296, 298.

33 From a letter to T. Mervyn Jones; it is worth noting that Rees spoke highly of the *Planet* pieces of Ned Thomas, the nationalist intellectual, and accepted a chapter of Thomas's *The Welsh Extremist* for publication in *Encounter*.

34 Benny Morris, *The Roots of Appeasement: The British Weekly Press and Nazi Germany during the 1930s* (London, 1991), 5, observes that of the literary intellectuals of the thirties drawn to developments in Germany, only Goronwy Rees and Richard Crossman gained editorial posts on the weeklies. Rees understood German nationalism in its various dimensions – he knew the language, was friendly with Adam von Trott, and had studied the *Freikorps* movement, those right-wing counter-revolutionaries who gave the Nazis much of their theory and practice.

Notes to Goronwy Rees's Writings

~

Notes to *A Bundle of Sensations*

p. 3 *is eternal, self-determined, and thinks*: from Green's refutation of David Hume on personal identity (*Works of Thomas Hill Green*, Vol. I, *Philosophical Works*, ed. R. L. Nettleship, 3rd edn (1894), 209). Green held to the notion of a fixed, unchanging personality.

p. 3 *Der Mann ohne Eigenschaften*: Robert Musil's long unfinished novel (1930–2), translated as *The Man Without Qualities*, projects its protagonist, Ulrich, not as an individual of settled personal identity but as a mutable embodiment of political and cultural forces.

p. 5 *Hume's chapter on Personal Identity*: Book I, section vi, of the *Treatise*; Elizabeth Bowen in *The Death of the Heart* (1938) has Eddie – a character partly based on Goronwy – declare that 'I suppose, that I'm I at all is just a romantic fallacy'.

p. 5 *who collects Mr Bain?*: the Scottish philosopher Alexander Bain (1818–1903) is remembered for his work in association psychology, which regards the self as a collection of disparate mental operations held together by the laws of association. F. H. Bradley's dismissal comes in a footnote to his *Ethical Studies* (2nd edn, 1927, 39), a stance he later modified.

p. 5 *H. W. B. Joseph*: 'a constant source of worry and anxiety' to Rees, H. W. B. Joseph (1867–1943), tutor in philosophy at New College, became a kind of father figure. 'It was not that I disliked Joseph; on the contrary, I was very fond of him. How could one have disliked anybody who was so interested in one's moral and intellectual welfare? But the burden of his concern sometimes weighed heavily on one who, like myself, was addicted to pleasure. Sometimes when I was enjoying myself most the thought would, absurdly, cross my mind: *What would Joseph think?*' (G.R., 'Memories of New College, 1928–1931', in John Buxton and Penry Williams (eds.), *New College, Oxford, 1379–1979* (1979), 124).

p. 5 *William of Wykeham*: Bishop of Winchester and Chancellor of England, William of Wykeham (1324–1404) founded both New College, Oxford, and Winchester College.

p. 6 *But curved in what?*: A. J. Ayer, Rees's contemporary and friend at Oxford, provides a similar picture of Joseph: 'He dealt above all in refutation and was ready to take on anything from Marx's economics to the theory of relativity. He was said to be a good tutor to men of ability who were content to follow along the lines that he had laid down, but his merits were over-shadowed by the severity with which he lit on any mistake, however trivial, and his intolerance of any approach which differed from his own. The great American pragmatist, William James, hit him off admirably when he wrote, in reply to some published criticism, "I feel as if Mr Joseph almost pounced on my words singly, without giving the sentences time to get out of my mouth"' (A. J. Ayer, *Part of My Life* (1977), 78).

p. 6 *Cook Wilson*: though John Cook Wilson (1849–1915) published little, his influence at Oxford was powerful, largely on account of his conscientiousness as a tutor. He spent his entire career within the University, becoming Wykeham Professor of Logic in 1889.

p. 9 *one place of worship for every two or three hundred people*: Rees was born 29 November 1909; *Kelly's Directory* for 1914 lists eighteen places of worship (excluding those for Pentecostals and Unitarians) for a town population of some 8,500.

p. 9 *a person of considerable importance in the town*: from 1903 to 1922 the Revd Richard Jenkin Rees (1868–1963) was minister of Tabernacl, a dominating chapel in Powell Street with a membership of some seven hundred. In 1894 he had married Apphia Mary James (1870–1931); Morgan Goronwy Rees (named after Goronwy Owen, the wayward eighteenth-century Welsh-language poet) was the youngest of their four surviving children.

p. 10 *the whole of the One Hundred-and-Nineteenth Psalm*: at 176 verses, comfortably the longest of the Psalms.

p. 10 *from the learned commentary of the Rev. Elias Jones, DD*: appearing before a Royal Commission in October 1907, the Revd R. J. Rees explained how through their Sunday schools the Calvinistic Methodists implemented a highly organized system of religious instruction. Three catechisms were employed, with *Y Rhodd Mam/The Mother's Gift* used for the youngest children. Substantial lessons, and commentaries on the historical books of the Old Testament, were also prepared by expert authorities within the Connexion. That for the Epistle to the Hebrews was the work not of Elias Jones but of the Revd Dr T. C. Edwards, first principal of the University College of Wales, Aberystwyth.

p. 12 *was always apparent*: 'It is of the kind that speaks neither to the mind nor the heart of his audience, but plays upon its nerves until they are strung to such a pitch of intensity that they shriek for release in action. It was the kind of oratory that, in my childhood, was capable of transforming an incurable alcoholic into a life-long teetotaller in the twinkling of an eyelid. But it can only be practised by one who has a profound and subtle understanding of the secret hopes and fears of his audience.' Rees is here describing Hitler's oratory, witnessed at the *Sportpalast* in Berlin in September 1932; everyone around him in the audience of 10,000 was a victim of its spell. 'Who knows, if I had not been inoculated in childhood against the tricks of oratory, I might have succumbed myself' (*Encounter* (November 1975), 44).

p. 13 *the chapter in the Acts*: Acts 2: 1–13.

p. 15 *I came across a poem*: D. H. Lawrence's 'Piano', first published in his *New Poems* (1908).

p. 16 *one of the greatest actors and exhibitionists of the Welsh pulpit*: almost certainly Philip Jones (1855–1945). It was Jones who caught the cold superiority of Tabernacl when pronouncing its members 'the cream of Aberystwyth – the ice-cream'.

p. 17 *a Professor of Philosophy at the University College*: W. Jenkyn Jones, Professor of Logic and Philosophy (1911–32) and an ordained Presbyterian minister, was seemingly related to Rees but not directly his uncle.

p. 17 *The Pavilion on the Links*: Robert Louis Stevenson's adventure story, published in *The New Arabian Nights*, vol. 2 (1882), prefigures *Treasure Island*.

p. 18 *Innocent Abroad*: the text of this chapter is as printed in *Encounter* (April 1956). Rees had also drawn upon his summer 1929 experiences as tutor to the son of a Prussian baron for chapter 2 ('A German Interlude') of his undergraduate novel, *The Summer Flood* (1932).

p. 18 *Brandenburg, Lowes Dickinson, and Sidney Fay*: books by these authorities had appeared in successive years: Lowes Dickinson's *The International Anarchy, 1904–1914* (1926), Erich Brandenburg's *From Bismarck to the World War: A History of German Foreign Policy, 1870–1914* (translated 1927), and Sidney Bradshaw Fay's *The Origins of the World War* (2 vols., 1928). Together they countered the viewpoint that Germany alone was responsible for the outbreak of war.

p. 18 *Maynard Keynes's Economic Consequences of the Peace*: Keynes was principal Treasury representative at the Versailles Peace Conference. His passionate disagreement with what he considered to be the unacceptably harsh clauses of the settlement led to *The Economic Consequences of the Peace* (1919), a powerful critique and one highly influential in Britain, where 'an entire generation had grown up to regard reparations as both a political crime and an economic blunder' (G.R., *The Great Slump: Capitalism in Crisis, 1929–33* (1970), 130).

p. 19 *the England of Mr Stanley Baldwin, Lord Birkenhead, and Sir William Joynson-Hicks*: Prime Minister Baldwin made much of his image as the plain provincial Englishman, out of sympathy with intellectuals and foreigners, while from the right of the Conservative Party the flamboyant Lord Birkenhead (Lord Chancellor, 1919–22) set his face against all liberal reform – 'the trouble with Lord Birkenhead is that he is so un-Christlike', remarked Margot Asquith. Sir William Joynson-Hicks, Home Secretary during the general strike of 1926, became the voice of class vindictiveness and repression ('for the police force he displayed a singular devotion', states his entry in the *Dictionary of National Biography*).

p. 19 *as produced by Sir Nigel Playfair and Lovat Frazer*: Nigel Playfair's 1920 revival of John Gay's *The Beggar's Opera*, with sets and costumes by C. Lovat Frazer, ran for 1,469 performances at the Lyric, Hammersmith. Brecht's German adaptation, *Die Dreigroschenoper* (*The Threepenny Opera*) was staged in 1928, with music by Kurt Weill.

p. 20 *Mr Issyvoo*: the camera-like observer of Christopher Isherwood's *Goodbye to Berlin* (1939).

p. 20 *in the summer vacation*: that is, summer 1929.

p. 20 *Wandervögel*: a German youth movement flourishing in the twenties.

p. 20 *Nachtlokal*: night-club.

p. 21 *Boguslavitz, bei Breslau, Schlesien*: with the division of Silesia between Poland and Germany, Boguslavitz and Breslau became Boguszow and Wroclaw respectively.

p. 21 *a famous German air-ace in the Great War*: Rees seems here to have had in mind the 'ace of aces', Baron Manfred von Richthofen ('the Red Baron'), who registered his eightieth aerial victory the day before he himself was shot down over the Somme (21 April 1918). No Reichendorf appears in the lists of German fighter aces of the First World War.

p. 21 *here was Modernismus, here was Baukunst*: *Modernismus* (modernism) and *Baukunst* (the art of building) were expressed in the Cologne railway station, designed by Georg Frentzen (1854–99) and completed by J. E. Jacob Stahl (1839–1902). An awesome, forward-looking structure, it was destroyed in the Second World War.

p. 22 *Kamchatka*: the remote Russian province on the edge of Siberia.

p. 23 *Heines, Gauleiter of Silesia*: Edmund Heines (1897–1934), a senior member of the brown-shirted SA (*Sturmabteilungen*), the Storm Troopers of the Nazi Party, was appointed district leader and police chief at Breslau in 1933. On 30 June 1934, at a lakeside hotel at Bad Wiessee, he and a young homosexual chauffeur were dragged from their bed and shot, first victims of the Night of the Long Knives.

p. 25 *and I was twenty*: actually nineteen; his twentieth birthday fell on 29 November 1929.

p. 26 *Mr Forster's famous words*: appearing in *Howard's End* (1910).

p. 26 *Die Grundlagen des neunzehnten Jahrhunderts*: the English-born Germanophile Houston Stewart Chamberlain published this, his major work, in 1899 (translated as *The Foundations of the Nineteenth Century* in 1910). An intellectual springboard for Nazism, it helped shape Alfred Rosenberg's *Der Mythus des 20. Jahrhunderts* (*The Myth of the Twentieth Century*), published in 1930.

p. 26 *Moeller van den Bruck*: a revolutionary conservative, Arthur Moeller van den Bruck (1876–1925) deeply influenced Hitler who seized on his *Das Dritte Reich* (*The Third Reich*) for its title and content, more especially the notion of a superior Nordic race and the mystical belief in a German national spirit.

p. 27 *Reichstagsabgeordneter*: Member of Parliament.

p. 27 *Kommt nicht in Frage*: out of the question!

p. 28 *the Deutschnationalen, and its leader Hugenberg*: head of the German National People's Party and press baron, Alfred Hugenberg crucially boosted Hitler's career when the two men united to oppose the Young Plan, a scheme designed to lessen the burden of the war reparations imposed on Germany under the settlement of Versailles. Together they recruited to their cause the most extreme racialist and nationalist elements (the embryo of a new dynamic Germany, as Hugenberg said of the six million who in the national plebiscite of December 1929 voted to reject the Plan). Hitler gained immensely from an alliance which, in Rees's words, 'almost overnight turned him into what he had hitherto never been, a national figure, with the aura of respectability which his association with the German nationalists conferred upon him' (*The Great Slump*, 43–4); appearing on a platform with Hugenberg was more important than conquering the streets.

p. 29 *Graf Westarp*: Kuno, Count von Westarp (1864–1945), led the German National People's Party between 1920 and 1925. A monarchist at odds with Hugenberg, he left to form the Conservative People's Party.

p. 29 *that poor Ludendorff!*: a prominent military strategist in the First World War, General Erich von Ludendorff (1865–1937) became President Paul von Hindenberg's chief of staff. He joined with Hitler in the unsuccessful Munich *putsch* against the Bavarian government (November 1923) and for a while represented the National Socialists in the Reichstag, but his increasingly eccentric views led to the leadership of his own minority party.

p. 31 *Die sind aber so schön*: But they're so beautiful.

p. 31 *Ostkämpfer in the Balticum*: the eastern combatants in the Baltic provinces, campaigning against the Russians, Letts and Estonians.

p. 31 *the most idealistic, of assassins and murderers*: the individuals here mentioned were mostly ex-officers of the *Freikorps*, counter-revolutionary nationalists of the ultra-right who, with the disbandment of their volunteer formations, found other outlets for violence, not least in street fighting and the assassination of Weimar politicians. General Georg Maercker (1865–1924) commanded the first *Freikorps* unit, which in 1919 put down the Spartacist Uprising in Berlin and crushed councils of the radical left throughout post-revolutionary Bavaria; Albert Leo Schlageter (1894–1923), following his execution for acts of sabotage, became a Nazi martyr; Captain Hermann Ehrhardt (1881–1971) aided Hitler in establishing the SA, a paramilitary force designed to clear the streets of Jews and Communists, and soon to be led by Franz Pfeffer (1888–1968). Erwin Kern (1898–1922) and Hermann Fischer (1896–1922) were indeed assassins: on 24 June 1922 they gunned down the German Foreign Minister, Walthur Rathenau. Kern lost his life while resisting arrest, which in turn caused Fischer to shoot himself (the Nazis marked the spot with a monument).

An accomplice to Rathenau's murder, Ernst von Salomon (1902–72) emerged from five years' imprisonment to a new career as writer, propagandist and historian. Rees knew his autobiographical novels (published 1930–2) and thought them valuable aids to an understanding of National Socialism. In 1954 Rees provided a lengthy preface to Constantine FitzGibbon's translation of *Der Fragebogen*, the published *Answers of Ernst von Salomon* to a questionnaire served by the Allied Military Government on those thought to be Nazi collaborators. Von Salomon, Rees concluded, was 'an outstanding example of the type of man of action as artist, or artist as man of action, which is one of the most characteristic products of this century, of men who can find complete satisfaction neither in art nor in action, and express in both the violence of their frustrations'.

p. 32 *the wholesale plundering of the Osthilfe funds*: to complement his financial reforms of April 1930, Brüning set up a government fund, the *Osthilfe* or Eastern Aid, designed for the relief of agriculture east of the Elbe. It came to be widely believed that the money was misappropriated, finding its way not to small farmers and peasants but into the pockets of large landowners: the President himself, and his family, were said to be implicated.

p. 33 *Grossartig!*: Terrific!

p. 33 *Sofort anrufen!*: Ring up immediately!

p. 34 *soldatesque*: soldierly. Stendhal's was to be a style eschewing everything that was rhetorical or superfluous.

p. 35 *from the novels of Karl May*: Karl May (1842–1912); his stories of American Indians after the manner of James Fenimore Cooper were immensely popular among German schoolboys; the young Hitler was addicted to them.

p. 36 *of the Stosstrupps and the Argonne, of the Freikorps and the Balticum*: in the Meuse-Argonne offensive of September 1918, German troops tenaciously defended their positions in front of the Argonne forest, east of Verdun.

Rees elsewhere elaborated on the importance of the *Freikorps*, the volunteer units of demobilized soldiers, students and freebooters, all violently anti-democratic, who in 1918 and 1919 opposed the communists in the Baltic and eastern provinces.

Rejecting all civilized norms, and obedient only to their leaders, they fought 'in a kind of ecstasy compounded of a patriotism which was akin to nihilism and of a conscious barbarism'. The *Freikorps* influence on National Socialism was deep and direct: 'it was largely responsible for supplying it with an ideology, a spiritual outlook, with a political and tactical technique, and to a very significant extent with its personnel' (G.R., preface to *The Answers of Ernst von Salomon* (1954), xi); as Rees saw it, the absence of a voice like Salomon's from most cultural histories of Weimar only reinforced the misguided impression that there was something surprising and inexplicable about Hitler's rise to power.

p. 39 *in the spring of 1939*: on 20 April 1939 Rees enlisted with the Royal Artillery Territorials and was posted to the 90th Field Regiment.

p. 39 *Les Caves du Vatican*: in Gide's story (published 1914), Lafcadio hurls Fleurisoire, a travelling companion who irritates him, through the door of a moving train; the impulsive, motiveless action satisfies a need for sensation.

p. 40 *Credo quia impossibile*: 'I believe because it is impossible', Tertullian's rule of faith. More than once in his writings Rees alluded to Richard Crossman's naïveté in this area (Crossman's biographer, on the other hand, sees him as more alert to the Nazi menace than the majority of his left-wing Oxford contemporaries). In the July 1932 Reichstag elections the Nazis won 230 seats on a staggering 13.5 million votes; the Social Democrats returned 133 delegates, and the KPD 89. Willi Münzenberg was the dedicated and extremely effective Communist publicist.

Rees in 'A Winter in Berlin' elaborates on continental socialist thinking and its process of abstract reasoning designed to uncover the purposes and thrust of history, by 'adjusting and adapting the events of the real world to its preconceived views of what ought to be, indeed must be, if one can penetrate to their deeper reality'. No matter the hunting down in 1934 of communists and socialists in the streets and cellars of the city – the Nazi terror was, if anything, proof that the German proletarian revolution was at hand: 'brown on the outside, red on the inside', Münzenberg assured his comrades of the SA thugs.

p. 40 *Of purgatorial pains*: [I have been unable to identify the source of this quotation – Editor.]

p. 41 *Joachim*: 'He is much better on historical problems than on constructive philosophy I think, and is really almost a genius, with respect to Aristotle': so wrote T. S. Eliot of Harold Henry Joachim (1868–1938), his tutor at Merton. Joachim succeeded J. Cook Wilson as Wykeham Professor of Logic but, according to A. J. Ayer, was no longer an active philosophical force by the time he and Rees arrived at Oxford.

p. 42 *Anima Mundi*: here Rees must mean *Spiritus Mundi*, a term he uses in a similar context in *A Chapter of Accidents* and which doubtless he took from Yeats's 'The Second Coming' ('a vast image out of *Spiritus Mundi* / Troubles my sight'). Yeats defined *Spiritus Mundi* as 'a general storehouse of images which has ceased to be a property of any personality or spirit'; whereas *Anima Mundi* ('world-soul') is 'an idea stemming from Plato's *Timaeus*, where the world is a living organism endowed with a soul by the Demiurge . . . it is a model for the restoration of harmony in the human soul' (*The Oxford Companion to Philosophy*, ed. Ted Honderich (1995), 36).

p. 42 *âmes damnées*: damned souls.

p. 42 *a children's hymn I had learned in the Sunday school in Wales*: the hymn was composed by Revd Thomas Levi (1825–1916), Calvinistic Methodist minister and author, and a predecessor of Goronwy's father at Tabernacl, Aberystwyth.

p. 42 *The Drill Hall was in the heart of Bloomsbury*: located in Handel Street, the Drill Hall was close to Tavistock Square (where the the Woolfs were near the end of their stay) and not far from Rees's *Spectator* office at 99 Gower Street.

p. 44 *Choctaw*: the language of one of the indigenous peoples of North America.

p. 45 *the historically timely, genuine social collectivity of the workers*: reflecting on the thirties, Rees remarked how it had sometimes seemed necessary to invent a different proletariat, and that Brecht had once ironically suggested to the East German government that since the people had proved unsatisfactory, they should be dismissed and another one appointed (*Encounter* (January 1974), 26).

p. 45 *Pollaiuolo's Martyrdom of St Sebastian*: 'The Martyrdom of St Sebastian' (*c.*1475), thought to be the collaborative work of the Pollaiuolo brothers, Antonio and Piero, hangs in the National Gallery, London. It is described as striking for its representation of the human body from a variety of viewpoints.

p. 53 *the way to acquire morale*: in a well-received *Spectator* article (18 August 1939, 241–2), Rees criticized Territorial leadership on the grounds that it was drawn from too narrow a social base. 'It can be said confidently that the reserve of talent and ability in the ranks is vastly higher than can be found among the officers, some of whom treat the TA as an extension of public school life . . . One of the most important artillery camps provides no means whatever by which the soldier after his day's work may reasonably rest, read, write or listen to the wireless, far less a technical library which many of the most eager would be glad to use.' The soldier's recreation is beer, one NCO had explained; 'and so apparently the War Office prefers that it should be'.

p. 55 *my landlord*: Major Dudley Ward, Regimental Adjutant, Welsh Guards (Jenny Rees, *Looking for Mr Nobody: The Secret Life of Goronwy Rees* (1994), 106).

p. 58 *Dis alter visum*: 'To the gods it seemed otherwise' (Virgil, *Aeneid* ii, 428).

p. 60 *a kind of Clausewitz*: Karl von Clausewitz (1780–1831), military theoretician and author of *Vom Kriege* (*On War*), was director of the General War School in Berlin, 1818–30.

p. 62 *not as loss but as gain*: 'Most men, and more women, are only too glad to be relieved of any claim to a personality of their own so long as you give them another in exchange – that is, a personality which belongs to a group and which they share only because they belong to the group. It's just a little trick of substitution; the whole art of government depends on it.' The speaker here is Marwitz, the SA officer in Rees's novel *Where No Wounds Were* (1950).

p. 63 *the world of a Marmeladoff*: in Dostoevsky's *Crime and Punishment* Marmeladoff is the masochistic drunkard whose whimpering family survives in misery and squalor; he dies after being run over by a horse and carriage.

p. 64 *francs-tireurs*: irregular combatants, guerrillas.

p. 66 *my college in Oxford*: All Souls, of which Rees was a fellow.

p. 67 *laissez-faire, laissez-aller*: letting people do as they think best.

p. 68 *a land of Cockaigne*: the medieval Utopian dreamland of idleness and plenty.

p. 69 *our Stammtisch*: regulars' table.

p. 70 *he made it unnecessary to read Fortescue*: Sir John William Fortescue (1859–1933), military historian, whose monumental *History of the British Army* (13 vols., 1899–1930) is particularly impressive on the Peninsular War.

p. 71 *from the pages of Ouida*: the pen-name of Marie Louise de la Ramée (1839–1908). Her hugely popular novels chronicled the romantic liaisons of upper-class military heroes.

p. 77 *maquis*: underground (force).

p. 82 *at Sandhurst after Christmas*: according to military records, Rees was posted to the 161st Officer Cadet Training Unit on 26 September 1939 and discharged on 22 March 1940, having been appointed to a commission in the Royal Welch Fusiliers.

p. 82 *the loudest voice in the British Army*: the legendary RSM Ronald Brittain, to whom it attributed such parade-ground explosions as 'You 'orrible little man!' and 'wake up there!'.

p. 83 *A Day at the Seaside*: serial rights to *A Bundle of Sensations* were purchased at 'a pretty stiff price' by the *Sunday Times*, which published two controversial extracts from this chapter under the title, '"Monty" and the Drama of Dieppe' (22 and 29 May 1960).

p. 83 *at GHQ Home Forces*: drafted into Army Intelligence in June 1940, Rees proved a most efficient staff officer. A. J. Ayer remembered how Rees, on the staff of the German Interrogation School at Cambridge in 1941, had instructed himself and Robin Zaehner in the interrogation of German prisoners of war (according to Cyril Connolly, it was Rees's experience of one particular prisoner that gave rise to *Where No Wounds Were*).

p. 83 *Henry Yorke*: the novelist Henry Green, about whom more is said in *A Chapter of Accidents*. Rees had become a friend in the mid–1930s, helping to place Green's *Party Going* with John Lehmann at the Hogarth Press.

p. 83 *where my brother was stationed at that time*: Goronwy's barrister brother Geraint, two-and-a-half years his senior, did service in the Welsh Guards.

p. 84 *I was to be transferred to HQ South-Eastern Command*: promoted Major, Rees moved from Whitehall to Reigate, 11 March 1942.

p. 86 *opéra bouffe*: comic opera.

p. 88 *with a priest than a general*: Nigel Hamilton, biographer of Montgomery, finds Rees's insight here remarkable, 'for there is no doubt that it was at this stage of his life that the posthumous figure of Bishop Montgomery [Monty's father] came more and more to influence Bernard in the conduct of high command' (*Monty: The Making of a General, 1887–1942* (1981), 518). Reviewers of *A Bundle of Sensations* were much taken by Rees's pages on Monty and Nigel Hamilton agrees: 'Anyone who ever served or worked with Montgomery will testify to the accuracy of this portrait.'

p. 90 *smiling rather grimly*: the Canadian officers were, respectively, Major-General John Hamilton ('Ham') Roberts and Lieutenant-Colonel Churchill Mann. Roberts had no experience of divisional combat command and Mann became his principal planning adviser.

p. 92 *a pure pyknic type*: in the classification of physical and temperamental types devised by the German psychiatrist Ernst Kretschmer, the pyknic type is of stocky physique with a rounded body and head; the related temperament is cycloid – that is, alternating between exhilaration and depression.

p. 92 *irretrievably a pongo*: Rees provided a gloss for *Sunday Times* readers (12 June 1960, 10): 'a naval term for anyone so misguided or unfortunate enough to be in the Army'; one reader thought the word was slang for army officers only, not for all army personnel.

p. 94 *the bombing of Dieppe*: one treatment of Dieppe cites this announcement to Rees as an example of Mountbatten's tendency to invoke the Prime Minister's name whenever things went badly for him. 'In fact at the time . . . the Prime Minister and the Foreign Secretary had already authorized the bombing of Dieppe. The reason for the misleading presentation was probably that Mountbatten did not want it known that he, titular member of the Chief of Staff Committee, did not have the clout to make Harris, who held them in complete disregard, bend' (Brian Loring Villa, *Unauthorized Action: Mountbatten and the Dieppe Raid* (1989), 152). Air Marshall Sir Arthur Harris insisted that his proposed large-scale air attacks on Germany left him with no bombers to spare for Dieppe; only a token force could be offered.

p. 94 *shameful not to respond to it*: Mountbatten's optimism was indeed infectious, and he remained convinced that the operation had a fair chance of success: 'like so many others with extraordinary egos, Mountbatten believed he had a Destiny and that no misfortune could come to him' (Villa, 207).

p. 95 *They were also bait*: Rees's verdict has been much debated. Villa (162) concludes that the responsible Air Chiefs, were they alive today, would argue that 'the compromises they made with *Jubilee* in order to keep alive the hope of a strategic bomber offensive were, in the harsh logic of warfare, the price that had to be paid to save the far greater number of lives than were lost at Dieppe. But what an appalling way to save lives.' Rees had come to the same conclusion: 'In the end, the justification for the dead men on the beaches of Dieppe is the still living ones who took part in the invasion of Normandy' (*Sunday Times*, 12 March 1961). In cold statistics, Allied losses in personnel amounted to 4,350 (with 1,179 dead and 2,190 taken prisoner); German losses numbered 591, including 311 dead and missing. In the aerial battle the Allies lost 106 aircraft and the Germans 48 (J. Rohwer and G. Hummelchen, *Chronology of the War at Sea, 1939–45: The Naval History of World War Two* (1992), 158).

p. 96 *suffered in the First World War*: on December 25 1941 Lieutenant-General Sir Bernard Paget became Commander-in-Chief, Home Forces, in succession to General Alan Brooke. Paget was wounded in the First World War, serving as a Brigade Major on the Western Front.

p. 96 *but the Army Commander seemed to give sense to it*: 'To a temporary soldier at least, plagued with the often aimless and feverish chaos of many higher headquarters, there was an almost classical simplicity in Field-Marshal Montgomery's conception of waging war, and in his gift for imposing order on the most confused (with one exception) of all human activities, in the calm with which he announced himself, and a certain dry and logical beauty in his passion for careful preparation and his implacable desire that his troops should be correctly launched into battle. One almost thought war was rational . . .' (G.R., *Spectator*, 7 January 1949, 6–7, reviewing Dwight D. Eisenhower, *Crusade in Europe*).

p. 97 *Doesn't know how to fight a battle*: the Admiral is taken to be Mountbatten.

p. 100 *our LCTs and LCPs and LCAs*: Landing Craft, Tank; Landing Craft, Personnel; Landing Craft, Assault.

p. 103 *in a month's time*: Operation Rutter was cancelled on 7 July 1942 and Operation Jubilee launched on 19 August 1942.

p. 105 *my club in London*: the Garrick. The biography was most probably Robert Emmons, *The Life and Opinions of Walter Sickert* (1941).

p. 105 *by which he judged any military operation*: Rees's antipathy towards war correspondents extended to Martha Gellhorn. 'Like most war correspondents', he wrote, 'she is not content only to tell what she saw, perhaps because what one really sees in war is so unutterably confused and chaotic that it refuses to compose any kind of picture: it would not, after all, encourage the old folks at home to be told that the only result of their efforts and sacrifices and sufferings is the meaningless shambles which is all the naked eye sees in a battlefield. So war correspondents nearly always tell us, not only what they see, but what they feel; it gives dignity to the proceedings. Even more, they tell us what *we* ought to feel' (*Encounter* (November 1959), 68–70).

p. 111 *Never glad confident morning again!*: from Robert Browning's 'The Lost Leader'.

p. 113 *their greatest victory over the West*: a reference to the battle of Teutoburg Forest (AD 9) in which an alliance of German tribes, led by Armibius, ambushed and destroyed three Roman legions.

p. 113 *of the Wilhelminischezeit*: the Wilhelmine period, the era of Kaiser William II (1888–1918).

p. 113 *elaborate white starched caps*: *Where No Wounds Were* (1950) conjures up a similar picture of the German countryside, the sanctified heart of the nation in National Socialist thinking.

p. 114 *the British Zone of occupation*: even before the Normandy landings, arrangements were in hand for the administration of a defeated Germany. In a four-power occupation, the country as a whole would be governed by the Allied Control Commission, with Britain, France, the USSR and the USA each taking responsibility for a separate geographical zone (the British sector comprised north-western Germany). The challenge was to manage German demilitarization, uproot the Nazi regime, and set in place some framework for democratic government.

p. 116 *as senior intelligence officer*: in August 1944 Rees was appointed instructor at the Control Commission School, planning and conducting courses for soldiers-turned-administrators; in April 1945 he took charge of political intelligence in the Political Division of the Commission (a kind of diplomatic mission), assisting Sir William Strang, Political Adviser to the Commander-in-Chief, Field Marshal Montgomery.

p. 118 *A week later we set off on our tour*: this six-day tour began on Sunday 1 July 1945, moving from Essen in the south, through the Rhine Province and the Ruhr, then northwards via Nienburg and Hamburg into Schleswig-Holstein (swollen with refugees and a million *Wehrmacht* prisoners).

p. 120 *the colossal fragments of a ruined world*: reviewing the *Carceri* (Prisons) drawings in the *Spectator* (7 July 1950), Rees made much of Piranesi's phantasmagorical world, a expression of 'some profoundly significant condition of the human mind'.

p. 122 *a kind of primitive justice?*: 'Revenge is a kind of wild justice' (Francis Bacon, 'Of revenge', *Essays* (1597)).

p. 122 *Erst kommt das Fressen, dann kommt die Moral*: from Brecht's *Die Dreigroschenoper* (1928); Rees's own translation was 'Grub first, morality later'.

p. 122 *Mr Morgenthau*: voicing the immediate post-war reaction against Germany, the American Henry Morgenthau contrived a plan that would render the country impotent by reducing it to an agricultural community. Rees took up this plan and the German 'problem' at a Liberal Party summer school of 1946:

It is impossible to create a democracy on a foundation of economic decay; the attempt to do so is folly, and this is the folly we are committing at present. The spectacle of well-fed administrators attempting to teach democracy to an audience of the undernourished and starving is one of nauseating hypocrisy and futility and the attempt can only end in discrediting democracy itself. There is only one solution to the problem of Germany – to lead her back as soon as possible into the normal current of production and exchange. This means permitting her an industrial establishment sufficient to allow her to stand on her own feet economically: it also means rejecting plans for the partition of Germany and all other arrangements whose real object is to prevent her economic recovery. (Text taken from the *Manchester Guardian*, 3 August 1946.)

p. 122 *beastly enough to the Germans*: Noel Coward's song, 'Don't Let's Be Beastly to the Germans', was composed near the close of the war.

p. 124 *Saint-John Perse's Anabasis*: Saint-John Perse was the pseudonymn of Alexis Léger (1887–1975). His long prose poem *Anabese* (1922) has as one of its themes the great historical transmigrations of peoples. The work appeared in English (*Anabasis*, 1930) in a translation by T. S. Eliot.

p. 124 *Völkerwanderung*: mass migration.

p. 125 *printed and circulated on Foreign Office green paper*: a copy is lodged at the Public Record Office; portions of Rees's diary are reprinted in Jenny Rees, *Looking for Mr Nobody*.

p. 126 *a quite exceptionally intelligent and efficient staff officer*: the assistant was Noël Annan, who provides a picture of Rees in his Berlin post: 'Routine business never passed Goronwy's desk, although occasionally it might be disfigured by a small sheet of paper. But he knew pre-war Germany well from his *Marxisant* days in the thirties . . . He had a journalist's nose for events that might give some clues about the state of Germany' (*Changing Enemies: The Defeat and Regeneration of Germany* (1995), 152).

p. 126 *faits-divers*: small news items.

p. 127 *neckulturny*: filthy types.

p. 127 *Bolshoi Narod!*: a great people!

p. 127 *Untermenschen and Unmenschen*: thugs and monsters.

p. 131 *Oberkommando der Wehrmacht*: the military high command.

p. 134 *The Great Good Place*: the text of this chapter is as printed in *Encounter* (August 1958), except that Rees drops the original subtitle, 'Recovery and Rediscovery'.

p. 134 *his sanity and health:* he also comes to recognize that 'everyone was a little someone else'; James too, like Rees, was much taken with the notion that we all harbour dual natures.

p. 134 *I had in fact been run over*: Rees landed in Heatherwood Hospital in early May 1957 following a serious motor accident at a garage in Littlewick Green, to the west of Maidenhead. He and his wife had stopped for petrol and Rees, walking to the back of their car, was hit by a passing minibus and dragged along the road. His injuries were severe; he needed a massive blood transfusion and thirty-five stitches to the face. His shattered left leg took sixteen months to mend; even so, for the rest of his life he walked with a slight limp.

p. 143 *immer bereit, immer rasiert*: always ready, always shaved.

p. 145 *or spoke Volapuk*: the artificial language invented by Johann M. Schleyer in 1879 as a means of international communication.

p. 151 *and practically no music*: Perry Como's version of 'Magic Moments' headed the charts throughout March and April 1958; 'Lollipop, Lollipop', by the Mudlarks, was prominent during April and May (challenged by a version from the Chordettes).

p. 152 *the Scaliger of the Turf*: Joseph Justus Scaliger (1540–1609), recognized as the greatest scholar of the Renaissance.

p. 152 *Lady Docker*: Lady Norah Docker, wife of the company director Sir Bernard Docker, was a celebrated socialite of the period; to her is attributed the comment, 'mink is so hot to sit on'.

Notes to *A Chapter of Accidents*

p. 162 *the East End of London*: Goronwy's grandparents, John and Catherine Rees, settled in Stepney Green, a crowded quarter off the Mile End Road. John Rees became deacon at New Jewin, the Welsh Calvinistic stronghold in the City.

p. 162 *a long line of tenant farmers*: the Reeses farmed Ruel Isaf, overlooking the village of Bow Street, a little inland from Aberystwyth.

p. 164 *becoming a doctor*: after training at Guy's, the younger son, Morgan James Rees (1875–1916), became medical officer for Aberdare and later, medical inspector under the Local Government Board at Whitehall. Commissioned in the RAMC, he died in the Somme offensive, while evacuating casualties at Thiepval.

p. 165 *the murderer Wainwright*: in 1874 Henry Wainwright, a brush-maker, shot Harriet Louisa Lane, with whom he lived at 215 Whitechapel Road. He was tried at the Old Bailey, found guilty of wilful murder, and hanged at Newgate, 21 December 1875.

p. 166 *to prepare himself for the ministry*: Goronwy's father had not at this stage settled on a career as minister. The Pauline call was received in August 1889 shortly before his twenty-first birthday. An Aberystwyth Classics graduate, he had embarked upon a University of London science degree in the hope of qualifying in medicine. However, failure in chemistry and his parents' disapproval of Apphia James, the young woman he was eventually to marry, threw him into despair. As his private journal records:

> Both of us were reduced to grief, and darkness seemed to be all around my path – we had got into the hollow amidst dark mountains with no seeming way of outlet. But it was God's way of bringing my life with its energies to him . . . In that mountain hollow whose steep sides seemed merciless and gave no hope of outlet, God showed me the narrow pass of choice and decision – I went through it, and passing through, I entered on a valley beautiful in the extreme.

p. 166 *the same narrow valley in which his parents had been born*: the Jameses occupied Tynrhos, another hillside farmhouse above Bow Street, on the opposite side of the valley to the Reeses at Ruel Isaf.

p. 167 *the great Professor Fleure*: H. J. Fleure, founder and first professor of geography at Aberystwyth, undertook extensive research into the anthropology of the Welsh, using measurements from some five thousand Welsh persons of ascertained localized ancestries.

p. 167 *as recently as 1878*: at Oxford almost all religious tests were abolished in 1871, and by 1882 some 200 Nonconformist undergraduates were studying there. Mansfield College, a predominantly Congregationalist institution, opened at Oxford in 1886; R. J. Rees entered it three years later, graduating with a first-class degree in theology in 1892.

p. 167 *a brief stay in Pwllheli*: in October 1894 the now married R. J. Rees moved from the English church at Ala Road, Pwllheli, not to Aberystwyth but to the Cardiff suburb of Roath. There he remained as minister of Clifton Street chapel until 1903 and his appointment at Aberystwyth. During their years in Cardiff the Reeses produced two daughters, Muriel and Enid.

p. 167 *Cantref Gwaelod*: the legend of the plain of Gwaelod and its inundation through Seithenyn's negligence was adapted by Thomas Love Peacock for his satirical romance, *The Misfortunes of Elphin* (1829). This is Rees's likely source: from the same book he later quotes the 'The War Song of Dinas Fawr'.

p. 168 *to reappear to him*: Geoffrey Grigson was the first to suggest that the sight of Hafod, Colonel Thomas Johnes's dramatically landscaped demesne set in the Cardiganshire hills twelve miles south-east of Aberystwyth, might have played a part in the genesis of 'Kubla Khan' (*Cornhill Magazine*, Spring 1947). On a walking tour of 1794, three years before the composition of the poem, Coleridge passed by Hafod, but there is no record of his actually having visited the estate.

p. 168 *beside*: 'beside' in the sense of 'in addition to' rather than 'by the side of'. Nanteos, the house in the valley, is three miles inland from Aberystwyth, and the abbey of Strata Florida some dozen miles further south-eastward on the edge of the Cambrian mountains. This paragraph refers to the Nanteos cup, a wooden drinking vessel which may once have belonged to the Cistercians of Strata Florida. Locally the story runs that the cup came into the possession of the Powells of Nanteos at the time of the dissolution of the monasteries: fearful of Thomas Cromwell's commissioners, seven monks fled to Nanteos bearing the holiest of relics – the cup used by Christ at the Last Supper (supposedly brought to Glastonbury by Joseph of Arimathea). Whatever its provenance – and the Strata Florida link is plausible – the cup was in regular use during the early years of this century, borrowed by those with faith in its miraculous healing powers.

p. 168 *Miss Jessie Weston*: Eliot famously begins his Notes to *The Waste Land* with, 'Not only the title, but the plan and a good deal of the incidental symbolism of the poem were suggested by Miss Jessie L. Weston's book on the Grail legend: *From Ritual to Romance* (Macmillan).'

p. 170 *he had made il gran rifiuto*: he had shirked his responsibility.

p. 170 *the Asquithian 'Wee-Free' Liberals*: nicknamed after the minority of the Free Church of Scotland who in 1900 stood apart from amalgamation with the United Presbyterian Church.

p. 172 *exerted on the other side*: in the Cardiganshire by-election of February 1921 the Lloyd Georgian Coalition Liberal, Captain Ernest Evans, defeated Llewelyn Williams, the Asquithian Independent Liberal, though not without Conservative support and (so it was said) a fleet of Tory motor cars.

p. 173 *das ewig Weibliche*: the eternal woman (from Goethe's *Faust*, pt. 2: '*Das Ewig-Weibliche zieht uns hinan*', 'Eternal woman draws us upward').

p. 175 *My family's move to Cardiff*: occasioned by R. J. Rees's appointment as general superintendent of the Forward Movement, the home-mission agency of the Presbyterian Church of Wales, which evangelized in the towns and valleys of the south.

p. 175 *took up a teaching post in Barry*: the elder sister Muriel (named after a character in Mrs Craik's *John Halifax, Gentleman*) took a degree in 1921 and taught history at Barry County Girls' School; as an undergraduate she married Eurwyn Robyns-Owen, later coroner for south Caernarfonshire and magistrates' clerk at Pwllheli.

p. 175 *to learn his way in the steel industry*: Enid, the younger sister, became Mrs Ernest Griffiths.

p. 175 *after taking their degree*: Geraint Rees (1907–86) took first-class degrees at Aberystwyth and Cambridge (St John's). He was called to the Bar in 1932 and became judge at the Central Criminal Court, Old Bailey.

p. 176 *some melancholy solitude together*: the Reeses lived at 39 Tydfil Place, a substantial property off Ninian Road, near Roath Park.

p. 177 *a liberal in theology*: not strictly the case: in the New Theology controversy of 1907 R. J. Rees spoke for the conservatives against the radicals, or 'new theologians', who closely identified with the socialist cause.

Elmer Gantry, Sinclair Lewis's novel of 1927, treats of a corrupted preacher who deals in sham religion.

p. 178 *Mr A. J.* Cook: Arthur J. Cook, general secretary of the Miners' Federation of Great Britain, whose Marxist convictions drew him away from the chapel. An electrifying public speaker, from 1924 to 1926 he won massive support from the miners for his brand of militant working-class politics.

p. 180 *the hideousness of its neighbour*: the fourteen-year-old Rees had expressed his disquiet at this street in Roath in the pages of his school magazine:

> Even at the outset of my walk [to school] I am plunged into a region of mystery and gloom, for Mackintosh Place is wrapt in stilly silence and dark melancholy. It is my own opinion that this street is an exile from its true country, for it was built by a Scotchman named Mackintosh who seems to have brought the spirit of these grey houses from the dark towns and moors of Scotland; which may account for its alien appearance in the flat plains of Cardiff.

p. 181 *a bright boy*: a pupil of the Board School, Alexandra Road (1916–21), Rees won an entrance scholarship to Ardwyn, the County School at Aberystwyth, heading the county list for his year. He attended Ardwyn for one academic year (September 1921–July 1922).

p. 183 *my Welsh master in school*: J. Ll. Williams, remembered in school circles as a north Walian in a Welsh tweed suit, passionately addicted to his home locality and to William Williams ('Pantycelyn'), the eighteenth-century hymnist. Williams lamented the paucity of students opting to study Welsh at a highly anglicized institution. As one master has recalled, it was a situation particularly distressing to Saunders Lewis, an occasional schools inspector in the late 1930s; on one visit to Cardiff High he was driven to scattering the stock of English classics across the school library floor (Jack Wanger interview, 1994).

p. 183 *I could not do it in Welsh*: the linking of such a decision with the passage of adolescence accords with Glyn Jones's comment that for the bilingual writer the language of adolescent awakening, 'the language in which ideas – political, religious, aesthetic – first dawn upon his mind, is the language likely to be the one of his creative work'.

p. 184 *a Welsh historian of the greatest distinction*: the teachers were S. Michaels (Classics), Vyvyan Evans (mathematics), R. T. Jenkins (history) and Dyfed Parry (English). Michaels possessed an Oxford first and Evans was a Cambridge wrangler; Dyfed Parry (who thought Goronwy the best English pupil he had ever taught) had been a lecturer at Aberystwyth before coming to Cardiff, while R. T. Jenkins left his post in 1930 to became professor of history at Bangor.

p. 184 *The headmaster*: J. R. Roberts governed some four hundred pupils and a staff of twenty-one. One teacher recalls him spelling out the autonomy of Cardiff High School: nobody interfered with it – no director of education, no local educational authority – 'We are our own world' (Jack Wanger interview, 1994).

p. 188 *jeunesse dorée*: gilded youth.

p. 189 *ewige Wiederkehr*: endless cycle.

p. 189 *Arthur Symons*: *The Symbolist Movement in Literature* (1895) by the poet and critic Arthur Symons was a hugely influential study.

p. 189 *the Secret Rose*: 'Surely thine hour has come, thy great wind blows, / Far-off, most secret, and inviolate Rose?' ('The Secret Rose', *The Collected Poems of W. B. Yeats* (1950), 77–8).

p. 189 *the Valley of the Black Pig*: ' . . . unknown spears / Suddenly hurtle before my dream-awakened eyes, / And then the clash of fallen horsemen and the cries / Of unknown perishing armies beat about my ears.' ('The Valley of the Black Pig', *The Collected Poems of W. B. Yeats* (1950), 73).

p. 191 *The Golden Bough*: Rees's reading of *The Waste Land* would have alerted him to this anthropological study by Sir James Frazer ('one which has influenced our generation profoundly', according to Eliot's Notes).

p. 191 *Sir John Rhŷs's Celtic Pantheon*: Sir John Rhŷs, Professor of Celtic at Oxford, wrote prolifically but published no book under this title; Rees might have had in mind his *Celtic Britain* (1882).

p. 191 *Spiritus Mundi*: see *A Bundle of Sensations*, note on *Anima Mundi* p. 42.

p. 191 *His name was Nagle*: J. Hugh Nagle, active in the Abbey Theatre during the 1919 season.

p. 194 *my joys lay there*: the opening of 'News', by Thomas Traherne.

p. 194 *Edward Garnett*: author and literary editor, appreciated for his sound advice and willingness to help young writers.

p. 194 *Yeats's lines*: from 'The Scholars'; Rees quotes an early version of the poem.

p. 195 *my history master*: R. T. Jenkins inspired an obituary tribute from Rees:

> I was a pupil of his for five years at the High School for Boys, Cardiff, and have counted this ever since as a very great privilege. As a teacher he could be severe and caustic, because of the high intellectual standards he imposed on himself and on others. But boys easily forgave his severity, because it was always illuminated by wit and humour and by his gift for treating history as if it were something one had just read about in the morning paper. His classes sometimes collapsed in laughter.
>
> His understanding of history was both broad and deep. His history course included, in addition to the normal syllabus, a class in Plato's *Republic*, which was an excellent introduction to philosophy, and one in universal history which to a

schoolboy opened up unusually wide perspectives. He was the best teacher of history I have ever known (*The Times*, 17 November 1969, 12).

p. 196 *as it actually existed*: a reference to the ideal of the historian's task, as propounded by Leopold von Ranke (1795–1886) in a famous dictum, 'our task is thus to discern what has really happened [*eigentlich geschehen ist*]'.

p. 199 *told me that they were not*: Jack Wanger, a former Cardiff High School teacher, has spoken of Rees, on the eve of university, as 'arrogant in the mind' – though aware that success at Oxford depended not solely on academic prowess (interview, 1994).

p. 199 *from a chair beside the fire*: in the year of his death Rees spoke affectionately of Warden H. A. L. Fisher, 'austere but benevolent, wistful and self-indulgent in recalling the days when he was a member of the Cabinet, presiding over the college in the same liberal and humane spirit that had inspired his Education Act, and somehow finding the time and interest to invite one to come for a walk once a term, when he would discuss affairs of state, or Renan and Taine, and gravely listen to anything one had to say oneself as if one really had something of value to contribute to the conversation'. Rees also remembered Sunday lunches at the Fishers, and his vision of their daughter Mary, 'at whom, yellow-haired like a Lorelei, I used to gaze on Sunday evenings in the chapel' ('Memories of New College, 1928–1931', in John Buxton and Penry Williams (eds.), *New College, Oxford, 1379–1979* (1979), 125).

p. 200 *The Loom of Youth*: broaching of public-school homosexuality, Alec Waugh's first novel (1917) was something of a *succès de scandale*.

p. 201 *a few years later*: in 1934.

p. 201 *Utopian dreams of revolution*: while not quarrelling with this picture of himself, Gaitskell and others, Richard Crossman strongly rejected the contention that politics were irrelevant to the Oxford of 1928: 'This was the period when Lindsay, Tawney and Cole were at the height of their powers and when the Labour Club was a power in the land. But Mr Rees dismissed it all as boring Wykehamist seriousness . . .' (*New Statesman*, 25 February 1972, 242).

p. 202 *a bump supper*: held to celebrate a rowing victory.

p. 203 *of playing games*: Rees played representative rugby and football and recalled how in the New College XV Richard Crossman used to exasperate him 'by his assumption that rugby was a matter of brute force rather than intelligence, which offended all my instincts as a Welshman'. The soccer XI contained Douglas Jay, Frank Pakenham and John Sparrow, the latter all elegance and style. 'He disapproved of my rather bustling methods as a centre-forward and would shake his head sadly if I scored a goal which did not come up to his exacting standards' (G. R. 'Memories of New College, 1928–1931', 123).

p. 205 *Do What Thou Wilt is the Whole of the Law*: 'In their rules there was only one clause. Do what you will' (*Gargantua*, Bk.1, Ch. 57, referring to the fictional Abbey of Thélème).

p. 205 *not a book, but a man*: Pattison's *Isaac Casaubon, 1559–1640* (1875) much influenced Rees. He made its observations – 'The scholar is greater than his books'; 'Knowledge is not the thing known, but the mental habit which knows' – the basis of his inaugural lecture as principal, University College of Wales, Aberystwyth.

p. 206 *in drunkenness and ecstasy*: from *Blick ins Chaos* (*A Glimpse into Chaos*), a passage quoted in the original by T. S. Eliot in his Notes to *The Waste Land*. Rees provides his own translation.

p. 206 *the Kellogg–Briand Pact*: the Pact of 1928 was jointly sponsored by Aristide Briand, Prime Minister of France, and Frank Kellogg, the American Secretary of State. Disclaiming war as an instrument of national policy, it was ratified by sixty-three nations. 'At the time it was regarded by millions of people throughout the world as the expression of a rational hope for the future, firmly based upon the immense improvement that had already taken place in international relations. As A. J. P. Taylor has said, there was never a time in history when an outbreak of war seemed less likely than in 1929, or when men could more reasonably look forward to the establishment of universal and permanent peace' (G.R., *The Great Slump*, 6).

p. 207 *sporting his oak*: a university colloquialism meaning, 'to shut the outer door of one's rooms as a sign that one is engaged' (*OED*).

p. 207 *which to me was wealth*: it is worth stressing that Rees at Oxford rarely felt the want of money; indeed he elsewhere repeats that his income from scholarships placed him at an advantage in relation to his New College contemporaries, many of whose parents were forced into considerable financial sacrifice.

p. 209 *the gulf between two nations and two cultures*: some have found this self-portrait unconvincing. 'My memory of him', wrote Richard Crossman, 'is of an extremely brilliant and handsome scholar who took Oxford society by storm and won as many admirers as Elizabeth Longford.' Other Oxford contemporaries have vouched for Rees's tremendous charm and conversational brilliance. Richard Wilberforce fell under his spell ('I was attracted – enchanted – by him – his looks, his cleverness, his reading – and this never left me'). Yet he and Patrick Reilly (both New College men) also detected an alien component in Rees: writing home at the time to his parents, Reilly spoke of his 'strong impression that the English he [Rees] was speaking was not his mother tongue' (Sir Patrick Reilly, letter to Jenny Rees, 27 January 1993), while Sir Richard Wilberforce writes that it was Rees's misfortune to have come 'detached' from Wales; the New College Wykhamists were luckier – 'we had families, school friends, professions, to hold us together' (letter to Jenny Rees, 2 May 1995).

p. 209 *an aristocratic and very beautiful young man*: Hamish St Clair Erskine, second son of the Earl of Rosslyn. See note to p. 222.

p. 209 *and with dons*: pre-eminently Maurice Bowra, of whose circle Rees by his third year was a well-established member. Isaiah Berlin saw Bowra as a major emancipating force upon the undergraduates of his day: he 'broke through some of these social and psychological barriers, and the young men who gathered round him in the 20s and 30s, stimulated by his unrestrained talk, let themselves go in their turn' (*Personal Impressions* (1982), 125).

p. 210 *nights spent in arguments and ignorant goodwill*: an allusion to Yeats's lines on Con Markiewicz ('Easter 1916'):

> That woman's days were spent
> In ignorant good-will,
> Her nights in argument
> Until her voice grew shrill.

p. 211 *the college chaplain*: Revd Robert Henry Lightfoot (1883–1953), author of *History and Interpretation in the Gospels* (1935); nervous of temperament and pedantic in manner, he found himself at odds with the more high-spirited New College undergraduates.

p. 213 *the adventures of Billy Bunter*: Reed wrote school stories for boys, most famously *The Fifth Form at St Dominic's* (1881); Frank Richards created Billy Bunter, the Owl of the Remove at Greyfriars.

p. 214 *for the foreseeable future*: this is not as it appeared to Keynes in 1919: 'We are thus faced in Europe with the spectacle of an extraordinary weakness on the part of the great capitalist class, which has emerged from the industrial triumphs of the nineteenth century, and seemed a very few years ago our all powerful master. The terror and personal timidity of the individuals of this class is now so great, their confidence in their place in society and in their necessity to the social organisation so diminished, that they are the easy victims of intimidation. This was not so in England twenty-five years ago, any more than it is now in the United States' (*The Collected Writings of John Maynard Keynes*, Vol. 2, *The Economic Consequences of the Peace* (1971), 150).

p. 215 *the South Wales Miners' Federation*: thus Rees in the *Bookman* (November 1934), 105: 'The South Wales miners have perpetually struck and fought, they have been brave, determined and seen the world as it really is; they have, by fighting, forced their will upon the world . . . The one noble and admirable force in Wales today are the South Wales workers and their perpetual struggle to revolutionize the life, not only of themselves and their families, but of the entire working class . . . It is the South Wales miners and steel-workers, their lives and problems and struggles, which still make a Welsh people possible; and among them we can find our nationality.'

p. 215 *I had learned in the chapel*: Rees was haunted by a Welsh hymn ('*Oll yn eu gynau, yn eu gynau gwynion*'), drawing on the seventh chapter of Revelation and its reference to the survivors of Armageddon, which he sang as a child: 'Who are those who are arrayed in white garments? / They are those who came out of great tribulation / And washed their clothes as white as snow . . .'

p. 215 *Die Weltgeschichte is das Weltgericht!* 'The world's history is the world's judgement!' (Schiller, *Resignation*).

p. 217 *An embryo musician*: the witty and attractive Martin Cooper would study with Egon Wellesz in Vienna and later work as music critic for the *London Mercury* and *Spectator*.

p. 219 *would carry highest*: Richard Crossman regularly headed the New College list, he being, in Rees's words, 'so efficiently organised for success'. Though the two did not always hit it off – 'I thought of him as a playboy on the make. He thought of me as a bore,' said Crossman (which provoked the reply, 'It would have been truer to say, I think, that I was on a different kind of make from his, and he had thought me frivolous') – Rees came to acknowledge Crossman as the best political journalist of his day. His strength as a writer was his weakness as a politician: 'The golden rule for a politician is never to have an idea which is obviously your own, and this was something to which Crossman could never resign himself' (*Encounter* (June 1974), 41).

p. 221 *not have existed*: Rees became particularly close to Maire Lynd (nicknamed 'B.J.'), daughter of Robert and Sylvia Lynd, and a much admired undergraduate at

St Anne's. Then in his final term at New College he got to know Shiela Grant Duff, bound for Lady Margaret Hall. Her autobiography, *The Parting of Ways* (1982), is fond and just on Goronwy (the two briefly contemplated marriage) and helps to pinpoint his movements in the early 1930s. It was in 1931, as a member of Maurice Bowra's circle, that he first seems to have met Elizabeth Bowen.

p. 222 *and almost aggressively so*: *The Summer Flood*, Rees's *roman-à-clef* of 1932, describes a brief homosexual affair between Owen Morgan and a fellow under-graduate, Sasha, a drunken, degenerate aristocrat. Their relationship is thought to mirror one of Rees's own Oxford entanglements, most probably with Hamish St Clair Erskine, second son of the Earl of Rosslyn; 'the most shimmering and narcissistic of all the beautiful butterflies' in his homosexual coterie, Erskine was sent down from New College at the end of Michaelmas term, 1930 (Selina Hastings, *Nancy Mitford* (1985), 61).

p. 223 '*Only connect*': in a fine essay on Lytton Strachey (*Encounter* (March 1968), 71–83), Rees returned to this theme, this time to stress the gulf between 'the saintly Moore' and those who interpreted his ethical philosophy in a selective and idiosyncratic way. For them, the final chapter of *Principia Ethica* (1903) provides a crucial text: 'By far the most valuable things, which we know or can imagine, are certain states of consciousness, which may be roughly described as the pleasures of human intercourse and the enjoyment of beautiful objects.' Rees quotes approvingly Keynes's comment that, compared with the unworldliness of the last pages of *Principia Ethica*, the New Testament is a handbook for politicians, but adds that even so, Keynes and his friends found within Moore's pages justification for their sexual proclivities: 'The almost hysterical admiration inspired by Moore in some of his Cambridge followers was based on the fact that he gave them philosophical reasons for doing what they in any case wanted to do on totally different grounds.'

p. 226 *the great embezzler Clarence Hatry*: 'Hatry, who built an industrial and financial empire on assorted enterprises which ranged from penny-in-the-slot machines to investment trusts, was reduced to forging share certificates in order to maintain his empire. His collapse caused widespread distress in Britain, and Hatry was sent to prison; after his release, the legend of his financial genius was still strong enough to find him backers who set him up in business again, but by then the magic had deserted him' (G.R., *The Great Slump*, 41).

p. 226 *opéra bouffe*: comic opera.

p. 227 *hortus conclusus*: enclosed garden, private retreat.

p. 229 *My philosophy tutor*: H. W. B. Joseph.

p. 229 *That summer my mother died*: Apphia Rees died of angina in 1931, shortly after her sixty-first birthday.

p. 229 *which was to take place shortly*: the chronology is not quite right. Rees's letters of the period make it clear that by summer 1931 he had decided to try for an All Souls fellowship. The history tutor who intervened was (Ernest) Llewellyn Woodward (1890–1971), author of *The Age of Reform, 1815–70* (1938), vol. 13 in the Oxford History of England.

p. 230 *that I had been elected to a fellowship*: younger fellows were recruited by a system of competitive examination and normally two prize fellows were elected each autumn. Rees gained the first prize fellowship of 1931. Writing to Jenny Rees (27 January 1993), Sir Patrick Reilly quotes from a letter to his parents written immediately before his own election to All Souls (1932). He is pessimistic about his prospects: 'they have not been taking men of my type recently, but much rather men, like Rees, who have made a real mark in intellectual Oxford Society, as much by the brilliance of their conversation as by their real ability'. Douglas Jay (himself prize fellow for 1930) placed the emphasis differently: 'though he [Rees] has lots of supreme talents which I have not got, he was actually elected for the moderate ones he shares with me and the interest in the truth we both care about . . . a desire for truth about the most important things and a determination not to be weak or lazy or dishonest in finding it.' Rees himself was characteristically self-denigrating, reporting to his father how Sir Charles Oman, Chichele Professor of Modern History, had opposed the election on the grounds that his history papers 'were the worst he'd ever read & it was an impertinence to offer them at a fellowship examination!'.

p. 230 *the editor of The Times*: the highly influential Geoffrey Dawson, for whom Rees briefly worked. Dawson's predecessor, George Buckle, was likewise a fellow of All Souls.

p. 230 *a matter for national self-congratulation*: the election was reported in the Welsh press and Cardiff High School granted itself a rare half-holiday. (Similarly, Michael Ignatieff mentions how the success of Isaiah Berlin, the first Jew to be elected to All Souls, was received with celebration throughout the whole Jewish community.)

p. 231 *luxe, calme et volupté*: 'luxury, peace and sensual indulgence' (Charles Baudelaire, 'L'Invitation au Voyage', *Les Fleurs du mal* (1857)).

p. 232 *the Warden of All Souls in his study*: F. W. Pember, Warden from 1914 to 1932.

p. 232 *pas trop de zèle*: don't overdo it.

p. 234 *later than I expected*: between the winning of an All Souls fellowship and his appointment in January 1936 to the assistant editorship of the *Spectator*, Rees was chronically restless and uncertain as to career. From Shiela Grant Duff's *The Parting of Ways*, we know that he was in Freiberg and Vienna during the spring of 1932 and that later that summer he returned to Germany, spending time at Wickersdorf, Berlin and Vienna again. In 1932 he and Shiela also made a trip to Russia, visiting Moscow and Leningrad. By the end of the year Rees was back in England, working on the *Manchester Guardian* as leader writer, a job first offered him in September 1931 when the editor C. P. Scott, looking for someone interested in foreign affairs and with 'an easy knack of writing', settled on Rees in preference to Rees's friend Isaiah Berlin (Michael Ignatieff, *Isaiah Berlin: A Life* (1998), 57–8). Rees abandoned Manchester early in 1933 and by the summer was once more travelling, this time to Czechoslovakia accompanied by Shiela and Isaiah. In January 1934 he began an extended stay in Berlin with the intention of working on a biography of Ferdinand Lassalle.

p. 234 *Guy Burgess*: Rees's memory plays him false on the date of his momentous first encounter with Burgess. Felix Frankfurter, the American jurist and future Supreme Court Justice, did not arrive for his academic year as George Eastman Visiting Professor at Oxford until June 1933. We have his account of the dinner party that brought Burgess to Oxford (besides Bowra, Burgess and Rees, others present included Isaiah Berlin, A. J. Ayer and his wife Renée, and Sylvester Gates, the lawyer and banker) – an 'almost excessively clever young crowd' observed Frankfurter, who does not date the evening precisely. It was most probably at the start of summer term 1934, for Rees mentions his tentative plan to visit Russia with Burgess during the summer vacation, a trip Burgess undertook in different company. It accords also with Rees's remark that at the time Burgess was helping to organize a busmen's strike in Cambridge; the dispute with the Eastern Counties Omnibus Company over union recognition and conditions of employment came to a head in October 1934.

p. 235 *in everything he had to say*: testimonies to Burgess's extraordinary personality and behaviour are plentiful, and many have additionally vouched for his remarkable qualities of mind. This latter must be taken on trust, for little evidence exists in the shape of published writings by Burgess. Elected a Cambridge Apostle in November 1932, he became the following year a postgraduate student at Trinity, undertaking research on the intellectual origins of the English bourgeois revolution. But he was pre-empted by Basil Willey's ground-breaking *The Seventeenth Century Background*, a book Burgess warmly welcomed in an impressive *Spectator* review (23 March 1934).

p. 235 *who was also both communist and homosexual*: the companion was Derek Blaikie who, according to Richard Deacon, published a Marxist analysis of modern literature and met his death in the Second World War. Rees in his *People* articles claimed that during this Russian trip of summer 1934 Burgess was recruited by Bukharin, last of the Bolshevik old guard and 'the darling of the party' (as Lenin described him). Rejecting Rees's assertion, Burgess's biographer Tom Driberg claimed that all Guy's meetings with communists in Moscow arose from introductions given to Blaikie by Rees himself (who had visited the Soviet Union two summers previously).

p. 237 *a leader writer on the Manchester Guardian*: in November 1934 Rees began a four-month spell with *The Times*. He had worked on the *Manchester Guardian* two years previously.

p. 238 *Forward from Liberalism*: originally announced as *Approach to Communism*, Spender's retitled book appeared in January 1937.

p. 239 *Lunarcharsky and Madame Kollantai*: Alexandra M. Kollantai (1872–1952), the world's first female ambassador, wrote frankly on sexuality and on women's position in society. Anotoly Lunarcharski (1875–1933), head of the Commissariat of Enlightenment (created after the Revolution), was associated with artistic freedom and experimentation.

p. 239 *political adviser to the House of Rothschild*: Rees explained to Andrew Boyle that during 1935–6 Burgess was being paid a handsome retainer by Mrs Charles Rothshild, the mother of Victor, to act as her adviser on financial investments (Boyle, *The Climate of Treason: Five Who Spied for Russia* (1979), 118).

p. 239 *the Right in action*: this particular German visit, subject of 'A Winter in Berlin', took place *before* his first meeting with Burgess (although Rees returned to the city later in 1934).

p. 240 *Märzhasen*: March hares, a term used derisively of those who stampeded towards the Nazis after Hitler's accession to power.

p. 242 *quite reasonable to call him a fascist*: Captain John Robert (Jack) Macnamara, a thirty-year-old ex-guards officer, elected Unionist MP for Chelmsford in 1935. A member of the influential Anglo-German Fellowship and of the Link (a more sinister pro-Hitler grouping), he and his friend Tom Wylie embarked with Burgess on their Rhine journey in the spring of 1936.

p. 243 *no doubt of his existence*: in fact he is named by Costello, *Mask of Treachery* (1988), 300, as the Venerable John Herbert Sharp, the Church of England's representative in South-Eastern Europe (within the Diocese of Gibraltar).

p. 243 *a particularly unhappy one*: again, the chronology needs clarification. Rees worked on *The Times* from 12 November 1934 to 16 March 1935. Later in 1935 he looked for new professional openings (with the *Evening Standard* and the BBC), progressed with a novel (*A Bridge to Divide Them*), met Shiela Grant Duff in Paris at Easter and went on with her to Spain. Summer was spent in Wales, writing WEA lectures on the Renaissance which he gave throughout the autumn. The break with Shiela ('the girl I was supposed to be going to marry') came in March 1936, by which time Rees was settled at the *Spectator*, with a flat in Ebury Street, SW1. Shiela confirms that Guy Burgess reappeared in Rees's life early in 1936.

Regarding his stint with *The Times*, we know that for four unhappy months he was employed as a sub-editor in the Home News department at a salary of £5 per week and that he left by mutual agreement on account of the paper's support for appeasement – a policy with which he violently disagreed. Yet Rees at the end of his life remembered with respect and affection the newspaper's sub-editing room: 'It was indeed a remarkable institution, which instilled into one habits of accuracy, respect for fact, and clarity of expression, which are indispensable to any journalist. It often used to remind me more of a research institution than a newspaper office' (*Encounter* (February 1979), 31).

p. 246 *Lulu Harcourt*: son of Sir William Harcourt, Lewis ('Lulu' or 'Loulou') Harcourt, 1st Viscount Harcourt (1863–1922), was himself a Liberal politician, particularly successful as Colonial Secretary.

p. 246 *for reviewing any books I chose*: Rees occupied the post from February 1936 to August 1939; as assistant to Wilson Harris, he provided a weekly leader, the occasional signed essay and a stream of book reviews.

p. 246 *I also fell in love with a girl*: Pamela de Bayou, the French-born painter married to the publisher Frederic Warburg. 'While she was not in any conventional sense pretty, she had the assurance of a woman accustomed to the attention of men', wrote Diana Trilling in her snapshot of 'the obstreperous Pamela' during the 1960s ('Goronwy – and Others: A Remembrance of England', *Partisan Review* (January 1996), 15–19). Rees nowhere mentions Elizabeth Bowen, whom he notoriously deserted for Rosamond Lehmann in September 1936 (Lehmann is alluded to, though not named).

p. 246 *choses vues*: *objets d'art*.

p. 247 *a show of reason*: though Rees was 'for the Republic', and well understood why the Spanish conflict had taken hold of the popular imagination, he argued for a policy of non-intervention by all outside governments in what was essentially a civil war. 'Callous as it may seem, the great issues which hang on the Spanish conflict must be entrusted to the courage and endurance of the Spanish people themselves' (*Spectator*, 7 August 1936, 225–6).

p. 247 *gathered in one room together*: in the second of his *People* articles (18 March 1956, 3), Rees had named these characters (excepting Anthony Blunt, 'the clever young English historian'). 'Ignatz', supposed colleague of the Hungarian communist leader, Béla Kun, is the Soviet agent Rudolph Katz (sometimes confused with the celebrated Otto Katz, executed following the show trial of 1952), 'Jimmy' is Burgess's young live-in boyfriend Jack Hewit (1917–97), and the anti-Nazi diplomat is Baron Wolfgang von und zu Putlitz. Edouard Pfeiffer, a notorious homosexual, was principal aide to Edouard Daladier, the French Minister of War who became Prime Minister, for the third time, in September 1938.

p. 248 *about the historian*: 'we still don't know for certain whether or not Blunt really was a communist through and through', writes Yuri Modin, last KGB London controller of the Cambridge spies. 'Having known him myself, I think that in his heart of hearts he wasn't, even though he shared certain Marxist opinions. He never advertised his beliefs' (Yuri Modin, *My Five Cambridge Friends* (1994), 70).

p. 248 *petit noyau*: small knot or nucleus; M. and Mme Verdurin are leading characters in Proust's *A la recherche du temps perdu*.

p. 249 *épater les bourgeois*: shock middle-class values.

p. 250 *the condition of the depressed areas*: the review was of James Hanley's *Grey Children: A Study of Humbug and Misery in South Wales* (1937). In it Rees spoke of the south Wales unemployed and of the industrial culture they had created: one in which the miner 'lived a strangely varied, violent and comprehensive life, ennobled by his desire for social progress and education' (*Spectator*, 5 November 1937, 806–7). The review's tone and argument are conveyed in the following extracts:

> The unemployed believe their misery is unjust and unnecessary, and that by sincere and determined efforts it can be remedied. In many cases they are told, in reply, that all that can be done has been done, that the misery which still exists is unavoidable, that the ruin and decay of South Wales is the result of inexorable processes which cannot be controlled; and this argument is applied in practice by encouraging large-scale emigration. The distressed area is being evacuated. It is a curious answer; if you tell men and women, already inclined by temperament and tradition to revolutionary opinions, that their sufferings are caused by an impersonal economic system, you leave them but one choice. Lenin could not do it better.

> To such men, whatever their poverty now, pity is an insult, and it is no cure for their condition. And it is a serious fault of Mr Hanley's book that it will arouse, above all, pity. It is inevitable that this should be so, given the method he uses. Unemployed men and women, as individuals, have nothing to show but the poverty of their homes, their loss of independence, their utter lack of resources, their absence of hope for the future. As individuals they are outcasts from society, objects of charity or philanthropy, the passive subjects of suffering. And indeed to some extent they are isolated, but less so than they seem or than they feel. For in fact they are not isolated. It is because their lives and their sufferings are so closely related to the working of modern society that they are a condemnation of it. Otherwise they might be treated as irrelevant.

p. 252 *carried more weight with me*: that person was Anthony Blunt, brought into the Cambridge network largely through the efforts of Burgess. Though experts contest certain details concerning the recruitment of the Cambridge spies, it is agreed that Kim Philby was the first to enlist, in the spring of 1934; he was joined before the end of the year by Donald Maclean and Burgess (both approached at Philby's suggestion). Anthony Blunt came next (no later than 1936) and after Burgess's crucial overture. John Cairncross followed Blunt, thus completing the

Cambridge Five, or the Magnificent Five, as the KGB later dubbed them. All were ideologists who accepted no payment, agents of the Communist International (the Comintern) united in the struggle against fascism, though by 1937 they were aware that they were working for the Soviet Union – the ultimate anti-fascist bastion (Nigel West and Oleg Tsarev, *The Crown Jewels: The British Secrets at the Heart of the KGB Archives* (1998), 132–3; Christopher Andrew and Vasili Mitrokhin, *The Mitrokhin Archive: The KGB in Europe and the West* (1999), 73–88; Yuri Modin, *My Five Cambridge Friends*, 61 ff., advancing somewhat earlier dates for the recruitment of Burgess and Blunt).

Rees's liking for Blunt comes as something of a surprise, given Blunt's reputation as a cold fish, aloof and uncomfortably severe. But another side to his personality was evident in the 1930s. Like Rees, he was a rebellious son of the manse, with, as Louis MacNeice saw it, an 'habitual contempt for conservative authorities' (Costello, *Mask of Treachery*, 70). Gavin Ewart remembered him as a cultured man, intelligent and entertaining, and something of a drinker, at least in the company of drinkers (Barrie Penrose and Simon Freeman, *Conspiracy of Silence: The Secret Life of Anthony Blunt* (1986), 136). Rees first met Blunt through Burgess and got to know him better when Blunt, then on the staff of the Warburg Institute, began to contribute *Spectator* articles seeking to apply Marxist principles to the history of art. 'It was curious', Rees reflected, 'how so obviously learned a man depended on the guidance of Guy Burgess in formulating his views for the printed page' (*Observer*, 13 January 1980).

p. 252 *So I promised*: 'Nevertheless, out of sheer curiosity, I resolved to approach "X" [Blunt]. Walking with him in a London park one day I suddenly said: "I gather you know what Guy is really up to?" "Yes", he replied curtly. And he made it quite clear that he did not want to talk any more about Guy Burgess and himself' (G.R., *People*, 18 March 1956, 3).

p. 252 *I was indeed not shocked*: fifty years later Rosamond Lehmann, the only person to whom Rees spoke about this conversation with Burgess, recalled how 'an awfully flustered and stressed' Goronwy had revealed the staggering news that Burgess was a Comintern agent who had tried to recruit him. Rees needed to tell somebody (and he and Rosamond were lovers), but he promised that if she let it go further he would strangle her. When she asked him whether he intended to work with Burgess, 'Goronwy gave me an ambiguous answer' (quoted in Costello, *Mask of Treachery*, 31).

p. 254 *a conference of the Writers' International in Paris*: the Paris conference of the International Association of Writers for the Defence of Culture actually took place in July 1938. Rees, accompanied by Rosamond Lehmann, attended as an executive committee member of the Association's British section; other committee members included Harold Laski, Rose Macauley, Kingsley Martin, Hugh Walpole and Rebecca West, with Cecil Day-Lewis as chairman (Sean Day-Lewis, *C. Day-Lewis: An English Literary Life* (1980), 110–11).

p. 254 *Willi Münzenberg*: of the great communist agitator and propagandist, Rees remarked that 'his activity was so multifarious and ubiquitous that in a sense it would be true to say that the great anti-Fascist crusade of the thirties was an invention of Münzenberg's' (G.R., '*Darkness at Noon* and "Grammatical Fiction"', in Harold Harris (ed.), *Astride Two Cultures: Arthur Koestler at 70* (1975), 107).

p. 255 *Hassliebe*: love–hate relationship.

p. 256 *galère*: set-up, set of people – in allusion to Molière's 'mais que diable allait-il faire dans cette galère?' ('but what the hell was he doing there?').

p. 256 *homme de confiance*: confidential agent.

p. 257 *in a café in the East End*: Rees also spoke of being taken by Burgess one Sunday morning to Limehouse for a Chinese meal. 'Burgess stopped outside a ship's chandler's shop and pushed something through the letter-box. From what I learned later this letter-box was also used by Blunt' (G.R., quoted in Richard Deacon, *The Greatest Treason: The Bizarre Story of Hollis, Liddell and Mountbatten* (1989), 157).

p. 260 *He was frightened*: the Nazi–Soviet pact of 23 August 1939 came as a thunderbolt to those who innocently imagined that the communist cause was wholly synonymous with anti-fascism. Burgess's defence and explanation mirrored the pro-Soviet line, that of neutrality between the Allies and Axis; the British and French, themselves unwilling to join a united front against Hitler's eastwards expansion, were luring Germany into a war against the Soviet Union. The pact, so Blunt later argued, was actually a tactical necessity designed to buy time for a programme of Russian rearmament. Interviewed by Robert Cecil in 1981, Blunt confirmed that, on hearing of the pact, he and Burgess had rushed home from holiday to find Rees so distressed at this turn of events that he was refusing to cooperate any further in their Comintern activity. Taking Cecil into the bathroom (and turning on the taps for fear that the other room might be bugged), Blunt whispered, 'I want to tell you that Rees was one of us and this was the time he quit' (Costello, *Mask of Treachery*, 336). Burgess had anticipated as much, and behind his rapid return to England was the wish to placate Goronwy, and thus try to keep him as a source (Blunt, in conversation with Sir Ellis Waterhouse, as quoted in Penrose and Freeman, *Conspiracy of Silence*, 213). Though Rees promised not to betray his erstwhile colleagues, henceforth Burgess and Blunt considered him untrustworthy, and potentially highly dangerous.

p. 260 *Now let's go and have a drink*: in one of her later interviews, Rosamond Lehmann mentions how, following the Nazi–Soviet pact, Rees reported that Guy had dropped his position as a Comintern agent. 'But they went on seeing each other a great deal. Guy got drunker and drunker as time went on. He and Goronwy used to argue all the time' (Penrose and Freeman, *Conspiracy of Silence*, 214).

In his *People* articles, and in conversations with Andrew Boyle, Rees recalls that at the outbreak of war Burgess spoke of being sorely tempted to defect altogether from communism and that Blunt seemingly had quit as a Comintern agent. The two spies did indeed persuade Rees that they were pulling out at this point, at the same time gaining an assurance that he would keep silent on their past activity. There was, however, a counter view, propagated by those close to Blunt, that even after the Nazi–Soviet agreement – and thus while in military intelligence – Rees continued wittingly to cooperate with Burgess.

p. 261 *Erst kommt das Fressen, dann kommt die Moral*: 'food comes first, then morals'.

p. 261 *in the spring of 1940*: Rees was actually discharged from Sandhurst in March 1940, having won a commission with the Royal Welch Fusiliers.

p. 261 *all-embracing reality of their time*: Rees's 'Letter from a Soldier', *Horizon* (July 1940), 467–71, argues his position passionately and persuasively:

The complement of your advice that the artist should ignore the war is that the soldier, who must die that the artist may live, will find no voice which may speak for him what he wishes all the world to know, even more, no imagination that may illuminate for him the experience he knows but cannot comprehend . . . His enormous sacrifice will have no interest for those who alone are worthy and capable of communicating it; his expense of spirit and blood, his patience and endurance, his dim confused consciousness of their significance, will speak and be spoken of only in the stale rhetoric of politicians and the falsehoods of war correspondents.

Horizon gave Rees's article the status of an editorial and subsequently modified its attitude to the war.

p. 262 *who was hardly out of school*: on 20 December 1940 Rees married Margaret Ewing Morris ('Margie'), daughter of a Liverpool underwriter. She was twenty years of age and he just turned thirty-one. Rees's intention to marry devastated Rosamond Lehmann; 'she [Margie] makes me happier than I've ever expected to be', he tried to explain to Rosamond, '& I know that my happiness isn't merely a temporary fancy. I need her as much as she needs me, & I can't think of myself without her any more.' Frances Partridge's diary confirms that Goronwy's defection was an 'incomprehensible' blow to Rosamond, who felt 'he still loved her though he didn't seem to realize it' (*Good Company* (1994), 31).

p. 263 *even more evasive than usual*: in January 1939 Burgess got a foothold in secret intelligence when he joined Section D of the War Office as propaganda expert. In July 1940 he was assigned to work in Moscow, using diplomatic cover, but the mission came to nothing, seemingly because the British ambassador, Sir Stafford Cripps, refused to countenance a posting over which he had not been consulted. In the *People* (25 March 1956, 3) Rees revealed that Burgess had been accompanied on this mission by a friend who knew nothing of his links with the Russians. That friend was Isaiah Berlin, a fluent Russian speaker recruited as a press attaché. When Burgess was recalled to London, Berlin remained at the British Embassy in Washington ('his brilliant despatches were favourite reading matter during the war at the Foreign Office', noted Rees). Berlin resented Goronwy's suggestion that he might unwittingly have been used by Burgess and wrote to tell him so (Ignatieff, *Isaiah Berlin*, 194).

p. 263 *Semiramis*: the Assyrian Queen Sammuramat (Greek: *Semiramis*), builder of Babylon, was famed for her beauty and courage.

p. 263 *proved impossible to dislodge*: Rees offered Andrew Boyle a little more: 'When on leave in London later in the war, I visited Guy from time to time in the large flat he'd rented from Victor Rothschild above the offices of *The Practitioner*, the medical newspaper, at 5 Bentinck Street, a few minutes' walk from Broadcasting House. Anthony Blunt [the scholar at MI5] was also in permanent residence, as were two highly placed girl secretaries engaged on important official work. Richard Llewelyn-Davies, the architect and another ex-Apostle from Trinity College, Cambridge, fell in love with one of them and then emulated the man-who-came-to-dinner by "hanging up his hat" and never leaving' (*Observer*, 13 January 1980). The women were Teresa Mayor, Rothschild's secretary at MI5 (and later his second wife), and Patricia Rawdon-Smith, née Parry ('Semiramis'), who upon divorce married Richard Llewelyn-Davies (Costello, *Mask of Treachery*, 195–6, 390–1).

p. 264 *the future possibilities of the peace*: Burgess's boyfriend, Jack Hewit, would sometimes insist that too much had been made of Rees's description of affairs at Bentinck Street – the presence of people from the office meant that parties there were fairly respectable. However, Malcolm Muggeridge's account of his only visit to Guy's Mayfair flat (he was received in its basement, a bomb shelter that doubled as a drinking den), lends support to Rees: 'Burgess gave me a feeling such as I have never had from anyone else, of being morally afflicted in some way. His very physical presence was, to me, malodorous and sinister, as though he had some consuming illness . . . There was not so much a conspiracy gathered around him as just decay and dissolution. It was the end of a class, of a way of life' (*Chronicles of Wasted Time*, Vol. 2, *The Infernal Grove* (1973), 107).

p. 264 *that immense operation*: in a television interview with John Morgan (1978), Rees recalled that Montgomery had asked him for an estimate of Allied casualties during the initial phase of the Normandy landings. The brief was daunting, but working day and night, Rees produced 'some really very elegant looking tables', and wrote on a sheet of paper the possible number of losses. Next day he was summoned before the C.-in-C.: '"Thank you, very good, very good", Monty began, "but you see, it won't do. If our casualties are as big as this, we can't do the operation at all. We haven't got the reserves to replace the casualties. Divide Major Rees's calculations by half."'

p. 264 *evidence of my own errors*: recounting the Dieppe fiasco, Rees told John Morgan that 'I really did have a very strong sense of guilt for very nearly the first time in my life . . . I felt partly responsible for the disaster . . . being heavily bombed from the air, straight onto the deck of the destroyer. I thought I might be killed, and indeed a great many people were, but I was lucky again – a very lucky man' (television interview, 1978).

p. 265 *fêtes galantes*: music, dancing and love-making (usually in a rural setting).

p. 266 *an extremely important member of the security services*: again a reference to Anthony Blunt. Rees's claim, that he did not seriously imagine that Burgess was continuing with his espionage activites after the Nazi–Soviet pact, was never accepted by Blunt (Penrose and Freeman, *Conspiracy of Silence*, 185).

p. 268 *I now had two small children*: Margaret Jane ('Jenny', the biographer), born 16 March 1942, and Lucy, born 21 December 1943. Jenny Rees explains that both names were taken from Brecht's *The Threepenny Opera*.

p. 268 *Ils sont dans le vrai!*: 'Theirs is the true path!'

p. 269 *the Alger Hiss case in America*: on 3 August 1948, Whittaker Chambers, then a senior editor of *Time* magazine, testified before the notorious House Committee on Un-American Activities in Washington that from 1934 to 1937 he had been an underground Communist agent, with the primary task of maintaining contact with a secret group of Communists in the service of the United States government. Among the members of the group whom he named was Alger Hiss, a brilliant young lawyer and State Department official. Hiss denied the allegations of Chambers, but before two grand juries was found guilty of perjury and given a five-year prison sentence. The Hiss case, in Rees's words, 'stripped America of its political innocence'. Chambers was not merely naming Hiss as a Communist agent; he was also appearing to prove that there existed a vast conspiracy to subvert the United States government and that the Communist Party had successfully infiltrated its agents into government positions of power.

p. 269 *The case fascinated me also*: Diana Trilling has noted its magnetic attraction for Rees, who would regularly question her husband Lionel about his novel, *The Middle of the Journey* (1947); Lionel Trilling had known Whittaker Chambers and had used him as a basis for Maxim, one of the characters in the book. It was about Chambers, and never Hiss, that Goronwy enquired, and implicit in all his references was the opinion that Chambers had been telling the truth. 'It was not debate about Hiss's guilt or innocence which moved Rees to question Lionel. On this point his mind was settled. What he sought from Lionel was personal information about Chambers, of a kind which was not contained in Lionel's book' (Trilling, 'Goronwy – and Others', 29).

Rees returned in print to the character of Whittaker Chambers, or rather, to his demonization by both American and British commentators. For if Alger Hiss was an angel, the all-American hero, there was something diabolical about Chambers, the rootless intellectual and spy-turned-informer. Rees strongly identified with Chambers, in the ex-communist's act of testimony and in his consequent sufferings. He rounded on Chambers's enemies (not least Conor Cruise O'Brien) who sought to destroy this testimony by a campaign of character assassination: Chambers might be smeared as a liar, a forger and a psychopath, but history would prove him right about Alger Hiss. Remembering Rees's pro-Chambers pieces (as in the *Spectator*, 20 February 1953), Robert Conquest remarked that 'his emotional exaltation of Whittaker Chambers's character caused more ill feeling on the pro-Hiss side than almost any other contribution' (review of *A Chapter of Accidents*, London Magazine (June–July 1972), 159).

p. 271 *proving too much for him*: Burgess's Soviet handler explains: 'The pressure he had carried so lightly during the war, when his country was fighting against Fascism in alliance with the Soviet Union, became more and more burdensome with the coming of peace – and the Cold War. I saw him weakening psychologically and physically, before my eyes' (Modin, *My Five Cambridge Friends*, 164–5).

p. 272 *the Minister of State, Hector McNeil*: as Burgess reported to the KGB, this appointment of December 1946 was 'not only an important promotion but one that can be put to valuable use'. As personal assistant to a senior Foreign Office minister in the new Labour government (second in command to the Foreign Secretary, Ernest Bevin), Burgess became an 'agent in place', privy to British policy towards Russia at the beginning of the Cold War, and a source of thousands of restricted documents passed to Soviet Intelligence during his time at the Foreign Office.

p. 272 *the Private Secretary*: Frederick Warner; 'he too was a notorious homosexual and one of Burgess's favourite drinking companions' (West and Tsarev, *The Crown Jewels*, 177).

p. 273 *chasse au bonheur*: search for pleasure; the good life.

p. 274 *Sexual Behavior in the Human Male*: published in 1948, the Kinsey Report became available in Britain in December of that year.

p. 275 *a pre-war musical by Beverley Nichols*: 'Little White Room', from *Floodlight* (1937).

p. 275 *a song of Peter Lind Hayes*: Carson Robinson's song, 'Life Gets Tee-jus' (1946), in the style of talking blues, was recorded by Hayes in 1948. The last line of the verse quoted actually runs, 'Just can't depend on nothin'.'

p. 280 *a strangely constituted quartet*: Rees (*Observer*, 20 January 1980) named the MI5 official as Guy Liddell.

p. 280 *the coulisses of politics*: behind the scenes in politics.

p. 282 *anything more serious than a reprimand*: 'This last point was in my view the most powerful. I know a good deal about the Foreign Office bureaucrats. They will do almost anything to avoid a formal board of enquiry, which takes up everybody's time, often involves bringing witnesses from long distances, and produces endless paper wrangles' (G.R., *People*, 11 March 1956, 5).

p. 282 *NKVD*: Narodnyi Kommissariat Vnutrennikh Del: People's Commissariat for Internal Affairs – later the KGB.

p. 282 *Le Boeuf sur le Toit*: a West End club; it was Fred Warner, the Private Secretary, who pushed Burgess down the stairs, apparently in the course of a friendly wrestling match.

p. 283 *the Foreign Office's Far Eastern Department*: on McNeil's advice Burgess moved to the Far East Department on 1 November 1948. The North African holiday took place a year later, in November 1949 (West and Tsarev, *The Crown Jewels*, 179–80).

p. 284 *in her own interests adopt*: 'It was a brilliant performance', wrote Rees of Burgess's Oxford lecture. 'For without disclosing his own sympathies, he made a very powerful case for British recognition of the new regime. Not long afterwards Britain did indeed recognise the Chinese Reds. Guy can claim that he played a significant part in that important act of policy' (*People*, 1 April 1956, 3).

p. 286 *which had gathered to say goodbye to him*: Rees's *People* articles named some of the guests at this legendary farewell party (held in July 1950 at Burgess's flat in Lower Bond Street), and others have expanded the list. Besides Hector McNeil and Kenneth Younger, also present were Guy Liddell, David Footman and Anthony Blunt ('the three distinguished members of the security services'); the novelist James Pope-Hennessy; Baron Wolfgang Putlitz; and the two secretaries from Bentinck Street days, Patricia Rawdon-Smith and Teresa Mayor (now married to Richard Llewelyn-Davies and Victor Rothschild, respectively). Describing the occasion to Andrew Boyle, David Footman related a subsequently much quoted exchange between McNeil and Burgess. The minister, on the point of leaving, offered Burgess a word of advice:

> 'There are three basic don'ts, Guy, to bear particularly in mind when you're dealing with Americans. The first is Communism, the second is homosexuality, and the third is the colour bar. Do please memorise them, won't you?' Burgess smiled his seraphic smile and at once quipped back: 'I've got it, Hector, so there, don't worry. What you're trying to say in your nice, long-winded way is – "Guy, for God's sake don't make a pass at Paul Robeson"' (Boyle, *The Climate of Treason*, 353).

p. 287 *moved from London to the country*: by the end of 1950 Rees had left St John's Wood for Falcon House at Sonning-on-Thames, midway between London and Oxford. In August 1951 he became non-resident Estates Bursar of All Souls – the preferred choice of Geoffrey Faber, who had held the post since 1923.

p. 288 *but you ratted*: in his *People* account Rees assigns this incident to October 1950. Maclean at the time had undertaken psychiatric treatment following the nervous collapse which ended his service at the British Embassy in Cairo. He was still prone to drinking bouts and other lapses of self-control.

p. 289 *he had enlisted me also*: Rees had earlier explained that the only meaning he could attach to the Gargoyle Club outburst 'was that Maclean believed I had "ratted" from the espionage organisation to which Guy Burgess had belonged' (*People*, 8 April 1956, 10).

p. 290 *Alan Nunn May*: the British atomic scientist, in 1946 found guilty of espionage and sentenced to ten years' imprisonment; he had been at Trinity Hall with Maclean.

p. 291 *was being sent home*: Guy's outrageous behaviour on his drive to Charleston and afterwards was part of a plan, devised in conjunction with Philby, to ensure his expulsion from Washington; back in London he would warn Maclean that MI5 was on his track and aid his flight across the Iron Curtain (Modin, *My Five Cambridge Friends*, 199).

p. 292 *on his recent visit to the United States*: Anthony Eden's American visit took place in November 1950. He became Foreign Secretary (for the third time) after the general election of October 1951. 'Grant's tomb' is the massive memorial honouring Ulysses Simpson Grant in Union Square, Washington.

p. 293 *a Third Secretary*: Burgess was in fact appointed a Second Secretary at Washington.

p. 294 *a leading national newspaper*: the offer, from Michael Berry, was for a job on the *Daily Telegraph*.

p. 294 *his paper's political views*: Rees would have had in mind his own journalism of the 1930s. The *New Statesman* not the *Spectator* was his natural political home but he was granted appreciable latitude in his opinions, sometimes more than the traditional readership of the *Spectator* could bear.

p. 297 *except one other person*: Rosamond Lehmann.

p. 298 *I telephoned to a friend*: David Footman, a highly placed MI6 officer whom Rees had first met through Burgess in 1943. Footman confirmed that, as stated here, he received Rees's telephone call on Sunday evening, 27 May 1951 (elsewhere Rees recollected having made the call on Saturday evening, 26 May, and on Monday morning, 28 May).

p. 299 *I also told another friend of Guy's*: Anthony Blunt. Richard Deacon comments: 'This may seem odd in view of the fact that Rees had already been told by Burgess that Blunt was, if not a spy, at least a supporter of the Soviet cause. But Rees knew that Blunt still had contacts with MI5 and he probably wanted to test his reactions' (*The Greatest Treason*, 157). It was Blunt whom Burgess contacted with his plans for Maclean immediately on disembarking from America. Though no longer employed by MI5, Blunt remained important in the Cambridge network, acting as an intermediary between Burgess and his KGB handler.

p. 299 *On Monday*: Rees's *Observer* interview has Blunt coming to see him one day earlier (on Sunday, not Monday).

p. 299 *E. M. Forster's famous statement*: 'if I had to choose between betraying my country and betraying my friend I hope I should have the guts to betray my country' (from 'Two Cheers for Democracy', an essay first published in 1938 and reprinted in Forster's *What I Believe* (1939)).

p. 300 *and made my way to MI5*: there is an obvious time-discrepancy here, first pointed out by Anthony Blunt. The MI5 interview could not have taken place 'the next day' (that is, Tuesday 29 May) if, as Rees claims at the end of the chapter, on emerging from the interview he saw newspaper headlines announcing the disappearance of the two British diplomats: the story did not break until 7 June. David Footman adds another version (*Encounter* (January 1981), 32): he recalls passing on Rees's message to MI5 'on the Monday morning [28 May]. Late that afternoon, following his interview with MI5, he came round to my flat in a state of complete nervous exhaustion.' Rees in 1951, confirming that it was David Footman who had made the initial approach, insisted that he was not then asked to tell his story to MI5 'until nine days later'.

p. 300 *who had also known Guy well*: talking with Andrew Boyle, Rees named the officer as Guy Liddell and made plain that it was Footman and Blunt whom he had telephoned on returning from Oxford. On his deathbed in Charing Cross Hospital Rees tried to put straight the chronology and, in doing so, offered a new explanation of MI5's inordinate delay. It seems that Guy Liddell, as requested by Footman, quickly telephoned Rees with the promise that he would get in touch again as soon as possible. But not until Friday 1 June was a move initiated. 'Guy Liddell asked me out to lunch. I was taken aback to see that he came accompanied by Anthony Blunt. The pair of them took up where Blunt had left off. They did their level best to convince me that I'd be wasting everyone's time if I went along and submitted the nebulous kind of evidence against Guy Burgess that I seemed determined to offer' (*Observer*, 20 January 1980). Rees was not warned off and in face of his persistence Liddell agreed to a formal debriefing. This was conducted by two MI5 investigators, Liddell himself and Dick White, head of counter-espionage and soon to become Director-General of MI5.

Rees speaks of two interrogations, the first taking place on Wednesday 6 June. Exactly what transpired at these meetings is still a matter of conjecture but Rees reports that the second, longer, encounter proved a gruelling affair ('They treated me as if I were a spy and a traitor with lots to hide'). He found Liddell 'discouraging, dismissive and even mildly threatening in the sense that he kept indicating that all this not only wasted MI5 time, but could be considered "mischievous to the cause of national security"' (Richard Deacon, *The Greatest Treason*, 157, drawing on private information from Rees). But this time Rees revealed the name of Anthony Blunt as the only other conspirator given to him by Burgess when he had asked for one. Years later a desperately defensive Dick White, friend of Blunt's and unwitting provider of numerous items of information, recounted the exchange rather differently:

> I thought he [Rees] was a four-letter man. If he had really known all these things why hadn't he come forward? Then he went into this explanation of how he thought we had known it all. So I said to Rees: 'You assume we knew? Burgess was working for the Russians and we did nothing about it? What can you mean?' He was slippery as an eel and had a violent antipathy to Blunt. He said, why don't you ask Blunt about these things. But he did not say that Blunt was our man. No, he said nothing resembling that. (quoted in Penrose and Freeman, *Conspiracy of Silence*, 356)

Perhaps the nearest we have to an official line is Margaret Thatcher's statement to the House of Commons, 15 November 1979, part of which runs: 'He [Blunt] first came under suspicion in the course of the inquiries which followed the defection of Burgess and Maclean in 1951 when the security service was told that Burgess had said in 1937 that he was working for a secret branch of the Comintern and that

Blunt was one of his sources. There was no supporting evidence for this. When confronted with it Blunt denied it . . .'

p. 302 *returning himself later?*: Burgess had assured Kim Philby that, having helped Maclean escape, he would himself stay put in London; if he were also to defect, it would point MI5 straight at Philby. But Burgess was persuaded by the KGB, who now judged him a security risk, to escort the distressed and vulnerable Maclean on part of his journey. At Prague airport the two were met by KGB agents and whisked into Soviet territory on Sunday evening, 27 May. Why Burgess had not turned back at Prague puzzled Yuri Modin; perhaps the KGB had assured him that his Moscow stay would be brief: 'Knowing the man's character, I believe he may have imagined he'd be given a few days to enjoy himself in Moscow, and then would drift back to London as if nothing had happened' (Modin, *My Five Cambridge Friends*, 209).

Guy spread the story of an Ischia visit: on 24 and 25 May 1951 he tried telephoning Auden, who was staying with the Spenders in London.

p. 303 *Browning's lines*: the opening of 'Waring' (*Dramatic Lyrics* (1842)). Stephen Koch writes approvingly of one touch in a BBC television dramatization of Burgess's and Maclean's defection, which has Burgess alerting Blunt to his intentions by mailing him a note containing no more than page references to Browning's ballad. Blunt reads the first stanza *sotto voce*, then, 'enraged – at once betrayed, bereft, and very much endangered – Blunt flings the book across the room' (*Stalin, Willi Münzenberg and the Seduction of the Intellectuals* (1995), 198–9).

p. 307 *an object of suspicion*: in two later interviews Rosamond Lehmann recalled that she had approached the security services immediately after the papers published news of the disappearance of 'two British government employees'; she believed, on the evidence of pre-war conversations with Goronwy, that Burgess was one of the defectors. Jim Skardom from MI5 pressed her hard about Burgess, and about 'A.B.' and 'G.R.'. 'He kept on asking: "What can you tell us about G.R.?"' To her it was obvious that they suspected Rees (Costello, *Mask of Treachery*, 568–9; Penrose and Freeman, *Conspiracy of Silence*, 362–3).

p. 308 *mutatis mutandis*: with the necessary changes.

p. 308 *in the ranks of the security services themselves*: besides Anthony Blunt's, Rees in 1951 offered MI5 the names of Stuart Hampshire and Robin Zaehner as possible members of a Burgess network; he had suspicions of Guy Liddell as well, and these only grew over time. The charges against Hampshire, the philosopher who had worked for MI5, and Zaehner, once an MI6 man in Tehran and afterwards a distinguished academic, proved unsustainable, while the mere suggestion of Guy Liddell's guilt roused the anger of Dick White, his long-standing colleague and friend. Even so, Rees could not but ponder Liddell's attempts to persuade him from volunteering any kind of information: the counter-intelligence officer's one-time membership of the Bentinck Street brotherhood and his continued close association with Burgess and Blunt seemed sinister rather than simply careless and indiscreet.

Jenny Rees provides the revealing background to Rees's naming of Stuart Hampshire. Shortly after the defection of Burgess and Maclean, an agitated Rees told Hampshire, a friend and former colleague of Burgess, that he had arranged to see MI5: what should he say? Should he mention that Burgess had told him that Blunt was an agent too? 'I'm afraid I gave him a very bad piece of advice,' Hampshire admitted; 'I said, "Look Goronwy, just do nothing. Let them find out what they want." I had been in MI5 myself and I told Goronwy that I knew how it worked. I did not think he ought to run round and volunteer anything. I thought that . . . if they interrogated him and said, well, what about Anthony Blunt? . . . then he might as well tell the truth, but otherwise do nothing . . . But what I did was not right and it played a very significant part in the whole story.' 'Indeed it did', comments Jenny Rees, 'because Rees equated his advice to do nothing with the advice he had received from Blunt' (*Looking for Mr Nobody*, 164).

p. 309 *the enemy espionage system*: Modin considers such questions in his assessment of the relative contributions of the Cambridge Five. All were stars, but Maclean vied with Philby for the title of spy of the century. Maclean 'gathered the political, economic and scientific intelligence that guided the strategy of our leaders for over ten years – and what years'. Yet Philby was perhaps even greater, and his appointment as head of the anti-communist section of SIS an unparalled masterstroke: 'In effect the British Secret Service had just named a Russian agent as head of the branch whose specific task was to spearhead the battle against Russian spies. This made Philby the most important operative we had anywhere in the world.' No wonder his reputation with the KGB was 'almost Godlike'.

Yet Guy Burgess, in Modin's eyes, had his own kind of pre-eminence. 'He held the group together, infused it with his energy and led it into battle, so to speak. In the 1930s, at the very start, it was he who took the initatives and the risks, dragging the others along in his wake. He was the moral leader of the group' (Modin, *My Five Cambridge Friends*, 270, 46, 254).

p. 312 *And God will save the Queen*: from '1887', the opening poem of A. E. Housman's *A Shropshire Lad* (1896).

p. 313 *which I found unexpectedly fascinating*: on demobilization Rees rejoined the *Spectator* (November 1945), only to submit his resignation in February 1946. He foresaw that over the next few years he would need to address continuously aspects of the Cold War, defending actions on the part of the United States that he did not wholly approve of: 'And I felt very averse to getting involved in this kind of argument and having to write about it all the time.' Rees remained co-director of Henry Pontifex Ltd, makers of brewers' machinery, for fully seven years, working largely from its London offices, though with regular trips to the factory in Birmingham. 'It was a new world to him, but all his life he was breaking fresh ground and finding it of absorbing interest. He invited me up to see it [the Birmingham factory] and his delight was infectious – the business itself, the personalities of the skilled craftsmen, the dogmas, procedures and mystique of the Coppersmiths' Union' (David Footman, *Encounter* (January 1981), 32).

What Rees understandably does not mention is his work at this time for the Secret Intelligence Service (SIS), or MI6, serving in Political Intelligence at the Russian and German desks. In *The Faber Book of Espionage* (1993), Nigel West, noting the high proportion of journalists, novelists and academics recruited by the British intelligence services, suggests that 'the skills of these professionals are ideally suited to the essential core activity of any security agency: the acquisition, collation, analysis and distribution of information'. Among friends at MI6 were David Footman, the leading Soviet authority who headed the Political Section, A. J. Ayer and a clutch of ex-*Spectator* men. On afternoons Rees slipped away from Pontifex to the SIS headquarters opposite St James's Park tube station – 'going to

The Office', as his wife described it. Rees was first approached about a job in SIS in November 1944, a move that alarmed Guy Burgess who concocted a fanciful alibi against any damaging talk by Rees about pre-war contacts with the Soviets. In the event, Burgess persuaded David Footman not to employ Goronwy (West and Tsarev, *The Crown Jewels*, 173). Rees's eventual berth at SIS particularly unsettled Burgess at the time of his North African indiscretions (November 1949): despite their close personal relations he thought Goronwy still capable of whispering about his past political unreliability.

p. 313 *I made of my time*: besides continuing to review for the *Spectator*, Rees in extended lunch hours worked on *Where No Wounds Were*, a full-scale novel of ideas published to considerable acclaim in June 1950.

p. 314 *as Estates Bursar of All Souls*: the Estates Bursar was the senior college officer, after the Warden and Sub-Warden.

p. 314 *a group of young philosophers*: Michael Dummett, Anthony Quinton and Bernard Williams, three fellows of the College in the early 1950s, developed an Oxford conception of linguistic analysis.

p. 314 *Hoti's business*: Robert Browning's grammarian is a Renaissance classical scholar whose students, in the act of burying him, praise his achievements ('A Grammarian's Funeral', *Men and Women* (1855)):

> So, with the throttling hands of death and strife,
>   Ground he at grammar;
> Still, thro' the rattle, parts of speech were rife:
>   While he could stammer
> He settled *Hoti's* business – let it be! –
>   Properly based *Oun* –
> Gave us the doctrine of the enclitic *De*,
>   Dead from the waist down.

(*Hoti, oun* and *de* are transliterations of three Greek particles.)

p. 316 *an absorbing and fascinating occupation*: Richard Wilberforce, Rees's successor in the post, judged him 'a *good* bursar – businesslike and quite imaginative. The farm tenants, of course, liked him a lot' (letter to Jenny Rees, 2 May 1995). Wilberforce confirmed his performance as bursar when Sir David Hughes Parry sounded him on Rees's suitability as Principal of University College, Aberystwyth ('frankly, I think he had doubts about you', Wilberforce wrote to Rees).

p. 316 *The War Song of Dinas Fawr*: Thomas Love Peacock's ballad, an original composition written for *The Misfortunes of Elphin* (1829), captures the manner of much early Welsh verse.

p. 317 *not entirely disinterested thought and deliberation*: one is reminded of Rees's old history teacher, R. T. Jenkins, when approached in 1930 regarding the vacant chair of history at Aberystwyth: ' "Beware the Greeks bearing gifts", was his instinctive reaction (and that of others, so he claimed), to any gambit by the Aberystwyth College authorities' (E. L. Ellis, *The University College of Wales, Aberystwyth, 1872–1972* (1972), 234).

p. 317 *as simple as it might seem*. Rees was the late recommendation of a selection committee convened to find a successor to Principal Ifor L. Evans, who had died in May 1952. Rejecting all internal applicants, Thomas Jones, the College's octogenarian President and chairman of the committee, began to sound out likely candidates in Oxford, Cambridge and London. One year later Rees's name came forward (backed by Maurice Bowra, John Sparrow and another fellow of All Souls, the banker Lord Brand) and, following an interview at Bristol, the committee unanimously decided to recommend him: Rees had intellectual distinction, administrative experience and a show of the third requirement for the post – that the candidate be fluent in Welsh (bilingual as a child, Rees promised to revive his spoken Welsh).

p. 319 *Je est un autre*: Rimbaud's dictum ('The I is another') comes from a letter to Paul Demeny, 15 May 1871, the so-called *lettre du voyant*, in which he develops his ideas on the subjective and objective in poetry.

p. 319 *my children*: besides Jenny and Lucy, the Reeses now had twin sons, Daniel Jenkyn and Thomas James, born at the beginning of 1948. In a letter to his father, Rees spoke of having given the boys 'good Welsh names' and mentioned that 'after the christening in the vestry, when the vicar was taking down particulars, he asked "Father's occupation", and I being somewhat dazed answered automatically *"Minister of the Gospel"*, as I always have. I have never seen such a look of disbelief and astonishment on anyone's face.'

p. 320 *had a certain justification*: from the beginning, Thomas Jones expected fierce opposition to Rees from the nationalists within the College and, sure enough, primed by Sir David Hughes Parry (Jones's elected successor as College President), they attacked him extravagantly at the Council meeting of 28 June 1953. Rees faced them 'with dignity and lucidity and humour' (Thomas Jones's words) and his appointment as College Principal was overwhelmingly approved. Jones felt relief and pleasure: Rees and Margie were 'a beautiful young pair, in the prime of their powers, facing their new adventure'.

p. 320 *a typically feckless family of Welsh squires*: the Richardes family of Plas Penglais, and pre-eminently Roderick Richardes (d. 1846), described as psychopathic and thoroughly objectionable. 'With some justification, Principal Goronwy Rees criticised the redevelopment [of the Plas] on the grounds that many of the older architectural features had been treated in a rather cavalier manner and that the rendering of the external walls was in questionable taste' (R. J. Colyer, 'Roderick Eardley Richardes and Plas Penglais, Aberystwyth', *Ceredigion*, 10, 1 (1984), 97–104).

p. 321 *a Daisy Miller*: heroine of Henry James's story of the same name.

p. 322 *haunted the mind of the college council*: such a moral climate told heavily on the Reeses. A. J. Ayer remembered how on his stays in Aberystwyth he had sometimes to buy their drink for them; 'it was not thought suitable that the Principal of the College or his wife should be seen in a place where liquor was sold' (*Encounter* (January 1981), 29).

p. 323 *when I first went there*: the students, for their part, kept faith with Rees and an emergency general meeting, called in face of attempts to remove him, revealed the depth of their support. The Principal 'had increased the prestige of the College throughout the country. He had increased the material amenities of the students and had proved a fine leader; he had fostered progressive ideas; his interests were wide and sympathetic. Nothing could be further from the truth than to say that he was unfitted to be a leader of students . . . [it was] an honour and a privilege for students to defend him' (report of a speech by the student president in the students' magazine, *The Courier*, 22 June 1956).

Mary Davies Parnell, an undergraduate at Aberystwyth at the time, well conveys the bond between the students and Rees (*Plateaux, Gateaux, Chateaux* (1997), 157):

> The students, especially the women, adored him. He mingled with the student body, went to Hall and College Balls and danced with the girl students; he supported Aber teams at inter-varsity games; he invited representatives of student groups, clubs and teams to tea at his large house . . . He appeared informal for a great man, far more congenial than some of the lecturers . . .
>
> In the summer [1956] the students at a General Meeting passed a resolution in support of him. It was about this time that Clement Attlee came to address the Union. He was applauded as he entered the Examinations Hall, applause which became thunderous on the appearance of the Principal behind him. It was a show of approval, the like of which I've never seen accorded to anyone and he was clearly moved by it.

p. 327 *King Charles's Heads*: an allusion to *David Copperfield*, where the simple-minded Mr Dick's compulsive writing of a memorial for the Lord Chancellor is continually blocked by his obsession with King Charles's beheading.

p. 328 *resolutely turned to the past*: in a radio talk, 'Returning to Wales' (28 September 1953). Rees's broadcast remarked on the persistence of the Welsh way of life and belief,

> an intense cultural and intellectual conservatism which shows itself sometimes in an almost Chinese reverence for what is established and sanctified by custom, a strange form of ancestor worship which is all the stranger because, as an articulate body of thought and belief, it is not more than a hundred and fifty years old. I would say, quite sincerely, that the most striking single impression I have received on returning to Wales is that of the strangely rigid and unchanging habit of thought and belief of the Welsh people today.

Such comment stirred up listeners, as did Rees's long-remembered use of lines from Gerard Manley Hopkins:

> Lovely the woods, waters, meadows, combes, vales,
> All the air things wear that build this world of Wales;
> Only the inmate does not correspond.

p. 330 *I had not thought a great deal about him*: at least not before 1955. In November of that year he spoke to Chatto & Windus about a book on Burgess which he was writing 'at great speed'.

p. 330 *its White Paper*: *Statement on the Findings of the Conference of Privy Councillors on Security, March 1956*, Cmd. 9715 (HMSO).

p. 331 *The God that Failed*: Richard Crossman's *The God that Failed: Six Studies in Communism* (1950) brought together essays by six intellectuals, describing their journey into communism and their subsequent disillusioned return. His contributors were Arthur Koestler, Ignazio Silone, Richard Wright, André Gide, Louis

Fischer and Stephen Spender. Crossman later declared that had he known his story, he would have recruited Rees, not Spender, to his gallery of ex-communists (review of *A Chapter of Accidents*, *New Statesman*, 25 February 1972, 242–3).

p. 332 *however evil its consequences might be*: as argued in the Introduction, a considerable exaggeration.

p. 332 *I must pay*: Rees considered the novel at length in an essay, '*Darkness at Noon* and "Grammatical Fiction"', published in a collection edited by Harold Harris, *Astride Two Cultures: Arthur Koestler at 70* (1975), 102–22. Nicolai Rubashov is modelled on Nikolai Bukharin, president of the Comintern, whose show-trial of March 1938 was a culmination, or *reductio ad absurdum*, of the Great Purge. Koestler's hero had become one of those 'people in prison who revalue their lives and discover they are guilty, though not of the crimes of which they are accused'.

p. 333 *Quis custodiet ipsos Custodes?*: 'Who is to guard the guards themselves?' (Juvenal).

p. 334 *Magna est veritas et praevalebit*: 'Truth is mighty, and will in the end prevail' (Vulgate Bible).

p. 334 *the third and fourth sections of this book*: Rees produced a version of the story sometime in 1955, for A. J. Ayer recalls having been shown a 'beautifully written' manuscript at a time when Rees had no intention of publishing it; David Footman read it also ('so fantastically unlike what *The People* printed a few months later'). Then on 12 February 1956 – the day after Burgess and Maclean reappeared in Moscow – Rees wrote to his literary agent David Higham enclosing the first few pages of 'a long story of what Burgess was actually about since his undergraduate days'; when completed, this account might run to 20,000 words and be publishable as it stood; or it could be expanded into a full-length book, or shaped as a series of articles. What did Higham advise? By 24 February Rees had accepted a commission, arranged through Higham's, for an expanded narrative to be serialized in the *People* (at a fee of 2,000 guineas); by 2 March he had provided Nat Rothman at the *People* with a text of around 28,000 words and some original sketches by Burgess for use as illustrations. In the event the newspaper articles amounted to fewer than 10,000 words.

p. 334 *and therefore gave my agreement*: the articles were published anonymously in the *People* on five consecutive Sundays (11 March–8 April 1956). John Morgan, a good friend of Rees's in later years, understood that Keidrych Rhys, editor of *Wales* and a columnist for the *People,* had a hand in the appearance of the articles, but there is no hard evidence of this. It seems that Rees sanctioned the rewriting and corrected weekly proofs; his decision to publish anonymously astonished Nat Rothman (then deputy editor of the *People*), given that the very first article unmistakably pointed to his authorship. Not to sign the articles seemed a cowardly act, and this, so Rothman thought, put people's backs up (Jenny Rees, *Looking for Mr Nobody*, 188). That Rees should have allowed a popular newspaper so to sensationalize his material struck his Oxford and London friends as utterly incomprehensible; had he spoken in his own voice, under his own name, in some reputable journal, they imagined he would not have suffered as he did.

p. 335 *the President of the college*: Sir David Hughes Parry, a former Vice-Chancellor of the University of London; his dislike of Rees was open, as was his determination that he be removed. The President in fact believed that over lunch with Rees at the lakeside hotel in Tal-y-llyn (10 April) he had secured the Principal's voluntary resignation: in the words of the Willink Report, 'The President was agreeably relieved by the Principal's readiness to give up his appointment.'

Rees did express a wish to leave the College, and confirmed it in writing shortly after Tal-y-llyn. Both he and the President envisaged his withdrawal by the end of September, before the 1956–7 session began. The President hoped for an early announcement to this effect, but this Rees firmly rejected: it would suggest he had been forced out of office, and further reduce his chances of finding another post.

p. 336 *in North Wales*: at a turbulent Council meeting of 29 June 1956 Rees spoke of the President's actions as having fostered among the Press the impression that he (the Principal) was about to resign, and also of the loyalty that had been shown him by members of the academic staff, and by the students particularly. Now an end could be put to 'the ordeal by insinuation, innuendo and malicious invention from which we have all suffered, and the College most of all, during the last three months'. A resolution to the effect that no further action be taken on the matter of the *People* articles was duly passed, by twenty-seven votes to twenty-one.

p. 336 *a committee of enquiry be appointed*: among the professorial staff, the prime movers against Rees were Lily Newton, Reginald Treharne and Richard Aaron, respectively Professors of Botany, History, and Logic and Philosophy. They and fifteen other heads of department signed a letter to the President (20 July 1956) urging that a committee of inquiry be immediately set up to examine 'the present situation in the College'. The tide had begun to turn against Rees with the public announcement, following the June meeting of Council, of some high-profile College resignations, including that of the Treasurer and of Sir Ifan ab Owen Edwards, senior Council member and a pillar of the Welsh establishment. Son of Sir Owen M. Edwards, brother-in-law to Sir David Hughes Parry, founder President of the Welsh League of Youth, Cymmrodorion Society medallist and one-time director of extra-mural studies at Aberystwyth, Sir Ifan spoke of being forced 'with deep regret' to sever his family's connection with the College, which had lasted from its earliest days. The special Council meeting of 27 July overturned the June resolution and called for an independent inquiry.

p. 336 *three gentlemen of impeccable social, professional and academic credentials*: the chairman Henry Willink QC, Master of Magdalene College, Cambridge, was an old Etonian who trained at the bar before becoming a Conservative MP and health minister; opposing Aneurin Bevan, Willink warned that the NHS 'will destroy so much in this country that we value'. Other committee members were Dr J. W. F. Hill, President of Nottingham University, and Dr Walter J. Warboys, Chairman of the Council of Industrial Design.

p. 336 *some eight months*: in responding to the Willink report, Rees stated his belief that, taken together, the deliberations of the Council and the proceedings of the committee of inquiry had occupied an inordinate amount of time, and that 'so protracted a procedure in itself constitutes a grave injustice to myself'. The Committee first met on 17 October 1956; its final Report is dated 8 February 1957.

p. 336 *might be open to criticism*: something of the nature of the attack on Rees can be gathered from an exchange between the President and Richard Aaron (August 1956). What questions should the Committee consider? Rees's private life was certainly a subject for scrutiny, though it was accepted that rumours of debts and drunkenness would be difficult to substantiate. The focus had to be on the *People* articles: 'malicious, salacious and sordid', they were a betrayal of the College; they had lowered its prestige and that of its teachers, and of the office of Principal itself. Nor were the students immune; Rees's articles had lowered the tone of student life ('this is the sort of life which the Principal and his friends lived – obviously the thing to do!'). One had to ensure, Aaron stressed to the President, that the articles were read, 'all five of them . . . If the Committee are honest men that of itself should settle the matter' (NLW, Richard I. Aaron Papers, 34).

p. 336 *The Vice-Principal of the college*: Professor R. M. Davies: 'genial and rotund, he had engaging traits: he invariably rolled his own cigarettes which he wrapped in liquorice paper, and as a built-in counter to the niggardliness of College equipment grants he coined the maxim, "*well i ni gael dau*" ("we had better have two")' (E. L. Ellis, *The University College of Wales, Aberystwyth, 1872–1972*, 267).

p. 337 *sacra arcana*: sacred mysteries.

p. 337 *The warden of an Oxford college*: Maurice Bowra, Warden of Wadham. Bowra came to regret this letter (which implied that Rees, not Burgess, was the traitor), and was troubled that *A Chapter of Accidents* might cast him in an unfavourable light. 'This is fair enough', Bowra wrote to Chatto & Windus sometime before its publication, 'as I wrote him a very nasty letter – though it was before the row broke out and he was really in trouble.' Rees was not alienated: 'Maurice is not litigious', he assured his editor, but 'a good hearted as well as an honourable man.'

p. 337 *A distinguished moral philosopher*: Stuart Hampshire, who 'wrote a very angry letter to Rees, which I have regretted ever since. I would never do such a thing again, but I was upset' (Jenny Rees, *Looking for Mr Nobody*, 186). In conversation with Jenny Rees, Hampshire recalled his sense of outrage at Rees's account of the Bentinck Street circle. The smearing of Victor Rothschild was particularly offensive, for Rees here was trading in innuendo and guilt by association. Isaiah Berlin added that he thought it reckless of Rees, in the post-McCarthy atmosphere, 'to write an article saying that people in the Foreign Office were communists and homosexuals'. The vilification of Burgess caused less pain – Guy was not everyone's favourite – but Goronwy as puritan rigourist, scourging the excesses of his erstwhile friend, mystified all who knew him. (A member of the Wolfenden Committee, he was at that very moment proving an effective advocate for liberalization of the law relating to homosexuality: partly because of him some effective homosexual spokesmen agreed to give evidence). As for Anthony Blunt – the unnamed presence in the articles – because of Rees's hints he became once more an object of speculation, but his friends rallied round him and continued their destruction of Rees as a credible witness.

On Rees's motives for publishing the articles an Oxford consensus emerged: it was by way of a pre-emptive strike. Burgess's sudden resurfacing in Moscow had provoked this panicky move designed to discredit any stories of past connections that Burgess might care to reveal. 'Guy is now a terribly dangerous man . . . capable of doing a great deal of harm to a great many people, some of whom . . . are friends of yours and mine', he wrote to Isaiah Berlin (Ignatieff, *Isaiah Berlin*, 194). 'What of course he [Rees] was out to do', reflected Noël Annan in a review of Boyle's *The Climate of Treason*, 'was to expose Blunt and – let the chips fall where they might – name numbers of those who were friends of the spies and might, or might not, also be hidden agents. He suffered obloquy and social ostracism for his pains and his career was blasted while Blunt sailed serenely on' (*TLS*, 7 December 1979, 85). Annan correctly surmised that for Rees the unmasking of Blunt vindicated his decision to publish what in 1956 was dismissed as 'hysterical nonsense': Rees's call for a public inquiry would likewise appear to have been justified, though Annan still doubted that such an inquiry would have caused the Establishment to crumble: as Annan himself had memorably written, 'The explosion detonated by these articles was atomic; but the blast-walls of the Establishment are so cunningly constructed that the person who was most hideously wounded was Mr Rees himself' (*TLS*, 11 February 1972, 142).

Burgess's own much quoted explanation for the articles was that Goronwy probably needed the money ('He always did'); as Rosamond Lehmann had predicted, Guy seemed to be the one person not too angered by Rees's behaviour.

p. 338 *salonfähig*: socially acceptable. A. J. Ayer recalls a chance meeting with Rees in a London restaurant at this time: 'When I went up to greet him, he said "What, are you still speaking to me?" "Of course", I said, "why shouldn't I?" "Well", he answered, "nobody else is . . ." This was some way from being true. There were others who stood by him, and of his critics some for whom he cared most soon forgave him' (*Encounter* (January 1981), 29).

p. 338 *R. C. Zaehner*: 'He was one of my oldest friends and boon companions', wrote Rees of the eccentric Spalding Professor of Eastern Religions and Ethics at Oxford (and another All Souls fellow); 'I feel sad that I shall never again sit up drinking with him all night until dawn reminded us that there was such a thing as bed' (*Encounter* (February 1975), 40).

p. 338 *F. W. Deakin, Douglas Young and David Footman*: F. W. (later Sir William) Deakin was Warden of St Antony's College, Oxford; he had a background in British Intelligence. Douglas Young was a chartered surveyor in the City; he and his wife were close friends of the Reeses. Another clergyman's son, David Footman joined MI6 in 1935 and in 1953 became a Fellow of St Antony's College, publishing four studies of Russian history to add to his early fiction and a biography of Ferdinand Lassalle; of Rees he wrote, 'Along with his warmth and his gaiety I was struck by his enormous capacity to be interested and his uncanny quickness at seizing the point' (*Encounter* (January 1981), 31).

p. 338 *had learned from their parents*: Rees complained before the College Council, 29 June 1956, of the 'atmosphere of suspicion, rumour, and insinuation directed not only at me but at my family – even my children, who at school are exposed to jeers because even their schoolfellows know, it appears, that I am to be dismissed'.

p. 339 *a vicious little mouse*: Rees's description is accurate in so far as the Willink Report (into 'the present situation in the College') attacked him vehemently on matters which he took to be minor. Having found no reason to question his 'financial probity, temperance, or sexual morality', nor his competence as a university administrator – on the contrary, 'The net effect of what we have read and heard leaves us with the impression of an academic community that was running well and smoothly' – the case against him had to rest on the publication of the *People* articles and his behaviour afterwards. On the matter of the articles, the report told heavily against Rees: 'In negotiating a remunerative contract with the *People*, the Principal offered material that was lewd and scandalous' (part of which, as he acknowledged, was 'exaggerated and unfair'), and in doing so he had shown 'a wanton disregard for the interests of the College'. Regarding Rees's subsequent actions, the Committee was equally damning: 'having on the 10 April made an agreement with the President [to resign], he went back on his word'; his moves to remain in office, and in particular to avoid any Committee of Enquiry, were 'discreditable', and his attitude to the President of the College 'not only discourteous and offensive, but also unfair'.

Accepting that his fate was sealed – that the report was no objective investigation but biased heavily against him on evidence that he had not been allowed to see – Rees's response to Willink was understandably brief. The *People* articles were the only grounds for an inquiry, and 'I cannot believe that the simple expression of the Committee's opinion that the articles are "scandalous" provides any sufficient justification for the protracted, laborious and expensive enquiry carried out by the Committee.' As for the 10 April meeting and the supposed offer of resignation, the Committee had complely accepted the President's word and entirely rejected his own; but this was entirely characteristic of its treatment of unfolding events after the appearance of the articles, where 'The contrast between the severity with which the Committee has condemned my actions, and the forbearance shown to others, is, it seems to me, striking.'

p. 340 *five young children to support*: a third son, Matthew, was born in October 1954.

p. 340 *A month later*: in early May 1957. On 15 March 1957 the College Council received the Willink Report, together with the Principal's resignation; by April the Reeses had left Aberystwyth.

Notes to *A Winter in Berlin*

p. 344 *Gleichschaltung*: forcing into line.

p. 344 *Solitudinem faciunt pacem appellant*: 'They make a wilderness and call it peace' (Tacitus, *Agricola*, ch. 30).

p. 344 *Gummiknüppeln*: rubber truncheons.

p. 344 *razzia*: raid.

p. 345 *Frederick Voigt*: the distinguished foreign correspondent had known and liked Goronwy during the latter's brief spell at the *Manchester Guardian* (1932–3).

p. 345 *von Prittwitz*: at odds with the Nazi regime, Friedrich Wilhelm von Prittwitz und Gaffron, an older Foreign Office diplomat, resigned as German Ambassador in Washington but unlike von der Schulenberg and von Hase he survived the Third Reich.

p. 345 *honoris causa*: with due respect.

p. 345 *the attempted assassination of Hitler?*: reviewing Terence Prittie, *Germans Against Hitler*, Rees recalled others involved in Operation Valkyrie, the conspiracy of 20 July 1944: 'Some of them I had known when young: Adam von Trott zu Solz, Helmuth von Moltke, Werner von Haeften. I had drunk with some of them in Berlin *Kneipen* [pubs], argued with them about Hegel and Marx, about Hölderlin and Stefan George and Moeller van den Bruck, all that delirium of the brave which so filled the minds of their generation. Who could have guessed then that it was to be their fate to be strung up like carcasses on butchers' meat hooks, objects of derision to both the Nazis and the Allies, targets for the jeers of Dr Goebbels and Dr Taylor [? A. J. P. Taylor] alike' (*Encounter* (August 1964), 64).

p. 346 *Machtübernahme*: seizure of power by Hitler in January 1933.

p. 346 *Kriegsministerium*: War Office.

p. 346 *if he had gone to the Bendlerstrasse?*: in December 1932 Kurt von Schleicher (1882–1934) was invited to form a government with himself as Chancellor and Minister of Defence. His regime lasted little more than a month; on 28 January the Schleicher cabinet resigned and two days later Hitler was confirmed as Chancellor. Schleicher was left with control of the *Reichswehr* (the Republic's defensive land forces) though a replacement had been found in Werner von Blomberg (1878–1946), commander of the East Prussian military area and military adviser to the German delegation at the Geneva Disarmament Conference. Rees alludes to rumours on the evening of von Blomberg's return of a possible *putsch* by the army, but Schleicher's power had ebbed to nothing and on 30 June 1934 he was murdered by an SS bullet. Von Blomberg, far from maintaining the army's distance from the Nazis (as Hindenberg might have expected), conceived the notion of an oath of personal loyalty to the Führer.

p. 347 *Gregor Strasse*: German politician (1892–1934), head of the Nazi Party organization, and a serious rival to Hitler. Like von Schleicher, he was murdered in 1934.

p. 348 *Hermann Oncken*: the immensely productive Oncken (1869–1946) published his political biography of Lassalle in 1904.

p. 348 *Preussische Staatsbibliothek*: among the world's greatest repositories for manuscripts, books and periodicals, the Prussian State Library was housed on Unter den Linden, east of the Brandenburg Gate.

p. 349 *coureur de femmes*: womanizer.

p. 349 *Philister*: philistine.

p. 350 *then Foreign Secretary*: later Chancellor of the Exchequer and a key appeaser in Chamberlain's cabinet. Rees occupied, in his absence, Simon's rooms at All Souls.

p. 350 *rus in urbe*: the countryside in the town (Martial, *Epigrams*).

p. 350 *Wilhelminisch*: Wilhelminian; pertaining to the reign of William II of Germany, 1888–1918.

p. 351 *not because I was English*: Rees in his autobiographical writings could be Welsh or English, depending on what mental or temperamental differences he was seeking to illustrate (later in this essay he makes reference to 'English habits of mind'). His occasional assumption of Englishness caused misunderstanding and resentment in Wales.

p. 352 *the Barn*: a feature of The Wharf, the Asquiths' Thames-side retreat near Oxford.

p. 353 *Erich Kästner's Herr Schmidt*: Kästner (1899–1974), author of *Emil and the Detectives* and other children's classics, was also a left-wing satirist banned in Nazi Germany; his 'sad and cynical' contemporary verses were, so Rees believed, a true guide to the reality of Berlin in the 1920s. Rees here quotes from the poem 'Kurt Schmidt, statt einer Ballade' (*Ein Mann gibt Auskunft* (1930)) and provides his own translation.

p. 354 *Hasso von Seebach*: an employee of the United Press, Hasso von Seebach emigrated to the United States, returning to Germany after the war (Klemens von Klemperer (ed.), *A Noble Combat: The Letters of Shiela Grant Duff and Adam von Trott zu Solz, 1932–37* (1998), 54).

p. 356 *follow where he led*: Adam von Trott zu Solz (1909–44), diplomat and member of the resistance, had been a Rhodes Scholar at Oxford where he and Rees enjoyed an 'essentially frivolous' relationship; 'they loved to make fun of each other, to ridicule each other's ideas and even appearance . . .' (Christopher Sykes, *Troubled Loyalty: A Biography of Adam von Trott zu Solz* (1968), 96–7). Later Trott followed Rees in his romantic attachment to Shiela Grant Duff.

Trott's intellectual make-up puzzled his English contemporaries, who found it hard to disentangle his legitimate German nationalism from Hitler's dreams of world domination. Trott therefore became distrusted and his role in the German resistance consequently called into question – so much so that when news of his death for his part in the plot against Hitler reached Oxford, Maurice Bowra exclaimed, 'That's one Nazi who was hanged' (Giles MacDonogh, *A Good German: Adam von Trott zu Solz* (1989), 5). As has been said, as late as 1972 Harri Webb could compare the Rees of *A Chapter of Accidents* with Adam Trott, 'an empty character, with no loyalty or sensibility'. Webb's review disgusted Rees, for whom Trott and his fellow conspirators, in their individual moral struggle against the dictates of patriotism and the oath of allegiance to Hitler, 'had dedicated to Germany a love which surpassed the love of country'.

p. 357 *von Gottes Gnaden*: by the Grace of God.

p. 357 *Büchner*: Rees and Stephen Spender collaborated on a translation of Büchner's *Dantons Tod* (*Danton's Death*), published by Faber in March 1939.

p. 357 *the Bauers*: actually the Mayers (as confirmed by Giles MacDonogh in correspondence with the editor). J. P. Mayer was a Jewish bookseller whose Berlin premises doubled as a socialist meeting-place. A friend of von Seebach and the Trotts, Peter Mayer edited the early humanistic writings of Marx and became a leading authority on Alexis de Tocqueville.

p. 358 *Hofjude*: Court Jew; cf. *Schutzjude*, a protected Jew.

p. 359 *the Warden took alarm*: W. G. S. Adams, Warden of All Souls, 1933–5.

p. 361 *Bonzen*: big shots; fat cats.

p. 363 *a matter of life and death*: Rees's own behaviour began to worry his brother Geraint, who gathered from a Welsh acquaintance recently returning from Berlin that Goronwy was involved in dangerous political activity.

Bibliography

~

Goronwy Rees: Principal Books and Translations

The Summer Flood (London, Faber & Faber, 1932). Novel.

A Bridge to Divide Them (London, Faber & Faber, 1937). Novel.

Danton's Death: A Play in Four Acts, by Georg Büchner; translated by Stephen Spender and Goronwy Rees (London, Faber & Faber, 1939).

Where No Wounds Were (London, Chatto & Windus, 1950). Novel.

Conversations with Kafka: Notes and Reminiscences by Gustav Janouch; translated with a Preface by Goronwy Rees (London, Derek Verschoyle, 1953); second edition, revised and enlarged: London, Deutsch, 1971.

A Bundle of Sensations (London, Chatto & Windus, 1960).

The Multi-Millionaires: Six Studies in Wealth (London, Weidenfeld & Nicolson, 1961).

The Rhine (London, Weidenfeld & Nicolson, 1967).

St Michael: A History of Marks and Spencer (London, Weidenfeld & Nicolson, 1969); revised edition: London, Pan Books, 1973.

The Great Slump: Capitalism in Crisis, 1929–33 (London, Weidenfeld & Nicolson, 1970).

A Chapter of Accidents (London, Chatto & Windus, 1972; New York, Library Press, 1972).

Brief Encounters (London, Chatto & Windus, 1974). A selection from Rees's *Encounter* journalism.

Dalgety: The History of a Merchant House (privately printed).

Goronwy Rees: Contributions to Books and Periodicals

No full-scale bibliography of Rees exists. Below are the major pieces used in preparing this edition.

'From a Welshman Abroad', *Bookman* (November 1934), 105–6.

'The Empirical Society', *Spectator*, 13 December 1935, 992. Review of Sidney and Beatrice Webb, *Soviet Communism*.

'Europe and Spain' [*Spectator*, 7 August 1936], in Charles Moore and Christopher Hawtree (eds.), *1936 as Recorded by The Spectator* (London, Michael Joseph, 1986), 91–3.

'What Then Must We Do', *Spectator*, 12 March 1937, 480. Review of George Orwell, *The Road to Wigan Pier*.

'The Russian Mystery', *Spectator*, 18 June 1937, 1132.

'In Defence of Welsh Nationalism', *Spectator*, 10 September 1937, 416–17.

'In the Valley', *Spectator*, 5 November 1937, 806–7. Review of James Hanley, *Grey Children: A Study of Humbug and Misery in South Wales*.

'News from America', *Spectator*, 18 March 1938, 457–8.

'The Liberal Life', *Spectator*, 25 March 1938, 501–2.

'Beyond the Dyke' [radio script, June 1938]; partly reprinted in Patrick Hannan (ed.), *Wales on the Wireless: A Broadcasting Anthology* (Llandysul, Gomer, 1988), 6–7, 133–4.

'Bolshevism and the West', *Spectator*, 9 September 1938, 397–8. Review of F. Borkenau, *The Communist International*.

'Fair Play for the Territorials', *Spectator*, 18 August 1939, 241–2.

'Letter from a Soldier', *Horizon* (July 1940), 467–71.

'A Poet Abroad', *Spectator*, 1 November 1946, 456. Review of Stephen Spender, *European Witness*.

'Supreme Commander', *Spectator*, 7 January 1949, 6–7. Review of Dwight D. Eisenhower, *Crusade in Europe*.

'Piranesi', *Spectator*, 7 July 1950, 22. Review of Aldous Huxley, *Piranesi*.

'The Informer and the Communist', *Spectator*, 20 February 1953, 206–7. On Whittaker Chambers and Alger Hiss.

'Returning to Wales [radio script, 28 September 1953]; partly reprinted in Patrick Hannan (ed.), *Wales on the Wireless: A Broadcasting Anthology* (Llandysul, Gomer, 1988), 180–1.

'Preface', in *The Answers of Ernst von Salomon to the 131 Questions in the Allied Military Government 'Fragebogen'*; translated by Constantine FitzGibbon (London, Putnam, 1954), vii–xii.

'Predicaments', *Welsh Anvil / Yr Einion*, 7 (1955), 18–31. Text of lecture delivered July 1954.

'Guy Burgess Stripped Bare!', *People*, 11 March 1956, 5. Continued: 18 March, 3; 25 March, 3; 1 April, 3; 8 April, 10.

'Two Faces of War', *Encounter* (November 1959), 68–70. Review of Martha Gellhorn, *The Face of War*, and Neil McCallum, *Journey with a Pistol*.

'The Dieppe Raid', *Sunday Times*, 5 June 1960, 33. An exchange between Rees and Brigadier Bernard Fergusson.

'From Another Country', *New Statesman*, 24 February 1961, 296, 298. On Wales.

'Lessons in Co-operation', *Sunday Times*, 12 March 1961, 32. Review of Bernard Fergusson, *The Watery Maze: The Story of Combined Operations*.

'Have the Welsh a Future?', *Encounter* (March 1964), 3–13.

'All the Conspirators', *Encounter* (August 1964), 64–5. Review of Terence Prittie, *Germans against Hitler*, and Roger Manvell and Heinrich Fraenkel, *The July Plot*.

'The Witness', *Spectator*, 22 January 1965, 105. Review of Whittaker Chambers, *Cold Friday*. Letter, *Spectator*, 12 February 1965, 198 (Conor Cruise O'Brien); reply, 19 February 1965, 229 (Goronwy Rees).

'A Case for Treatment: The World of Lytton Strachey', *Encounter* (March 1968); reprinted in Goronwy Rees, *Brief Encounters* (London, Chatto & Windus, 1974), 69–86.

'Dr R. T. Jenkins', *The Times*, 17 November 1969, 12. Rees remembers his history teacher at Cardiff High School for Boys.

'William Foster meets Goronwy Rees', *Scotsman*, 12 December 1972. Interview.

'Introduction', in John McVicar, *McVicar by Himself*, edited by Goronwy Rees (London, Hutchinson, 1974), 11–28; revised edition: London, Arrow Books, 1979.

'Were the Intellectuals Duped?', *Encounter* (January 1974), 25–7.

'Richard Crossman', *Encounter* (June 1974), 41.

'*Darkness at Noon* and "Grammatical Fiction"', in Harold Harris (ed.), *Astride Two Cultures: Arthur Koestler at 70* (London, Hutchinson, 1975), 102–22.

'Albert Speer', *Encounter* (November 1975), 42–4.

'Arms and the Man', *New Statesman*, 16 April 1976, 508–9. Review of Alun Chalfont, *Montgomery of Alamein*.

'Back to the Boathouse', *TLS*, 29 April 1977, 505. Review of Paul Ferris, *Dylan Thomas*, and Daniel Jones, *My Friend Dylan Thomas*.

'Spies and their Society', *TLS*, 23 December 1977, 1496. Review of John Fisher, *Burgess and Maclean: A New Look at the Foreign Office Spies*.

'Memories of New College, 1928–31', in John Buxton and Penry Williams (eds.), *New College, Oxford, 1379–1979* (Warden and Fellows of New College, 1979), 120–6.

'*The Times*', *Encounter* (February 1979), 31.

'Odd Man Out Among the Spies', *Observer*, 13 January 1980, 33, 35. Interviewed by Andrew Boyle. Continued: *Observer*, 20 January, 35.

Goronwy Rees: Biography and Criticism

Rees's life has been excellently covered in Jenny Rees, *Looking for Mr Nobody: The Secret Life of Goronwy Rees* (London, Weidenfeld & Nicholson, 1994); the paperback reissue (London, Phoenix, 1997) reprints as an appendix four letters from Rees to Rosamond Lehmann, 1940–1. Note also:

Ellis, E. L., 'The Man of *The People*: Goronwy Rees and the Aberystwyth Episode', *New Welsh Review*, 29 (1995), 44–7.

Encounter (January 1981), 27–36: reminiscences of Rees by A. J. Ayer, Donald McCormick ('Richard Deacon'), David Footman, John Morgan and Jonathan Power.

Harris, John, *Goronwy Rees* (Cardiff, University of Wales Press, 2001).

—— 'Any One There? In Search of Goronwy Rees', *Planet*, 110 (1995), 14–21.

—— 'A Journalist in the Thirties', *New Welsh Review*, 29 (1995), 31–8.

Jones, Richard, 'Fiction Which Foreshadows Foolishness', *New Welsh Review*, 29 (1995), 39–43.

Morgan, John, 'Goronwy Rees', in *John Morgan's Wales: A Personal Anthology* (Swansea, Christopher Davies, 1993), 47–51. Based partly on conversations with Rees.

Norton-Taylor, Richard, 'Both Perfect Prey and Perfect Foil', *New Welsh Review*, 29 (1995), 48–50. On Rees and the Cambridge spies.

Rowse, A. L, 'Elizabeth Bowen; Goronwy Rees', in his *Memories and Glimpses* (London, Methuen, 1986), 417–32. See also Rowse's *All Souls in My Lifetime* (London, Duckworth, 1993).

Trilling, Diana, 'Goronwy – and Others: A Remembrance of England', *Partisan Review* (January 1996), 11–47. An absorbing and sympathetic appraisal.

Rees makes an appearance in a number of memoirs of the period (as listed by Jenny Rees). Most important by far is Shiela Grant Duff's *The Parting of Ways: A Personal Account of the Thirties* (London, Peter Owen, 1982), which quotes from Rees's letters and is our best guide to his movements in the early 1930s. A. J. Ayer's two volumes of autobiography, *Part of My Life* and *More of My Life* (London, Collins, 1977; 1984) also have some pages on Rees; Ayer wrote Rees's *Times* obituary (14 December 1979, 16) and his *Dictionary of National Biography* entry.

The literature on the Cambridge spy ring is extensive and most studies make some reference to Rees. The following have been particularly helpful:

Andrew, Christopher and Vasili Mitrokhin, *The Mitrokhin Archive: The KGB in Europe and the West* (Harmondsworth, Penguin, 1999).

Annan, Noël, 'The Cambridge Spies', in his *Our Age: Portrait of a Generation* (London, Weidenfeld & Nicolson, 1990), 224–44.

Bowyer, Tom, *The Perfect English Spy: Sir Dick White and the Secret War, 1935–90* (London, Heinemann, 1995).

Boyle, Andrew, *The Climate of Treason: Five Who Spied for Russia* (London, Hutchinson, 1979). Reviewed: *TLS*, 7 December 1979, 83–5 (Noël Annan).

Cecil, Robert, 'The Cambridge Comintern', in Christopher Andrew and David Dilks (eds.), *The Missing Dimension: Governments and Intelligence Communities in the Twentieth Century* (London, Macmillan, 1984), 169–98.

Costello, John, *Mask of Treachery* (London, Collins, 1988). On Anthony Blunt.

Costello, John and Oleg Tsarev, *Deadly Illusions* (London, Century, 1993).

Deacon, Richard, *The Greatest Treason: The Bizarre Story of Hollis, Liddell and Mountbatten* (London, Century, 1989).

Koch, Stephen, *Stalin, Willi Münzenberg and the Seduction of the Intellectuals* (London, HarperCollins, 1995).

Modin, Yuri, *My Five Cambridge Friends* (London, Headline, 1994).

Penrose, Barrie and Simon Freeman, *Conspiracy of Silence: The Secret Life of Anthony Blunt* (London, Grafton, 1986).

Rees, Jenny, *Looking for Mr Nobody: The Secret Life of Goronwy Rees* (London, Weidenfeld & Nicholson, 1994). Includes a lengthy interview with Oleg Tsarev on the nature of Rees's co-operation with Burgess.

West, Nigel and Oleg Tsarev, *The Crown Jewels: The British Secrets at the Heart of the KGB Archives* (London, HarperCollins, 1998).

Wright, Peter, *Spycatcher* (New York, Viking, 1987).

Other Printed Sources

Annan, Noël, *Changing Enemies: The Defeat and Regeneration of Germany* (London, HarperCollins, 1995).

Berlin, Isaiah, *Personal Impressions* (London, Oxford University Press, 1982).

Day-Lewis, Sean, *C. Day-Lewis: An English Literary Life* (London, Weidenfeld & Nicolson, 1980).

Hamilton, Nigel, *Monty: The Making of a General, 1887–1942* (London, H. Hamilton, 1981).

Hastings, Selina, *Nancy Mitford* (London, H. Hamilton, 1985).

Hynes, Samuel, *The Auden Generation: Literature and Politics in England in the 1930s* (London, Bodley Head, 1976).

Ignatieff, Michael, *Isaiah Berlin: A Life* (London, Chatto & Windus, 1998).

Klemperer, Klemens von (ed.), *A Noble Combat: The Letters of Shiela Grant Duff and Adam von Trott zu Solz, 1932–37* (Oxford, Clarendon Press, 1998).

MacDonogh, Giles, *A Good German: Adam von Trott zu Solz* (London, Quartet, 1989).

Morris, Benny, *The Roots of Appeasement: The British Weekly Press and Nazi Germany during the 1930s* (London, Frank Cass, 1991).

Partridge, Frances, *Good Company: Diaries, January 1967–December 1970* (London, HarperCollins, 1994).

Sykes, Christopher, *Troubled Loyalty: A Biography of Adam von Trott zu Solz* (London, Collins, 1968).

Villa, Brian Loring, *Unauthorized Action: Mountbatten and the Dieppe Raid* (Toronto, Oxford University Press, 1989).

West, Nigel, *The Faber Book of Espionage* (London, Faber & Faber, 1993).

Non-Printed Sources

Rees, Goronwy, 'Beyond the Dyke' (June 1938), 'Returning to Wales' (September 1953), 'A Child in the Chapel' (January 1955) [Radio scripts]. BBC Written Archives Centre, Reading; National Library of Wales (NLW), Aberystwyth.

—— Letters to Revd R. J. Rees. Calvinistic Methodist Archive, NLW, Aberystwyth.

—— Letters to Shiela Grant Duff, Douglas Jay, T. Mervyn Jones and Maire Lynd. Private collections.

'Goronwy Rees: A Man of His Time', HTV Wales, 1978 [television interview with John Morgan]. NLW, Aberystwyth.

Chatto and Windus Archive. Reading University Library.

Richard I. Aaron Papers, NLW, Aberystwyth.

Rees, Revd R. J., Diary. Calvinistic Methodist Archive, NLW, Aberystwyth.

Reilly, Sir Patrick, Letter to Jenny Rees, 27 January 1993. Private collection.

Wilberforce, Sir Richard, Letter to Jenny Rees, 2 May 1995. Private collection.

[Willink Report.] *Report of the University College of Wales, Aberystwyth, Committee of Enquiry, 1956–57* (1957). University of Wales, Aberystwyth.